RECREATING ANCIENT HISTORY

RECREATING ANCIENT HISTORY

*Episodes from the Greek and Roman Past in the Arts
and Literature of the Early Modern Period*

EDITED BY

KARL ENENKEL, JAN L. DE JONG

JEANINE DE LANDTSHEER

WITH THE COLLABORATION OF

ALICIA MONTOYA

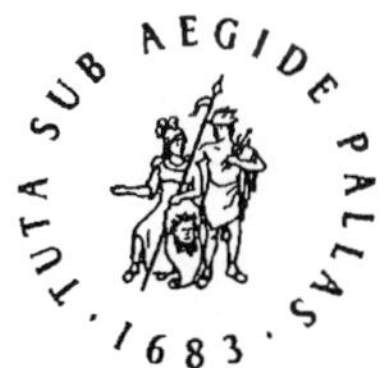

BRILL ACADEMIC PUBLISHERS, INC.
BOSTON • LEIDEN
2002

Library of Congress Cataloging-in-Publication Data

Recreating ancient history : episodes from the Greek and Roman past in the arts
and literature of the Early Modern Period / edited by Karl Enenkel, Jan L. De Jong,
Jeanine De Landtsheer ; with collaboration of Alicia Montoya.
        p. cm.
    Originally published: Leiden ; Boston : Brill, 2001.
    Includes bibliographical references and index.
    ISBN 0–391–04129–0
        1. History in art. 2. Civilization, Classical, in art. 3. Arts, Modern. I.
Enenkel, K. A. E. II. Jong, Jan L. de. III. Landtsheer, J. de (Jeanine) IV.
Montoya, Alicia.

    NX650.H5 R43 2002
    700'.458—dc21

                                                                    2002066268

ISBN 0–391–04129–0

PRINTED IN THE UNITED STATES OF AMERICA

TABLE OF CONTENTS

Preface.. vii

*The Representation of History in Artistic Theory in the Early
Modern Period* 1
    Anton BOSCHLOO (Leiden)

*Universals and Particulars. History Painting in
the "Sala di Costantino" in the Vatican Palace* 27
    Jan L. DE JONG (Groningen)

Theatrum Hodiernae Vitae: *Lipsius, Vaenius and the Rebellion
of Civilis* 57
    Mark MORFORD (Leeds, Mass.)

Strange and Bewildering Antiquity: Lipsius's Dialogue
Saturnales sermones *on Gladiatorial Games (1582)* 75
    Karl ENENKEL (Leiden)

Justus Lipsius's De militia Romana: *Polybius Revived or
How an Ancient Historian was Turned into a Manual of
Early Modern Warfare* 101
    Jeanine DE LANDTSHEER (Leuven)

*"The Grandeur that was Rome": Scholarly Analysis and
Pious Awe in Lipsius's* Admiranda 123
    Marc LAUREYS (Bonn)

*Civic Self-Offering: Some Renaissance Representations of
Marcus Curtius*... 147
    Maria BERBARA (Rio de Janeiro)

Montaigne, Plutarch and Historiography 167
    Paul J. SMITH (Leiden)

Plutarch's Lives *and* Coriolanus: *Shakespeare's View of Roman History* 187
    Bart WESTERWEEL (Leiden)

The Reception of Plutarch in the Netherlands: Octavia and Cleopatra in the Heroic Epistles of J.B. Wellekens (1710) 213
    Olga VAN MARION (Leiden)

The Reception of Plutarch in Friedrich Schiller's Lectures on Solon and Lycurgus's Legislation 235
    Sjaak ONDERDELINDEN (Leiden)

Marc Anton ironisch? Zu Form und Erfindung seiner Leichenrede in Shakespeares Julius Caesar 253
    Wilfried STROH (Munich)

The Uses of Ancient History in the Emblems of Joannes Sambucus (1531–1584) 269
    Arnoud VISSER (Leiden)

The Emperor Hadrian as an Artist in Karel van Mander's Schilder-boeck 287
    Francesca TERRENATO (Rome)

Tyrant or Stoic Hero? Marc-Antoine Muret's Julius Caesar 303
    Jan BLOEMENDAL (The Hague)

Caesar the Father in Marie-Anne Barbier's La mort de César *(1709)* 319
    Alicia MONTOYA (Leiden)

The Dutch Republic between Hauteur and Greed — Lambert van den Bosch and his Drama L. Catilina 339
    Bettina NOAK (Berlin)

List of Illustrations 357

Index 363

List of Contributors 373

PREFACE

Two feature films released during the last twenty years caused excited debates on the historical accuracy of their themes. One was the famous film *Amadeus* from 1984 (originally a theatre play by Peter Shaffer, who was personally involved in reworking it into a film), and the other *Artemisia* by Agnès Merlet, from 1998. To quote just two opinions, H.C. Robbins Landon wrote in his *1791. Mozart's last Year*: '[…] it may prove difficult to persuade the public from the current Shafferian view of the composer as a divinely gifted drunken lout, pursued by a vengeful Salieri. By the same token, Constance Mozart, she (in the film) of extraordinary décolleté and fatuous giggle, needs to be rescued from Shaffer's view of her.'[1] Sheila Farr wrote about the way the Italian painter Artemisia Gentileschi (1593–1652) was recreated in the film of the same name: 'why […] are the few documented facts ignored and the artist's life boiled down to a syrupy, sensational fantasy? Truth is a hundred times more interesting than the fiction that French director Agnès Merlet concocts from the life of seventeenth-century Italian painter Artemisia Gentileschi'.[2]

A similar debate would have been unthinkable in the early modern period, because the attitude towards history then was different from what it is nowadays. History was not considered as a series of events from the past that had to be reconstructed as completely and accurately as possible, but as a rich field of raw material, that could be used, recycled and adapted to new needs and purposes.

The two examples show that film producers — just like writers of historical novels, playwrights and artists in general — still make free use of history to find themes that fit their artistic ideas, and that if these themes do not completely fit, they freely rework and adapt them till they do. This makes the question, whether or not a work of art gives a correct presentation of history, basically irrelevant. And yet the main criterion of a number of critics and a large part of the audience seems to be: is this film, or novel, or theatre play, or work of art, a cor-

---

[1] Robbins Landon H.C., *1791. Mozart's Last Year* (London: 1988) 181.
[2] Farr S., *Lusty For Life* (http://www.film.com/film-review/1998/10493/732/default-review.html).

rect reconstruction of the past?[3] Not only does this criterion not do justice to the artistic intentions of the makers, but it also implies the assumption that it is actually possible to recover history precisely as it was.

In the early modern period the criterion for judging works of art was not the extent to which they illustrate the past correctly. It is true that a correct representation of 'reality' could be an important — although ambiguous — criterion, but it was applied to history in a way that was different from what a large part of the present-day audience would expect. The reason is that the general sense of history was different then from ours.

The essays collected in this volume do not discuss the view on history or the development of history as a science in the early modern period. The theme of this book is: how did historians and artists — writers, playwrights, and painters — represent history, or rather — as it has already become clear that they did not aim at an 'exact' rendition — how did they *recreate* history?

To answer this question, the realm of history has been focused on that of classical Antiquity. There are several reasons for doing so. First of all, the history of the Greeks and Romans had never ceased to appeal to men's imagination and to provoke men's admiration, in particular because the Greeks and Romans themselves had recorded and cultivated their history in an unprecedented way. To those living in the early modern period it offered many stimulating examples and new points of view. For this and other reasons, ancient history acquired a renewed charisma and urgency. Persons and institutions from the classical past were seen and studied as examples for the present. A strong feeling of identification with Antiquity developed, and tracing one's roots and origins to people or events from ancient history was viewed as somehow partaking in their glory and renown. This was not only true for individual persons or families, but also for cities and institutions. Ancient history was not just studied out of interest for

---

[3] From this point of view Robbins Landon's remarks on *Amadeus* are understandable: he is writing as an historian, and it worries him that the impact of the film will make the general public think of Mozart rather as 'a divinely gifted drunken lout' than as the more 'normal' person which he really seems to have been. Robbins Landon does not deny the filmmakers the right to represent Mozart differently from the historical personality or blame them for that. He sees (p. 194) the Mozart biography by Wolfgang Hildesheimer from 1977 as the source of Shaffer's Mozart as 'a divinely gifted drunken lout' and of Constance as a woman 'of extraordinary décolleté and fatuous giggle'.

the past, but also as a way of legitimizing the present. And where the ancient past did not offer a direct link with or a legitimization for the present, it often was created. In this context historical myths like the Batavian Revolt or the Donation of Constantine were developed or cultivated.

Another reason for focusing on the history of classical Antiquity is that it offered more artistic freedom than biblical and Christian history. The field of religion was Church territory, where — officially — artists were not allowed to add or change things that did not agree with the text of the Bible or the teachings of the Church. The degree to which this rule was observed changed from time to time and from place to place, but especially since the Council of Trent (1545–1563) it was quite strictly maintained for at least some fifty years.

Yet, even though the history of classical Antiquity constituted a province which to some extent was outside the reach of the Church, there was no absolute freedom there either. Men of the early modern period realized very well that the historians from classical Antiquity had written their works according to certain historical and stylistic conventions. Scholars of the early modern period adopted these conventions and turned them into 'new' standards for writing history. Artists such as playwrights and painters, however, could not simply adopt these conventions. Yet they too strove for 'new' standards, within their own artistic medium. To do so, they also studied examples from classical Antiquity, such as Aristotle's *Poetics* for writing drama, Pliny's account of Greek sculpture and painting in his *Natural History* for the visual arts, Horace's *Ars Poetica* with its famous dictum that painting is like poetry ('ut pictura poesis'), and a host of other writings and surviving works of art. Fascination with and knowledge of classical history grew enormously, and new fields of interest and points of view were opened up. Yet the study of history was never seen as an attempt to reconstruct the past as neutrally, completely and accurately as possible. In some cases ancient history may indeed have been 'reconstructed', yet it was practically always very consciously recreated. It is this process of recreation that forms the topic of this book.

In dealing with the question how scholars, writers and artists recreated ancient history, the contributors of this volume have addressed a number of important, common issues, so as to obtain some unity within a wide range of subjects extending from fifteenth-century Italian painting to the teaching of Greek history in eighteenth-century Germany. All contributors discuss the sources which scholars, writers and artists used, and consider if — and why — they preferred one source over another. This leads to questions such as: did they consult these sources in their original language or in translation? To which extent did they make use of commentaries, explanations, and later adaptations? Were they aware that classical historians and authors like Sallust, Cicero, Livy and Plutarch had not produced 'objective descriptions' but had reworked and manipulated their material? How did they themselves manipulate their sources, and can that be explained in relation to the specific circumstances? Did they perhaps contribute to or consciously create historical myths? What was the audience they were addressing, who were their patrons and what was their influence? What were the literary and artistic conventions they had to respect, and did they really do so? What was their vision of ancient history and what did they want to 'show' with the events they represented and recreated?

Each contributor to this volume has worked with these and similar questions as his or her starting point. Their papers have been arranged in more or less chronological order, which has sometimes been interrupted in order to group together papers which deal with related topics, such as Justus Lipsius as a scholar of ancient history, William Shakespeare as an author of historical drama, or the works of Plutarch as a popular source of ancient history. Together, these papers attest to the general appeal of ancient history in the early modern period, and offer descriptions of the wide range of the ways in which it was studied and recreated.

The volume opens with Anton Boschloo's survey of recommendations and rules for representing ancient history in art treatises of the early modern period. He shows that, even though there were no specific rules for representing scenes from ancient history, the authors of treatises would almost without fail come up with events from Greek or Roman history when it came to giving examples. Obviously, then, this realm of history was considered abundant in deeds and actions that were worth remembering and recreating. To this end, according to Boschloo, 'the representation of history as such was subordinated'. And even though, as time progressed, the demand for historical accuracy in all kinds of details such as costumes and backgrounds grew stronger, painters retained their freedom to adapt history to their artistic ends.

The contribution of Jan L. de Jong focuses on representations of the historical myths which had originated around the life and deeds of Constantine the Great. Various historians of the fifteenth century, however, began to distrust their authenticity, in spite of the claims of the Roman Catholic Church. Against the background of these doubts and the rapid spread of Protestantism, the Pope had some crucial events from the life of the 'first Christian emperor' painted in his audience hall so as to underscore the papal claims of supremacy. According to De Jong, the painters of the Constantine scenes strove to persuade the observers of the truth of the historical myth by representing history 'as it should have been'. Following the ideas voiced by Aristotle in his *Poetics*, they tried to raise the 'particulars' of 'real' history to a 'poetic' level of 'universal truths'.

The paper of Marc Morford also deals with events of obscure authenticity, namely the Batavian revolt. Against the background of the Low Countries' striving for independence from the Habsburg empire, this marginal episode acquired enormous importance. In the *Batavorum cum Romanis bellum* Otto van Veen, following Justus Lipsius, turned it into an important historical event, thus using it as a means to legitimize the political *status quo* of the Twelve Years' Truce between the Netherlands and Spain.

Justus Lipsius also plays an important role in the contributions of Karl Enenkel, Jeanine De Landtsheer and Marc Laureys. This attests to the importance for classical scholarship of Justus Lipsius, who raised the historical discourse of antiquarian studies to a level that had never been reached before. Karl Enenkel, examining Lipsius's first monograph on cultural history — the *Saturnales sermones* — shows how this great humanist disclosed some of the unknown and strange aspects of antique culture, namely the cruel and almost inhuman gladiatorial combats. Thus he created a new notion of Antiquity which was not adapted to contemporary values, but which revealed its alterity. Jeanine De Landtsheer, on the other hand, shows how Lipsius's antiquarian discourse could also be translated into very practical results. Lipsius's study of the work of Polybius was exploited by the Dutch stadholder Maurits van Nassau, who used it as a manual for modern warfare. Marc Laureys studies Lipsius's last extensive monograph on cultural history, the *Admiranda*, and elaborates on its specific function within the context of pilgrims' literature. Wondering what brought about Rome's former 'grandeur', Lipsius presents the Roman empire as an example for the Habsburg empire.

Maria Berbara concentrates on a particular topic: that of human self-sacrifice. In Antiquity sacrificing oneself for the common good was considered one of the highest forms of heroic and virtuous behavior. This view changed, however, in the early Christian centuries, in particular through the influence of St Augustine. The example of Marcus Curtius illustrates how from the fifteenth century onwards opinions on the merit of human self-sacrifice turned positive again. Marcus Curtius was ranged among the exemplary heroes of Antiquity and his self-sacrifice was even paralleled with the sacrifice of Christ. This made him a perfect hero, in both the antique and the Christian sense.

The following papers, by Paul J. Smith, Bart Westerweel, Olga van Marion and Sjaak Onderdelinden, all illustrate Plutarch's impact as a historiographer in the early modern period. Paul Smith discusses how Plutarch's specific way of writing history, interspersed with digressions and biographical details, was taken up and cleverly elaborated upon by Montaigne in his *Essais*. The paper by Bart Westerweel shows how Shakespeare found Plutarch's biographical way of dealing with history very stimulating for his historical plays, even if it did not meet the traditional demands of the genre of drama, as appears from his *Coriolanus*. Olga van Marion deals with efforts to create a 'Plutarchus moralizatus' which would fit in with the moral needs of the developing bourgeois society of the Dutch Republic. Thus J.B. Wellekens, in his *Heroic Epistles*, presents the characters of Octavia and Cleopatra quite differently from how they had originally been sketched by Plutarch. Sjaak Onderdelinden describes how Plutarch's account of Solon and Lycurgus impelled Friedrich Schiller in his lectures to think about cultural progress and social dynamics.

In his paper on Shakespeare's *Julius Caesar* Wilfried Stroh touches on aspects similar to those discussed by Bart Westerweel, but from a different approach. He demonstrates how Shakespeare, in constructing Marc Antony's famous funeral oration, was inspired by Cicero's *Philippica* and used the devices of classical rhetorics. Therefore, according to Stroh, the relevant device is not, as is widely accepted, irony (*ironia*), but the *oratio figurata*.

Arnoud Visser focuses on the Hungarian humanist Johannes Sambucus, showing how he exploited ancient history in his search for morally edifying examples, which he could turn to good use in his emblems. Francesca Terrenato traces the origins of the 'historical myth' of the emperor Hadrian as a practising artist. She demonstrates how antique references to Hadrian's interests in the arts were in the course of time augmented and specified, leading to his inclusion as a practising painter and sculptor in Karel van Mander's *Schilder-boeck* of 1604. Of course this myth did not originate in an inaccurate reading of the antique sources, but it was coined in order to raise the status of the visual arts.

Jan Bloemendal and Alicia Montoya both focus on one of the most prominent and intriguing personalities of ancient history, Julius Caesar, and describe how he was 'recreated' as a dramatic character. Bloemendal discusses a didactic play which Marc-Antoine Muret wrote for the pupils of the Collège de Guyenne. Muret presented Julius Caesar as a wise ruler and a stoic hero: a combination of the 'actual' Julius Caesar and the mythological hero Hercules. Alicia Montoya describes the specific problems that female writers were confronted with in late seventeenth-century France. She demonstrates how Marie-Anne Barbier in her play of 1709 very carefully stuck to the classical sources so as to give it a 'male' character, while at the same time infusing it with typically 'female' elements.

Bettina Noak, on the other hand, concentrates on a Roman hero with a negative reputation, the 'degenerated' nobleman Catiline. Noak reconstructs the political background of the Dutch Republic that may have inspired the Dutch playwright and schoolmaster Lambert van den Bosch in shaping this dramatic character.

The papers collected in this volume offer a wide but far from exhaustive range of examples and strategies of recreating ancient history. They show that it was not considered a 'dead' era which had come to a definite end. Ancient history was, on the contrary, seen as a period which was still teeming with life, with power to absorb and with inspiring examples, and with an aura that still cast its rays over the early modern period. It was an era that did not ask for neutral reconstruction, without personal commitment, but one that stimulated active involvement and creative responses. The papers of this volume testify to this.

THE REPRESENTATION OF HISTORY IN ARTISTIC THEORY IN THE EARLY MODERN PERIOD

Anton Boschloo

Since the Renaissance, subjects from Greek and Roman history have frequently been depicted. Did artists have clear indications about how they should set to work? Did artistic theory in the Renaissance formulate specific conditions concerning the depiction of Greek and Roman history? When we try to answer this question, it quickly becomes clear that the depiction of events from classical Antiquity was part of a much wider field, a field where art achieved its highest aims, the field of *historia*. The concept *historia* encompasses all depictions of narrative events, whether or not they originate in (classical) history, mythology, literature or the Bible. Artistic theory constantly discussed how an artist could develop into an exemplary historical painter, or, in more general terms, how he should represent 'history'. This article will investigate the interpretations of *historia* between the fifteenth and the eighteenth centuries, and what effect they may have had on how the history of Antiquity was represented.

From Alberti to Bellori

In 1435, in his tractate on painting, Leon Battista Alberti was the first person to discuss the *historia* in detail. In the second book, he mentions a number of conditions to which a representation of the deeds of a number of people must conform.[1] When depicting the human figure, the artist must ensure that the correct proportions are used; physical imperfections must be corrected as far as possible.[2] Poses, gestures and movement must all be in agreement with the capacity and function of the person depicted in the action and with his state of mind. For example, in a depiction of the dead Meleager being borne away, the dead weight of the body must be visible in all of the limbs.[3] It was not

---

[1] Alberti, *De pictura*, § 35 ff.
[2] Ibid., § 36; 40.
[3] Ibid., § 37; 42.

only the correct relationship between the limbs of each separate figure that was very important, the relationship of the figures to each other and of the figures to the space around them also had to be correct.[4] The entire representation had to be characterised by harmony, grace and dignity. It had to please the viewer with abundance and variety, for example in the richness of its motifs, but also in the depiction of different ages, facial expressions, poses and types of clothing. Every repetition of pose or gesture was to be avoided. At the same time, however, the artist had to be careful not to be extravagant, which would conflict with the worthiness and elegance of the representation. He should aim for moderation.[5] Thus he should also avoid any excessive movements when depicting his figures.[6] If all these conditions are met, then the result is a *historia* whose convincing presentation of the people involved and their emotions will touch the soul of the viewer, while at the same time be pleasing to look at because of the variety and harmony of composition and colour. Thus both the educated and the illiterate viewer shall be entertained for a longer period of time.[7]

Alberti provides general guidelines for the *historia* in painting, and thus also for the depiction of events from Greek and Roman history, which remained valid for a very long time. The first person to develop his ideas further, but who also interpreted them in his own way, was Leonardo da Vinci. Leonardo, too, wanted to touch the viewer by means of a convincing depiction of emotions. He also wanted abundance and variety ('copia' and 'varietà') to beguile the eye, but he went much further than Alberti. He advised the artist to place opposites that strengthen each other beside each other, thus creating more effect: the beautiful next to the ugly, the large next to the small, the old man next to the young one, the strong next to the weak. In order to be able to give facial expressions that essential variety, the artist must practise by sketching what he sees in the street, just as he must try to master the unprecedented richness of nature by observing and drawing.[8] The variety that must characterise the work of an artist was important to Leonardo because the painter would then be able to successfully challenge the poet-writer: whereas a poet must demand patience from a reader to plumb the subtleties of his story, a painter

---

[4] Ibid., § 39.
[5] Ibid., § 40.
[6] Ibid., § 44.
[7] Ibid., § 40; 41.
[8] Leonardo, *Treatise*, §§ 267-74.

can instantly affect and beguile the viewer with the myriad of motifs, emotions, movements and actions he is able to collect into a single representation.[9] For Leonardo, the strength of painting lies in the fact that it can show all the aspects of an event or action to the viewer at once. This also implies that the artist must aim for maximum conviction so that there can be no misunderstanding about the meaning and scope of the action he is depicting. Just like Alberti, Leonardo was mainly concerned with the persuasiveness of the representation. In order to achieve that persuasiveness, the artist is permitted to make use of every artifice at his disposal, including the introduction of suggestive contrasts, so long as he does not violate nature.

Neither Alberti nor Leonardo posed themselves the question that would concern later writers about art, namely the historical reliability of the painted *historia*, in the sense of a detailed reconstruction of time, place and action. The artist, called a second god ('secondo dio') by Leonardo, had to have higher ambitions. He had to depict an event from the past in such a way that it was no longer bound to time and place, but acquired a more general, exemplary meaning. Leonardo himself visualised his *Battle of Anghiari* in the Palazzo della Signoria in Florence, not as an event from Florentine history that could be accurately identified and localised, but rather as the prototype of a heroic cavalry battle in a timeless environment.[10] Half a century later, however, the freedom of the artist when depicting an event from the past was no longer self-evident. In his *Dialogo della pittura* from 1557, the Venetian Lodovico Dolce formulated his thoughts as follows. The invention of a *historia* by the artist is fed by the material ('la materia') of the story on the one hand, and by his own imagination ('ingegno') on the other. To be completely in control of the material, he must first be familiar with the stories ('istorie') and fables ('favole') of writers and poets. The presentation of the story in a picture is then the fruit of his imagination. This presentation, that is, the representation of the events, should be well organised and appropriate.[11] The artist may not

---

9 For Leonardo's comparison of painting and poetry, see ibid., §§ 20-42.

10 *The Battle of Anghiari*, not completed by Leonardo, is still only known from a few copies. See Heydenreich, *Leonardo da Vinci*, I, 49-54 and II, figs. 58-64.

11 Dolce, *Dialogo*, 171: 'Per quello che s'è detto appare che la invenzione vien da due parti: dalla istoria e dall'ingegno del pittore. Dalla istoria egli ha semplicemente la materia, e dall'ingegno, oltre all'ordine e la convenevolezza, procedono l'attitudini, la varietà e la (per così dire) energia delle figure; ma questa è parte comune col disegno'. For the required familiarity with the 'istorie' and 'favole', see ibid.,170.

be nonchalant about any part of his invention at all. However, just like the poet, he is permitted some freedom, but always within limits.[12] Thus far according to Dolce. The field of tension that will continually appear and reappear in the views of art theoreticians about the *historia* is revealed here, however casually, namely the field of tension between the two extremes of text and artistic invention, of 'materia' and 'ingegno'. To which of the two the author in question attached the most weight depended on his position, background and intentions.

Just how influential considerations other than artistic ones could sometimes be when defining a good *historia* in painting is illustrated by the guidelines of Giovanni Andrea Gilio in his *Dialogo degli errori* [...] *de' pittori* from 1564. Gilio was a cleric and his primary concern was that the stipulations of the Council of Trent concerning religious art be put into practice. In order to promote this, his treatise explains in detail which rules an artist had to follow. Just as Dolce differentiated between 'istorie' and 'favole', Gilio sometimes calls an artist 'puro istorico', sometimes 'puro poeta' and sometimes 'misto', sometimes a historian, sometimes a poet, and sometimes something in between.[13] Religious subjects fell within the scope of the 'pittore istorico' and demanded great discipline from him because he had to stick closely to the available texts when depicting them.[14] Precisely because of this responsible duty, Gilio ranked the 'pittore istorico' above other types of artist. After all, through his pictures he is the one who familiarises the ignorant with biblical history, the events from the lives of Mary, Christ and the saints. He must not permit himself to follow the example of the many who have let their fantasies run wild, they only want to show off their abilities; he must illustrate the pure, simple truth of the story with his brush, just as a historian does with his pen.[15] Even a 'pittore istorico' was permitted a certain amount of freedom in the details, but only those that are irrelevant to the meaning of the story.

---

[12] Ibid., 171: 'E perché abbiamo ristretto il pittore sotto queste leggi, sì dell'ordine come della convenevolezza, non è che alle volte egli, come il poeta, non possa prendersi qualche licenza, ma tale che non trabocchi nel vizio'.

[13] Gilio, *Dialogo*, 15: 'Perché doverebbono sapere che il pittore a le volte è puro istorico, a le volte puro poeta, et a le volte è misto'.

[14] Ibid., 24: 'e molta più considerazione vuole l'istoria che la poesia, perché quella è sciolta et ampia, e questa è ristretta in un termine che a niuno è lecito passarlo'.

[15] Ibid., 25: 'e che non sia meno ubligato a mostrare la pura e semplice verità il pittore col pennello, che si faccia l'istorico con la penna'. Gilio regrets that this so rarely happens: 'Circa l'istorie, pochi sono fedeli e puri demostratori de la verità del soggetto' (ibid.).

His duty was to carefully familiarise himself with the subject of the *historia* to be painted, the time and the place where the action occurred and the people who were involved, and then to produce a considered presentation in which everyone is given his rightful place.[16]

Gilio deals in great detail with the mistakes made by the many painters, first and foremost Michelangelo, who did not stick to the rules for 'pittore istorico'.[17] This strict attitude towards historical painters fits perfectly into the climate of the Counter-Reformation. In the decades following the Council of Trent, other writers, even those who were not representatives of the Church, adopted this attitude. Thus Raffaello Borghini in his *Riposo* from 1584 not only approvingly cited Gilio's differentiation between the 'pittore istorico', the 'pittore poeta' and the 'pittore misto', but even required painters who depicted the inventions of poets, the 'pittore poeta', not to permit themselves too much freedom by adding things.[18] The artists themselves usually had other ideas. Vasari, for example, who was a great admirer of Michelangelo's *Last Judgement*, condemned by Gilio, did not fail to point out the importance of the artist's own powers of invention.[19] As a painter of *historia*, he had of course to obey certain rules and make use of the knowledge of writers and scholars, but that need not impede his creative spirit. A contemporary of Vasari, the sculptor Vincenzo Danti, is of the opinion that the true artist actually manifested himself in what his spirit added to the incompleteness of what exists, as does the poet, but unlike the historian.[20]

---

[16] Ibid., 26: 'Ma prima d'ogni altra cosa si deve informare del soggetto de l'istoria che egli dipingere disegna; dopo del tempo, del luogo, de le persone, e non confondere ignorantemente l'uno con l'altro, ma ordinatamente dare ad ognuno il suo proprio, acciò si servi in ogni cosa il decoro'.

[17] The title of his treatise speaks volumes in this context: *Dialogo nel quale si ragiona degli errori e degli abusi de' pittori circa l'istorie*. The subtitle specifically mentions the *Last Judgement* by Michelangelo.

[18] Borghini, *Il Riposo*, 53-5.

[19] For Vasari's ode to the *Last Judgement* by Michelangelo and his implicit defence of it against criticism, see Vasari, *Le vite*, VII, 209-15.

[20] Danti, *Trattato*, 252-3: 'Perciocché lo imitare et il ritrarre intendo io che abbiano tra loro la differenza che ha la poesia con la storia. L'istoria scrive propriamente le cose come elle sono successe, verbigrazia, descrivendo la vita d'un particolare, la racconta apunto come ell'è stata, e questo è il proprio della storia, dire le cose per apunto come l'ha sentite o vedute. E la poesia non solamente le dice come l'ha viste o sentite, ma le dice come arebbono a essere in tutta perfezzione; e discrivendo essa poesia la vita d'un particolare, la racconta come arebbe avuta a essere, con tutte le virtù e perfezzioni che se l'appartengono', and ibid., 266: 'E per questo si può dire che sia tanto differente il ritrarre all'imitare, quanto è differente lo scrivere istorie dal far poesie, come dissi di sopra; e che tanto più sia nobile e di più considerazione l'artefice

None of these views explicitly discussed the depiction of events from Greek and Roman history. They always spoke of the *historia* in general, and if a certain category was singled out, then it was religious subjects, the field on which all the attention of the spokesmen of the Counter-Reformation was concentrated. If the history of Antiquity is occasionally referred to, then it is never because depiction of it had to conform to specific conditions, but rather because that history formed such a rich source of inspiration for the artist's inventions. That, at least, is the opinion of the Milanese painter-writer Gian Paolo Lomazzo, which he expressed in his *Trattato dell'arte della pittura* from 1584. In this tractate, Lomazzo paid a lot of attention to the question of which type of representation is suited to which location.[21] After all, paintings should not only be in harmony with the function of the space for which they are intended, but also strengthen that function. Lomazzo stated that the reception rooms in the prominent *palazzi* of princes, where the visitor must be impressed by the intrepidity and grandeur of the prince, were eminently suitable for heroic feats of arms from the past. The viewing of the great and honourable deeds of great princes and famous commanders-in-chief would elevate the spirit and evoke a desire for honour and fame.[22] Heroic commanders-in-chief from classical Antiquity were the perfect choice for the protagonists. In addition, Charlemagne and Charles V, whose heroic deeds had given them fame equal to that of the Roman emperors, could also be considered.[23] Suitable subjects included military deliberations, bloody battles, victories, and triumphal processions. It did not matter so much which victory or triumphal procession was chosen.

Lomazzo was concerned with the exemplary, elevating aspect of a battle, sea battle, siege or triumphal procession as such, and not with the depiction of a once-off event (similarly, Leonardo's *Battle of Anghiari*

---

che usa l'imitare, di quello che usa il ritrarre, quanto senza comparazione è più nobile et in maggior grado il poeta che non è l'istorico'.

[21] Lomazzo, *Trattato*, VI, 22-28, 294 ff.

[22] Ibid., VI, 25, 299 "Quali pitture siano proporzionate a palazzi reali, case di principi et altri luochi solari": '[...] in cui riguardando pare che gli animi nostri si sollevino a pensieri e desideri d'onore e di grandezza'.

[23] However, the deeds of the exemplary figures depicted in the rooms of a *palazzo* had to be more or less of the same level; that is, no 'fatti' of a Caesar next to those of a small *condottiere*: 'Perciò che disdirebbe che, per essempio, appresso i fatti di Cesare et altri grandi eroi e capitani si collocassero i fatti di qualche picciolo duca, o conduttier d'essercito' (ibid., VI, 25, 299).

could have taken place anywhere and at any time).[24] In a long series of chapters about the way that battles, sea battles, ambushes, offering scenes, triumphal marches and many other subjects should be painted, he is always describing a prototype,[25] concentrating on the poses, movements and emotions of the (groups of) figures required for the various subjects, and on the desired effects of light and colour. The actual entourage could then be adapted time and again to the historical circumstances of the action to be depicted. This does not mean that Lomazzo did not think that the presentation of the depiction was important, but it was of secondary importance in his instructions to the artist. For example, in his chapter on battle scenes he deals in detail with the differences in army deployment, uniforms, armour, and ways of riding horses between the various peoples, but then concluded that the most important thing was that the soldiers' bodies be well proportioned and muscular, and that they appear large and strong.[26] In his discussion of representations of attacks and sieges he remarked that whatever type of attack the artist wanted to depict, all he had to do was vary the instruments used by the soldiers.[27] The crucial factors were the emotions and movements of the attackers and the attacked, that is what an artist should concentrate on.[28] In order to acquire the necessary information about classical Antiquity and the events of that time he should read the stories ('istorie') and study the classical triumphal arches and other antiquities ('anticaglie') and medals.[29]

---

[24] Lomazzo was probably thinking of this famous cavalry battle when he mentioned Leonardo as the first of the 'primi inventori' in his discussion of perspective in battle scenes. Ibid., VI, 29, 308 ("Composizioni delle guerre e battaglie").

[25] Ibid., VI, 29 ff., p. 306 ff.

[26] Ibid., VI, 29, 306-7 ("Composizioni delle guerre e battaglie").

[27] Ibid., VI, 37, 322 ("Composizione d'assalti"): 'E qualunque sorte d'assalti occorre dipingere, solamente ne gl'instromenti si ha da variare e secondo quelli far che i soldati s'adoprino, come i Greci a Troia per il cavallo ripieno d'uomini armati'.

[28] Ibid., 323: 'Sopra ogni cosa si voglion mostrar i moti de gl'assalitori fieri e degl'assaliti svelti e spediti, mentre che cercano di schermirsi con passo dubbioso et incerto, non altrimenti che Cesare quando fu assalito da Bruto e Cassio, o Gioab all'altare, e Senacherib da' suoi figliuoli proprij inanzi a gl'idoli'.

[29] Lomazzo recommends that the painter read texts to gain knowledge about the way in which the various peoples dressed: 'ancora che il pittore si reggerà però in questa parte dietro la consuetudine delle nazioni del vestire, la quale facilmente s'impara leggendo le istorie' (308). The study of the visible remains of classical Antiquity is discussed in chapter 43, 347 ("Composizione di trionfi"): 'E chi vuole sapere piú accuratamente [sic] di questi trionfi, vegga ne gli archi trionfali e nelle altre anticaglie di Roma, dove vederà la superba forma delle carrette discoperte, e parimente ne' rovesci delle medaglie antiche e de gli instrumenti sopra quali si portavano le armi e i trofei', as Giulio Romano, Rosso, Perino del Vaga, Primaticcio, Cambiaso and Carlo Urbini also did.

In 1587, some years after Lomazzo's dissertation, Giovanni Battista Armenini, an artist of limited talents from Faenza, published *De' veri precetti della pittura* in Ravenna. He, too, was extremely concerned with the question of which types of depictions were suitable for which spaces.[30] Stories with subjects concerning moral virtues belonged in the rooms of powerful and high-ranking people because they teach us to be reasonable, just, courageous and moderate.[31] Numerous examples of such virtues are known from Roman history ('istorie romane') in particular, but illustrious deeds from the family history of the commissioner could also be considered. A combination of both was also highly commendable. Thus Armenini was very impressed with the decoration of a room in the Palazzo Doria in Genoa which has five representations of the most remarkable deeds of great Romans who defended their country, while painted on the walls are twelve heroes from the house of Doria.[32] When selecting a subject, the virtue and dignity ('virtù' and 'dignità') of the various inhabitants of a *palazzo* should be taken into account. For the women's quarters, for example, the stories of famous women, both Greek and Roman, were ideal subjects, whereas in the youths' quarters the stories of famous heroes like Mucius Scaevola, the Horatii, Marcus Curtius and Scipio were suitable because they would inspire youthful hearts to magnificent and honourable deeds.[33] To be able to paint all this well, artists had to keep studying books about Roman history, if not in Latin then in the vernacular. Armenini particularly recommended Plutarch, and then Livy, Appian, Valerius Maximus, Petrarch and Boccaccio. Books about 'istorie romane' were good because they dealt with events that had actually happened and were full of excellent examples worthy of consideration.[34]

---

[30] Armenini, *De' veri precetti*, III, 1 ff. In II, 11, 153 ff., Armenini goes in great detail into the way that a *historia* should generally be painted.

[31] Ibid., III, 8, 199-203. See also III, 10, 212-3: 'Ma i soggetti che ci vanno dentro delle istorie (per quanto io conosco) non mi ci par meglio che di cose appartenenti alle virtù morali, acciò s'impari a esser prudente, giusto, temperato e forte in ogni sua azzione e, nell'essequirle, destrezza'.

[32] Ibid., III, 9, 207.

[33] Ibid., III, 10, 213: 'E dove dimorano i giovani, vi si facciano l'istorie di quei Muzii, di gli Orazii, de' Scipioni e de' Curzii, che ci sono notissime per l'istorie loro; e questi acciò si sveglino in parte e si rimovano da quelle viltà, pigrizie, avarizie et ociosità delle quali il mondo è pieno, et i lor cuori s'infiammino a far cose magnanime e generose'.

[34] Ibid., III, 15, 236: 'E circa alle materie profane, bonissimi sono i libri i quali trattano dell'istorie romane, come di cose che sono vere e piene d'essempi ottimi e profittevoli, e massime quelli che sono descritte da Plutarco; e dietro a questi vi è Tito

The representation of the history of Greek and Roman Antiquity in painting was mainly interpreted by art theoreticians in the fifteenth and sixteenth centuries as a good opportunity to display exalted and elevating actions from the classical past, sometimes in combination with actions from a more recent past, but always with an exemplary function to which the representation of history as such was subordinated. For some time to come, this approach remained characteristic of the opinions about historical painting in art literature. The influential publication by the authoritative Roman art theoretician Giovanni Pietro Bellori, *Le vite de' pittori, scultori e architetti moderni* (Rome: 1672), is a good example of this. Bellori was a very respected antiquarian; he published articles and books about classical statues, paintings, coins, cameos and epigraphs, and about the reliefs on the columns of Trajan and Marcus Aurelius. Among other things, he was Queen Christina of Sweden's antiquarian.[35] However, when he wrote about more or less contemporary paintings with subjects from Roman history in *Le vite*, none of his archaeological knowledge is evident, neither in a critical nor an admiring sense. Questions about the historical accuracy of the events depicted were just not asked. Bellori confined himself to the artistic qualities of such representations, paying particular attention, just like his predecessors, to the depiction of emotions. For him, the persuasiveness of a painting was the most important factor, and that depended in the first instance on a telling depiction of the right emotions, attitudes and movements of the protagonists. Thus would the viewer be convinced of the moral virtues of the classical heroes.

From Félibien to Reynolds

The ideas about the presentation of events from Greek and Roman Antiquity in contemporary painting briefly presented here are not confined to Italian art theory. In the second half of the seventeenth century, French theoreticians began to hold their own in no uncertain terms with their Italian predecessors and contemporaries, and their

---

Livio, Appiano Alessandrino, Valerio Massimo, gli Uomini Illustri del Petrarca, le Donne Illustri del Boccaccio [...]'. Then follows a list of works for studying 'le favole'.

[35] See 'Cronologia della vita e delle opere principali di Giovan Pietro Bellori', in Bellori, *Le vite*, LXI-LXIV.

observations display a similar approach. A case in point is the description of Poussin's *Death of Germanicus* from 1628 in the *Entretiens sur les [...] plus excellens Peintres* (Paris: 1666–1668) by the well-known academic and antiquarian André Félibien. In these *Entretiens*, created in the circles of the Académie Royale de Peinture et de Sculpture, Poussin's famous painting is discussed a number of times, but only in the light of the consummate expression of the main characters' noble feelings of pain.[36] Just like Bellori, who was also an admirer of this painting, Félibien concentrated on the power of the emotions which the artist used to depict the death of Germanicus, without paying any attention to the question of the historical accuracy of the portrayal. What concerned him was making the drama of a 'soggetto tragico' (Bellori) tangible.[37]

Within the academic climate of the time, however, within which Félibien's *Entretiens* also saw the light, opinions were developing that bear witness to a changing attitude towards the *historia* in painting. These new opinions can be clearly traced in the official discussions carried on at the Académie about works of art from the royal collection, and were reflected in the *Conférences* by that selfsame Félibien. As had previously happened in Italy, here, too, the freedom of the artist in his interpretation of an event from the past was coming under discussion. Characteristic of this are the critical comments — despite all the appreciation — about Poussin's *The Gathering of the Manna* in the sixth *Conférence* (1667).[38] Poussin had differentiated different stages in the reactions of the Israelites to the wonderful rain of manna, and expressed them in a wide variety of actions and emotions (surprise, thankfulness, eagerness and aggression). He had permitted himself as a painter to collect a number of successive moments from the story into one picture, thus impressing the viewer as far as possible with the range of the event. In fact, Poussin was the latest in a long tradition

---

[36] Félibien, *Entretiens*, VIII, 82: 'Peut-on concevoir une idée plus belle et plus noble de la mort d'un grand Prince, que l'idée qu'il doit avoir eûë de la mort de Germanicus, lorsqu'il l'a representé dans son lit, environné de sa femme affligée, de ses enfans éplorez, et de ses amis dans une profonde tristesse?' Quoted from the facsimile of the 1725 edition in Pace, *Félibien's Life*, 109 ff. See further Félibien, *Entretiens*, VIII, 18 and Pace, *Félibien's Life*, 153-4, note 18.2.

[37] Bellori, *Le vite*, 427: 'ed egli [Poussin] si elesse di rappresentare la morte di Germanico, soggetto tragico, con forza di affetto e di colorito il piú eccellente, come riporteremo nel fine'.

[38] Félibien, *Conférences*, VI, 58-82. For the criticism see ibid., 78-9. Poussin's painting is in the Louvre. See Blunt, *Poussin*, cat. no 21.

within painting, even though his depiction of the differences in reactions and emotions is extremely suggestive and succinct. Now, however, critics within the Académie were demanding that the artist respect the unity of time, place and action. The reactions of those present to the finding of the manna should only be depicted in their mutual simultaneity, because otherwise the painter was violating reality.[39]

Indicative of the strict opinions of some academics is that even Poussin, who was highly regarded by them, was posthumously called to order. In the discussion of his work, the dilemma arose of the degree to which one painting can tell a story, illustrate an event, and how much space should be assigned to the imagination and fantasy of the artist. The rather dogmatic attitude in the Académie Royale towards the duty of the (historical) painter laid a number of restrictions on painting which involuntarily recall Gilio's strict rules of a century earlier. The major difference is that whereas Gilio formulated his rules as the spokesperson of the church and clergy, in the Académie it was representatives of painting itself who led the discussions. The paintings discussed in the Académie were usually religious representations, but the criticism put forward could also be applied to the *historia* in general and thus also to the depiction of events from Greek and Roman history.

Academic criticism in France of the excessive freedoms of the historical painter was not without effect. Once included in the extensive arsenal of the now authoritative French art theory, during the later seventeenth and eighteenth centuries it permeated thinking about art and the relationship between text and image, between story and representation. This is also true for Dutch art literature, on the development of which French theoreticians had great influence. Representative of this development is the *Groot Schilderboek* by Gerard de Lairesse

---

[39] The anonymous critic pointed out that the manna had fallen during the night and had been found by the Israelites in the morning, whereas Poussin made it seem as if the manna had fallen during the day in the presence of the Israelites. Further, the urgent need for food and the extreme misery, depicted by Poussin in the woman and child, was completely without foundation, given that the worst hunger had already been stilled by the quails which had covered the camp the night before (*Exodus* 16: 11-5). (Félibien, *Conférences*, VI, 78). Le Brun discusses this comment at length, with the starting point being 'qu'il n'en est pas de la Peinture comme de l'Histoire', that is, that the painter sometimes has to summarise 'beaucoup d'incidens qui ayent précedé' in order to clearly depict the subject he wants to paint (ibid., 79 ff.).

from 1707. In Chapter 3 of Book II, in which great attention is paid to the 'ordonnance of Histories', the author advises the painter of a historical piece to first make a sketch and then 'de beste en nauwkeurigste schryver over die zaak opmerkelyk [te] lezen' ('to carefully read the best and most accurate writer about the event') and then to return to the drawing and to pay attention to the country in which the event took place, the time of the year and of the day, the environment — inside or outside, rich or poor — and the quality and dignity of the people.[40] To gain sufficient knowledge of all of this, the artist must read a lot and have a good supply of books. If he doesn't know enough about something, he must search out information. De Lairesse himself assisted the artist with regard to the depiction of Greek and Roman history by providing a large amount of information about 'Roman Laurel Wreaths' and 'Honour Symbols', 'Roman Triumphs and Triumphal Pageantry', 'Greek Games', 'War Clothing and Weaponry' of the Greeks and Romans, and 'Trophies and Escutcheons'.[41] Later on, when he describes the various types of rooms and the decoration suitable to each, he directs the painter — not the first to do so — to visual examples for the reproduction of clothing and weaponry 'gelyk men in de prenten der Kolom van Trajanus en in andere overblijfselen der Oudheid vind' ('like those found in the prints of Trajan's Column and in other remains of Antiquity').[42] The last chapter in Book II demonstrates that De Lairesse could at times adopt a pronounced academic standpoint: 'Noodzaakelyke Waarnemingen in het beschilderen der Zaalen, Gaanderyen, en andere plaatsen, alwaar men gezint is een Geschiedenis in verscheidene Stukken te vervolgen' ('Essential Observations when painting the Chambers, Galleries and other places where one intends to pursue a History in various Parts'). In this chapter, he exhorts the artist to bear the passage of time in mind when depicting a series of events involving one person: the artist must show the changes in the age of the protagonist involved in the story, because the deeds of people like Romulus, Caesar, Scipio or Alexander took place over a long sequence of years.[43]

De Lairesse pointed out many mistakes in depictions of the 'Histo-

---

[40] Lairesse, *Groot Schilderboek*, vol 1, II, 3, 47 ff. ("Het Ordineeren der Geschiedenissen"). He expands on this elsewhere: III, 1, 167 ff. ("Onderscheid tusschen 't Antiek en 't Modern").

[41] Ibid., vol 2, XI, 4-8.

[42] Ibid., vol 2, VIII, 12, 116.

[43] Ibid., vol 1, II, 21, 160-1.

ries of Antiquity'. Not only had he seen a Queen Sophonisba 'dressed in modern clothing' in 'a room papered with gold leather', but — even worse — a Dido in an interior with a map in the background 'zynde de nieuwe vergrooting van Amsterdam, die men kan zien dat by Allard op den Dam gedrukt is' ('of the new enlargement of Amsterdam, which you can see has been printed by Allard op den Dam').[44] Dutch painting of the seventeenth century provided many examples of such freedoms in the interpretation of classical subjects, and that De Lairesse with his classical orientation was offended by them is not surprising. However, his criticism also applied to less visible transgressions of the rules of historical veracity. In a list of 'mishits' (cf. Gilio's 'errori') in the depictions of battle dress and weaponry, he pointed out both an Achilles with a Roman helmet and an Aeneas with a Greek helmet.[45] And in a print based on the above-mentioned *Death of Germanicus* by Poussin, he was surprised by the presence of Greek and Roman morions.[46] Forty years earlier, this criticism did not occur to Bellori and Félibien.

Despite the importance of knowing about the clothing, weaponry, objects, buildings, etc. in Antiquity to be able to accurately depict events from Greek and Roman history, the main thing in the eighteenth century remained the ability of the artist to present the essence of the deed and its implications to the viewer in a penetrating manner and in magnificent style. Historical reliability continued to play second fiddle to persuasiveness, even in academic circles. This is again stated very explicitly in the art theoretical views of Sir Joshua Reynolds,

---

[44] Ibid., vol 1, 196-7.

[45] See vol 2, XI, 7, 331 ff.: *Van de Krygskleederen en Wapenrustingen der byzondere Volkeren, doch voornamentlyk van die der Grieken en Romeinen.* Lairesse observed the Achilles with a Roman helmet in a print by Testa, in which Achilles is dragging the body of Hector around the walls of Troy. Aeneas with a Greek helmet was one of Lairesse's own youthful mistakes in a representation of Aeneas being given weapons by Venus (ibid., 332). Lairesse had earlier admitted having made mistakes himself: 'Niet dat ik door anderer Meesters misslagen op te haalen de myne zoek te verschoonen: geensins. Ik heb myne gebreken zo wel gehad, en misschien veel arger, als een ander: want ik weet, dat ik, zelfs in myn besten tyd, eenige groote misslagen begaan heb, die my tegenwoordig moeijen, en welke ik niet zoude durven verhaalen, alhoewel ik doorgaans in dit Werk deze en geene aantoon' (ibid.).

[46] Ibid., 332. Lairesse parries possible criticism of his remarks about such a great artist as follows: 'Zommige zullen mogelyk zeggen, dat wy zulke beroemde Meesters ongelyk doen wanneer men hunne konst zo naauwkeurig onderzoekt. Doch men moet weeten, dat de meening niet anders is als om zich daar aan te spiegelen, en uit eens anders misslagen te leeren d'onze te verbeteren'.

whose *Discourses* (1769–1790) may be regarded as authoritative for the way that art was regarded in the art academies in the second half of the eighteenth century. Some passages from the fourth *Discourse* (1771), as well as others given at the prize-giving ceremony at the Royal Academy in London, clearly illustrate Reynolds's standpoint. In this *Discourse*, Reynolds deals with the concept of invention, as well as the duty of the historical painter. First, the artist should choose subjects that are in the public interest and will affect people[47] — top of the list are subjects like 'the great events of Greek and Roman fable and history'. Whenever these great events are related, as with 'the capital subjects of scripture history', every person conjures up a picture in his mind of the event and the expressions of the persons involved in it. The ability of the artist to render that mental picture onto canvas is, according to Reynolds, what we call invention. In that image, elements such as clothing, furniture, and situation are less important, and the artist must ensure that they do not distract the attention.[48] In his plea for a historical art characterised by grandeur, by magnificent style, Reynolds went to an extreme because he thought that, where necessary, the artist should sacrifice historical reliability to that higher ideal:

> But it is not enough in Invention that the Artist should restrain and keep under all the inferior parts of his subject; he must sometimes deviate from vulgar and strict historical truth, in pursuing the grandeur of his design.[49]

As an example, he refers to Raphael, who gave the apostles noble and worthy appearances in his famous cartoons, even though the Bible and other sources indicate that this was actually sometimes very different. Famous men from Antiquity should be dealt with in just the same way by artists.[50] More than three centuries earlier, Alberti had exhorted the painter to abandon or disguise the ugly;[51] Reynolds goes even

---

[47] Reynolds, *Discourses*, 57.

[48] Ibid., 58.

[49] Ibid., 59.

[50] Ibid., 60: 'Alexander is said to have been of a low stature; a Painter ought not so to represent him. Agesilaus was low, lame, and of a mean appearance: none of these defects ought to appear in a piece of which he is the hero'.

[51] Alberti, *De pictura*, § 40. Alberti points approvingly at those painters and sculptors who do not depict Pericles with an uncovered head, but rather with a helmet because he was said to have had a long, ugly head. He also recalls how Plutarch relates the habit of painters in Antiquity when painting kings with a physical defect not to ignore the defect, but to correct it as far as possible while maintaining the resemblance.

further by explicitly stating that the artist must sometimes depart from unattractive historical truth. He also explains why he thinks that an artist must do this. Unlike the poet and the historian, a painter cannot dwell on his heroes; he cannot relate that they sometimes had unpretentious appearances, but did great deeds and had noble characters. The artist has to show everything at once:

> He has but one sentence to utter, but one moment to exhibit. He cannot, like the poet or historian, expatiate, and impress the mind with great veneration for the character of the hero or saint he represents, though he lets us know at the same time, that the saint was deformed, or the hero lame.[52]

The artist can only suggest nobility of spirit by its external manifestation: 'He cannot make his hero talk like a great man, he must make him look like one'. In so doing, he is not actually distorting the truth, on the contrary, he is confronting the viewer with a higher truth by rightly making use of poetic license.[53]

The discussion above deals very generally with the opinions about the *historia* in art as developed in art theory from the middle of the fifteenth until deep in the eighteenth century. Greek and Roman history is discussed in various ways, but not because different demands should be made on depicting it than, for example, for representations of events from more modern history. The attention to the history of Antiquity is more a result of the fact that during the Renaissance, it came to form one of the most important thematic fields for the visual arts and from the conclusion that it contained ideal deeds and events that could inspire virtue. The ideas about the *historia* during this long stretch of time were characterised by a large degree of continuity. Most of the authors were primarily concerned with the persuasiveness of the representations, which had to be based on a succinct presentation of the crux of the story. To achieve this, the artist had to continually strive to select the most significant events from the story and to convey the related emotions in all their intensity to the viewer. Only twice in all that time was the importance of historical reliability and accuracy specifically dealt with, in the context of the Council of Trent and in that of the Académie Royale in Paris. At the former, opinions were almost entirely confined to religious art; at the latter

---

[52] Reynolds, *Discourses*, 60.
[53] Ibid.: 'All this is not falsifying any fact; it is taking an allowed poetical license'.

they concerned *historia* in general, even though the discussions in the French academy were mainly concerned with paintings of religious subjects.

Theory and practice: academy drawings

How do the views of the theoreticians relate to actual art? The precepts of Gilio and his like certainly affected the development of religious art, but very indirectly and circuitously. He himself was too far removed from actual art practice to be paid much attention by artists. In the Académie Royale — and other art academies — it was a different matter. There, artistic theory and actual art naturally went hand in hand. The combination of the two, regarded as essential for the development of a young artist, was in fact one of the raisons d'être of the academies. Theoretical education was heavily promoted from above in the Académie Royale so that with its help artists would be able to develop their art in the desired direction. The Paris academy and other academies are thus ideal material for research into the degree to which the guidelines developed during theoretical discussions for the depiction of an event from the past were observed by young artists. More than anything else, the drawings produced by the students for the annual drawing competitions in the academies should provide insights. Such *concorsi* were documented in the Accademia di San Luca in Rome from as early as 1663. Usually, not only the winning drawings have been preserved, but also the sometimes very detailed descriptions of the subjects to be depicted. Below, attention will be paid to a number of these drawings in the Accademia di San Luca, the authoritative art academy in Italy in the seventeenth and eighteenth centuries, the academy which stood model for the founding of the Paris Académie Royale de Peinture et de Sculpture. This was also the academy where Bellori aired his art theoretical views.

Once a year, the Accademia di San Luca chose subjects for the students to depict in mutual competition, one for each of the three classes of painting and sculpture. Several entries from each class could be awarded prizes, and they subsequently became the property of the academy. A jury made the decision and the winners were honoured in a solemn session of the academy, lustre being added by a high-flown speech. The first time that not only the description of the subject from classical history but also some of the drawings depicting it were preserved was after the 1677 competition.[54] The subject for the painting was *Alexander the Great cuts the Gordian knot*. After a short description of the event to be depicted, the prospective participants were told that they were to depict Alexander surrounded by Macedonians in Greek armour opposite the Phrygians in Trojan costume. The wagon to which the yoke was tied with the famous knot had to be a simple one, 'because King Gordius was called to the throne from the plough'. The artists do not appear to have been unduly bothered by the details of Greek or Trojan equipment in their entries, but they have obeyed the injunction that the wagon must 'not be rich nor of gold'. For the rest, the two surviving prize-winning drawings differ greatly from each other [figs. 1 and 2].[55]

The next time that a subject from classical history was chosen was 1682. The first class had to draw *The Meeting between Alexander the Great and the Mayor of Susa*, the second class *Polystratus finds the dying King Darius*. The task for the third class was the copying of classical reliefs. The copying of reliefs or statues from classical Antiquity appears to have been a regular part of the *concorsi*, reserved for the third class. The subjects this time were very summarily indicated without any tips for entourage or how the representations should be worked out,[56] which makes the marked similarities between some of the representations all the more striking. This is particularly true of the entries from the second class, whose subject was *Polystratus finds the dying King Darius*. Three of the drawings show such remarkable similarities in their presentation of the event that it is hard to imagine that the artists worked independently of each other [figs. 3 and 4]. However, strict supervision ensured that this was the case. It is possible that strong image types were developed in the academy for certain actions and motifs and the up-and-coming artists automatically fell back on them, thus unintentionally creating similar results. What is more probable, however, is that the three drawings all have a common prototype.

----

[54] For detailed information about the subjects, the participants and the prize-winning drawings, with illustrations, see Cipriani – Valeriani, *I disegni di figura*, I-III.

[55] Ibid., I, 63-6, figs. A.37-38. The instruction to the participants that follows the description of the subject is: 'Si potranno fingere intorno ad Alessandro i suoi Macedoni armati all'uso greco, allegri per la felicità del Re loro et dall'altra parte i Frigii in atto di maraviglia vedendo sciorre il fatal nodo, vestiti nel loro habito troiano. Il carro non sarà né ricco, né d'oro; poiché Gordio dall'aratro fu assunto al regno' (63).

[56] Ibid., 99-107, figs. A.67-75.

A similar relationship between the structure and presentation in the depictions can be found in the two drawings of *Hannibal crossing the Alps* which won the prizes for the first class in 1683, even though the specification of the subject was very summary: 'draw how Hannibal, the Carthaginian, crossed the Alps with his army to enter Italy' [figs. 5 and 6]. The drawings for the subject *Roman soldiers kill Archimedes while he is writing* which won the prizes in the second class, on the other hand, once again differ dramatically from each other.[57] In all four preserved drawings, the scene is portrayed against a background of classical columns and arches, but each of them has chosen a different solution for the ordonnance and attitudes of the figures. On the other hand, the weaponry of the Roman soldiers in all the drawings conforms to a set standard. The students have undoubtedly learned how to do weaponry from copying Roman reliefs, a set part of the curriculum and of the competitions — as noted above, it appeared regularly as the task for the third class.

What the young artists at the academy learnt about depicting 'historical' events thus appears to have corresponded closely to what was being formulated in the field of art theory: pursuit of an exemplary portrayal of a certain action with at the forefront a convincing interpretation of the reactions and emotions of the protagonists. Just how exemplary the portrayal was depended on the control and application of tried and trusted formulas for the ordonnance and scene-setting of groups of figures in certain situations, for example a (dramatic) meeting, a confrontation, an attack, etc., and for the expression of the required emotions using poses and gestures. Motifs and attributes worked out in more detail could then refer to a specific event from the past. In the same way, Lomazzo gave very general instructions about how the artist should set to work on the depiction of, for example, the siege of a city, with all its associated confusion, emotions, poses and gestures; then the representation could be further embellished in accordance with the historical event in question. That the academy students

---

[57] Ibid., 109-17, figs. A.79-80 (*Hannibal crossing the Alps*), A.81-2, A.84 and A.86 (*Roman soldiers kill Archimedes while he is writing*). That the artists did indeed sometimes study the classical texts as they had been advised is demonstrated by one of the two depictions of *Hannibal crossing the Alps*, drawn by Francesco Boccaccini (A.79). In the background, men can be seen stoking a fire; this is consistent with the description by Livy of how soldiers when quarrying stone first made a fire and then poured vinegar on the hot stone to soften it (Livy, *Ab urbe condita*, XXI, 37). My thanks to Jan de Jong for pointing out this reference to me.

were trained to use standard scenes for the depiction of certain actions may be assumed from the repeated similarities in the visual interpretations of the subjects chosen for the *concorsi*. In 1704, for example, when the first class had to draw *Romulus killing King Amulius*, the majority of the entries use the same composition for the picture: in the middle, and slightly in the background, Romulus is holding King Amulius fast and has his dagger raised; the space in front of the throne is open in front and to the left and right of the middle are groups of fiercely fighting figures; the throne itself, raised, with a few steps and emphasised by a baldachin or heavy curtains, is placed against a background of monumental, classical architecture [figs. 7 and 8].[58] The prize-winning drawings from the second class, whose subject was *Romulus and Remus chase away the cattle thieves*, are remarkable in that the pose of one of the brothers, the one shaking his stick at the thieves, is always more or less the same, despite slight differences in the placement of the figure in the space.[59] There are also strong affinities in the construction and execution of the compositions between the drawings of *The Rape of the Sabine Women* and *The Building of Rome* from 1705, as well as in some of the entries for the 1706 competition, with the subjects *The Sabine Women among the fighting Romans and Sabines* and *Tarpeia's Punishment*.[60]

The general similarities in the presentation of certain subjects may be the result of a common training with clear guidelines. Sometimes, however, as we have seen, the points of similarity between two entries are so striking that there must be a different explanation. This is also the case with the interpretations of the subject chosen for the first class in the *concorso* of 1707, the *Battle between the Horatii and the Curiatii*. The assignment was to depict the climax of the fight between the three young warriors representing the two armies, as described by Livy.[61] Although the six preserved entries are comparable in various respects, two drawings, by Masucci and Calandrucci, are extremely closely related to each other [figs. 9 and 10].[62] To the left, a commander on horseback depicted at an angle from behind, and accompanied by a

---

[58] Ibid., II, 41-54, figs. A.157, 159, 161-3.

[59] Ibid., figs. A.166-9.

[60] Ibid., 55-69, figs. A.176-80 (*The Rape of the Sabine Women*); figs. A.181-3 (*The Building of Rome*); and 71-86, figs. A.188-9, 191-4 (*The Sabine Women among the Fighting Romans and Sabines*); figs. A.195, 197-9 (*Tarpeia's Punishment*).

[61] Ibid., 87-102, figs. A.204, 206-7, 209, 211-2.

[62] Agostino Masucci: pencil and red chalk, 520 x 760 mm, Accademia di San Luca (fig. A.204); Giovanni Battista Calandrucci: red chalk, 510 x 750 mm, Accademia di San Luca (fig. A.209).

young shield bearer, draws the gaze towards six fighting men in the middle. Four of them are shown standing, in a complicated but nonetheless orderly combination of various battle poses; in addition, a half-prone warrior is trying to defend himself from the violence of his attacker. Further to the right, another mounted commander with a shield bearer, once again on a slightly raised part of the terrain, rounds off the picture. The two armies are shown in the background as a cordon of standing soldiers with helmets, lances and shields, with in the middle two army commanders on horseback with their swords drawn, flanked by standards and trophies. Assuming that the drawings were created independently of each other, here, too, the unavoidable conclusion is that they both draw on the same prototype. This is exactly what the organisers of the *concorso* wanted to avoid. Apparently aware of the tendency of the participants in the competition to lean on an authoritative example, they explicitly stated that it was not permitted to imitate the composition and poses of the fresco with the same subject by Giuseppe Cesari in one of the rooms on the Capitol.[63] Remarkably, precisely this fresco seems to have nevertheless been chosen by the two winning artists, and the one who kept most closely to Cesari's fresco, Agostino Masucci, was awarded first prize.[64]

The subjects from Roman history chosen for the various *concorsi* were very variable in nature. Usually, they were subjects from the permanent repertoire of the visual arts, but events which had seldom or never before been depicted were also chosen. This meant that the participants in the competition were not always able to orientate themselves with an authoritative example. Sometimes the subject itself was rather obscure, for example in 1708, when events from the time of the

---

[63] The directions for the participants were as follows: 'Si rappresenti dunque i due eserciti Romano ed Albano, l'uno incontro l'altro schierati e nell'amplo spazio divisorio s'esprima i sei giovani eletti alla crudel tenzone che stiano nell'atto piú fiero dell'orribil zuffa, con avvertenza precisa di non immitare questa medesima istoria con le attioni e le dispositioni fatte dal cav. Giuseppe Cesari d'Arpino e depinte in una delle sale del Campidoglio perché non saranno in conto alcuno ricevute né approvate, ma in tutto e per tutto dovrà farsi nuova inventione da potervisi riconoscere una total diversità et osservanza di ciò che ne dice Tito Livio nella prima deca della sua istoria al Primo Libro' (ibid., 89).

[64] Cesari's fresco, which depicts the battle between the last two of the three Horatii and Curiatii, is in the Sala Grande of the Palazzo dei Conservatori. Pagani M., *Dialogo della Vigilanza* [...] (Rome: 1623), gives a very favourable description of Cesari's frescoes in the Palazzo dei Conservatori. He particularly praises the precision with which Cesari follows Livy's text, unlike others who just fantasised something themselves. See Waźbiński, Z., *Il cavaliere d'Arpino*, 349-53.

third and fourth Roman kings were chosen, for which there was no tradition at all.[65]

Sometimes it was not the subject itself that was unusual, but rather the moment to be portrayed. This was the case, for example, in the *concorso* of 1707, already discussed above. The organisers clearly wanted a subject for the second class that was related to that for the first class, and chose the next moment from the fight between the Horatii and the Curiatii — the heroic actions of the last of the three Horatii, who had to tackle three wounded Curiatii, and succeeded in killing his three opponents in turn. The participants were told exactly how they were to depict this battle. From a high perspective, they had to depict the two dead Horatii between the two armies in the background 'con tratti leggeri'; before that, they had to show in three different plans how the last of the Horatii kills the first, the second and then the third of the Curatii, emerging as the sole victor of the confrontation.[66] This was an almost impossible task for the artists; not only did they have to draw three consecutive deeds by one and the same person, difficult enough at the best of times, but also deeds which were virtually identical to each other so that it was almost impossible to avoid a certain monotony in the representations. The only prize-winning entry to be preserved shows that the young artist, Alessandro Discenet, chose his own solution which differed somewhat from the rather complicated task.[67]

The two moments from the fight between the Horatii and the Curiatii chosen as subjects for the first and second classes in the 1707 competition appear to have been part of a long-term project. The subjects set for the competitions from 1704 on often included events chosen to illustrate successive different phases from early Roman history: *Romulus killing King Amulius* and *Romulus and Remus chase away the Cattle Thieves* (1704), the *Rape of the Sabine Women* and *The Building of Rome* (1705), the *Sabine Women among the fighting Romans and Sabines* and *Tarpeia's Punishment* (1706), two moments from the *Battle between the Horatii and the Curiatii* (1707), the *Punishment of Mettius Fufetius* and *An Eagle flies away with the Helmet of Lucumo (Tarquinius Priscus), son of Demeratus of Corinth* (1708).

---

[65] Ibid., 103-18. The subjects for the first class were: *The punishment of Mettius Fufetius* (figs. A.218-9, 221, 223, 225-6), and for the second class: *An Eagle flies away with the Helmet of Lucumo (Tarquinius Priscus), son of Demeratus of Corinth* (figs. A.227-8, 230).

[66] For the detailed description of the subject to be portrayed, see ibid., 89.

[67] Ibid., fig. A.213.

That it was indeed the intention of the organisers of the *concorsi* to pass the events of early Roman history in review in the wake of Livy is also demonstrated by the formulation of the last task. The description of the task begins as follows: 'The events from Roman history, already depicted up to the deeds between the Horatii and the Curiatii, shall now be continued by [...]', followed by an explanation of the battle between Rome and Alba Longa, as described in Livy, culminating in the title of the subject to be portrayed, the punishment of Mettius Fufetius by Tullus Hostilius, the third king of Rome. The explanation accompanying the task for the second class first tells how things were going for King Tullus Hostilius before the event to be depicted from the reign of the fourth king of Rome, Ancus Marcius, was presented.[68] Finally, in the 1709 *concorsi*, the seventh and last king of Rome, Tarquinius Superbus, takes centre stage after a short description of his two predecessors, Tarquinius Priscus and Servius Tullius.[69]

After six years (1704–1709) when events from the times of the Roman kings were dealt with in chronological order, the years 1710 and 1711 covered more independent subjects from later Roman history, while in 1716 the theme of the classical triumphal march was chosen. For several years after that, mainly biblical subjects were set. The classical theme only reappeared among the subjects for the *concorsi* in 1768; however, it was no longer the history of Rome by Livy that was central, but individual subjects instead. The extensive descriptions which provided an explanation of the subjects in the early years of the eighteenth century were also dispensed with. This probably did not make all that much difference to the artists who participated in the competitions, however, because the concrete directions concerning the way in which the subjects were to be depicted were extremely summary, even in the early descriptions. These directions were confined to a short description of the actions of the main figures and the related emotions, sometimes with the addition of 'as described by Livy in the first decade of his first book', or with the reference 'Iliad, book 18'. Only by exception was any attention paid to how the action should be staged, and the same was true for the minor figures and the entourage.

The young artists in the academy, who had to demonstrate their competence in depicting subjects from Greek and Roman history, were

---

[68] Ibid., 105.
[69] Ibid., 119-27, figs. A.236-9, 241-2.

expected to produce a meaningful presentation of an event from an impressive past, usually characterised by drama and heroism, by means of a convincing portrayal of the people involved in their relationship to each other, something which was also considered important in the theoretical views. The setting of the representation had to be fitting, which meant that the clothing and armour of the protagonists and the entourage had to match the picture that had developed of the Roman world. This picture was strongly influenced by the tangible remains of classical Antiquity, buildings, statues, reliefs, coins and medals, and later also paintings. Artists who had studied these objects would effortlessly be able to create convincing evocations of that heroic world in their representations. This was why Lomazzo recommended that painters study the triumphal arches and antiquities of Rome, as well as Roman coins and medals. Vasari even called *The Battle of Constantine* by Giulio Romano a 'shining example [...] for anyone who after him wants to paint such battles', because this fresco bears witness to the great knowledge of the painter: 'He had learned so much from the ancient columns of Trajan and Marcus Aurelius in Rome, he learned a lot about what the soldiers wore, their armour, standards, bastions, city walls, battering rams and all kinds of implements of war'.[70] If artists were not able to study the remains of Antiquity in Italy themselves, then they could also make very profitable use of prints to develop the essential knowledge of this field. Hence the remark by De Lairesse in his description of clothing and weaponry in a representation of Horatius killing his sister: 'just as is found in the prints of Trajan's column and in other remains from Antiquity'. Whether the artists really did delve into books by Plutarch, Livy and other classical authors in order to gain better insight into the 'istorie romane', as Armenini recommends and which the organisers of the *concorsi* clearly expected, is certainly questionable. Their artistic ability was sufficiently developed by the study of the visual traditions of Antiquity — or by images inspired by it — to be able to satisfy the expectations of their principals in full. However, some artists were certainly aware of the works of different classical authors — driven by the old ambition to be considered on an equal footing with educated scholars, writers and poets.

---

[70] Vasari, *Le vite*, V, 529-30.

Even when a growing interest in archaeology in the second half of the eighteenth century led to an increasingly critical search for the 'true face' of Antiquity, the freedom of the artist when representing history remained intact. More than ever before, the artist was expected to make the great events of history tangible to such a degree that they would touch the viewer deeply and elevate his spirit. In France in 1754, La Font de Saint-Yenne made a plea for paintings with classical themes which could form 'une école des moeurs'. He absolutely did not mean mythological representations, which he regarded as immoral, but rather events from Greek and Roman history, events which illustrated 'the virtuous and heroic actions of great men, exemplars of humanity, generosity, grandeur, courage, disdain for danger and even for life itself, of passionate zeal for the honour and safety of the country'.[71] It was a plea with a long history. After all, had Armenini not written as early as 1587 that paintings of impressive events from the past in the large halls of *palazzi* should elevate the viewer, and events from Roman history were ideal subjects because of their 'virtù morali'? Armenini's 'virtù morali' and La Font de Saint-Yenne's 'école des moeurs', that was what the representation of Greek and Roman history was all about. If the historical painter could emphasise the moral qualities with a maximum of eloquence, he was assured of success. This was also true of the most celebrated historical painter of the late eighteenth century, Jacques-Louis David, despite the distance he put between himself and current opinions about the presentation of *historia* from classical Antiquity. When he exhibited his *Oath of the Horatii* in 1785, the painting evoked all sorts of questions among antiquarians about the historical reliability of this event and about various details in the portrayal and in the setting of the representation. However, these critical noises were completely swamped by the wave of approval that met the *Oath of the Horatii*, and which turned it into one of the most admired paintings during the French Revolution.[72] Once again, poetic freedom had triumphed over historical reliability. That this could happen is a direct result of the power of conviction of the artist's creativity.

---

[71] Quoted in Honour, *Neo-classicism*, 44.

[72] See Haskell, *History and its Images*, 395-7. For an analysis of David's break with tradition and the vehement and often contradictory reactions evoked by his *Oath of the Horatii*, see Crow, *The Oath of the Horatii*, 424 ff.

Selective bibliography

ALBERTI L.B., *De pictura*, ed. C. Grayson, *On Painting and on Sculpture. The Latin Texts of "De pictura" and "De statua"* (London: 1972)

ARMENINI G.B., *De' veri precetti della pittura* [Ravenna: 1587], ed. M. Gorreri – E. Castelnuovo (Turin: 1988)

BELLORI G.P., *Le vite de' pittori, scultori e architetti moderni* [Rome: 1672], ed. E. Borea – G. Previtali (Turin: 1976)

BLUNT A., *The Paintings of Nicholas Poussin. A Critical Catalogue* (London: 1966)

BORGHINI R., *Il riposo* [Florence: 1584], ed. M. Rosci, 2 vols (Milan: 1967)

CIPRIANI A. – VALERIANI E., *I disegni di figura nell'Archivio Storico dell'Accademia di San Luca*, 3 vols (Rome: 1988–1991)

CROW T., "*The Oath of the Horatii* in 1785. Painting and pre-Revolutionary radicalism in France", *Art History* 1 (1978) 424-71

DANTI V., *Il primo libro del trattato delle perfette proporzioni* [Florence: 1567], in *Trattati d'arte del Cinquecento fra Manierismo e Controriforma*, ed. P. Barocchi, 3 vols (Bari: 1960–1962) I, 207-69

DOLCE L., *Dialogo della pittura* [Venice: 1557], in *Trattati d'arte del Cinquecento fra Manierismo e Controriforma*, ed. P. Barocchi, 3 vols (Bari: 1960–1962) I, 141-206

FÉLIBIEN A., *Conférences de l'Académie Royale* [Paris: 1669] (London: 1705)

GILIO G.A., *Dialogo [...] degli errori e degli abusi de' pittori* [Camerino: 1564], in *Trattati d'arte del Cinquecento fra Manierismo e Controriforma*, ed. P. Barocchi, 3 vols (Bari: 1960–1962) II, 1-115

HASKELL F., *History and its Images. Art and the Interpretation of the Past* (New Haven–London: 1993)

HEYDENREICH L.H., *Leonardo da Vinci*, 2 vols (Basle: 1954)

HONOUR H., *Neo-classicism* (Harmondsworth: 1988)

LAIRESSE G. DE, *Het groot schilderboek* [Amsterdam: 1707] (Haarlem: 1740)

LEONARDO DA VINCI, *Treatise on Painting [Codex Urbinas Latinus 1270]*, transl. and annot. by A.P. McMahon, introd. by L.H. Heydenreich, 2 vols (Princeton, N.J.: 1956)

LOMAZZO G., *Trattato dell'arte della pittura* [Milan: 1584], in *Gian Paolo Lomazzo. Scritti sulle arti*, ed. R.P. Ciardi, 2 vols (Florence: 1973)

PACE C., *Félibien's Life of Poussin* (London: 1981)

REYNOLDS J., *Discourses on Art*, ed. R. Wark (New Haven–London: 1975)

VASARI G., *Le vite de' più eccellenti pittori, scultori e architettori* [Florence: 1568], ed. G. Milanesi, 9 vols (Milan: 1878–1885)

WAŹBIŃSKI Z., "Il cavaliere d'Arpino ed il mito accademico. Il problema di autoidentificazione", in *Künstler über sich in seinem Werk. Internazionales Symposium der Bibliotheca Hertziana*, ed. M. Winner (Rome: 1989) 317-63.

Figures 1-10 belong to *The Representation of History in Artistic Theory in the Early Modern Period* by Anton Boschloo.
Figures 1-16 belong to *Universals and Particulars. History Painting in the "Sala di Costantino" in the Vatican Palace* by Jan L. de Jong.

FIGURES 1-10 (Boschloo)

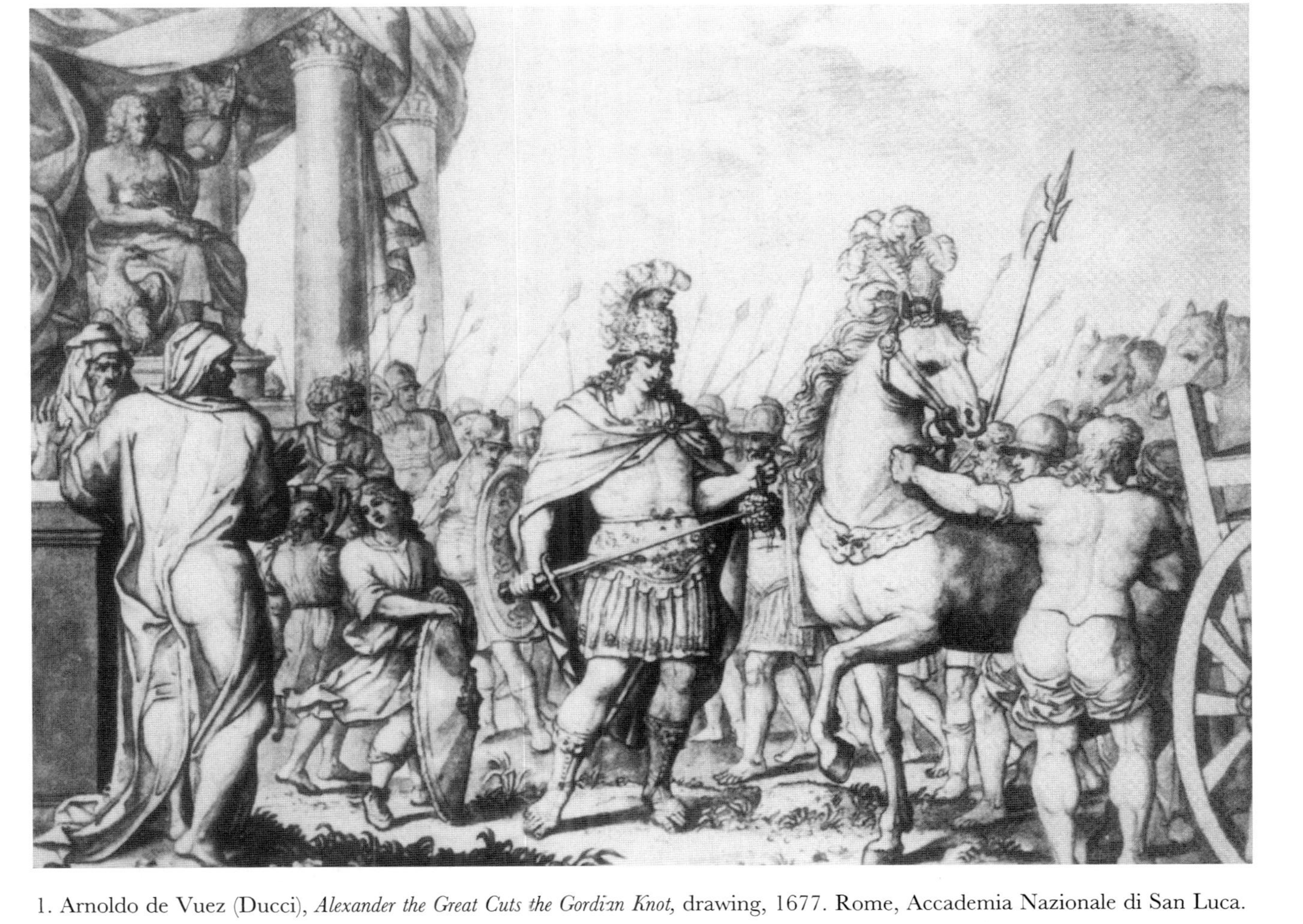

1. Arnoldo de Vuez (Ducci), *Alexander the Great Cuts the Gordian Knot,* drawing, 1677. Rome, Accademia Nazionale di San Luca.

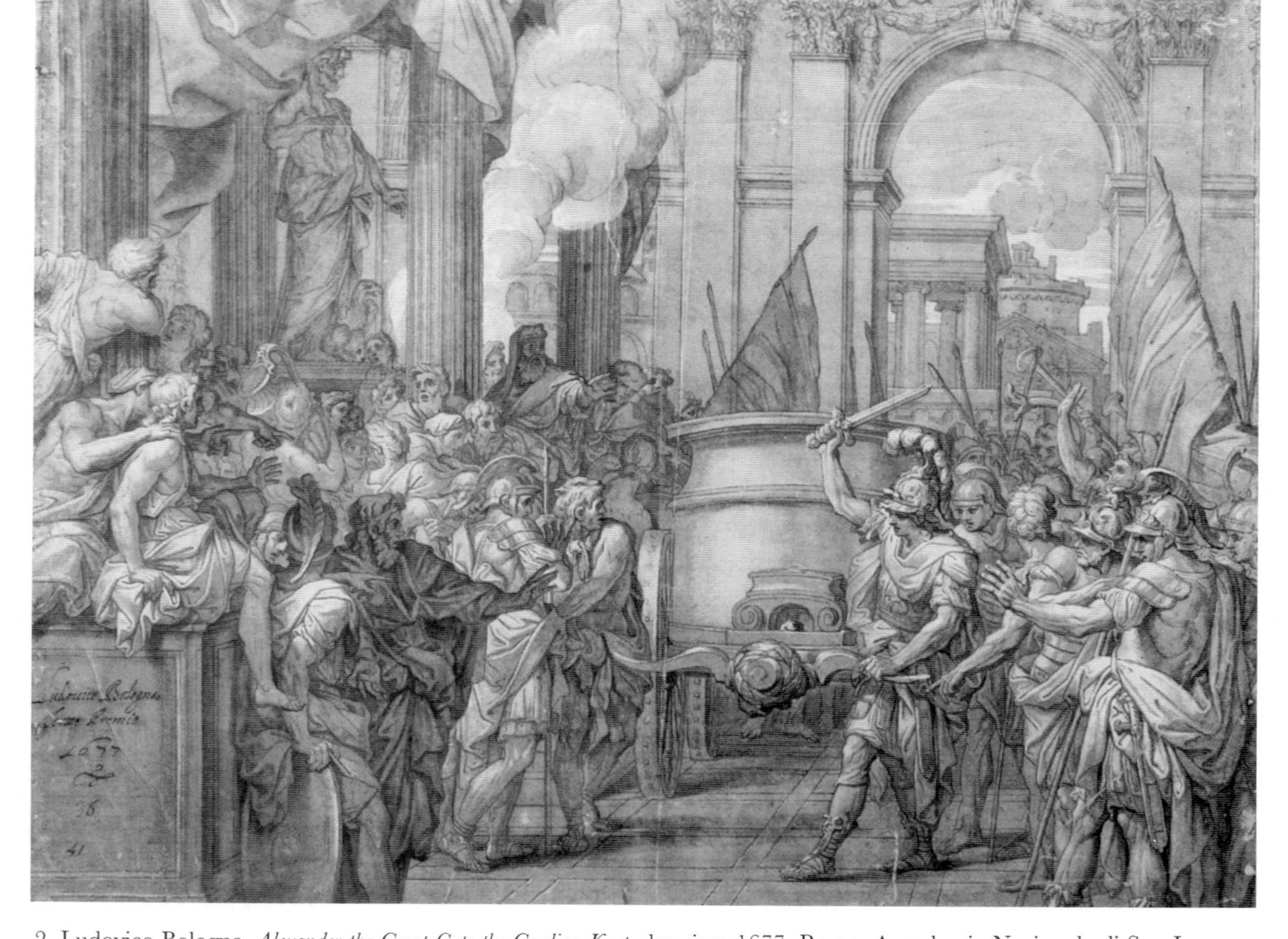

2. Ludovico Bologna, *Alexander the Great Cuts the Gordian Knot*, drawing, 1677. Rome, Accademia Nazionale di San Luca.

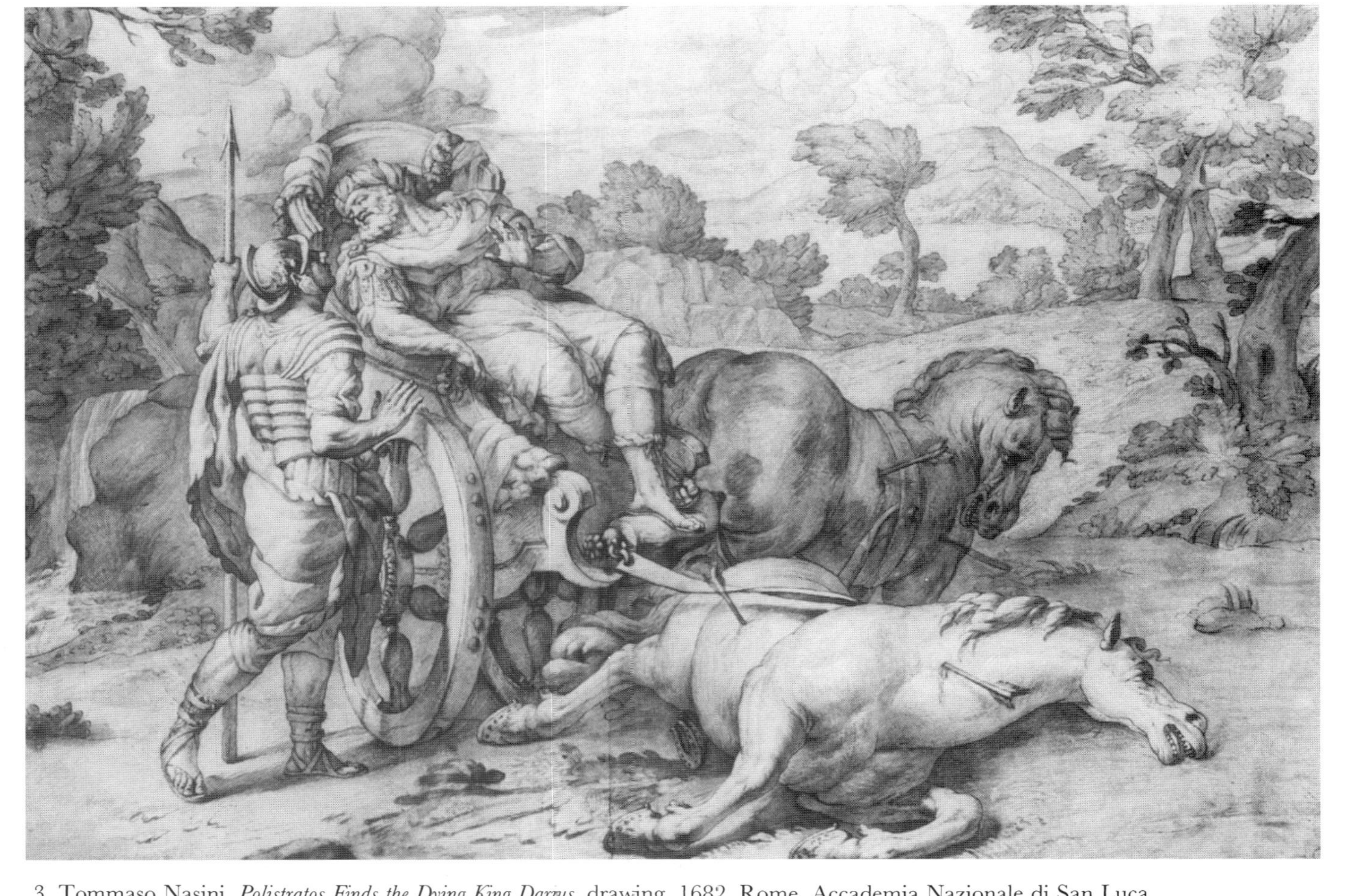

3. Tommaso Nasini, *Polistratos Finds the Dying King Darius*, drawing, 1682. Rome, Accademia Nazionale di San Luca.

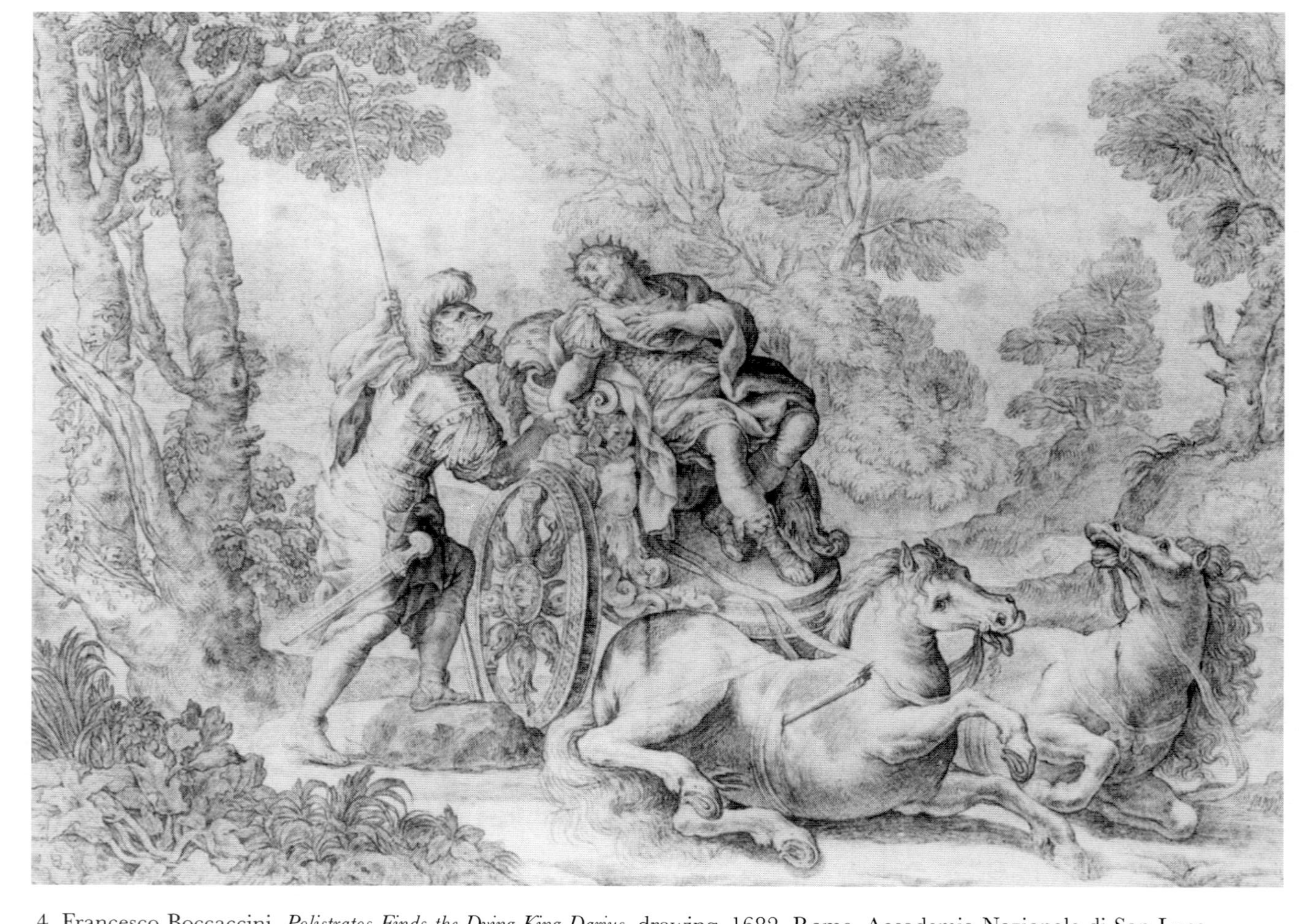

4. Francesco Boccaccini, *Polistratos Finds the Dying King Darius*, drawing, 1682. Rome, Accademia Nazionale di San Luca.

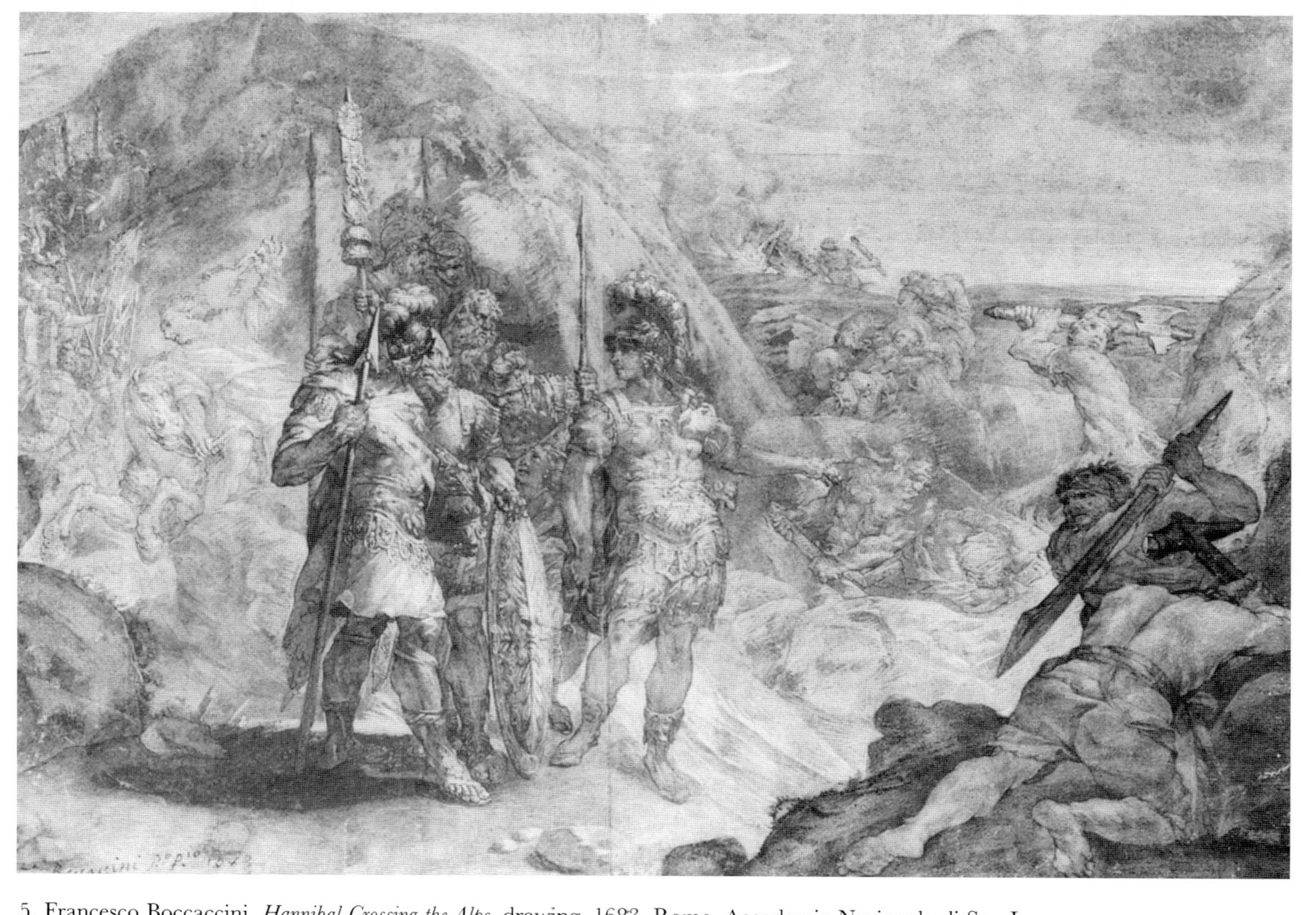

5. Francesco Boccaccini, *Hannibal Crossing the Alps*, drawing, 1683. Rome, Accademia Nazionale di San Luca.

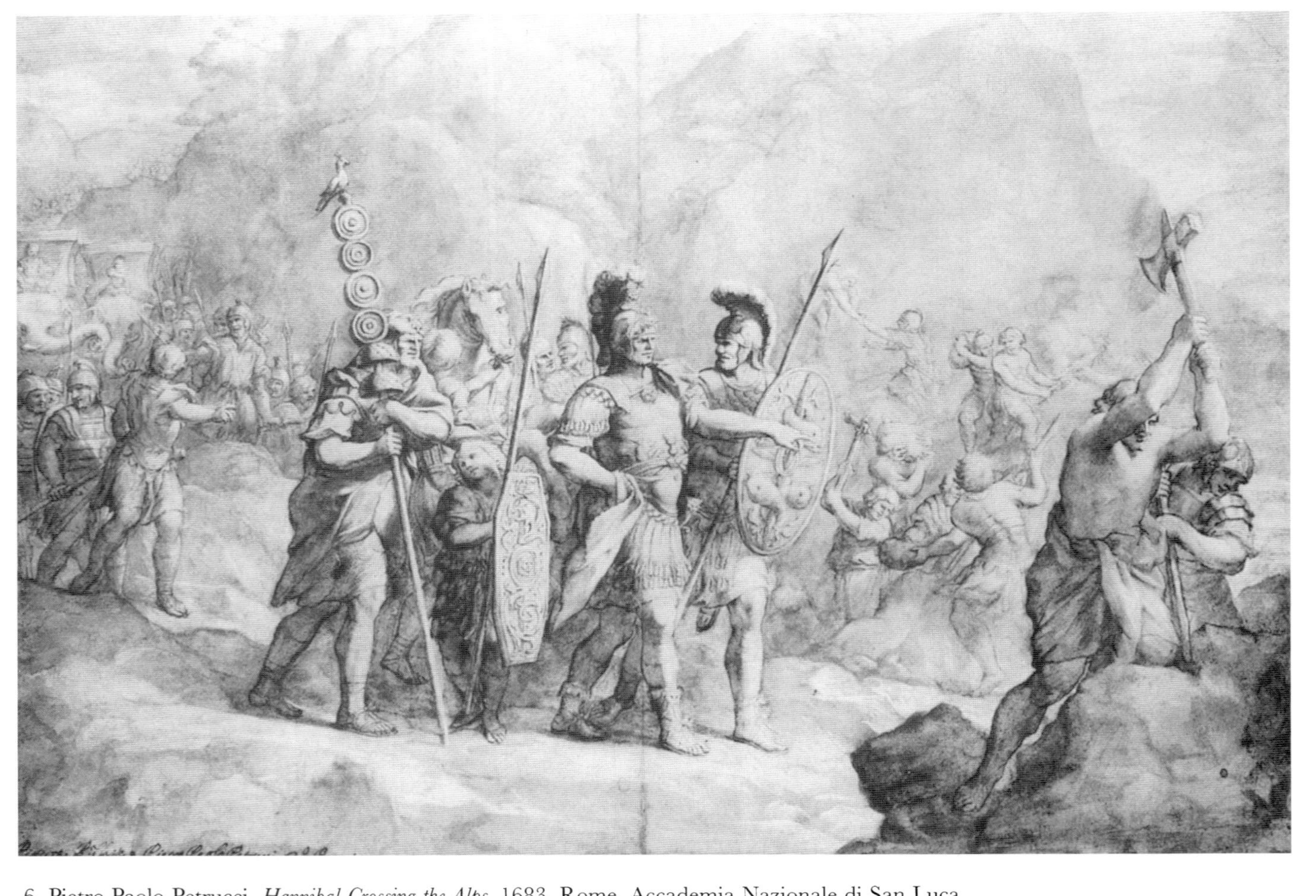

6. Pietro Paolo Petrucci, *Hannibal Crossing the Alps*, 1683. Rome, Accademia Nazionale di San Luca.

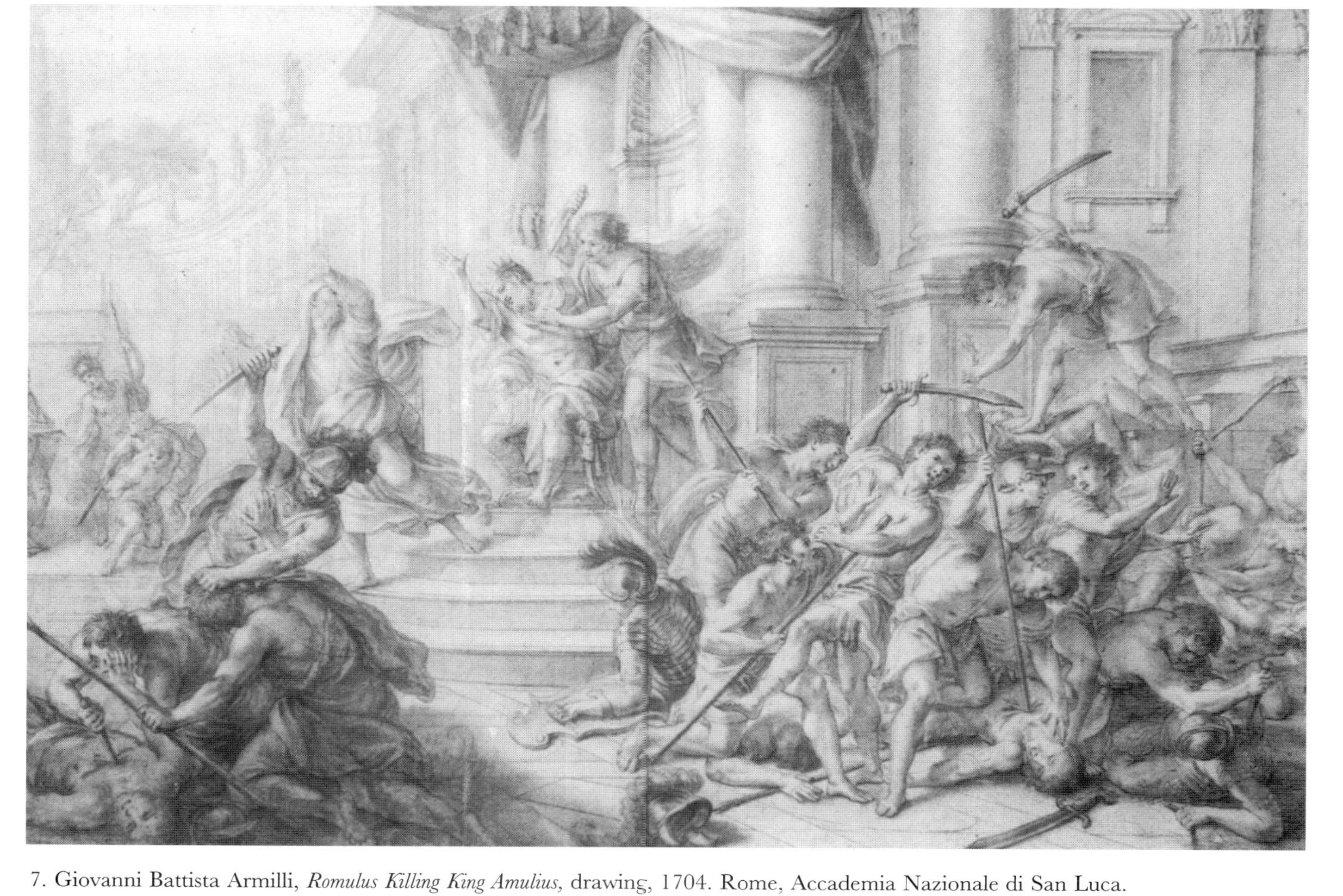

7. Giovanni Battista Armilli, *Romulus Killing King Amulius*, drawing, 1704. Rome, Accademia Nazionale di San Luca.

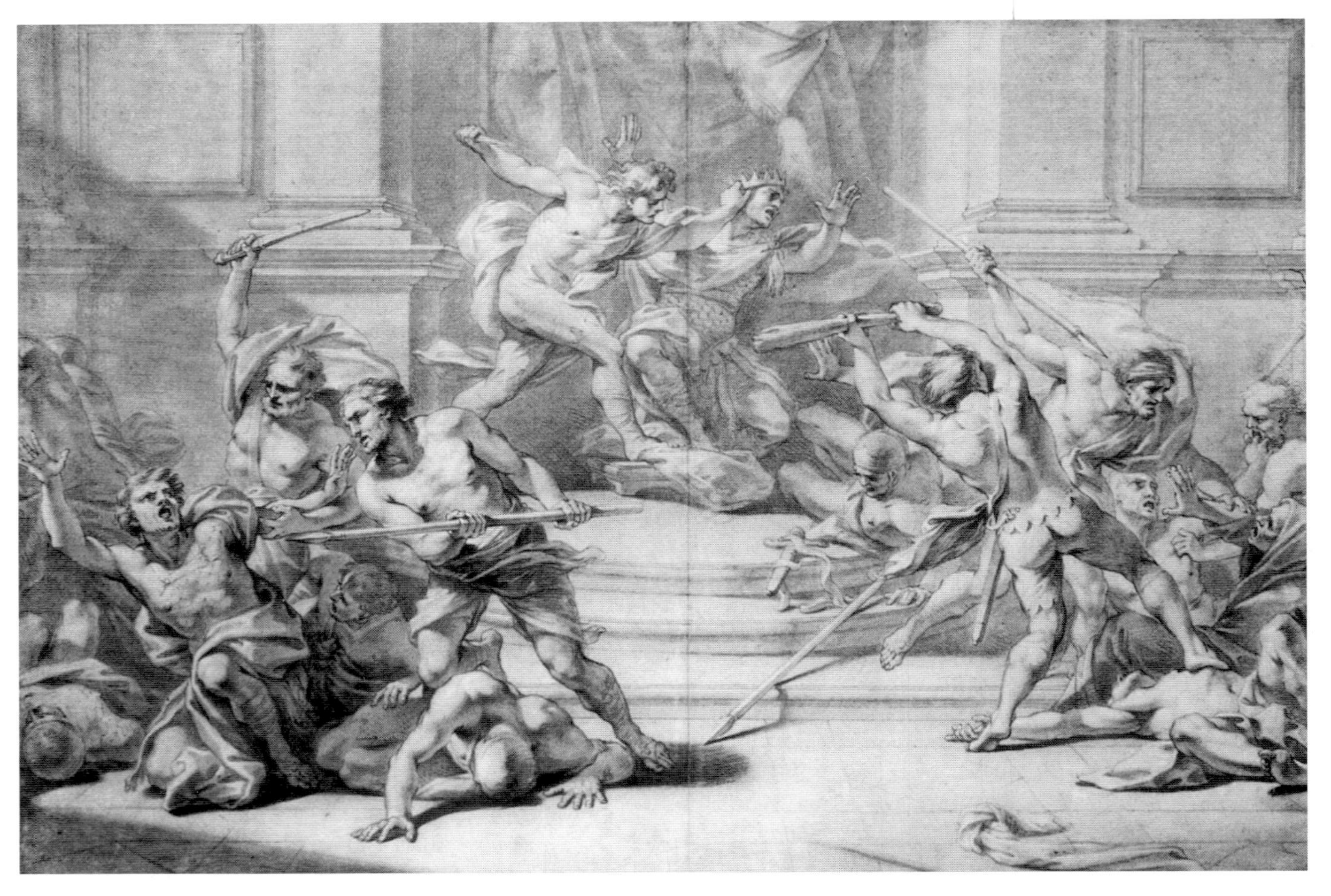

8. Angelo de Coster, *Romulus Killing King Amulius*, drawing, 1704. Rome, Accademia Nazionale di San Luca.

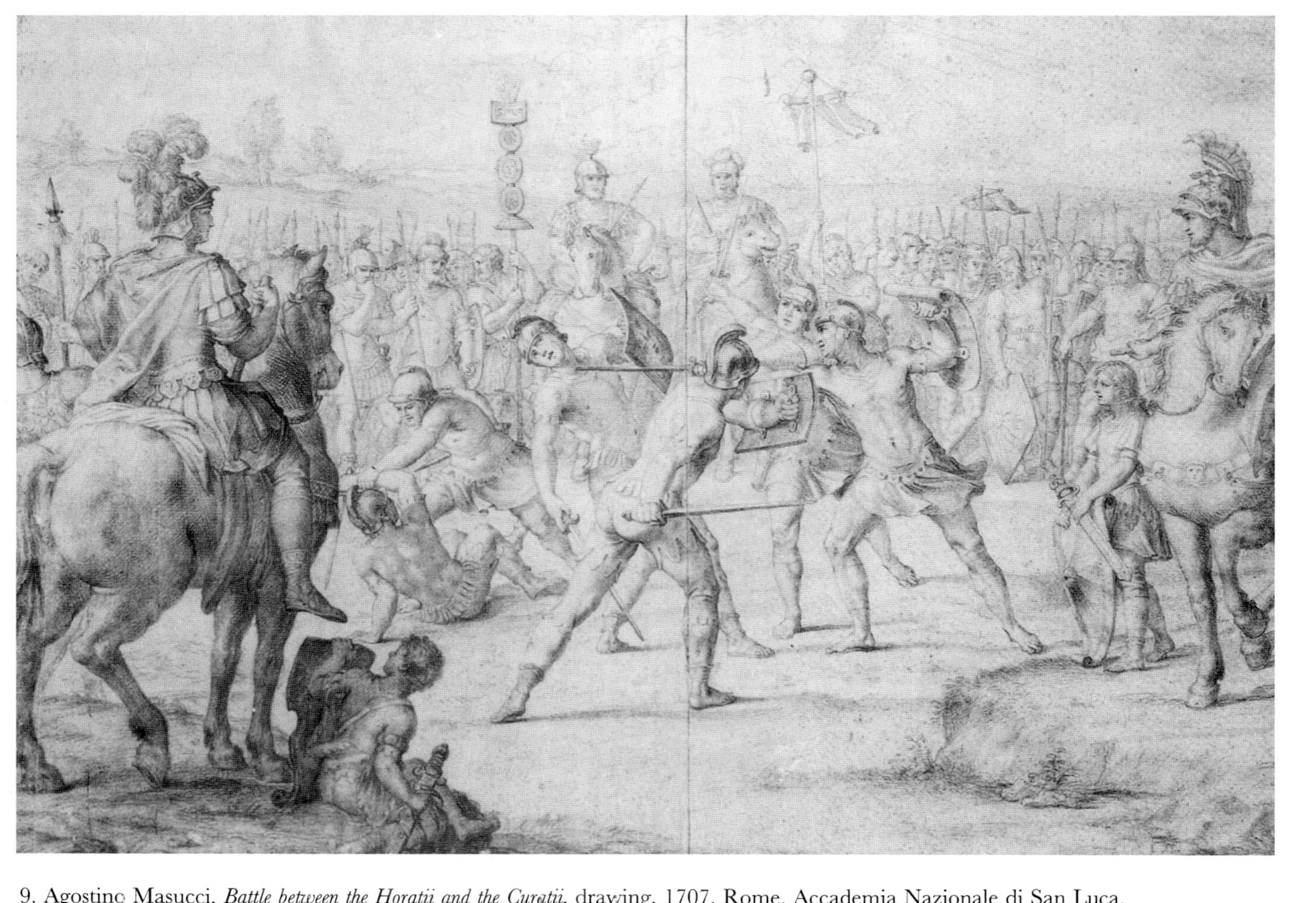

9. Agostino Masucci, *Battle between the Horatii and the Curatii*, drawing, 1707. Rome, Accademia Nazionale di San Luca.

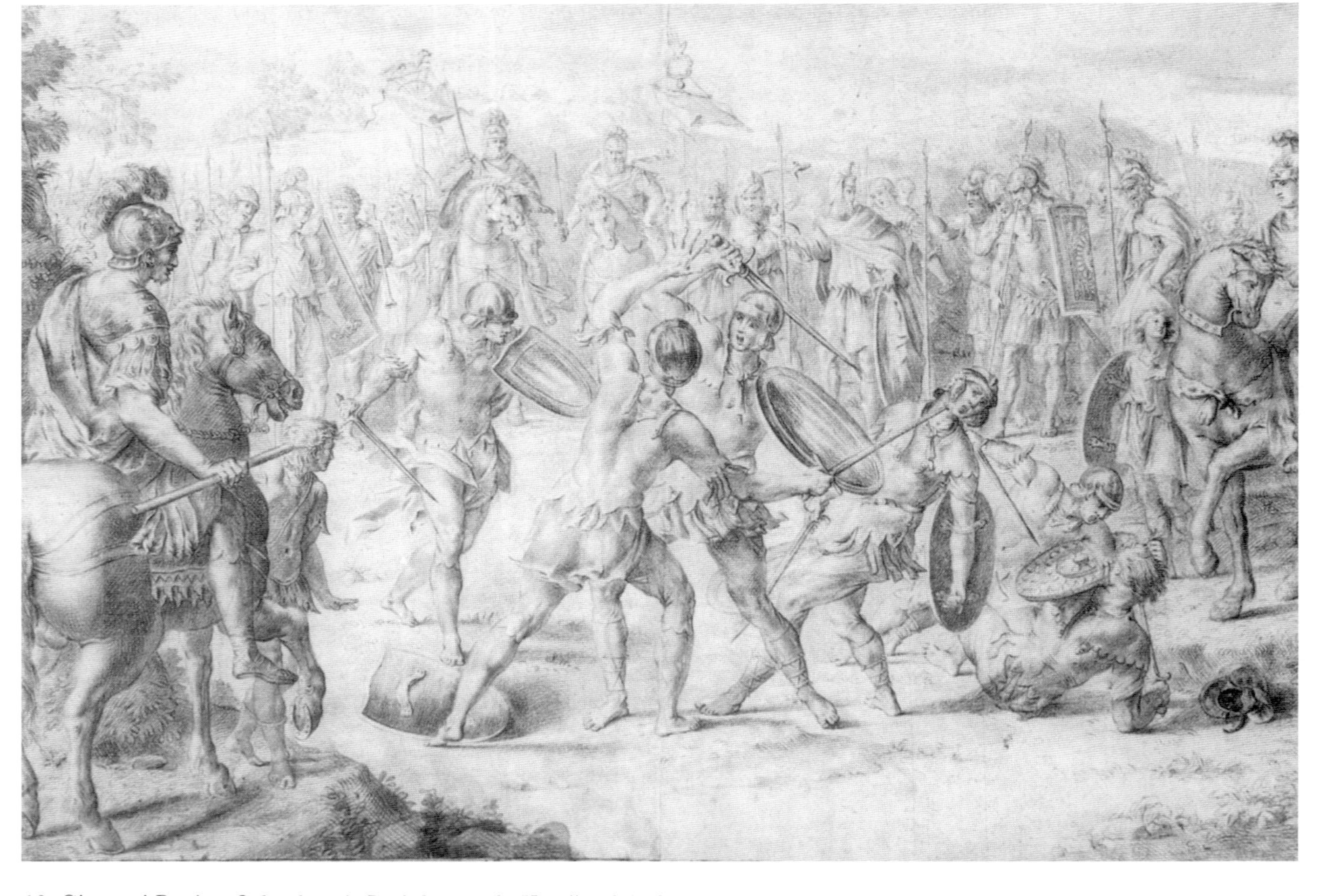

10. Giovanni Battista Calandrucci, *Battle between the Horatii and the Curatii*, 1707. Rome, Accademia Nazionale di San Luca.

FIGURES 1-16 (De Jong)

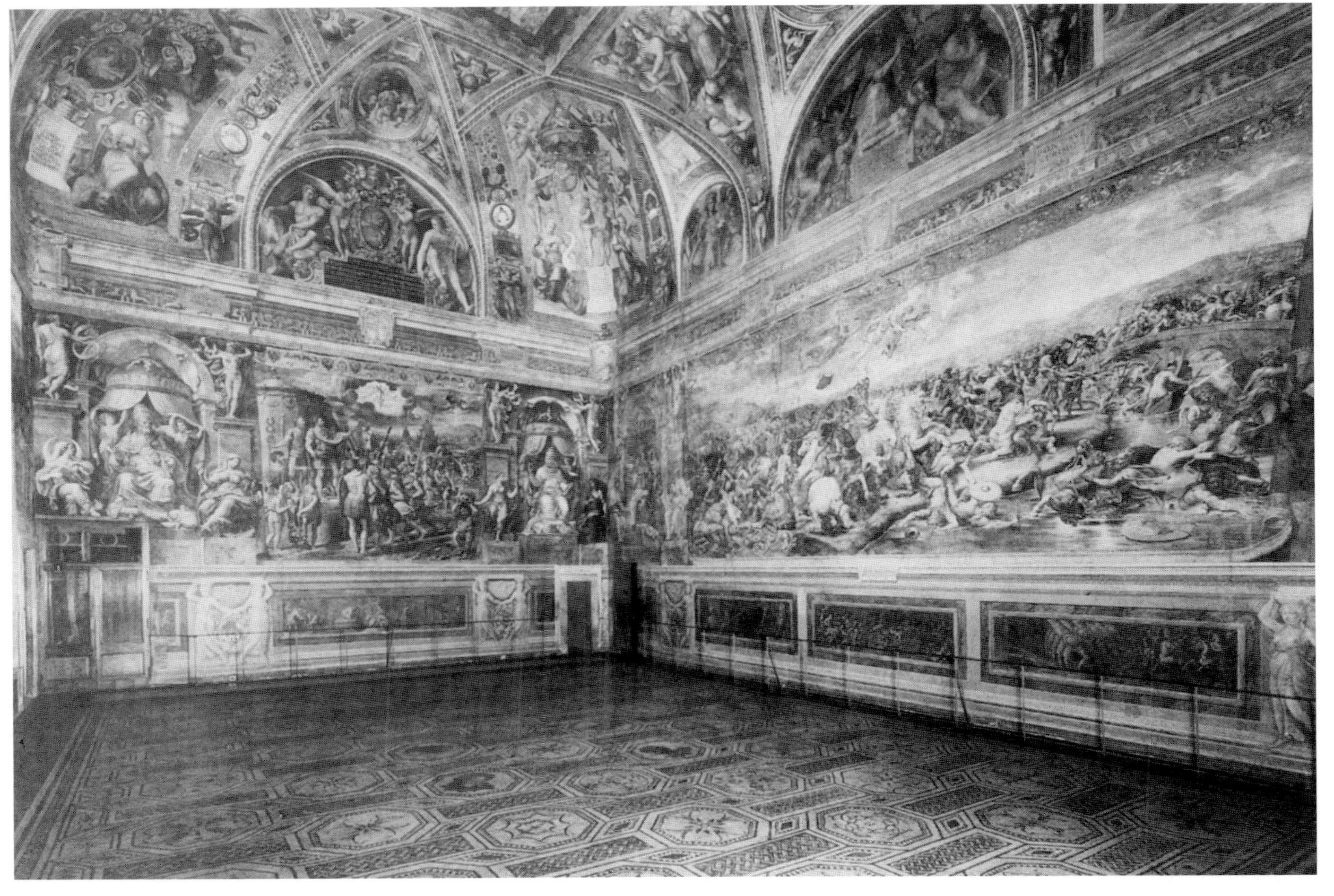

1. Sala di Costantino. Vatican Palace, Rome.

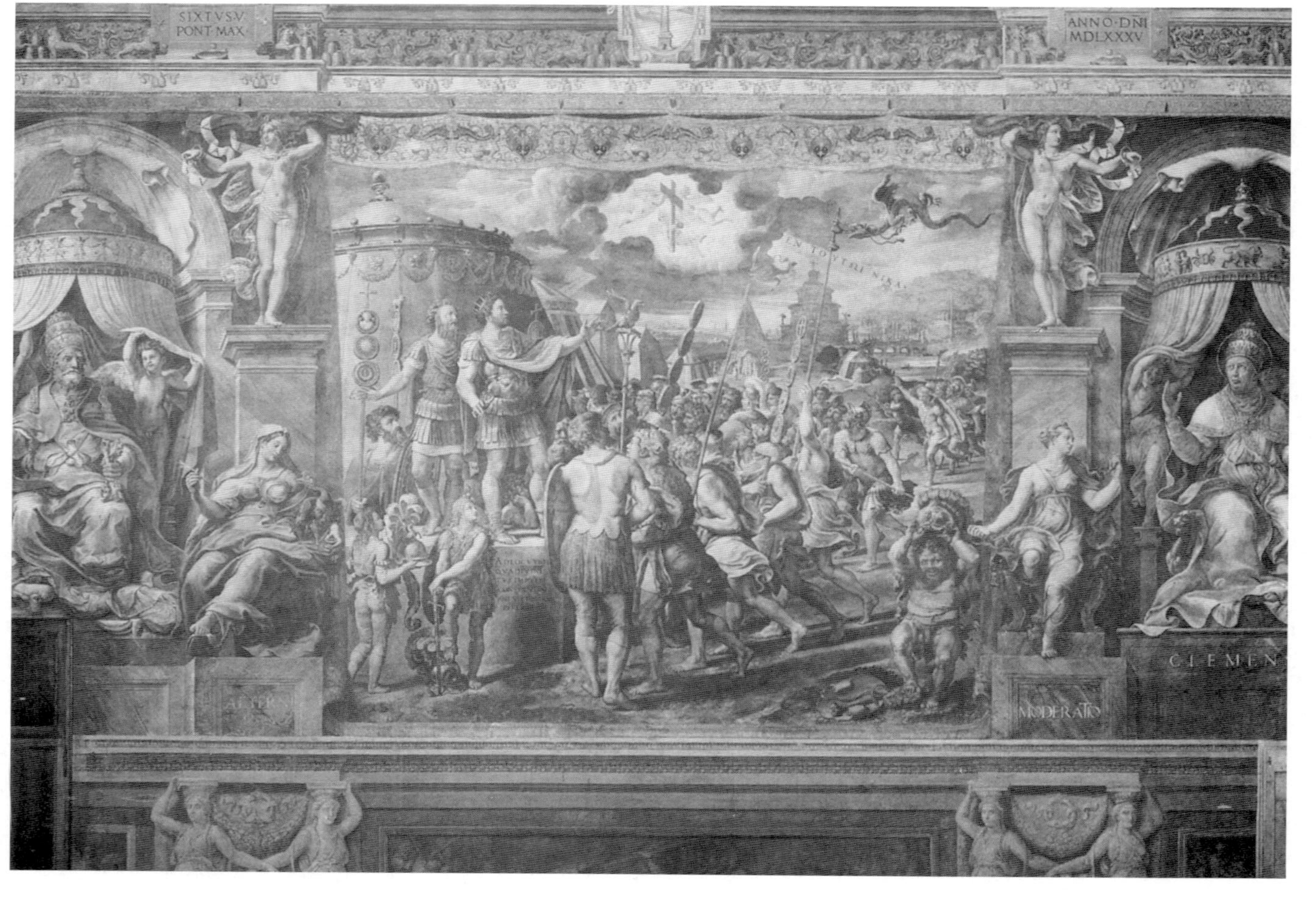

2. Raphael, *The Apparition of the Cross*, 1519–1520. Sala di Costantino, Vatican Palace, Rome.

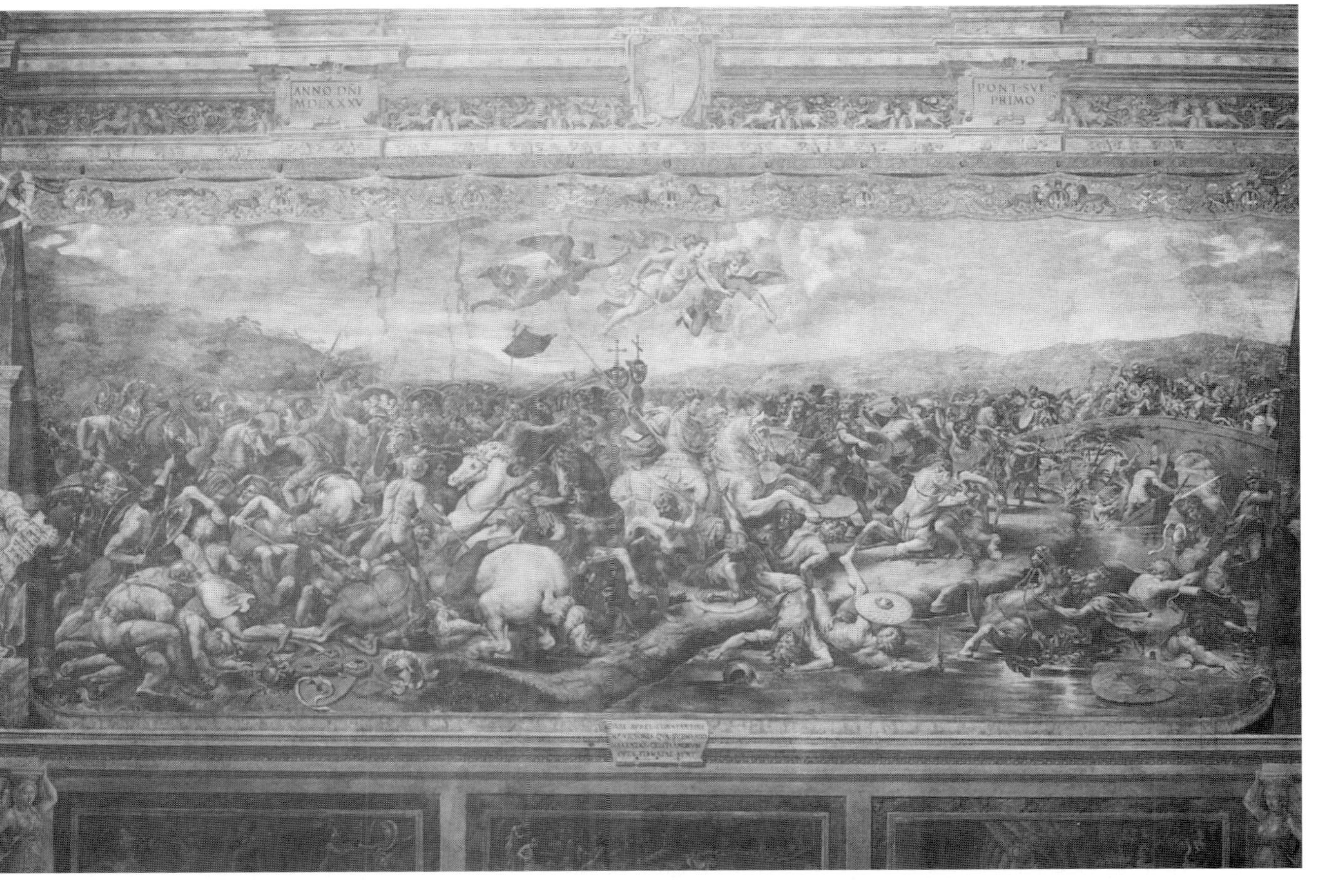

3. Raphael, Giulio Romano and Gianfrancesco Penni, *The Battle at the Milvian Bridge*, ca. 1520. Sala di Costantino, Vatican Palace, Rome.

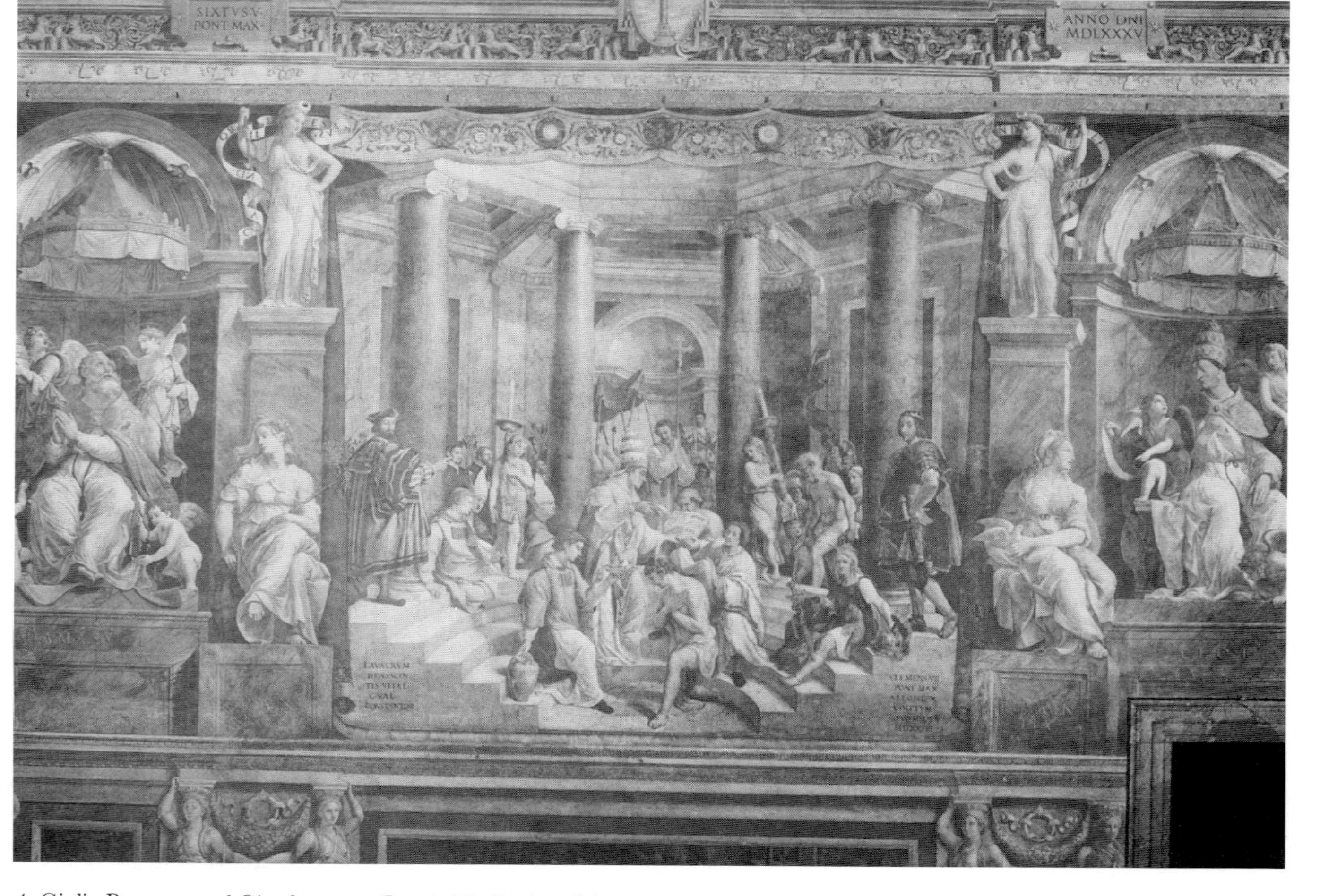

4. Giulio Romano and Gianfrancesco Penni, *The Baptism of Constantine*, ca. 1523–1524. Sala di Costantino, Vatican Palace, Rome.

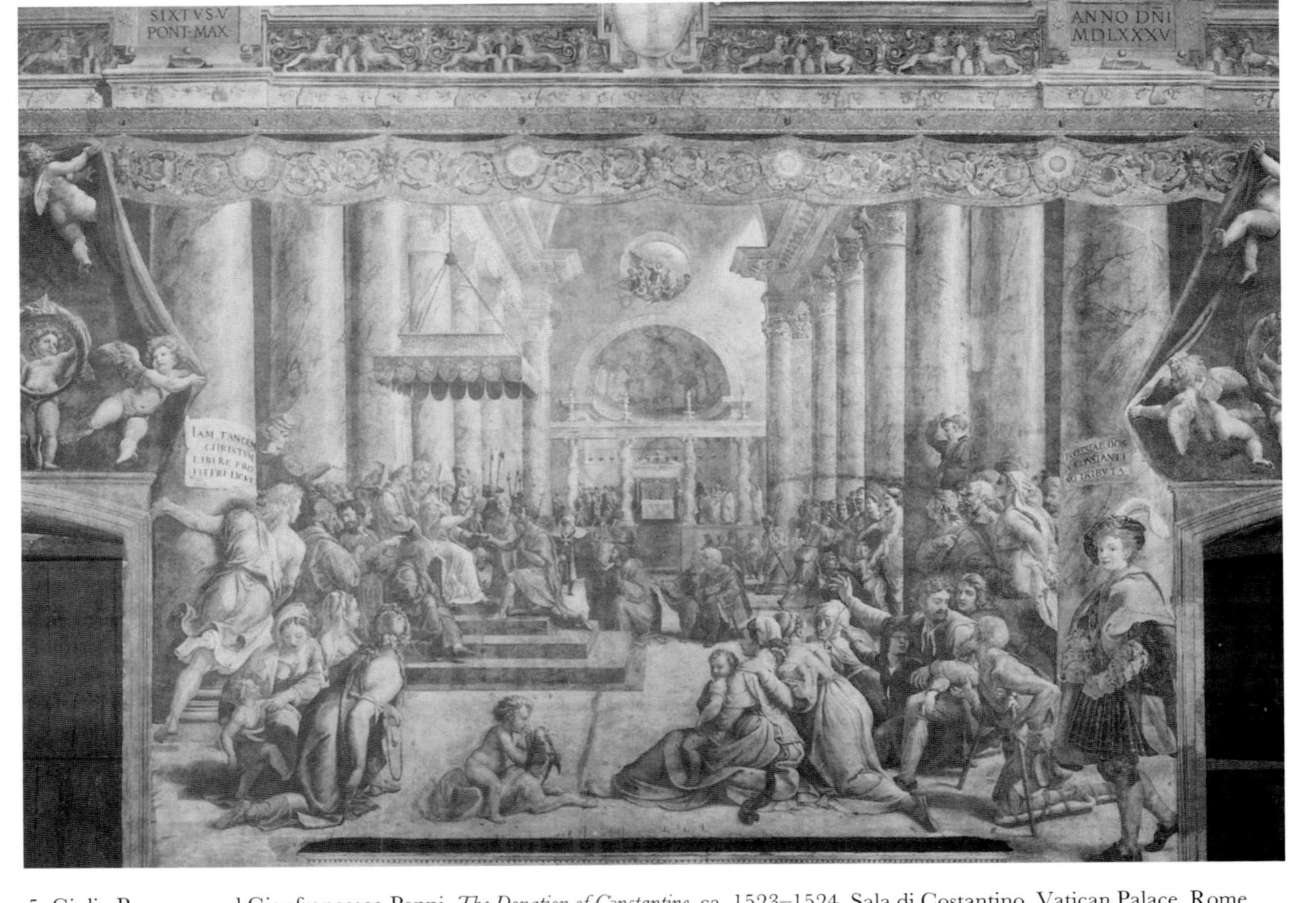

5. Giulio Romano and Gianfrancesco Penni, *The Donation of Constantine*, ca. 1523–1524. Sala di Costantino, Vatican Palace, Rome.

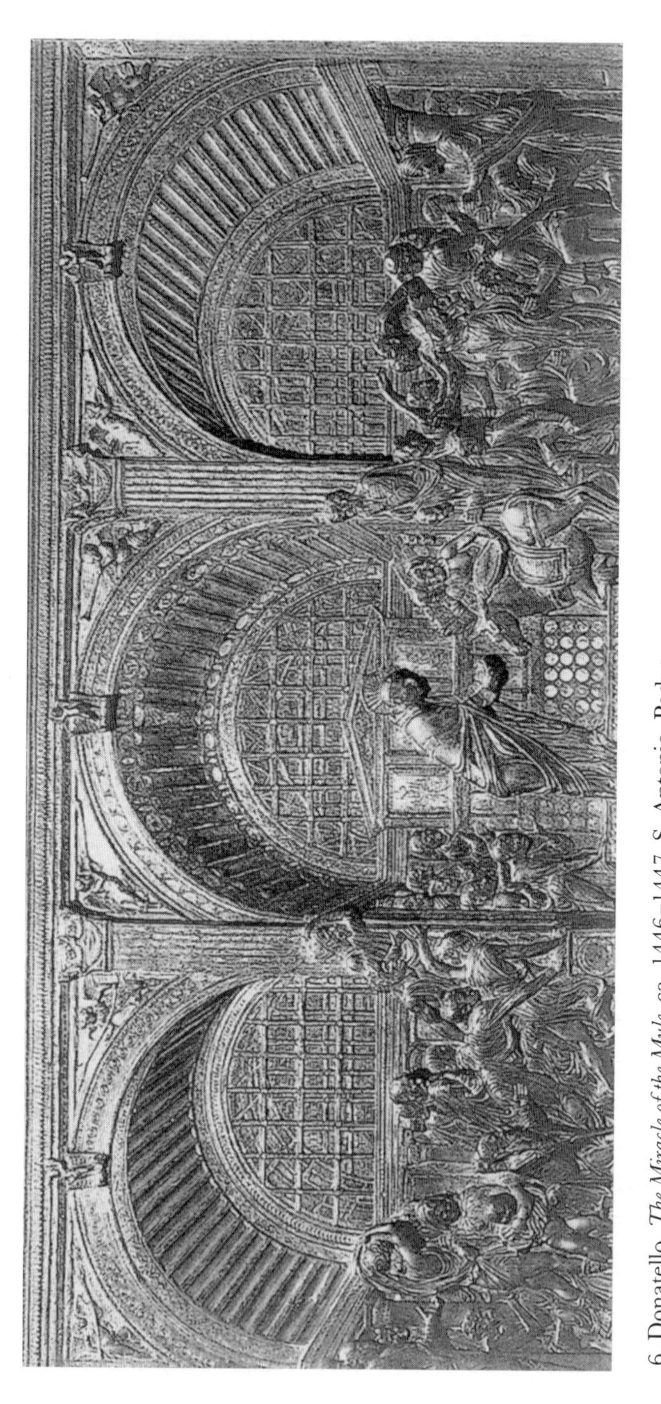

6. Donatello, *The Miracle of the Mule*, ca. 1446–1447. S. Antonio, Padua.

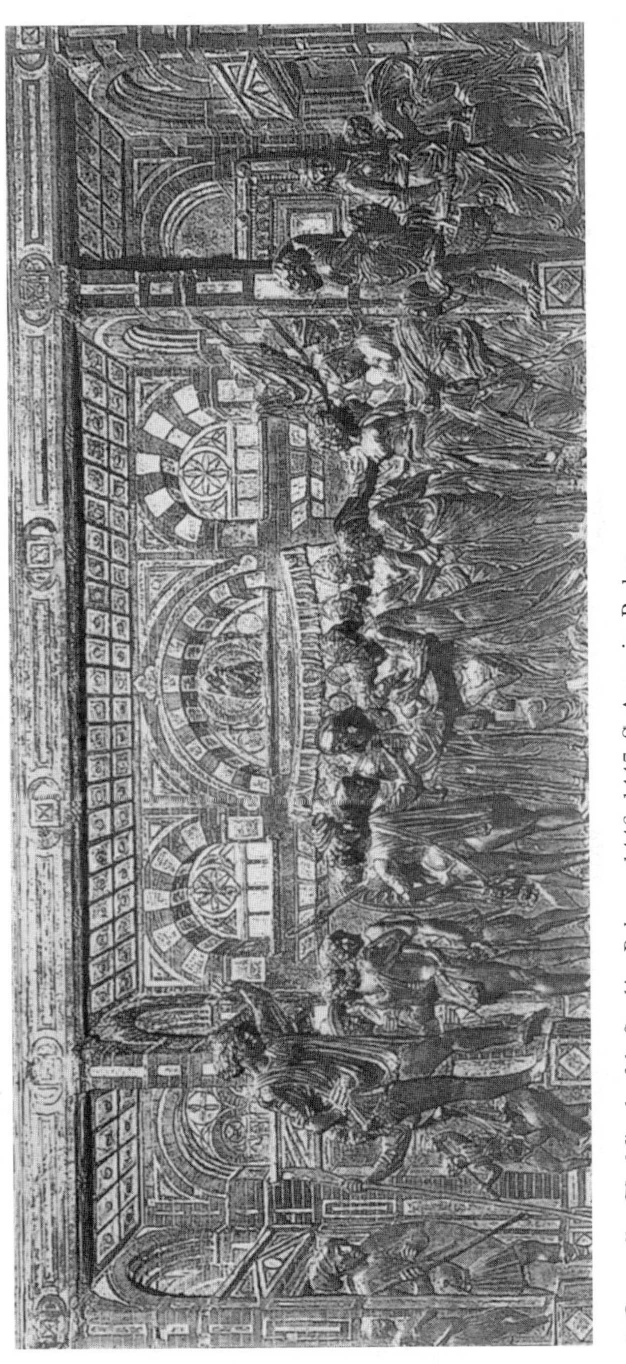

7. Donatello, *The Miracle of the Speaking Babe*, ca. 1446–1447. S. Antonio, Padua.

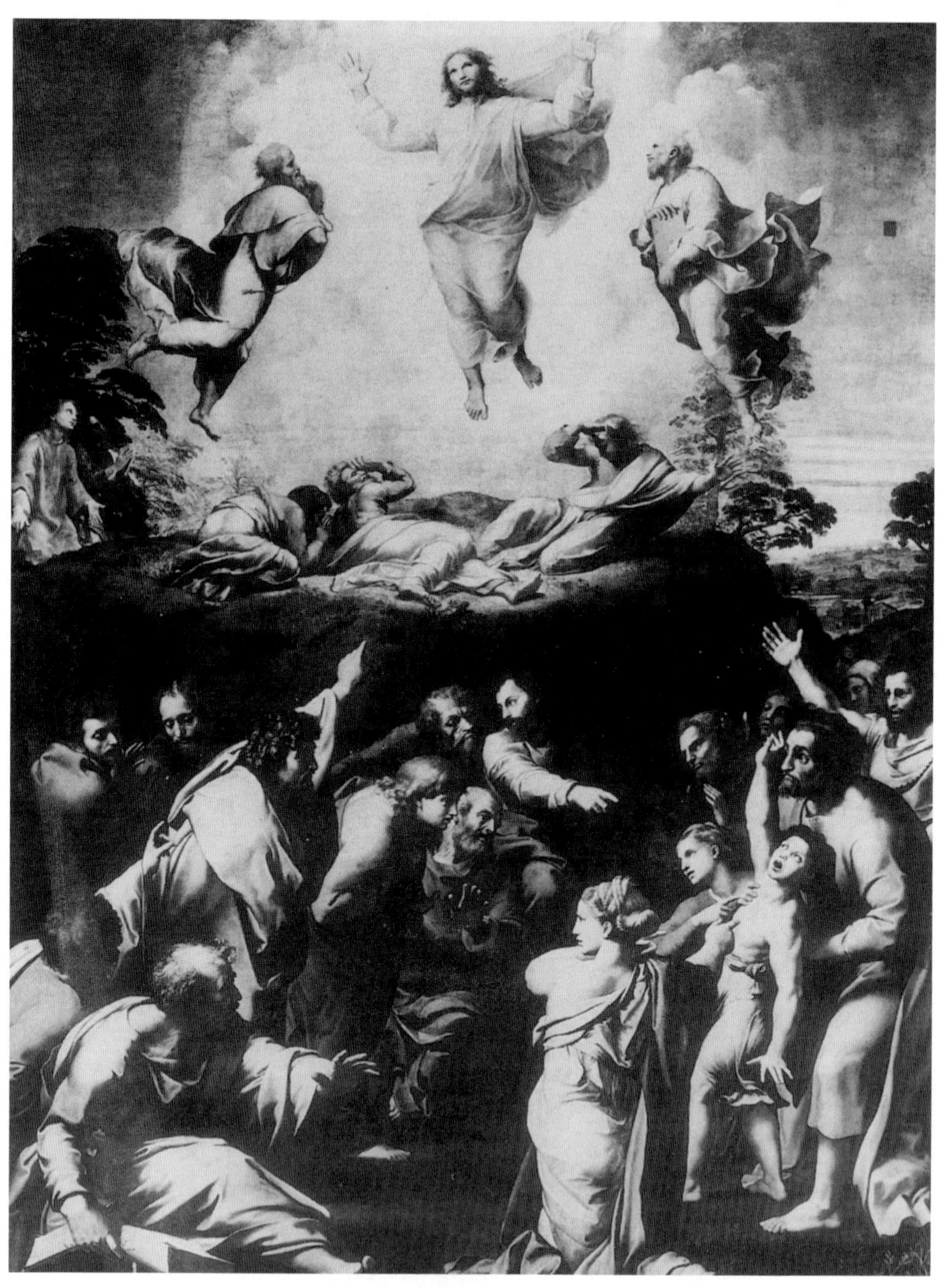

8. Raphael, *The Transfiguration*, ca. 1518–1520. Rome, Pinacoteca Vaticana.

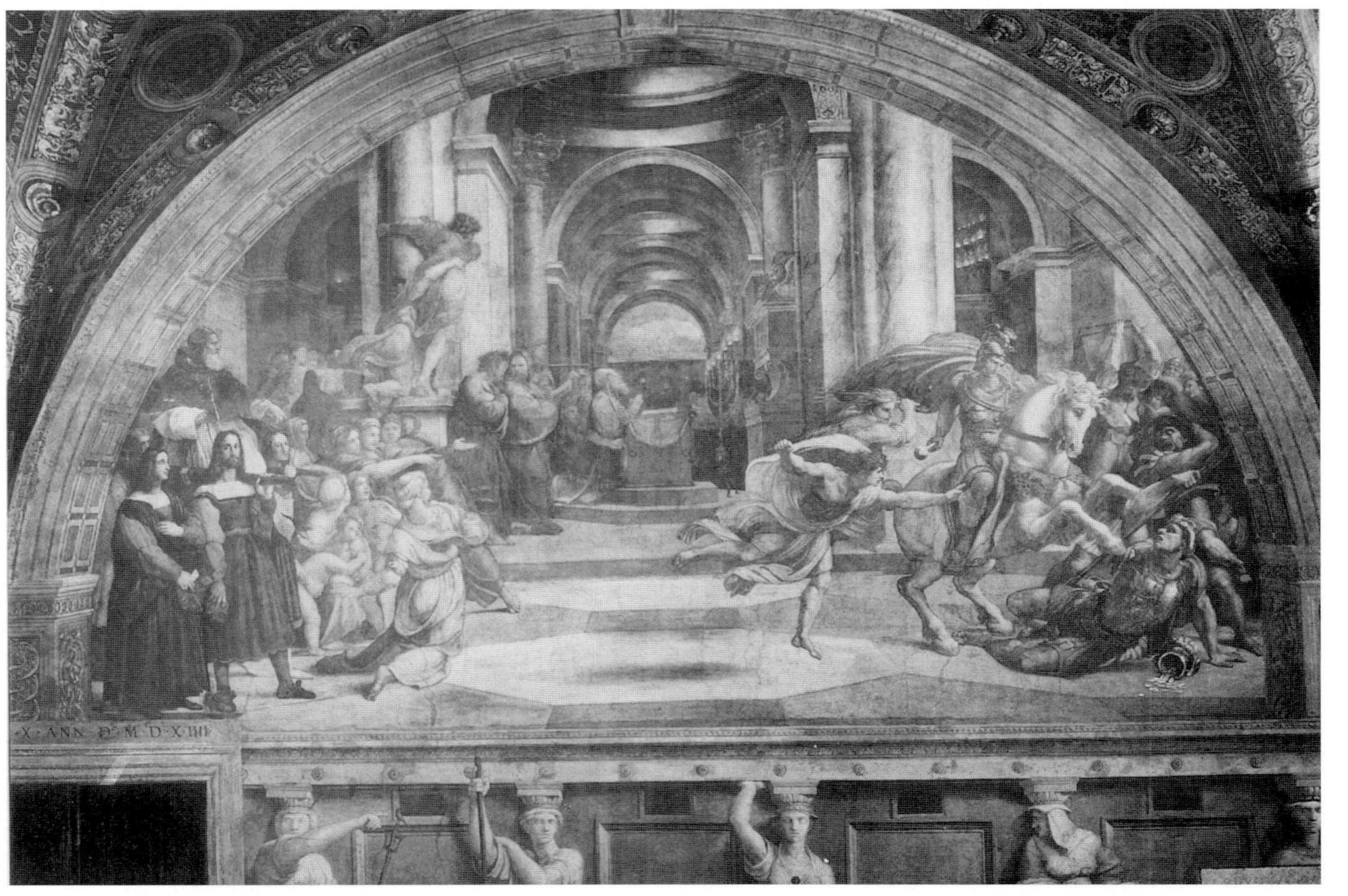

9. Raphael, *The Expulsion of Heliodorus*, ca. 1512–1513. Stanza di Eliodoro, Vatican Palace, Rome.

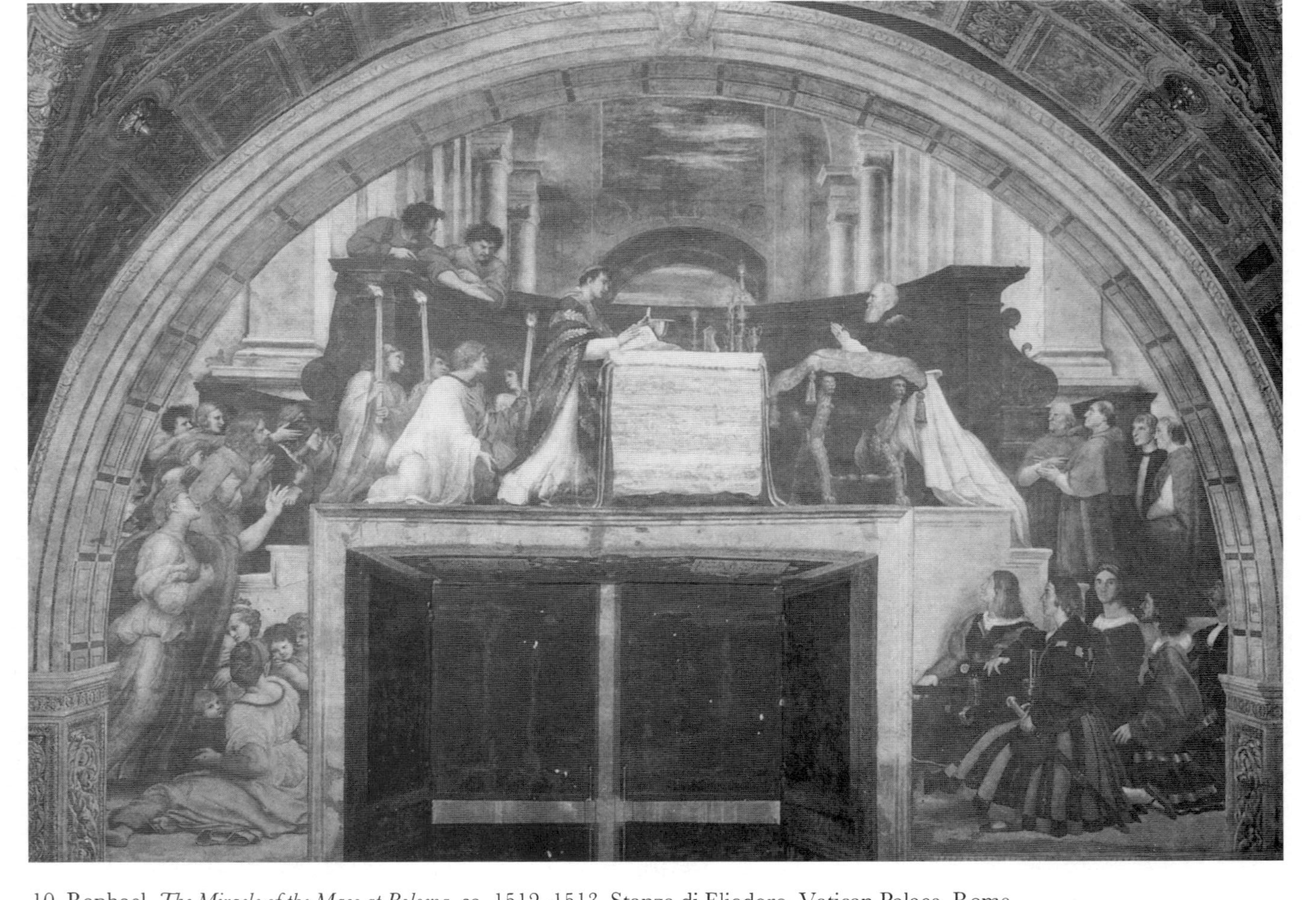

10. Raphael, *The Miracle of the Mass at Bolsena*, ca. 1512–1513. Stanza di Eliodoro, Vatican Palace, Rome.

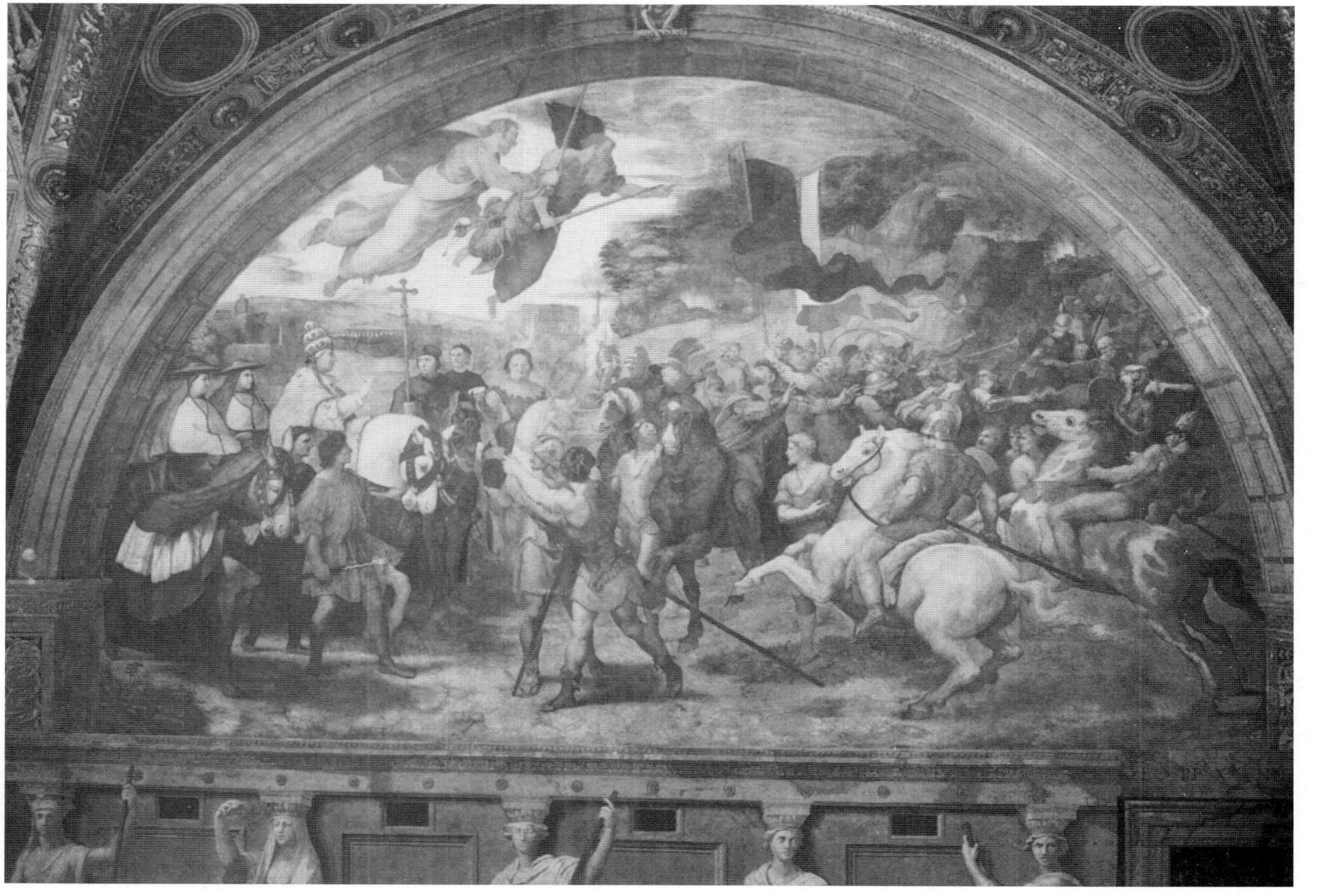

11. Raphael, *Pope Leo III Repelling Attila*, ca. 1513–1514. Stanza di Eliodoro, Vatican Palace, Rome.

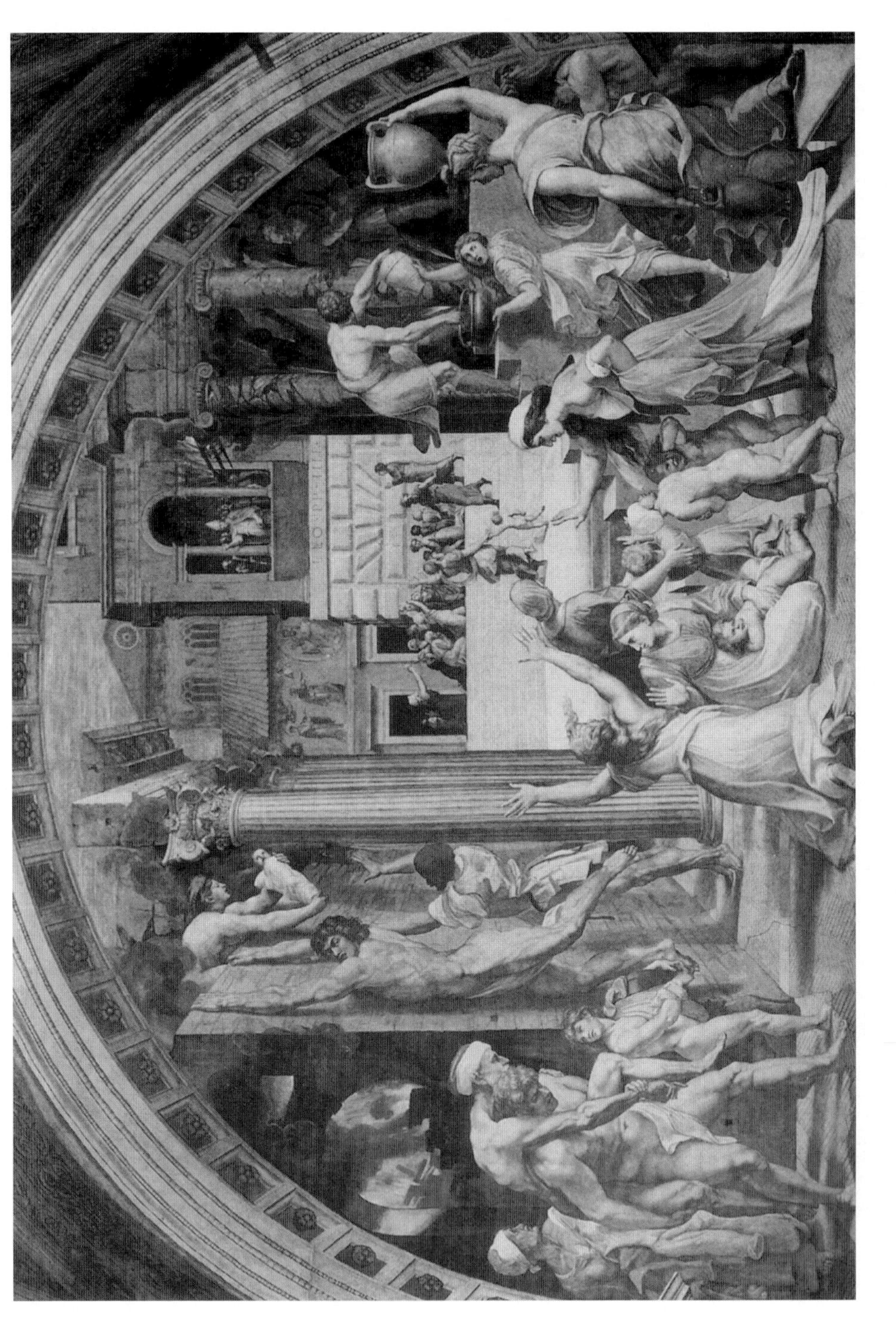

12. Raphael, *The Fire in the Borgo*, ca. 1516–1517. Stanza dell'Incendio, Vatican Palace, Rome.

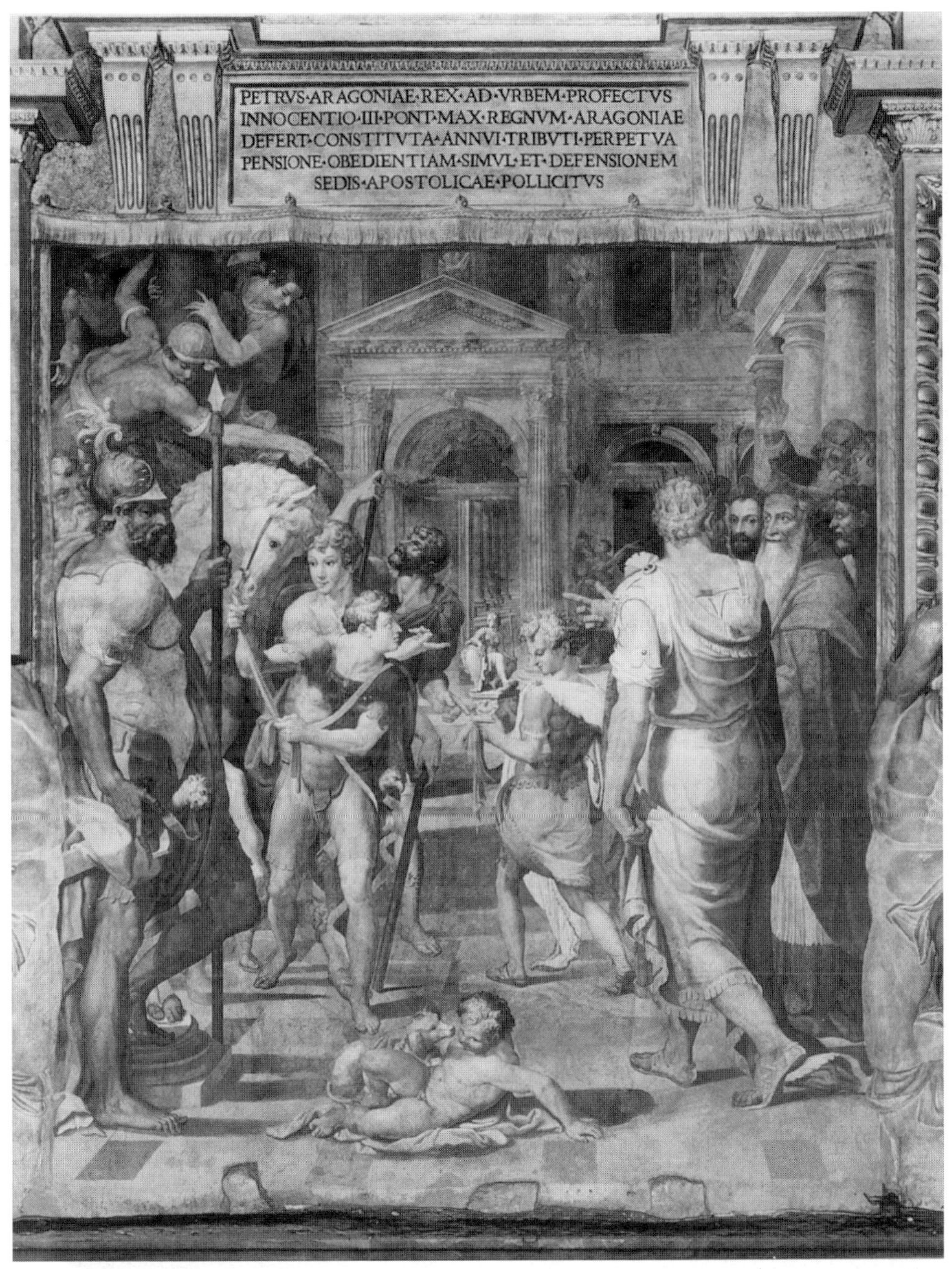

13. Livio Agresti, *King Peter of Aragon Offering His Kingdom to Pope Innocent III*, ca. 1564. Sala Regia, Vatican Palace, Rome.

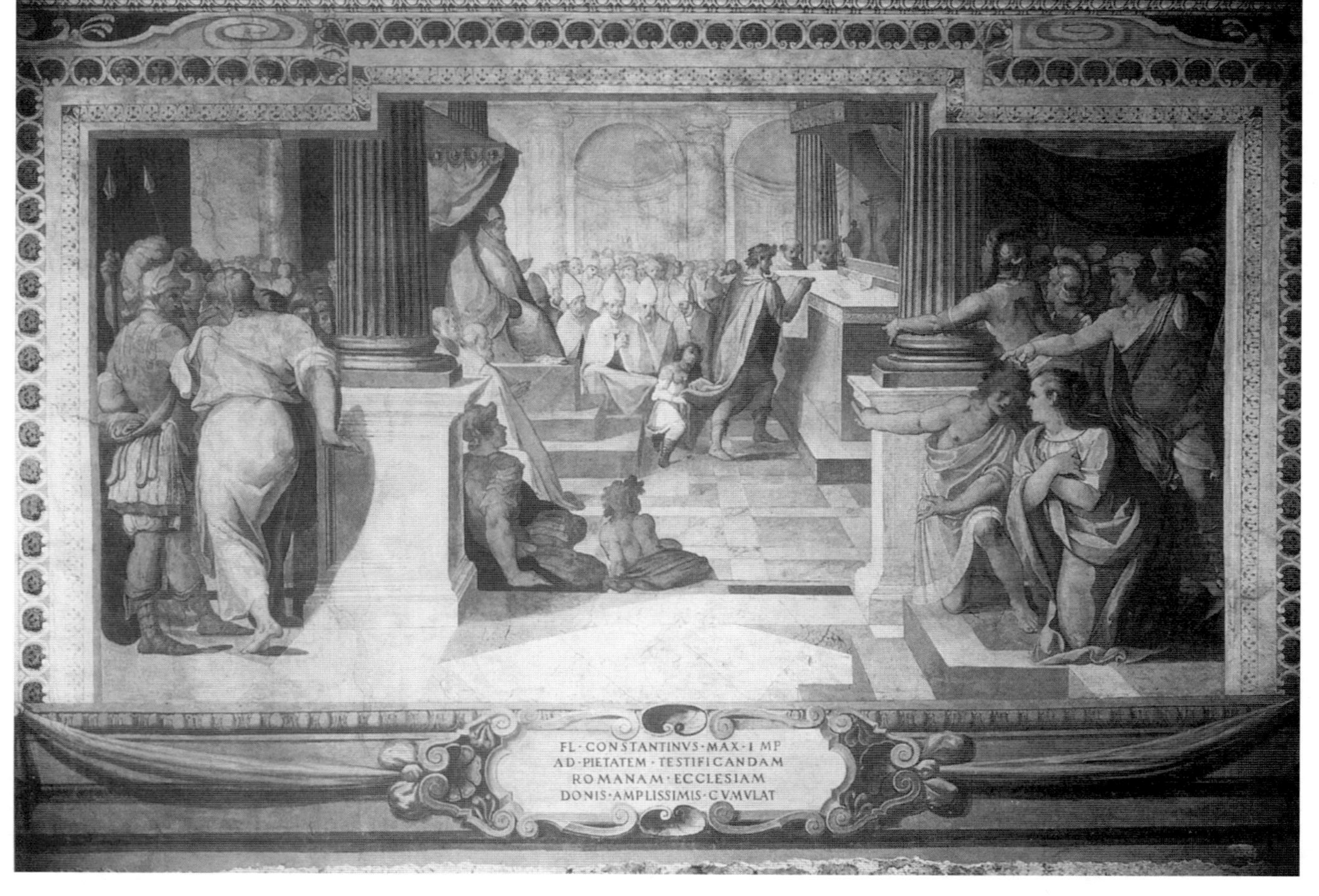

14. Cesare Nebbia and Giovanni Guerra, *The Donation of Constantine*, ca. 1588. Sala di Costantino, Lateran palace, Rome.

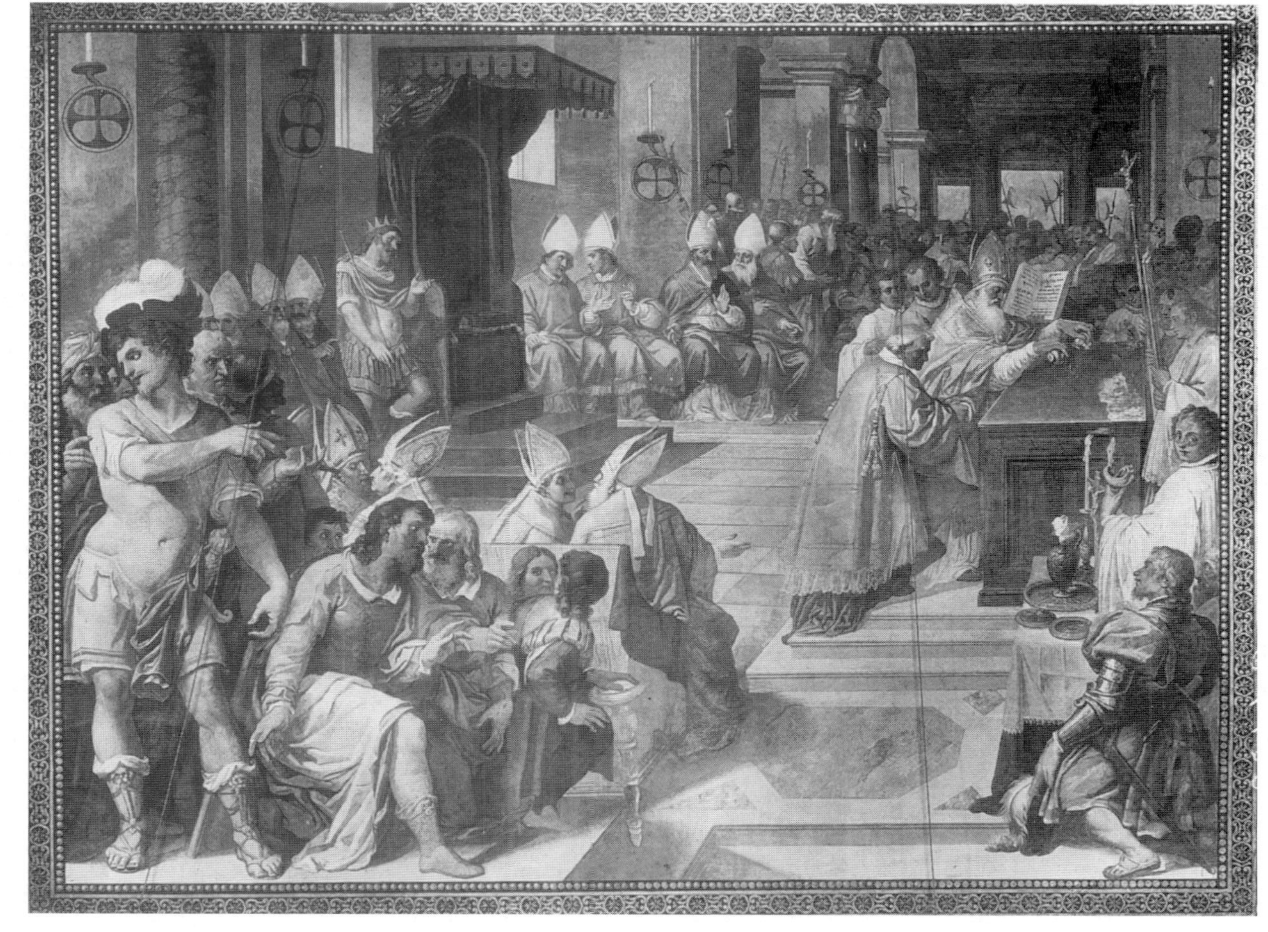

15. Giovanni Battista Ricci, *Pope Sylvester Consecrating the High Altar of the Lateran*, ca. 1599–1600. St John in Lateran, Rome.

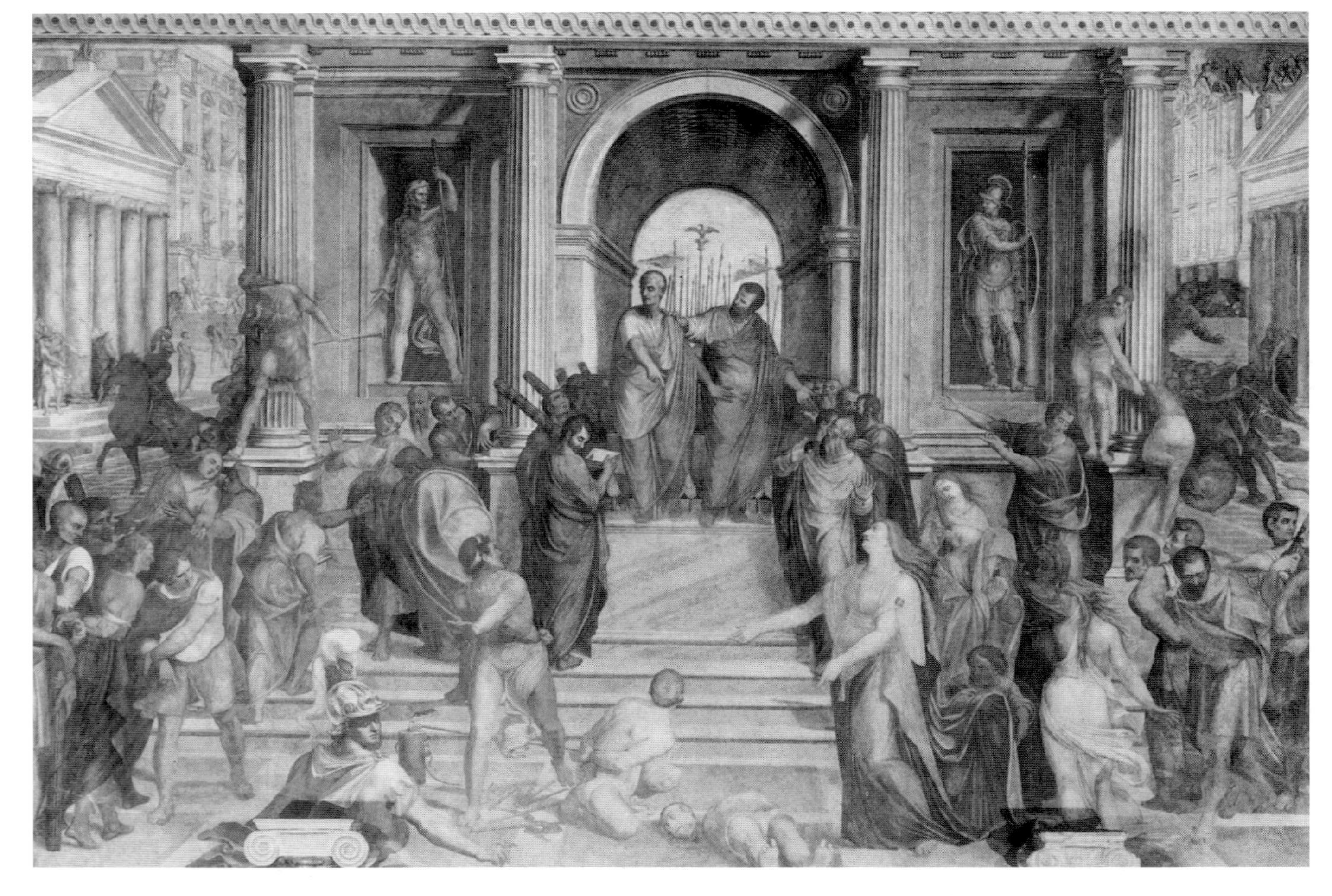

16. Tommaso Laureti, *The Justice of Brutus*, ca. 1586–1592. Sala dei Capitani, Conservators' Palace, Rome.

UNIVERSALS AND PARTICULARS.
HISTORY PAINTING IN THE "SALA DI COSTANTINO"
IN THE VATICAN PALACE*

Jan L. de Jong

In the spring of 1519 Pope Leo X (1513–1521) commissioned the painter Raphael to decorate his audience hall with scenes from the life of the first Christian Emperor, Constantine the Great. Neither Leo nor Raphael lived to see the project finished. In 1524 it was completed by Raphael's pupils Giulio Romano and Gianfrancesco Penni, by order of Leo X's cousin, Pope Clement VII (1523–1534).

The audience hall, now usually called "Sala di Costantino" because of the theme of its decoration, is situated on the second floor of the Vatican Palace, next to the papal apartment with the famous *stanze* that Raphael painted between 1508 and 1517 [fig. 1]. Thanks to a number of recent studies the history of its decoration and the reasons why Constantine the Great and Pope Sylvester were chosen as its theme, are well known.[1] The room was meant — and indeed functioned — primarily as an audience hall, which the Holy Father could enter from the papal apartment. Originally it had a wooden ceiling with gilded decorations, which after some fifty years threatened to collapse and was therefore replaced by the present stone ceiling in 1581.[2] The floor also looked different from what it does now: it was covered with tiles showing the motto of Pope Leo X. The present floor comes from the famous *Domus Aurea* of the Emperor Nero and was laid in 1854.[3] The walls still

---

* I am very grateful to Anton Boschloo, Karl Enenkel, Victor Schmidt, Henk van Veen and Lyckle de Vries for their valuable comments and suggestions, and to my wife Elizabeth for correcting my English.

[1] By far the most complete is Quednau R., *Die Sala di Costantino im Vatikanischen Palast. Zur Dekoration der beiden Medici-Päpste Leo X. und Clemens VII.*, Studien zur Kunstgeschichte 13 (Hildesheim–New York: 1979), with the history of the decoration in particular 80-95. A brief but useful summary of the known information on the Sala, with good colour illustrations, is presented in Cornini G., Strobel A.M. de and Serlupi Crescenzi M., "La sala di Costantino", in Jacks P.J. (ed.), *Raffaello nell'appartamento di Giulio II e Leone X* (Milan: 1993) 167-201.

[2] In the same year it was painted with the scene which is still *in situ* by Tommaso Laureti; see Rossi's remarks in Madonna M.L. (ed.), *Roma di Sisto V. Le arti e la cultura* (Rome: 1993), 91-2.

[3] The original floor had already been replaced by a new one in 1726; Quednau, *Die Sala di Costantino*, 40.

look more or less the same as they originally did, although some extra doors were inserted in the course of time.[4] The upper part of each of the four walls is decorated with a large history scene, flanked by representations of Popes, sitting in full *pontificalia* on a throne under a canopy. Each Pope is accompanied on either side by a woman personifying some virtue or concept. The lower parts of the walls are decorated with painted caryatids and monochrome scenes imitating bronze reliefs. Just like the large history scenes above them, these scenes represent episodes from the life of Constantine.[5] On special occasions, however, the lower parts of the walls were covered with expensive tapestries showing playing *amorini* and the *imprese* of Leo X. This may indicate that these monochrome scenes were considered less important.[6]

The cycle of the four large scenes from the life of Constantine the Great, which have been made to look like tapestries, starts at the entrance wall on the east side of the room. The first scene shows the sign of the Cross appearing in the sky on the eve of Constantine's battle against Maxentius [fig. 2]. The next scene, on the long south wall, shows Constantine triumphing over his adversary at the Milvian bridge [fig. 3]. The cycle continues on the west wall — through which one enters the papal rooms — with a representation of Pope Sylvester baptizing the emperor [fig. 4], and it ends with the scene between the windows on the north wall, showing how the Pope receives the famous donation from the hands of Constantine [fig. 5].

The series of Popes flanking these history scenes starts with St Peter at the left side of *The Apparition of the Cross*. The following Popes are not simply St Peter's first seven successors, but are Popes from various centuries, up to Gregory the Great (590–604) on the right side of *The Donation of Constantine*. The exact reasons for selecting these specific eight Popes are not clear, but the general meaning is obvious. Just like

---

[4] Quednau, *Die Sala di Costantino*, 41-2.

[5] These scenes have been damaged in the course of time and some of them have totally been repainted; for their history and the identification of their subjects, see Quednau, *Die Sala di Costantino*, 472-93.

[6] The tapestries were designed by Raphael's assistant Tommaso Vincidor, and woven in Brussels. They are now lost. I am not sure if they are the ones described in 1580–1581 by an anonymous visitor to Rome: 'Sono alla sala di Costantino molte pitture, tutta essendone coperta, eccetto il basso dove stanno panni di seta e d'oro continuamente, fatti a Fiorenza da papi de Medici […]' (Vatican Library, *cod. Barb. lat.* 2016, published by Lanciani R., "Il Codice barberiano XXX, 89, contenente frammenti di una descrizione di Roma del secolo XVI", *Archivio della società romana di storia patria* 6 (1883), 459).

the Popes who were painted around 1482 between the windows of the Sistine Chapel, they represent the uninterrupted link running from the past to the present. During an audience this link is seen to be continued personally by the living Pope.[7]

In this paper I will not go into the details of the monochrome scenes or the representations of the Popes, but concentrate on the four large history scenes, and discuss in particular the way in which their painters have represented the 'historic' events from the fourth century.

Changes Around 1520

Rolf Quednau, in 1979, observed acutely that the interruption in the work on the decoration of the Sala, caused by the death of first Raphael and then Pope Leo X, resulted in more than simply a change of painters.[8] After Raphael had passed away the Pope decided that not the renowned and experienced painter Sebastiano del Piombo would continue the decoration project, but the still young assistants of Raphael, using the preparatory drawings and cartoons of their deceased master. Soon afterwards, however, Leo X himself died, and his immediate successor, Hadrian VI, had neither the money nor the desire to finish the project. But he died within two years after his election and his successor Clement VII, a nephew of Leo X, had the work resumed almost immediately. However, he did not continue it according to the original plans.

From a letter written by Sebastiano del Piombo, on 6 September 1520, when Leo X was still alive, we can infer that the decoration of the first and the second wall of the Sala was in progress by the time of Raphael's death, and that it was to be continued on the remaining two walls with scenes showing Constantine releasing captured prisoners, and the preparation for Constantine's bath in the blood of innocent children.[9] How far the decoration had proceeded by the time of Leo's

---

[7] As some of the inscriptions under the Popes were lost and not restored correctly, it has become impossible to identify each of them accurately. This much is clear, though, that Clement I (on the right side of *The Apparition of the Cross*) is a portrait of the then reigning Pope Leo X, and that Leo I (right of *The Baptism of Constantine*) is a portrait of Clement VII. See, in detail, Quednau, *Die Sala di Costantino*, 157-326.

[8] Quednau, *Die Sala di Costantino*, 384 ff. and 447 ff.

[9] Published in Quednau, *Die Sala di Costantino*, 844-66, esp. 846. According to Quednau, 373-4, there is no literary source for the scene with the release of captured

death is not quite clear, but in 1523 Pope Clement must have decided to maintain Raphael's assistants without, however, sticking to the original plans for the decoration. It is true that Constantine would remain the protagonist of the decoration, but in a less prominent way. In the two remaining scenes he would be shown subservient to the Pope: on his knees to be baptized, and again kneeling while donating the territory of Rome to the Church.[10] How can this change of emphasis be explained?

Already before the death of Leo X the impact of the Reformation was becoming a serious threat. Not only purely theological issues were at stake, other issues also played a role. One of them was the authority and the position of the Pope. Martin Luther's doubts about the institution of the papacy, based on theological grounds, were embraced for political and nationalistic reasons by Ulrich von Hutten. In 1519 or 1520 Von Hutten published a number of writings by various authors who all attacked the position of the Pope, in particular his claims of representing the divine power on earth (the Pope as *Vicarius Christi*) and, therefore, his being elevated above temporal lords. These claims were not only based on a specific reading of biblical texts, but also on the historical tradition according to which the Emperor Constantine had donated the western, Roman half of his empire to Pope Sylvester. Several scholars from the fifteenth century, in particular Lorenzo Valla, had proved that the text of this donation, the so-called *Constitutum Constantini*, was not an authentic document written in the fourth century. At first these findings did not cause much of a stir, but the combination of Luther's doubts about the position of the Pope, together with Von Hutten's edition of the various reputations of the *Constitutum*'s authenticity, formed a major threat to the Holy See. Even Luther himself was shocked by what he learned from Von Hutten's edition, as appears from a letter from 24 February 1520:

---

prisoners; it may therefore have been inspired by classical reliefs showing a similar subject. The bathing scene is based, according to Quednau, 374-5, on various medieval legends of St Sylvester.

[10] For the literary sources of these scenes, see Quednau, *Die Sala di Costantino*, 448-50. He remarks that both scenes are based on 'apokryphen Textvorlagen' and that they were 'im Schrifttum des 15. und 16. Jahrhunderts gleichermassen umstritten'. Cf. Freiberg J., "In the Sign of the Cross: the Image of Constantine in the Art of Counter-Reformation Rome", in Lavin M.A. (ed.), *Piero della Francesca and His Legacy*, Studies in History of Art 48 (Hannover–London: 1995) 68.

> I have at hand Lorenzo Valla's proof [included in Von Hutten's edition] that the Donation of Constantine is a forgery. Good heavens, what darkness and wickedness is at Rome. You wonder at the judgment of God that such unauthentic, crass, imprudent lies not only lived, but prevailed for so many centuries, that they were incorporated in the canon law [...] and became as articles of faith. I am in such a passion that I scarcely doubt that the Pope is the Antichrist expected by the world, so closely do their acts, lives, sayings, and laws agree.[11]

The papal reaction to Von Hutten's publication was immediate: already in 1520 Pope Leo X ordered the burning of heretical books, among which those by Von Hutten were explicitly mentioned.[12]

It is in the context of these attacks on the position of the papacy that the changes in the decoration of the Sala di Costantino should be seen. Two events based on sources which were already suspect in the fifteenth century, were inserted to show how the Emperor Constantine, out of gratitude for his victory 'in the sign of the Cross', converted to the Christian faith and handed over half of his territory to the Pope.[13] Rolf Quednau has formulated this very aptly: 'Beide Fresken kommen einer Affirmation der illustrierten Ereignisse gleich, d.h. zwei umstrittene Sachverhalte wurden durch ihre Verbildlichung als historische Wahrheit sichtbar gemacht'.[14]

In what follows I will discuss how Raphael, but especially Giulio Romano and Gianfrancesco Penni, who executed the scenes of *The*

----

[11] Letter from Luther to Georg Spalatin, 24 February 1520, quoted after the translation in Partridge L., *The Renaissance in Rome 1400–1600* (London: 1996) 159. The original text reads: 'Ich habe [...] die durch Laurentius Valla widerlegte Schenkung Constantins in Händen, [...]. Lieber Gott, welch ein grosse Finsternis oder Nichtswürdigkeit der Römlinge! und, worüber du dich in Gottes Gericht wundern kannst, dass unter die Decretalen so unreine, so grobe, so unverschämte Lügen gesetzt worden sind und (damit nichts an dem greulichsten Greuel fehle) die Stelle von Glaubensartikeln eingenommen haben. Ich werde so in die Enge getrieben, dass ich fast nicht zweifle, dass der Pabst recht eigentlich der Antichrist sei, den nach der allgemein angenommenen Meinung die Welt erwartet; so sehr stimmt alles dazu, was er lebt, thut, redet und ordnet'. J.G. Walch (ed.), *Doktor Martin Luthers sämtliche Schriften*, vol 21 (*Briefe von 1507–1532*), Brief 265 (Gro Oesingen: 1986), quoted after the German translation of L. Partridge's book *Renaissance in Rom. Die Kunst der Päpste und Kardinäle* (Cologne: 1996) 158. See also Quednau, *Die Sala di Costantino*, 454-5.

[12] See, most extensively, Quednau, *Die Sala di Costantino*, 448 ff. Also very informative are Epp S., *Konstantinszyklen in Rom. Die päpstliche Interpretation der Geschichte Konstantins des Grossen bis zur Gegenreformation*, Schriften aus dem Institut für Kunstgeschichte der Universität München 36 (Munich: 1988) 32-8 and Chastel A., *The Sack of Rome. 1527* (Princeton, N.J.: 1983) 63-4.

[13] See above, n. 10.

[14] Quednau, *Die Sala di Costantino*, 458.

Baptism [fig. 4] and *The Donation* [fig. 5], tried to present these controversial events as 'historical truth'.

Painting History

What may strike the observers of the Constantine scenes most, is the large amount of details and additions to the main story. The foregrounds of *The Baptism* [fig. 4] and *The Donation* [fig. 5] in particular are occupied by emotionally engaged bystanders, and their backgrounds offer carefully reconstructed views of respectively the Lateran Baptistery and the church of St Peter. The main story is not situated prominently in the foreground, but somewhere in the middle zone of the picture. The same is basically true for *The Apparition* [fig. 2] and *The Battle* [fig. 3]. Many soldiers reacting emotionally to the apparition of the Cross occupy the foreground of the first scene, while the amount of fighting soldiers in the second scene makes the observers almost lose sight of Constantine himself.

All four scenes are full of details: archeologically interesting ones, like the costumes and arms of the soldiers, topographically involving ones, such as the carefully reconstructed backgrounds, engaging ones like the bystanders reacting to what is happening and the contemporarily dressed persons staring out of the picture, tragic ones such as the father clasping the dead body of his son in the left corner of *The Battle* [fig. 3], touching ones like the little boy playing with his dog in *The Donation* [fig. 5], unaware of the importance of what is going on, and amusing ones like the dwarf in the right foreground of *The Apparition* [fig. 2].

In short: there is a great variety of details. What may strike the observers also, is the wide range of emotions shown especially by the bystanders in the pictures. They all react to or seem to comment on what is going on, each in his or her own way. The soldiers in *The Apparition* [fig. 2] look to their commander, waiting for his reaction. In *The Donation* [fig. 5] some people climb on the columns and others push away the guards, all trying to see the Pope and the emperor, while mothers are explaining to their children what is going on.

Another striking feature is the presence of contemporary persons and elements in these historical scenes. The man on the left foreground of *The Baptism* [fig.4] is wearing sixteenth-century clothes, and his face looks as if it were portrayed from life. He is staring at the observers and seems to point out what is going on. A contemporary person also occupies the right foreground of *The Donation* [fig. 5], while the dwarf in *The Apparition* [fig. 2] could just as well be a portrait of a sixteenth-century person.[15]

Those observers who take some time to think over the pictures, may be struck by some details which, in spite of the general archaeological accuracy, cannot be correct. In the background of *The Apparition* [fig. 2], for instance, can be seen the mausoleums of the Emperors Augustus and Hadrian, and the pyramid of Romulus. This situates the scene in the *Ager Vaticanus*. Yet it is not probable that the emperor had his troops stationed on that spot on the day before the battle: that implies that he had only one night to move them to the Milvian Bridge where the battle took place. But the *Ager Vaticanus*, and more exactly the spot where Constantine is staring at the apparition of the Cross, is symbolically very significant, as it is the place where St Peter was buried, where the church in his honor would arise and where, from c. 1450 on, the Pope would reside.[16] The view of the interior of St Peter's in *The Donation* [fig. 5] is obviously anachronistic, as the construction of this church started only after Constantine's conversion (supposedly c. 315). At the moment of the donation (whenever that was supposed to have taken place) the building and its furnishing can not possibly have been in such a complete state as the painting shows.

Inscriptions explain the scenes, but sometimes in more than a straightforward way.[17] In *The Donation* [fig. 5] one inscription tells what the scene shows ('Ecclesiae dos a Constantino tributa'), while the other comments on it: 'now finally people can freely confess their faith in Christ' ('Iam tandem Christum libere profiteri licet'). In *The Baptism* [fig. 4] one inscription tells in words with biblical reminiscences that through his baptism Constantine is reborn: 'Lavacrum renascentis vitae C. Val. Constantini', echoing the words of St Paul's *Epistle to Titus* (3, 5): 'lavacrum regenerationis et renovationis Spiritus Sancti'.

---

[15] Already in 1568, in his *Vita* of Giulio Romano, Vasari made suggestions about the identity of these persons (V, 60-1; transl. II, 122-3). For the possible identification of these assumed portraits, see Quednau, *Die Sala di Costantino*, 344-5, 412-3 and 442-5. See also n. 32.

[16] Preimesberger R., "Tragische Motive in Raffaels *Transfiguration*", *Zeitschrift für Kunstgeschichte* 50/1 (1987) 108; Fehl P.P., "Raphael as a Historian: Poetry and Historical Accuracy in the Sala di Costantino", *Artibus et Historiae* 14/28 (1993) 22.

[17] All the inscriptions are transcribed and commented on by Quednau, *Die Sala di Costantino*, 345-6, 414-8, 445-6 and 852-3.

The other inscription explains that 'today salvation is come to Rome and the empire' ('Hodie salus urbi et imperio facta est'). These words repeat what Christ said to Zacheus when he donated half of all he possessed to the poor: 'Hodie salus domui huic facta est' (*Luke* 19, 9). In this way Constantine's baptism acquires almost biblical dimensions, which is visually underscored by the fact that the composition is based on representations of the baptism of Christ.

The various features discussed may make it clear that the paintings do not illustrate the historical events in a straightforward manner, but with a certain rhetoric.[18] They all show bystanders who are emotionally involved and in this way — and also through other means — the observers are invited to also get involved. Backgrounds and inscriptions are used to confer on the events a dimension which makes them seem important for all times and more than just something which happened in the past.

The paintings in the Sala di Costantino, therefore, are not literal illustrations of historical events, in spite of the general archaeological accuracy. They must consciously have been manipulated in such a way, that their significance would seem to range further than just the fact that they had occurred in the past, and that they would look like examples from history which will serve as lessons for the future.

Already Aristotle (384–322 BC) in his *Poetics* had made a distinction between history dealing with mere facts or particulars, and — on a higher level — history dealing with notions of a more general kind, which he described as belonging rather to the realm of poetry:

> the function of the poet is not to say what *has* happened, but to say the kind of thing that *would* happen, i.e. what is possible in accordance with probability or necessity. The historian and the poet are not distinguished by their use of verse or prose [...]. The distinction is this: the one says what has happened, the other the kind of things that would happen. For this reason poetry is more philosophical and more serious than history. Poetry tends to express universals, and history particulars.[19]

What Raphael and after him Giulio Romano and Gianfrancesco Penni seem to have tried to do, was to express not just particulars but uni-

---

[18] For the sake of completeness I must say that none of the written sources — as far as they were available (see above, n. 10) — gives enough information to enable the painters to make a 'literal' illustration. Yet it is clear that the scenes were composed according to well-thought-over principles.

[19] IX, 1451a-b (Penguin Classics, transl. by M. Heath (Harmondsworth: 1996) 16).

versals, elevating history to the level of poetry and universal truths. This was not uncommon in sixteenth-century painting. Later in the century, in 1564, this practice was discussed in a treatise by Giovanni Andrea Gilio. Referring to well-known sixteenth-century paintings in Rome, he wrote:

> A painter sometimes is a pure historian, sometimes a pure poet, and sometimes he is a mixture of both. When he is a pure poet, I think that he is allowed to paint whatever his fancy dictates him, with those gestures however, and with those exertions, which are appropriate to the character he makes.

The 'mixture of both' (*pittura mista*) is, many pages later, explained as follows:

> We will call him a 'mixed painter' (*pittore misto*), who creates a charming mixture of things which are true and which are invented, and who sometimes adds fabulous things for the sake of beauty. But when he wants to practice this genre, he should bring these things together in such a mode that they land on the appropriate place, either through his own fancy or through imitation, and that they seem to have been born from one and the same body, so that the beginning does not disharmonize with the middle, nor the middle with the end, but that they are so linked together, that all parts respond to each other. In this way the observer will experience the things which are fabulous and invented as true and appropriate, and will find that without them the work has neither beauty nor excellence. We can find an example of this in the work of Homer and Vergil, who created in their poems such a sweet, pleasant, graceful and beautiful mixture, that the more one reads them, the more they please, and if the world would last in eternity, they would please in eternity and they would always be esteemed.[20]

---

[20] *Due dialoghi di M. Giovanni Andrea Gilio* [Camerino: 1564] in: Barocchi P., *Trattati dell'arte del Cinquecento fra Manierismo e Controriforma*, 3 vols (Bari: 1960–1962) II, 15 and 89: 'Il pittore a le volte è puro istorico, a le volte puro poeta, et a le volte è misto. Quando è puro poeta, penso che lecito gli sia dipingere tutto quello che il capriccio gli detta, con quei gesti, con quei sforzi sieno però convenevoli a la figura che egli fa. [...] Chiameremo noi pittore misto quello che fa una leggiadra mescolanza di cose vere e finte et a le volte per vaghezza de l'opera v'aggiunse le favolose. Ma quando ei vuol in questo genere esercitarsi, deve di maniera consertarle, che cadano a propogito, o sia per proprio capriccio o per imitazione, e paiano nate d'un istesso corpo, in modo che il principio non discordi dal mezzo, né 'l mezzo dal fine, ma sieno in modo concatenate insieme, che si rispondano tutte proporzionatamente: acciò chi le vede giudichi le cose favolose e finte vere e proprie, e che, senza quelle, l'opera non avesse né vaghezza né bontà. Del che l'esempio potiamo pigliare da Omero e da Virgilio, i quali ne' loro poemi fecero sì dolce, vaga, leggiadra e bella mescolanza, che quanto più si leggono, tanto più piacciono, e se 'l mondo in eterno durasse, in eterno piacerebbono e sarebbono in pregio'.

As an example is mentioned how Vergil in the *Aeneid* had combined various historical events which took place at different moments, such as Aeneas meeting Dido, even though she lived — according to Gilio — more than 140 years after him.[21] Vergil also introduced personifications like Horror and Furor, and predictions of the future through the 'historical' scenes on the shield of Aeneas.[22] Michelangelo, Raphael and other artists following their lead — according to Gilio — have applied these and similar means to painting:

> Well, here you see in which way painters can gracefully use metaphors and metonymies, and also many other tropes, which, if one knows how to arrange and combine them well, will make an elegant and beautiful mixture.[23]

If we try to classify the paintings in the Sala di Costantino, they seem to belong to the category of *pittura mista* – the more so, as they compare very well with the examples of *pittura mista* in Rome that Gilio mentions: Giorgio Vasari's scenes from the life of Pope Paul III in the Palazzo della Cancelleria (1546), Francesco Salviati's scenes from the history of the Farnese family in the Palazzo Farnese (1552–1563); and the paintings in the Sala Regia of the Vatican Palace (which were being executed at the time Gilio was writing; fig. 13).[24] The latter ones

---

[21] *Aen.* I and IV.

[22] *Aen.* VIII, 618-731.

[23] Barocchi, II, 102: 'Or ecco in che modo i pittori possono usare le metafore e le metonimie vagamente, e molt'altre figure ancora, che, se uno le saprà ben ordinare et accompagnare, farà una vaga e bella mistura'. Gilio makes some interesting remarks about *pitture miste*. They are meant for a learned public, as he states while discussing Vasari's paintings in the Palazzo della Cancelleria in Rome (see n. 24): 'suchlike things are made for men of letters and gentlemen, and not for ignorants and plebeians, as these are not sacred figures' ('simil cose si fanno per letterati e gentiluomini, e non per ignoranti e plebei, conciossia che queste non sono figure sacre', ibid., 100). Also, the history itself should not be covered by so many embellishing elements, that it seems an allegory or *favola* rather than a scene from history: 'nor do I praise a painter who inserts in his admixture things that are so fabulous that they absorb what is true, and removes the decorum and the beauty from the story, and reduces it to a fiction or a fable' ('né lodo che il pittore frametta tra le sue misture cose tanto favolose che assorbano il vero, e lievi il decoro e la bellezza a l'istoria, e la riduca in finzione o in favola', ibid.). One should realize that Gilio was writing in exactly the same year that the Council of Trent decreed that religious pictures should be an exact illustration of the text of the Bible or that which is taught by the Church, and that everything that could lead to distraction was to be avoided. Gilio therefore wanted religious pictures to be plain and straightforward and warned that *pitture miste* should not be used for churches or for religious purposes: 'Mixed paintings really should not be installed in churches nor amongst sacred objects' ('Le miste pitture veramente non si doverebbono mettere ne le chiese né fra le cose sacre', ibid., 114).

[24] After Salviati's death in 1563, the paintings in the Palazzo Farnese were complet-

are especially relevant, as they depict events that are comparable to the ones in the Sala di Costantino: kings and emperors showing obedience to the Pope and donating their territory to him, or, in Gilio's words: 'Catholic emperors who have done some great benefit to the Church of Rome, to the Pope or to the Christian faith'.[25]

In the Sala di Costantino the painters have tried to raise the history scenes to the level of 'poetry', and 'to express universals' instead of 'particulars'. We have already noted some of the means they used to this end, but we will now take a closer look and study these means in detail.

Painting and Poetry

Many motifs and details of the paintings in the Sala di Costantino are based on a wide range of visual examples, among which the reliefs of the Arch of Constantine in Rome stand out in particular.[26] But rather than tracing individual examples, it is relevant for our purpose to study *how* the various visual elements were used.

It will come as no surprise that the *Constantine* paintings continue developments in Raphael's earlier works. The source of many motifs is accordingly to be found in the history paintings which Raphael executed in the adjoining *stanze*, and in other history paintings like *The Transfiguration* [fig. 8]. These motifs were noticed and admired by contemporary observers of the paintings, as appears from the descriptions

---

ed by Taddeo and Federigo Zuccaro. On Vasari's paintings in the Palazzo della Cancelleria and those of Salviati in the Palazzo Farnese, see Kliemann J., *Gesta dipinte. La grande decorazione nelle dimore italiane dal Quattrocento al Seicento* (Milan: 1993) 37-55. On the Sala Regia, see Partridge L. – Starn R., "Triumphalism and the Sala Regia in the Vatican", in B. Wisch and S.S. Munshower (ed.), *'All the World's a Stage [...]'. Art and Pageantry in the Renaissance and Baroque, I: Triumphal Celebrations and the Rituals of Statecraft*, Papers in Art History from the Pennsylvania State University 6 (University Park, PA: 1990) 23-81; Böck A., *Die Sala Regia im Vatikan als Beispiel der Selbstdarstellung des Papsttums in der zweiten Hälfte des 16. Jahrhunderts*, Studien zur Kunstgeschichte 112 (Hildesheim: 1997) and Jong J.L. de, "Papal History and Historical Invenzione. Vasari's Frescoes in the Sala Regia", in Jacks P.J. (ed.), *Vasari's Florence: Artists and Literati at the Medicean Court* (Cambridge: 1998) 220-37. Gilio mentions the Palazzi della Cancelleria and Farnese on p. 15, and the Sala Regia on p. 114 of Barocchi's edition.

[25] Gilio, *Due dialoghi*, 114: 'catolici imperatori c'hanno fatto qualche gran giovamento a la Romana Chiesa, al Pontefice overo a la cristiana religione'.

[26] Quednau, *Die Sala di Costantino*, passim, exhaustively lists the visual examples in his discussion of the individual scenes; Fehl, "Raphael as a Historian", esp. 17 ff., stresses the importance of the reliefs on Arch of Constantine as a visual source.

by Giorgio Vasari, who wrote and rewrote Raphael's biography in respectively 1550 and 1568. However, pointing out similar motifs in earlier scenes by Raphael does not really provide an answer to the question how he developed the various means to raise history painting from the level of expressing 'particulars' to 'universals': it only pushes the question forward. For where did Raphael get his inspiration from?

To answer this question, one should consider both visual and literary sources, even though it is hard to make a neat distinction. One may assume that as a painter, Raphael was in the first place susceptible to visual examples. Yet the specific way in which he used his visual means betrays acquaintance with art theoretical writings and classical literary theories. To start with Raphael's visual models, by far the most important ones seem to have been a few specific works of one particular artist: Donatello's bronze reliefs from c. 1446–1447 on the high altar of the church of S. Antonio in Padua, showing four miracles performed by St Anthony [fig. 6, 7]. In each composition Donatello has represented the saint in the center, surrounded by crowds of amazed, emotionally reacting people. They climb on the columns of the encompassing architecture to get a better view of the miracle performing saint, they discuss with each other, try to explain what has happened and lift their arms up in the air. Some motifs and combinations were almost 'literally' adopted by Raphael and his pupils in the paintings of the Sala di Costantino (particularly in *The Baptism* [fig. 4] and *The Donation* [fig. 5]) and, earlier, in the *stanze* [figs. 9, 10, 11, 12].[27] Donatello may have found some examples for the

---

[27] For a detailed discussion of the various motifs that Raphael adopted, and of the question how Raphael knew Donatello's reliefs (Raphael never was in Padua, so he must have known them only through copies), see Vöge W., *Raphael und Donatello* (Strasbourg: 1896); Dunkelman M.L., *Donatello's Influence on Italian Renaissance Painting* (Ph. D., New York University: 1976) (Ann Arbor, Mi.: 1979) 119-42; and Kecks R., "Assistenzfigur und Architekturkulisse: zur Entwicklung eines Bildmotivs bei Donatello und Raffael", *Mitteilungen des Kunsthistorischen Institutes in Florenz* 33/2-3 (1989) 257-300, 278-80. Giorgio Vasari admiringly described Raphael's use of figures climbing on the pedestals of columns in *The Expulsion of Heliodorus* [fig. 9]: 'Veggonsi oltra ciò, per bel capriccio di Raffaello, molti saliti sopra i zoccoli del basamento, et abbracciatisi alle colonne, con attitudini disagiatissime stare a vedere; et un popolo tutto attonito in diverse e varie maniere, che aspetta il successo di questa cosa' [IV, 182] ('Besides this, through a beautiful fancy of Raffaello's, one sees many who have climbed on to the socles of the column-bases, and, clasping the shafts, stand looking in most uncomfortable attitudes; with a throng of people showing their amazement in many various ways, and awaiting the result of this event' [transl. I, 727]). In *The Miracle of the Mass at Bolsena* [fig. 10], women point out to each other and to their children what is happening to the sceptical priest who is celebrating mass. Vasari described

motif of people climbing on the pedestals of columns in fourteenth-century Italian painting, but the individual emotional reactions and the specific structure of the compositions were his own invention.[28]

Raphael must also have been acquainted with written sources. One of them may have been the treatise on painting by Leon Battista Alberti, from 1435–1436.[29] Amongst other things, Alberti advised to include portraits and gesticulating persons in history paintings, so as to catch the attention of the observers and make them feel involved.[30]

---

them in the following words: 'Fecevi Raffaello intorno molte varie e diverse figure [...] e alterate dalla novità del caso fanno bellissime attitudini in diversi gesti [...] fra le quali ve n'ha una che a piè della storia da basso siede in terra tenendo un putto in collo, la quale sentendo il ragionamento che mostra un'altra di dirle del caso successo al prete, maravigliosamente si storce mentre che ella ascolta ciò, con una grazia donnesca molto propria e vivace' [IV, 178-9] ('Round him [the priest] Raffaello made many figures, all varied and different [...] and all, bewildered by the strangeness of the event, are making various most beautiful movements and gestures [...]. Among the women is one who is seated on the ground at the foot of the scene, holding a child in her arms; and she, hearing the account that another appears to be giving her of the thing that has happened to the priest, turns in a marvellous manner as she listens to this, with a womanly grace that is very natural and lifelike' [transl. I, 725]). Vasari described the reacting people in *The Donation of Constantine* [fig. 5] as follows: 'Fece Giulio in questa storia molte femine che ginocchioni stanno a vedere cotale cerimonia, le quali sono bellisime; et un povero che chiede la limosina; un putto sopra un cane, che scherza; et i lanzi della guardia del Papa che fanno far largo e star indietro il popolo, come si costuma' [V, 61] ('In this scene Giulio painted many women kneeling there to see that ceremony, who are very beautiful; a beggar asking for alms; a little boy amusing himself by riding on a dog; and the Lancers of the Papal Guard who are making the people give way and stand back, as is the custom' [transl. II, 123]). Cf. Vasari's description of Raphael's *Transfiguration* [fig. 8]: 'Èvvi una femina fra molte, la quale è principale figura di quella tavola, che inginocchiata dinanzi a quegli, voltando la testa loro e coll'atto delle braccia verso lo spiritato, mostra la miseria di colui' [IV, 203] ('Among many women is one, the principal figure in that panel, who, having knelt down before the Apostles, and turning her head towards them, stretches her arms in the direction of the maniac and points out his misery' [transl. I, 740]).

[28] See Greenhalgh M., *Donatello and his Sources* (London: 1981) 159-62, who can only come up with examples for individual motifs but not for the combination of the various motifs or the compositional devices. For fourteenth-century examples of the motif of people standing on the pedestals of columns, and Donatello's use of them, see Kecks, "Assistenzfigur und Architekturkulisse", 257-66.

[29] Alberti originally wrote the treatise in Latin, in 1435; he translated it into Italian in 1436 and added a few details. Only more than a century later did it first appear in print, in Basel in 1540, in Latin. The first printed edition in Italian — a translation from the Latin by Lodovico Domenichi — appeared in Venice in 1547. It was followed by an Italian translation by Cosimo Bartoli, in *Opuscoli morali di Leon Battista Alberti* (Venice: 1568). See Kemp M., "Introduction", in *Leon Battista Alberti. On Painting*, Penguin Classics (Harmondsworth: 1991) 23 and 28.

[30] *De pictura* III, 56 (p. 98-101): 'Quae res [*sc.* ab ipsa natura omnia suscipere] in picturis quam sit optanda videmus, nam in historia si adsit facies cogniti alicuius hominis, tametsi nonnullae praestantioris artificii emineant, cognitus tamen vultus

This was a device which was widely applied in fifteenth century paint-ing, but it seems to have originated in the fourteenth century.[31] Raphael and his pupils used it extensively in the Sala di Costantino, as, for instance, in *The Baptism* [fig. 4] and *The Donation* [fig. 5]. In con-trast to the 'historical' persons, some individuals in these scenes are wearing sixteenth-century clothes, which makes them stand out as contemporary personages and suggests that they were portrayed from life.[32] The man on the left foreground in *The Baptism* [fig. 4], for instance, stares at the observers and seems to point out what is going on, in accordance with Alberti's advice:

> I like there to be someone in the *historia* who tells the spectators what is going on, and either beckons them with his hand to look, or with fero-cious expressions and forbidding glance challenges them not to come near, as if he wished their business to be secret, or points to some dan-ger or remarkable thing in the picture, or by his gestures invites you to laugh or weep with them.[33]

---

omnium spectantium oculos ad se rapit, tantam in se, quod sit a natura sumptum, et gratiam et vim habet' ('We can see how desirable this [*sc.* taking everything from Nature] is in painting when the figure of some well-known person is present in a 'his-toria', for although others executed with greater skill may be conspicuous in the pic-ture, the face that is known draws the eyes from all spectators, so great is the power and the attraction of something taken from Nature').

[31] Gesticulating figures can already be seen in the works of Giotto (c. 1277–1337), and according to Vasari's *Vita*, Giotto included several portraits of contemporaries in his works. Well-known fifteenth-century examples of portraits in history scenes include the works of Benozzo Gozzoli, Domenico Ghirlandaio and Sandro Botticelli; see also below, n. 33.

[32] For possible portraits in the *Constantine* scenes, see Quednau, *Die Sala di Costantino*, 344-5, 412-3, and 442-5; see also above, n. 15.

[33] *De pictura* II, 42 (p. 80-3): 'Tum placet in historia adesse quempiam qui earum quae gerantur rerum spectatores admoneat, aut manu ad visendum advocet, aut qua-si id negotium secretum esse velit, vultu ne eo proficiscare truci et torvis oculis minite-tur, aut periculum remve aliquam illic admirandam demonstret, aut ut una arrideas aut ut simul deplores suis te gestibus invitet'. Fifteenth-century examples of similarly gesticulating figures include the large man on the right foreground of Paolo Uccello's *Flood* of c. 1440 (Florence, S. Maria Novella, Chiostro verde), and the large central figure in Filippo Lippi's *Banquet of Herod* of c. 1460 (Prato, Duomo).

[34] II, 40 (p. 78-9): 'Primum enim quod in historia voluptatem afferat est ipsa copia et varietas rerum. [...] Dicam historiam esse copiosissimam illam in qua suis locis per-mixti aderunt senes, viri, adolescentes, pueri, matronae, virgines, infantes, cicures, catelli, aviculae, equi, pecudes, aedificia, provinciaeque; omnemque copiam laudabo modo ea ad rem de qua illic agitur conveniat'. Cf. Leonardo da Vinci, no 268, I, 110-1: '"Della varietà nelle istorie": Dillettesi il pittore ne componimenti dell'istorie della copia e varietà e fuga il replicare alcuna parte che in essa fatta sia accio ch'ella novita e abbondantia attraga a se e diletti l'occhio d'essa riguardatore, dico che nella istoria si richiede e ai loro lochi accadendo misti li homini di diverse effigie con diverse etta e abbiti in sieme misti con donne fanciulli cani cavagli ediffici campagne e colli'

As another device to make the observers feel involved, Alberti stressed the importance of showing a great variety of details and people reacting to what is going on in the picture:

> The first thing that gives pleasure in a *historia* is a plentiful variety. [...] I would say a picture was richly varied if it contained a properly arranged mixture of old men, youths, boys, matrons, maidens, children, domestic animals, dogs, birds, horses, sheep, buildings and provinces; and I would praise any great variety, provided it is appropriate to what is going on in the picture.[34]
>
> [...]
>
> A *historia* will move spectators when the men painted in the picture outwardly demonstrate their own feelings as clearly as possible. Nature provides — and there is nothing to be found more rapacious of her like than she, — that we mourn with the mourners, laugh with those who laugh, and grieve with the grief-stricken.[35]

Similar ideas were voiced by Raphael's contemporary Leonardo da Vinci in his unpublished notes for a treatise on painting.[36] Especially relevant is his remark about the importance of showing people reacting to what is happening in the story:

> The elements of narrative paintings ought to move those who look at or contemplate them in the same way as him who the narrative painting represents. That is, if the narrative painting represents terror, fear, flight, sorrow, weeping, and lamentation; or pleasure, joy, laughter and similar conditions, the minds of those who view it ought to make their limbs move so that they seem to find themselves in the same situation which the figures in the story represent. If they do not do so, the skill of the painter is in vain.[37]

("'Of variety in narrative paintings': The painter takes pleasure in the abundance and variety of the elements of narrative paintings, and avoids the repetition of any part that occurs in it, so that novelty and abundance may attract and delight the eye of the observer. I say that, depending on the scene, a narrative painting requires a mixture of men of various appearances, ages, and costumes, and also mixed with women, children, dogs, horses, buildings, fields, and hills').

[35] *De pictura* II, 41 (p. 80-1): 'Animos deinde spectantium movebit historia, cum qui aderunt picti homines suum animi motum maxime prae se ferent. Fit namque natura, qua nihil sui similium rapacius inveniri potest, ut lugentibus conlugeamus, ridentibus adrideamus, dolentibus, condoleamus'. There are many more places in Alberti's treatise where these advices are repeated or worked out in greater detail and illustrated with examples.

[36] See n. 34. Leonardo's notes existed in various manuscripts and were published for the first time only in 1817, by Guglielmo Manzi in Rome; see the 'Introduction' by L.H. Heydenreich to A.P. McMahon's translation of Leonardo's *Treatise on Painting* and Pedretti C., *Leonardo da Vinci on Painting. A Lost Book* (Berkeley–Los Angeles: 1964).

[37] Leonardo da Vinci, no 267, I, 110: "Delle componimenti dell istorie": Li componimenti delle istorie depinte debbono movere li risguardatori e contemplatori

Other details cannot be explained by referring to art treatises, but only by assuming that Raphael had at least some acquaintance with classical literature. An example are the angels flying above Constantine in the *Battle*-scene. They are fighting in favor of Constantine's army, even though nobody on the battlefield seems to see them. This motif strongly resembles similar events in Vergil's *Aeneid*, for instance in II, 604-23 where Venus shows to Aeneas how — invisible to mortal men — the Gods are battling on the side of the Greeks and are helping them to destroy Troy.[38] Raphael had used this device earlier in *The Expulsion of Heliodorus* [fig. 9] in the Stanza d'Eliodoro, where an avenging horseman is seen by Heliodorus but not by the other people in the scene. Vasari very aptly described it as follows:

> one sees the furious onset of an armed man on horseback, who, accompanied by two on foot, and in an attitude of the greatest fierceness, is smiting and riding down the proud Heliodorus, who is seeking [...] to rob the Temple of all the wealth stored for the widows and orphans. Already the riches and treasures could be seen being removed and taken away, when, on account of the terror of the strange misfortune of

---

di quelle a quello medesimo effeto che è quello per il quale tale istoria e figurata cioè se quella istoria rapressenta terrore paura o fuga overamente dolore pianto ellamentatione, o piaccere gaudio e riso e simili accidenti ch'elle menti dessi consideratori movino le membra con atti che paiono ch'essi sieno congionti al medesimo caso di che esse istorie figurate sonno rapresentatrici e se cosi non fano l'ingegnio di tale operratore è vano'.

[38] Vergil, *Aen.* II, 604-23; similar events in *Aen.* X, 633-88 and XII, 843-86, and in the works of Homer, for instance *Il.* VIII and XVI. One could also think of some episodes in the Bible, for instance the story of Balaam and his donkey (*Numbers* 22, 22-35), the blinding of Saul (*Acts* 9, 3-9), and the account of Pharaoh and his troops pursuing the Israelites (*Exodus* 14, 9-28), when 'the angel of God which went before the camp of Israel, removed and went behind them; and the pillar of the cloud went from before their face, and stood behind them'. Eusebius, by the way, in his *Life of Constantine* (I, 38) of c. 343, described the Battle of the Milvian Bridge in terms of a re-enactment of the Crossing of the Red Sea. The motif of helping gods or saints, who have been depicted but are not visible to the persons in the scenes, was also used in 1572 by Vasari in his painting of *The Battle of Lepanto* in the Sala Regia in the Vatican Palace; see De Jong, "Papal History and Historical Invenzione", 235. Raphael must have been fairly familiar with the work of Vergil. Not only did he add a very clear Vergilian detail to his painting of *The Fire in the Borgo* (Aeneas and his son and father escaping from the burning city of Troy), already mentioned by Vasari in 1550 (IV, 193; [fig. 12]), he was also involved in designing prints with scenes from the *Aeneid*, which were executed by Marcantonio Raimondi: one illustrating the plague at Crete, the so-called *Morbetto*, of c. 1512–1513 (*Aen.* III, 130-91; Bartsch A., *Le peintre graveur* (Vienna: 1803–1821) XIV, 17) and the so-called *Quos ego* of c. 1518, illustrating several episodes grouped around the five lines of Vomanius (a rather obscure author who lived during the Roman Empire) which summarize the content of *Aen.* I (Bartsch XIV, 352).

Heliodorus, so rudely struck down and smitten by the three figures mentioned above (*although, this being a vision, they are seen and heard by him alone* [my italics]), behold, they are all dropped and upset on the ground, those who were carrying them falling down through the sudden terror and panic that had come upon all the following of Heliodorus.[39]

Another motif which points to acquaintance with classical literature occurs in the *Battle at the Milvian Bridge* [fig. 3]. In the left foreground an old soldier clasps the dead body of a young man. In 1695 Giovanni Pietro Bellori described this fragment as follows:

in the midst of the combat and the massacre, fierceness turns into the compassion of an old father, who has recognized his young son to be a dead page now, stretched out with his insignia, and bending down with one knee on the ground he embraces the inanimate body, so as not to leave it unburied.[40]

This motif may have been suggested to Raphael by the similar theme of an old man carrying his drowned young son on his shoulder in Michelangelo's painting of *The Flood* in the Sistine Chapel of c. 1510.[41] But it may also have been inspired by passages from Vergil's *Aeneid*, for instance Mezentius weeping over his dead son Lausus, or Evander crying over the death of Pallas.[42] Against the setting of fight-

---

[39] Vasari, transl. I, 726; IV, 180-2: 'se vede la furia d'uno armato a cavallo, il quale, accompagnato da due appiè, con attitudine ferocissima urta e percuote il superbissimo Eliodoro, che [...] vuole spogliare il tempio di tutti i depositi delle vedove e de' pupilli: e già si vede lo sgombro delle robbe et i tesori che andavano via, ma per la paura del nuovo accidente di Eliodoro abbattuto e percosso aspramente dai tre predetti — che per essere ciò visione, da lui solamente sono veduti e sentiti —, si veggono tutti traboccare e versare per terra, cadendo chi gli portava per un subito orrore e spavento che era nato in tutte le genti di Eliodoro'.

[40] *Descrizzione delle imagini dipinte da Rafaelle d'Urbino nelle camere del Palazzo Apostolico Vaticano* (Rome: 1695), 56; the description continues: 'One can well sense the weight and the burden of the limbs falling down while the father, raising the shoulder, is lifting him from under his side. The naked arm hangs down while the head rests on the other arm, stretched on the ground, the fingers of the hand releaving their grasp of the insignia' ('frà le stragi, e 'l conflitto cangiasi la fierezza nella commiserazione di un vecchio Padre, il quale avendo ricinosciuto il figliuolo giovane Alfiero morto, e disteso con l'insegna, piegasi con un ginocchio à terra, ed abbraccia il corpo esangue, per non lasciarlo insepolto e ben s'intende la gravezza, e 'l peso delle cadenti membra, mentre il padre nel sollevarlo di sotto il fianco, alzandosi la spalla, pende il braccio ignudo, e si abbandona la testa sù l'altro braccio disteso à terra, rallentante le dita della mano nel ritenere l'insegna').

[41] Fehl, "Raphael as a Historian", 47.

[42] Resp. *Aen.* X, 833-908, and XI, 139-81; cf. *Aen.* IX, 473-502, where the death of Nisus and Euryales is lamented by their mother.

ing and killing, a motif like this lends a tragic, 'human' note to the scene.[43]

This stylistic device was recommended by Quintilian in his *Institutio Oratoria* of c. 90. Using the example of the storming of a town, he tells how a report of it can increase the impact on the audience by highlighting stirring details:

> the mere statement that the town was stormed, while no doubt it embraces all that such a calamity involves, has all the curtness of a dispatch, and fails to penetrate to the emotions of the hearer. But if we expand all that the one word 'stormed' includes, we shall see the flames pouring from house and temple, and hear the crash of falling roofs and one confused clamour blent of many cries: we shall behold some in doubt whither to fly, others clinging to their nearest and dearest in one last embrace, while the wailing of women and children and the laments of old men that the cruelty of fate should have spared them to see that day will strike upon our ears. Then will come the pillage of treasure sacred and profane, the hurrying to and fro of the plunderers as they carry off their booty or return to seek for more, the prisoners driven each before his own inhumane captor, the mother struggling to keep her child, and the victors fighting over the richest of the spoil. For though, as I have already said, the sack of a city includes all these things, it is less effective to tell the whole news at once than to recount it detail by detail. And we shall secure the vividness we seek, if only our descriptions give the impression of truth, *nay, we may even add fictitious incidents of the type which commonly occur* [my italics]. The same vivid impression may be produced also by the mention of the accidents of each situation [...].[44]

Quintilian is, of course, talking about rhetorical means, but his advice can just as well be used for paintings. In fact, according to the descrip-

---

[43] Preimesberger, "Tragische Motive in Raffaels *Transfiguration*", 112-3, connects this detail with Aristotle, *Poetica* 1453 a.

[44] VIII, 3, 61-70 (Loeb Classical Library, transl. by H.E. Butler (London–Cambridge, Mass.: 1920–1922) 244-51): 'Sine dubio enim, qui dicit expugnatam esse civitatem, complectitur omnia quaecunque talis fortuna recipit, sed in adfectus minus penetrat brevis hic velut nuntius. At si aperias haec, quae verbo uno inclusa erant, apparebunt effusae per domus ac templa flammae et ruentium tectorum fragor et ex diversis clamoribus unus quidam sonus, aliorum fuga incerta, alii extremo complexu suorum cohaerentes et infantium feminarumque ploratus et male usque in illum diem servati fato senes; tum illa profanorum sacrorumque direptio, efferentium praedas repetentiumque discursus et acti ante suum quisque praedonem catenati et conata retinere infantem suum mater et, sicubi maius lucrum est, pugna inter victores. Licet enim haec omnia, ut dixi, complectatur eversio, minus est tamen totum dicere quam omnia. Consequemur autem, ut manifesta sint, si fuerint versimilia; et licebit etiam falso adfingere quidquid fieri solet. Contiget eadem claritas etiam ex accidentibus'.

tion of Pliny, a similar stylistic device was used long before Quintilian by the Greek painter Aristides in his rendering of the capture of a city:

> a picture of a mother lying wounded to death in the sack of a city; she appears conscious that her babe is creeping towards her breast, and afraid lest, now that her milk is dried up, he should suck blood.[45]

Through Pliny's description Raphael certainly was aware of this device of adding 'fictitious incidents' so as to intensify 'the impression of truth', as he used it in the foreground of his design for a print showing *The Plague in Crete*.[46] This raises the question if Raphael knew and used more stylistic devices recommended in classical literature.

Again it is hard to decide whether Raphael knew certain stylistic principles through visual examples or through personal knowledge of classical literary sources, but it is striking that the stylistic means he used seem to form a direct illustration of the recommendations of authors such as Aristotle, Cicero and Quintilian. The foreground of *The Donation* [fig. 5], for instance, includes a group of women, men and children, reacting to the main event that is taking place in the middle ground. In this way, common people are contrasted with historically important people. The way in which these common people are grouped and in which they behave — talking, gesticulating, turning to each other — forms a contrast to the solemn way in which the emperor kneels before the Pope and makes his donation. A similar use of contrasts or *contrapposti* can be observed in the other scenes. In *The Apparition* [fig. 2], Constantine reacts composedly to the appearance of the Cross, while his men around him behave excitedly.[47] In *The Battle* [fig. 3] the emperor is shown victoriously riding his rearing white stallion, in contrast to his adversary, who is desperately grabbing his horse in the water, in the middle of general chaos and confusion.

---

[45] *Naturalis historia* **XXXV**, 98: 'oppido capto ad matris morientis ex volnere mammam adrepens infans, intellegiturque sentire mater et timere ne emortuo lacte sanguinem lambat' (transl. after Jex-Blake K. – Sellers E., *The Elder Pliny's Chapters on the History of Art* (Chicago: 1968) 132-5).

[46] See n. 38.

[47] See the pertinent remarks by Preimesberger, "Tragische Motive in Raffaels *Transfiguration*", 108-10, about the contrast in reactions and emotions between the 'common people' on the foreground and the apostles in the middleground of Raphael's *Transfiguration* [fig. 8], esp. 109: 'der kontrollierten und edel gedämpften Affektgestik der Apostel, die so deutlich dem Decorum gehorcht, [ist] die in Körperhaltung, Mimik und Gestik ungedämpfte Affektäusserung des 'vulgus' entgegengesetzt'.

Contrasting opposites as a compositional device was already recommended by Aristotle in his *Rhetoric*, because 'contraries are easily
understood and even more so when placed side by side, and also
because antithesis resembles a syllogism; for refutation is a bringing
together of contraries'.[48] Similar ideas were later voiced by Leonardo
in relation to painting:

> In *istorie* one ought to mingle direct contraries so that they may afford a
> great contrast to one another, and all the more when they are in close
> proximity; that is, the ugly next to the beautiful, the big to the small, the
> old to the young, the strong to the weak; all should be varied as much as
> possible and close together.[49]

As can be inferred from this quote, contrasts are not only used so as to
make certain things stand out very clearly. There are also contrasts for
the sake of variety. Within the group of common people on the foreground in *The Donation* [fig. 5], for instance, are various contrasts: a
strong young father is sitting next to a cripple old man, a young
woman in a yellowish dress talks to an old lady, a child on the left is
picked up by his mother so as to see what is going on, while the boy in
the center keeps playing with his dog, unaware of the importance of
what is happening. The contemporarily dressed person on the right,
looking out of the picture to the observers, is contrasted to the intensely involved person on the left, who has climbed on the base of a column. Similarly, the two young armour-bearers in the lower left corner
of *The Apparition* [fig. 2] are contrasted with the dwarf in the opposite
corner. It would take too long to point out all the contrasts in *The Battle* [fig. 3]. A similar use of contrasts can also be related to classical literature. Cicero, for instance, recommended it at several places as a
means of embellishment:

> in speeches the purpose of which is to give pleasure there are various
> methods of arrangement. For we either keep to chronological order or
> to arrangement in classes; or we ascend from smaller matters to larger
> or glide down from larger ones to smaller; or we group these with com-

---

[48] *Rhetoric* 1410a (Loeb Classical Library, transl. by J.H. Freese (Cambridge,
Mass.–London: 1991) 392-3. I owe most of the references to matters relating to contrasts or *contraposto* to the very instructive article by Summers D., "Contrapposto: Style
and Meaning in Renaissance Art", *The Art Bulletin* 59/3 (1977) 336-61.

[49] No 271, I, 111: 'Dico che nelle istorie si debbe mischiare insieme viccinamente i
retti contrari per che dano gran parangone l'uno al'altro e tanto più quanto saranno
più propinqui cioè il brutto viccino al bello el grande al piccholo el vechio al giovane il
forte al debolo e cosi si varia quanto si po e più viccino'.

plete irregularity [*inaequabilis varietas*], intertwining small matters with great ones, simple with complicated, obscure with clear, cheerful with gloomy, incredible with probable, all of these methods falling under the head of embellishment.[50]

Still more classically inspired stylistic means may be observed within the groups of bystanders in the scenes. Some of them do see what is going on, but do not seem to realize the significance of it.[51] This may be a means to set off the momentum of the main event, just as in Ovid's description of Daedalus and Icarus flying through the air:

> Some fisher, perhaps, plying his quivering rod, some shepherd leaning on his staff, or a peasant bent over his plough handle caught sight of them [Daedalus and Icarus] as they flew past and stood stock still in astonishment, believing that these creatures who could fly through the air must be gods.[52]

At the same time these groups of bystanders form a demonstration of the process of 'recognition', as it was described by Aristotle in his *Poetica*.[53] This is especially clear in *The Donation*, where the people in the

---

[50] *De partitione oratoria* IV, 12: 'Quia quibus in orationibus delectatio finis est varii sunt ordines collocandi. Nam aut temporum servantur gradus aut generum distributiones, aut a minoribus ad maiora ascendimus aut a maioribus ad minora delabimur: aut haec inaequabili varietate distinguimus, cum parva magnis, simplicia coniunctis, obscura dilucidis, laeta tristibus, incredibilia probabilibus inteximus, quae in exornationem cadunt omnia'. Text and translation quoted after the Loeb edition by H. Rackham (London–Cambridge, Mass.: 1968) 320-1.

[51] Cf. Vasari's descriptions of Raphael's *Mass at Bolsena* [fig. 10], quoted in n. 27.

[52] *Metamorphoses* VIII, 217-20: 'Hos aliquis tremula dum captat harundine pisces, / aut pastor baculo stivave innixus arator / vidit et obstipuit, quique aethera carpere possent / credidit esse deos'. Transl. after Innes M.M., Penguin Classics (Harmondsworth: 1974–1978) 185.

[53] *Poetica* 1452a-b and 1454b-55a (Penguin Classics, transl. by M. Heath (Harmondsworth: 1996) 17-9 and 26-7); it is a matter of speculation if and how Raphael was familiar with Aristotle's *Poetica*. According to Weinberg B., *A History of Literary Criticism in the Italian Renaissance* (Chicago: 1961) 422: 'Beginning with Valla's translation into Latin in 1498, a whole series of documents soon became available to the Renaissance reader: the Greek text of 1508, the reprinted Valla and Averroës in 1515, Erasmus's Greek text of 1532, Pazzi's text and translation of 1536 (rpt 1537 and 1538), and finally Segni's translation into Italian of 1549'. See also Buck A., *Die Rezeption der Antike in den romanischen Literaturen der Renaissance*, Grundlagen der Romanistik 8 (Berlin: 1976) 148-53. According to Preimesberger, "Tragische Motive in Raffaels *Transfiguration*", 111-2, Raphael may have known the content of the *Poetica* through his literary friends, notably Janus Lascaris, the editor of the Greek edition of 1508 (Venice). Preimesberger suggests (p. 112): 'Sollte also die staunenswerte kreative wie rezeptive Intelligenz Raffaels, rascher und zielgerichteter als die Gelehrten Leos X., sich ähnlich wie auf die Wiedergewinnung der antiken architektonischen Gestalt Roms auch auf den Versuch sichtbarer Wiederherstellung der antiken Tragödie im Medium moderner theatralischer Malerei gerichtet haben?'

foreground are in various stages of recognizing the consequences of
the emperor's action. According to Aristotle, 'recognition is a change
from ignorance to knowledge'. It comes about 'as a result of what has
happened before, out of necessity or in accordance with probability'.
A recognition of this kind 'will involve pity or fear, and it is a basic
premise that tragedy is an imitation of actions of this kind. Moreover,
bad fortune or good fortune will be the outcome in such cases'.[54] The
people in the scene are starting to realize that what they are witnessing
is a change of their fortune for the better — and the observers of the
scene are supposed to join them in realizing this. The inscription on
the left column makes it clear what this change of fortune involves:
now finally people can freely confess their faith in Christ ('Iam tandem
Christum libere profiteri licet').[55] In order to make the observers feel
involved, Raphael tried to express various sorts of reactions and emotions, in accordance with contemporary art theory.[56] But here too he
may have drawn inspiration from Aristotle's *Poetics*, adapting his recommendations for a theater play to painting:

> When constructing plots and working them out complete with their lin-
> guistic expression, one should so far as possible visualize what is hap-
> pening. By envisaging things very vividly in this way, as if one were
> actually present at the events themselves, one can find out what is
> appropriate, and inconsistencies are least likely to be overlooked. [...]
> One should also, as far as possible, work plots out using gestures.[57]

One could consider *The Apparition* [fig. 2] in the same way, although
the aspect of recognition is already included in the story itself. Still, in
the various reactions of the soldiers and of Constantine himself,
Raphael has tried to represent their growing recognition of the changing fortune.[58]

Also some details show the aspect of recognition, for instance the
old father embracing his dead son in *The Battle* [fig. 3]. Although the
army in which he is fighting is gaining a victory, his fortune has

---

[54] *Poetica* 1452a-b (Penguin Classics, transl. by M. Heath (Harmondsworth: 1996)
18-9).

[55] See above, n. 17.

[56] See above, n. 35 and 37.

[57] *Poetica* 1455a (Penguin Classics, transl. by M. Heath (Harmondsworth: 1996) 27).

[58] In this case one could make a link with the — according to Aristotle, *Poetica*
1454b (Penguin Classics, transl. by M. Heath (Harmondsworth: 1996) 26) — 'least
artistic kind [of recognition]', viz. 'by means of tokens'. Of this kind of recognitions,
those which 'are used only for confirmation are less artistic [...]; recognitions which
arise out of a reversal [...] are better'.

reversed for the worse now that he recognizes the dead body of his son.[59] Maxentius, too, drowning in the river, recognizes his changing fortune, now that he realizes that Constantine, assisted by divine intervention, is the glorious victor of the decisive battle.[60]

The various events from Constantine's life all take place against an accurately reconstructed background. *The Baptism* [fig. 4] is situated in the baptistery of St John in Lateran, and *The Donation* [fig. 5] in St Peter's which, at the time of the painting's execution, was being demolished to make room for the new building. *The Apparition* [fig. 2] and *The Battle* [fig. 3] show carefully rendered topographical sites and archaeologically correctly dressed soldiers and accouterments. Giorgio Vasari admiringly wrote:

> He himself [Giulio Romano] learned so much from the ancient columns of Trajan and Antoninus that are in Rome, that he made much use of this knowledge for the costumes of soldiers, armour, ensigns, bastions, palisades, battering-rams, and all the other instruments of war that are painted throughout the whole of that Hall.[61]

The setting of these historical events demanded, of course, an historical background. Yet Raphael and his assistants may have had more in mind than just an appropriate and accurate framework.[62] The classical setting formed an appropriate, venerable backdrop to the momentous events taking place, and created a fitting majestic air. This concurs with Quintilian's recommendation about the use of old words:

> Words are *proper, newly-coined* or *metaphorical*. In the case of *proper* words there is a special dignity conferred by Antiquity, since old words, which not everyone would think of using, give our style a venerable and majestic air: this is a form of ornament of which Vergil, with his perfect taste, has made unique use. For his employment of words such as *olli, quianam, moerus, pone* and *pellacia* gives his work that impressive air of Antiquity which is so attractive in pictures, but which no art of man can

---

[59] See Belfori, cited in n. 40; Preimesberger, "Tragische Motive in Raffaels *Transfiguration*", 112-3, and Fehl, "Raphael as a Historian", 46.

[60] Cf. Preimesberger, "Tragische Motive in Raffaels *Transfiguration*", 113, and Fehl, "Raphael as a Historian", 34-8.

[61] Vasari, *Lives of the Painters*, II, 122; V, 60: 'Il quale [Giulio Romano] imparò tanto dalle colonne antiche di Traiano e d'Antonino che sono in Roma, che se ne valse molto negl'abiti de' soldati, nell'armadure, insegne, bastioni, steccati, arieti, et in tutte l'altre cose da guerra che sono dipinte per tutta quella sala'.

[62] For the degree in which the background of *The Apparition* [fig. 2] is accurate, see above, n. 16. Also the other backgrounds contain details that are obviously not correct, for instance the Villa Madama in the left background of *The Battle* [fig. 3]; the villa's construction started only in 1518. See Quednau, *Die Sala di Costantino*, 351-2.

counterfeit. But we must not overdo it, and such words must not be dragged out from the deepest darkness of the past.[63]

In Raphael's time, a similar advice was given by Baldassare Castiglione in his *Libro del Cortegiano*:

> Therefore in writing I believe that it is right to use Tuscan words, and only those employed by the ancient Tuscans, because that is a convincing proof, tested by time, that they are sound and effective in conveying what they mean. Furthermore, they possess the grace and dignity which great age imparts not only to words but also to buildings, statues, pictures and to everything that is able to endure.[64]

From these consideration it appears that the paintings in the Sala di Costantino were not meant as an accurate illustration of a historical event. Consciously the painters tried to raise the history scenes to the level of 'poetry', and 'to express universals' instead of 'particulars'. To do so they used and combined visual examples and devices from classical literary theory, and added their own inventions, even if they could not be justified by historical sources. That, however, did not diminish the general admiration. If the painters' own inventions were

---

[63] *Institutio oratoria* VIII, 3, 24-5 (transl. H.E. Butler, 224-5): 'Cum sint autem verba propria, ficta, translata, propriis dignitatem dat antiquitas. Namque et sanctiorem et magis admirabilem faciunt orationem, quibus non quilibet fuerit usurus, eoque ornamento acerrimi iudicii P. Vergilius unice est usus. *Olli* enim et *quianam* et *moerus* et *pone* et *pellacia* aspergunt illam, quae etiam in picturis est gratissima, vetustatis inimitabilem arti auctoritatem. Sed utendum modo, nec ex ultimis tenebris repetenda'.

[64] *Libro del Cortegiano* I, 30: 'Però nello scrivere credo io che si convenga usar le parole toscane, e solamente le usate dagli antichi Toscani; perché quello è gran testimonio ed approvato dal tempo che sian bone e significative de quello perché si dicono; ed oltra questo hanno quella grazia e venerazion che l'antiquità presta non solamente alle parole, ma agli edificii, alle statue, alle pitture e ad ogni cosa che è bastante a conservarla' (quoted after Cordié C. (ed.), *Opere di Baldassare Castiglione, Giovanni della Casa, Benvenuto Cellini*, La letteratura d'Italia. Storia e testi, 27 (Milan–Naples: 1960) 53; transl. after Bull G., *Castiglione. The Book of the Courtier*, Penguin Classics (Harmondsworth: 1976) 72). Just like Quintilian, Castiglione adds that the use of old words should not be indiscriminate (I, 33, 58): 'E, perché voi dite che le parole antiche, solamente con quel splendor d'antichità, adornan tanto ogni subietto, per basso ch'egli sia, che possono farlo degno di molta laude, io dico che non solamente di queste parole antiche ma né ancor delle bone faccio tanto caso ch'estimi debbano senza 'l suco delle belle sentenzie esser prezzate ragionevolmente; perché il divider le sentenzie dalle parole è un divider l'anima dal corpo: la qual cosa né nell'uno né nell'altro senza distruzione far si po' ('to your claim that antique words, simply because of their ancient splendour, enhance every subject so greatly that, no matter how trivial it is, they make it praiseworthy, I reply that I do not judge even good let alone antique words so uncritically as to believe that they should be valued even if they lack the substance of good sense. Because to divorce sense from words is like divorcing the soul from the body: in neither case this can be done without causing destruction', transl. after Bull, 76).

in accordance with the tenor of the story, they were rather a source of delight. This appears clearly from Vasari's description of Raphael's painting in the Stanza d'Eliodoro, showing *Pope Leo III repelling Attila* [fig. 11], in which Raphael included a detail similar to the angels flying in the air in *The Battle at the Milvian Bridge* [fig. 3]:

> In this scene Raffaello made St Peter and St Paul in the air, with swords in their hands, coming to defend the Church; and while the story of Leo III says nothing of this, nevertheless it was thus that he chose to represent it, perchance out of fancy, *for it often happens that painters, like poets, go straying from their subject in order to make their work the more ornate, although their digressions are not such as to be out of harmony with their first intention* [my italics].[65]

History Painting

The paintings in the Sala di Costantino were very successful. Although present-day appreciation of them varies, and *The Baptism* [fig. 4] and *The Donation* [fig. 5] in particular receive limited appreciation because of their supposedly 'weak' execution, they offered a standard for future history paintings. The devices employed by Raphael and his assistants became stock elements to express the historical importance of an event. Bystanders discussing what is going on, children innocently playing without being aware of the importance of the situation, people climbing on columns — they became the standard attributes of any history painter, even to the point where they have lost their original impact. Already around 1550 one can observe this 'iconographic inflation'. The scene painted by Livio Agresti in the Sala Regia in the Vatican Palace around 1564, is an example. The painting shows an obscure event from papal history that is comparable to the donation of Constantine, namely the Spanish King Peter of Aragon offering his kingdom to Pope Innocent III in 1204 [fig. 13].[66] The scene shows bystanders pointing and gesticulating, and some standing on the pedestals of columns. A boy on the foreground is play-

---

[65] Vasari, *Lives of the Painters*, I, 727-8; IV, 183: 'Fece Raffaello in questa storia San Pietro e Paolo in aria con le spade in mano che vengono a difender la Chiesa: e se bene la storia di Leon III non dice questo, egli nondimeno per capriccio suo volse figurarla così, come interviene molte volte che così le pitture come le poesie vanno vagando per ornamento dell'opera, non si discostando però per modo non conveniente dal primo intendimento'.

[66] See above, n. 24; Böck, *Die Sala Regia im Vatikan*, 37-8.

ing with a dog, seemingly unaware of what is going on. But in this painting the bystanders and other elements from the entourage have become so dominant, that the main event is more or less lost amongst them. A little boy with a statuette symbolizing the king's donation walks in the center, hardly noticed by any of the bystanders.[67] King Peter is seen on the back talking to some cardinals.[68] In short, what originally was 'historical entourage' here seems to have become the subject of the scene.[69] This means that a detail such as the little boy with the dog has completely lost its original function. In *The Donation* [fig. 5] this detail sets off the solemnity of the historical event.[70] Now the boy and his dog are mainly in the way of the man leading the horse, making the observers wonder whether the boy will get trampled on, or if the dog will manage in time to scare the horse away. The only function of this group seems to be closing off the composition of the painting at the bottom. It is no wonder that in his *Discourse on Sacred*

---

[67] The motif of a statuette symbolizing the king's donation is derived from the *Donation* scene in the Sala di Costantino [fig. 5], which is described by Vasari as: 'Gostantino a' piedi ginocchioni, il quale gli [*sc.* il Papa] presenta una Roma d'oro fatta come quelle che sono nelle medaglie antiche: volendo per ciò dimostrare la dote che esso Gostantino diede alla Chiesa Romana' [V, 61] ('Constantine kneeling at his [*sc.* the Pope's] feet and presenting to him a figure of Rome made of gold in the manner of those that are on the ancient medals, by which Giulio intended to signify the dowry which Constantine gave to the Roman church' [*Lives of the Painters*, II, 123]).

[68] According to Böck, *Die Sala Regia im Vatikan*, 38, the person on the right represents Pope Innocent III. This seems to me, however, impossible, as he is wearing cardinal's clothes. I do agree with Böck, ibid., that he has the portrait traits of Pope Paul III (1543–1549).

[69] Similar remarks could be made of many of the paintings in the Sala Regia, especially of the *soprapporte*, executed c. 1564 by Giovanni Battista Fiorini, Girolamo Siciolante da Sermoneta and Orazio Sammachini. The paintings by Giorgio Vasari in the same Sala, executed c. 1572, also offer interesting examples of re-using inventions of Raphael and his assistants; see De Jong, "Papal History and Historical Invenzione".

[70] Vasari's description of it has been quoted in n. 27. Fehl, "Raphael as a Historian", 54, interprets the boy and the dog as 'an allegory of the Christian faith'. Other possible interpretations are suggested by Quednau, *Die Sala di Costantino*, 440-2. It should be added that Agresti's scene is a *pastiche* of various examples, which makes one wonder if the painter did not adopt the motif of the boy and the dog for the same reason as he adopted other motifs, namely to fill the composition with well-known figures. The soldier partly seen on the back, on the left side, for instance, is adopted from the figure of St Paul in Raphael's *St Cecilia*-altarpiece of c. 1513–1516 (Bologna, Pinacoteca); this figure was later also used by Vasari in 1546, on the left in his scene of *Pope Paul III distributing Honours* in the Sala dei Cento Giorni (Rome, Palazzo della Cancelleria); the boy leading the horse was copied after the figure of St John the Baptist in Michelangelo's *Last Judgement* in the Sistine Chapel, of 1536–1541. The group on the right, with King Peter and the two cardinals, is copied after the group on the right in Raphael's *School of Athens* in the Stanza della Segnatura of 1510–1512.

and Profane Images of 1582, cardinal Gabriele Paleotti warned against
the use of similar details:

> Some create still another disproportion in regard to the whole, when
> they insert in pictures that have a predominantly religious or solemn
> subject, other things which are out of place within the context and have
> nothing to do with the main theme. The Greeks call these πάρεργα:
> such as […] *a little boy playing with a dog* [my italics], birds fighting, or a
> peasant catching frogs, or other similar things which painters concoct,
> with no regard whether it complies with the topic they are working on.[71]

Other examples include the various paintings in the palace and the
church of St John in Lateran in Rome. In the *Constantine* series in the
Sala di Costantino, executed by Cesare Nebbia, Giovanni Guerra and
a host of assistants around 1588, the influence of the Vatican frescoes
can clearly be seen.[72] In the scene showing *The Donation of Constantine*
[fig. 14] the emperor appears as a little figure almost in the background, while the foreground is occupied by people talking and standing on the pedestals of columns, on places and in positions from
where, logically spoken, they can hardly see what is going on. This
makes that the connection between them and the main event is missing, and thus that their original function is lost.[73] The same is true for
the Constantine frescoes in the transept of the Lateran church, painted in the years around 1599–1600 by various painters supervised by
Giuseppe Cesari d'Arpino.[74] The scene showing *Pope Sylvester consecrating the High Altar of the Lateran* [fig. 15], to mention only the most obvi-

---

[71] Paleotti G., *Discorso intorno alle imagini sacre e profane* (Bologna: 1582) 28, quoted
after Barocchi II, 378: 'Un altra sproporzione ancora rispetto al tutto pongono alcuni,
quando con le imagini massimamente sacre, o di cose gravi, s'aggiongono altre che
sono fuori di quello soggetto e che non hanno a fare punto con l'opera principale; le
quali i Greci chiamano πάρεργα: come […] un putto che scherza con un cane, o una
battaglia d'uccelli, o un contadino che pesca ranocchi, o altre simil cose che s'imagi-
nano i pittori, non havendo risguardo se cio risponde a quello che hanno per le mani'.
Examples of scenes with birds fighting and chasing each other through the air can be
found in the works of the fifteenth-century(!) painters Domenico Ghirlandaio
(1449–1494) and Bernardo Pintoricchio (c. 1460–1513).

[72] On these paintings, see Mandel's remarks in Madonna, *Roma di Sisto V*, 94-103
and 116; Freiberg J., *The Lateran in 1600. Christian Concord in Counter-Reformation Rome*
(Cambridge: 1995) 23-30, esp. 28 and idem "Sign of the Cross", 75.

[73] It may be clear that Freiberg's comments on this scene ("Sign of the Cross", 75)
are only partially correct: 'The event is cast as recorded in the text of the Donation,
the document placed by the Emperor "above the venerable body of the blessed
Peter", that is, upon the high altar of Saint Peter's. Constantine's pious bequest is no
longer cast in symbolic terms as it has been in the Vatican; rather it is depicted as a
binding instrument of law'.

[74] Freiberg, *The Lateran in 1600*, 81-129.

ous example, also contains an extensive entourage at the cost of the main event, without an obvious link between the two.[75]

A final example to demonstrate how active the tendency of 'iconographic inflation' was, and how it also affected history paintings other than scenes from the life of Constantine, is offered by the frescoes executed by Tommaso Laureti between 1586 and 1592 in the Sala dei Capitani in the Conservators' Palace, on the Capitol in Rome [fig. 16].[76] They show moments from the early history of Rome and they are clearly inspired by Raphael's frescoes in the Vatican *stanze*. However, here too the entourage has increased along the indicated lines, with the result that it is not always immediately clear who the protagonists of the scene are.[77]

In the Sala di Costantino in the Vatican, the relationship between the theme and the entourage is well balanced. Bystanders serve a function and they are more than just a device to fill the scene. They set off the importance of the historic event and make the observers feel involved. This way of creating a functional entourage was developed by Raphael in his slightly earlier history paintings in the adjacent *stanze*, but it was expanded and put to full use in the Sala di Costantino. The artists, in particular Giulio Romano and Gianfrancesco Penni who painted *The Baptism* [fig. 4] and *The Donation* [fig. 5], must have done this consciously. They were confronted with the task of depicting events of which hardly anything was known and which were increasingly subject to doubts and criticism about their truthfulness. In this context of growing scepticism their strategy was not to make an attempt at reconstructing the particulars of an historic event, which was doomed to fail. Instead they strove for a depiction of what would have happened, in accordance with probability and necessity. Using stylistic devices from the realm of artistic traditions, art theory and classical literary theories, they tried to raise the discussion from the level of particulars about the Emperor Constantine and Pope Sylvester to that of universals about the relation between secular pow-

---

[75] The composition is clearly based on Raphael's *Coronation of Charlemagne*, of c. 1516–1517, in the Stanza dell'Incendio in the Vatican.

[76] On these paintings, see Tittoni's remarks in Madonna, *Roma di Sisto V*, 165-7.

[77] From around 1600 on, artists working in the so-called Baroque style kept using these same means but in a different way. By arranging gesticulating persons in a (often diagonal) line leading to the protagonist(s) of the scene, and by using light effects to direct the attention of the observers, they were able to create more clarity and a renewed emotional appeal.

er and spiritual authority. Constantine is not shown as the great emperor who, in the first half of the fourth century, donated part of his realm to Pope Sylvester I. He has been represented as the primary representative of secular power in his conduct towards spiritual authority. The particulars of his baptism and donation do not matter: the universals do.

Selective Bibliography

ALBERTI L.B., *On Painting and On Sculpture. The Latin Texts of 'De Pictura' and 'De Statua'*, ed. and transl. by C. Grayson (London: 1972)

BADT K., "Raphael's *Incendio del Borgo*", *Journal of the Warburg and Courtauld Institutes* 22 (1959) 35-59

BAROCCHI P., *Trattati dell'arte del Cinquecento fra Manierismo e Controriforma*, 3 vols (Bari: 1960–1962)

BUCK A., *Die Sala Regia im Vatikan als Beispiel der Selbstdarstellung des Papsttums in der zweiten Hälfte des 16. Jahrhunderts*, Studien zur Kunstgeschichte 112 (Hildesheim: 1997)

EPP S., *Konstantinszyklen in Rom. Die päpstliche Interpretation der Geschichte Konstantins des Grossen bis zur Gegenreformation*, Schriften aus dem Institut für Kunstgeschichte der Universität München 36 (Munich: 1988)

FEHL P.P., "Raphael as a Historian: Poetry and Historical Accuracy in the Sala di Costantino", *Artibus et Historiae* 14/28 (1993) 9-76

FREIBERG J., *The Lateran in 1600. Christian Concord in Counter-Reformation Rome* (Cambridge: 1995)

FREIBERG J., " In the Sign of the Cross: the Image of Constantine in the Art of Counter-Reformation Rome", in Lavin M.A. (ed.), *Piero della Francesca and His Legacy*, Studies in History of Art 48 (Hannover–London: 1995) 67-87

JONG J.L. DE, "Papal History and Historical Invenzione. Vasari's Frescoes in the Sala Regia", in Jacks P.J. (ed.), *Vasari's Florence: Artists and Literati at the Medicean Court* (Cambridge: 1998) 220-37

KECKS R., "Assistenzfigur und Architekturkulisse: zur Entwicklung eines Bildmotivs bei Donatello und Raffael", *Mitteilungen des Kunsthistorischen Institutes in Florenz* 33/2-3 (1989) 257-300

LEONARDO DA VINCI, *Treatise on Painting [Codex Urbinas Latinus 1270]*, transl. and annot. by A.P. McMahon, introd. by L.H. Heydenreich (Princeton, N.J.: 1956)

MADONNA M.L. (ed.), *Roma di Sisto V. Le arti e la cultura* (Rome: 1993)

PREIMESBERGER R., "Tragische Motive in Raffaels *Transfiguration*", *Zeitschrift für*

Kunstgeschichte 50/1 (1987) 88-117

QUEDNAU R., *Die Sala di Costantino im Vatikanischen Palast. Zur Dekoration der beiden Medici-Päpste Leo X. und Clemens VII*, Studien zur Kunstgeschichte 13
(Hildesheim–New York: 1979)

VASARI G., *Le vite de' più eccellenti pittori, scultori et architettori* ([Florence: 1550],
2nd ed. Florence: 1568), ed. P. Barocchi – R. Bettarini (Florence: 1966 ff.)

VASARI G., *Lives of the Painters, Sculptors and Architects*, transl. by Gaston du C. de
Vere, introd. and notes by David Ekserdjian (London: 1996).

THEATRUM HODIERNAE VITAE:
LIPSIUS, VAENIUS, AND THE REBELLION OF CIVILIS

Mark Morford

In 1612 Otho Vaenius (Otto van Veen) published an illustrated version of Tacitus's narrative of the revolt of Julius Civilis against the Romans in 69–70 BC. The full title of Vaenius's book was *Batavorum cum Romanis bellum a Corn. Tacito lib. IV et V Hist. olim descriptorum figuris nunc aeneis expressum.* In the Dutch version the addition of the words 'Oude Hollandtsche' identified the Dutch with the Batavi: *De Batavische of oude Hollandtsche oorloghe teghen de Romeynen* [fig. 1]. The book consists of an allegorical frontispiece [fig. 2] and thirty-five engravings by Antonio Tempestà of scenes from Books IV and V of Tacitus's *Histories.* Beneath each engraving are two captions, one in Latin and the other a Dutch paraphrase, often with significant additions or omissions. On the opposite page is the Latin text of the passage of Tacitus on which the engraving is based. The Latin text is not faithfully transcribed, and sometimes Vaenius supplements it with his own Latin. At the end of the book he provides a text in Dutch that paraphrases, and occasionally adds commentary on, Tacitus's text. Here the speeches are included (for example, that of Petilius Cerialis at *Hist.* IV, 73-4 on p. xx, the text for plate 26), and Vaenius adds his own notes on questions of tribal or topographical identifications. The Dutch text is printed in Gothic font, which adds to the antiquity that Vaenius claims for the Batavi. On the other hand, the subject-matter is made more immediate by the use of contemporary names and titles. Roman *legati* are *colonnelen* (p. v and *passim*); Mumius [*sic*] Lupercus is *colonel en sergeant maioor* (p. iv); the *Britannica classis* of *Hist.* IV, 79 becomes *d'Enghelsche armade* (p. xxii). The ancient names for peoples and places are given their modern equivalents — perhaps the most striking way in which the text is given contemporary meaning: the Sequani become *de Bourgoignons* and the Gallic chieftains assemble at *Reims in Champaigne* in the text for plates 22 and 23 (p. xvii), while Vaenius identifies tribes, rivers and towns in Holland and Belgium. Thus the Dutch text is significant for Vaenius's first purpose: to relate the most important episode in the heroic early history of the Netherlands to his own times. His second goal (it can safely be inferred) was to take advantage of a profitable market three years after the initiation of the Twelve Years' truce of 1609.[1]

Vaenius was born in 1556 in Leiden, where his father became Burgomaster in 1560. He studied art first at Leiden under Isaac van Swanenburgh, and when he was seventeen, he moved to Liège to study under the humanist, poet and artist, Dominicus Lampsonius (1532–1599).[2] Since 1558, Lampsonius had been secretary to successive Prince-Bishops of Liège: he was a member of a circle of influential Catholics who confirmed Vaenius's loyalty to the Catholic church. Also in the circle were the Archdeacon of Brabant, Laevinus Torrentius (Lieven van der Beke) — diplomat, scholar, humanist, and church leader — and the learned Canon, Charles de Langhe (Langhius). Torrentius put the greatest pressure on Lipsius to return to the Catholic church in 1591, and he secured the offer for him of the chair of history at the University of Leuven in 1592.[3]

Thus Vaenius was familiar with the Catholics who influenced Lipsius, and his sojourn in Liège was probably as important for his friendship with Lipsius as his connection with Leiden. He left Liège in 1575 and spent the next five years in Rome, returning to Leiden in 1583, and in 1584 to Liège. In 1585 he moved to Brussels, where he served the Governor of the Spanish Netherlands, Alessandro Farnese, Duke of Parma. For twenty years (1592–1612) he lived in Antwerp, moving in 1612 back to Brussels, where he died in 1629.[4]

Vaenius was prominent among Antwerp artists, and his use of the Latinised name is an indication of his claim to high social status. He was

---

[1] For the truce and its effects, see Parker G., *Europe in Crisis. 1598–1648* (Ithaca, N.Y.: 1979) 131-45, especially 135-7. For Vaenius's profit-motive, see Müllers W., *Der Bataveraufstand 69–70 n. Chr.: Zerstörung und Schlacht von Vetera*, 2 vols (Cologne: 1978) II, 22: 'eine marktorientierte und -gezielte Publikation'.

[2] See A. Roersch, "Lampsonius, Dominicus", in *Bibliotheca Belgica. Bibliographie générale des Pays-Bas*, ed. F. Van der Haeghen; rpt ed. M.-T. Lenger (Brussels: 1964–1975) III, 662-7. Lampson is the first person not a member of Vaenius's family to be recorded in his *Album amicorum*. In his poem (p. 24) Lampsonius says of himself: 'Post superos patriamque et utrumque, o amice, parentem / primus amicorum merito tibi ponor in albo'. Vaenius's portrait of Lampson appears on the opposite page. The correspondence between Lipsius and Lampsonius published by Burman P., *Sylloges epistolarum a viris illustribus scriptarum* (Leiden: 1727) I, 123-44, is especially illuminating.

[3] For Torrentius, see Morford M., *Stoics and Neostoics* (Princeton: 1991), 102-7 and 119-23. For Langhius, *ibid.*, 64-6 and 161-8. Torrentius spent thirty years in Liège (1557–1587) before occupying the episcopal throne at Antwerp, where he died in 1595. Langhius is the principal speaker in Lipsius's *De constantia* (1584), a dialogue set in Liège in 1572.

[4] He was appointed *praefectus monetae* by the Archdukes Albert and Isabella.

the teacher of Pieter Paul Rubens, who worked with him in 1596–1600, before going to Italy. Vaenius was an expert in the use of emblem and allegory, and he published several books of emblems, of which the best known is *Q. Horatii Flacci Emblemata*.[5] He had important roles in the *Joyeuses Entrées* of 1594 and 1599, by means of which Antwerp proclaimed its devotion to its rulers and its hopes for the future. He should be given credit for teaching Rubens (who directed the designs for the *joyeuse entrée* of 1635) the uses of moral and political allegory.[6]

Vaenius was loyal to the Catholic and Spanish causes, but he also was influenced by the Neostoicism of Lipsius. In his book of Horatian emblems he quotes Lipsius three times, referring to him as the 'Phoenix of our age', and he interprets the Epicurean Horace in Stoic terms.[7] The first evidence for their friendship dates from 1584, when Lipsius contributed an entry to Vaenius's *Album amicorum*, focusing on the stoic ideal of friendship:

> We dedicate this memorial to white-haired Good Faith, which from now on we want to preside over Love and Friendship, and with which I follow you, Otho Vaenius, young man with most cultivated intellect and hand, and will follow you to the very end: wherever God will lead you, wherever God will lead me. I, Justus Lipsius, wrote this at Leiden on June 2nd, 1584.[8]

Lipsius was a devoted teacher of younger men who were to become prominent in the service of church or state, and he valued their friendship. Like the distinguished humanists, Abraham Ortelius and Franciscus Sweertius, he saw in Vaenius scholarly learning as well as artistic ability.[9] The entry in the *Album* was written perhaps on the day on

---

[5] Antwerp, Verdussen: 1607.

[6] The scholarly restraint of Rubens (and before him Vaenius) contrasts with the excesses of the three-day *Joyeuse Entrée* of Marie de Medicis into Amsterdam in 1638: see Barlaeus C., *Medicea Hospes* (Amsterdam: 1638).

[7] Cf. Morford M., "L'Influence de Juste Lipse sur les Arts", in Mouchel C. (ed.), *Juste Lipse en son Temps*, Actes du Colloque de Strasbourg 1994 (Paris: 1996) , 238. The reference to Phoenix is a pun on the name of the mythical bird and of the Homeric hero who was tutor to the young Achilles.

[8] See Gheyn J. van den, *Album amicorum de Otto Venius* (Brussels: 1911) 55. The Latin text reads: 'Hoc monumentum CANAE FIDEI SACRAMUS, quam praeesse AMORI ET AMICITIAE hinc volumus qua te, OTHO VENI, cultissimae mentis et manus adolescens, prosequor et ad extremum prosecuturus sum: quocumque te, quocumque me Deus trahet. Scripsi ego, IUSTUS LIPSIUS, Lugduni Batavor. postridie Kal. Iun. M.D.LXXXIV'. For specifically stoic ideas in Lipsius's theory of friendship, see Morford, *Stoics and Neostoics*, 14-28.

[9] For Ortelius, see the entry in Vaenius's *Album amicorum*, 46-7, and in his own *Album amicorum*, facsimile ed. J. Puraye, *De Gulden Passer* 45 (1967) 123. For Sweertius, see the entry on p. 57, and his entry on Vaenius in his *Athenae Belgicae* (Antwerp: 1628) 590-1.

which Vaenius left Leiden for Liège. Two days earlier Lipsius wrote to
Lampsonius at Liège commending Vaenius: 'Otho Vaenius is leaving
us to my regret. He is a young man whose character and artistic ability is outstanding. He could have been very helpful to me in illustrating
many objects from Antiquity'.[10] So in the first part of his *Poliorceticon*,
when Lampsonius (the interlocutor) suggests that the technical
descriptions be illustrated, they both regret the unavailability of Vaenius, 'a young man created for the Muses and the Graces', who is
away in the service of Parma.[11] Evidently Lipsius saw plenty of Vaenius after his return to the Spanish Netherlands in 1591. In May,
1601, he commissioned a painting of the Roman heroine Arria, in
whom Lipsius saw an *exemplum Fidei et Amoris*, precisely the virtues
highlighted in the entry in the *Album* seventeen years earlier.[12]

Vaenius himself espoused the attributes of Ciceronian stoicism — love
of country and parents. Thus in his *Album* (p. 19) he quotes Cicero:

---

[10] ILE II, 84 05 31, 23-25 (*Ep. misc.* I, 60): 'Otho Venius [sic] a nobis abit, sed invitis: insignis moribus et arte adolescens, et cuius manus usui mihi esse poterat ad multa
Antiquitatis illustranda'. In 1588 Lampson writes to Lipsius, referring to Vaenius as
Otho meus (ILE 88 07 00 = Burman, *Sylloges* I, 126: July, 1588). A year later he reports
the grave illness of Vaenius's father, 'alone, of all men, the best and most cultivated
man' (ILE 89 09 00 = Burman, *Sylloges* I, 127: September 1589; undated, but replying
to ILE III, 89 08 14 = *Ep. misc.* II, 86 [= II, 90 in the 1590-edition]). Although Gerlo –
Vervliet included ILE 88 07 00 and ILE 89 09 00 in their appropriate place in their
Inventaire de la correspondance de Juste Lipse, 1564–1606 (Antwerp: 1968) both undated letters were omitted in ILE III (1588–1590). This omission will be corrected in ILE IV
(1591).

[11] *Poliorceticon* (Antwerp: 1596) I, Dial. 6 (*Opera Omnia* (Antwerp: 1637) III, 273).
The reference to Vaenius's service under Parma indicates a dramatic date for the dialogue before 1592. See *Bibliotheca Belgica* III, 1037-38. The illustrations were engraved
by Peeter vander Borcht and Lipsius implies that Lampsonius designed them (cf. their
separate grouping in the 1605 edition on the pages following Dialogue 6; in the *Opera
Omnia* (Antwerp: 1637) they are divided between pp. 273 and 274). The *Poliorceticon*
was dedicated to Ernest of Bavaria, Archbishop of Cologne and Prince Bishop of
Liège. Lampsonius served him as his secretary in Liège (and lists his vices in ILE 91 06
04 = Burman, *Sylloges* I, 134).

[12] *Ep. ad. Belg.* III, 83 (= ILE 01 05 22): see Morford, "L'Influence de Juste Lipse
sur les Arts", 235-6. In 1602 he writes to Oultremannus thanking him for his approval
of the commission (*Ep. misc.* IV, 14 = ILE 02 07 09): see ILE 02 08 19 for Oultremannus's reply. Vaenius's portrait of Lipsius is the subject of the long poem by Oultremannus printed in Burman, *Sylloges* II, 95-9 (ILE 03 00 00 O¹), to which Lipsius
replied in *Ep. misc.* IV, 89 (= ILE 04 02 01 O). The portrait is not listed in Thieme-
Becker 34, 176-7, in the catalogue of Vaenius's surviving works, but the engraving by
Cornelius Boel from Vaenius's design exists: see S. Leman in *Justus Lipsius en het Plantijnse Huis*, ed. R. Dusoir, J. De Landtsheer and D. Imhof (Antwerp, Museum Plantin
Moretus: 1997), 221 (no 99).

'Dear are [our] children, relatives and friends. But for everyone our country alone includes all our loyalties. What good man would hesitate to die for his country if he could benefit it [by doing so]?'[13] Later (p. 27, following the portrait of Lampsonius), he writes: 'We are not born for ourselves alone, but our country claims part [of our loyalty] for itself, our parents claim part, and our friends claim part'.[14] The editor of the *Album*, J. van den Gheyn, rightly comments: 'Deux idées principales sont développés dans les pièces de l'*Album*, celle de patrie et celle d'amitié. La première est surtout traitée par Otto Venius lui-même'. It is hardly surprising then, that Lipsius described Vaenius as *insignis moribus*, for he himself had consistently taught the stoic doctrines of love for friends and of the individual's duty towards the universal community, human and divine.[15] The patriotism of Vaenius, however, was both more local and more consistent than that of Lipsius, whose successive changes of local, political and religious loyalties led to a more fluid idea of patriotism. Lipsius himself works out a solution to this problem in *De constantia* I, 8-11, in which he (as a young man, the dramatic date being 1572) argues the Ciceronian point of view, while Langhius (representing the mature Lipsius of 1583) shows him that the true *patria* is Heaven: 'but heaven is [the mind's] true and proper fatherland'.[16]

To understand the political and moral complexities of Vaenius's *Batavorum cum Romanis bellum* we have to understand the nature of his patriotism. Born at Leiden in the Dutch Netherlands, he spent his adult life in the service of Catholic princes, and his formative years were those in Liège. Lipsius's devotion to the church and state of the Spanish Netherlands was that of a prodigal son, who had returned to his

---

[13] *De officiis* I, 17, 57 (Cicero's text actually reads 'cari sunt parentes, cari liberi [...]'): 'chari sunt liberi, propinqui, familiares, sed omnes omnium charitates patria una complexa est, pro qua quis bonus dubitet mortem oppetere, si ei sit profuturus?'. Van den Gheyn, *Album amicorum*, 81, wrongly transcribes Vaenius's heading above the quotation, 'Cicero', as 'puero'.

[14] 'Non solum nobis nati sumus, sed ortus nostri partem sibi vindicat patria, partem parentes, partem amici'.

[15] 'Magnus hic orbis est, sed una civitas', *Ep. misc.* IV, 40 (= ILE 02 11 04 G), letter to his great-nephew, Willem de Greve (aged 9!).

[16] *De constantia* I, 11: 'At caelum vera illi [sc., hominis animo] germanaque patria est'. Langhius's argument disinguishes between *caritas* (the proper feeling towards parents or *patria*) and *pietas* (the proper attitude towards God). In this way Lipsius (through the persona of Langhius) both evades the problem of loyalty towards one's *patria* and attempts to reconcile stoicism with Christianity.

fatherland after sojourning among the Lutherans at Jena and the Calvinists in Leiden. Hence the subtleties of his arguments for the universal *patria* in the *De constantia*, written while he was at Leiden, which failed to deceive Torrentius.[17] Vaenius had no need for such prevarication. The very first entry in his *Album amicorum* is a painting of *PATRIA*, a woman seated in a *hortus inclusus* holding a shield emblazoned with the lion *gueules* of Belgium. Outside the fence patrols Neptune (a reference to sea-power, whether Dutch or Spanish), and below is a four-line quotation from Ovid on the attractive power of one's *patria*.[18] Vaenius sought to reconcile his loyalty to the Spanish Netherlands with the expectations of his Dutch readers in a work that glorified both rebellion against and reconciliation with an imperial power.

In 1612 the magistrates at the Hague paid Vaenius's brother, Peter, £32 and 8 shillings for twelve copies of *Batavorum cum Romanis bellum*. Evidently they saw a parallel between the heroic resistance of Civilis to the Romans and their own resistance to the power of Spain. In the following year they bought twelve paintings by Vaenius on the same subject, which now are all in the Rijksmuseum at Amsterdam.[19] Thus Tacitus's account of the rebellion, known in the Netherlands not least from Lipsius's editions of Tacitus, was given a visual interpretation in the two series by Vaenius. Lipsius, especially through his *Politica*, first published in 1589, had taught his contemporaries how to use ancient texts for contemporary purposes. For example, in his dedication to the *Ordines Bataviae* of his Commentary on Tacitus' *Annales* he says:

> And not all [historical narrative] is equally useful to us. The most valuable, in my opinion is that in which there is the greatest likeness to and portrayal of our own times. Just as in a portrait we recognise more easily a familiar face, so in history we recognise more readily examples of familiar behaviour.[20]

---

[17] See Morford, *Stoics and Neostoics*, 102-6 and 118-22.

[18] *Epistulae ex Ponto*, I, 3, 35-8. In Vaenius's prayer (*Album amicorum*, 21) he lists [lines 7-10], as objects of his love, *Patria*, parents, teachers, and the friends named in the *Album*. The second entry in the *Album*, after *Patria*, is the double portrait of his parents.

[19] The two purchases are reported by Waal H. van de, *Drie Eeuwen Vaderlandsche Geschied-Uitbeelding*, 2 vols (The Hague: 1952) I, 210 and II, 98. The paintings are nos 2432-43 in the *Katalog der Gemälde* [...] *im Reichsmuseum zu Amsterdam* (Amsterdam: 1920) 418.

[20] Dedication of the *Liber Commentarius* (Antwerp: 1581): the key phrase is 'similitudo et imago plurima temporum nostrorum' (ILE I, 81 00 00 H, 25-6).

Lipsius ends the dedication by instancing the revolt of Civilis as an example of Tacitean narrative that illuminates his own times:

> To Tacitus you [the States of Holland] owe the true and ancient description of Batavia; to him you owe [that of] the Chatti and your own origins. To him alone you owe Civilis and the wars fought against the most powerful people in the world — wars which even now excite envy and can scarcely be believed, even though they were written truthfully. Blest are you, o Batavians, in this glorious history, for you were the only corner of Europe that dared to challenge long ago Roman power and fifteen legions. Not without the hidden law of destiny, you were even then the defenders and champions of liberty. Yet your reward of that eternal glory would have perished if this writer [Tacitus] had perished.[21]

These words were written when Lipsius was secure, confident and grateful in his residence at Leiden. They are very different from the circumspect dedication to Maximilian II of his first edition of Tacitus in 1574, while they avoid the outspoken rhetoric of his second Jena oration.[22] The ambiguities in Lipsius's approach to the revolt of Civilis become clear in the later editions of his Tacitus, for the dedication written for his Protestant benefactors was omitted once he had left Leiden and returned to the Spanish Netherlands.[23] Nevertheless, the words of the 1581 dedication gave the authority for a patriotic reading by the Dutch of Tacitus's *Historiae*, while Lipsius's own shifting loyalties gave precedent to those who, like Vaenius, sought to appeal to readers in both the Dutch and the Spanish Netherlands.

Tacitus's account of the rebellion of Civilis has been vindicated by Peter Brunt.[24] Civilis was both a Batavian prince and a Roman citizen and army officer. He knew Vespasian (indeed, he claimed to be his friend), and the early stages of the rebellion were masked by the events of the civil war between Vitellius and Vespasian.[25] Tacitus showed

---

[21] Lipsius's Latin here (too long to quote in full) rises to heights of eloquence: note especially the phrase 'vindices et adsertores publicae libertatis'. The words from 'cum principe' to 'Europae' were plagiarized by Pieter Schrijver, *Batavia Illustrata* (Leiden: 1609), 3. In his dedication Schrijver explicitly compares the ancient Batavian heroes to his contemporaries: 'nec hodierni Batavi degeneres', etc.

[22] See Morford , *Stoics and Neostoics*, 153-5.

[23] Printed in the *Curae Secundae* (Leiden: 1589), but not in the 1607 Tacitus.

[24] Brunt P.A., "Tacitus on the Batavian Revolt", *Latomus* 19 (1960) 494-517. See also the commentary of Heubner H., *Tacitus: Die Historien. Kommentar: Bücher IV und V* (Heidelberg: 1976 and 1982, the latter with W. Fauth) especially IV, 33-6.

[25] *Hist.* IV, 13: '[Civilis] Vespasiani amicitiam studiumque partium praetendit'; V, 26: 'erga Vespasianum vetus mihi [sc., Civili] observantia'.

that Civilis was motivated principally by the cruelty of the Roman troops, the unjust execution of his brother, Paulus, by Fonteius Capito (legate of Lower Germany in 68), and his own arrest and transportation to Rome (followed by his acquittal by Galba and his return to the Rhine). For Tacitus the intention of Civilis was always to revolt from Rome and restore the freedom of the Batavi to lead their lives according to their ancestral customs.[26] Hence the importance of the feast in the *sacrum nemus* (Schakerbos) and the swearing of the oath of loyalty to the leadership of Civilis (*Hist.* IV, 14-5) .[27]

Tacitus divides his narrative into three parts. The first (*Hist.* IV, 12-37), illustrated in nos 2-17 of Tempestà's engravings, focuses on the early successes of Civilis, climaxing in the siege of the Roman legionary fortress of Vetera. The section ends with the murder (at Novaesium) of the ex-consul Hordeonius Flaccus, legate *pro praetore* of Upper Germany, by his own soldiers (*Hist.* IV, 36), and the escape of Dillius Vocula, legate of Legio XXII, to whom Hordeonius Flaccus had delegated his authority (*Hist.* IV, 25). The section closes (*Hist.* IV, 37) with scenes of demoralisation and confusion in the Roman legions.

The second part of the narrative (*Hist.* IV, 54-79, corresponding to nos 18-28 of the engravings) opens with the Gallic leaders Julius Classicus, Julius Tutor and Julius Sabinus (*Hist.* IV, 55), joining Civilis. The surrender and sack (against the orders of Civilis) of Vetera (*Hist.* IV, 60) is the zenith of Civilis's fortunes, for they began to fade with the arrival of Cerialis (*Hist.* IV, 68), a Flavian leader and a relative of Vespasian's, appointed as legate of Lower Germany. His forces were augmented by eight legions from Rome, Britain and Spain, and he quickly restored Roman morale by vigorous activity. Tacitus recognises his leadership in the speech at *Hist.* IV, 73-4 arguing for the advantages to the German and Gallic tribes of inclusion within the Roman empire. The section ends with the capture of Civilis's camp (*Hist.* IV, 76-8) and the handing over of his wife and sister (with the daughter of Julius Classicus) to the Romans.[28] Thus the tide had turned decisively against Civilis.

In the third section (*Hist.* V, 14-28, corresponding to nos 29-36 of

---

[26] Rossum J.A. van, "Julius Civilis en het Germaanse Gevaar", *Lampas* 25 (1992) 184-97, however, sees the origins of the revolt within the civil war between Vitellius and Vespasian.

[27] For Civilis's speech, see Keitel E., "Speech and Narrative in *Histories* IV", in *Tacitus and the Tacitean Tradition*, 46-9.

[28] *Hist.* IV, 79: they had been left by Civilis as hostages (pignora societatis) after winning the alliance of the people of Colonia Agrippinensis (IV, 63-5).

the engravings) Tacitus narrates the defeat of Civilis at the battles in the marshes outside Vetera and at the bridge over the Rhine. After various skirmishes and a night attack by Civilis on the Roman camp (*Hist.* V, 19-22), Cerialis ravages the countryside of the Batavi, sparing only Civilis's holdings (*Hist.* V, 23). The Batavi begin to murmur against Civilis (*Hist.* V, 24-5), who sees that a Roman victory is inevitable. He confers with Cerialis on a bridge over the 'Nabalia' (which has not been identified with any certainty), and the *Historiae* break off with the opening words of his speech (*Hist.* V, 26).

The commentary of Lipsius on Tacitus's narrative is almost entirely concerned with the establishment of correct readings and *explication de texte*. With one notable exception (the speech of Cerialis at *Hist.* IV, 73-4), he avoids political judgements. These he made elsewhere, in the 1581 dedication to the *Ordines Batavorum*, and in the *Politica* and the *Monita et exempla*, in which he repeatedly counselled submission to higher authority in the interests of peace and order.[29] In *Politica* VI, 4 he describes (unfavourably: 'detestatur' is his word in the table of contents) the origins and progress of rebellion, weaving into the chapter some thirty-five quotations from Tacitus. In the next chapter (*Politica* VI, 5) he argues against revolution, even when the king is a tyrant, for (and here he quotes Tacitus, *Hist.* IV, 8, 4) 'even the most exemplary rulers set limits to liberty'. Thus, he concludes, 'ferenda regum ingenia' ('we must be patient with the characters of kings'). In the next chapter (*Politica* VI, 6) he considers whether the *Sapiens* should take part in rebellion or civil war. While he praises Cato (whose stoic principles led him to take part in the Civil War between Caesar and Pompey), he praises Atticus still more, for he avoided taking sides in the war. For himself, Lipsius concludes:

> But those same people [i.e., those who are eager for war] should consider my way of life: and let them know that 'my policy is favourable to peace and civil pursuits, and it is not one of armed warfare'.[30]

---

[29] For *prudentia* in the *Politica*, see Morford M., "Tacitean *Prudentia* and the Doctrines of Justus Lipsius", in *Tacitus and the Tacitean Tradition*, ed. T. J. Luce – A. J. Woodman (Princeton: 1993) 129-51.

[30] 'Sed iidem illi vitam meam cogitent: sciantque "consilia nostra pacis ac togae socia, non belli atque armorum esse"'. The quotation is from Cicero, *Pro Marcello*, 14. The same quietism permeates *Monita et exempla politica* II, 1, 4, published in 1605, sixteen years after the *Politica*.

It is significant that in this chapter Lipsius quotes Tacitus only once and Cicero fourteen times. For the scholar who wished to be inconspicuous when difficult (and possibly fatal) political choices had to be made, Cicero was a safer guide than Tacitus. Lipsius had withdrawn by 1589 (the date of publication of the *Politica*) from the revolutionary attitude of the 1581 dedication. By the time of his return to Leuven (1592) he neither would nor could praise Civilis as the *vindicator libertatis*.[31]

Vaenius, however, less than three years after the Truce of Antwerp, was able to use the text of Tacitus to appeal to the patriotism and pride of both the contemporary Batavi (the Dutch) and the modern equivalent of the Roman empire (the Habsburg monarchy). Readers on both sides would feel pride in their ancestors' struggle for liberty or in the magnanimity of the imperial power. Vaenius announces himself as *Lugduno-Batavus* (he was born in Leiden) on the title-page, and so identifies with the Dutch.[32] Yet his political sympathy with the Spanish rulers of the Southern Netherlands is made clear in the even-handed treatment given to Civilis and Cerialis and, above all, in the reconciliation between the Batavi and the imperial powers portrayed in the frontispiece [fig. 2]; in the Latin caption to plate 36 [fig. 4]; in the Latin commentary added to the text of Tacitus opposite plate 36. Further, Vaenius ends his Dutch paraphrase (p. xxvii) by pointing out that the Batavi not only were restored to their former condition under Vespasian and his successors, but were also considered to be *amici et fratres Romanorum*, 'so that it is well to assume, as Tacitus sufficiently implies, that the war was ended by an accord'.[33] Thus Vaenius had it both ways. His book appealed both to the Dutch and to his Catholic readers in the Spanish Netherlands. Van de Waal is only partly right to say that 'the work glorified the revolt of the Batavians', and that its contemporary reference was to 'the heroic

---

[31] Lipsius, nevertheless, praised the free spirit of the speech of Calgacus in *Agricola*, 31-2 (the lemma is "nos terrarum ac libertatis"): 'animosa et alta haec oratio Galgaci [*sic*]'.

[32] He signs himself as *BatavoLugdunen.* in the *Album amicorum* of Ortelius, see n. 9.

[33] 'Soo ist wel te presumeren. dat dese oorloghe (ghelijck uut Tacitus selve ghenoegh verstaen wert) by accoort te neder gheleyt is'. Schrijver, *Batavia Illustrata*, 193-5, supports his case for the heroic stature of the ancient Batavi with a spurious inscription written in *literae praegrandes*: Gens Batavorum amici et fratres Romani Imperii. It was said to have been carved over the entrance to the *praesidium* of the legionary camp of 'Romaeoburgum' (i.e., Roomburg near Leiden). The ancient name of the camp was Matilo.

struggle of the Water-Beggars',[34] for it equally stressed the reconciliation of the Batavi with the Romans and that of the Southern Netherlands with the Habsburg monarchy.

Vaenius's name alone appears on the 1612 title-page of *Batavorum cum Romanis bellum* [fig. 1], while Tempestà's signature appears on the first plate [fig. 2] with the date 1611. An edition of *Romanorum et Batavorum societas* was published by Tempestà at Rome in 1611, containing the same illustrations and captions (in Dutch and Latin), but without the Dutch commentary.[35] The engravings were prepared a year previous to the 1612 publication in Antwerp, and Tempestà published them immediately for the Roman market. Vaenius then used them for his own publication (without giving credit to Tempestà, beyond the signature or monogram [AT] on some of the engravings). The Catholic censor's *imprimatur* is dated Antwerp, 25 November 1611. We can conclude that Tempestà took advantage of the Italian market, while Vaenius wished to present Tacitus in a way that would appeal to both sides in the Netherlands. The engravings show common features of Tempestà's style — elongated figures, a prominent figure in the foreground to lead the viewer's eye into the scene, and monumental horses.[36] It is possible that Vaenius may have done no more than choose the scenes and sketch the outlines, being responsible principally for the antiquarian features of armour, siege-engines, and fortresses, in which he was, as Lipsius had said in the *Poliorceticon*, an expert. It is impossible to say with any certainty whether the twelve paintings followed the publication of *Batavorum cum Romanis bellum*, or were undertaken while Tempestà was completing his engravings.[37]

---

[34] Waal H. van de, "The Iconological Background of Rembrandt's Civilis", in Nordenfalk, *Rembrandt's Claudius Civilis*, 12-3, enlarging on Van de Waal, *Drie Eeuwen Vaderlandsche Geschied-Uitbeelding*, 2 vols (The Hague: 1952) 210.

[35] According to the *Notes* to the catalogue entry for the copy in the Houghton Library of Harvard University, 'these engravings were reused as illustrations in Otto van Veen's *Batavorum cum Romanis bellum*, published in Antwerp: 1612'.

[36] Bartsch A., *Le Peintre Graveur*, 21 vols (Vienna: 1803–1821) XVII, 125-6, refers to Tempestà's preference for 'les batailles, les chasses, les marches et les combats', and he comments on variety of stances ('attitudes') and movements of his horses, and especially the noblesse of their heads. For an example, see plate 31 [fig. 3]. Tempestà's engravings (Bartsch XVII, 560-95), are reproduced in Buffa S., *The Illustrated Bartsch*, 35, 1 (New York: 1984) 288-324.

[37] See Van de Waal, *Drie Eeuwen Vaderlandsche Geschied-Uitbeelding*, 210-5 (partly repeated, in English, in Idem, "The Iconological Background of Rembrandt's Civilis", 12-6).

The first thing that the reader comes upon in Vaenius's book is *Totius Historiae Argumentum* and *Inhoudt ende cort begrijp van dese naevolgende Historie*, printed in parallel columns, the Latin in Roman font and the Dutch in Gothic. The Latin opens with the dogmatic statement 'inter ceteros populi Rom. socios principem facile locum olim tenebant Batavi' ('the Batavians held by far the first place among all the allies of the Roman people'), amplified in the following lines. The Dutch column begins 'De Bataviers oft Hollanders werden hier voortijts van de Romeynen voor het verbondt met hen ghemaecht', and continues also with the military virtues of the ancient Batavians (who, as 'Hollanders' are easily identified with the participants in the Dutch Revolt). At the end Vaenius says that the reader can read fully 'the whole history of this war translated into *Nederlandtsch*'. Thus the political thrust of the work is set forth immediately. Vaenius makes the virtues of the ancient Batavi, and the respect that the Romans had for them, accessible to contemporary Batavi in their own language.

Opposite the Introductions is the first engraving [fig. 2], a circular medallion showing Roma and Batavia (the latter holding a shield emblazoned with the Belgian Lion, as in the picture of *Patria* in the *Album amicorum*): they clasp hands in concord and alliance, while the gods of the Tiber (with Romulus and Remus), the Maas, and the Rhine are shown below. In the background the Batavi (whose excellence as horsemen and swimmers is emphasized in both the Latin and the Dutch texts opposite) are riding away across the Rhine, while (to the left) the Roman emperor enters Rome in triumph as Victoria holds the wreath of victory over his head. In monumental lettering around the scene is the inscription: *ROMANORVM ET BATAVORVM SOCIETAS*. Thus Vaenius's ambiguous political attitude is made clear at the very beginning. His work celebrates the heroism of the Batavian prince and his people; he depicts the equality of the Batavi with the Romans and, through the scenes in the background, shows that after the war each side resumed its ways — the Romans with their empire intact, the Batavians with their liberty and way of life maintained.[38] The double meaning for the contemporaries of Vaenius is obvious.[39]

---

[38] The seer, Veleda, as Lipsius points out in his commentary on *Germania*, 8, 2 (p. 438 of the 1607 Tacitus), was captured and displayed in the triumph for the campaign of 77–78 AD (see Heubner H., *Tacitus: Die Historien*, IV, 61, 2), as indicated by Statius, *Silvae* I, 4, 90: 'captivaeque preces Veledae'. Her future fate does not affect her importance in Tempestà's plate 21, but it does detract from Vaenius's implication that everything returned to normal after the revolt.

[39] Lipsius justly estimates the relative power of the Batavi and the Romans in his

The extant text of Tacitus's *Histories* breaks off in the middle of the speech of Civilis at the conference on the bridge, when he and Cerialis faced each other. In the engraving (plate 36 [fig. 4]) Tempestà shows Civilis (on the further side of the gap, facing the viewer) and Cerialis (from the rear) addressing each other with vigorous gestures. The massed troops behind each leader and in the background emphasize the martial setting, which is confirmed by the broken pieces of the bridge in the river and the group of four Roman soldiers and a mounted cavalryman in the foreground. Quite different is Vaenius's painting of the same scene [fig. 5], in which the commanders' positions are reversed and only Civilis speaks. Behind him in the foreground are eight Batavian warriors more ready for a parade than for battle, while Cerialis's troops are lightly sketched in the background. The river flows in the background between peaceful towns, undamaged by war and rich with towers and spires. Behind the Romans a tree is in full leaf, in contrast to the ruins of the bridge that are so conspicuous in the engraving. The painting focuses more on the blessings of peace, which, it is implied, will be the result of the treaty agreed upon by the two leaders.

Tacitus does not state as a fact that such a treaty was made, and Vaenius himself, in the last words of his book (quoted above), admits that he is making an inference.[40] Nevertheless, thirty years after these events Tacitus describes the Batavi (*Germania* 29, 1) as 'virtute praecipui' among the tribes along the lower Rhine and exceptional in being exempt from tribute. They were called upon to support Rome only in time of war by supplying conscript troops. The special status of the Batavi, says Tacitus, was 'their continuing privilege and a distinguishing sign of their long-standing alliance' ('manet honos et antiquae societatis insigne'). In fact, their geographical position made it hardly worthwhile for the Romans to attempt to subjugate them. Instead, their exceptional military prowess was recognised and used when needed. Their naval skills were not great: plate 33 [fig. 6] shows the abortive naval battle of *Hist.* V, 23, without suggesting that a par-

---

commentary on *Hist.* IV, 12, 3 'nec opibus Romanis, societate validiorum, attriti' (in the 1607 edition p. 397; the text differs from that of Heubner, who reads *rarum in societate*): 'sententia est. quamquam Romanis socii et foederati Batavi, quae societas apud potentiores plerumque in servitutem transit: tamen non ita iis factum. Libertatem tenuere [...]'.

[40] See n. 33; cf. Heubner's commentary *Tacitus: Die Historien* V, 26 (p. 178). As for Civilis, nothing more is known of his fate.

allel be drawn with contemporary Dutch naval power. The focus is rather on the Romans and their curiosity that Civilis should make such an ambitious attempt: 'Cerialis miraculo magis quam metu derexit classem' ('Cerialis steered his fleet more out of wonder than out of fear'). Lipsius comments: 'nondum in mari aut aquis, quales nunc miramur' ('the Batavian sailors, on the sea or inland waters, were not yet as skilled as those whom we now admire').[41]

We return now to the scene of the swearing of the oath to Civilis in the *sacrum nemus* (plate 4 [fig. 7]). Van de Waal has plausibly suggested that the first of the two feast scenes in the series of paintings [fig. 8] was the starting-point of the whole series, and that it preceded the engraving, which itself was followed by the second feast scene [fig. 9].[42] The first scene is a garden-feast (*tuinfeest*) in the Venetian style, having nothing to do with Tacitus's narrative beyond drawing attention to the contrast between the peaceful, courtly scene, and the oath-taking at the feast narrated by Tacitus (*Hist.* IV, 13). The second focuses on Civilis as orator (as Tacitus narrates), and it is accurate in such details as the two tables, respectively for the *primores gentis* and the *promptissimos vulgi* of Tacitus. But Tempestà's engraving totally lacks dramatic or historical interest.[43] It shows a series of elderly men shaking the hand of Civilis, who is not even the focal point of the composition.[44]

In both the engravings and the paintings the dress of the Romans and Batavi is significant. Generally Roman military dress and armour are

---

[41] In the 1607 edition, p. 432; Heubner, *Tacitus: Die Historien* on V, 23 (p. 173), paraphrases 'miraculo' as 'aus Neugier'; Vaenius, *Batavorum cum Romanis bellum*, p. xxv, as 'om de Hollanders te doen verwonderen'.

[42] Van de Waal, "The Iconological Background of Rembrandt's Civilis", 13-7, repeating Idem, *Drie Eeuwen Vaderlandsche Geschied-Uitbeelding*, 213-5. For the failings of Tempestà's engraving see Carroll M.D., "Civic Ideology and its Subversion: Rembrandt's *Oath of Claudius Civilis*", *Art History* 9 (1986) 17.

[43] In contrast, in Rembrandt's *Claudius Civilis* [fig. 17] Civilis is the dominating figure, while Rembrandt has included details from Tacitus, such as Civilis's blind eye (Tacitus's 'oris dehonestamentum') and the touching of swords to confirm the oath. See Carroll, "Civic Ideology and its Subversion", criticising Van de Waal, *Drie Eeuwen Vaderlandsche Geschied-Uitbeelding* and "The Iconological Background of Rembrandt's Civilis". The painting, submitted as a decoration for the new Town Hall of Amsterdam in 1663, was rejected.

[44] Vaenius enlarges on the text of Tacitus in his Dutch commentary (p. ii). Besides the contemporary terms (*Colonnelen, Capiteynen*, etc.) he adds the supposed words of the oath, which in Tacitus are vague (*patriis exsecrationibus*): they swear 'van lijf ende leven voor t'vaderlandt gewillichlijck te wagen'.

shown accurately, but Civilis is portrayed in Renaissance dress and the women are shown in Burgundian clothing with the high conical headdress of the late Middle Ages, as can be seen in the engraving of the women stationed behind the Batavian troops as 'hortamenta victoriae' [fig. 10].[45] Here the dress, the gestures, and the activities of the women are totally at variance with the significance of the women in Tacitus. In the corresponding painting [fig. 11] Vaenius dispenses with the Burgundian dress and portrays the scene more in accordance with *Germania* 7, 2, where 'the men bring their wounds to their mothers and wives, who are not afraid to count them and demand [*sc.* that their menfolk be wounded]'. The Burgundian dress, perhaps, is meant to convey an idea of a timeless past, while the Renaissance clothing of the men brings the ancient Batavi closer to Vaenius's own time.

In these details Vaenius was taking sides in contemporary controversy about the life and clothing of the ancient Batavi and Germans.[46] For Tacitus the Batavi were a German tribe, but Vaenius is careful to distinguish between the Batavi, whom he calls 'Het Hollandtsch crygsvolck' or 'De Hollanders', and the Germans, who are 'De Duytschen'. For example, the Germans get drunk and rashly attack the legionary fortress of Vetera (plate 13 [figs. 12 and 13]), in contrast to the courage and skill shown by the Batavi (plate 14 [fig. 14]). The distinction was significant. In 1611 Philipp Clüver (Cluverius), a former student of Scaliger's at Leiden, published his *Commentarius de III Rheni alveis*, in which he argued that the Batavi were part of Gaul and were not Germans.[47] In 1616 he published his *Germaniae antiquae libri tres*, which gave a much more primitive view of the ancient Batavi than that of Vaenius and sought to prove that they were democratic [fig. 15].[48]

---

[45] *Hist.* IV, 18, 2; cf. *Germ.* 7, 2. Lipsius, commenting on the former passage (in the 1607 edition, p. 400), notes the importance of the *feminarum ululatus*.

[46] See Schöffer I., "The Batavian Myth during the 16th and 17th Centuries", in *Britain and the Netherlands*, vol 5: *Some Political Mythologies*, ed. J.S. Bromley – E.H. Kossmann (The Hague: 1975), especially 91-5.

[47] He makes the same argument in *Germaniae antiquae libri tres*, 473-80.

[48] Cluverius P., *Germaniae antiquae libri III* (Leiden: 1616; 1631² quoted) I, 38 ("De democraticis rebuspublicis cum principatu"), 265-6, 'corrects' Tacitus's 'Iulius Civilis [...] regia stirpe' (*Hist.* IV, 13, 1), by saying that Civilis was a *princeps* (i.e., first among equals). His discussion "De cultu corporum atque vestitu" is at I, 16, 104; twelve figures of ancient Germans and Batavi come after p. 120, with German warriors illustrated after p. 304. See also Carroll, "Civic Ideology and its Subversion", 18-20. Hugo Grotius's *Liber de antiquitate Reipublicae Batavicae*, was published at Leiden in 1610. Cluverius's principal opponent was Johannes Pontanus, who attacked him in

Vaenius, then, distinguished the ancient Batavi from the Germans
and the Gauls. They were the ancestors of the Dutch, and their home
was north of the Waal and more or less in the area of the Holland of
his day.[49] Nevertheless, he sought also to satisfy his readers in the
Spanish Netherlands, especially by depicting the reconciliation of the
Batavi and the Romans. We have discussed the programmatic frontispiece [fig. 2], and we turn now to the scene (plate 26 [fig. 16]), in
which Cerialis receives back the legionaries who had gone over to the
side of Civilis (*Hist.* IV, 72, 2-4). The gestures and the words (in the
Latin and the Dutch) are generous and noble. The message is clear:
the imperial power is merciful to those who ask for mercy.

Vaenius did not include an illustration of an equally significant
episode that followed, Cerialis's speech to the Treveri and Lingones
(*Hist.* IV, 73-4).[50] Cerialis argued that if the Roman empire were to
collapse only tribal warfare would follow. Here is the commentary of
Lipsius on this passage:

> An oracular saying, whose truth [our] ancestors saw. And we, too, see it
> and will see it, so long as Europe is divided amongst so many masters
> and does not obey the reins of the one Charioteer. Plutarch rightly,
> then, has written that 'the Roman empire is, as it were, the anchor for a
> world adrift'.[51]

These words, which first appeared in the Notes to the *Histories* in the
Curae Secundae of 1588,[52] express precisely the dilemma that Lipsius
sought to avoid and Vaenius to exploit. In 1589 Lipsius had argued in
the *Politica* magisterially (indeed, brutally) for the principle of *una religio*

---

books published in 1614 and 1617, and in a letter to Grotius (Molhuysen P.C.,
Briefwisseling van Hugo Grotius, vol 1, Rijksgeschiedkundige Publikatiën 64 (The Hague:
1928) 439, letter of 1 December 1615, by which time Cluverius's *Germaniae antiquae libri III* must have been published, despite its publication date of 1616).

[49] Precisely defined by Ortelius A., *Synonymia Geographica* (Antwerp: 1578) 57: 'ea
pars Hollandiae quae hodie inter veterem Rhenum et Vahalum fluvios, a Lobico ad
Oceanum usque, quasi duobus brachiis constringitur'. He says that the name *Betuwe*
keeps the old name.

[50] See the critical analysis of the speech by Keitel, "Speech and Narrative in *Histories* IV", 51-7.

[51] In the 1607 edition, p. 420 (the lemma is 'Quid alia quam bella'): 'Oraculum
cuius fidem proavi viderunt: et nos videmus, videbimusque, quamdiu secta in tot
dominos Europa non audiet unus Aurigae habenas. Putarchus [*sic*] igitur vere,
Imperium Romanum velut anchora esse scripsit fluctuanti mundo'.

[52] The comment is not printed in the *Notes* to the 1585 edition of Tacitus. Lipsius's
marginal note on the speech is: 'Cerialis, ita me Deus, facunda et sapiens oratio'.

in uno regno.[53] In adding this passage to his commentary on the *Histories* he made clear that the revolt of Civilis, however heroic, was praiseworthy only in so far as it ended in the reconciliation of the Batavi and the Romans. Vaenius combined both points of view.[54]

Selective Bibliography

BARTSCH A., *Le Peintre Graveur*, 21 vols (Vienna: 1803–1821)

BRUNT P.A., "Tacitus on the Batavian Revolt", *Latomus* 19 (1960) 494-517

BUFFA S., *The Illustrated Bartsch*, 35, 1 (New York: 1984)

BURMAN P., *Sylloges epistolarum a viris illustribus scriptarum* (Leiden: 1727)

CARROLL M.D., "Civic Ideology and its Subversion: Rembrandt's *Oath of Claudius Civilis*", *Art History* 9 (1986) 12-35

GHEYN J. VAN DEN, *Album amicorum de Otto Venius* (Brussels: 1911)

GROTIUS H., *Liber de antiquitate Reipublicae Batavicae* (Leiden: 1610)

ILE: *Iusti Lipsi Epistolae*, ed. A. Gerlo and others (Brussels: 1978–)

HEUBNER H., *Tacitus: Die Historien. Kommentar: Bücher IV und V* (Heidelberg: 1976, 1982)

KEITEL E., "Speech and Narrative in *Histories* IV", in *Tacitus and the Tacitean Tradition*, ed. Luce T.J.–Woodman, A.J. (Princeton: 1993) 39-58

LUCE T.J. – WOODMAN A.J. (ed.), *Tacitus and the Tacitean Tradition* (Princeton: 1993)

MOLHUYSEN P.C., *Briefwisseling van Hugo Grotius*, vol 1, Rijksgeschiedkundige Publikatiën 64 (The Hague: 1928)

MORFORD M., *Stoics and Neostoics* (Princeton: 1991)

MORFORD M., "Tacitean *Prudentia* and the Doctrines of Justus Lipsius", in *Tacitus and the Tacitean Tradition*, ed. Luce T.J.–Woodman, A.J. (Princeton: 1993) 129-51

MORFORD M., "L'Influence de Juste Lipse sur les Arts", in *Juste Lipse en son Temps*, Mouchel C., Actes du Colloque de Strasbourg 1994 (Paris: 1996) 235-45

---

[53] *Politica* IV, 3-4: these chapters led to the controversy with Coornhert and eventually played a part in Lipsius's departure from Leiden. See Morford, *Stoics and Neostoics*, 106-18.

[54] While Vaenius omits the speech of Cerialis from the engravings, he does give a full version in his Dutch commentary on plate 26 (p. xx), translating 'Quid aliud quam' [...] as: 'Wat isser anders te verwachten dan en onderlinghe oorloghe tusschen alle natien'.

MÜLLERS W., *Der Bataveraufstand 69–70 n. Chr.: Zerstörung und Schlacht von Vetera*, 2 vols (Cologne: 1978)

NORDENFALK C., *The Batavians' Oath of Allegiance* (Stockholm: 1982)

NORDENFALK C., *Rembrandt's Claudius Civilis* (= *Konsthistorik Tidskrift* 25-6) (Stockholm: 1956)

PARKER G., *Europe in Crisis. 1598–1648* (Ithaca, N.Y.: 1979)

ROSSUM J.A. VAN, "Julius Civilis en het Germaanse Gevaar", *Lampas* 25 (1992) 184-97

SCHÖFFER I., "The Batavian Myth during the 16th and 17th Centuries", in *Britain and the Netherlands*, vol 5: *Some Political Mythologies*, ed. J.S. Bromley – E.H. Kossmann (The Hague: 1975) 78-101

SCHRIJVER P., *Batavia Illustrata* (Leiden: 1609)

TEMPESTÀ A., *Romanorum et Batavorum Societas* (Rome: 1611)

VAENIUS O., *Batavorum cum Romanis bellum* (Antwerp: 1612)

VAENIUS O., *Q. Horatii Flacci Emblemata* (Antwerp: 1607)

WAAL H. VAN DE, *Drie Eeuwen Vaderlandsche Geschied-Uitbeelding*, 2 vols (The Hague: 1952)

WAAL H. VAN DE, "The Iconological Background of Rembrandt's Civilis", in Nordenfalk, *Rembrandt's Claudius Civilis*, 11-25.

Figures 1-16 belong to '*Theatrum Hodiernae Vitae*': *Lipsius, Vaenius and the Rebellion of Civilis* by Mark Morford.
Figures 1-10 belong to *Strange and Bewildering Antiquity: Lipsius's Dialogue 'Saturnales sermones' on Gladiatorial Games (1582)* by Karl Enenkel.

FIGURES 1-16 (Morford)

BATAVORVM
CVM ROMANIS
BELLVM,

à Corn. Tacito lib. IV. & V. Hist. olim descriptum,
figuris nunc æneis expressum,

Auctore OTHONE VÆNIO Lugdunobatauo.

DE BATAVISCHE
Oft OVDE HOLLANDTSCHE OORLOGHE
teghen de Romeynen.

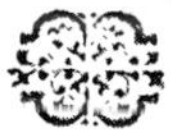

ANTVERPIÆ,
Apud Auctorem væneunt.
M . DC . XII .
Cum Gratia & Priuilegio,

1. Otho Vaenius, *Batavorum cum Romanis Bellum* (Antwerp: 1612), Title-Page.

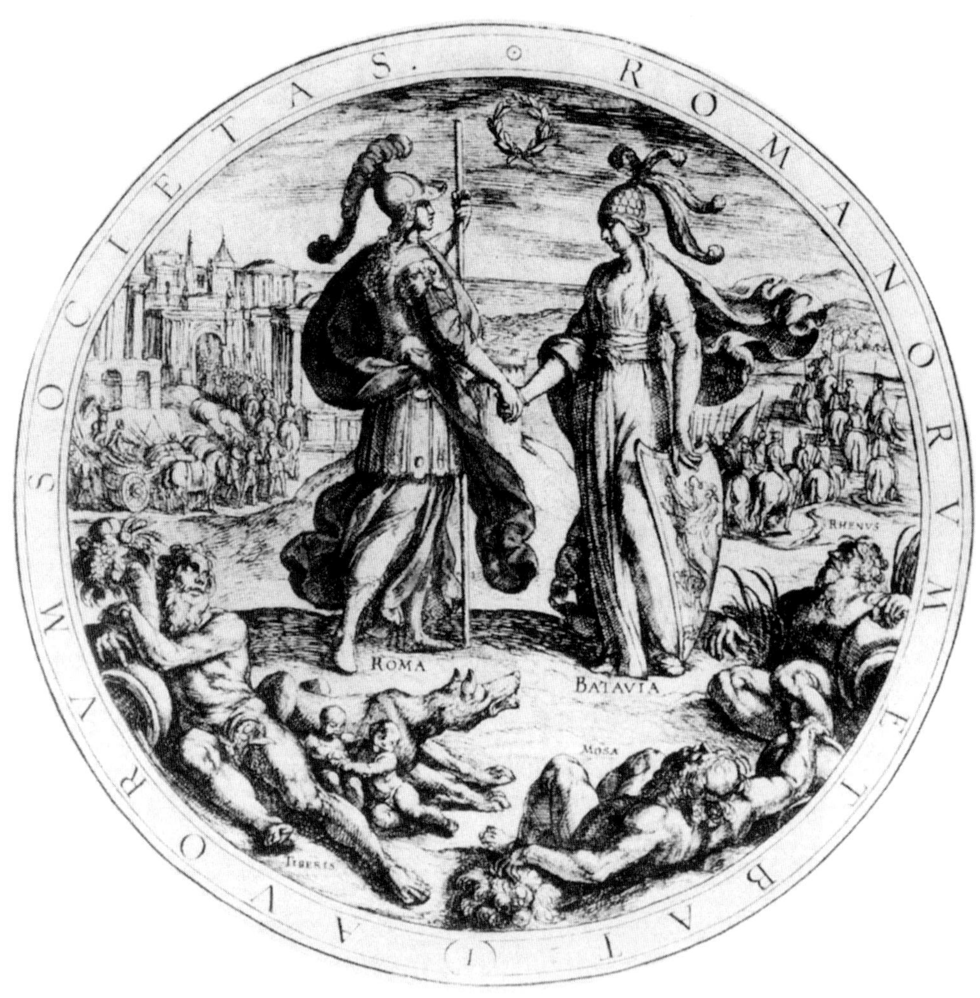

2. Antonio Tempestà, *Romanorum et Batavorum Societas* (Rome: 1611).

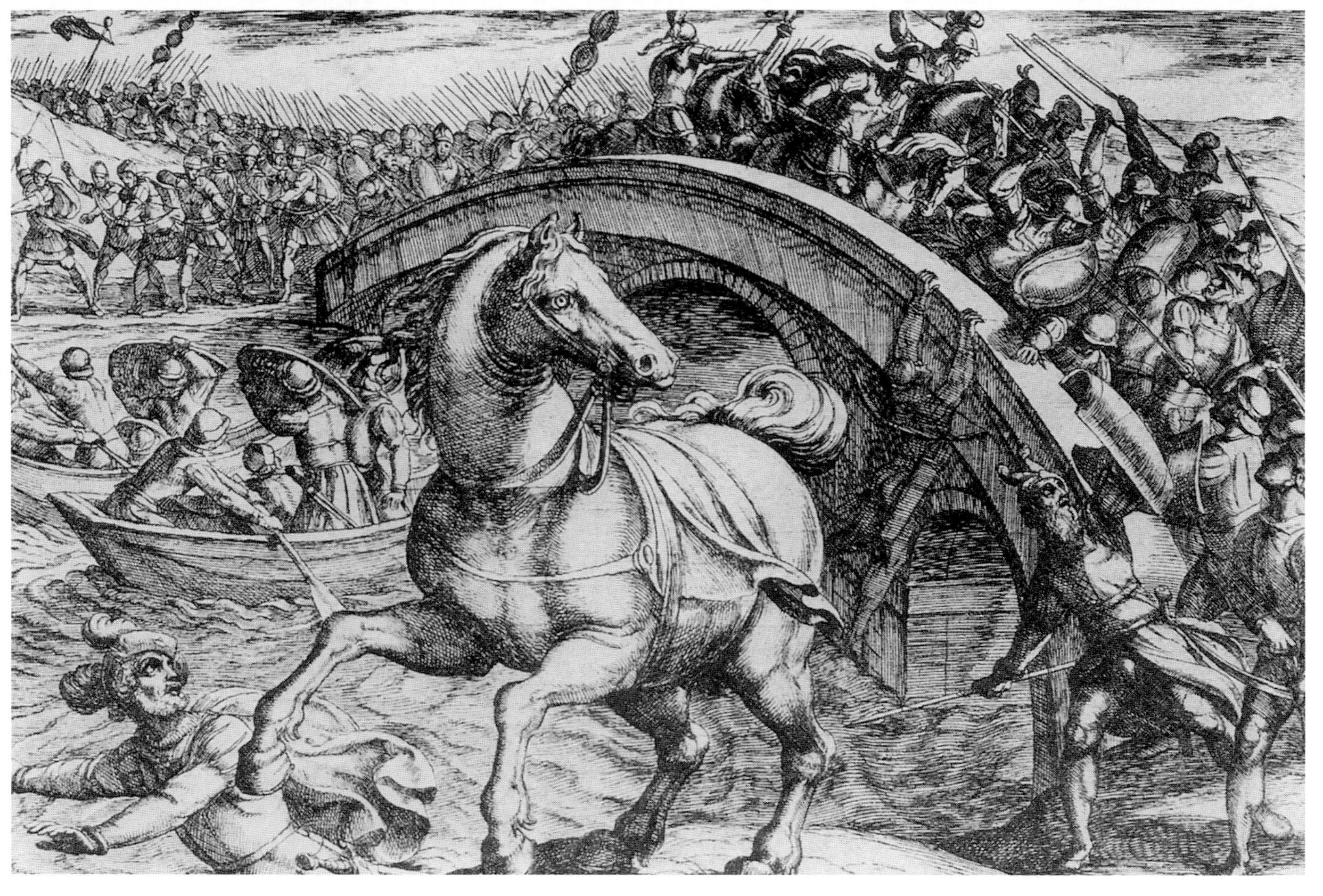

3. *Battle at the Bridge*. Antonio Tempestà, Plate 31, *Romanorum et Batavorum Societas* (Rome: 1611).

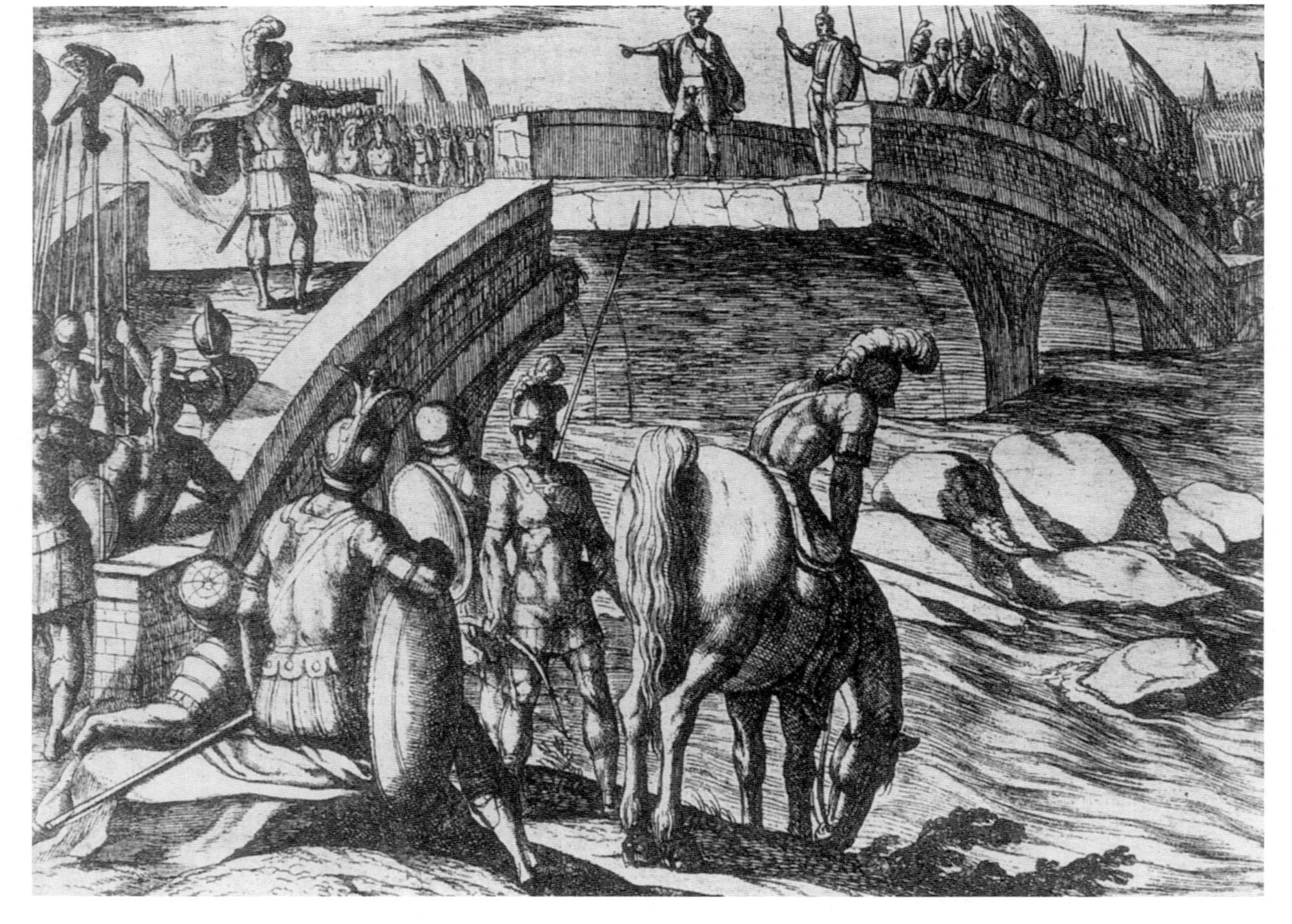

4. *Cerialis and Civilis at the Bridge*. Antonio Tempestà, Plate 36, *Romanorum et Batavorum Societas* (Rome: 1611).

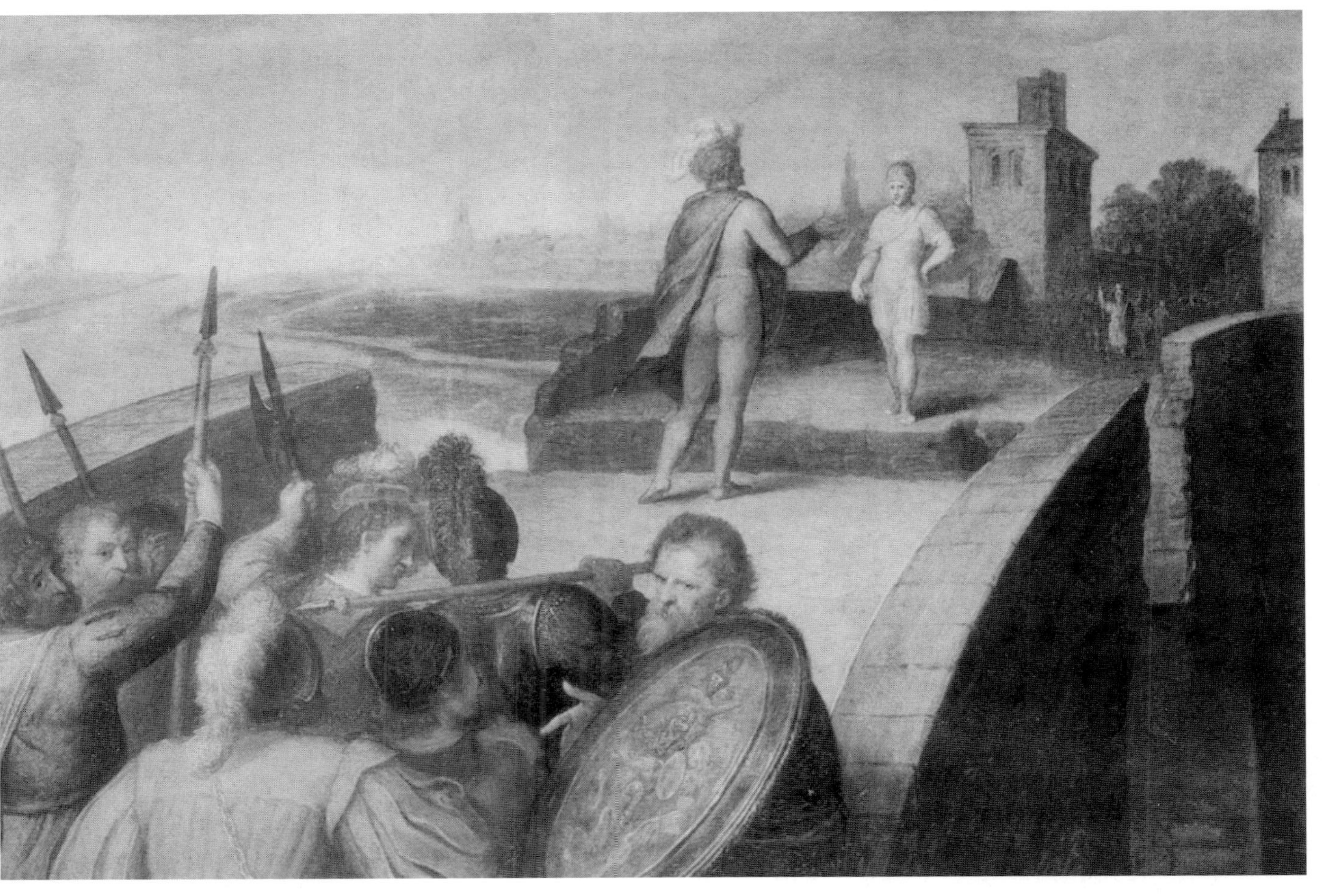

5. Otho Vaenius, *Cerialis and Civilis at the Bridge.*

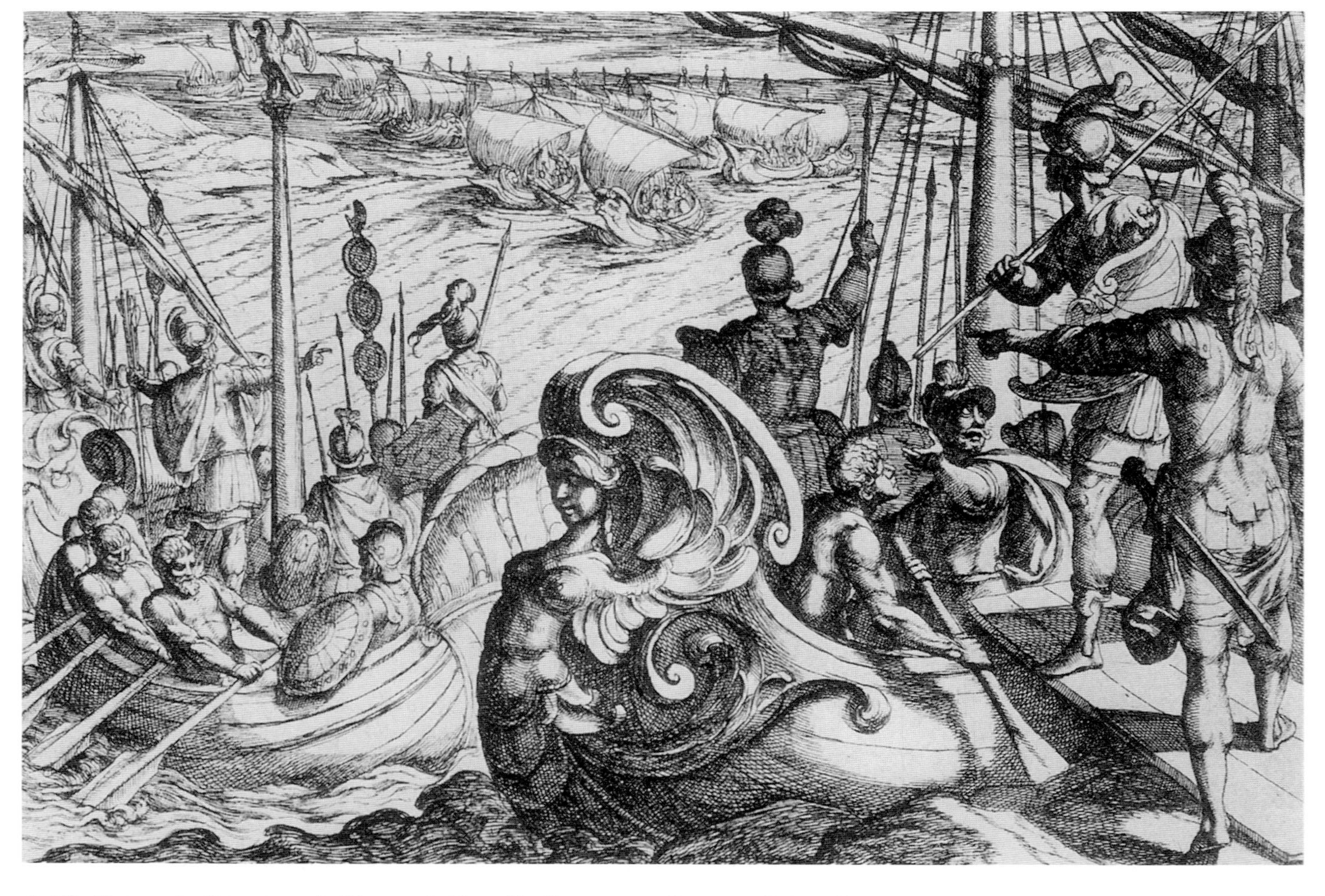

6. *The Fleets on the Rhine*, Antonio Tempestà, Plate 33, *Romanorum et Batavorum Societas* (Rome: 1611).

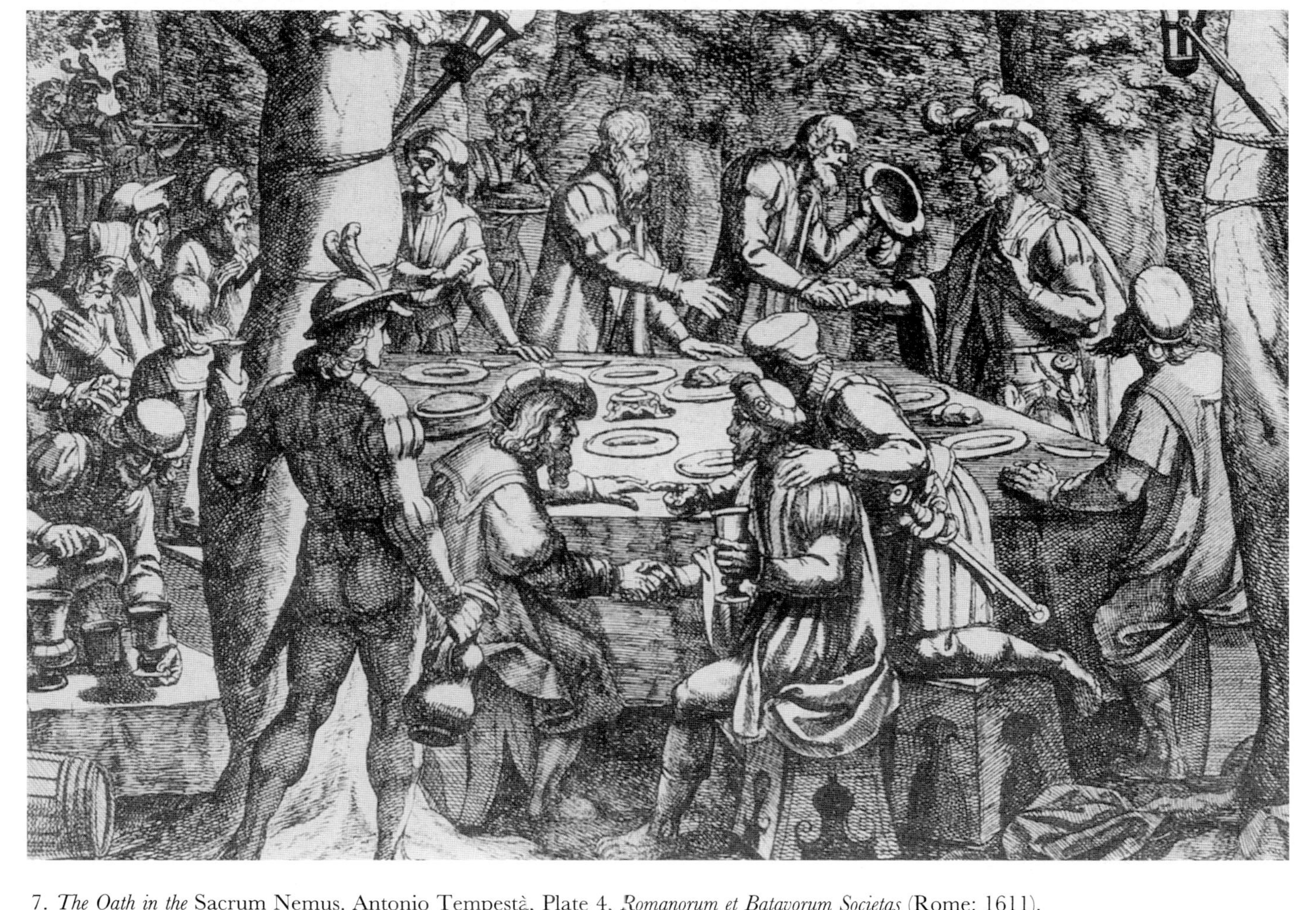

7. *The Oath in the* Sacrum Nemus. Antonio Tempestà, Plate 4, *Romanorum et Batavorum Societas* (Rome: 1611).

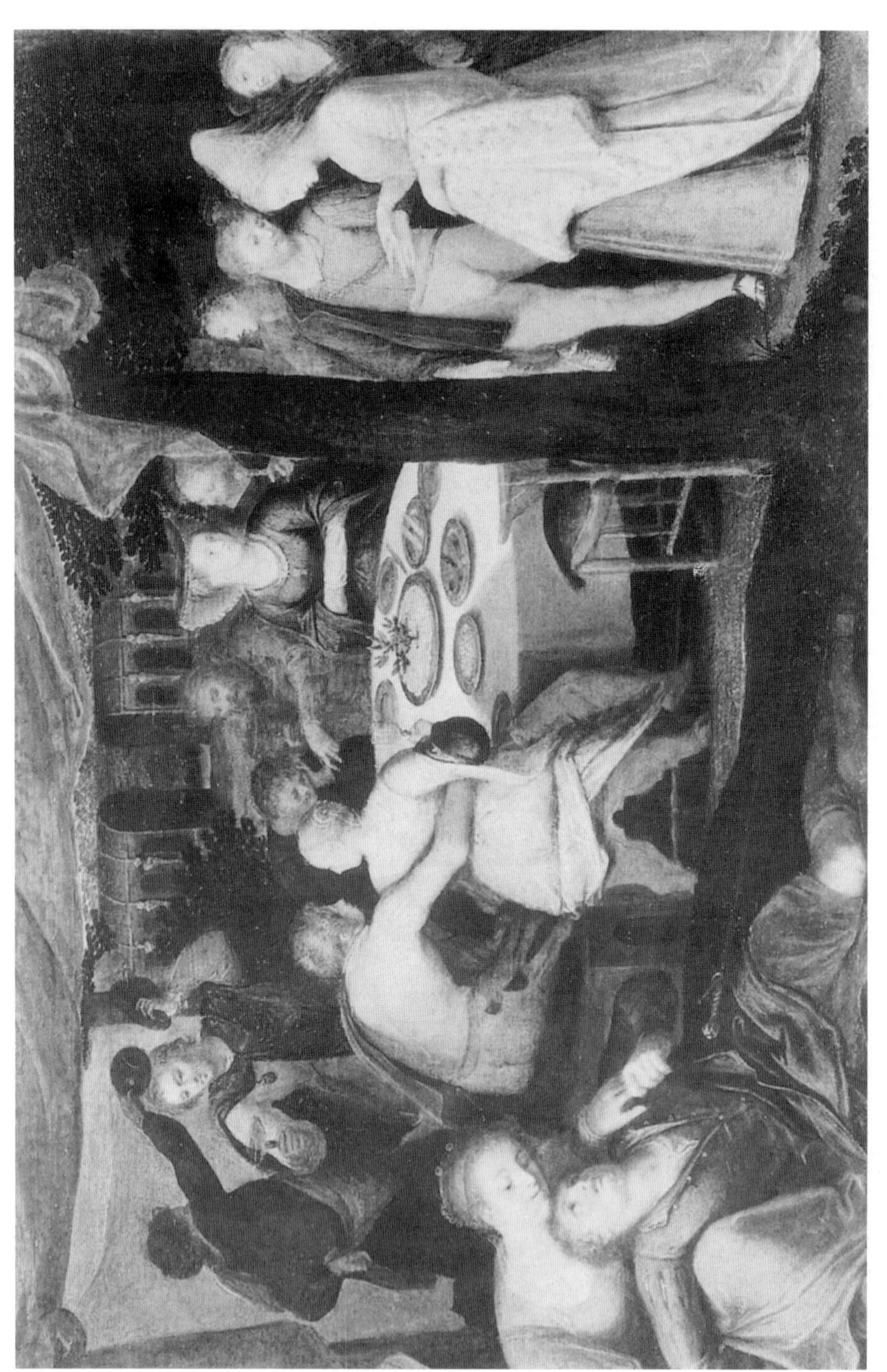

8. Otho Vaenius, *The Feast in the Garden.*

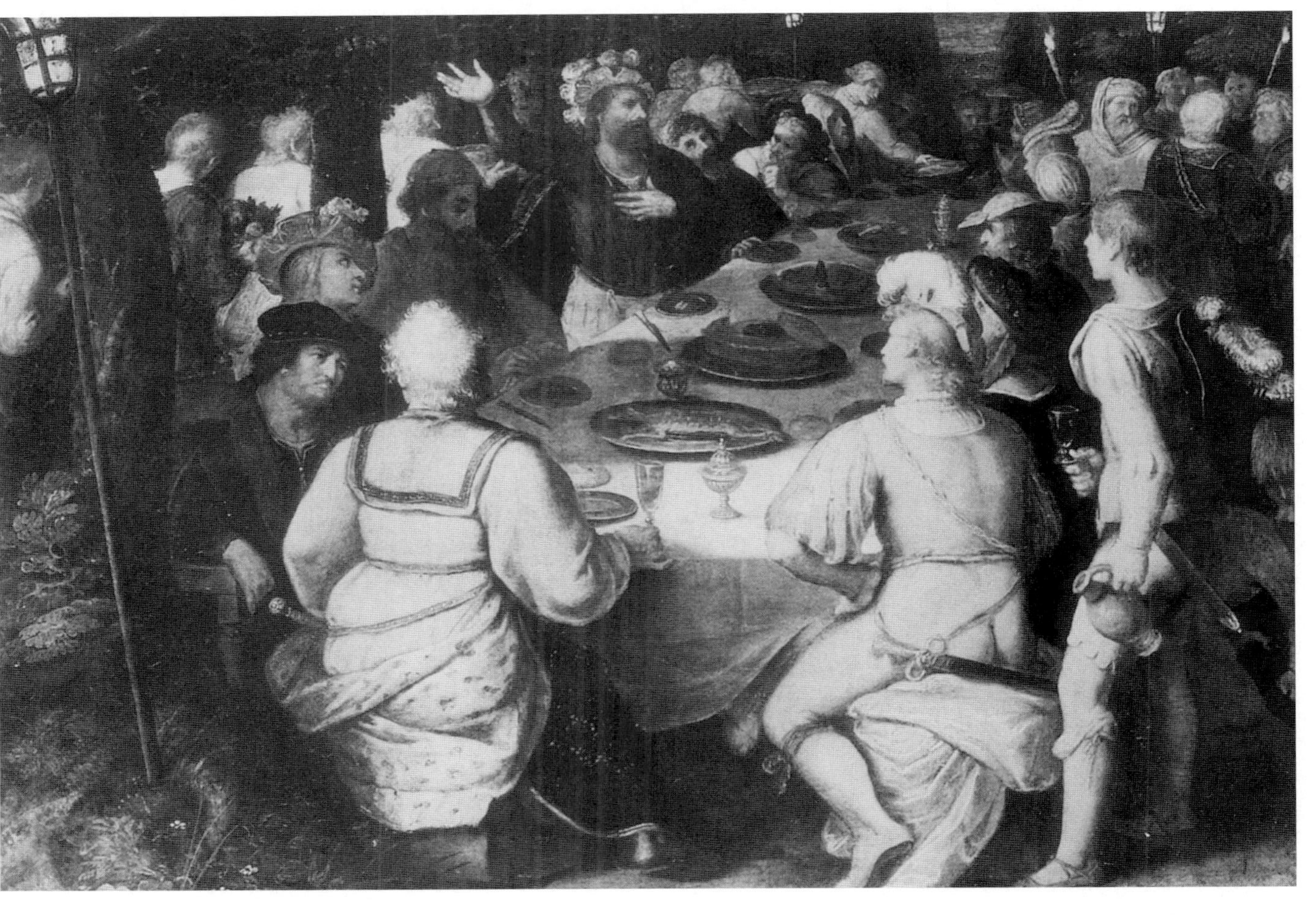

9. Otho Vaenius, *The Oath in the Sacrum Nemus.*

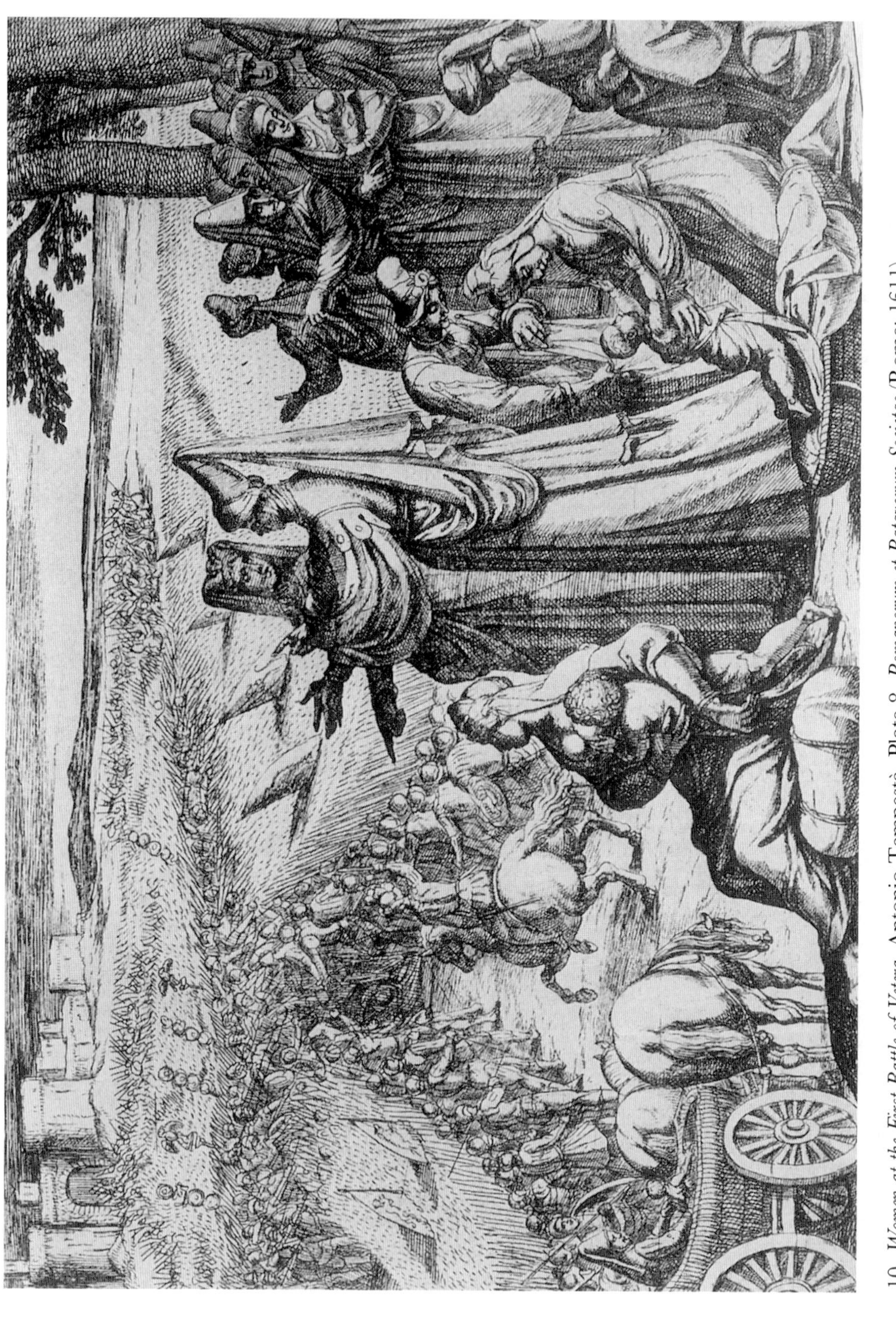

10. *Women at the First Battle of Vetera.* Antonio Tempestà, Plate 8, *Romanorum et Batavorum Societas* (Rome: 1611).

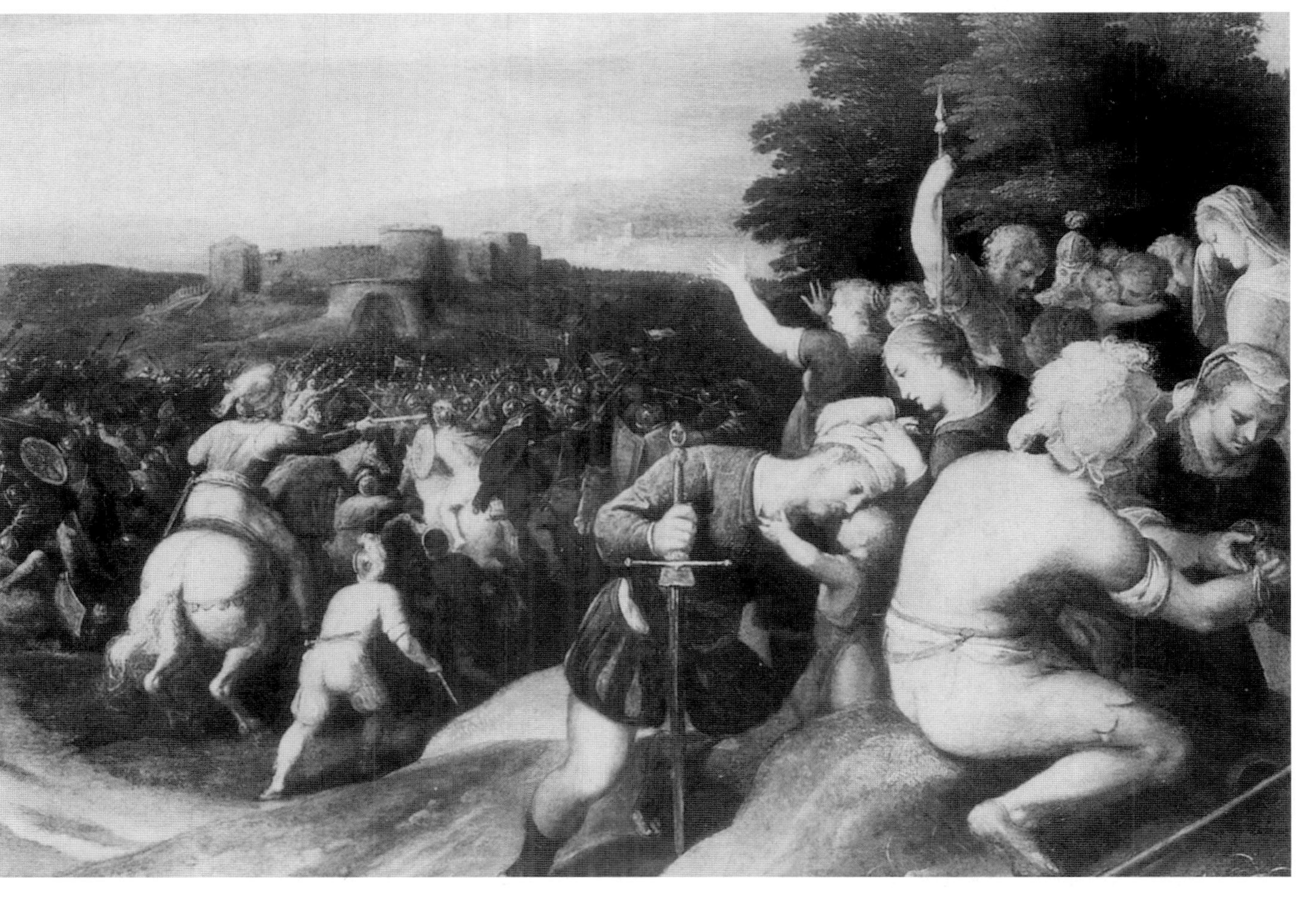

11. Otho Vaenius, *Women at the First Battle of Vetera.*

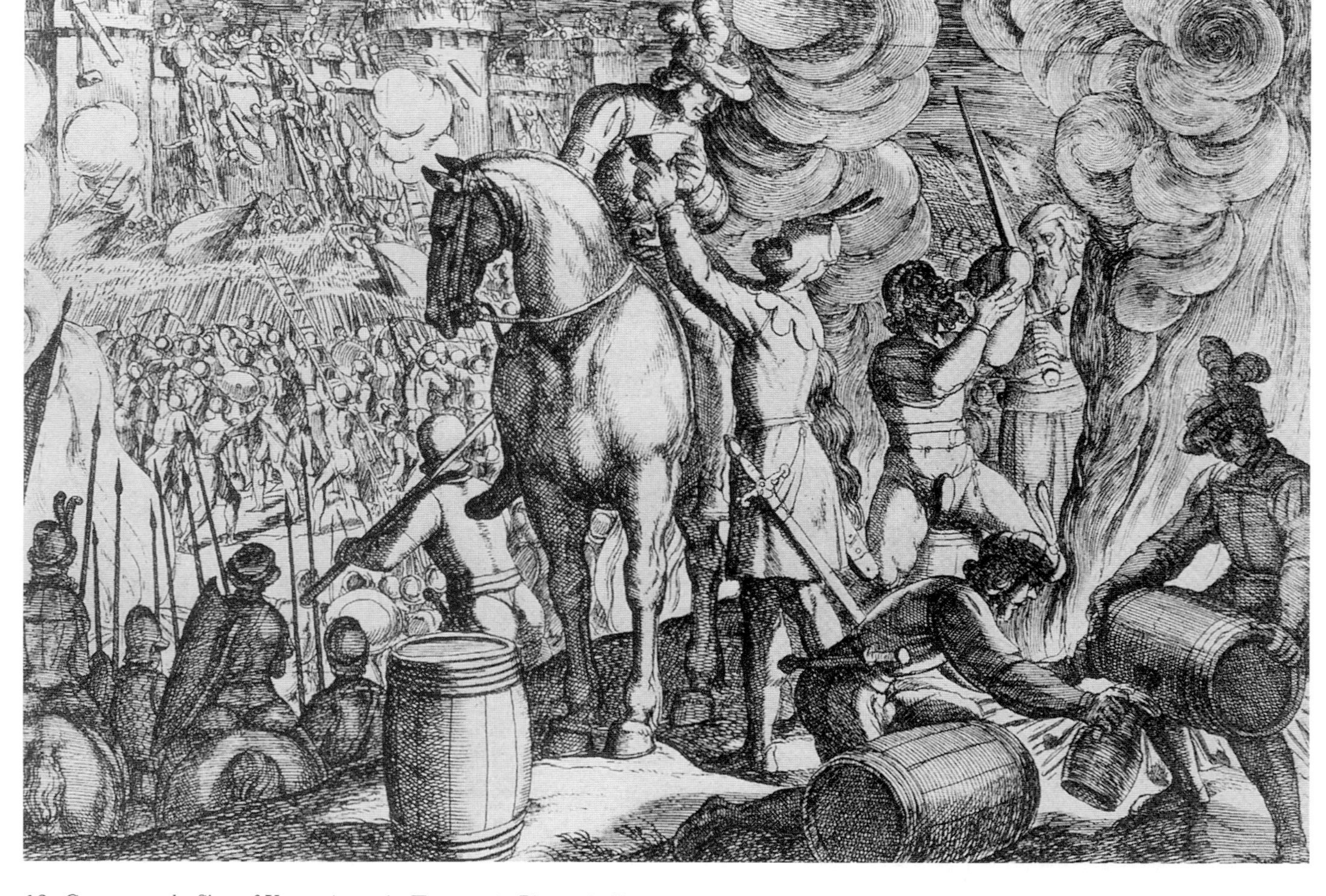

12. *Germans at the Siege of Vetera.* Antonio Tempestà, Plate 13, *Romanorum et Batavorum Societas* (Rome: 1611).

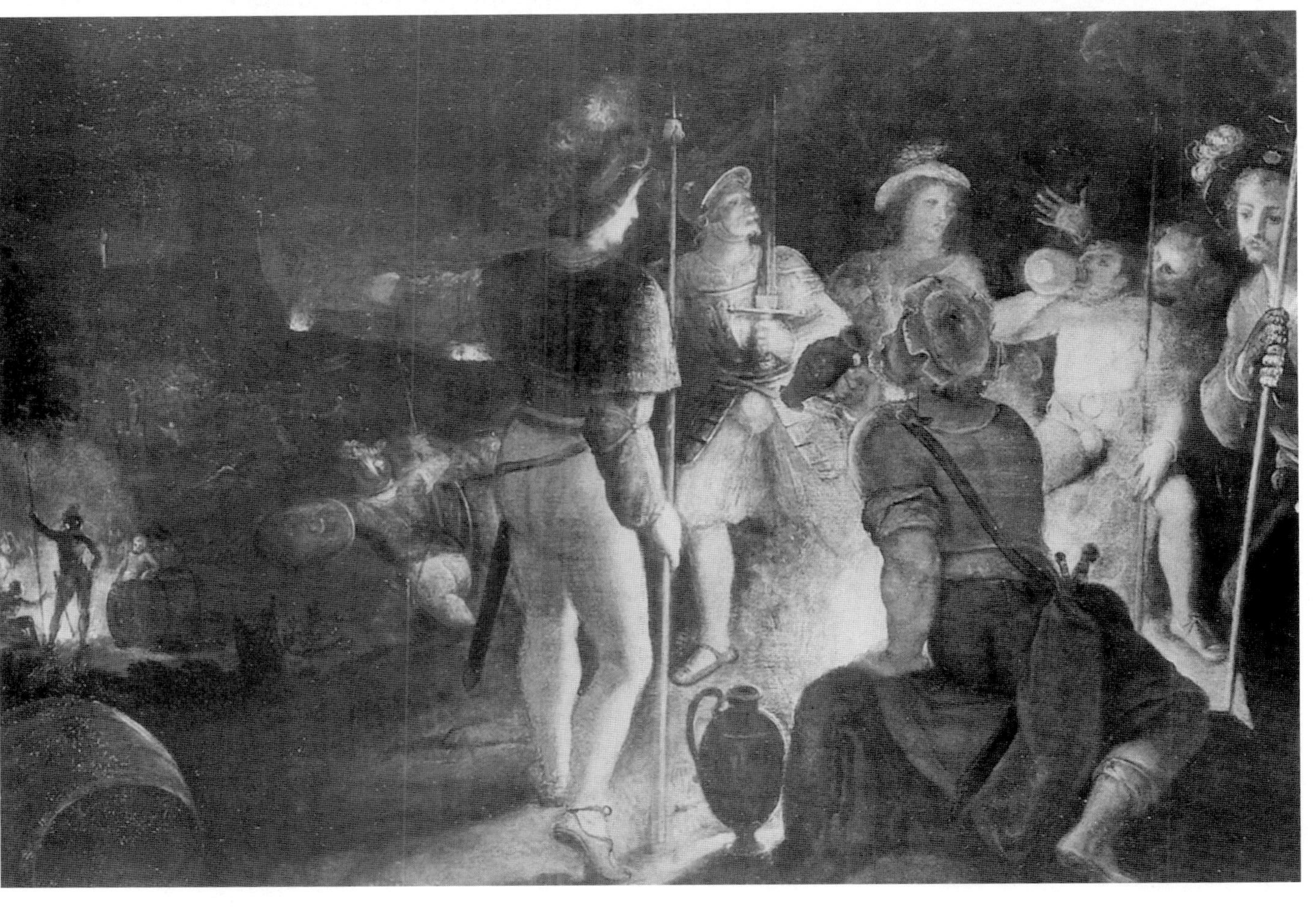

13. Otho Vaenius, *Germans at the Siege of Vetera*.

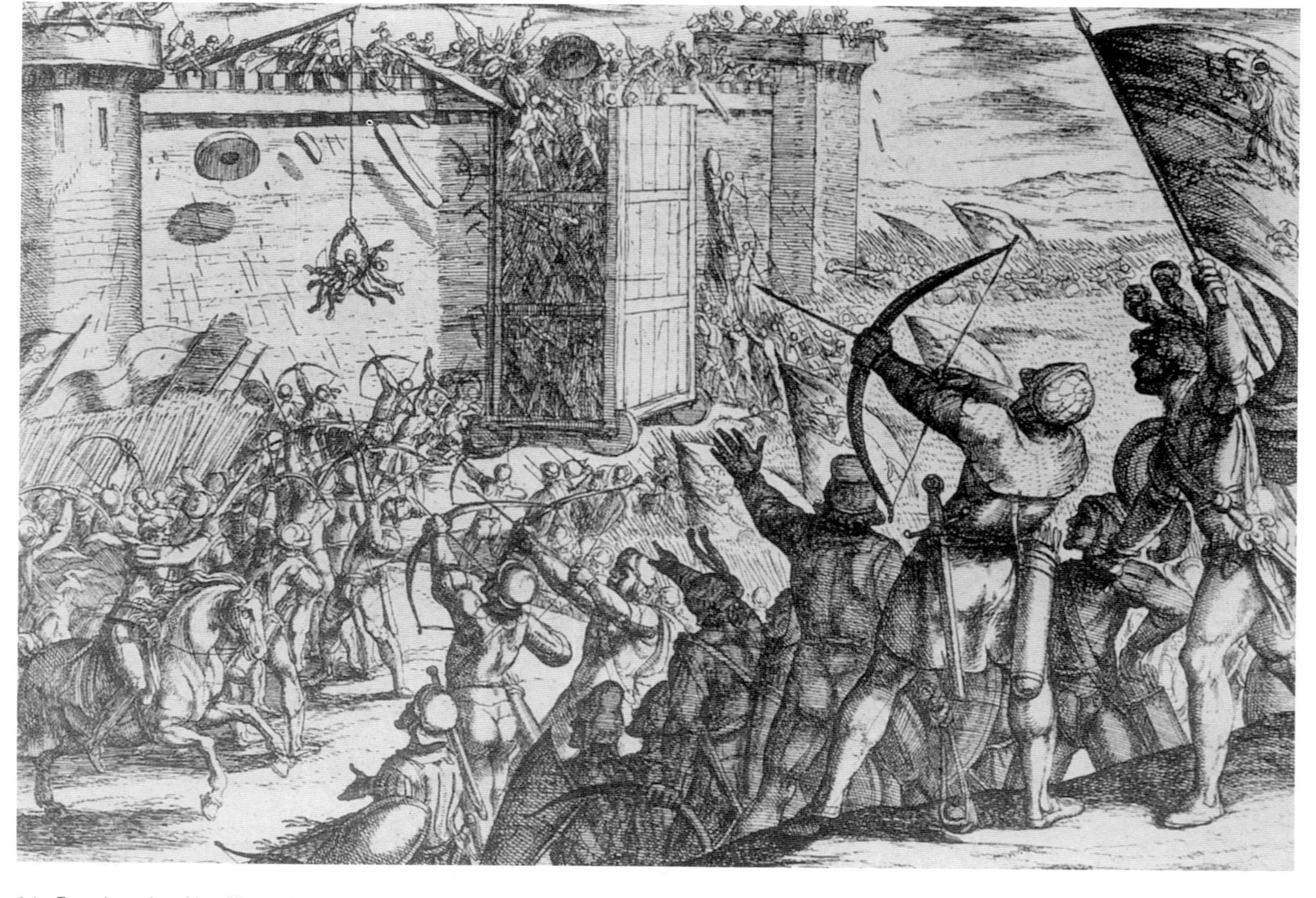

14. *Batavians Attacking Vetera.* Antonio Tempestà, Plate 14, *Romanorum et Batavorum Societas* (Rome: 1611).

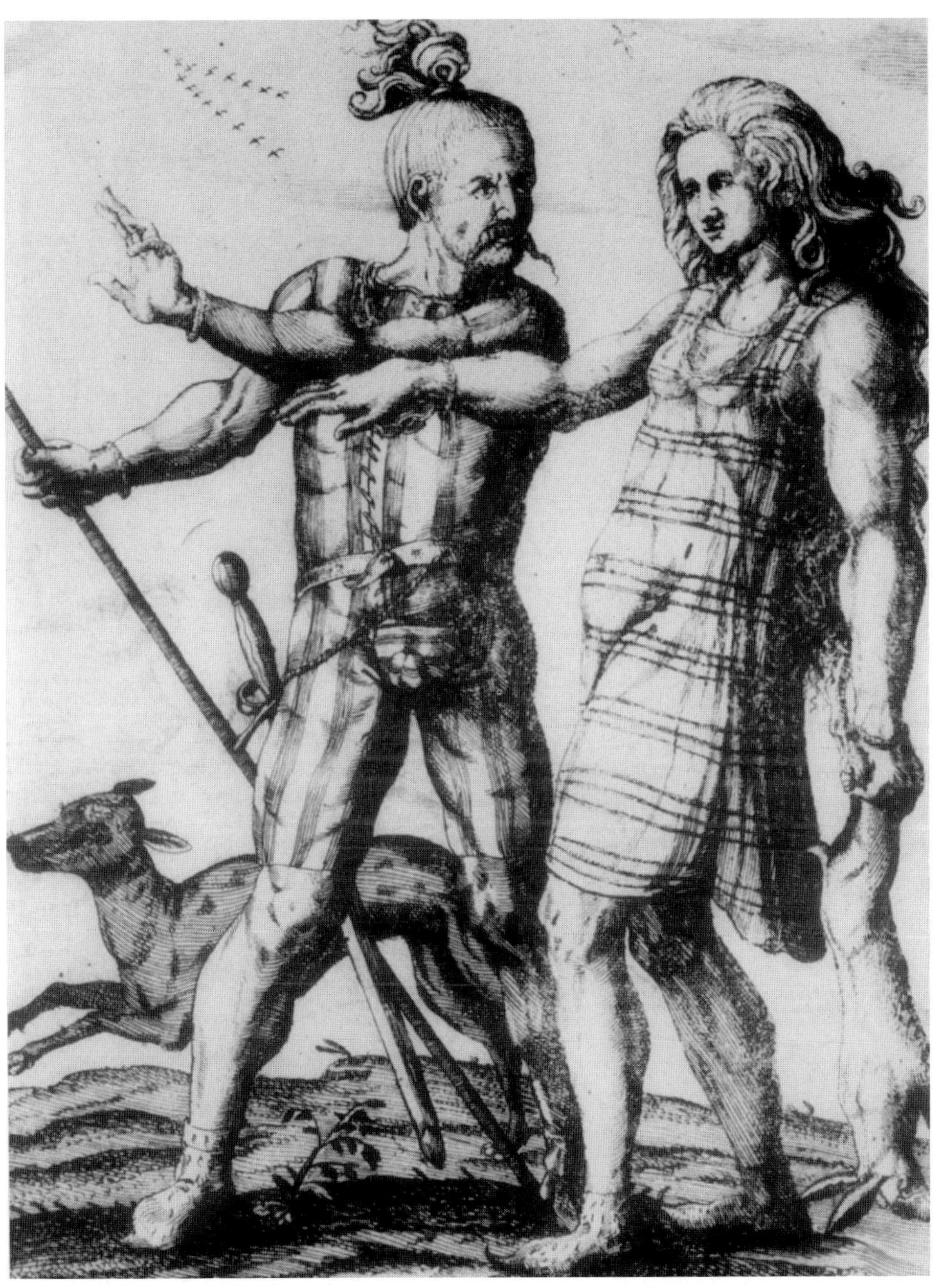

15. Cluverius, *A Batavian Man and Woman.*

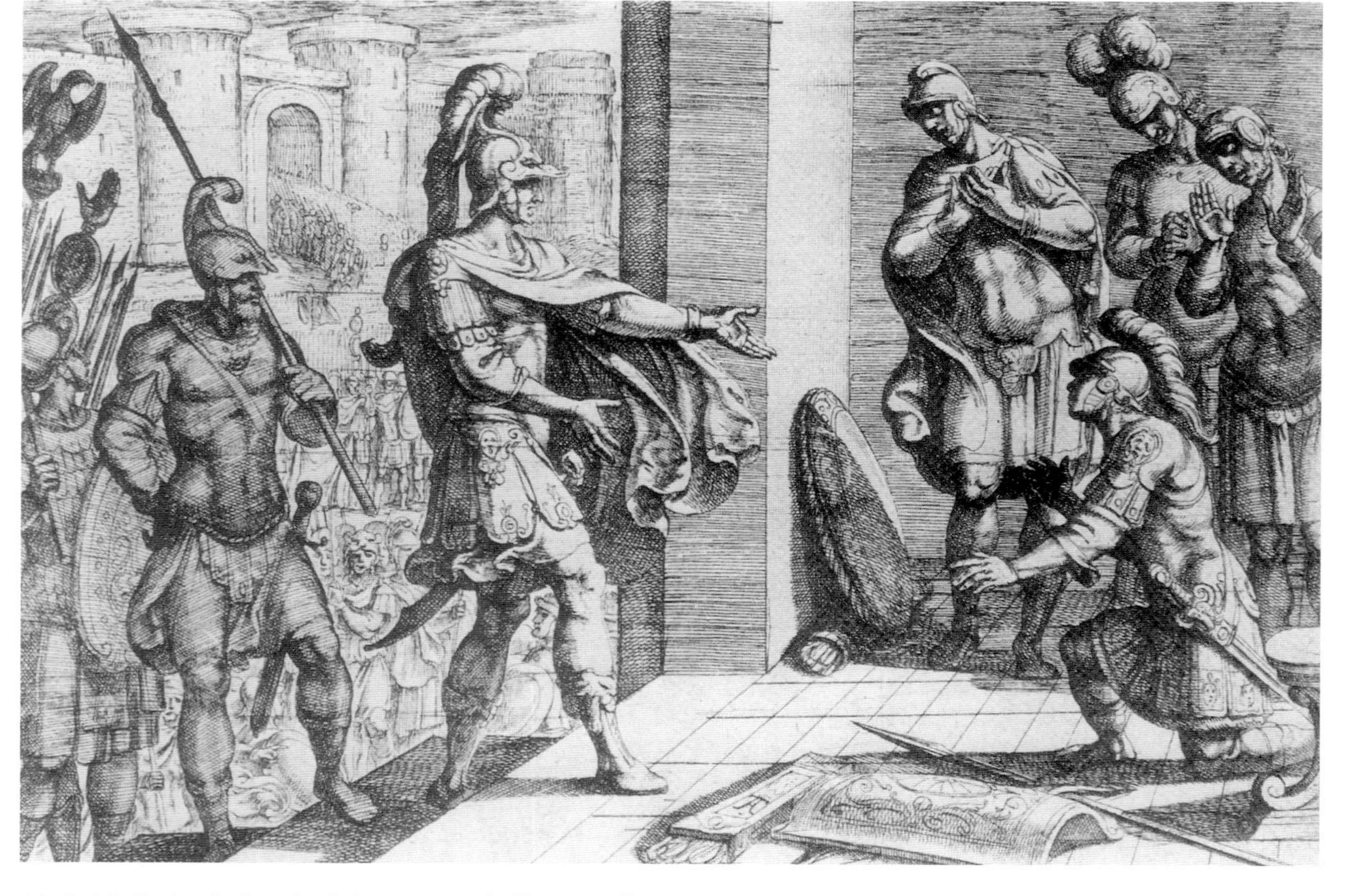

16. *Cerialis Receives the Returning Legionaries*, Antonio Tempestà, Plate 26, *Romanorum et Batavorum Societas* (Rome: 1611).

FIGURES 1-10 (Enenkel)

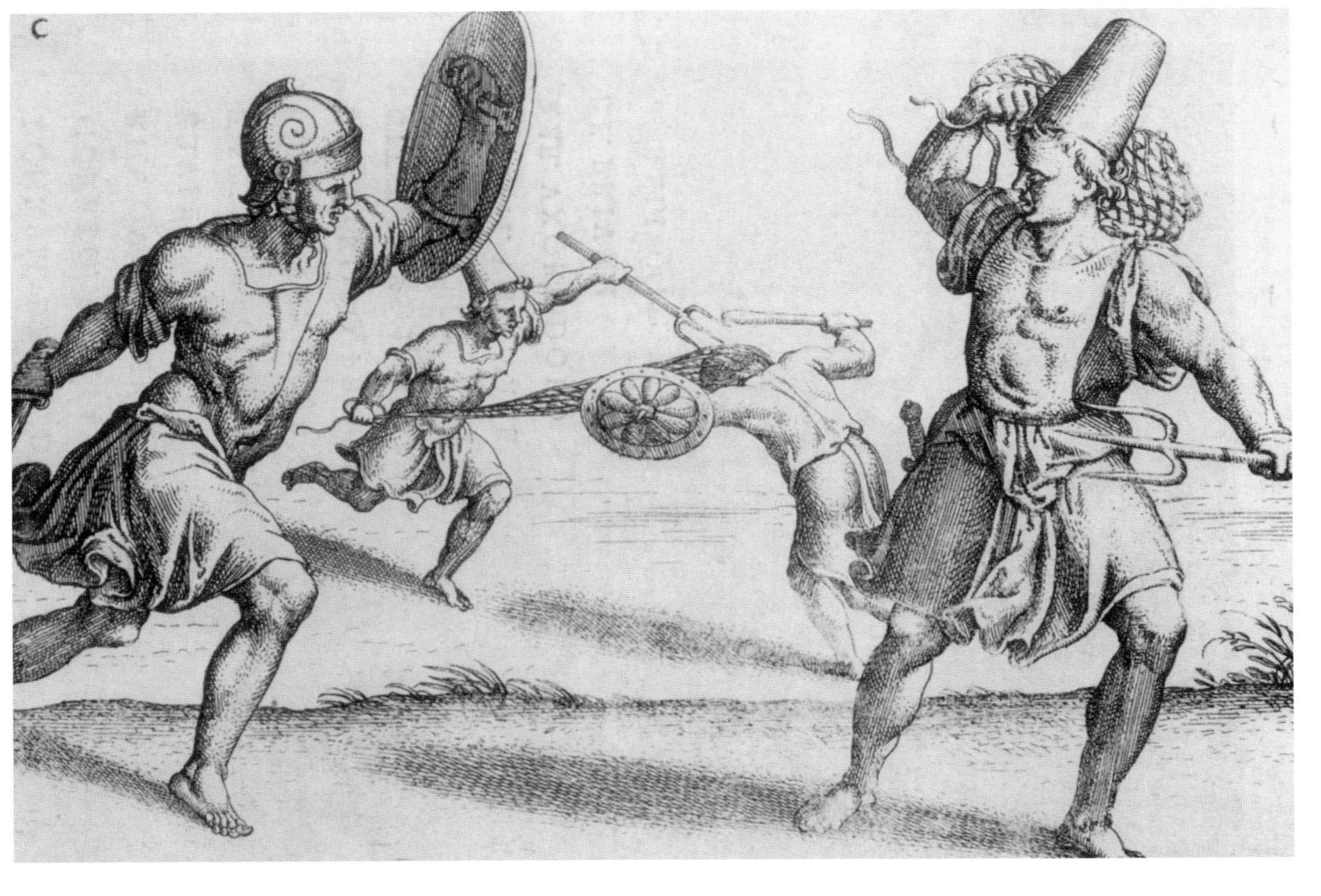

1. *Retiarius and Secutor*. Lipsius, *Saturnalium sermonum* [...] ⟨Antwerp: 1585⟩.

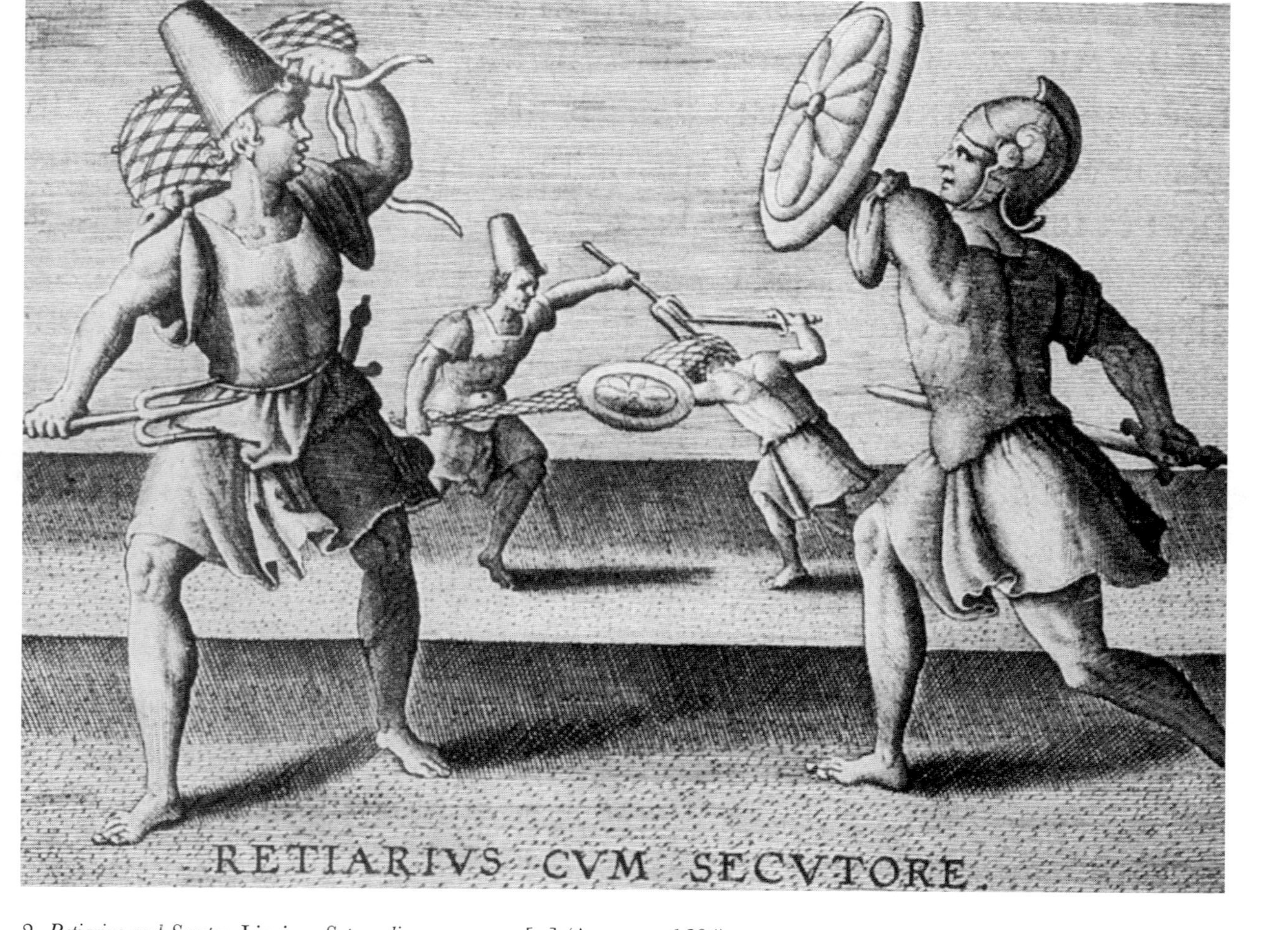

2. *Retiarius and Secutor*. Lipsius, *Saturnalium sermonum* [...] (Antwerp: 1604).

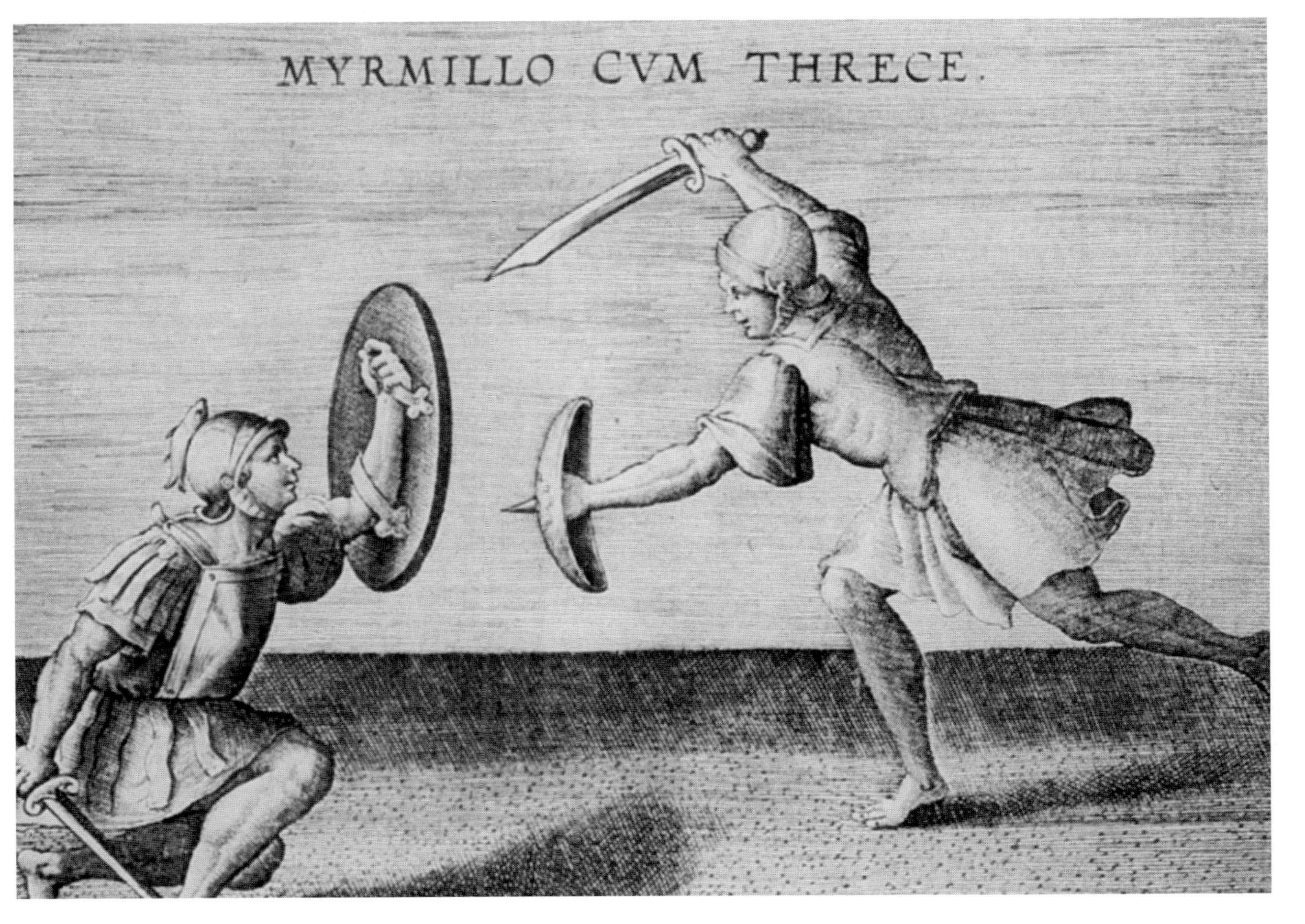

3. *Myrmillo and Thr[a]ex.* Lipsius, *Saturnalium sermonum* [...] (Antwerp: 1604).

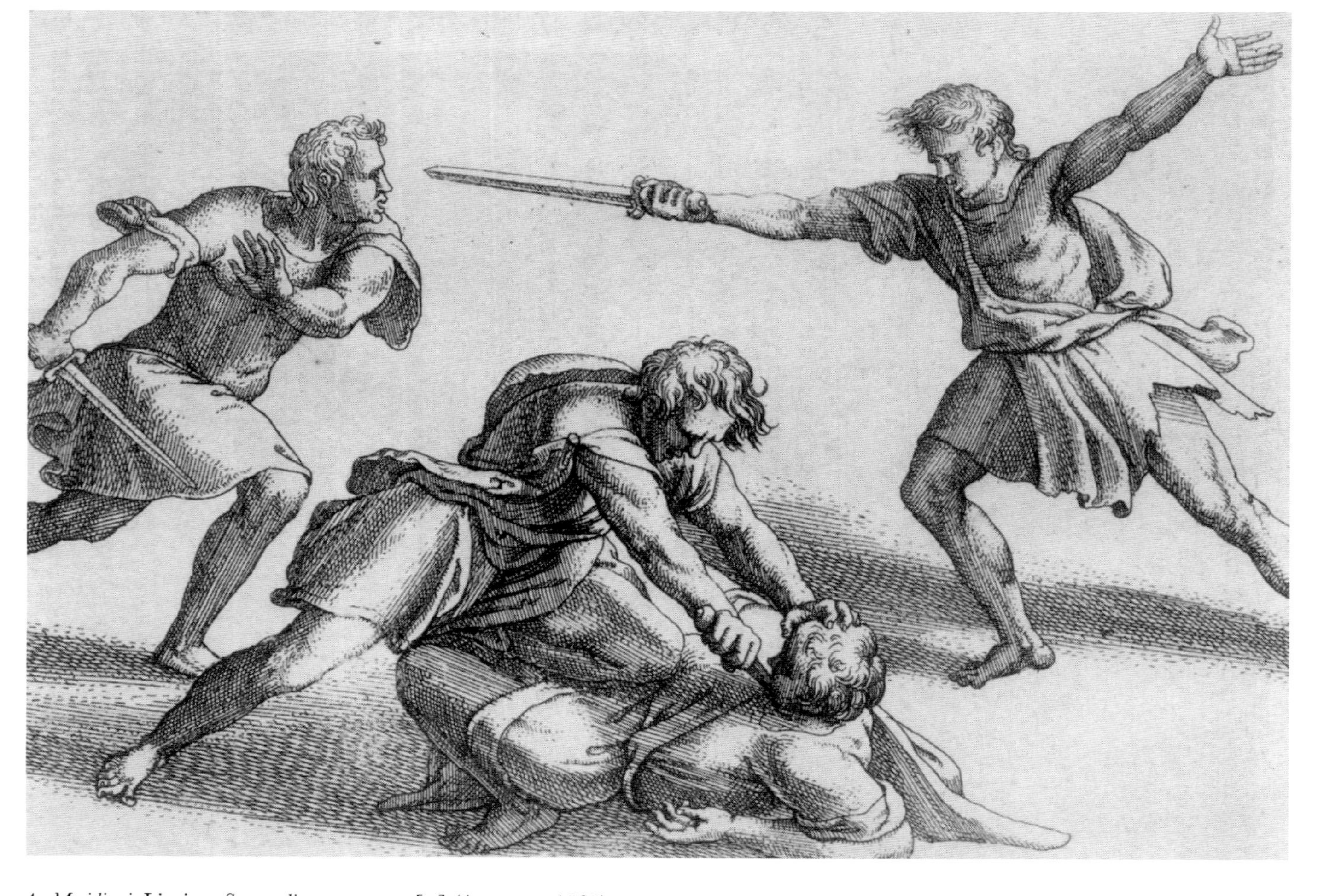

4. *Meridiani.* Lipsius, *Saturnalium sermonum* [...] (Antwerp: 1585).

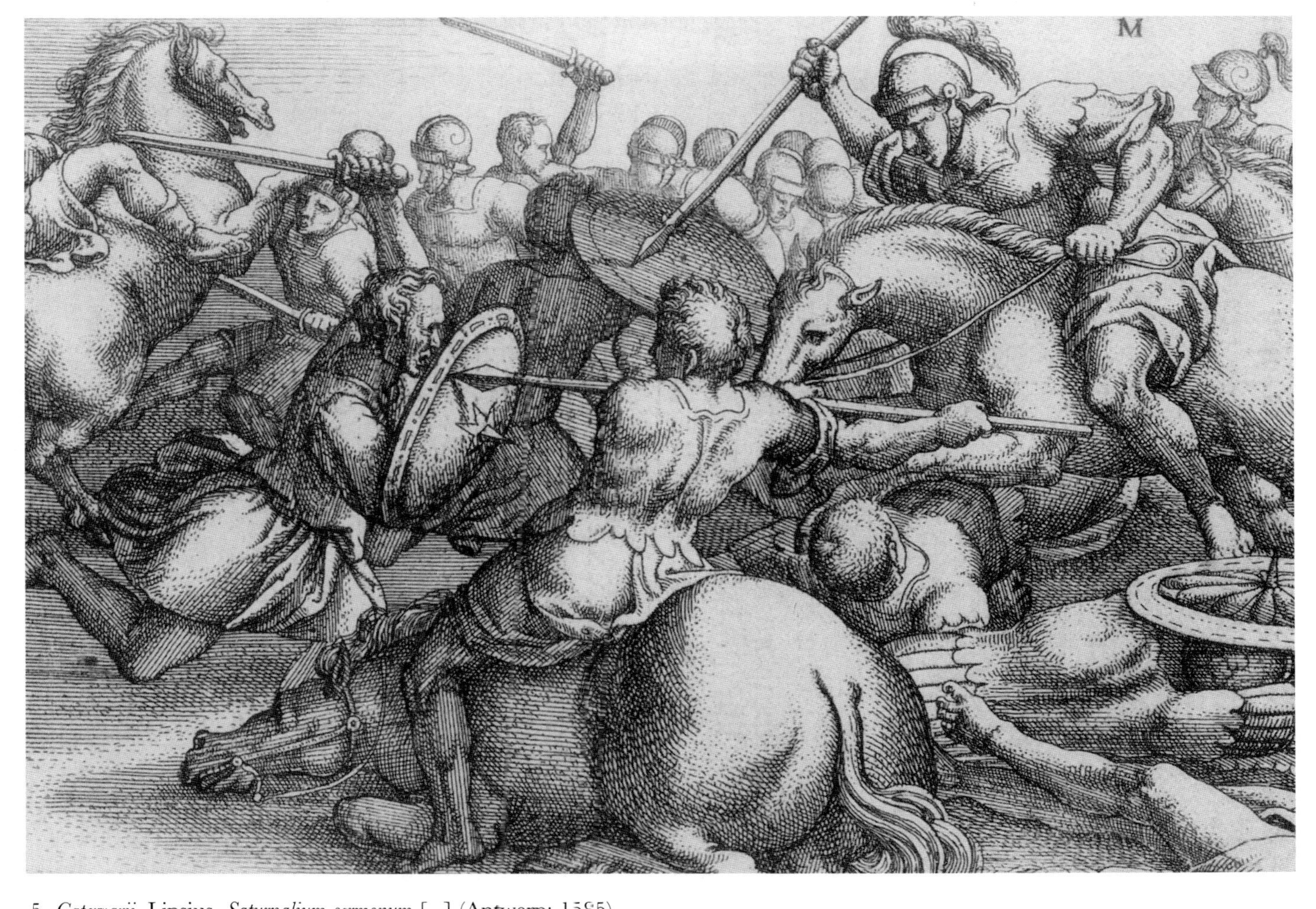

5. *Catervarii*. Lipsius, *Saturnalium sermonum* [...] (Antwerp: 1585).

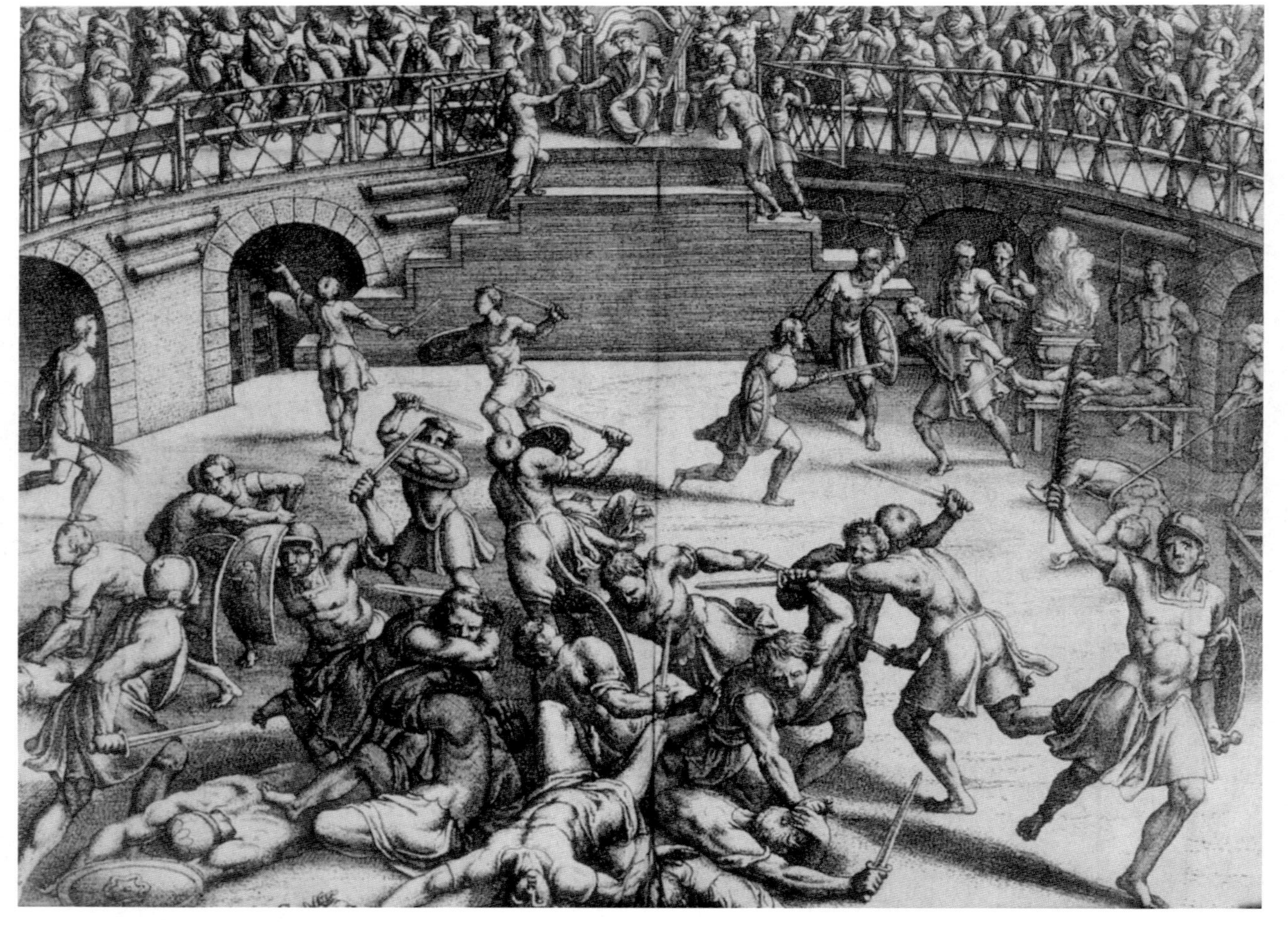

6. *Big Battle Scene*. Lipsius, *Saturnalium sermonum* [...] (Antwerp: 1585).

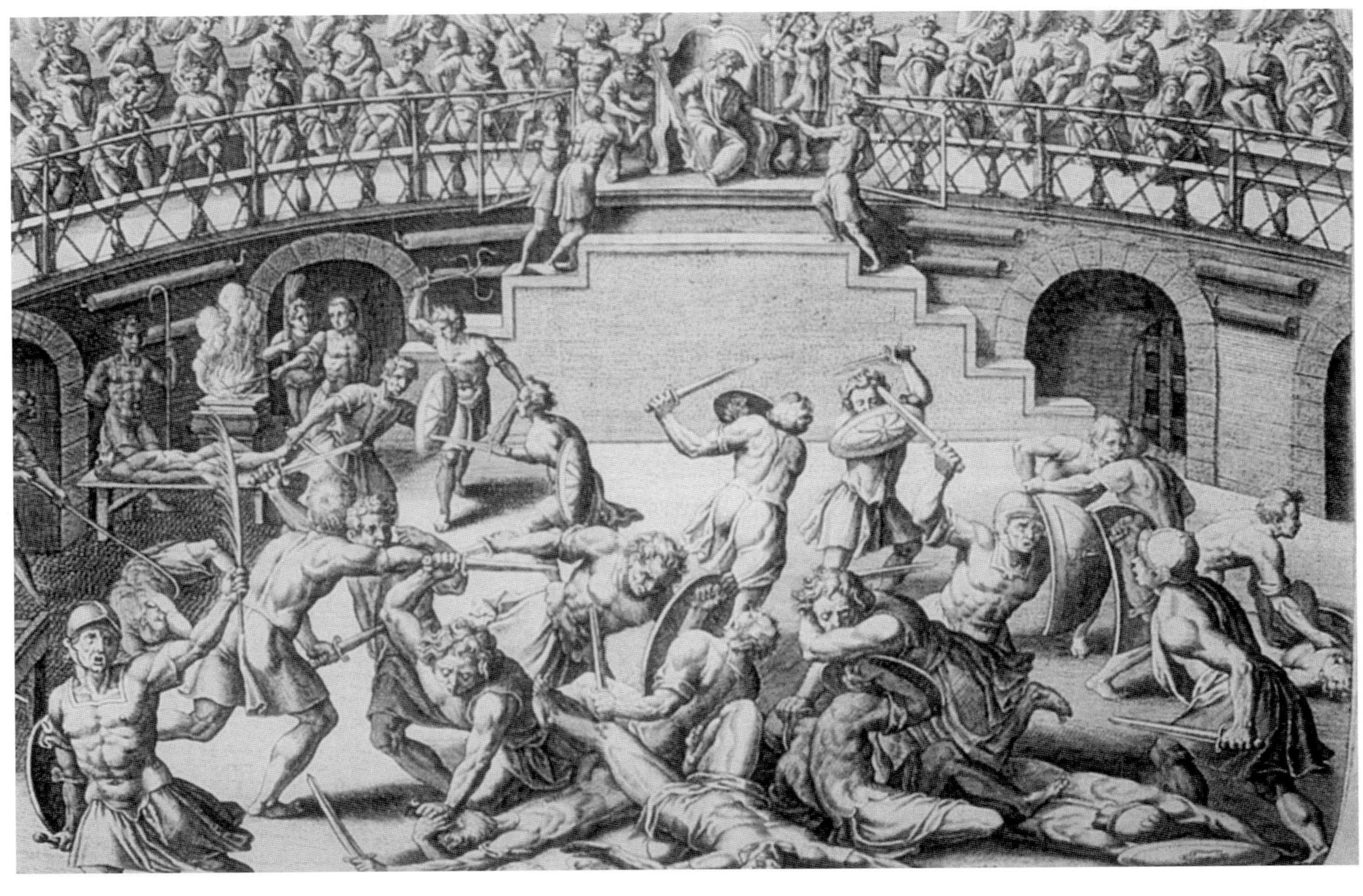

7. *Big Battle Scene.* Lipsius, *Saturnalium sermonum* [...] (Antwerp: 1604).

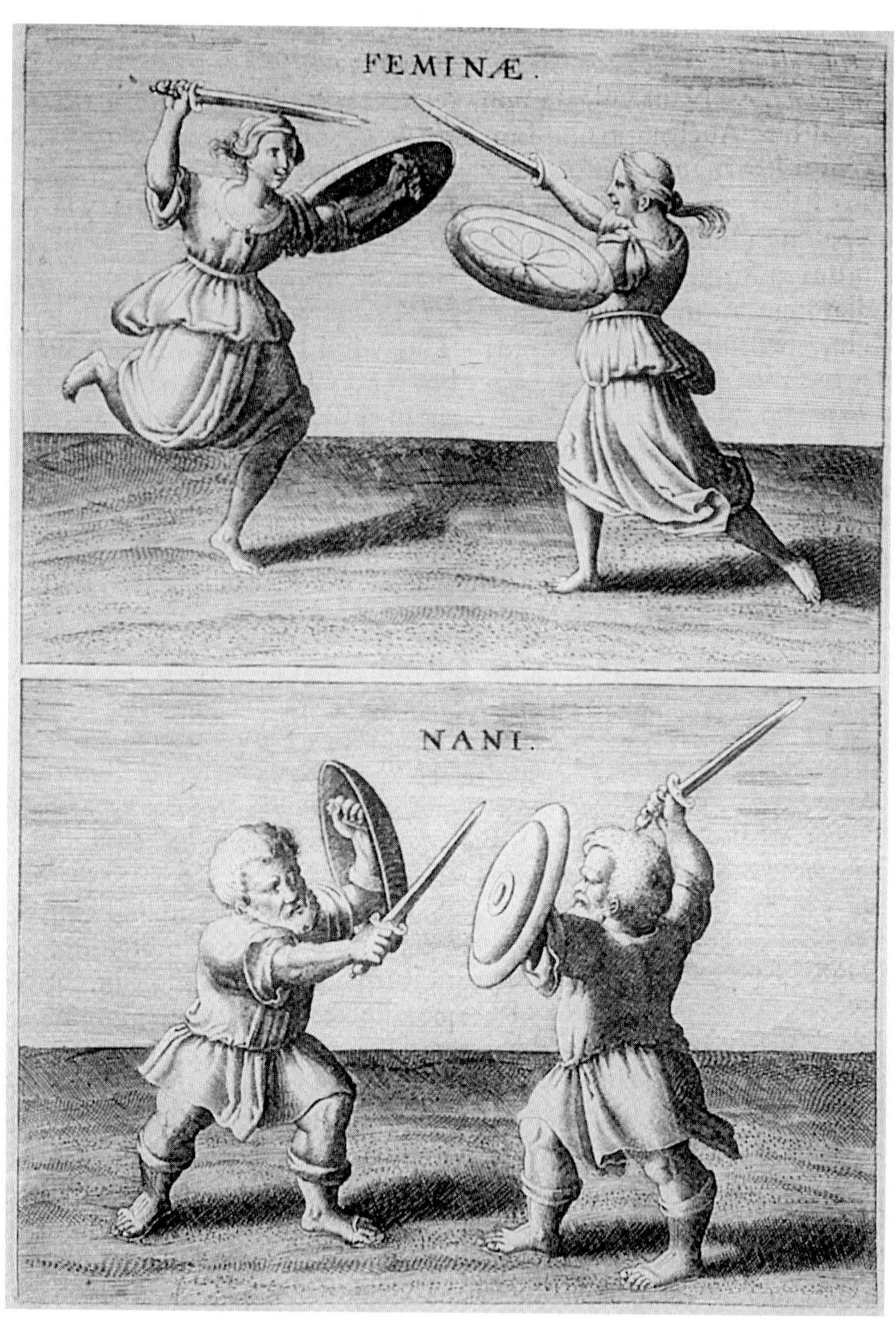

8. *Women and Dwarfs Fighting as Gladiators.* Lipsius, *Saturnalium sermonum* [...] (Antwerp: 1604).

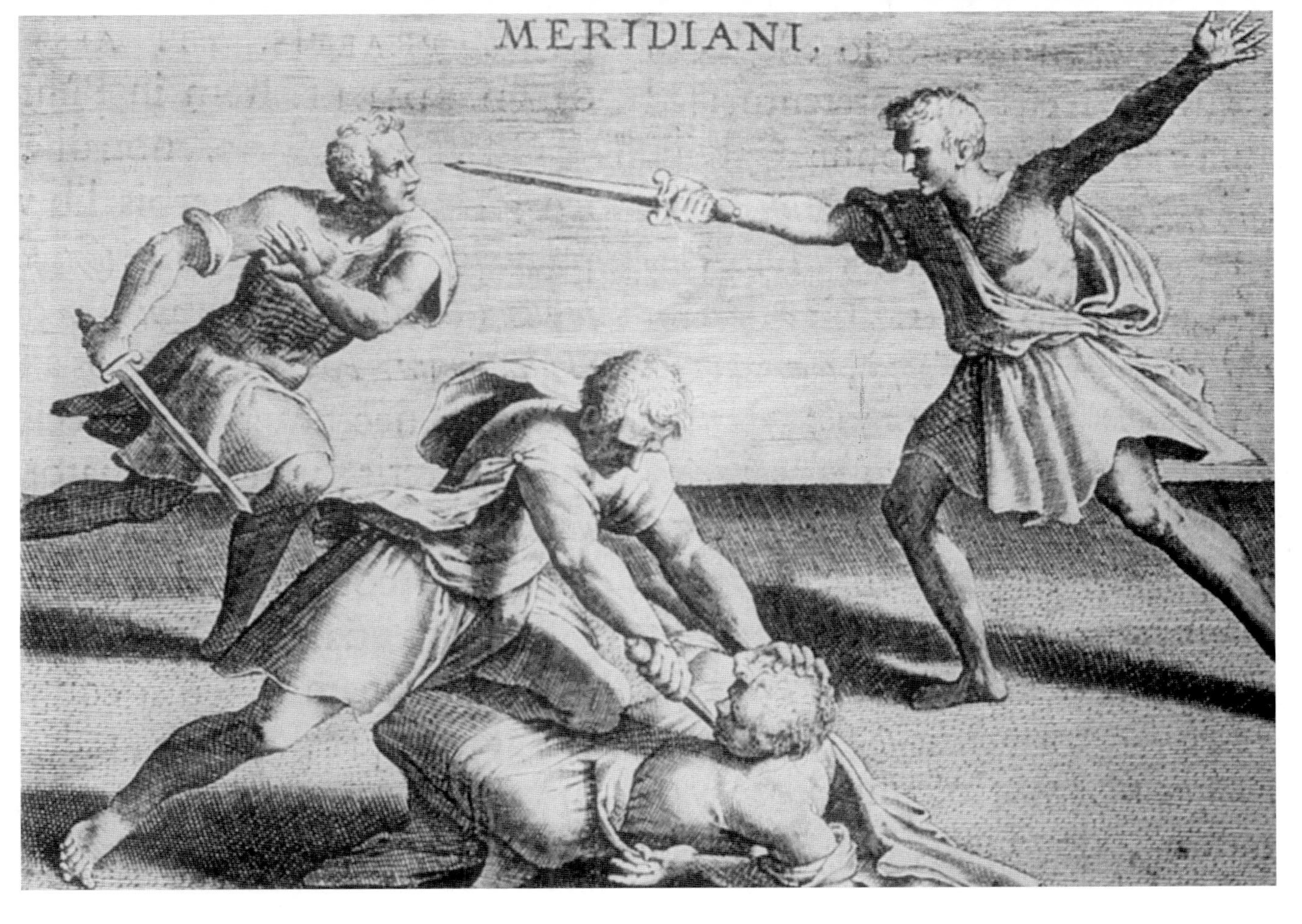

9. *Meridiani.* Lipsius, *Saturnalium sermonum* [...] (Antwerp: 1604).

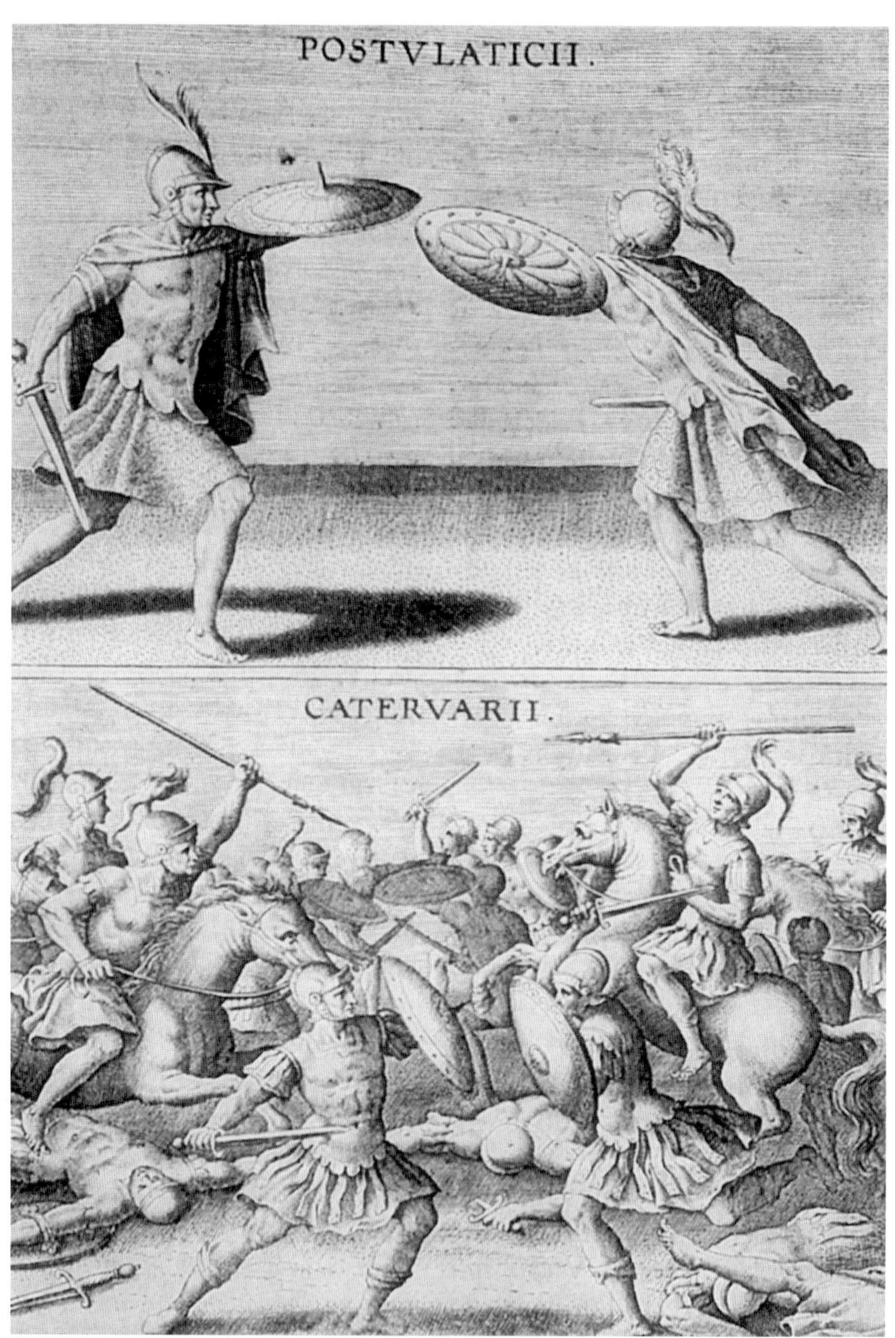

10. *Postulaticii and Catervarii*. Lipsius, *Saturnalium sermonum* [...] (Antwerp: 1604).

STRANGE AND BEWILDERING ANTIQUITY:
LIPSIUS'S DIALOGUE *SATURNALES SERMONES* ON
GLADIATORIAL GAMES (1582)

Karl Enenkel

A source of education, learning, civilisation, and an inexhaustible reservoir of moral examples: these are the terms in which ancient history was interpreted throughout the Middle Ages and the early Renaissance. This interpretation was coupled with a static conception of history.[1] Ancient history was used as a means to confirm the status quo in culture, literature, political thinking, and as a model of cultural identity. Roman heroes, like Scipio Africanus, Horatius Cocles and Cato the elder were seen as prefigurations of 'timeless', but in fact contemporary virtue. In this mainstream of medieval and early Renaissance interpretation ancient history was to a high degree adapted to contemporary values. Consequently, certain aspects of Antiquity were suppressed or entirely neglected.

One of these aspects was the thirst for blood, cruelty, *crudelitas*, the lust for killing and watching the killing of people, in Roman life most spectacularly present in gladiatorial combat. In fact we have here the exact reverse of the Christian virtue of *misericordia*, compassion. That is of course not to say that cruelty was not present in the Middle Ages and in the early Renaissance (one might suspect the opposite), but it was, in literature and the arts, suppressed by Christian values. Given the fact that Antiquity functioned in the first place as a moral example, medieval and early Renaissance interpreters were not inclined to consider it cruel and bloodthirsty. Consequently, medieval or early Renaissance authors hardly ever talked about the Roman gladiatorial combats.

In the course of the fifteenth century, however, some changes in the attitude towards Roman history took place. Or should one rather call them changes in focus and interest? The godfather of this new interest and attitude is the Italian historian Flavio Biondo.[2] He

---

[1] Cf. Moos P. von, *Geschichte als Topik. Das rhetorische Exemplum von der Antike zur Neuzeit und die historiae im "Policraticus" Johanns von Salisbury* (Hildesheim–Zurich–New York: 1988) 7 ff.

introduced a new style of historical works called antiquarian.[3] A Renaissance antiquarian writer is interested in (Roman) Antiquity not only as a source of moral examples and topical embellishments; in his eagerness to reconstruct Antiquity he is interested in various aspects of Roman culture even if they do not fit contemporary values. In his *De Roma triumphante* (finished 1459),[4] for example, Biondo among other aspects examines Roman religion (books one and two), Roman warfare (books six and seven) and the phenomenon of Roman triumph (book ten). There is no need here to demonstrate that Roman religious habits did not fit Christian religion. Biondo, moreover, made not the slightest attempt to bring Roman religion closer to Christianity. What did interest him was the reconstruction of the religious habits of the Romans by bits and pieces, based on his vast reading of Latin authors. Biondo's presentation, however, is not exactly what modern readers might expect of a cultural history: it is a huge collection of facts and quotations from Roman authors, thus resembling a source book more than a cultural history.[5] The important thing is, however, as Angelo Mazzocco has demonstrated, Biondo's new scientific approach. He clearly dismissed a purely static conception of history and was very well aware of the changes that took place between Roman Antiquity and his own time. He was convinced that all segments of human life, public and private, profane and religious, habits and institutions, had undergone far-reach-

---

[2] For Biondo cf. Fubini R., art. "Biondo Flavio da Forli", in *Dizionario biografico degli Italiani* X (1968) 536-59; Masius A., *Flavio Biondo, sein Leben und seine Werke* (Leipzig: 1879); Hay D., *Flavio Biondo and the Middle Ages* (London: 1960); Cappelletto R., *Recuperi ammianei da Biondo Flavio* (Rome: 1983).

[3] Cf. Mazzocco A., "Biondo Flavio and the Antiquarian Tradition", in *Acta Conventus Neo-Latini Bononiensis*, ed. R.J. Schoeck (New York: 1985) 124-36; Idem, "Some Philological Aspects of Biondo Flavio's *Roma Triumphans*", *Humanistica Lovaniensia* 28 (1979) 10-5; Idem, "Linee di sviluppo dell'antiquaria del Rinascimento", in *Poesia e poetica delle rovine di Roma. Momenti e problemi*, ed. V. De Caprio, Quaderni di Studi Romani, n. s. 1, 47 (Rome: 1987) 55-71; Robathan D.M., "Flavio Biondo's *Roma instaurata*", *Medievalia et Humanistica* 1 (1970) 203 ff.; Witt R.G., "Biondo's *Italia illustrata* — Summa oder Neuschöpfung? Über die Arbeitsmethoden eines Humanisten", *Renaissance Quarterly* 45 (1992) 836 ff.; Biondo's antiquarian works include *De Roma triumphante*, *Roma instaurata* and *Italia illustrata*.

[4] *Biondi Flavii Foroliviensis De Roma triumphante libri decem* ([Brixiae]:[1503]); Idem, together with the *Romae instauratae libri tres* and the *Italia illustrata* (Basle: 1531; Paris: 1532 and 1533).

[5] As Mazzocco, "Biondo Flavio and the Antiquarian Tradition", 129, correctly remarks: 'The quotations from classical texts are so extensive and widespread that at times the *Roma triumphans* does in fact become a reproduction of classical works'.

ing transformations and that it was worthwhile to focus his audience's attention on them.[6]

Biondo's treatment of the gladiatorial combats, however, is neither distinct nor very explicit. We find small sections on them in the second book about religion.[7] The context shows that Biondo was not particularly interested in them: he actually elaborated on various feasts (*Consualia, ludi Troiani, ludi Capitolini, Lectisternium, ludi Apollinares* etc.), adding a passage on the engagement of various Roman emperors in organizing and financing the games. With respect to the feasts Biondo's *inventio* depended on the Roman feast calendar, most prominently transmitted in Ovid's *Fasti* (*Feasts*),[8] with respect to the emperors' engagement on Suetonius's *Biographies of the Roman Emperors*[9] and on

---

[6] Mazzocco, "Biondo Flavio and the Antiquarian Tradition", 128 and passim. Biondo wrote his antiquarian works in the ambience of the papal court. This does not mean, however, that he had to censure himself too severely. The Popes of this period, Nicholas V (1447–1455; Tommaso Parentucelli), Callistus III (1455–1458; Alfonso Borgia) and Pius II (1458–1464; Enea Silvio Piccolomini) were very well-disposed towards humanism, Parentucelli and Enea Silvio being famous humanists themselves. So when Biondo at times pointed to the usefulness of his historical (antiquarian) works, this does not mean that he turned away from his new historical and scientific approach. Rather, his claim that his contemporaries should learn from highly developed Roman society with regard to the organisation of life and to their moral attitude, functioned as an advertisement for his antiquarian enterprises. In this interpretation I differ a bit from Marc Laureys, whose article in this book, " 'The grandeur that was Rome' " emphasizes the more traditional aspects of Biondo's work (cf. p. 123-46).

[7] In the Paris edition: 1532–1533, f. 65v-76r.

[8] Ovid's feast calendar is chronologically structured; for Ovid's *Fasti* see P. Ovidii Nasonis *Fastorum libri sex*, rec. E.H. Alton, D.E.W. Wormell, E. Courtney, Bibliotheca Teubneriana (Leipzig: 1978); idem, *Fasti = Festkalender*, lateinisch – deutsch [...], neu übers. und hrsg. von N. Holzberg, Tusculum-Bücherei (Darmstadt: 1995); idem, *Fasti*, rec. J.-B. Pighi (Paravia: 1973); idem, *Die Fasten*, hrsg., übers. und kommentiert von F. Bömer (Heidelberg: 1957–1958); idem, *Fasti, book IV*, ed. with comm. by E. Fantham (Cambridge: 1998); Herbert-Brown G., *Ovid and the Fasti: an Historical Study* (Oxford: 1994); Miller J.F. et alii, *Reconsidering Ovid's Fasti* (Baltimore, Md.: 1992); idem, *Ovid's Elegiac Festivals: Studies in the Fasti* (Frankfurt a. M.: 1991); for the Roman feast calendar in general see Radke G., *Fasti Romani: Betrachtungen zur Frühgeschichte des römischen Kalenders* (Münster: 1990); *Fasti Capitolini*, rec. praef., indd. instr. A. Degrassi (Paravia: 1954).

[9] The emperors' biographies of both Suetonius and the *Historia Augusta* are divided into thematic lemmas. In each biography there is a lemma on the emperor's engagement in public feasts. For Suetonius's *Biographies of the Roman Emperors* see Suetonius, with an Engl. trsl. by J.C. Rolfe, Loeb Classical Library (London: 1914; rev. 1951); idem, *De caesaribus*, ed. C. Ihm, Bibliotheca Teubneriana; Wallace-Hadrill A., *Suetonius: The Scholar and his Caesars* (New Haven–London: 1983); Gugel H., *Studien zur biographischen Technik Suetons*, in *Wiener Studien*, Beiheft 7 (Vienna: 1977); Mouchova B., *Studie zu Kaiserbiographien Suetons*, Prague 1968 (in *Acta universitatis Carolinae: Reihe der phil. und hist. Monographien*); Steidle W., *Sueton und die antike Biographie* (Munich: 1951, rpt 1963); Bradley K.R., "The Rediscovery of Suetonius", *Classical Philology* 80 (1985)

the *Historia Augusta*.[10] A number of digressions from this scheme show that Biondo was not altogether uninterested in the various types of games: theatre-games, hunting shows (*venationes*), animal fights and horse races, to each of which he devoted a paragraph or so. Biondo did not, however, devote such a paragraph to the gladiatorial games.

Similar features can be discovered in one of the most influential antiquarian works, the *Romanae antiquitates* of the German humanist and schoolteacher Johannes Rosinus (Roßfeld), written nearly at the same time as Lipsius's *Saturnales sermones* and first published a year later, in 1583.[11] In this work Rosinus, like Biondo, unfolded the whole of Roman civilisation; he also followed Biondo in dividing the work into ten books and in elaborating on the same subjects, even in a similar order. The gladiatorial games are again treated only shortly in the context of the Roman games. Like Biondo, Rosinus clearly is interested much more in other types of games, especially theatre performances. To these he dedicated seven pages, to the gladiatorial games only three quarters of a page.[12] In his short sketch of the gladiatorial games, Rosinus seems to be most pleased by their cessation. Because 'what is more uncivilised than to condone people for slaughtering each other?'.[13] Altogether, Rosinus was not inclined to underline the

---

254-65; Anna G. d', *Le idee letterarie di Suetonio* (Florence: 1954); Funaioli G., art. "Suetonius", in Pauly-Wissowa, *Realencyclopädie der Classischen Altertumswissenschaft* II, 7 (1931), col. 593-641; Idem, "I Cesari di Suetonio", in *Studi di letteratura antica. Spiriti e forme, figure e problemi delle letterature classiche* (Bologna: 1947) II, vol 2, 147-72; Lewis R.G., "Suetonius' *Caesares* and their Literary Antecedents", in *Aufstieg und Niedergang der Römischen Welt* II, 33.5 (1991) 3623-74; Townend G.B., "Suetonius and his Influence", in *Latin Biography*, ed. T.A. Dorey (London: 1967) 79-111.

[10] For the *Scriptores Historiae Augustae* see ed. E. Hohl, add. et corr. C. Samberger and W. Seyfarth, Bibliotheca Teubneriana (Leipzig: 1971); *The Scriptores Historiae Augustae*, with Engl. trsl. by D. Magie (London: 1960–1961); Lippold A., *Die Historia Augusta: eine Sammlung römischer Kaiserbiographien aus der Zeit Konstantins*, hrsg. von G.H. Waldherr (Stuttgart: 1998); Scheithauer A., *Kaiserbild und literarisches Programm: Untersuchungen zur Tendenz der Historia Augusta* (Frankfurt a. M.: 1987); Kolb F., *Untersuchungen zur Historia Augusta* (Bonn: 1987).

[11] *Romanarum antiquitatum li. X* (Basle: 1583); I used the augmented edition by Thomas Dempster (Amsterdam: 1743). For Rosinus see *Allgemeine deutsche Biographie* 29 (1889) 237-9; for the *Romanae antiquitates* cf. Mazzocco, "Biondo Flavio and the Antiquarian Tradition", 124-5.

[12] Rosinus, *Romanae antiquitates* IV, 24 (ed. Dempster), 351-2.

[13] *Romanae antiquitates* IV, 24 (ed. Dempster), 352: 'Quid enim immanius quam vitam dare hominibus, ut eam ipsi mutuis caedibus ab sese auferant?' This is another rendering of Tertullian's sharp criticism of the gladiatorial shows in *De spectaculis*, 12, 3: 'Itaque quos paraverant armis, quibus tunc et qualiter poterant eruditos, tantum ut occidi discerent'. Lipsius, interestingly enough, left out exactly this sentence in his rendering of Tertullian's passage in the *Saturnales sermones*. See below.

importance of the gladiatorial games for Roman life. He considered them as something perverse, worthy of being forgotten.

If one takes into consideration that the most important antiquarians were not fond of dealing with the gladiatorial shows, it seems rather surprising that Lipsius dedicated a whole work, in two books, to this tricky subject, and all the more suprising that he chose it as the subject of his first historical work in the full sense.[14] Lipsius worked on the *Saturnales sermones*[15] during the first years of his Leiden professorship.[16] The framework of the genesis of the text can be reconstructed from Lipsius's letters:[17] the plan appears at the very beginning of his Leiden period, in October 1578.[18] Interestingly enough, the plan was obviously different at that time: Lipsius wanted to compose a more extended work on Roman games, *De spectaculis Romanorum*. The title,

---

[14] On Lipsius as a historian, see Nordman V.A., *Justus Lipsius als Geschichtsforscher und Geschichtslehrer* (Helsinki: 1932). The *Saturnales sermones* are mentioned on p. 37. Lipsius treated some historical details in his philological works, for example on the emendation of various authors, the *Variarum lectionum libri I* (Antwerp: 1569), in his *Antiquarum lectionum commentarius* (Antwerp: 1575) and in his *Electorum liber I* (Antwerp: 1580). The *Saturnales sermones*, however, is his first historical monograph (pace Nordman, who deals with Lipsius's philological works in his chapter on "Justus Lipsius als Historiker", 34-36). The above-mentioned works are more plausibly classified as philological writings in *Lipsius en Leuven*, ed. G. Tournoy–J. Papy–J. De Landtsheer (Leuven: 1997) 55 ff. ("Lipsius' filologisch werk"). For the *Variae lectiones*, see the article by G. Tournoy, ibid., 55-8; for the *Antiquae lectiones* cf. the article by G. Tournoy, ibid., 58-9; for the *Saturnales sermones* cf. my article ibid., 84-8.

[15] *Saturnalium sermonum li. II, qui de gladiatoribus* (Antwerp: 1582); *Saturnalium sermonum li. II, qui de gladiatoribus. Noviter correcti, aucti, et formis aeneis illustrati* (Antwerp: 1585) (for example Leiden, University Library 181 D 5); *Saturnalium sermonum li. II, qui de gladiatoribus. Adiecta est hac editione graecorum locorum conversio, quae in Antverpiensi desyderabatur* (Antwerp: 1585); *Saturnalium sermonum li. II, qui de gladiatoribus. Adiecta est hac editione graecorum locorum conversio, quae in Antverpiensi desyderabatur* (Paris: 1585); *Saturnalium sermonum li. II, qui de gladiatoribus. Editio ultima, auctior et ornatior. In qua quid distincte praestitum sit, pagina altera docebit* (Leiden: 1590); *Saturnalium sermonum li. II, qui de gladiatoribus. Editio ultima et castigatissima. Cum aeneis figuris* (Antwerp: 1598) (for example Leiden, University Library 575 B 5); *Saturnalium sermonum li. II, qui de gladiatoribus. Editio ultima et castigatissima. Cum aeneis figuris* (Antwerp: 1604). Furthermore, during Lipsius's lifetime, editions of the work also appeared in his *Opera omnia*.

[16] For Lipsius's Leiden period see *Lipsius in Leiden*, ed. K. Enenkel and C.L. Heesakkers (Voorthuizen: 1997), especially the articles by R.J. van den Hoorn, "On Course for Quality: Justus Lipsius and Leiden University", 73-92 and by K. Enenkel, "Humanismus, Primat des Privaten, Patritismus und Niederländischer Aufstand: Selbstbildformung in Lipsius' Autobiographie", 13-45; Mout M.E.H.N., "In het schip: Justus Lipsius en de Nederlandse Opstand tot 1591", in *Bestuurders en geleerden*, ed. S. Groenveld – M.E.H.N. Mout – I. Schoeffer (Amsterdam: 1985) 55-64; eadem, " 'Heilige Lipsius, bid voor ons' ", *Tijdschrift voor geschiedenis* 97 (1984) 195-206.

[17] See Enenkel, "Justus Lipsius, *Saturnalium sermonum libri duo* [...]" in *Lipsius en Leuven*, 84-8, especially 86.

[18] ILE I, 78 10 27.

80   KARL ENENKEL

On Roman Games, might suggest that Lipsius's plan was very close to the
treatment of the subject in other antiquarian writings, which means
that theatre performances would have held the most prominent place.
Nevertheless, this was not the case. Lipsius already focussed at that
early stage on the 'visual' games: horse races, hunting shows and
above all, gladiatorial combats.[19] A first draft of the work, then called
Iusti Lipsi Saturnaliorum[20] *dies quinque sive spectacula Romanorum*, is preserved in Lipsius's Leiden manuscripts. In this first draft the work is
subdivided into three parts: 1. *gladiatores*; 2. *venatio*; 3. *circenses*. These
parts exactly refer to the three 'visual' games: gladiatorial fights, animal huntings and horse races.[21] From the fragments it can be deduced
that Lipsius had a work of five books in mind;[22] fragments are actually
preserved of four books. As far as we can surmise, the first two books
should have been dedicated to the gladiatorial games, the third to the
amphitheatre, the fourth to the hunting shows and the fifth, consequently, to the horse races. In the course of his work, however, he
decided to deal exclusively with the gladiatorial games. This choice
was remarkable indeed. What inspired him to work out exactly this
odd aspect of Roman culture? The letters, unfortunately, do not give
us any clue in this respect. Before we try to answer this question,
therefore, we must first go into detail and understand in which way
Lipsius treated the subject, and return to it at the end of the article.

But how to deal with such an embarrassing subject? First of all, Lipsius
decided to write a scholarly treatise. It is evident that, in this, he was
inspired by Flavio Biondo and other antiquarian writers like Carlo
Sigonio.[23] At the time of writing, the antiquarian discourse was already
an accepted historical genre. Since Biondo's groundbreaking work,
more than 120 years had passed, so at least the humanist segment of
Lipsius's audience must have felt perfectly at ease with this choice of
form. If one compares the *Saturnales sermones* to Biondo's work, one can

---

[19] This is already indicated by the letters regarding the *Saturnales sermones*, in which
Lipsius talks about hunting shows (*venationes*) and circus performances (*circenses*), but
never about theatre performances. On his emphasis on 'visual games' with regard to
the Roman games, see below.

[20] In the first draft Lipsius clearly chose the form *Saturnaliorum*, which is also possible; see Macrobius, *Saturnalia* I, 4: 'Certum est licito et Saturnalium et Saturnaliorum
dici' ('It is certainly allowed to say Saturnalium and Saturnaliorum as well').

[21] Leiden, University Library, Ms. Lips. 19.

[22] Each book should reflect the discussions of one of the five days.

[23] Cf. Nordman, *Justus Lipsius als Geschichtsforscher und Geschichtslehrer*, 35.

observe that Lipsius improved on the antiquarian genre in various
ways, in terms of handling the sources, methodical presentation, philological criticism and literary merits as well. One might even suspect
that Lipsius must have been rather disappointed by Biondo's lack of
structure and his imprecise, erroneous and ill-located quotations, and
that he deliberately wanted to surpass him in these respects.

The *Saturnales sermones*, however, excel by their clear presentation:
Lipsius analyses the subject methodically, dividing it into two books
and subdividing it into chapters (34 in total), each dedicated to one or
more specific issue: When do gladiatorial combats first appear? Where
do they come from and what was their original meaning? In which
context did they take place? For what reason were gladiatorial combats
staged? In which areas of the Roman empire were they staged and during which period? What about the organisation, what about the spectators? What about the equipment of gladiators? Etc. The chapters are
indicated by extended title descriptions. Furthermore, the *Saturnales sermones*, like Biondo's work before, are marked by a large number of quotations from ancient authors. Lipsius's treatment of the theme is dominated by the presentation (and interpretation) of evidence. The quotations are indicated very precisely for a sixteenth-century work. Furthermore, the quotes are clearly marked by the choice of different letter
types.[24] We will return later on to the scholarly merits of the *Saturnales
sermones*. What is important at the moment are the psychological side-
effects of this presentation for the reader: he is confronted with an
embarrassing subject, but the way in which it is treated seems to comfort him. The reader is convinced that here is an author at work who
first of all wants to inform him in a correct and careful manner and to
present to him evidence from ancient authors. This last aspect especially seems to comfort him, because of the enormous belief in the authority of the ancient authors.

Furthermore, the choice of literary form makes the reader feel at
ease. Lipsius deliberately adapted the favorite genre of Renaissance
prose writers, the dialogue,[25] to his antiquarian enterprise. The dia-

---

[24] Quotes from Latin authors are indicated by italics; quotes from Greek authors
are presented in the original language (italic types). In the 1585 edition Lipsius carefully added translations to the Greek quotations, also indicated by italics.

[25] For the humanist dialogue, see Burke P., "The Renaissance Dialogue", *Renaissance Studies* 3 (1989) 1-12; Enenkel K., sections "Der Dialog im lateinischen Humanismus der frühen Neuzeit" and "Eine humanistische Dialogpoetik: Carolus Sigonius *De
dialogo*", in Idem, *Kulturoptimismus und Kulturpessimismus in der Renaissance. Studie zu Jacobus*

logue was considered the most 'civilised' genre; it enabled humanists
to express at the same time their life-style, good manners, social position, their love of Antiquity, and their learning. The dialogue form of
the *Saturnales sermones* goes back mainly to two ancient examples:
Cicero's dialogues and Macrobius's *Saturnalia*. Cicero's dialogues
excel in their elaborate dialogue setting, in which he carefully explains
when, under which circumstances and where a dialogue was held.
Modern readers may wonder why Cicero took such pains to explain
all this, but it was necessary, given the morality of the Roman upper
class, the members of which were allowed to participate in literary
activities only in their spare time or on holidays. Thus, when they
wrote literary works, they always had to apologize and to justify themselves. Moreover, Cicero's dialogues excel in their civilized manner of
conversation. His dialogue partners all belong to the upper class, they
treat each other as gentlemen and they never lose their politeness and
social decorum.

In his *Saturnales sermones*, Lipsius imitates the Ciceronian type of dialogue. He elaborates on the dialogue setting and justifies the conversation, even doubly so: firstly the dialogue takes place during a holiday
period (in December) and, secondly, when Lipsius has fallen ill.[26]
Similarly to some of Cicero's dialogues, for example *De oratore*, friends
arrive on a holiday to pay him a visit. In the *Saturnales sermones* Lipsius's
friends Victor Giselinus and Janus Lernutius visit him in order to
inquire about his health, and later the humanists Stephanus Pighius
and Janus Dousa, who came all the way from Leiden, also join the
company. Furthermore, in the *Saturnalia*, the Ciceronian background
of civil war is also present. Dousa brings with him bad news from the
war between the Dutch and the Spanish (conceived of as a civil war by
Lipsius). Lipsius's (the dialogue persona's) reaction reminds us of the
situation in Cicero's dialogues characterized by despair about the
state. As in Ciceronian times, in their discussions Lipsius and his
friends create an atmosphere suggestive of another reality, a private
and artificial one as well, in order to flee from the cruel reality of
political life. The artificial reality is dominated by Antiquity. It func-

---

Canters Dyalogus de solitudine [...] (Frankfurt a. M.: 1995) 137-43 and 152-62; Snyder J.
R., *Writing the Scene of Speaking. Theories of Dialogue in the Late Italian Renaissance* (Stanford:
1989); *Le dialogue au temps de la Renaissance*, ed. M.T. Jones-Davies (Paris: 1984); Marsh
D., *The Quattrocento Dialogue. Humanist Tradition and Humanist Innovation* (Cambridge,
Mass.: 1980).

[26] *Saturnales sermones* I, 1: 'Occasio et origo horum sermonum'.

tions as an intellectual asylum, as a place of peace and beauty. To deal with Antiquity is to make a statement: Lipsius and his humanist comrades withdraw from the despair of daily life.

Furthermore, as the title suggests, Lipsius's *Saturnales sermones* go back to the dialogue *Saturnalia* by the fifth-century Roman politician and philologist Ambrosius Macrobius Theodosius.[27] Macrobius's dialogue characters, like Cicero's, belong to the upper class, being politicians (the famous Symmachus and Nicomachus) or intellectuals (Servius, the commentator of Vergil). Macrobius gave his dialogue the title *Saturnalia* because the fictional conversations took place on the first three days of the *Saturnalia*, the Roman holidays held in December. Macrobius was also inspired by Cicero's dialogue technique. The conversations have a polite character and, in a pleasant atmosphere, erudite men exchange their thoughts. Macrobius's *Saturnalia*, however, display even more erudition than Cicero's dialogues. In fact, the work is a learned commentary on Vergil's *Aeneid*.[28] Lipsius took from Macrobius not only the dialogue setting of the *Saturnalia*, but also the very learned nature of the work and the exegetic, philological and antiquarian interest displayed by the dialogue characters.[29]

Like Macrobius's dialogue characters Symmachus, Nicomachus and Servius, Lipsius's characters are very much occupied with the past. Mentally, it seems, they live in Antiquity. Even in simple talks about daily subjects they use ancient terms. For example, when they inquire about Lipsius's health, they refer to Hygeia, the Greek goddess of health; Lipsius, the dialogue character, says to his servant: 'Hey servant, our table is profane. You forgot the salt vessel',[30] which refers to the ritual salt vessel present in ancient Roman houses. The very starting point of the discussion is derived from this mental attitude. When Lipsius gets angry at his slow servant, Dousa says: 'Please forgive him. Today is the feast of the slaves [...] Don't you know, that today is the

---

[27] For Macrobius's *Saturnalia*, see Flamant J., "La technique du banquet dans les *Saturnales* de Macrobe", *Revue des Etudes Latines* 46 (1968) 303-19; Türk E., *Macrobius und die Quellen seiner Saturnalien* (Freiburg: 1961); Albrecht M. von, *Geschichte der römischen Literatur* (Munich: 1994) II, 1179-83.

[28] Cf. Sinclair B.W., "Vergil's *sacrum poema* in Macrobius' *Saturnalia*", *Maia* N. S. 34 (1982) 261-3; Santoro A., *Esegeti virgiliani antichi (Donato, Macrobio, Servio)* (Bari: 1964).

[29] It is noteworthy that in Lipsius's dialogue, as in Macrobius's *Saturnalia*, the dialogue characters never have the function of merely corroborating or contradicting the main character's monologue, but that all of them play a significant part in developing the scholarly theme.

[30] *Saturnales sermones* I, 2, p. 9.

feast of the *Saturnalia*?'[31] Of course, in Lipsius's house no ancient Roman ritual salt vessel was present nor were *Saturnalia* celebrated in his days. But Lipsius chose these details to give to the dialogue an ancient Roman flavour and to express the fervent humanist interest of his circle in Antiquity. To have such conversations was a matter of lifestyle in the sixteenth century. It symbolizes the atmosphere of learning, humanism and civilisation. Thus, bewildering and embarrassing Antiquity, with its terrible face of slaughter and mass murder, gently enters via the back door, in a pleasant, calm and civilized atmosphere.

What picture did Lipsius draw of the Roman gladiatorial combats? In which way did he interpret his sources? If one takes into account the civilized atmosphere and his deep love of Antiquity, one might expect that Lipsius would do his best to 'save Antiquity' by minimizing the cruelty of the gladiatorial games, by explaining and excusing them, or, at least, by reducing their size and frequency.

Roman gladiatorial combats, especially in the last decade, have drawn a lot of attention, resulting in a series of groundbreaking monographs and articles.[32] Thus our understanding of the games has improved greatly, as has our knowledge of all sorts of details, archeological and historical as well. This recently acquired knowledge can be useful in estimating Lipsius's construction of history in a better way. What is startling, however, is that the number of literary sources in modern studies is not much bigger than in Lipsius's work, which means, that in collecting the sources, Lipsius did a great job. All the more astonishing is that in modern studies on gladiatorial combats, Lipsius's work is hardly ever mentioned.

In his interpretation, Lipsius seems, at first sight, not to be far off from modern studies. The similarities are partly due to the same literary sources, among others Tertullian's *De spectaculis*, Livy, Suetonius,

---

[31] I, 2, p. 10.

[32] Wiedemann T., *Emperors and Gladiators* (London–New York: 1992); Plass P., *The Game of Death in Ancient Rome. Arena Sports and Political Suicide* (Madison–London: 1993); Auguet R., *Cruauté et civilisation: Les jeux romains* (Paris: 1970) (English translation *Cruelty and Civilisation. The Roman Games* (London–New York: 1994²)); Golvin J.-C., *L'amphithéâtre Romain* (Paris: 1988); Idem and Landes C., *Amphithéatres et gladiateurs*, CNRS 1990; Grant M., *The Gladiators* (Harmondsworth: 1970); Barton C.A., *The Sorrows of the Ancient Romans. The Gladiator and the Monster* (Princeton: 1993); Villes G., *La gladiature en occident des origines à la mort de Domitien* (Paris–Rome: 1985 [manuscript]); Weismann W., art. "Gladiator", in *RAC* XI (1981), col. 23-45; Hopkins K., "Murderous Games", in Idem, *Death and Renewal* (Cambridge: 1983) 1-30; Shotter D., "Gladiators", *The Classical Review* 54 (1994) 127-8; Wistrand M., *Entertainment and Violence in Ancient Rome. The Attitudes of Roman Writers of the First Century A.D.* (Göteborg: 1992).

Cassius Dio, the *Historia Augusta* and Servius. The most detailed ancient account is found in Tertullian's *De spectaculis* (*On Games*).[33] Since the Christian Tertullian was not such a fan of gladiatorial combats, *De spectaculis* is a polemic pamphlet against the Roman games, written in an aggressive and gloomy mood, in which Tertullian argues that no good Christian should be allowed to attend the games. Interestingly enough Tertullian's main argument to condemn the gladiatorial shows is not so much dependent on their cruelty and inhumanity but on the fact that they were embedded in Roman — 'pagan' — religion. In this respect, one can understand why he takes such pains to explain the origins of the gladiatorial combats: this helps him to prove that gladiatorial combats were totally intermingled with pagan religion, whereas in his days this was not so much the case any longer. Through his account of their origin, Tertullian enables himself to put forward his condemning judgement: 'The amphitheatre (where the gladiatorial combats took place) is consecrated to more and to more horrible deities than the Capitolium (the very centre of Roman Paganism): IT IS THE SANCTUARY OF ALL DEMONS'.[34]

Lipsius, although he quotes Tertullian in extenso, did not agree with this total demonisation of gladiatorial combats. In a programmatic note, he declares that his aim is not to condemn, but to describe and to explain (*explicare*), and in this, he follows Suetonius, not Tertullian.[35] This different writer's intention can be seen even when Lipsius

---

[33] Ed. (introduzione, testo crit., commento e traduzione) E. Castorina (Florence: 1961, rpt 1973); Tertullian, *Apology. De spectaculis. With an English translation by* T.R. Glover (London: 1931); *De spectaculis — über die Spiele*, Lateinisch-Deutsch, übers. und hrsg. von K.-W. Weeber (Stuttgart: 1988); Biglmair A., *Die Beteiligung der Christen am öffentlichen Leben* (Munich: 1902); Chase R.M., "*De spectaculis*", *Classical Journal* 23 (1927) 107 ff.; Köhne J., *Die Schrift Tertullians "Über die Schauspiele" in kultur- und religionsgeschichtlicher Beleuchtung* (thesis Münster: 1929); Nat P.G. van der, "Tertullianea II: the structure of the *De spectaculis*", *Vigiliae Christianae* 18 (1964) 129 ff.; Sider R. D., 'Tertullian. On the shows: an Analysis', *Journal of Theological Studies* 29 (1978) 339 ff.; Waszink J.H., "Pompa diaboli", *Vigiliae Christianae* 1 (1947) 15 ff.; Weismann W., *Kirche und Schauspiele. Die Schauspiele im Urteil der lateinischen Kirchenväter unter besonderer Berücksichtigung von Augustin* (Würzburg: 1972).

[34] *De spectaculis*, 12, 7: 'Pluribus enim et asperioribus nominibus amphitheatrum consecratur quam Capitolium: omnium daemonum templum est'.

[35] *Saturnales sermones* I, 7 (p. 24). Lipsius says that there are two authors on gladiatorial combats, Suetonius (the work is lost now) and Tertullian. 'Sed causa scribendi iis finisque non una. Ille, ut explicaret, noster ut damnaret descenderunt in hanc arenam. Et sane plerique Theologi e priscis passim invecti in eos [...]. Et bene illi nec male nunc ego, qui per Suetonii vestigia iens ritus illustrabo prisci et nobis ignoti aevi' ('But they have not the same goal in writing. The first author enters the arena of writing in order to explain; our author, on the other hand, to condemn. And certainly

quotes Tertullian. He is inclined then to weaken sharp and strong evaluations, especially the condemnation of gladiatorial combats. So in the story about the origins of the gladiatorial combats Lipsius leaves out Tertullian's sarcastic remark that the old Romans trained the slaves in fighting very well only for the purpose of learning to die.[36] Lipsius's attitude towards Tertullian might confirm our expectations that his predominant goal was 'to save Antiquity'. Nevertheless, as we will see, it is doubtful whether this indeed was the case. Possibly Tertullian's *De spectaculis* plays a more important role than that of a mere source book for interesting historical details.

If we look at Lipsius's account of the historical development, the function and the extension of gladiatorial combats, it appears that he did not try to save Antiquity by minimizing the games. On the contrary: he stressed their importance, size, frequency and geographical extension. He maintained that gladiatorial games were the most important and frequent kind of Roman games, much more important than theatrical performances and horse races.[37] Although even nowadays it is not easy to quantify the number of days a year during which Romans might have been able to watch gladiatorial combats, Lipsius's view can hardly be sustained. It is clear that there were far more feast days on which theatrical performances and horse races were given. By the time of Augustus there were 65 official feastdays (state *ludi*) in total: 48 were reserved for theatrical performances, 13 for chariot races, and only 4 (!) for gladiatorial combats. These proportions remained valid throughout Antiquity: in 354 AD there were 176 feastdays in total, 102 reserved for theatrical performances, 64 for chariot

---

the majority of the old theologians attacked them [...]. What they did was right, but what I will do is also not wrong when I will follow Suetonius's footsteps and explain the habits of a remote age, unknown to us').

[36] *De spectaculis*, 12, 3: 'tantum ut occidi discerent'; cf. *Saturnales sermones* I, 8 (p. 28).

[37] For example, I, 7, p. 24-5: 'Spectaculorum apud Romanos quadrigas constituo: Gladiatores, Venationem, Circenses, Scenam. Tria ex iis ad oculos maxime, unum pertinuit ad aures. Quae ad oculos, propria fere Romanorum; aut si in alia gente, tenuia prae istis et dictu parum digna [...]. Dicam de gladiatoribus [...] quod inter omnia scire vos volo celeberrimum fuisse frequentissimumque Romae' ('I think that the Romans knew four types of games: gladiatorial games, hunting shows, horse races and theatre performances. Three of them appeal predominantly to the eyes, one of them to the ears. The three of them which appeal to the eyes are typically Roman. If they appear among other people, they are unimportant compared to the Roman and not even worth mentioning [...]. I will talk about gladiatorial games. I want you to know that they attracted the biggest audience and were performed in Rome most frequently').

races and only 10 days for gladiatorial combats and animal huntings.[38] Although it might have been difficult for Lipsius to get to these figures, it was certainly possible for him to see that among the state *ludi* about which there was abundant evidence, gladiatorial games formed only a small minority.[39] But apparently he was not inclined to draw such a conclusion.

Lipsius, furthermore, very much underlined the official character of the gladiatorial games, from the very beginnings on for the whole period of the Roman Republic. According to him, the games were then either organized as public and official events or were directly under state control. This situation he considered normal and in accordance with the state of virtue which he also otherwise ascribed to the Roman Republic.[40] The Roman Principate, on the other hand, could not, according to him, live up to this moral standard: gladiatorial combats became more and more private and, as a result of this, increased in number to a spectacular degree. All classes of private persons, Lipsius maintains, organized gladiatorial games,[41] even such low-ranked people as shoemakers.[42] Moreover, whereas gladiatorial games functioned during the Roman Republic in their religious context, during the Principate they were organized just for fun (*voluptas*), to satisfy people's desire to watch the killing of fellow men.[43]

---

[38] See T. Wiedemann, *Emperors and Gladiators*, 12.

[39] He also could have realized that the name for the gladiatorial games, *munera*, is not the same as for the other games (*ludi*). He correctly works out the term *munera* in I, 7 (p. 25): 'Spectaculum hoc appellatum proprie, *Munus*'.

[40] See, for example, *Admiranda* IV, 7 (p. 194), where he says that he admires the heroes of the Roman Republic, the Fabricii, Curii, Quinctii, for the virtue which declined later on, because of the growth of wealth and luxury. This is a widespread argument found also in Roman writers of the first century AD.

[41] I, 8 (p. 29): 'Sed paullatim, ut res solet, res increbuit a tenui canali in mare quoddam [...]. Dare enim coeperunt vulgo etiam privati et plerisque ea cura in testamentis' ('But slowly, as it happens, they became more frequent and out of a small channel they became a whole sea. For even private persons began to organize them').

[42] This surprising information Lipsius drew from Martialis, *Epigrammata* III, 16, 1-2: 'Das gladiatores, sutorum regule, cerdo, / Quodque tibi tribuit subula, sica rapit' ('You, king of the shoemakers, give gladiatorial games and what you gained by the awl you lose by the dagger'). Martialis indeed puns at a shoemaker, who lived in Bologna (*Bononia*) and who gained a fortune so that he was able to provide gladiatorial games. Cf. Friedländer's commentary ad locum: *M. Valerii Martialis Epigrammaton libri. Mit erklärenden Anmerkungen von L. Friedländer* (Amsterdam: 1967 [originally Leipzig: 1886]) 290. Lipsius used this information as evidence that in the empire gladiatorial combats were so privatized that even shoemakers organized them. Martialis's indignant pun, however, only makes sense if it was quite exceptional in those days for shoemakers to organize games.

[43] *Saturnales sermones* I, 9: *Praeter funus et religionem, etiam voluptatis causa dati gladiatores.* The examples given in this chapter are derived from the Principate.

Now Lipsius's theory about the development of gladiatorial shows, as shifting from official (in the Republic) to private events, is difficult to sustain in the light of modern insights. In fact, to a certain degree the contrary was the case. When the shows appeared, in 264 BC, they were precisely private initiatives: sons of noblemen gave them in honour of the death of their fathers. In general, during the Republic gladiatorial combats were never under state control. This is true even for the late Republic: as Wiedemann correctly remarks, 'the idea of publicly provided gladiatorial shows in the late Republic has to be dismissed'.[44] The first Roman emperor, Augustus, on the other hand, put the gladiatorial combats under state control. According to his regulation, only the *praetores* were allowed to organize them, only two times a year, and could never present more than 120 gladiators. If another person wanted to give gladiatorial combats, a special decree of the Roman Senate was required.[45] From Augustus on, nearly every emperor tried to control the gladiatorial combats in some way or another. In other words, during the Principate, private initiatives to organize gladiatorial shows were, at least in the capital, very limited.

Of course Lipsius, who eagerly excerpted Cassius Dio and Tacitus, must have been aware at least of the evidence indicating these facts.[46] He used the evidence, however, in the opposite way: Cassius Dio's account of Augustus's restrictions was presented as proof that *all sorts* of magistrates, '*even praetores*', organized gladiatorial games, which means, *as a proof for the extension of the games*. Chapter I, 9, indeed, is entitled and set up in such a way that one gets the impression that fairly every Roman magistrate had the power to organize gladiatorial games: besides *praetores* also *aediles, quaestores, consules, sacerdotes, aerarii* and last not least *imperatores* (emperors). The title of the chapter runs as follows: 'Besides as part of religious beliefs and burial rites, gladiatorial games were also given just as entertainment (*voluptatis causa*) by many magistrates, even priests, financial ministers (here the text of Lampridius is corrected), emperors'. Why did Lipsius interpret the sources in such a peculiar way?

Another interesting point is Lipsius's opinion about the spreading of the gladiatorial combats in the provinces of the Roman Empire. Of course, for the modern historian too, it is difficult to get a very precise

---

[44] Wiedemann, *Emperors and Gladiators*, 7.
[45] Cf., for example, Cassius Dio, *Roman History* LIV, 2, 4.
[46] The evidence of Cassius Dio is quoted in *Saturnales sermones* I, 9 (p. 31).

and detailed picture. This is partly due to the fact that Roman historiography is very much Rome-centred so that events in the provinces only appear cursorily. What we have therefore is scattered information which one has to interpret very cautiously. The general outlines, however, are clear. Gladiatorial shows were a typically Roman phenomenon, and their spread in the provinces must be considered a part of Romanisation. Thus their spread is the result of a complex process. Gladiatorial combats were at the same moment as much present in deeply Romanised provinces (like the Provence) as in Italy, and, in other provinces like Greece, almost absent.

Lipsius, however, suggested that there was a fairly steady spread in the whole empire. According to him, the development ran parallel to the development in the capital: first, gladiatorial combats were organized as official events by kings and cities, and, later, by private persons.[47] He interpreted the scattered information provided by the Roman historiographers, for example, from Livy and Flavius Josephus, as facts representing a steady development. In Livy, for instance, he found the report that King Perseus of Macedonia (179–168 BC) was the first in Greece to give gladiatorial shows.[48] Lipsius suggests that this was the beginning of a habit: the Greeks took over the Roman shows. Lipsius does not make much of Livy's hint that Perseus's fellow Greeks considered the shows horrible and strange (in fact in Greece gladiatorial shows never had the same success as in Italy). He even concludes that other kings and princes organized them: 'Beyond doubt other kings and princes too, gave them in their kingdoms'.[49] The chronological gap of more than 150 years between Perseus of Macedonia and Herod Lipsius did not consider noteworthy. He used the example of Herod to prove that not only pagans organized gladiatorial shows but also Jews. To this he ascribed an

---

[47] *Saturnales sermones* I, 10 (p. 33-34). Lipsius summarized his view lucidly in the title of the chapter: 'Nec Romae solum, sed in provinciis. Ubi reges dabant praesidesque. Paulatim in coloniis et municipiis increbruit mos; ubi minores magistratur dabant. Postea promiscue privati, vario praetextu' ('Gladiatorial combats were not only given in Rome, but also in the provinces. There the habit slowly became more frequent in the cities with the status of a *colonia* and in municipalities. There they were organized by the minor magistrates. Later on, without any system, by private persons, on different occasions').

[48] Livy, *Ab urbe condita* XLI, 20, 11; Lipsius, *Saturnales sermones* I, 10 (p. 33).

[49] Lipsius, *Saturnales sermones* I, 10 (p. 33). As evidence Lipsius presents the report in Flavius Josephus about king Herod of Juda (born in 22 BC) who built amphitheatres and organized gladiatorial shows (Flavius Josephus, *History of the Jews* XIX, 336).

especially embarrassing effect: even the people of the Old Testament God were so cruel and bloodthirsty as to enjoy gladiatorial shows! One must conclude that Lipsius did not do his best to limit the geographical extension of gladiatorial combats. On the contrary, he made them universal. Their huge extent added to their importance and their impact. Strange and bewildering Antiquity became, in Lipsius's account, even more embarrassing and bewildering.

This is certainly true for the number of casualties caused by gladiatorial shows. Lipsius presents them as a true *catastrophe for the whole world*.[50] He maintains that the shows caused more casualties than all wars together. During the Principate, he says, every month 20,000 or 30,000 gladiators died.[51] Thus, every year 240,000 or 360,000 people were killed in gladiatorial shows! Needless to say, Lipsius confronts us with figures which are hardly credible. If they were true, the Roman Empire would have been a wasteland within half a century.[52]

Thus Lipsius drew a horrible picture of this cultural phenomenon, demonstrating that it was spread throughout the Roman Empire and beyond, emphasizing its frequency, its importance, the bloodshed and the enormous loss of life involved. One may wonder, given his love of Antiquity and the Christian context in which he wrote, what purpose he had in mind in constructing history in such a way. One thing is sure: he did not do it in order to condemn his beloved Antiquity. Also, it never was his aim to use the historical sources in a wrong or even malicious way, although his interpretation may seem biased to us. We must not forget that after more than four hundred years of scholarship we are in a better position to understand certain historical phenomena of Antiquity, and that Lipsius was the first to deal in extenso with the gladiatorial combats.

Lipsius's book, in a way, draws an entirely new picture of the Roman games in the framework of antiquarian studies. A theme that

---

[50] *Saturnales sermones* I, 12.

[51] *Saturnales sermones* I, 12 (p. 38): 'Mentior, si non unus aliquis mensis Europae stetit vicenis capitum millibus aut trecenis' ('I would lie, if there were one month in Europe in which did not 20,000 or 30,000 people die').

[52] One may wonder how Lipsius came to such figures. He encountered in Roman historiographers various numbers of gladiators presented in shows. In chapter I, 11 he based himself on extremely high figures concerning the games Titus organized in celebration of his victory against the Jews, which lasted 100 days, and Trajanus's games celebrating the victory against the Dacians, which lasted 123 days and during which 10,000 gladiators were presented. Such figures, however, were very rare exceptions; cf. *Saturnales sermones* I, 11 (p. 37).

especially interested him was 'strange and unknown Antiquity'. He did not believe in the medieval and early Renaissance feeling of historical continuity. He was aware of the fact that the world had changed profoundly, and that Roman Antiquity formed an essentially different, unknown world: it was a 'priscum et nobis ignotum aevum'.[53] He considered it as his task to discover this new intellectual continent and to transmit his knowledge to a wider audience of interested laypeople. He wanted to be their guide, to bring light into the darkness of ignorance.[54] Lipsius developed the idea of the *Fax historica* (*Torchlight of historical reading*), a kind of lexicon in which important concepts of Roman history are explained.[55] In an opening passage of the *Saturnales sermones*, he says that he is indeed following Suetonius, 'to shed light on the rites of Antiquity, an age unknown to us'.[56] If we take into account the function Lipsius ascribed to himself, we can better understand why he was inclined to emphasize the 'alterity' of Antiquity, to underline strange and embarrassing aspects. It makes his function more important. If Antiquity were more or less the same as the sixteenth century, what would a guide be required for?

In his attempt to underline strange and embarrassing Antiquity Lipsius did not stand alone in his age. It can be observed that in the course of the sixteenth century the interest in antiquarian treatises in strange and remote aspects of Antiquity was ever growing. This was surely the result of scholarly development, of progress in science, but not exclusively. It was also the result of a change in taste and esthetic judgement. One may observe a similar interest in literature and in the visual arts, and its predilection for the horrible, strange, irrational and miraculous.[57] 'The true subject of the poet, and in fact his only subject, is the miraculous', Torquato Tasso said in his *Discorsi dell' arte poetica*, and: 'Horror turns out to be beautiful'.[58] The same is to be seen in the visual arts: horrible subjects, such as the head of the Medusa or decapitation scenes, as when Salome presents the head of John the Baptist, are

---

[53] *Saturnales sermones* I, 7 (p. 24).

[54] Cf. *Saturnales sermones* I, 7 (p. 24): 'Ut omittam scripta omnia profana, quibus immitenda lux ab hac narratione' ('Not to mention all the pagan works on which I must shed light in this treatise').

[55] Cf. the Lipsian manuscripts at the Leiden University Library, ms. Lips. 14.

[56] *Saturnales sermones* I, 7 (p. 24): 'Nec male nunc ego, qui per Suetonii vestigia iens ritus illustrabo prisci et nobis ignoti aevi'.

[57] Cf. for example Hocke G.R., *Manierismus in der Literatur. Sprachalchemie und esoterische Kombinationskunst* (Hamburg: 1959).

[58] Ibid., 159.

favourite themes of paintings.[59] Lipsius's treatise on gladiatorial shows perfectly fits this esthetic taste. As one of the dialogue characters of the *Saturnales sermones* remarks: 'These games are beautiful and pleasant'.[60] One might hold that, among other purposes, Lipsius adapts Antiquity to mannerist taste. Interestingly enough, in his other antiquarian studies too, Lipsius stuck to the idea of the strange, horrible and miraculous. He wrote two more treatises concerned with gladiatorial combats, *On the amphitheatre* (on the Colosseum) and *On amphitheatres outside Rome*;[61] the subject of his next major historiographical monograph, *De cruce libri III* (written in 1592, printed in 1593/4), is *crucifixion*, the most horrible form of death penalty in Antiquity.[62] In this work, Lipsius does his best to bring all sorts of horrible details before the reader's eyes: where exactly were the nails driven through, was it the palms or more precisely the wrists? What exactly did crucified people die of? A parallel with the *Saturnales sermones* is that Lipsius also mentions an enormous number of crucified people in *De cruce*.[63] A few years later he published a treatise on Roman war technique.[64] His last voluminous antiquarian treatise is called *Admiranda sive De magnitudine Romana* (*On Admirable Things or on Roman Greatness*).[65] In this monograph on Roman culture Lipsius again underlines the astonishing and the incredible: the enormous size of the Roman empire, its immense population, its miraculous growth, its unbelievably rich resources etc.

Now in the *Saturnales sermones*, Lipsius's emphasis on the strange and embarrassing is to be seen not only in his theoretical treatment of the subject. In a considerable part of the work he tries to visualize the gladiatorial games, to show all the details a Roman spectator would see.

---

[59] Cf. Hofmann W. (ed.), *Zauber der Medusa. Europäische Manierismen* (Wien: 1987) passim; Hibbard, H., *Caravaggio* (New York: 1983) passim.

[60] II, 25 (p. 116): 'Pulchri isti et oblectantes ludi'.

[61] *De amphitheatro* (Leiden: 1584); *De amphitheatris quae extra Romam libellus. In quo Formae eorum aliquot et typi* (Leiden: 1584). Cf. Enenkel, art. "Justus Lipsius. De amphitheatro [...]", in *Lipsius en Leuven*, 88-92.

[62] *De cruce libri III ad sacram profanamque historiam utiles* (Antwerp: 1593); cf. Landtsheer J. De, art. "Justus Lipsius. De Cruce [...]", in *Lipsius en Leuven*, 92-5; Pickering E.P., "Justus Lipsius' *De cruce libri tres* (1593) or the Historian's Dilemma", in *Festgabe für L.L. Hammerich, aus Anlaß seines siebzigsten Geburtstages* (Copenhagen: 1962) 199-214; Zaninotto G., *Il supplizio della Croce* (Rome: 1987) 14-30; Landtsheer J. De, "Justus Lipsius's *De Cruce* and the Reception of the Fathers", *Neulateinisches Jahrbuch* 2 (2000) 97-122.

[63] Cf. the article by D. Imhof in *Justus Lipsius (1547–1606) en het Plantijnse Huis*, 174-5.

[64] *Poliorceticon sive De machinis, tormentis, telis libri quinque* (Antwerp: 1596). See the article by Jeanine De Landtsheer in this book, 101-22.

[65] See the article by Marc Laureys in this book, 123-46.

He shows the place where the games took place (I, 17), the clothes the spectators wore, the organizers, the gladiators (II, 18; II, 7 ff.). He brings before the reader's eye the different types of gladiators, the terrible *Secutor* (the man with the sword and the shield) [figs. 1 and 2], the horrible *Retiarius* (the man with the trident and the net) [figs. 1 and 2], the *Thrax* [fig. 3], the *Myrmillo* [fig. 3], the *Samnites* and so on (II, 7-16). In the concluding chapters he shows the combats themselves, what is going on, how the gladiators fight, and how the defeated are killed (II, 20-23). Lipsius here directly appeals to the senses of his readers, as one can see from the opening lines of chapter II, 20 (*The Description of the Combat itself*): 'Please give me now your eyes and ears. I will show you the combat [...]. Behold, the gladiators prepare themselves, they pick up their weapons: good God!, what skill to defend themselves, to attack others!'[66]

Visualisation is an important mode of presentation in the *Saturnales sermones*. In the introductory letter to Christopher Plantin Lipsius remarks programmatically: 'I made the audience not only want to hear about the games, but I put them before their eyes'.[67] This striving for visualisation occurs many times in the *Saturnales sermones*. One of its functions is to stir up the emotions of the reader; to make him feel the horror that is evoked by deliberate and senseless killing. This is underlined sometimes by the emotional exclamations of the dialogue partners: 'Please spare my eyes here, I said. I am not able to watch this with dry eyes. These are wolves, no human beings!'[68]

This purpose of Lipsius is also emphasized by the illustrations, which appear from the 1585 edition on. There are, during Lipsius's lifetime, two sets of illustrations. The first set of fifteen illustrations for the 1585 edition was made by an unknown artist, possibly by Pieter vander Borcht or an engraver close to him [figs. 1; 4-6].[69] In 1604 (maybe because the original plates were worn out) the Plantin press

---

[66] II, 20: "Pugnae ipsius descriptio": 'Quaeso oculos mihi nunc date et aures. Pugnam vobis ostendam [...]. Ecce componunt se gladiatores et colligunt in arma: Deus bone!, quanta arte curaque sui defendendi, alterius petendi!'

[67] '[Spectacula] proposui non auribus solum, sed oculis'.

[68] II, 23 (p. 112).

[69] The style of the drawings shows similarities with the style of Peeter vander Borcht, who worked for the Plantin House; cf. *Justus Lipsius (1547-1606) en het Plantijnse Huis*, 169. Hollstein's *Dutch and Flemish Etchings, Engravings and Woodcuts ca. 1450–1700*, vol 32, compiled by G. Luijten, ed. by D. de Hoop Scheffer (Roosendaal: 1988) 182 ff., consider them 'anonymous after Otto van Veen'. Surprisingly, Luijten–De Hoop Scheffer reproduce the engravings of the 1604 (or later) edition, but attribute them to the 1585 edition (p. 182).

ordered new illustrations. They were engraved after the example of the original ones, but the design was made anew [figs. 2; 3; 7-10], inscriptions were added in the engravings to indicate which type of gladiator is depicted, but above all, Lipsius was consulted.[70] Now in these engravings it is precisely the horrible scenes which are shown: the fight for life and death between various types of gladiators [figs. 1-4; 8-10],[71] views of big battle scenes in the amphitheatre [figs. 5-7],[72] maiming and killing.

On engraving C (p. 106) the terrible *Retiarius,* who has caught his opponent and pierces to his neck with his trident, can be seen [figs. 1 and 2]. On engraving K [fig. 4; p. 132] a battle is shown in two stages: first a violent attack of two gladiators pitted against one another, and — in the foreground, even more brutally — one gladiator mercilessly kills a comrade lying in the sand by stabbing a sword (or dagger) into his throat. Engraving M shows an even more violent battle scene (visualizing the *catervarii*) with some seventeen people involved, some of them on horseback [fig. 5, p. 137]. Killed fighters and horses lie on the ground, fighters attack each other, relentlessly stabbing men and horses alike with swords and spears. A big wounded horse can be seen in the centre, its rider still sitting on it and pushing a spear towards the

---

[70] Lipsius obviously was not totally pleased with the illustrations of the 1585 edition. The reason was not that he would have been either against illustrations in general or against illustrated editions of his antiquarian works. When the artist and humanist Otto van Veen (Vaenius) left Leiden he remarked that Van Veen left to his great regret because he could have been useful to him as an illustrator of his antiquarian studies. Cf. Lipsius, *Ep. Misc.* I, 60 (31 May 1584): 'Otho Vaenius a nobis abit, sed invitis: insignis moribus et arte adolescens, et cuius manus usui mihi esse poterat ad multa Antiquitatis illustranda'. On Otto van Veen and Lipsius, cf. the article by Mark Morford in this book. Thus Lipsius was probably not pleased with the way in which the illustrations were executed. If one compares engraving K of the 1585 edition (p. 132) with the one on p. 101 of the 1604 edition, one can see that the dress of the soldiers is rendered in a much more precise way in the latter. I think that Lipsius was also very much disturbed by the rendering of grass on the ground of the amphitheatre in the 1585 edition, for example in the *Retiarius* illustration on p. 106 [fig. 1]. He must have felt ashamed because of such an historical fault: of course, in the arena of a Roman amphitheatre no grass was to be found. In the *Retiarius* illustration of the 1604 edition, which was made with Lipsius's consent, interestingly enough, the grass on the ground is left out [fig. 2]. The same thing happens with engraving D (p. 112) of the 1585 edition and the *Myrmillo-cum-Threce* illustration of the 1604 edition (p. 84 [fig. 3]). On the *laquerarii* engraving of the 1585 edition (engraving I, p. 125) stones suddenly appear in the sand of the arena. Not surprisingly, in the illustration of the 1604 edition (p. 92) the stones are left out [fig. 3].

[71] Engraving A (p. 89), B (p. 91), C (p. 106 [fig. 1]), D (p. 112), E (p. 116), F (p. 119), H (p. 123), I (p. 125), K (p. 132 [fig. 4]), L (p. 135) and M (p. 137 [fig. 5]).

[72] Engraving ('Falttafel') between pp. 140 and 141, and between 152 and 153 [fig. 6].

attacker. Three of the fighters have lost their helmets, so that one can imagine what will happen next. The large illustration between p. 152 and 153 again shows a most cruel fighting scene: no less than twenty-four gladiators fight with each other at the same time [figs. 6 and 7]. Several horrible killings are presented to the spectator: perhaps the most horrible is the dead man in the very centre of the foreground: his head has fallen back and his closed eyes are directed towards the spectator, while his hand which has been cut off, lies next to the body. Just as terrible is the view of a gladiator slightly to the right of the centre [fig. 6], who stares at the spectator while he receives a deadly stroke to his body. Equally shocking is the dead body in the right corner [fig. 6; in the left corner fig. 7] which is drawn out of the arena by a long hook. The first illustration of the set (engraving A) is a fighting scene which must have shocked the readers for other reasons: in it, two women attack each other with sword and shield [fig. 8].

Although Lipsius adapted Roman Antiquity to late sixteenth-century taste, this was certainly not his only goal. He truly wanted to inform the reader and to teach him about an important aspect of Roman culture. In Roman literature, he argues, references to gladiatorial combats appear on almost every page, in historical texts as well, as in orations and poetry. Very many metaphors, similitudes and images are derived from gladiatorial combats.[73] How can one understand Roman literature without a clear knowledge of gladiatorial games? With this goal in mind, he deliberatly chose, in contrast to Tertullian's *De spectaculis*, an informative mode of presentation.

Which audience did he have in mind? In the dedication letter to Busbequius Lipsius says that the *Saturnales sermones* are meant not for specialists, scholars of classical Antiquity, but for more ordinary users, the interested layman or student.[74] At first sight this argument sounds not implausible. But if one looks closer, it is not so clear wether one should believe him. His specific way of presenting the subject indicates that he also had specialist scholars in mind. I already mentioned the enormous amount of evidence Lipsius gave. This has to do of course with Lipsius's intentions: he wanted his work to be an exhaustive

---

[73] *Saturnales sermones* I, 6 (p. 21-2): 'Quae historia ab hac commemoratione gladiatorum, quis orator, quis poeta abstinuit? Et quidem pleraeque metaphorae, similitudines, imagines, alii flores orationis sunt ab istis'.

[74] 'Quamquam huic ipsi operae aliquod pretium fortasse erit apud eos, qui veteri germanaque doctrina non perfusi sunt, sed tincti'.

account, a true scholarly 'Fundgrube' on the subject. The reader
should be able to find all available information and quotations on
gladiatorial combats. This scholarly presentation means that history
takes the shape of a collection of evidence. Moreover, the historical
work is at the same time a *philological work,* history *more philologico.* Lipsius does not only present (and interpret) fragments from classical
authors, but he also looks critically at the transmission of the text. He
always focusses on the quoted classical texts themselves: he wants to
emendate them and to explain their meaning. From the paratextual
level one can see that he considered this a very important goal indeed
of his work, for in the chapter titles he often indicates explicitly the
result of his textual criticism. Some examples: in the title of I, 2 he
announces 'Arnobius explained; a vulgate reading of Livy defended
[...]; Seneca emended and explained [...]; Festus and Cicero emended
[...]; Plautus explained; Petronius and Dio corrected'; in I, 3: '[the text
of] Ausonius healed; Varro healed and explained'; I, 5: 'Tibullus and
Tertullian explained'; I, 7: 'Tacitus corrected'; I, 8 : 'Cicero explained
[...]; Ausonius explained and emendated [...]' and so on. In fact, in
nearly every chapter the title promises the results of textual criticism.
This is emphasized once more by marginal notes that guide the reader
directly to the textual emendations. These paratextual advertisements
show that Lipsius was very proud of his philological endeavour and
that he wanted his readers to pay special attention to it. It means at
the same time, that he certainly wrote the *Saturnales sermones* for scholars too. He wanted to impress and to inform his philologist colleagues.
Traces left by users of classical texts show that Renaissance scholars
indeed paid attention to Lipsius's textual criticism in the *Saturnales sermones.* A Renaissance user, for instance, of the Basle edition of Pliny's
Naturalis historia (1554) wrote in the margin: 'Melius liber vetus, nisi
naturam, spectaculum sibi ac paria componentem. Lips. satur. l. 2. c.
XIX' ('the old book has the better reading *nisi naturam.* [See] Lipsius,
Saturnales sermones, book two, chapter nineteen').[75]

With his scholarly and philological method Lipsius is far indeed
from Tertullian's *De spectaculis* which is dominated by an evaluative
and apologetic mode of presentation. The surprising fact is, however, that Lipsius's theory about the origin, development and func-

---

[75] C. Plinii Secundi *Historiae mundi libri XXXVII* [...] (Basle: 1554) (exemplar of the
Leiden University Library 763 A 5) 129, lines 7 ff. (ad *Naturalis historiam* VIII, 34). The
annotation in all probability was made by Jacobus Tollius.

tion of the gladiatorial games goes back to exactly this author. In the early days, Tertullian states, the games were embedded in burial rites. Later on the element of entertainment/lust increased. Thus the games were separated from burials and given in honour of the living. One can even show that the *inventio* of *Saturnales sermones* I, 8-9 directly depends on Tertullian's account in *De spectaculis* 12. I remarked above that in I, 9 Lipsius strangely interprets the restrictions of the emperors as evidence for the opinion that in the empire all classes of persons organized gladiatorial combats. In I, 9 Lipsius works out the different categories of magistracies that organized gladiatorial shows. In *De spectaculis* 12, 5 we read: 'And even if this kind of games were transferred from the honour of the dead to the honour of the living, I mean to the holders of quaestorships, magistracies and priestships [...]', a passage quoted also by Lipsius in the first part of the chapter. This means that Lipsius searched for evidence in various classical authors in order to illustrate what Tertullian said.

But, as we saw, Lipsius did not take over Tertullian's theological condemnations. Interestingly enough, the *Saturnales sermones* end up with a totally anti-Tertullianic chapter in praise of the gladiatorial combats![76] Lipsius argues that gladiatorial combats were useful from a moral point of view because they made people virtuous. The Romans, he says, were 'people born to fight' ('gens nata ad arma'). Thus it is appropriate that they lived up to this peculiarity even in their pas times. To watch fights which pitted man against man was very useful, because it made them brave. Sometimes they organized gladiatorial combats before they went to war in order to increase the courage of the soldiers. Even from the philosophical (stoic) point of view the games are useful: they teach people how to despise death. Lipsius compares the bravery of the Romans in facing death with the weakness and decadence of his days: 'You, degenerated man, will not take them as an example? Should you not say to yourself: this futile man (a gladiator) without education, without (stoic) philosophical training is able to despise death, the most extreme aspect of human affairs. And I am afraid of exile and of migrating to another country. This man, without losing his good mood, sheds blood. And I shed tears, when I loose my unimportant belongings?' This is, of course, a rhetorical tour

---

[76] II, 25 (p. 116-9): 'Quid pro Romanis proque his ludis dici possit' ('What one can say in favour of the Romans and of these games').

de force.[77] In this passage Lipsius drives strange and embarrassing Antiquity to its climax.

Thus this final chapter, although some of its arguments stem from authors like Cicero, is set up to strike the reader with complete astonishment. The values familiar to him are turned upside down. The new and wide perspective forces him to rethink the whole book and to admire Lipsius's mental power in being able to open up this new intellectual horizon.

Selective Bibliography

AUGUET R., *Cruauté et civilisation: Les jeux romains* (Paris: 1970) (English translation *Cruelty and Civilisation. The Roman Games* (London–New York: 1994²))

BARTON C.A., *The Sorrows of the Ancient Romans. The Gladiator and the Monster* (Princeton: 1993)

BURKE P., "The Renaissance Dialogue", *Renaissance Studies* 3 (1989)

ENENKEL K., *Kulturoptimismus und Kulturpessimismus in der Renaissance. Studie zu Jacobus Canters Dyalogus de solitudine* [...] (Frankfurt a. M.: 1995)

ENENKEL K., "The Theatre of *Fortitudo* and Death: On the Evaluation of the Gladiatorial Combats by Roman Authors", in Andreia. Penn–Leiden–Papers 1 (2001) (forthcoming)

HOPKINS K., "Murderous Games", in Idem, *Death and Renewal* (Cambridge: 1983) 1-30

MAZZOCCO A., "Biondo Flavio and the Antiquarian Tradition", in *Acta Conventus Neo-Latini Bononiensis*, ed. R.J. Schoeck (New York: 1985) 124-36

MAZZOCCO A., "Linee di sviluppo dell'antiquaria del Rinascimento", in *Poesia e poetica delle rovine di Roma. Momenti e problemi*, ed. V. De Caprio, Quaderni di Studi Romani, n. s. 1, 47 (Rome: 1987) 55-71

NORDMAN V.A., *Justus Lipsius als Geschichtsforscher und Geschichtslehrer* (Helsinki: 1932)

PLASS P., *The Game of Death in Ancient Rome. Arena Sports and Political Suicide* (Madison–London: 1993)

---

[77] In a way, Lipsius plays a safe card by putting these thoughts in the mouth of another person, Janus Lernutius. So, if people were offended by the argument, he could always maintain that they were not his words. This does not mean, however, that the historical Lipsius disagreed. In the whole of the *Saturnalia* he puts the arguments in the mouth of different persons.

SIDER R.D., "Tertullian. On the shows: an Analysis", *Journal of Theological Studies* 29 (1978) 339 ff.

SNYDER J.R., *Writing the Scene of Speaking. Theories of Dialogue in the Late Italian Renaissance* (Stanford: 1989)

WEISMANN W., *Kirche und Schauspiele. Die Schauspiele im Urteil der lateinischen Kirchenväter unter besonderer Berücksichtigung von Augustin* (Würzburg: 1972)

WEISMANN W., art. "Gladiator", in *RAC* XI (1981), col. 23-45

WIEDEMANN T., *Emperors and Gladiators* (London--New York: 1992)

WISTRAND M., *Entertainment and Violence in Ancient Rome. The Attitudes of Roman Writers of the First Century A.D.* (Göteborg: 1992).

JUSTUS LIPSIUS'S *DE MILITIA ROMANA*:
POLYBIUS REVIVED OR HOW AN ANCIENT HISTORIAN
WAS TURNED INTO A MANUAL OF EARLY MODERN
WARFARE[*]

Jeanine De Landtsheer

Polybius (c. 200–c. 118 BC), the 'Greek historian of Rome's rise to Mediterranean dominion and of the world in which that happened',[1] became a politician like his father Lycortas.[2] When the Romans defeated the Greeks at the battle of Pydna in 168 BC, they took 1,000 prominent Achaeans as hostages to Italy, among them Polybius. He was detained in Rome, but soon became a welcome guest and friend of grecophile leading citizens, especially of P. Cornelius Scipio Africanus. When seventeen years later the barely three hundred surviving Achaeans were finally allowed to return home, Polybius lingered with his Roman friends for five more years and Scipio took him with him on his military campaigns in Africa. The Roman general highly appreciated his Greek friend's military skills and tactical insight concerning sieges.[3] During these campaigns Polybius became an expert on Roman army practice too. When he wrote his *Histories* after his return to his native country (shortly after 146 BC), he could rely on this profound practical experience. The *Histories*, divided into forty books, covered the period between 264 BC, the beginning of the First Punic War, to 144 BC, two years after the destruction of Carthage and Corinth, when Rome had fully established its supremacy in both the Western and the Eastern part of the Mediterranean.

According to Polybius the historian's primary task was explanation:

---

* I am indebted to Toon Van Houdt and Karl Enenkel with whom I discussed this contribution in an earlier stage.

[1] On Polybius, see, among others, *The Oxford Classical Dictionary* (Oxford: 1996³) 1209-10; *Paulys Realencyclopädie der classischen Altertumswissenschaft*, ed. G. Wissowa – K. Ziegler (neue Bearbeitung), 83 vols (Stuttgart: 1893–1980) XXI, 2, 1140-578; Walbank F.W., *Polybius* (Berkeley–Los Angeles–London: 1972); Idem, *A Historical Commentary on Polybius*, 3 vols (Oxford: 1957) I, 1–16. The quotation comes from *The Oxford Classical Dictionary*, 1209.

[2] In 170–169 BC he was appointed *hipparchos*, one of the top positions of the Achaean Confederacy.

[3] Polybius was also the author of a now lost treatise *On Tactics*.

'The mere statement of a fact may interest us, but is of no benefit to us; but when we add the cause of it, the study of history becomes fruitful. For it is the mental transference of similar circumstances to our own times that gives us the means of forming presentiments of what is about to happen'.[4] Thus Polybius had a double purpose with his *Histories*: 'to provide useful training and experience for the practical politician, and at the same time to teach the reader how to bear the vicissitudes of Fortune, by describing those that have befallen others', as Walbank has phrased it.[5]

For his explanations Polybius also used digressions obligatory in ancient historical works. Interestingly enough, he seemed to emphasize these digressions more than his predecessors. In the sixth book, for instance, he elaborated on the Roman constitution and on Rome's military organization.[6] This book will be of special importance for this article, since it includes the text that inspired Lipsius for his treatise *De militia Romana*.[7]

Of Polybius's *Histories*, only books I-V, about four fifth, have survived;[8] of the rest we can only get an impression from excerpts and fragments.[9]

In the Middle Ages, the text of Polybius was fairly unknown in the Latin West. In the middle of the fifteenth century, he aroused the interest of Florentine humanists, such as Leonardo Bruni. The latter used Polybius I-II, 35 for his history of the first Punic and the subse-

---

[4] Polybius XII, 25b. Translation quoted from W.R. Paton's edition with translation in Loeb Classical Library (Cambridge, Mass.–London: 1960) IV, 371.

[5] Walbank, *Commentary* I, 6-7, referring to Polybius I, 1, 2.

[6] On composition, revision and publication of the *Histories*, see Walbank, *Polybius*, 13-5; Idem, *Commentary* I, 292-7. The course of events which Polybius described and in which he took an active part made him rethink and extend his original plan.

[7] *Iusti Lipsi de militia Romana libri quinque. Commentarius ad Polybium. E parte prima historicae facis* (Antwerp: 1595–1596). The treatise was reissued by the *Officina Plantiniana* in 1598 (*Editio nova, aucta varie et castigata*) and 1602 (both on 1,500 copies), 1614 (1,050 copies) and 1630 (775 copies). On the *editio princeps* and later editions, see Vander Haeghen F., *Bibliotheca Belgica: Bibliographie générale des Pays-Bas*, ed. M.-Th. Lenger (Brussels: 1964–1975) III, 1002-5 (L 369-75).

[8] On the resurgence of Polybius, see Momigliano A., "Polybius' Reappearance in Western Europe", in *Sesto Contributo alla storia Degli Studi Classici e del mondo antico*, Storia e letteratura. Raccolta di studi e testi 149 (Rome: 1980) 103-23; Burke P., "A survey of the Popularity of Ancient Historians 1450-1700", *History and Theory* 5 (1966) 135-52. See also Röck C., *Studien zur Rezeption der griechischen, römischen und byzantinischen Kriegsschriftsteller im 16. Jahrhundert* (diss. Heidelberg, forthcoming).

[9] Among others in an encyclopaedic collection made at the behest of Emperor Constantine VII Porphyrogenitus (905–959).

quent Illyrian and Gallic Wars, a period missing in Livy.[10] A further step towards the recognition of Polybius occurred in the middle of the fifteenth century, when Pope Nicolas V (1447–1455) encouraged the translation of the most prominent Greek historians into Latin. Polybius's books I-V were entrusted to Niccolò Perotti, a scholar who was in the service of Cardinal Bessarion.[11] In that period Polybius was merely valued as a historian. This situation changed when Niccolò Machiavelli composed his *Discorsi*,[12] for he recognised Polybius's worth as a political thinker. In his treatise on the art of war a few years later,[13] he made use of Polybius's knowledge of the Roman army as well. From then on the military aspect too became more and more prominent and several translations of book VI, 19-42 were made, for example by Machiavelli's disciple Bartolomeo Cavalcanti.[14] Moreover, in 1529 Janus Lascaris published the Greek text of the fragmentary sixth book, together with a Latin translation.[15] In 1583 Francesco Patrizi composed a book on the Roman army based on ancient historians: *La militia Romana di Polibio, di Tito Livio e di Dionigi Alicarnaseo* (Ferrara). In this work, Polybius's fragmentary sixth book held a prominent place.[16] For the propagation of the Roman warfare in the Netherlands and the German Empire, Justus Lipsius[17] played an

---

[10] *Leonardi Aretini de bello Italico adversus Gothos* (c. 1420).

[11] This translation was criticized by sixteenth-century scholars, in particular by Isaac Casaubon.

[12] *Discorsi sopra la prima deca di Tito Livio* (Rome: 1531). Machiavelli must have completed his *Discorsi* in 1519, although they were only published four and a half years after his death. See *Niccolò Machiavelli. Discorsi. Gedachten over Staat en Politiek*. Vertaald, ingeleid en toegelicht door Paul van Heck (Amsterdam–Antwerp: 1997) 28-9; 65-8.

[13] *Arte della guerra* (Florence: 1521).

[14] Cavalcanti, an exile from Florence, translated Polybius's chapters on the Roman army for his lord, Duke Ercole II of Ferrara, who was looking to improve his army. Cf. Momigliano, "Polybius' Reappearance", 115-6.

[15] *Liber ex Polybii historiis excerptus de militia Romanorum et castrorum metatione inventu rarissimus. Ipso etiam Graeco libro adiuncto* (Venice: 1529). On the manuscript tradition of Polybius, see Moore M., *The Manuscript Tradition of Polybius* (Cambridge: 1965).

[16] From then on, interest in Polybius also extended beyond the borders of Italian humanism: the Greek text of books I-V was edited by Vincentius Opsopaeus (Hagenau: 1530). In 1574 Guilielmus Xylander provided a German translation.

[17] On Justus Lipsius, see *Biographie Nationale* (Brussels: 1866 ff.) XII, 239-89; *Nationaal Biografisch Woordenboek* (Brussels: 1964 ff.) 10, 403-15, and more recently *Lipsius en Leuven. Catalogus van de tentoonstelling in de Centrale Bibliotheek te Leuven, 18 september – 17 oktober 1997*, ed. G. Tournoy – J. Papy – J. De Landtsheer, Supplementa Humanistica Lovaniensia 13 (Leuven: 1997); *Justus Lipsius (1547–1606) en het Plantijnse Huis*, ed. R. Dusoir – J. De Landtsheer – D. Imhof, Publicaties van het Museum Plantin-Moretus en het Stedelijk Prentenkabinet 37 (Antwerp: 1997); *Justus Lipsius in Leiden. Studies in the Life and Works of a great Humanist*, ed. K. Enenkel – C.L. Heesakkers (Voorthuizen:

important part with his *De militia*. He recognized Patrizi explicitly as his predecessor: in the preface of this treatise he wrote:

> My labour has brought into the open something which has been highly demanding for many who came upon it. For this entire treatise of Polybius is — as a whole — most complex and veiled, and it needs not only an industrious, but also a shrewd mind to penetrate it. I hope, yes I declare that this is what I have realized for part of it, without any predecessors to help me, with the exception of the Italian Franciscus Patritius, the only one, as far as I know, who has walked this path.

Moreover, both Patrizi and Lipsius were convinced that the organisation of contemporary armies, in its technical and in its moral aspects, might greatly be improved by putting Polybius's information on the Roman army into practice. In his dedication to Duke Alfonso II d'Este Patrizi had stressed the point that the Roman military organisation and tactics would be the only way to cope with the Ottomans.[18]

Lipsius's correspondence sheds light on the genesis of *De militia*.[19] He had already made up his mind to compose an historical treatise called

---

1997); *The world of Justus Lipsius: A contribution towards his intellectual biography. Proceedings of a colloquium held under the auspices of the Belgian Historical Institute in Rome (Rome, 22-24 May 1997)*, ed. M. Laureys, Bulletin van het Historisch Instituut te Rome 68 (1998); *Justus Lipsius, Europae Lumen et Columen. Proceedings of the International Colloquium Leuven, 17-19 September 1997*, ed. G. Tournoy – J. De Landtsheer – J. Papy, Supplementa Humanistica Lovaniensia 15 (Leuven: 1999).

[18] This topic has been discussed by Momigliano A., "Polybius between the English and the Turks", in *Sesto Contributo alla storia Degli Studi Classici e del mondo antico*, Storia e letteratura. Raccolta di studi e testi 149 (Rome: 1980) 125-41.

[19] Of the *Iusti Lipsi Epistolae*, the following volumes are available: I (1564–1583), ed. A. Gerlo – M.A. Nauwelaerts – H.D.L. Vervliet (Brussels: 1978); ILE II (1584–1587), ed. M.A. Nauwelaerts – S. Sué (Brussels: 1983); ILE III (1588–1590), ed. S. Sué – H. Peeters (Brussels: 1987); ILE V (1592), ed. J. De Landtsheer – J. Kluyskens (Brussels: 1991); ILE VI (1593), ed. J. De Landtsheer (Brussels: 1994); ILE VII (1594), ed. eadem (Brussels: 1997); ILE XIII (1600), ed. J. Papy (Brussels: 2000). Volumes VIII (1595), ed. J. De Landtsheer and IX (1596), ed. H. Peeters, are forthcoming. In quoting Lipsius's letters, the abbreviation ILE is used, followed by a chronological number of three pairs of Arab numerals to indicate the year, month and day. When more letters were written on the same day, the first letter(s) of the correspondent's name is (are) added. For the correspondence not yet published in the ILE-series, the same system is used, following Gerlo A. – Vervliet H.D.L., *Inventaire de la correspondance de Juste Lipse, 1564–1606* (Antwerp: 1968). When referring to letters from 1591, I made use of S. Sué, *Justus Lipsius op de terugweg. Tekstkritische uitgave van de correspondentie van het jaar 1591, met commentaar en een biografische studie* (unpubl. diss. Brussels: [1974]), 2 vols (to appear as ILE IV). I checked Sué's text against the original sources.

Fax historica, when he was still in Leiden: on 13 January 1591 he wrote
to the Antwerp cartographer Abraham Ortelius:

> I am now postponing all other worries and am concentrating on my *Fax
> historica* which will come by useful to elucidate all historiographers, even
> all authors in a clear and easy way. It will dwell on all aspects of Antiq-
> uity: customs of both private and public life, religious and mundane, of
> military and legal practices and, moreover, also on the more specific
> vocabulary and idioms.[20]

In the course of 1593 the project of the *Fax historica* took a more realistic and definite shape: in March, Lipsius informed his Antwerp friends
Abraham Ortelius and Franciscus Sweertius that he would first of all,
by way of introduction to the intended editions, prepare a treatise on
the Roman army, as warfare was an ever-recurring and important
part of history.[21] Half a year later he wrote that he had nearly finished
his treatise.[22] Much too optimistically, as it turned out, for in December of the same year he was apparently still busy with the fifth book,
On discipline. He explained that he was totally absorbed by his *De Militia* and that he was amazed by the sharp contrast between the organisation of the army in Rome and the awful mess their own contemporaries were making of it.[23] In the spring of 1594 the treatise was finished.[24] While the work was at the printer's Lipsius continued with
what he considered its second part, viz. the *Poliorceticon, sive de machinis,
tormentis, telis libri quinque. Ad historiarum lucem* (Antwerp: 1596), on
devices and engines used at sieges. This sequel was nearly finished in
June 1595, when *De militia* came from the press. According to the pref-

---

[20] See ILE 91 01 13 O. A similar explanation was sent on the same day to printer
Johannes Moretus: 'I am now focusing on another and quite important project, and if
I can accomplish it, I dare say that for many years nothing has been edited that was
more useful to the literary world. I call it *Fax historica, Torchlight of History*; it will be a
clearly structured commentary on all historiographers, even on all authors of Antiquity' (ILE 91 01 13 M).

[21] ILE VI, 93 03 04 O, 5-10; 93 03 04 S, 14-6. In the latter Lipsius also promised a
study of the Roman magistrates and priests.

[22] ILE VI, [93] 09 22 B.

[23] ILE VI, 93 12 21, 1-11.

[24] Lipsius came to Antwerp to discuss some final details, the illustrations and the lay-
out of his treatise, with printer Johannes Moretus. On 25 May, Lipsius was in Antwerp,
for in his account book Moretus noted: *Ad 25 maij compté avec mons[ieu]r Lipsius, estant
p[ré]sent en Anvers* [...] Cf. Antwerp, Museum Plantijn Moretus, Arch. 21, f. 223 (= *Document 32* in Gerlo A. – Vervliet H.D.L. – Vertessen I., *La correspondance* [further abbreviated as GVd] 245-99). Yet in the following months he would add a small part of 'Analecta
sive observationes reliquae ad militiam et hosce libros', a further commentary of some
passages and quotations in *De militia*, see, for instance, ILE VII, 94 07 20 SC.

ace of *De militia* Lipsius had planned a third part, *De triumphis*, about the triumphal processions which rewarded a successful campaign. However, this was never realised, although the first draft of a few chapters is preserved in the Leiden University library.[25]

De militia was available from 11 June 1595 on, for according to Moretus's book of accounts, on this day he had six copies dispatched to Lipsius in Leuven. This same source provides us with the names of many more acquaintances who were sent a copy.[26] Lipsius's new work was published in an edition of 1,500 copies in quarto in five 'books' (parts), subdivided into a number of 'dialogues' (chapters) and concluded by a schematic summary, a 'tabula' or 'breviarium'. An appendix with supplementary annotations completed the treatise. In the *editio princeps* the treatise was divided into two almost equal parts, thus accentuating the importance of the fifth book, on discipline. The first part ([8] f. + p. 1-330) contained the dedication, the preface and books I-IV. After a blank page came a new title-page announcing the fifth book, another title-page and the *Analecta sive observationes*; the whole was concluded by two folia with *errata* in two columns (Greek and Latin), the ecclesiastical approbation and the privileges of Emperor Rudolph II and of the Spanish king, Philip II (p. 1-292 + [4] f.).

In his dedicatory letter to the Spanish crown prince, the future Philip III, Lipsius pointed out that a good leader had to be an expert general as well.[27] Philip would inherit an immense realm, with just one formidable adversary, the Ottomans. The disunited Christian world was keeping its eyes on him, full of hope or dread. To him, military art would be of vital importance to consolidate his power. Other nations too were improving their armies. With regard to the art of war, the Prince could learn a lot from Roman history, for going through it, he would come accross innumerable examples of virtue and would be given advice in matters of peace and war.

To present — and to enliven — his subject, Lipsius chose the form of a dialogue.[28] Each book represents the conversation of one day. In the

---

[25] Leiden, University Library, ms. Lips. 10, f. 53-6.

[26] Cf. Antwerp, Museum Plantijn Moretus, Arch. 21, p. 258 (= GVd 279-80, no 33). In the margin is pointed out explicitly that 77 copies were sent.

[27] Cf. *De militia* (Antwerp: 1595–1596), f. *2-**1v; an annotated and critical edition can be found in ILE VIII, [95 04 21] P.

[28] The sequel to *De militia*, the *Poliorceticon*, takes place in the country seat of the Liège Prince Bishop Ernest of Bavaria, to whom the treatise was dedicated, and was

opening section of the first book Lipsius sets the scene and explains the purpose of his treatise.[29] As Lipsius is enjoying a stroll, he is stopped by an eager student who urges him to expound on the army, as Lipsius had promised to do. First Lipsius tries to find an excuse, but the student insists: it is a holiday so that there is plenty of time. Moreover, war is the main topic in all conversation; 'How satisfactory would it be, in these circumstances, to understand the military practice of Antiquity, and even to glean something that might be useful in our day'. Lipsius pokes fun at the young man: 'What do you mean, "to glean something": you do not know this age or you must be feigning, for our present war-heroes despise all that, laughing it off as nursery songs and child's play!'. The young man perseveres: 'Perhaps because they are poorly instructed'. And he adds that he himself is longing to get a more detailed knowledge of the topic. Lipsius's efforts will possibly have a double effect: first, he insists, the discussion of military matters will be enlightening, a real 'torchlight of history' for every scholar who focuses on ancient history, as war and battles are the treatise's principal material.[30] A second effect might be that better knowledge of the ancient army might provide the modern commanders-in-chief with some useful suggestions. The combination of the Roman army (recruiting, discipline, and organisation) and, on the other hand, modern artillery, should create an invincible army.

Lipsius himself, in the outlines of the second chapter, points out his method. His starting point is Polybius, whom he calls the only relevant author on the Roman army.[31] Yet he will rearrange Polybius's text in an order more suitable to his purpose. For Lipsius intended to give a more methodical description of the Roman army, according to the definition 'multitudo apta et composita in armis, ad vim faciendam aut arcendam, sub certa lege' ('a suitable and well-structured crowd, provided with weapons to cause violence or to defend against it,

---

also presented as a fictitious conversation, this time between Lipsius and some of his Liège friends, Johannes Furius, Jacques de Carondelet, Petrus Oranus, Dominicus Lampsonius and Carolus Billaeus, cf. *Poliorceticon* I, dial. 1.

[29] *De militia* (Antwerp: 1595–1596), 1-4.

[30] This is a reference to the 'general title' of Lipsius's project, as well as a play on words, because the Latin *materia* in its literal sense means *fuel*.

[31] Lipsius did not appreciate Vegetius, whom he censured to have no substance and to mix up the customs of his own age and those of previous ones. On Flavius Vegetius Renatus (transition fourth – fifth century AD), cf. *The Oxford Classical Dictionary*, 1584. His *Epitoma rei militaris* (four books) is the only account of Roman military practice to have survived intact. Lipsius's criticism is not unfounded.

according to strict rules'). Lipsius distinguishes five elements, each of which will be the theme of one of *De militia*'s books: recruiting (*dilectus*), divisions (*ordo*), armament (*arma*), battle-array (*acies*) and discipline (*disciplina*). These themes will be discussed mainly by commenting on the corresponding sections in Polybius. Additionally, Lipsius will use other ancient sources on *militia*. In explaining Polybius, Lipsius always quotes the Greek text from the edition of Janus Lascaris, together with a Latin translation made by himself. He criticizes Lascaris's Latin translations which he considers are not always concise and pithy.[32]

Thus, Lipsius's *De militia* excels in its clear structure: first the army's recruitment, secondly its divisions and the commanders, next come the soldiers' equipment and the order of battle. In elaborating on these topics Lipsius always discusses first the infantry (lightly-armed before heavily-armed), then the cavalry and finally the auxiliaries. In his fifth book he dwells on the aspects which largely contributed to the Roman army's superiority, namely the strict and smooth organisation of their camps (*castra*) and the camp duties (*munia*), the training (*exercitia*) divided into *onera* (order of marching, luggage), *opera* (works preparing a siege) and drilling exercises, and finally the military 'contract' (*leges*): payment, rewards and penalties, and the discharge. A comparison between the Roman army's practice and that of his contemporaries concludes the five books.[33]

Notice should be drawn to the typography as well. By his careful lay-out, Lipsius tried to facilitate the reader's use of the text.[34] Each chapter is indicated by a title in small capitals and a one-line summary of its contents in italics. In the main text the speaker is indicated in small capitals (abbreviated); occasionally a relevant word is emphasized by using italics. The definition of *militia*, summing up the subject of each book, was printed in small capitals too; the five elements, which it contains, will return in small capitals at the beginning of each book. In the margin each new step is summarized in a smaller, italic font. Quotations are italicized; Greek citations are translated into Latin either in the margin (preceded by an asterisk, in a smaller font and in italics), or in the main text. Nearly always the sources are

---

[32] Occasionally Lipsius even points out an error in Lascaris's translation, see *infra*.

[33] In the appendix I have reproduced the table of contents of the five books with their 'dialogues' together with the corresponding chapters in Polybius, or the reference to fragments from other authors which Lipsius has called upon to explain aspects not dicussed by Polybius.

[34] Cf. Karl Enenkel's article in this book, 75-99, esp. 81.

named either as part of the main text, or sometimes in the margin (in a smaller font and in Roman characters). Often Lipsius lists the author's name (and title of the work) in the text and adds the exact book and chapter in the margin (in a smaller font and in Roman characters). Polybius's fragments are printed in two columns — Greek and Latin —, in a larger font and in italics. When Lipsius is commenting on longer quotations from Livy or Flavius Josephus, the ancient source is printed in a larger font and in italics as well, but in a single column. Lipsius's commentary is once more in the usual font and in Roman characters; the lemma is in italics, preceded by a quotation mark and a blank space, and concluded by a bracket.[35]

The text was illustrated with fifteen wood and thirteen copper engravings, most of the latter made by Peeter vander Borcht, a life-long faithful collaborator of the *Officina Plantiniana*. The woodcuts are nearly all representations of ancient coins; the illustration of the ordinary battle-array (*iconismus aciei vulgatae*), a copper engraving inspired by Patrizi, is outsized and was inserted between the pages.

A close examination proves that Lipsius commented almost on the whole text of Polybius VI, 19-42. Only a few sentences are left out.[36] One fragment, Polybius VI, 24, 3-5 (on the maniples) has been used twice.[37] Presumably Lipsius was not aware of this repetition, for he made a new translation with even a few slight alterations. Polybius's order was strictly respected in books I and III.[38] In books II[39] and V[40] Lipsius preferred to adjust Polybius's order to his own structure, as he had anounced. In book V the fragments usually run much longer before they are interrupted by Lipsius's commentary. Book IV of *De militia* is entirely based on other sources, because Polybius's chapters dealing with this subject are lost.

In a few cases Lipsius points out problems with the Greek text,

---

[35] For this system of layout, cf. the first two pages of *De militia* I, 2.

[36] This is the case with Polybius VI, 20, 8 (the transition between the recruitment of the infantry and that of the cavalry); VI, 24, 9 (a statement that the captains should be natural born leaders, calm and steady of character, and no foolhardy daredevils); VI, 32, 1-2 (given the exact numbers, everyone can calculate the total circumference of the camp) and VI, 37, 2-6, the largest passage (on cudgelling as a penalty for a lapse in guard duty).

[37] Scil. in *De militia* II, 2 and II, 8

[38] Respectively Polybius VI, 19, 1-21, 5 and Polybius VI, 22, 1-25, 11.

[39] Polybius VI, 21, 6-10; 24, 1 - 26, 9.

[40] Polybius VI, 26, 10-42.

proposing emendations which he motivates in his commentary.[41] More often Lipsius draws attention to errors in Lascaris's translation. This is, for instance, the case in *De militia* III,1 where he attracts his companion's attention to the fact that Lascaris always translates γροσφομάχους as *pilanos* (armed with a javelin, the third line of the heavily-armed), instead of as *velites* (lightly-armed skirmishers). To prove his point, he cites Polybius himself as evidence, as well as Livy and Ovid:

> Yet, why do I translate γρόσφους (this is the Greek word) as *hastas*? Why not by *pila*, as in Lascaris? Because this is refuted by reason and by Polybius in person, who will soon give a description of *pila* [in *De militia* III, 4]. And this is also suggested by examples taken from Livy.[42]

In his commentary, Lipsius either elucidates (parts of) Polybius's sentences, or illustrates them with quotations from other sources, mostly historiographers, both Latin and Greek.

Time and again Lipsius praises Polybius and he seldom has doubts about his information. On the Roman camp, for instance, Lipsius remarks:

> Polybius does not extoll the Roman camp vaguely or lightly, but he calls it 'the aspect that most of all is worthy of being known'. And who is Polybius? The author who, more than anyone else, is sound of judgement, and nobody is more familiar with the subject or more experienced.

Nonetheless Lipsius also took into consideration the possibility that a situation might have changed since Polybius's age.

> That was what usually happened in those times, and each of the consuls was entrusted with two legions. [...] But later, with the expansion of the empire, when especially created *praetores* were sent to the provinces, and often also to the battle-fields, there is evidence confirming that more than four legions were recruited. Yet, why this 'later'? The same hap-

---

[41] In *De militia* I, 2 (= Polybius VI, 19, 2), Lipsius rightly presumed that the text was corrupt; he did not agree with the interpretations of his predecessors Carolus Sigonius and Nicolaus Grucchius and emendated the text into *twenty* years. Yet modern editors adopt Casaubon's solution, namely that ordinary military service lasted *sixteen* years. Cassius Dio might illuminate the question: until Augustus the full term was sixteen years (Cassius Dio XLIV, 25, 6), but this was increased to twenty years afterwards (Cassius Dio XLV, 23, 1).

[42] A similar example can be found in *De militia* III, 6 where Lipsius rejects Lascaris's translation of καρδιοφύλακα as 'cordituum' as 'quite learned, but far-fetched' and proposes 'pectoral' as a more common substitute.

pened even before Polybius's time, whenever the situation was perilous or seemed to be so.[43]

Lipsius confirms his observations by two examples from Livy.[44]

> Yet [he continues], during the second Punic War, when so many citizens' lives were lost, Livy even speaks of eighteen legions[45] and immediately afterwards of twenty-three legions.[46] However, when the Romans dreaded war with the Gauls, the Romans and their allies in Italy — according to Pliny III, 20[47] — gathered an army of 80,000 cavalry and 700,000 infantry, without any help from outside Italy, and even without Gallia Transpadana [the northern part of Italy, between the Alps and the river Po].

In conclusion, however, Lipsius states that he considers Polybius as the most trustworthy author.[48]

On rare occasions the Leuven humanist criticized Polybius, albeit in a rather mild way. With regard to VI, 19, 3 he reproaches Polybius for being obscure, notably when he states that everyone has to serve his full term 'with the exception of those whose census is below 400 drachmae, all of whom are employed in naval service'.[49] Lipsius points out that the situation as described by Polybius is different from Servius's conception.[50] The 400 drachmes (= 4,000 *asses*) were indeed the minimum property census for admission into the fifth class, but only considerably later. Lipsius presumes that the adaptation took place under the influence of the Punic Wars, when it would have been foolish to refuse such a large number of people wanting to serve in the army. According to Lipsius, a subdivision in three categories was

---

[43] *De militia* I, 3 where Polybius's information is completed by Livy *Ab urbe condita* X, 25, 16 and III, 8, 4.

[44] *Ab urbe condita* II, 30, 7 and IX, 19, 2 (*10 legions*).

[45] *Ab urbe condita* XXIV, 11, 2, instead of book XXIII as in the margin of *De militia*.

[46] *Ab urbe condita* XXV, 3, 7, instead of book XXIV as in the margin of *De militia*.

[47] *Naturalis historia* III, 20, 138.

[48] 'But Polybius, the most trustworthy author in these matters, after having summed up each nation's contribution, reaches a conclusion that is almost the same as Pliny's. Look it up if you want' (Polybius II, 24 on the Roman and the Italian forces in 225 BC). See Walbank, *Commentary* I, 196-9 where a detailed account and further bibliographic references are given.

[49] On this passage, see Walbank, *Commentary* I, 698.

[50] As tradition has it, Servius Tullius, the sixth king of Rome (middle of the sixth century BC), made a first attempt at military organisation by dividing the citizens into categories according to their wealth. The weapons they could afford determined their function in the army and thus the richest were enlisted as cavalry.

made in the fifth class, also dependent on the census, a thesis proved by a passage from Aulus Gellius. The ones who paid a lower census were not allowed in the army, but could enlist in the navy.

Elsewhere, Lipsius reproves Polybius for being superficial and incomplete. This is for instance the case in *De militia* V, 5 on the quadrangular form of the Roman camp (= Polybius VI, 31, 10):

> This is the only information our teacher gives about the camp's exterior appearance; he is rather superficial, yes even negligent, if I may say so. For though three aspects of the camp's exterior should be discussed — trench, rampart and gates — he only touches on the former two, without a single word on the third!

Next Lipsius discusses Polybius's first point of information, viz. that the Roman camp was quadrangular. Lipsius notes the difference with the Greeks who often preferred a circular form[51] and quotes Flavius Josephus[52] as evidence of the quadrangular Roman form. A few sentences further Lipsius remarks that Polybius does not give a single detail about the tents themselves and he fills this gap with evidence from Caesar, Festus, Flavius Josephus, Tacitus etc.[53] The same topic is discussed in the Greek army too, with references to Xenophon, Quintus Curtius and even the historian Procopius.

All in all, those moments of criticism are rare. Lipsius adopts an attitude of benevolence towards his main source without being overindulgent. He will complement, yet seldom correct him. There is a striking difference in the humanist's kind admonitions to Polybius and the severe reproaches he heaps upon Livy, as it becomes clear from the examples given.

In his final section of *De militia* Lipsius compares Roman military practice as described by Polybius to the contemporary situation.[54]

---

[51] With a citation of Xenophon, *Laced.* XII, 1.

[52] *Bellum Iudaicum* III, 77. Lipsius further refers to Vegetius III, 8 to prove that in the late Empire circular and even oblong forms had been known, depending on the circumstances. Vegetius's information is confirmed by other examples.

[53] Polybius VI, 31, 14.

[54] A somewhat overlooked English translation of this final chapter had been published by Johannes Bingham under the title *A Comparison of the Romane Manner of Warre with this of our Time, out of the End of the Fifth Booke of Iustus Lipsius, De militia.* Bingham added it as an appendix to his *Xenophon: the Historie of Xenophon* (London: 1623), recently reissued as *The English Experience. Its Record in early printed Books published in facsimile,* no 704 (Amsterdam – Norwood, N. J.: 1974).

Lipsius was categorical: even considering weaponry, the practice of the Ancients superseded the modern by far. The system of *recruitment* enabled the Romans to pick out the best and most honest men, which can hardly be said about the armies of the modern age. Lipsius strongly recommends that sovereigns call upon their subjects, instead of upon foreign mercenaries, to defend their country.[55] As to the *divisions*, Lipsius merely contented himself with sounding Antiquity's praises in a few sentences: there was nothing too much, nothing wanting, nothing for pomp or burden. The third aspect, the *armament*, is by far the most elaborated, probably because the Leuven professor had to prove the highly questionable thesis that slings, darts and arrows might, indeed, surpass or even be equal to the far-ranging and lethal sixteenth-century guns. He only granted to his presumed opponents that the modern weaponry was certainly more noisy: 'but whom does it terrify? Birds? For I cannot think that true soldiers would be moved by their sound or fiery sight, unless perhaps at the very first'. Lipsius also firmly believed that the Roman war engines could match modern heavy artillery. Fourthly, the *battle-array* seemed highly recommendable as well, because the three lines of battle (called *hastati, principes* and *triarii*), surrounded by the *velites* and the cavalry, were meant to gradually exhaust the enemy, while each Roman group was allowed to mount an attack and to retreat safely afterwards, protected by the other categories, and to regain its forces. In his final point, about *discipline*, the humanist directed scathing criticism against his contemporaries:

> Whichever way one esteems the discipline of the Ancients, now there is none at all, as the very soldiers will acknowledge. O shame! O dishonour! Even barbarians and Scythians outdo us in this aspect, for at least, they have some kind of standards; we have none!

As to the soldiers' duties, he particularly, although totally unrealistically criticized the fact that the modern soldiers did no longer retreat into the famous Roman camps. According to Lipsius the soldiers were ashamed to be labourers and they considered using a spade an

---

[55] Lipsius also referred to his *Politica*, particularly to V, 9 where the subject had been discussed. The idea that a state's army should be recruited from its subjects was advocated also by Machiavelli in his *Arte della guerra*. Foreign soldiers would still be needed, but they should only be used to support the regular army, as was the case in the Roman army.

ignominy. And he continues, sarcastically: 'You would think them of royal blood and men of great riches, yet if you look upon them, they are fairly the most abject of all, whom need and desperation forced into service'. Exercises do not exist any more:

> The drum sounds: they assemble, have their name put in the muster-books, they make a few changes to their attire, assume a forbidding look, play the ruffians and lose themselves in boozing: here comes the army!

Need it be said that the military code of honour is totally lacking as well? Especially in this final aspect Lipsius's high esteem of the ancient army becomes more than evident, for, according to him, the Roman discipline was 'not merely good, but the best of what was and ever will be, a true example from heaven'.

If one approaches this final chapter from the perspective of a present-day reader, one is inclined to dispose of Lipsius's conclusion as the weakest — although masterfully written — part of the whole treatise, because Lipsius preferred to draw a black-and-white picture of an over-idealized Roman army, and a haphazard cocktail of undisci-plined ruffians, such as he characterized the late sixteenth-century army. The awe-inspiring abundance of accurate information, supported by numerous quotations from authors throughout Antiquity, is exchanged for a whole arsenal of rhetorical tricks to underline the out-rageousness of the contemporary situation. Yet, the very fact that Lipsius was now using a totally different approach, as well as the rhetorical refinement of his style reveal that he considered this by far the most crucial part of the whole treatise.

Lipsius did, indeed, want to provide his readers with an exhaustive antiquarian's description of what the Roman army was like in all its aspects, but, above all, this strong accent on the needs of discipline and of a smoothly run army was inspired by the unremitting confrontation with the disorganisation and the explosive military situation in the Southern Netherlands.[56] According to Lipsius, the answer to this prob-

---

[56] The constant military troubles in the Southern Netherlands notwithstanding, Lipsius's point of view needs to be corrected: one should not forget the financial aspect — the poor and highly irregular payment —, nor the fact that even within mutinying troops a very strict organisation was respected. See on this subject Parker G., *The Army of Flanders and the Spanish Road 1567–1659. The Logistics of Spanish Victory and Defeat in the Low Countries' Wars* (Cambridge: 1972) esp. 25-49 ("Mobilisation") and

lem was discipline, not in the sense of harsh, severe punishments motivated by outrage, but as a concept of 'a strict training of a soldier to strength and virtue'[57], as it was defined and expounded in *Politica* V, 13.[58] Strength could be secured by *exercitium*, frequent drill — daily weapon practice, marching, digging of fortifications —, and *ordo*, strict regulations; virtue, on the other hand, by *coerctio* or self-discipline as a means to restrain licence and unruliness. *Coerctio* was interpreted with the help of the basic concepts of the Roman Stoa: *continentia* (self-control), *modestia* (moderation) and *abstinentia* (abstinence). Hence, what was theoretically stated in the fifth book of the *Politica*, was worked out with the practical example of the Roman military system in *De militia*. Oestreich even points out a parallel with the Jesuit system:

> The methodical ideas of Loyola the soldier thus find their way into the modern army. Daily exercise and hierarchic organisation, blind obedience and strict dicipline determine the spirit of military life as it was revived by Lipsius; its models were provided by the Jesuit champion of the *ecclesia militans* and by the Roman legions.[59]

In fact, this combination of Roman military expertise — both skills and regulations — and Stoic ethos made Lipsius's *De militia* a highly innovative treatise intended as a remedy for the failing military system of his contemporaries.

The rediscovery of Polybius as an historian, politician and military expert had been of considerable influence on sixteenth-century scholars. Yet this was not limited to study-rooms or libraries alone. Hardly had Lipsius's *De militia* come off the press in the middle of June 1595, than it found its way to the army of a reforming Prince, as foretold by the *auditor* in the opening dialogue. This sovereign proved, however, another one than the Spanish Crown Prince to whom the work was dedicated.[60]

185-206 ("Life in the army and Mutiny"). For instance, once the revolt was decided upon, the mutiners elected a leader to govern them and life within their strongholds was strictly regulated by a number of appropriate laws which had to be observed.

[57] Scil. 'severam conformationem militis ad robur et virtutem' in *Iusti Lipsi Politicorum sive civilis doctrinae libri sex. Qui ad principatum maxime spectant* (Leiden: 1589).

[58] In fact, the theories on a state's army as put forward in the fifth book of the *Politica* are highly clarifying for a correct and complete interpretation of *De militia*'s final chapter.

[59] Oestreich G., *Neostoicism and the Early Modern State*, ed. B. Oestreich and H.G. Königsberger, transl. D. McLintock (Cambridge: 1982) 54.

[60] See on this subject Hahlweg W., *Die Heeresreform der Oranier und die Antike* (Berlin:

116   JEANINE DE LANDTSHEER

Soon after the treatise's appearance the States General of the Northern Netherlands offered a copy to their commander-in-chief Count Maurits of Nassau, Prince of Orange, who had studied for three semesters at Leiden University (1583–1584). This present was well-chosen, because the Prince of Orange and his half brother, Willem Lodewijk, Stadholder of Friesland, had been working on their armies' reform for about ten years. Confronted with a many years' war against the mighty Spanish King, they wanted to improve their military efficiency and protect civil society from disruption by soldiers, who had become a real plague in the Southern Netherlands during the 1590s.[61] From 1590 on, a code of military conduct was frequently reprinted; its articles were read aloud to all recruits and repeated every year at the outset of the campaigning season. Breaches of discipline, even when entering conquered cities, were severely punished. On the other hand, the soldiers could count on a steady payment at relatively small intervals.[62] Troops in fixed garrisons were submitted to regular military exercises and duties to keep them from making themselves a nuisance to their civilian neighbours; the growing complexity of warfare, including the development of new and more sophisticated arms and tactics necessitated new forms of drill. Moreover, the frequent exercises, demonstrations of skills, agility and extreme coordination, made a profound impression on the civilians who watched their progress. Numerous accounts of this training have been preserved. Willem Lodewijk was the first to insist on an offensive war and to experiment with various types of military exercises to prepare his troops for it.[63] Studying ancient authors, he admired the vari-

---

1941); Idem, *Das Kriegsbuch des Grafen Johann von Nassau-Siegen, 1561–1623* (Wiesbaden: 1973); Oestreich G., "Der römische Stoïzismus und die oranische Heeresreform", 11-34; Israel J., *The Dutch Republic. Its Rise, Greatness, and Fall (1477–1806)* (Oxford: 1995) 267-75.

[61] See a survey in Parker, *The Army of Flanders*, 185-206, and a survey of the mutinies between October, 1570 – November, 1607, 290-2; Wynans G., "Les mutineries militaires de 1596 à 1606", *Standen en Landen* 39 (1966) 105-21.

[62] The delay — sometimes more than two years — in the pay had been the main problem behind the many mutinies in the Spanish army.

[63] Cf. Reyd E. van, *Oorspronck ende Voortganck vande Nederlandtsche Oorloghen* (Amsterdam: 1644) 250-1 (Van Reyd was Willem Lodewijk's secretary). At the beginning of 1589 the Stadholder addressed the States General 'om de Staten te beweghen dat sy niet als dus langh des vijandts aenval verwachten ende nae syne gheleghentheyt sich richten, maer selfs hem aentasten ende eenighe steden belegheren soude'. See also *Journaal van Anthonis Duyck, Advokaat-Fiskaal van den Raad van State (1591–1602)*, ed. L. Mulder, 3 vols (The Hague–Arnhem: 1862-1866) I, xvi-xvii.

ation of battle-arrays which were described in them, as well as the swiftness of movement: turning to and fro, opening and closing smoothly and without breaking ranks at a simple command. Thus he divided the cumbersome square formations into smaller, more agile units and started practicing in group fights and man-to-man combat, in the open and in more limited spaces, and trained his men to exacting standards. The first attempts were painful and seemed ridiculous to both spectators and the enemy.[64] It is a popular story that Willem Lodewijk had try-outs of the exercises to which he subjected his army, at home the evening before, on which occasions he substituted tin soldiers for his troops![65] In 1594 he proposed the 'volley' technique with successive lines of infantry moving through each other's ranks, firing volleys in succession, which was in fact an adaptation of what the Roman *hastati* (heavily-armed soldiers) did with their javelins. Of course, the new technique could only be successful if the soldiers were able to load and reload their guns, take up their positions and fire in well-synchronized movements, which was another aspect of their drill. The exercise-masters even made use of illustrations; some of them were collected in highly popular manuals by Jacob de Gheyn in 1607 and by Adam van Breen in 1619.[66] Even the appropriate commands for every movement were given!

Soon Willem Lodewijk's example was followed by Maurits.[67] On 16 July 1595, Gerardus Sandelinus, who had left Lipsius and Leuven University at the end of April and had returned to Leiden, informed his mentor:

---

[64] Van Reyd, *Oorspronck ende Voortganck*, 252.

[65] See for instance Japikse N., *De Geschiedenis van het Huis van Oranje-Nassau* (The Hague: 1948) I, 138-9.

[66] Gheyn J. de, *Wapenhandelinghe van Roers, Musquetten ende Spiessen. Achtervolghende de ordre van Syn Excellentie Maurits Prince van Orangie Grave van Nassau etc.* (Amsterdam: 1608); Breen A. van, *De Nassausche Wapen-handelinge van Schilt, Spies, Rappier ende Targe* (The Hague: 1618). Van Breen refers to Vegetius in his preface and to Lipsius's *De militia* III, 2 in another passage; see also Israel, *The Dutch Republic*, 269.

[67] 'Sijn Excellentie dede een derden deel van tvolck vuyte trancheen voeren op tvelt ende dede die in verscheyden slachordren stellen, keeren, wenden, swencken, breecken ende maecken, bijenvougen ende separeren, om tvolck te wennen heure fylen ende gelederen te houden ende om tbreecken, veranderen ofte swencken vande slachordre wille die niet te verlaeten ofte haer daerinne niet te confunderen, welcke exercitie in tijden van noot seer dienstelijck soude konnen wesen'; *Journaal van Anthonis Duyck* II, 635 (9 August 1595).

> In the meantime, now that our Count has some leisure in The Hague,
> he has been training his soldiers to fight in the Roman way: sixty heavi-
> ly-armed infantry with spears on one side and forty on the other armed
> with Roman shields, according to the ancient customs. There is a fight
> and for a while the party provided with shields is able to keep its posi-
> tion against its opponents, but finally it must yield to their adversaries'
> force and agility, though not without demonstrating its merit. Maurits,
> who is most inquisitive about such matters, has been brought to such
> experiments by information he found in Fabricius. It was quite a spec-
> tacle with the sound of a drum to accompany the soldiers' fervour.[68]

Similar exercises were observed on 6 August and were described by
Anthonis Duyck in his *Journaal*.[69] Lipsius reacted promptly:

> I am pleased to hear about Prince Maurits's military sense. It is a very
> good occasion, but — in my opinion — he should deploy his troops
> otherwise: he should not put one section, that is sixty soldiers, against
> sixty others, but a good number of maniples. For it is combined action
> and the mutual support, which grant power, as do the beams in a build-
> ing. The Roman legions have always defeated the phalanxes, but with
> joined forces. If you had deployed only a limited number of Roman
> warriors against a limited number of Macedonians, the outcome would
> have been different! All this, and other aspects, are clearly and expertly
> explained by Polybius. Nothing is better than the Thessalian cavalry,
> but taken as a whole body. If you break them up in smaller parties, they
> are unfit for war.[70]

The exercises happened in summer, winter and autumn; according to
Anthonis Duyck there were fifteen of them between August and October 1595. On 20 December 1595 Maurits had the forethought to provide the companies which were fighting with guns with an extra ration
(one third) of gunpowder for the time of their training. Another witness was Arend van Buchell, who noted in July 1598:

---

[68] ILE VIII, 95 07 16 S.

[69] Cf. Van Reyd, *Oorspronck ende Voortganck*, 252: 'Maer insonderheydt is het by
Graef Maurits seer behertight die syn krygsvolck daerinne neerstelyck dede oefenen
ende daer na is het by verscheydene Natien ook ghevolcht'. Duyck, *Journaal* II, 635
gives a description: 'Sijn Excellentie [Maurits] hadde overlange eenige groote
schilden ofte targes laeten maecken op de Romeynsche faecoen om te sien off men
daer mede een bataillon piecken soude konnen breecken, d'welc hij tot meermaelen
in den Haege hadde doen besoucken ende bevonden tot dien eynde van goede effecte
te wesen, waeromme hij deselve mede op desen dach in tleger onder de Engelsen
dede besoucken, die wel mette piecke vechten, ende bevont tselve mede alsoe, omdat
de targes door alle de piecken doordrongen'.

[70] ILE VIII, 95 08 04 S.

> The recruits meet twice or three times a week to learn how to keep their ranks, to change directions suddenly, to turn and to stride as soldiers. This is called *drillen*, a word with Anglo-Saxon roots, I think. This kind of training was quite frequent among the Romans, even in time of peace.[71]

In addition to the military practices, new techniques were established and scientifically reinforced by mathematicians such as Simon Stevin. Maurits even granted his officers and engineers the occasion to study at Leiden University. So the impulse for reforms, given by Willem Lodewijk and reaching back to the Roman army, was soon taken up by Prince Maurits, who gave the military reform the necessary scientific foundations and support. Thus Lipsius's reworking of Polybius's sixth book, which is perhaps surprising to modern readers, exercised great influence on the military practice of the House of Orange in the late sixteenth and seventeenth century. Subsequently the Dutch system was imitated on a larger scale by strategists in other European states until far into the seventeenth century.[72]

Appendix: Index of the dialogues with reference to Polybius VI
(or other basic texts)

Book I: The recruiting

Dial. 1: Introduction and praise of the Roman army
Dial. 2: Method and order of the treatise; on levy, commanders and payment
    (= Polybius VI, 19, 1-4)
Dial. 3: Enrolment procedures, assignment of the tribunes to the legions etc.
    (= Polybius VI, 19, 5 - 20, 7)
Dial. 4: Sudden levy, punishment for not answering the call, exemptions
Dial. 5: Enrolment of the cavalry (= Polybius VI, 20, 9)
Dial. 6: Taking of the oath of allegiance (= Polybius VI, 21, 1-3)
Dial. 7: Selection of the allies. Distinction between the auxiliaries (= Polybius VI, 21, 4-5)
Dial. 8: The volunteers: meaning of name, numbers, ranks

---

[71] Buchell A. van, *Diarium, 1560–1599*, ed. G. Brom–L.A. van Langeraad, Werken uitgegeven door het Historisch Gezelschap gevestigd te Utrecht III, 12 (Amsterdam: 1907) 470.

[72] See Röck C., "Römische Schlachtordnungen im 17. Jahrhundert?" in *Tradita et inventa: Beiträge zur Rezeption der Antike*, ed. M. Baumbach, Bibliothek der Klassischen Altertumswissenschaften, N.F., 2nd series, vol 106 (Heidelberg: 2000) 165-86.

Dial. 9: Recruiting officers, soldiers appointed by their masters, tattoos

Book II: The sections and their commanders

Dial. 1: Introduction, four categories: lightly-armed soldiers and the three lines of heavily-armed troops (= Polybius VI, 21, 6-10)
Dial. 2: The maniple: number – Greek names (= Polybius VI, 24, 3-5)
Dial. 3: Confrontation of Polybius and Livy, *Ab urbe condita* VIII, 8, 2-8 with corrections
Dial. 4: The *cohors*: number, first *cohors*, the general's *cohors*
Dial. 5: The legion and how it was gradually enlarged
Dial. 6: Composition of the cavalry, the *turma*, their number (= Polybius VI, 25, 1a)
Dial. 7: Division of the allies, the auxiliaries (= Polybius VI, 26, 6-9)
Dial. 8: The captains (*centuriones*): numbers, rank and prerogatives (= Polybius VI, 24, 1-8)
Dial. 9: The higher officers (military tribunes): election, distinction, duties, *insignia*
Dial. 10: The leaders of the allies (= Polybius VI, 25, 1-2; 26, 5)
Dial. 11: The official assistant assigned to a general (*legatus*)
Dial. 12: The general (*imperator*)

Book III: The arms

Dial. 1: The lightly-armed soldiers: origins, equipment: type of sword, spear, shield, helmet (= Polybius VI, 22, 1-4)
Dial. 2: The heavily-armed soldiers: the oblong shield (*scutum*; dimensions, origin, examples) (= Polybius VI, 23, 1-5)
Dial. 3: The Spanish sword (origin, use, quality) (= Polybius VI, 23, 6-7)
Dial. 4: The javelin (length, form, strength, evolution) (= Polybius VI, 23, 8-11)
Dial. 5: The helmet and different types of crests (= Polybius VI, 23, 12-3)
Dial. 6: The leather cuirass (*lorica*) and its different types (= Polybius VI, 23, 14-6)
Dial. 7: The leggings; the cavalry's arms (= Polybius VI, 25, 3-11)
Dial. 8: Numidian cavalry

Book IV: The battle-array

Dial. 1: Disposition of the army and the usual battle-array (= Livy, *Ab urbe condita* VIII, 8, 9-13)
Dial. 2: Position of the lightly-armed troops, idem of cavalry and allies
Dial. 3: Standards and banners: definition, position
Dial. 4: Location of commanders and soldiers; penalty for breaking the order

Dial. 5: Different types of standards, esteem
Dial. 6: Double and triple battle-arrays
Dial. 7: Some other types
Dial. 8: Example of some fights (Crassus, Manlius, Caesar with Afranius, Caesar with Pompeius) (Plutarch, *Crassus* 23, 3-4; Livy, *Ab urbe condita* VIII, 9, 2-3; Caesar, *Bellum civile* I, 83, 1-2; Caesar, *Bellum civile* III, 88, 1-5; Caesar, *Bellum civile* III, 89, 1-4)
Dial. 9: Address of the troops before the fight; the troops' approval or disapproval
Dial. 10: Trumpets, horns and other military musical instruments
Dial. 11: War- and battle-cries
Dial. 12: Battle-signal; the red battle-banner

Book V: The discipline

Dial. 1: The Roman camp (= Polybius VI, 26, 10-2)
Dial. 2: The general's tent (= Polybius VI, 27, 1-2)
Dial. 3: Quarters for the officers and the special troops (= Polybius VI, 27, 3-7; 31, 1-9)
Dial. 4: Quarters for ordinary troops and allies (= Polybius VI, 28, 1-30, 6)
Dial. 5: Tents, trenches, ramparts, gates (= Polybius VI, 31, 10-4; 34, 1-2)
Dial. 6: Camp-duties: trenches, ramparts, watches; exemptions
Dial. 7: Enlarged or double camps (– Polybius VI, 19, 32, 3-8)
Dial. 8: Functions of tribunes, cavalry and others (= Polybius VI, 33, 3-12)
Dial. 9: Organisation and inspection of sentries, watch-words, rounds (= Polybius VI, 34, 7-12; 35, 1-7; 35, 8 - 37, 1)
Dial. 10: Management of the camp (= Polybius VI, 34, 3-6)
Dial. 11: Luggage
Dial. 12: Marching order, army train; the camp's marking off (= Polybius VI, 40, 1 - 42, 5)
Dial. 13: Examples of military work preparing a siege
Dial. 14: Drilling (marching – weapons) (Flavius Josephus *Bellum Iudaicum* III, 71-75)
Dial. 15: Theft within the camp; booty (= Polybius VI, 33, 1-2)
Dial. 16: Soldier's pay (origin and rise); rations of corn and barley (= Polybius VI, 39, 12-5)
Dial. 17: Rewards (weapons, bracelets, necklaces, medals, spoils) (= Polybius VI, 39, 1-11)
Dial. 18: Penalties (by whom inflicted, various types), disgrace (= Polybius VI, 37, 7-13; 38, 1-4)
Dial. 19: Discharge from service (four types: honourable, on account of ill health, through favour, through disgrace); profits
Dial. 20: Conclusion of the five books. Short comparison between ancient and contemporary army practices.

Selective Bibliography

Exercise of Arms. Warfare in the Netherlands, 1568–1648, ed. M. van der Hoeven (Leiden: 1997)

GERLO A. – VERVLIET H.D.L. – VERTESSEN I., *La correspondance de Juste Lipse conservée au Musée Plantin-Moretus* (Antwerp: 1967)

HAHLWEG W., *Die Heeresreform der Oranier und die Antike* (Berlin: 1941)

HAHLWEG W., *Das Kriegsbuch des Grafen Johann von Nassau-Siegen, 1561–1623* (Wiesbaden: 1973)

ISRAEL J., *The Dutch Republic. Its Rise, Greatness, and Fall (1477–1806)* (Oxford: 1995)

ILE: *Iusti Lipsi Epistolae*, ed. A. Gerlo – M.A. Nauwelaerts – H.D.L. Vervliet and others (Brussels: 1978 ff.)

Journaal van Anthonis Duyck, Advokaat-Fiskaal van den Raad van State (1591–1602), ed. L. Mulder, 3 vols (The Hague–Arnhem: 1862–1866)

LIPSIUS J., *De militia Romana* (Antwerp: 1595–1596)

MOMIGLIANO A., "Polybius between the English and the Turks", in *Sesto Contributo alla storia Degli Studi Classici e del mondo antico*, Storia e letteratura. Raccolta di studi e testi 149 (Rome: 1980) 125-41

MOMIGLIANO A., "Polybius' Reappearance in Western Europe", in *Sesto Contributo alla storia Degli Studi Classici e del mondo antico*, Storia e letteratura. Raccolta di studi e testi, 149 (Rome: 1980) 103-23

OESTREICH G., *Neostoicism and the Early Modern State*, ed. B. Oestreich and H.G. Königsberger, transl. D. McLintock (Cambridge: 1982)

OESTREICH G., "Der römische Stoïzismus und die oranische Heeresreform", in *Geist und Gestalt der frühmodernen Staates* (Berlin: 1969)

PARKER G., *The Army of Flanders and the Spanish Road 1567–1659. The Logistics of Spanish Victory and Defeat in the Low Countries' Wars* (Cambridge: 1972)

REYD E. van, *Oorspronck ende Voortganck vande Nederlandtsche Oorloghen* (Amsterdam: 1644)

WALBANK F.W., *A Historical Commentary on Polybius*, 3 vols (Oxford: 1957)

WALBANK F.W., *Polybius* (Berkeley–Los Angeles–London: 1972).

"THE GRANDEUR THAT WAS ROME": SCHOLARLY ANALYSIS AND PIOUS AWE IN LIPSIUS'S *ADMIRANDA**

Marc Laureys

In memory of Jozef IJsewijn,
who found Rome in Rome

The cultural-historical monograph about ancient Rome, *Admiranda sive de magnitudine Romana libri IV*, published by Justus Lipsius (1547–1606)[1] in 1598, has not always been correctly understood by modern scholars. The treatise, for example, heads the long list, assembled by A.H. Luijdjens,[2] of descriptions of Italy and Rome written or published in the Low Countries. It is followed there by such works as the *Iter Italicum* of Arnoldus Buchelius, the *Itinerarium Italiae* of Franciscus Schot-

---

* This article is a revised version of my part of the essay I co-authored with Jan Papy in the exhibit catalogue *Justus Lipsius (1547–1606) en het Plantijnse huis*, ed. R. Dusoir–J. De Landtsheer–D. Imhof (Antwerp: 1997) 129-37.

[1] Lipsius studies are thriving as never before since the numerous scholarly events and initiatives connected with the 450th anniversary of his birth in 1997. A good idea of current tendencies in the research on Lipsius, as well as relevant bibliography, can be gained from the following: *Juste Lipse en son temps*, ed. C. Mouchel, Colloques, congrès et conférences sur la Renaissance 6 (Paris: 1996) (on pp. 523-34 one finds a "Bibliographie des ouvrages critiques concernant Juste Lipse"); *Lipsius en Leuven. Catalogus van de tentoonstelling in de Centrale Bibliotheek te Leuven*, ed. G. Tournoy – J. Papy – J. De Landtsheer, Supplementa Humanistica Lovaniensia 13 (Leuven: 1997); *Lipsius in Leiden. Studies in the Life and Works of a Great Humanist on the Occasion of his 450th Anniversary*, ed. K. Enenkel–C.L. Heesakkers (Voorthuizen: 1997); *Justus Lipsius en het Plantijnse huis*; *The world of Justus Lipsius: A contribution towards his intellectual biography*, ed. M. Laureys, with the assistance of C. Bräunl – S. Mertens – R. Seibert-Kemp [=*Bulletin de l'Institut Historique Belge de Rome* 68] (Brussels–Rome: 1998) (especially 15-42 R. De Smet, "Les études lipsiennes 1987–1997: état de la question"). *Justus Lipsius, Europae Lumen et Columen. Proceedings of the International Colloquium Leuven, 17-19 September 1997*, ed. G. Tournoy – J. De Landtsheer – J. Papy, Supplementa Humanistica Lovaniensia 15 (Leuven: 1999); The older survey of his life and works by Bouchery, "Waarom Justus Lipsius gevierd?", *Mededelingen van de Koninklijke Vlaamse Academie voor Wetenschappen, Letteren en Schone Kunsten van België*, Klasse der Letteren 11, 8 (Brussels: 1949) 9-70 is still invaluable.

[2] Luijdjens A.H., "Chronologische lijst van beschrijvingen van Italië en Rome tot 1900 in de Nederlanden geschreven of verschenen", *Mededelingen van het Nederlands Historisch Instituut te Rome*, 2nd *series*, 1 (1931) 206. A few addenda are found in the exhibit catalogue *Herinneringen aan Italië. Kunst en toerisme in de 18de eeuw*, ed. R. de Leeuw (Zwolle: 1984) 259-61.

tus and the *Italia antiqua* of Philippus Cluverius. Similar misinterpretations can be found elsewhere, too.[3] They are probably inspired by the fact that Lipsius published his *Admiranda* shortly before the Holy Year 1600. Before and during such Holy Years, the production of guides to and descriptions of Rome traditionally reached a peak. In 1600, moreover, Lipsius's work was used for propaganda purposes in the wake of the Holy Year. In that year Lipsius's *Admiranda* appeared (in its second, slightly revised edition, which Lipsius had published the year before) in Rome, joined under the same cover with Thomas Stapleton's[4] *Vere Admiranda seu de magnitudine Romanae ecclesiae*, posthumously published in 1599. The new volume bore the telling subtitle: *Libri omnibus Christianis, maxime Romam adeuntibus, tam necessarii quam utiles* (*Books both necessary and useful for all Christians, most of all those going to visit Rome*). This joint publication had been instigated by the papal finance minister Bernardinus Paulinus and was carried out by the caustic convert Kaspar Schoppe (1576–1649).[5] His frenetic zeal for the Catholic cause pushed him to state his aim much more strongly in the preface to this double edition than he had done in his previous correspondence with Lipsius on the issue:[6] Lipsius and Stapleton were presented as gladiators against the heretics and ideal guides for pilgrims in the Holy Year.

Lipsius himself, however, had no intention of writing a manual or guide for travellers to Rome. In fact, Lipsius's views on the journey to Rome had always been somewhat ambivalent. In 1578 he had written an enthusiastic letter to the young nobleman Philippe de Lannoy, who was about to depart for an educational journey to Italy.[7] The epistle contained so much useful advice that it quickly acquired a

---

[3] See for example Etter E.-L., *Tacitus in der Geistesgeschichte des 16. und 17. Jahrhunderts*, Basler Beiträge zur Geschichtswissenschaft 103 (Basle–Stuttgart: 1966) 115, n. 114. Her appraisal of the *Admiranda* as a reflection of Lipsius's impressions of Rome misses the essence of the treatise completely; Lipsius recalls his stay in Rome only in passing (III, 2).

[4] Thomas Stapleton (1535–1598), an English Catholic theologian and controversialist, who worked mainly in Douai and Leuven; see O'Connell M.R., *Thomas Stapleton and the Counter-Reformation*, Yale Publications in Religion 9 (New Haven–London: 1964).

[5] Schoppe had adopted the Roman Catholic faith in 1598 and became one of the most effective papal publicists of his time. For a recent appraisal see the articles collected in *Kaspar Schoppe (1576–1649). Philologe im Dienste der Gegenreformation*, ed. H. Jaumann, Zeitsprünge. Forschungen zur Frühen Neuzeit, vol 2, 3/4 (Frankfurt a. M.: 1998).

[6] Schoppe realized that Lipsius had had different objectives and a different public in mind for his *Admiranda*; see ILE XIII, 00 01 07.

[7] ILE I, 78 04 03 (= *Cent. misc.* I, 22).

programmatic status and enjoyed a wide circulation in separate editions — not only in Latin, but also in translations into Dutch, French, and English —, as well as in collective volumes of travel literature.[8] For all his excitement about De Lannoy's voyage, however, Lipsius was careful to warn against the moral dangers such a trip would entail. A young man could easily fall victim to the many allurements for which Italy was notorious, the female charm of Mediterranean beauties being among the most formidable traps. Time and again Lipsius repeated these concerns; in a letter from 1587 to the young Dutch student Johannes Duystius, for example, he referred explicitly to the counsel given to De Lannoy.[9] In the preface to his *De amphitheatris quae extra Romam libellus* (*On amphitheatres outside Rome*, 1584), addressed to Abraham Ortelius,[10] Lipsius even declared that an educational journey to Italy was fruitful only for well-prepared adults and posed too great a risk at a youthful age. At the same time he minimized the benefit reaped from his own stay in Rome (1568–1570); looking back on those years, he said he had only gained superficial impressions. Lipsius's critical reflections came at a time when the educational value of travel was intensely debated. The moral hazards of travel, to be sure, had been a stock criticism since the Middle Ages, and were instilled into the minds of (prospective) travellers through the ever expanding medium of travel guides, in which these perils were often discussed. The popular *Guida romana* for foreign visitors, for example, contained a chapter called *Delle donne romane*;[11] Lipsius may have had this text in mind when he cautioned Philippe de Lannoy.[12] But travel was also questioned more substantially. In *The Scholemaster* (1570) Roger Ascham denounced extensively the moral risks connected with the journey to Italy. Joseph Stradling added to his English translation (1592) of Lipsius's letter to De Lannoy so

---

[8] For the transmission of this letter in print see *Bibliotheca Belgica* III, 1086.

[9] ILE II, 87 06 01 D (= *Cent. misc.* II, 32).

[10] ILE II, 84 01 05 O.

[11] This guide was first printed in 1557 as an appendix to *Le cose maravigliose dell'alma città di Roma* and reissued in several later editions of the *Cose maravigliose*; see Schudt L., *Le guide di Roma. Materialien zu einer Geschichte der römischen Topographie* (Vienna–Augsburg: 1930) 28-31 and 198-206. The entire text is transcribed in Baskerville E.J., *The English Traveller to Italy 1547–1560* (Ph.D. diss., Columbia University: 1967) 281-93.

[12] Lipsius's warnings were not purely academic, though. In his *Epistolicae quaestiones* IV, 12, he relates the fatal outcome of a liaison a friend of his had had in Naples. This text is pointed out by Papy J., "*Italiam vestram amo supra omnes terras!* Lipsius' Attitude towards Italy and Italian Humanism of the Late Sixteenth Century", *Humanistica Lovaniensia* 47 (1998) 266.

many rather critical considerations of his own that it hardly conveyed the exalted tone of the original. From these strictures it was but a small step to Joseph Hall's *Quo vadis? A just censure of travell* (1617), in which travel was condemned outright as a pernicious pastime.[13]

Lipsius's wavering attitude vis-à-vis the journey to Italy should be considered against the background of these contemporary discussions, but may have been accentuated by the stringencies he experienced during his final tenure at the University of Leuven (1592–1606), after he left Leiden rather spectacularly and returned to the Catholic fold. Over many years he systematically turned down the numerous invitations he received from prestigious institutions in Italy and elsewhere, while at the same time regularly complaining to the local authorities about his all too modest salary, which made it that more difficult to decline the generous offers from abroad. In 1599 this dilemma reached a climax, when he started planning a visit to Rome for the Holy Year 1600,[14] after he had received an invitation from Cardinal Francesco Sforza,[15] to whom he had offered a copy of his *Admiranda*. Although he announced his intention to a number of his friends and seemed resolved to depart, he changed his mind some months later and cancelled the whole project. The reasons he gave to justify this sudden decision, his bad health and a plague epidemic in Italy, do not seem to tell the whole story, and at times he shrouded the entire incident in rather cryptic terms. In the *Admiranda*, too, he expressed his desire to return to Rome, but in spite of the obvious opportunities that had come his way, he felt resigned to accept the impossibility of that wish (III, 2): 'First my fate withheld me, soon also the King, the former by a hidden resolution, the latter by open generosity. In sum, I see I have to die in the Low Countries as a native of this land, even if I do not despair of visiting Rome again in passing'.[16] We may reason-

---

[13] For a discussion of these texts see Warneke S., *Images of the Educational Traveller in Early Modern England*, Brill's Studies in Intellectual History 58 (Leiden–New York–Cologne: 1995); see also Schoneveld, C., "De vleesgeworden duivel? Het beeld van de reiziger in de Engelse literatuur van de Renaissance", in *Reizen en reizigers in de Renaissance. Eigen en vreemd in oude en nieuwe werelden*, ed. K. Enenkel – P. van Heck – B. Westerweel (Amsterdam: 1998) 59-67.

[14] For a detailed account of this whole episode (with references to all of Lipsius's letters connected with it) see Papy, "*Italiam vestram amo*", 249-54.

[15] See *Sylloges epistolarum a viris illustribus scriptarum tomi V*, ed. P. Burmannus (Leiden: 1724–1727) II, 39-40, *epistula* 752.

[16] 'Fatum meum primo me tenuit, mox et rex, illud occulto decreto, hic aperta benignitate. Ad summam, video Belgae mihi in Belgis moriendum, etsi de revisenda ea obiter non despero'. A similar phrase can be found in ILE 00 01 14 B (= *Cent. misc.*

ably assume that Lipsius, after he decided to return to his old university, was watched rather carefully in Leuven and that the authorities were anxious not to lose this widely renowned and highly publicized professor again. Already in 1593 it had been made clear to him that he should not count on unlimited freedom to travel abroad.[17] No wonder, then, that Lipsius repeatedly and emphatically begged the counsellors of the Spanish king in Brussels for permission to go to Rome. On the other hand, Lipsius certainly considered his move from Leiden to Leuven a return home and often in later years voiced his deep affection for his native Brabant, and Leuven in particular, both as a safe Catholic haven and an ideal resting-place after the many journeys that had marked his life and career.[18] Various factors, therefore, such as political pressure, Stoic resignation, Catholic conviction, and local patriotism, were at work in the curious affair of the failed visit to Rome. All these elements were intimately connected with Lipsius's previous career, and carefully weighed and expressed in the pertinent letters he chose to publish in his *Centuriae*.[19] They add, moreover, particular poignancy to the complex relationship with Italy that Lipsius shared with almost every cultured Northern European of the sixteenth and seventeenth centuries, marked as they all were by the stark and even painful contrasts between classical and modern Italy in general and Rome in particular, which resulted in a constant tension between Italophilia and Italophobia.[20]

III, 54): 'Fatalem vim magis et magis in dies agnosco, in publicis, in privatis, in me ipso. Ratio omnis vellet fortasse non peregrinari me, sed adire; tamen maneo et video divinitus decretum Lipsium in Belgis mori' ('I recognize ever more from day to day a fatal power, in matters public and private, and in myself. Every reason would have wanted me perhaps not to travel around [through Italy], but to visit [Rome]; yet I stay and see that it has been decreed from heaven that Lipsius die in the Low Countries'). I thank Jan Papy for drawing my attention to this passage. Still in the same vein, Lipsius blamed the goddess of Fate in a letter from 1603 (ILE 03 03 16 B [= *Cent. misc.* V, 18]): 'Quid tamen tenuit? Mala illa Parca, quae filum mihi nevit haud abire, quae filum mihi nevit hic obire' ('What kept me, though? That bad goddess of Fate, who made it my destiny not to go away, who made it my destiny to die here').

[17] ILE VI, 93 06 19: 'Respondit te Belgam et Regis subditum esse, patriam non debere relinquere, ut te ad exteras nationes conferas' ('[The Counsellor Christophe d'Assonleville] answered that you are a native of the Low Countries and a subject of the King, and that you ought not to leave your fatherland to go to foreign countries').

[18] See Papy, "*Italiam vestram amo*", 274-6.

[19] Papy, "*Italiam vestram amo*", 267-70 discusses the *Centuria ad Italos et Hispanos* from this perspective.

[20] I borrow these terms from Burke P., "The Uses of Italy", in *The Renaissance in National Context*, ed. R. Porter – M. Teich (Cambridge: 1992) 13. Italy was perceived more and more as a vast but dead repository of ancient wisdom and culture. For the

The *Admiranda sive de magnitudine Romana*, then, as Lipsius conceived them, do not belong to the genre of travel literature concerning Rome. The mere title shows that Lipsius approached Rome from a quite different viewpoint in this treatise. He did not just want to describe Rome, but aimed to capture and elucidate the essence of its greatness. For both these objectives, interpretation as well as description, Lipsius found inspiration in traditions that hark back to classical Antiquity itself.

Admiranda is attested as a book title in Roman literature. Pliny the Elder (*Naturalis historia* XXXI, 12 and 51) and Columella (III, 8, 2) refer to a work with this title, allegedly composed by Cicero. Although the few secondary quotations remaining hardly suffice to reconstruct the contents of this lost (and totally forgotten) treatise of Cicero, scholars have presumed it might have been a collection of wondrous phenomena and tales, inspired by Hellenistic examples, such as a composition by Theopompus.[21] More relevant than this book title, however, is a related concept that runs through the history of the perception of Rome and expresses the sense of awe and wonder people have always experienced at the sight of the Eternal City.[22] According to Lucan, Caesar marvelled at the walls of Rome when he returned from his military campaigns in Gaul (Lucan, *Pharsalia* III, 90: 'miratusque suae [...] moenia Romae'). Ammianus Marcellinus recounts in a famous passage of his *Res gestae* (XVI, 10, 1-7) how the Emperor Constantius

---

French point of view in a slightly later period, see Waquet F., *Le modèle français et l'Italie savante. Conscience de soi et perception de l'autre dans la république des lettres (1660–1750)*, Collection de l'École française de Rome 117 (Rome–Paris: 1989) especially 41-62 and 253-96. Renaissance poets expressed this tension with the topos of 'the (difficult) quest for Rome in Rome'; for a rich and suggestive discussion in a wide range of texts see Tucker G.H., *The Poet's Odyssey. Joachim du Bellay and the* Antiquitez de Rome (Oxford: 1992) especially 55-104 (but much of the rest of this book is highly relevant to this topic as well). Lipsius, too, evoked this theme in an elegy, addressed to his friend Janus Lernutius and entitled *De Urbe Roma* (verses 21-2); here again he elaborated on the dangerous pitfalls crafted by Roman women (verses 23-52). See Crombruggen H. van, *Janus Lernutius (1545–1619). Een biografische studie*, Verhandelingen van de Koninklijke Vlaamse Academie voor Wetenschappen, Letteren en Schone Kunsten van België, Klasse der Letteren 17, 23 (Brussels: 1955) 21; for a new edition and discussion see Papy J., "Justus Lipsius, Rome en de Romereis: zoektocht naar een oude mythe?", *Kleio* 26 (1997) 120-6.

[21] Teuffel W.S. – Kroll W. – Skutsch F., *Geschichte der römischen Literatur*, vol 1 (Leipzig: 1916⁶) 423-4; Schanz M. – Hosius C., *Geschichte der römischen Literatur*, vol 1, Handbuch der Altertumswissenschaft VIII, 1 (Munich: 1927⁴) 534-5.

[22] For a discussion of this concept in classical Latin literature, see Edwards C., *Writing Rome. Textual Approaches to the City* (Cambridge: 1996) 96-109.

II on a visit to Rome in 357 was filled with reverence and amazement while gazing at the remains of the ancient city, silent witnesses to a glorious past. Nearly two centuries later, Cassiodorus called the entire city one great *miraculum* (*Variae* VII, 15, 5)[23]. Especially during the Middle Ages, however, Rome became a city of wonders (*mirabilia*), pagan and Christian alike, in the eyes of the countless pilgrims who visited the city. This perception gradually grew so dominant that it also influenced the more learned descriptions, like the *Mirabilia Urbis Romae*, usually attributed to Benedictus Canonicus and dated to the middle of the twelfth century. In the *Mirabilia* Rome is presented as a texture of timeless relics that transcend the earthly sphere and point to the heavenly Kingdom. In this supernatural context the remains of the pagan legacy of Rome are sublimated as well.[24]

It is important to realize how strongly these ideas continued to colour the discourse on Rome during the Renaissance. Not only were the *Mirabilia* themselves printed and translated dozens of times, but new descriptions of Rome were composed after their model, such as Francesco Albertini's *Opusculum de mirabilibus novae et veteris urbis Romae* and Fra Mariano da Firenze's *Itinerarium urbis Romae* (both early sixteenth century). Even in the scholarly literature on ancient Rome, furthermore, this basically a-historical approach left its traces. Particular ly in fifteenth-century Roman humanism, marked by the papal Curia, the 'pilgrim perception'[25] largely conditioned the way in which Rome was understood. The Roman humanists, active as they were in an eminently clerical milieu, tried to harmonize the age-old contrast between pagan and Christian Rome by emphasizing the timeless and exemplary aspects of the Eternal City. The ruins spread out over the city were the most enduring vestiges of Rome's glorious past. Antiquarian studies, therefore, always constituted one of the essential components of Roman humanism. Even though the *Roma instaurata* and the *Roma triumphans* of Flavio Biondo (1392–1463)[26] immensely

---

[23] Lipsius quotes the testimonies of Ammianus Marcellinus and Cassiodorus in *Admiranda* III, 5.

[24] For the 'sacro-historical topography' of the *Mirabilia*, see Kinney D., "*Mirabilia Urbis Romae*", in *The Classics in the Middle Ages*, ed. A.S. Bernardo – S. Levin, Medieval and Renaissance Texts and Studies 69 (Binghamton, NY: 1990) 209.

[25] I borrow this term from Stinger C.L., *The Renaissance in Rome* (Bloomington: 1985) 34 and 43; on the persistence of this pilgrim perception in the Renaissance, see ibid., 31-46; on its impact on Renaissance antiquarian scholarship, see ibid., 59-72.

[26] The best brief account of the life and work of this luminary of Roman humanism is Fubini R., "Biondo Flavio", in *Dizionario biografico degli Italiani* X (1968) 536-9.

advanced the knowledge of the topography and the antiquities of Rome, the Rome he wanted to reconstruct was not a historical entity, but rather a model of virtue rising above time and space:

> Thus we have begun to try and see if we will be able to set and lay out before the eyes and mind of our fellow men who have superior talents and knowledge the mirror, the model, the image, the wisdom of all virtue and principle of good, sacred and propitious living, the flourishing city of Rome that blessed Augustine desired to see triumphant.[27]

Ideas such as these regained a particular prominence during the Counter-Reformation. Once again the popes strenuously promoted an image of Rome as a reborn holy city,[28] in which all traces of the pagan past had been entirely assimilated by the Christian tradition. In the sacred oratory of the second half of the sixteenth century this concept was elaborated in various forms by curial orators,[29] who in this way continued some basic themes of their fifteenth-century predecessors,[30] even if the essence of the relationship between pagan and Christian Rome was now more often interpreted quite militantly as a triumph of Christendom over the pagan heritage, rather than as a harmonious symbiosis of the two realms. At any rate, what was deemed particularly important now was to convey this concept of Rome to as wide an audience as possible. Just as the Baroque art of the Counter-Reformation aimed to imprint upon the minds of the beholders the fundamental truths of post-Tridentine Catholic faith, ways were sought to transmit as efficiently as possible this renewed image of Rome to the thousands who came and visited the city. In this process the Holy Years received

---

[27] 'Ita coepimus tentare si speculum, exemplar, imaginem, doctrinam omnis virtutis et bene, sancte ac feliciter vivendi rationis, Urbem Romam florentem ac qualem beatus Aurelius Augustinus triumphantem videre desideravit, nostrorum hominum ingenio et doctrina valentium oculis et menti subicere ac proponere poterimus'. The text is quoted by Stinger, *Renaissance in Rome*, 70 and 350, n. 202. It is unclear to which passage in Augustine's works this reference might apply. There is a good chance that the source text lies hidden in a medieval commentary to *De civitate Dei*.

[28] See Gamrath H., *Roma sancta renovata. Studi sull'urbanistica di Roma nella seconda metà del sec. XVI con particolare riferimento al pontificato di Sisto V (1585–1590)*, Analecta Romana Instituti Danici, supplementum XII (Rome: 1987) especially 123-64.

[29] See McGinness F.J., "The Rhetoric of Praise and the New Rome of the Counter-Reformation", in *Rom als Idee*, ed. B. Kytzler, Wege der Forschung 656 (Darmstadt: 1993) especially 167-90; Idem, *Right Thinking and Sacred Oratory in Counter-Reformation Rome* (Princeton, N.J.: 1995).

[30] See O'Malley J.W., *Praise and Blame in Renaissance Rome. Rhetoric, Doctrine, and Reform in the Sacred Orators of the Papal Court, c. 1450–1521*, Duke monographs in medieval and Renaissance studies 3 (Durham, N.C.: 1979) 207-25.

a new significance. The first Holy Year after the conclusion of the
Council of Trent especially, 1575, was meticulously prepared by Pope
Gregory XIII with a view to celebrating the hallowed status of the
Eternal City. In numerous pious publications the unique position of
Rome was explained and the special character of a voyage to Rome as
a spiritual experience was emphasized. The most widely circulating
text of this kind was a pastoral letter written by Cardinal Carlo Borromeo and appended to a number of editions of the *Cose maravigliose* of
1575. In this letter he admonished the pilgrims as follows:

> With similar affection and devotion, beloved sons, you should take this
> voyage upon yourselves, leaving behind every sort of worldly curiosity
> and vanity, for this would be travelling for the world and not for Christ.
> Nor should you be satisfied solely by going to Rome to visit those
> churches and relics of the saints, but to this you should add true and
> perfect penitence, so as to make this trip in the grace of God and with
> such a repression of your flesh and senses that it also serves for the
> atonement of our sins.[31]

Exhortations such as these did not miss their effect, as we can gather
from several travel accounts composed by pilgrims. An interesting testimony is provided by the German chaplain Jakob Rabus, who wrote
up his experiences on his visit to Rome in 1575. He clearly had not
conceived his trip to Rome just as a spiritual purification, but had also
shown interest for the monuments of classical Rome. This is how he
defended himself:

> Wo ich dann sieh, daß diese meine Arbeit dem günstigen Leser nit gar
> mißfallen wird, will ich mich zu Beschreibung der alten Monumenten
> und Antiquitäten, so in der h. Stadt Rom zu sehen, hiermit auch
> erboten haben. Denn obschon wohl Ablaß das Fürnehmst sein soll,
> darnach der Pilgram trachten soll, jedoch und dieweil man zwischen
> dem, daß man zu Erhebung des Anlaß eilt und zeucht, auf den Straßen
> allenthalben solche Antiquitates sehen kann, kann es so gar nit scha-
> den, wann einer schon weiß, wo er gehe oder stehe, und also ein Er-
> kenntnis schöpft der alten Welt und sich darneben der Unbeständigkeit

---

[31] "Lettera pastorale di Monsignor [...] Card. Borromeo", in *Le cose maravigliose dell'
alma città di Roma* (Rome: 1575) f. 101r-v: 'Con simile affetto et divotione dovete, figliuoli diletti, ricevere questa peregrinatione, lasciando ogni sorte di curiosità et vanità
mondana, che per ciò saria peregrinare per il mondo et non per Christo. Ne vi dovete
solamente contentare di andare a Roma a visitare quelle chiese et reliquie dei Santi,
ma a questo dovete coniungere vera e perfetta penitenza, di modo che facciate questo
viaggio in gratia di Dio et con tal mortificatione della carne et sensi vostri che serva
anco per la satisfattione delli nostri peccati'.

derselben dabei erinnert, indem er sieht, daß die ungeheuristen, aller-
stattlichsten Gebäu der Römer, die sie doch Aeternitati und der
Ewigkeit aufgeweiht und unzerstörlich zu sein vermeint haben, mittler-
weil zerfallen und zu grund gangen sein.[32]

Fascination with ancient Rome is reshaped into a moral lesson about
the frailty of earthly glory, a topic that became particularly popular
during the Counter-Reformation, as it demonstrated the ultimate triumph of the Christian realm over the pagan legacy of Rome.[33] Others, however, did not argue at all, and simply confessed their varying
interests. Hilarius Pyrckmair, for instance, the author of a *Commentario-
lus de arte apodemica seu vera peregrinandi ratione* (1577),[34] had visited Rome
in 1575, too. Even if he asserted that God should lie at the basis of
every journey (f. 11v-12r), he still admitted to having gazed at the
pagan remains of ancient Rome 'with utmost admiration and bewil-
derment' ('summa cum admiratione et stupore': fol. 4v).

Pyrckmair's *admiratio* brings us back to Lipsius's *Admiranda*. Although
Lipsius's knowledge and understanding of ancient Rome was of course
vastly superior to the stealthy curiosity Pyrckmair confessed to two
years after his visit to Rome, still the sense of stupefaction at the sight of
Rome, which both of them express in their own way, also has some
common traits. Lipsius, too, admits several times throughout the *Admiranda* to being filled with wonderment while studying the antiquities of
ancient Rome (see for example II, 4; II, 10; II, 13; III, 1); he, too, is
struck with awe, when he discusses topics such as the donations of the
emperors (II, 12: 'non inter admiranda, sed stupenda' ['among things
that should provoke not admiration, but stupefaction']) or the famous
revolving dining room of Nero[35] (III, 14: 'Quod mihi quidem stuporem
incutit non dissimulo, et iam lingua haeret' ['And I do not conceal that
this strikes me with amazement, and my tongue now sticks']). Even
more important is the fact that for Lipsius, too, the splendour of
ancient Rome obtains its final sense only in the even greater glory of
Christian Rome and therefore ultimately refers to God. The old Rome

---

[32] *Rom. Eine Münchner Pilgerfahrt im Jubeljahr 1575, beschrieben von Dr. Jakob Rabus, Hofprediger zu München,* ed. K. Schottenloher (Munich: 1925) 190.

[33] For a splendid discussion of this idea in Baroque poetry surrounding Rome, see
Rehm W., *Europäische Romdichtung* (Munich: 1960²) 135-54.

[34] About this work, one of the first apodemic treatises or writings on the theory of
travel, see Stagl I., *A History of Curiosity. The Theory of Travel 1550–1800,* Studies in
Anthropology and History 13 (Chur etc.: 1995), particularly chapter 1: "The
Methodising of Travel in the 16th Century", 47-94.

[35] See Suetonius, *Nero* 31, 2.

lives on in the new; the pope and his cardinals are the rightful successors to the ancient dictators and the senate.[36] Here again Lipsius picks up a theme that had been popular in fifteenth-century Roman, curial humanism; Flavio Biondo had concluded his *Roma triumphans* with a carefully elaborated image of Christian Rome as the fortress of a Christian state, in which the tent of the commanding general (*praetorium*) was the Basilica of Saint Peter, the consul the pope, the chief of the soldiers (*magister militum*) the emperor, the senators the cardinals and the various inferior officers the kings and other dignitaries of Europe.

The lesson that Lipsius draws from this subordination of ancient Rome is not unlike the sentiment voiced by pilgrims, such as Jakob Rabus. The ruins make the contingency of all earthly glory apparent and urge mortals, himself included, to turn humble in the face of God. When he recalls the remains of the huge ancient country estates he had inspected near Ostia and Ardea, he muses (III, 14): 'O Deus, quae mutatio? Quam haec cogitatio me ad te trahit, infirma et incerta haec omnia humana spectantem et spernentem' ('My God, what a change? How much this thought draws me to you, while I observe and spurn all these human creations, weak and uncertain as they are').

Many years earlier, in a chapter of *De constantia* (1583), similar reflections on the transient nature of all earthly glory, as evidenced by the rise and fall of lustrous cities and even empires, made him brand Rome a 'falsely Eternal City' (I, 16: 'falso Aeterna Urbs'). On the other hand, particularly for the antiquarian, ruins were of course ambivalent signs. They demonstrated the irrevocable fate of even the greatest of mankind's achievements and therefore drove men to restraint and modesty, but they also evoked the splendour of old and could be filled with life and meaning, perhaps not to the eye, but certainly to the mind. In the opening chapter of *De amphitheatro* (1584) Lipsius recounts a conversation he had had in Rome with Nicolaus Florentius.[37] Upon

---

[36] See the preface *Ad lectorem*. It ends with an apostrophe to the City, in which Lipsius eloquently sums up his sentiment: 'Gaude igitur non maior, sed melior iam Roma, non cultior, sed sanctior' ('So rejoice, Rome, not larger, but better now, not more cultivated, but more sacred'). In similar terms Lipsius expressed his joy at hearing the news of the safe arrival in Rome of one of his students in 1603 (ILE 03 03 16 B [= *Cent. misc.* V, 18]): 'Gaudeo Romam venisse, illam olim magnam, augustam, superadmirandam, nunc sanctam, religiosam, venerandam' ('I am glad that you have arrived in Rome, that city once great, majestic, to be marvelled at above all others, now holy, hallowed, to be venerated').

[37] On Nicolaus Florentius, Lipsius's guide in Rome, see the introductory note to ILE I, 69 00 00.

the sad sight of the dilapidated remains of ancient Rome, Florentius had reassured Lipsius: 'Scilicet haec ipsa ruta et caesa spirant etiam Romam veterem et velut scintillas emittunt prisci splendoris. Ex parietinis ecce istis et ex lapidibus imago statim animo oboritur urbis, quae una fuit ab omni aevo, una erit' ('This very rubble and wreckage still breathe, to be sure, ancient Rome and sends forth sparks, as it were, of pristine splendour. Look, from these walls and stones rises instantly in our mind an image of the city, that was unique in all ages and will be so in the future').[38]

For the rulers of the world, too, the ruins were meaningful witnesses to ancient grandeur that carried, moreover, not merely a scholarly but even a political message. It is significant that Lipsius chose to dedicate this work to Archduke Albert of Austria, Governor of the Spanish crown in the Low Countries. In his dedicatory address Lipsius stressed that earthly reigns and dominions reflect divine power and providence and that worldly rulers act as 'trustees and substitutes' ('curatores et vicarii') of God on earth. In that way sovereigns, and especially those who belong to the Habsburg dynasty, the true successors to the Roman empire, have a role to fulfill in God's salvational design and thus carry a great moral responsibility. To Lipsius's mind, therefore, Archduke Albert is no less than the logical dedicatee of a treatise on the greatness of Rome.

In this way we have arrived at the second component in the title of Lipsius's monograph, which clarifies the actual scope and purpose of his work. Lipsius aimed at elucidating the quintessence of the grandeur of ancient Rome. The nature of Roman excellence had been contemplated since classical Antiquity itself. The philosopher Poseidonius and the historian Polybius had pondered the question, and Augustine had analyzed the matter incisively in Book V of his *De civitate Dei*. In Lipsius's own time the discussion had been raised to a general level and approached from a mainly demographic viewpoint by Giovanni Botero (1544–1617) in his *Delle cause della grandezza delle città* (1588).[39] Lipsius, however, takes an entirely different stance in the *Admiranda*, not just with respect to his predecessors and contempo-

---

[38] For comments on this text, see Grafton A., "The Renaissance", in *The Legacy of Rome. A New Appraisal*, ed. R. Jenkyns (Oxford: 1992) 102; Nativel C., "Justus Lipsius, Belga Romae hospes", in *Justus Lipsius en het Plantijnse huis*, 41-2.

[39] For the life and work of this Italian political writer, see especially Chabod F., *Giovanni Botero*, in Idem, *Scritti sul Rinascimento*, *Opere* II (Turin: 1967) 271-458.

raries, but even in comparison to his own previous scholarship on Rome. In his preface *Ad lectorem* he explains that he had in the past been too much concerned with details and that he was now going to focus on essentials. For the study of ancient civilization in all its particles, as he had pursued it in his earlier monographs, had only a limited value:

> Ah, what benefit is gained from that? Life and morals should prevail, and then prudence, but also a certain elegance, should come next, this last element with measure, though. In time past we, too, perhaps sinned, but now with the change of time my mind has changed as well, and I cry out freely: there are some things I prefer to ignore rather than to learn.[40]

These thoughts throw light in two ways on Lipsius's conception of antiquarian research and spell out the specific cast of mind with which he explored the grandeur of Rome. First of all, Lipsius consistently continued to concentrate on the practical relevance of his antiquarian studies for his own time. This orientation, based on the principle of 'similitudo temporum' ('resemblance of [ancient and modern] times') and emphatically defended in the dedication of his edition (1574) of and commentary (1581) on Tacitus,[41] had always been the hallmark of Lipsius's philological and antiquarian pursuits. Lipsius was convinced that an adequate analysis of ancient culture could provide the necessary clues to save the contemporary society of its many political, social, and religious problems. How far he was prepared to take this approach, becomes evident in the *Admiranda*, where he unambiguously advocates the Roman system of colonies (I, 6) and the displacement of whole tribes to new locations (I, 7) as policies that deserve to be imitated by contemporary kings in the light of successful applications by the Spanish rulers in the New World. Possible objections, which one presumes would have occurred to Lipsius, are brushed aside as irrelevant in comparison to the public benefit (I, 6): 'The great public benefit dissolves or absorbs, here as in other cases, this minimal injustice'.[42] This was the price that Lipsius had to pay for consistently maintaining his concept of classical studies as a practical discipline that offers solutions for contemporary problems.[43]

---

[40] 'Ah, quis fructus est? Vita et mores praeeant, tum prudentia, sed et elegantia quaedam accedat, tamen ultima haec cum modo. Peccavimus et nos fortasse olim, sed nunc cum aliis annis mens est alia, et clamo libere: quaedam esse quae malo ignorare quam discere'.

[41] See ILE I, 74 07 00 M and 81 00 00 H respectively.

[42] 'Utilitas publica magna, ut in aliis, exiguum hoc iniquum diluit vel absorbet'.

[43] See Grafton A., "Portrait of Justus Lipsius", *American Scholar* 56 (1987) 390.

Secondly, he strove more systematically and conscientiously than in his earlier writings not just to gather and sum up a mass of documentation culled from literary and archaeological sources, but to select the cardinal pieces of evidence and order them according to a system of thematic categories. Antiquarian studies, to be true, had always been by nature thematically, rather than chronologically organized. Classical history did not need to be rewritten, since the ancient historians had recorded it so superbly that it was not only unnecessary, but even inappropriate to try to do their work over again. Therefore, Renaissance antiquarians focused on reconstructing the many material facets of ancient civilization. The fourfold division, namely in 'antiquitates sacrae, publicae, militares, privatae' ('sacred, public, military, private antiquities'), adopted by Flavio Biondo in his *Roma instaurata* and *Roma triumphans*, the first comprehensive survey of Roman antiquities, remained the standard one for all subsequent studies in the field.[44]

In the humanists' perspective antiquarian studies thus consisted of extended footnotes to the works of the ancient historians or other writers, as one can deduce from the mere titles of many antiquarian monographs or manuals.[45] Conversely, these categories of antiquarian research could offer a guideline for reading classical texts as efficiently as possible, so that the information drawn from that reading could be collected and assimilated as systematically as possible. In the sixteenth century, furthermore, several treatises were produced in which a

---

[44] See Momigliano A., "Ancient History and the Antiquarian", in Idem, *Contributo alla storia degli studi classici*, Storia e letteratura 47 (Rome: 1955) 73-5; Mazzocco A., "Linee di sviluppo dell'antiquaria del Rinascimento", in *Poesia e poetica delle rovine di Roma. Momenti e problemi*, ed. V. De Caprio, Quaderni di Studi Romani, series 1, 47 (Rome: 1987) 61-3. Momigliano's widely accepted idea that Varro's *Antiquitates rerum humanarum et divinarum* stood model for Renaissance antiquarians has been questioned by Wrede H., *Römische Antikenprogramme des 16. Jahrhunderts*, in *Il Cortile delle Statue. Der Statuenhof des Belvedere im Vatikan*, ed. M. Winner – B. Andreae – C. Pietrangeli (Mainz: 1998) 83, n. 1-2.

[45] Three examples connected with Lipsius may suffice: a collective volume (1592) containing some minor antiquarian writings, based on Lipsius's teaching, was given the title *Tractatus ad historiam Romanam cognoscendam apprime utiles* (*Treatises Most Useful for Learning Roman History*); Lipsius's monograph on the Roman army (1595–1596) was conceived as a commentary on Polybius, as he makes clear in the title: *De militia Romana libri quinque. Commentarius ad Polybium* (*Five books on the Roman Army. A Commentary on Polybius*). See the article of J. De Landtsheer in this book. Lipsius explains in the preface to his edition of Seneca (1605) that he devised his ambitious *Fax historica* (*Torchlight of History*), of which *De militia Romana* was to be a part, as a general commentary not just on ancient historians but on all of ancient literature.

method for reading history was proposed.[46] This reading strategy was in fact nothing more than a specific application of the humanist reading method in general, which aimed at a meticulous imitation of the idiom of the best classical authors and prescribed to that end the registering of famous sayings, brilliant turns of phases, or useful thoughts in notebooks.[47] Again the basis was laid in Antiquity itself: a sophisticated concept of imitation is already found in the classicizing theory of style developed by Dionysius of Halicarnassus[48] and a thematic reading method was recommended by the best and most authoritative rhetoricians and pedagogues, such as Quintilian.[49]

Along these lines Lipsius devised a set of categories in order to facilitate the perusal of historiographical literature. The most detailed and explicit instructions in this regard are contained in a famous letter to a student of his, Nicolas de Hacqueville.[50] Lipsius advised his pupil to assemble four notebooks according to four main categories, namely *Memorabilia* (facts and situations that surpass the ordinary), *Ritualia* (sacred and profane rites and customs in public and private life), *Civilia* (public institutions), and *Moralia* (human virtues and vices), each further divided into numerous smaller items. We encounter some of these rubrics in the *Admiranda*, although the structure of the treatise does not correspond to the system he laid out in his letter to De Hac-

---

[46] See Franklin J.H., *Jean Bodin and the Sixteenth-Century Revolution in the Methodology of Law and History* (New York: 1963) 83-8.

[47] See Bolgar R.R., *The Classical Heritage and its Beneficiaries from the Carolingian Age to the End of the Renaissance* (Cambridge: 1954) 265-75; Buck A., "Die 'studia humanitatis' und ihre Methode", in Idem., *Die humanistische Tradition in der Romania* (Bad Homburg – Berlin–Zürich: 1968) 141-50. Lipsius's own three preserved collections of thematically arranged quotations and references are briefly described by Waszink J., "Inventio in the Politica: Commonplace-books and the shape of political theory", in *Lipsius in Leiden*, 145. The central role played by these *loci communes* (commonplaces), not just in humanist reading but also beyond, has been treated comprehensively by A. Moss in her *Printed commonplace-books and the Structuring of Renaissance Thought* (Oxford: 1996); see also her "The *Politica* of Justus Lipsius and the Commonplace-book", *Journal of the History of Ideas* 59 (1998) 421-36. The use of commonplace-books in the field of natural history has been discussed in detail by Blair A., *The Theater of Nature. Jean Bodin and Renaissance Science* (Princeton, N.J.: 1996).

[48] See Fuhrmann M., *Die Dichtungstheorie der Antike. Aristoteles-Horaz-Longin. Eine Einführung* (Darmstadt: 1992²) 193-6.

[49] See Marrou H.-I., *Histoire de l'éducation dans l'Antiquité* (Paris: 1965⁶) 408-10.

[50] ILE XIII, 00 12 03 H (= *Cent. misc.* III, 61). Just as the letter to Philippe de Lannoy mentioned earlier, this epistle was also reprinted as an independent document, outside of Lipsius's letter collections; see *Bibliotheca Belgica* III, 1091. The text is summarized and discussed by Nordman V.A., *Justus Lipsius als Geschichtsforscher und Geschichtslehrer. Eine Untersuchung*, Annales Academiae Scientiarum Fennicae 38, 2 (Helsinki: 1932) 52-9.

queville. Lipsius rather seems to have chosen those of his thematic categories that to his mind were best suited to characterize the excellence of Rome.[51] Two topics, namely *Potentia* (belonging to the *Memorabilia*) and *Virtus* (belonging to the *Moralia*), are selected as main rubrics and systematically analyzed. Rome's power (*Potentia*) is based on the vastness of its territory (*a finibus*),[52] its troops (*a copiis*), its resources (*ab opibus*) drawn from various taxes and flowing back to the people through different kinds of donations, and its military and civil buildings and constructions (*ab operibus*). Its moral strength (*Virtus*) lies first in the force of its male citizens (*viri*), among whom Lipsius strictly separates the state leaders (*capita rei publicae*), namely members of the senatorial and equestrian order, from the common folk (*minora membra, id est populus*), and secondly in their military and civil virtues (*virtutes*). In the penultimate chapter (IV, 11), just before the conclusion of the treatise, Lipsius adds to the two main categories, *Potentia* and *Virtus*, a third one, *Tempus* (Time), explained as *Diuturnitas Romani imperii* (Durability of the Roman empire). The Roman empire, he argues, never ceased to exist, and lives on in the Habsburg monarchy, the Holy Roman Empire. Lipsius thus manages to link the end of the *Admiranda* to the dedication and prologue.

The *Admiranda* can be linked to the letter to De Hacqueville from a further angle. In the first part of the letter he outlines a carefully structured survey of world history and lists the most valuable historians for each of the periods and categories he distinguishes. This universal-historical perspective was also in Lipsius's mind when he conceived his *Admiranda*, for he did not just intend to write about the grandeur of Rome, but wanted to devote a similar study to the Hebrew, Egyptian, Spanish, and French empires. These *Admiranda Judaica, Aegyptiaca, Iberica*, and *Gallica*, however, about which we hear in a letter from 1603, were never completed.[53] A fragment of the *Admiranda Judaica* is preserved in the cod. Harleianus 4122 of the British Library in London.[54] A

---

[51] A detailed survey of the structure and content of the *Admiranda* can be found in the first Appendix to this paper.

[52] In this section Lipsius compares the extent of the Roman empire with that of the Turkish and Spanish empires. I transcribe this interesting and truly prophetic passage in the second Appendix to this paper.

[53] They are announced in ILE 03 03 17 GO (= *Cent. misc.* IV, 64; *Epistolario*, 360). Earlier that year Lipsius confessed he had been planning to write about *Admiranda veteris aevi*, but had managed to compose only a small part of it (ILE 03 02 14 S [= *Cent. misc.* V, 16]).

[54] The main rubrics correspond to those of the Roman *Admiranda*: *copiae, opes, opera,*

part of the *Admiranda Aegyptiaca* is said to be kept in Lipsius's papers, the *Musaeum Lipsianum*, in Leiden.[55] A few years earlier, furthermore, Lipsius had envisaged the continuation of his *Admiranda* in yet another way. In a letter of 1597 he explained that he wanted to add two sequels to his Roman *Admiranda*, on the one hand a study about the grandeur of other nations, such as the Jews, the Egyptians, the Persians, the Macedonians, and the Spanish,[56] on the other hand a volume entitled *Admiranda in virtutibus et vitiis*, in which he wanted to deal with the material treated in his *Monita et exempla politica*, but presented from a different viewpoint.[57]

Even before he published his *Admiranda*, then, Lipsius clearly imagined this treatise in a much broader historical and ethical context which in the final years of his life sadly did not materialize beyond the conceptual stage. This ambitious framework shows, nonetheless, how Lipsius abandoned his exclusive focus on Rome in his scholarly work and tried to probe new areas of research. But Lipsius did not only look for new fields and subject matter, he also modified his approach to classical studies in a number of ways. Surely this change of perspective was at least in part prompted by the need to align his concept of practical erudition more carefully with the notions of Catholic orthodoxy defended by the partisans of the Counter-Reformation, who kept a close eye on him after his return to Leuven. That pressure, however, made it all the more difficult to maintain a uniform and harmonious concept in his scholarship.[58] The very first treatise he published after he left Leiden, *De cruce* (*On the Cross*), is marred by a peculiar dichotomy between the actual topic discussed in the body of the work, crucifixions and other forms of punishment in classical Antiquity, and the distinctly Catholic framework, consisting of a militant preface to the reader and a devout *Laudatiuncula crucis*, which concludes the treatise.[59]

---

and *virtutes*. See especially Crombruggen H. van, "Een onuitgegeven werk van Justus Lipsius, *De magnitudine Hebraea*", *De Gulden Passer* 25 (1947) 280-5, but the text had already been pointed out in Reiffenberg F. de, *De Justi Lipsii vita et scriptis commentarius* (Brussels: 1823) 103. A critical edition has been announced by J. De Landtsheer.

[55] See Nordman, *Lipsius als Geschichtsforscher*, 43. From Nordman's reference it is not clear whether he actually saw the text or only quoted from a secondary source. At any rate, no one after him ever referred to this piece again.

[56] This series is, interestingly enough, not identical to the later one in four parts, mentioned earlier.

[57] See ILE 97 11 15 (= *Sylloge*, I, 545, *epistula* 520).

[58] See Laureys M., "Lipsius and Pighius: The Changing Face of Humanist Scholarship", in *The world of Justus Lipsius*, 341-2.

[59] See Jehasse J., *La renaissance de la critique. L'essor de l'humanisme érudit de 1560 à 1614* (Saint-Étienne: 1976), 352-4.

The mere choice of this polyvalent theme at this critical moment in his professional life was probably no coincidence.[60]

In the *Admiranda*, Lipsius even distanced himself explicitly from his earlier studies, in the sense that he intended to focus more on essentials, as noted earlier. This change of attitude, however, affects his treatise in a fundamental way. First of all, just as in the *De cruce*, the body of the work does not entirely harmonize with the dedication and the preface. Whereas Lipsius devotes the study itself exclusively to classical Rome, he underlines in the introductory texts the prevalence of the Christian over the pagan city. But, what is more, the thematic prism through which Rome is presented on the basis of evidence gathered from different historical contexts and even epochs tends to point in that same direction. The picture of Rome that emerges cannot in its entirety be located in a single historical framework or followed through a historical evolution,[61] but rather works like a static and monolithic ideal that lived on through the ages and contributed to strengthening the even greater brilliance of its Christian successor. For the Habsburg rulers, as Lipsius pressed upon the mind of his dedicatee Albert of Austria, the greatness of Rome was a part of their own history and thus represented a challenge to live up to.[62]

It has been argued that due to the attitude of the Counter-Reformation the Roman Catholic historiography of post-Tridentine Italy was primarily systematic and rational, not historical, since discussion of origins and development seemed misplaced in a world of eternal

---

[60] Lipsius's last antiquarian monograph, *De Vesta et Vestalibus* (1603), has a similar double face, as noted by Jehasse, *La renaissance de la critique*, 422-3. By contrast, his small treatise on ancient libraries (*De bibliothecis*), published the year before, shows a conspicuously irenic orientation, rising above the different churches; see Nelles P., "Juste Lipse et Alexandrie: les origines antiquaires de l'histoire des bibliothèques", in *Le pouvoir des bibliothèques. La mémoire des livres en Occident*, ed. M. Baratin – C. Jacob (Paris: 1996) 224-42.

[61] Grafton, *The Renaissance*, 122 observed the same phenomenon in *De militia Romana*.

[62] This positive appeal of the *magnitudo Romana*, embedded in the theme of the durability of the Roman empire, addressed in the chapter preceding the final conclusion (IV, 11), seems to me the fundamental argument of the *Admiranda*, pace Nativel, "Justus Lipsius, Belga Romae hospes", 45-7, who reads the treatise as a fragmentary and imperfect reconstruction of a destroyed Rome, reduced to an icon of human vanity and left at the mercy of God. Although there are certainly many texts in Lipsius's antiquarian writings that underscore this sentiment, it seems to me necessary to differentiate between varying concerns and purposes in Lipsius's antiquarian scholarship over the entire course of his career.

verities.[63] In this sense, the *Admiranda* can certainly be said to be coloured by the exacting intellectual climate of the Counter-Reformation. But in dealing with the city of Rome particularly, this approach was rooted in a much longer tradition, for the Eternal City had never lent itself easily to scholarly analysis without a due dosis of pious awe.

Appendix 1: Structure and Content of the Admiranda

Lipsius's description of the *magnitudo Romana* is based upon the following conceptual framework:

1. *Potentia* (Power):

1.1 *a finibus* (derived from the territory)
1.2 *a copiis* (derived from the troops)
1.2.1 *copiae* (troops):
1.2.1.1 *copiae provinciales*: *legiones, cohortes, alae* (troops of the provinces: legions, cohorts, wings)
1.2.1.2 *copiae urbanae*: *praetoriani, evocati, Batavi* (troops of the city of Rome: praetorian guards, veterans, Batavians)
1.2.1.3 *copiae classicae* (naval forces):
1.2.1.3.1 *in ipso mari* (in the open sea):
1.2.1.3.1.1 *praetoriae*: *Misenensis, Ravennas* (praetorian fleets: of Misenum, of Ravenna)
1.2.1.3.1.2 *minores*: *Foroiuliensis in Gallia, in Ponto, Ostia* [this last one doubted by Lipsius] (minor fleets: of Fréjus in Gaul, in the Black Sea, at Ostia)
1.2.1.3.2 *in fluminibus*: *Germanica in Rheno, in Danubio, in Euphrate* [this last one supposed by Lipsius] (on the rivers: the German fleet on the Rhine, on the Danube, on the Euphrates)
1.2.2 *coloniae* (settlements)
1.3 *ab opibus* (derived from the resources)
1.3.1 *opes publicae* (public resources):
1.3.1.1 *vectigalia prisca*: *e decumis, e pastionibus, e portoriis* (tolls of old: on tithes, on public pastures, on freight)

---

[63] See Bouwsma, W.J., "Three Types of Historiography in Post-Renaissance Italy", *History and Theory* 4 (1965), 307.

1.3.1.2 *tributa* (taxes)

1.3.1.2.1 *in agros* (on lands)

1.3.1.2.2 *in corpora: homines, animalia* (on bodies: persons, animals)

1.3.1.3 *e metallis* (from mines and quarries)

1.3.1.4 *vectigalia nova: aerarium militare, vectigal urinae, vectigal meretricium* (new tolls: military treasury, toll on public bathrooms, toll on prostitution)

1.3.1.5 *e triumphis* (from military triumphs)

1.3.1.5.1 *manubiae* (revenues from the sale of booty)

1.3.1.5.2 *aurum coronarium* (golden crown [or other present of gold] collected in the provinces for a victorious general)

1.3.1.6 *liberalitates aut erogationes* (donations and expenditures):

1.3.1.6.1 *impensae publicae* (public expenses):

1.3.1.6.1.1 *necessariae: in militem, in magistratus urbanos, in magistratus provinciales, in populum: frumentatio* (necessary expenses: for soldiers, for magistrates of Rome, for magistrates of the provinces, for the people: i.e. distribution of corn)

1.3.1.6.1.2 *arbitrariae: in ludos, in opera, in dona* (voluntary expenses: for games, for constructions, for gifts)

1.3.2 *opes privatae* (private resources)

1.4 *ab operibus* (derived from the constructions)

1.4.1 *opera temporaria* (temporary constructions):

1.4.1.1 *in militia* (in military practice):

1.4.1.1.1 *terrea: fossae, valli, aggeres* (made of earth: trenches, palisades, mounds)

1.4.1.1.2 *materialia: turres, testudines, musculi, vineae* (made of timber: towers, turtle-shaped protective screens, mantelets, movable shelters for siege operations)

1.4.1.2 *extra militiam: ludicra: theatra, amphitheatra, circi* (outside the military: stage constructions: theatres, amphitheatres, circuses)

1.4.2 *opera diuturna sive perpetua* (lasting or permanent constructions):

1.4.2.1 *publica: oppida* (public constructions: cities)
qualities to be treated: *altitudo, spatium, decor aedificiorum* (height of the buildings, size of the city, beauty of the buildings)
excerpta quaedam: templa, fora civilia, fora venalia, balnea thermaeque, rostra, statuae, viae, aquaeductus, cloacae, Traiani pons in Danubio (some chosen samples: temples, public places, market-places, baths and springs, speakers' platform, statues, roads, aqueducts, sewers, Trajan's bridge over the Danube)

1.4.2.2 *privata: domus, villae* (private constructions: houses, farms)

2 *Virtus* (excellence):

2.1 *viri* (men):

2.1.1 *capita reipublicae: senatores, equites* (heads of the state: senators, knights)

2.1.2 *minora membra, id est populus* (minor members, i.e. the people)

2.2 *virtutes* (talents):

2.2.1 *virtutes militares* (military talents):

2.2.1.1 *iustitia* (righteousness)

2.2.1.2 *fortitudo* (fortitude):

2.2.1.2.1 *milites*: *in opere, in agmine, in acie* (soldiers: in their work, in their marches, in combat)

2.2.1.2.2 *duces* (generals)

2.2.2 *virtutes civiles* (civil talents):

2.2.2.1 *pietas* (sense of duty)

2.2.2.2 *probitas* (honesty), to which are added: *abstinentia, continentia, modestia* (freedom from covetousness, self-restraint, discipline)

2.2.2.3 *constantia* (steadfastness)

2.2.2.4 objection of Lipsius's dialogue partner: *contra probitatem, contra abstinentiam, contra continentiam* (examples illustrating dishonesty, covetousness, lack of self-restraint)

2.2.2.5 defence of Lipsius centring on: *saevitia, luxus mensarum aut vestium* (cruelty, extravagance in eating and clothing)

Appendix to Part 2: *doctrina* (learning)

   a. *doctrinae studia* (pursuit of learning)

   b. *salaria in doctores* (salaries paid to teachers)

3. *Tempus*: *diuturnitas Romani imperii* (Time: permanence of the Roman empire).

Appendix 2: Lipsius's Comparison of the Extent of the Roman, Turkish, and Spanish Empires (Admiranda I, 3)

LIPSIUS: Pulchra autem ista facies et non nisi a Providentia sic ordinata et ornata, quam mecum vide. Utrimque ad hoc mare Mediterraneum provinciae se porrigunt et extendunt, ipsum in medio, tot portubus et insulis distinctum, quasi via et limes est, per quem commerciis iungantur. Nec aliud mihi pulchrius commodiusque videtur in hoc imperio, quam iste velut in medio corpore balteus, bullis insularum interstinctus, qui et dividit simul et constringit. Dabis mihi aliud tale et tantum? Non dabis.

AUDITOR: Immo, Lipsi, Turcicum et Regis quoque nostri Hispanicum imperium haud longe absunt.

LIPSIUS: De Turcico fatendum est in Asia et Africa late se extendisse, sed in validissima Europa nostra quid habet aut potius non habet? Certe vel sola Italia, Hispania, Gallia iunctae opibus viribusque pares sint aut superent illum hostem. O si Deus daret! Adeo nec provinciae illae orientales pro opibus et frequentia prisca sunt, et nostrae istae florem nunc habent et vigorem. Quid de Germania dicam? Illa olim horrida et rerum inops, quam artibus, oppidis copiisque exculta est et abundat!

AUDITOR: Mirifice, et haec tamen imperio tuo etiam deest.

LIPSIUS: Non sic, ut opinare. Nam si terminos meos cogitas, videbis ad Danubium usque Raetias, Noricum, Carnos, Pannones inclusos, et parte

altera ad Rhenum Helvetios, Rauracos, Argentoratenses, Nemetes, Van-
gionas, Treviros, Ubios, Menapios, Batavos ad Oceanum ipsum. Quae
pleraque omnia Germaniae hodiernae nomen et linguam et leges etiam
habent, at detracta vides quam eam artent et pulcherrimis membris spoli-
atam relinquant. Certum autem haec postrema omnia cis Rhenum Galli-
ae fuisse olim accensa, itaque sub iugo Romano. Sed de Hispanico imperio quod aiebas, id sane, spatia terrarum si consideras, praesertim in
Novo illo orbe et insulis, Romanum longe vel superat, sed iunctio et
devinctio provinciarum, viri et copiae quam deficiunt et delinquunt!
Nunc quidem, nam postea quid futurum sit nescio; florebunt, crescent
fortasse, et sensum meum tibi dicam? Nescio quo Providentiae decreto
res et vigor ab Oriente (considera, si voles) in Occasum eunt.

LIPSIUS: Surely a beautiful appearance, by nothing else than Providence
shaped and adorned in this way. Look at it together with me. Its
provinces are stretched out and extend on both sides of the Mediterranean sea, which itself lies in the middle, decorated by so many harbors
and islands, a road and passage-way, as it were, through which they are
joined in their commercial activities. Nothing seems to me more beautiful
and convenient in this empire than that sort of belt in the middle of the
body, which is marked off with the islands as studs, and at the same time
separates them and ties them together. Will you present me something of
similar quality and size? No, you won't.
STUDENT: Yes, I will, Lipsius; the Turkish empire and also the Spanish
empire of our King are serious competitors.
LIPSIUS: As for the Turkish empire, one ought to acknowledge that it has
covered a wide surface in Asia and Africa; but what does it own, or rather
not own, in our mighty Europe? For surely the mere union of Italy, Spain
and France should be equal in resources and power or even superior to
that enemy. O if God would only grant that! So true is it that those Eastern territories for all their present wealth and abundance have no tradition, and that our lands are now blooming and thriving. What should I
say about Germany? Once rude and without any potential, how has it
been developed and is now flourishing with culture, cities, and resources!
STUDENT: Amazing indeed, but still, this country, too, is not part of your
empire.
LIPSIUS: It is not like you think. For if you consider my boundaries, you will
find up to the Danube Raetia, Noricum, Carinthia, and Pannonia included, and on the other side towards the Rhine Central Switzerland, North-
west Switzerland, Alsace, the areas around Speyer, Worms, Trier,
Cologne, Flanders, and Holland, very much down to the ocean. Nearly all
of these territories carry the name, use the language, and abide by the laws
of present-day Germany; but if you take them away, you see how they
make it shrink and leave it robbed of its finest members. There is no
doubt, however, that all these last territories on this side of the Rhine were
once reckoned to Gaul and thus fell under Roman rule. But as to what you
said about the Spanish empire, true, if you consider the extent of its lands,
especially in that New World and its islands, that empire surpasses the

Roman empire by far. But how much the union and bond of those territories, the men and forces are lacking and failing! At least now, for I do not know what the future will bring; perhaps they will flourish and grow, and may I tell you what I feel? By some hidden decree of Providence momentum and might (please think about it) shift from East to West.

Selective Bibliography

BASKERVILLE E.J., *The English Traveller to Italy 1547–1560* (Ph.D. dissertation, Columbia University: 1967)

BOUWSMA W.J., "Three types of Historiography in Post-Renaissance Italy", *History and theory* 4 (1965) 303-14

BURKE P., "The Uses of Italy", in *The Renaissance in National Context*, ed. R. Porter – M. Teich (Cambridge: 1992) 6-20

CHABOD F., *Giovanni Botero*, in Idem, *Scritti sul Rinascimento, Opere* II (Turin: 1967) 271-458

CROMBRUGGEN H. VAN, "Een onuitgegeven werk van Justus Lipsius, *De magnitudine Hebraea*", *De Gulden Passer* 25 (1947) 280-5

EDWARDS C., *Writing Rome. Textual Approaches to the City* (Cambridge: 1996)

FRANKLIN J.H., *Jean Bodin and the Sixteenth-Century Revolution in the Methodology of Law and History* (New York: 1963)

FUBINI R., "Biondo Flavio", in *Dizionario biografico degli Italiani* X (1968) 536-9

GAMRATH H., *Roma sancta renovata. Studi sull'urbanistica di Roma nella seconda metà del sec. XVI con particolare riferimento al pontificato di Sisto V (1585–1590)*, Analecta Romana Instituti Danici, supplementum 12 (Rome: 1987)

GRAFTON A., "Portrait of Justus Lipsius", *American Scholar* 56 (1987) 382-90

GRAFTON A., "The Renaissance", in *The Legacy of Rome. A New Appraisal*, ed. R. Jenkyns (Oxford: 1992) 97-123

Herinneringen aan Italië. Kunst en toerisme in de 18de eeuw, ed. R. de Leeuw (Zwolle: 1984)

ILE: *Iusti Lipsi Epistolae*, ed. A. Gerlo et alii (Brussels: 1978 ff.)

Kaspar Schoppe (1576–1649). Philologe im Dienste der Gegenreformation, ed. H. Jaumann, Zeitsprünge. Forschungen zur Frühen Neuzeit 2, 3/4 (Frankfurt a. M.: 1998)

KINNEY D., "*Mirabilia Urbis Romae*", in *The Classics in the Middle Ages*, ed. A.S. Bernardo – S. Levin, Medieval and Renaissance Texts and Studies 69 (Binghamton, N.Y.: 1990) 207-21

LAUREYS M., "Lipsius and Pighius: The Changing Face of Humanist Scholarship", in *The world of Justus Lipsius: A contribution towards his intellectual biography*, ed. M. Laureys, with the assistance of C. Bräunl – S. Mertens – R.

Seibert-Kemp [= *Bulletin de l'Institut Historique Belge de Rome* 68] (Brussels–Rome: 1998) 329-44

Luijdjens A.H., "Chronologische lijst van beschrijvingen van Italië en Rome tot 1900 in de Nederlanden geschreven of verschenen", *Mededelingen van het Nederlands Historisch Instituut te Rome*, 2nd *series*, 1 (1931) 205-29

Mazzocco A., "Linee di sviluppo dell'antiquaria del Rinascimento", in *Poesia e poetica delle rovine di Roma. Momenti e problemi*, ed. V. De Caprio, Quaderni di Studi Romani, series 1, 47 (Rome: 1987) 55-71

McGinness F.J., "The Rhetoric of Praise and the New Rome of the Counter-Reformation", in *Rom als Idee*, ed. B. Kytzler, Wege der Forschung 656 (Darmstadt: 1993) 277-97

McGinness F.J., *Right Thinking and Sacred Oratory in Counter-Reformation Rome* (Princeton, N.J.: 1995)

Momigliano A., "Ancient History and the Antiquarian", in Idem, *Contributo alla storia degli studi classici*, Storia e letteratura 47 (Rome: 1955), 67-106

Nativel C., "Justus Lipsius, Belga Romae hospes", in *Justus Lipsius en het Plantijnse huis*, ed. R. Dusoir – J. De Landtsheer – D. Imhof (Antwerp: 1997) 39-48

Nelles P., "Juste Lipse et Alexandrie: les origines antiquaires de l'histoire des bibliothèques", in *Le pouvoir des bibliothèques. La mémoire des livres en Occident*, ed. M. Baratin – C. Jacob (Paris: 1996) 224-42

Nordman V.A., *Justus Lipsius als Geschichtsforscher und Geschichtslehrer. Eine Untersuchung*, Annales Academiae Scientiarum Fennicae, 38, 2 (Helsinki: 1932)

O'Connell M.R., *Thomas Stapleton and the Counter-Reformation*, Yale Publications in Religion 9 (New Haven–London: 1964)

O'Malley J.W., *Praise and Blame in Renaissance Rome. Rhetoric, Doctrine, and Reform in the Sacred Orators of the Papal Court, c. 1450–1521*, Duke monographs in medieval and Renaissance studies 3 (Durham, N.C.: 1979)

Papy J., "Justus Lipsius, Rome en de Romereis: zoektocht naar een oude mythe?", *Kleio* 26 (1997) 111-26

Papy J., "*Italiam vestram amo supra omnes terras!* Lipsius' Attitude towards Italy and Italian Humanism of the Late Sixteenth Century", *Humanistica Lovaniensia* 47 (1998) 245-77

Rehm W., *Europäische Romdichtung* (Munich: 1960²)

Rom. Eine Münchner Pilgerfahrt im Jubeljahr 1575, beschrieben von Dr. Jakob Rabus, Hofprediger zu München, ed. K. Schottenloher (Munich: 1925)

Schoneveld C., "De vleesgeworden duivel? Het beeld van de reiziger in de Engelse literatuur van de Renaissance", in *Reizen en reizigers in de Renaissance. Eigen en vreemd in oude en nieuwe werelden*, ed. K. Enenkel – P. van Heck – B. Westerweel (Amsterdam: 1998) 57-77

Schudt L., *Le guide di Roma. Materialien zu einer Geschichte der römischen Topographie* (Vienna–Augsburg: 1930)

Stagl J., *A history of Curiosity. The Theory of Travel 1550–1800*, Studies in Anthropology and History 13 (Chur etc.: 1995)

Stinger C.L., *The Renaissance in Rome* (Bloomington, Ind.: 1985)

Waquet F., *Le modèle français et l'Italie savante. Conscience de soi et perception de l'autre dans la république des lettres (1660–1750)*, Collection de l'École française de Rome 117 (Rome–Paris: 1989)

Warneke S., *Images of the Educational Traveller in Early Modern England*, Brill's Studies in Intellectual History 58 (Leiden–New York–Cologne: 1995).

CIVIC SELF-OFFERING:
SOME RENAISSANCE REPRESENTATIONS
OF MARCUS CURTIUS

Maria Berbara

Saluti patriae et christianae gloriae[1]

Marcus Curtius can certainly be placed among the most celebrated *exempla* of Roman civic self-sacrifice known to us. According to Livy,[2] in 362 BC the ground gave way in the middle of the Forum, leaving an immensely deep chasm that could not be filled, in spite of the earth everyone threw into it. The soothsayers, consulted on the matter, announced that in order to close the chasm and to guarantee the endurance of the Roman Republic, it would be necessary to offer up, at that same spot, that 'quo plurimum populus Romanus posset'. Varro adds that the reason why the earth had yawned was a forgotten vow, namely that the bravest Roman citizen be offered to the God of the Dead.[3] Having heard this, Marcus Curtius, a young Roman soldier, asked whether any blessing were more Roman than arms and military virtue. He then solemnly devoted himself to death, mounted a superbly adorned horse and, fully armed, hurled himself down the chasm. It is believed, states Livy, that the *Lacus Curtius*, the Curtian Lake, is named after him.[4]

The legend finds parallels in that of other Roman heroes such as Publius Decius Mus, the Roman consul who devoted his life to the gods of the underworld in order to guarantee the victory of the Roman army over the Latins at Veseris. The act of devotion was repeated, according to the legend, both by Decius's son and by his

---

[1] Inscription on the column upon which David stands next to the decapitated head of Goliath, in Ghirlandaio's Sassetti Chapel in Florence.

[2] *Ab urbe condita* VII, 6 (Loeb Classical Library, ed. and transl. B.O. Forster, III (London–Cambridge, Mass.: 1967) 372-5).

[3] *De lingua Latina* V, 148 (Loeb Classical Library, ed. and transl. R.G. Kent, I (London–Cambridge, Mass.: 1967) 138-41).

[4] In Antiquity there were two other explanations, however, for the name of the lake. See Richardson L., *A new Topographical Dictionary of Ancient Rome* (London–Baltimore: 1992) 229 (s.v. "Lacus Curtius").

grandson. The bravery of these men, their scorn for death and their readiness for sacrifice motivated their inclusion in the Roman gallery of *exempla virtutis*. The writings of Cicero and Seneca cite them as models conveying moral instruction, and Valerius Maximus includes them in his famous collection of exempla, the *Factorum et dictorum memorabilium libri novem*.[5]

These examples of Roman *devotio* have some common characteristics. Firstly, the hero is a virtuous person, most commonly a noble and courageous warrior. Secondly, his sacrifice is completely voluntary. Thirdly, the self-offering occurs during a situation of either war or natural catastrophe. Finally, the hero is usually armed and mounted on his horse at the moment of his sacrifice. If we exclude this last point, all the elements involved in the Roman self-offering are ultimately identifiable with those connected to the death of Christ and the Christian martyrs. In the third century, Origen noticed this parallel when he wrote that Jesus

> accepted his death willingly for the human race, like those who died for their country to check epidemics of plague, or famines or stormy seas. For it is probable that in the nature of things there are certain mysterious causes which are hard for the multitude to understand, which are responsible for the fact that one righteous man dying voluntarily for the community may avert the activities of the evil demons by expiation, since it is they who bring about plagues or famines or stormy seas or anything similar.[6]

The idea of one person having to pay to save the rest, allowing himself to be killed to re-establish a state of lost equilibrium, as well as that of the lesser value of a single man's life, are present both in Christian martyrdom and in the Roman civic self-offering. An abnegated death is an external sign of inner spiritual strength and virtue, valid in both symbolic universes.

---

[5] Curtius is mentioned by Valerius Maximus in V, 6, 2 (Collection G. Budé, ed. and transl. R. Combès, II (Paris: 1997) 118). Other famous *exempla* of bravery and devotion to the fatherland are Horatius Cocles, who held the Sublician bridge against the army of Lars Porsenna until it could be demolished, and Mucius Scaevola, also connected to the war against Porsenna, who, having been taken prisoner by the king, demonstrated his scorn for pain and death by burning his right hand. Contrary to Curtius, however, these heroes managed to escape death.

[6] *Contra Celsum* I, 31 (ed. H. Chadwick (Cambridge: 1980) 31-2).

The differences between both sacrificial models, however, outweigh the similarities. It is true that Curtius was included among the noblest *exempla* of fortitude, a virtue that was particularly praised among the Christians (one of the four cardinal virtues). Furthermore, he could not be blamed for inflicting pain upon himself in order to actually escape death (an accusation often raised against Scaevola), nor could his sacrifice be reputed to be ultimately sinful or useless, as for instance Lucretia's sacrifice in the name of chastity and honour.[7] Moreover, Curtius does not seem to have anything to gain by throwing himself into the chasm, and his sacrifice is necessary in order to guarantee the safety of his countrymen.

Despite the apparent Christian characteristics of his sacrifice, Curtius, together with other Roman heroes, was more often criticized than praised by early Christian writers.[8] The most elaborated criticism comes from St Augustine. When comparing the death of Roman heroes — including Curtius — to that of the Christian martyrs, he constantly seeks to emphasize the absolute superiority of the latter. St Augustine argues, in the first place, that the torture of the martyrs was 'not self-inflicted, but they bore tortures that were inflicted by others'.[9] This is, indeed, an important difference: both Christ's and the martyrs' death are passively undertaken, not actively determined; Curtius, on the other hand, brings himself to death, he is the one who takes the initiative to perform his own sacrifice. Secondly, and more importantly, the Roman hero died in order to save the earthly city, whereas the Christian martyrs were sacrificed in the name of the celestial kingdom. Since there was no eternal life for the former, he must have acted purely in search of glory among men. It was only the desire to be

---

[7] Although Lucretia was also praised by some Christian writers such as St Jerome and Tertullian, her suicide was considered to be sinful by others. St Augustine does not understand why a woman who has actually been a victim of rape should feel obliged to take her own life. He believes that if she had not committed any sin in her soul, she was free of guilt, and therefore did not have to die in order to efface it. Her suicide constitutes, moreover, an unforgivable act of murder. In Christian times, as noticed by Donaldson, the Roman concept of honour was often replaced by that of conscience; the culture of shame by that of guilt (see Donaldson I., *The Rapes of Lucretia* (Oxford: 1982) 33 f.).

[8] Nevertheless, Orosius's version of the story does seem to betray a certain admiration for the hero, while Minucius Felix, a cultivated Roman lawyer converted to Christianity who wrote in the first half of the third century, speaks of the honour due to his devotion (respectively *Histories Against the Pagans* III, 5,1-3, and *Octavius* VII, 3).

[9] *De civitate Dei* V, 14 (Loeb Classical Library, ed. W.M. Green, II (London–Cambridge, Mass.: 1963) 214-5).

praised, and not true virtue, that impelled him to offer up his own life.[10]

In the particular case of Curtius, St Augustine makes one other remark: it was in men and arms that the Romans excelled, and for this reason Curtius could consider himself as the best thing they — the Romans — had; accordingly, he had to perish fully armed. What would be his merit, however, if he had not decided to die voluntarily, but had been sent to death by an enemy of his faith? Despite all Augustine's negative criticisms, however, the idea of those Roman heroes as being a sort of 'competitive example' to Christians is also implicit in some of his comments:

> Yes, it was through that [Roman] empire, so far reaching in time and in space, so famous and glorious for the deeds of its heroes [...], that we have before us such models [*exempla*] to remind us of our duty. If in serving the glorious city of God we do not cling to the virtues that they clung to in serving the glory of the earthly city, let us be pricked to our hearts with shame.[11]

Similarly, St Jerome compares the sacrifice of Christ to that of Curtius and other renowned heroes, stressing the superior power of the former:

> Certainly if we trust the accounts of the pagans that Codrus, Curtius and the Decii by means of their death checked plagues, famine, and wars of cities, how much more can we believe that the Son of God by the shedding of His blood cleansed not one city but the whole world![12]

Again, Roman and Christian sacrifices are paralleled only in order to emphasize the superiority of the latter. The implicit value of the Roman self-offering is not denied, but pales by contrast with Christ's definitive sacrifice.

---

[10] *De civitate Dei* V, 18 (Loeb edition II, 225 f.). Lactantius, *Divinae Institutiones* III, 12, 22, went in a similar direction by stating that 'men who voluntarily sacrificed their life for the safety of their country, such as [...] Curtius and the two Decii at Rome, would never have preferred death to the advantages of life unless they had thought that they would achieve immortality through the esteem of their fellow-citizens'. The desire for praise was, thus, an implicit desire for immortality — but for false immortality, since it was to be guaranteed solely by other men.

[11] *De civitate Dei* V, 18 (Loeb edition II, 225 f.). This kind of argument 'from the lesser to the greater', according to which the Christians are exhorted to surpass the heroic deeds of the Pagans, is to be found in many other passages by Christian theologians. See Carlson M.L., "Pagan Examples of Fortitude in the Latin Christian Apologists" *Classical Philology* 43 (1948) 96.

[12] Commentary *In Ephesios* I, 1, 7 [386 A.D.]. See Carlson, "Pagan Examples", 100.

The criticism expressed by the Church Fathers is not only a matter of rhetorical rivalry, as it might seem at first, but indicates some irreconcilable characteristics of the Roman self-offering and the Christian sacrifice. As stated above, the former is most often performed in order to save the hero's earthly country, whereas the latter is dedicated to the eternal City of God. The concept of Roman self-offering was not so much connected to religion as it was to patriotism, which was, for the Romans, a moral duty of the highest order. Cicero seems to summarize a quite general opinion when he states that

> there is no social relation [...] more close, none more dear than that which links each one of us with our country. Parents are dear; dear are children, relatives, friends; but one native land embraces all our loves; and who that is true would hesitate to give his life for her, if by his death he could render her a service?[13]

As noted by Lecky, 'patriotism and military honour were indissolubly connected in the Roman mind. They were the two sources of national enthusiasm, the chief ingredients of the national conception of greatness [...]. Patriotism, in the absence of any strong theological passion, had assumed a transcendent power'.[14] The high appeal of patriotism, on the one hand, and the often dubious moral conduct of Roman gods, on the other, would explain why, for the Romans themselves, heroes such as Curtius, and not the gods, were the true *exempla virtutis* they were supposed to follow — a fact which not unsurprisingly is mentioned by St Augustine.[15]

Contrary to the Romans, on the other hand, Christians ignored the appeal of the homeland. As pointed out by Tertullian, their indifference to civic matters was absolute: 'Nec ulla magis res aliena quam publica'.[16] Not their countrymen, but the saints and Christ himself — thus either a supernatural being or men who were connected to super-

---

[13] *De officiis* I, 57 (Loeb Classical Library, ed. and transl. W. Miller (London–Cambridge, Mass.: 1975) 58-61). According to Cicero, the highest moral obligation is due to one's country; the second to one's parents, and the following to the children and the whole family.

[14] Lecky W.E.H., *History of European Morals from Augustus to Charlemagne* (New York: 1876) I, 181-2.

[15] See, for example, *Letter* 91, 4 (Loeb Classical Library, ed. and transl. J.H. Baxter (London–Cambridge, Mass.: 1953) 156-9).

[16] *Apologeticus* 38, 3 (Loeb Classical Library, ed. and transl. T.R. Glover (London–Cambridge, Mass.: 1984) 173). As summarized by Warde Fowler, while in ancient Rome the connection between religion and morality was a loose one, 'the new religion was itself morality' (Warde Fowler W., *The Religious Experience of the Roman People* (London: 1911) 466).

natural beings[17] — were their moral ideals; not a country, but the City of God, was worth living and dying for.

While the early Christian Fathers had more arguments against Curtius than in favour of him, later literary and iconographical sources would 'redeem' him of his possible sin of pride and include him in the gallery of Christianized ancient figures.[18] In the *Gesta Romanorum*, perhaps the most widely read medieval collection of *exempla*, Curtius typologically alludes to Christ closing the chasm of Hell.[19] Petrarch includes him in the *Triumphus Famae*[20] and Armannino Giudice in his *Fiorita d'Italia*. According to the latter, Curtius threw himself not into a chasm, but into the cave of a dragon that had been sent as a chastisement for the sins of the Romans. Here, thus, his death also has an expiatory value.[21]

It is in the visual arts, however, that the doubts regarding Curtius's character and virtue vanish completely. In paintings, reliefs, sculptures, engravings, majolicas and cassoni, the hero appears free from any ambiguity of character, and often pervaded by the same spiritualized pathos as the Christian martyrs themselves.

The moment chosen to represent Curtius is usually that of his

---

[17] Lecky, *History of European Morals* I, 183.

[18] In early modern literature, Curtius's name was very often transformed or sometimes even completely changed. In Fazio degli Uberti's *Dittamondo*, for example, it becomes *Marco Curio*; in the *Fiorita d'Italia*, *Metello*. In Jean d'Outremeuse's *Myreur des Histoires* he is referred to as *Marcus Tuitius*; in the *Kaiserchronik* as *Iovinus*, and in the German edition of the *Mirabilia Urbis Romae* as *Martinus*.

[19] Book XLIII. In many medieval sources, the chasm into which Curtius threw himself is called 'Hell', such as for instance in the *Dittamondo* ('Inferno'), the *Mirabilia* ('infernus'), and the *Kaiserchronik* ('Helleloch'; see Graf A., *Roma nella memoria e nelle immaginazioni del Medio Evo* (Turin: 1923) 177, n. 98, and Massmann H.F. (ed.), *Die Kaiserchronik*, 3 vols (Quedlinburg–Leipzig: 1854) III, 623). The last two sources also indicate that a church to St Antony was built in the same place in which the earth had yawned. The connection of the *Lacus Curtius* with the underworld seems to have had its origins as early as in Roman times. Suetonius, *Augustus* 77, 1 tells that the Romans used to throw coins into the lake in fulfilment of a vow for Augustus's welfare, and in Ovid's *Fasti* VI, 403-4 it is said that altars had been built in that spot.

[20] Chapter 1, 70-2. The poet enumerates a series of noble Roman heroes, whose devotion he praises, and then adds: 'Curzio venia con lor, non men devoto,/che di sé e de l'arme empié lo speco/in mezzo il Foro orribilmente voto'.

[21] Chapter 28. Graf, *Roma nella memoria*, 177, n. 98, sees an identification between this version of the story and the legend of St Sylvester.

death, when, mounting his horse, he jumps into the chasm.[22] He appears either all alone, or, more often, amidst the watching crowd. During the Middle Ages Curtius is hardly ever represented; it is from the end of the fifteenth century onwards that the image of the armed Roman knight jumping into the chasm begins to appear frequently both in Italy and in southern Germany.

On German soil, Curtius's popularity was mainly connected to his representation in woodcuts — one of the oldest examples being the frequently reproduced woodcut from the Latin edition of Schedel's *Weltchronik* (1493), in which the hero is depicted, dressed in the manner of a medieval knight, almost half submerged in the chasm[23] — and the so-called *Gerechtigkeitsdarstellungen,* painted on the façade of public buildings or palaces,[24] where the image of Curtius is usually combined with that of other Roman heroes. In the cycle of *viri illustres* commissioned by Wilhelm IV of Bavaria for his residence in Munich, a canvas showing the death of Curtius — painted by Ludwig Refinger in 1540 and now in Munich's Alte Pinakothek[25] — stood side by side not only with representations of Roman heroes, but also of figures belonging to the Judaic tradition, both groups being meant to illustrate moral *exempla.* In Refinger's painting, one distinguishes three iconographical elements suggesting a parallel between Curtius and Judaeo-Christian martyrs: the palm leaves carried by Curtius's countrymen (traditionally connected to Christ's arrival in Jerusalem and to the martyrdom of Christian saints); the broken column with the coats of arms of Bavaria and Baden in the foreground; and the arch in ruins and the fragmentary statue on the left. Both the broken column and the ruins appeared often in representations of saints who were martyred in Rome, where they alluded to the topos of the victory of Christianity over Paganism and the *Renovatio Romae.* These elements put us in mind of, for example, the representations of St Sebastian by Liberale da Verona in the Kaiser Friedrich Museum (Berlin),

---

[22] Some sixteenth-century majolicas, however, simply depict his portrait in profile. See for example Giacomotti J., *Catalogue des majoliques des Musées Nationaux* (Paris: 1974) no 961.

[23] As noticed by E.W. Braun in the *Reallexikon zur Deutschen Kunstgeschichte,* the horse with his bent forelegs seems to derive from the type of Paul's horse at the moment of the saint's conversion.

[24] In these works, Curtius is usually depicted among Cocles and Scaevola. For examples, see Braun, *Reallexikon zur Deutschen Kunstgeschichte.*

[25] See Moormann E.M. – Uitterhoeve W., *Van Alexandros tot Zenobia* (Nijmegen: 1989) 99.

Antonello da Messina in the Gemäldegalerie (Dresden), Perugino in the Louvre, Amico Aspertini in the National Gallery of Washington, or Mantegna in the Louvre and the Kunsthistorisches Museum of Vienna.[26]

This tendency to draw a parallel between Roman heroes and Christian martyrs originally came from Italy, where the representation of a 'Christianized' version of Curtius became increasingly popular from the second half of the Quattrocento onwards. The Christian connotation of Curtius's story was achieved by various means: it could be suggested through the hero's gestures and pose; indicated by symbolic elements — as in the case of the aforementioned German painting — or implied by the general meaning of the iconographical programme in which Curtius was inserted.

The latter proved to be the case in one of the earliest Italian versions of Curtius's story in modern times, namely Pintoricchio's fresco in the Roman palazzina della Rovere-Colonna at the Piazza SS. Apostoli.[27] Cardinal Giuliano della Rovere, the future Pope Julius II, had commissioned the palazzina around 1484. In 1507 he gave it to his niece Lucrezia Gora and to Marcantonio Colonna on the occasion of their marriage, and the palazzina has remained the property of the Colonna family ever since. Vasari tells that Pintoricchio painted 'nel palazzo di Sant'Apostolo alcune cose per Sciarra Colonna'; later, he attributes these paintings to Perugino.[28] As noted by Schmarsow, the attribution of the work to Perugino is mistaken, as is the name Sciarra. The frescoes must have been commissioned by Giuliano della Rovere himself sometime between the construction of the palazzina and 1492 — when the Cardinal left Rome — and executed by Pintoricchio.[29]

Pintoricchio's paintings are situated on the palazzina's ground

---

[26] For Mantegna's paintings, see Caldwell J.G., "Mantegna's *St. Sebastian* – Stabilitas in a Pagan World", *Journal of the Warburg and Courtauld Institutes* 36 (1973) 373-7. For the representation of the 'symbolic ruin', see Panofsky E., *Early Netherlandish Painting*, 2 vols (Cambridge, Mass.: 1953) II, 135 f.

[27] I would like to thank Daniela Cabrera for sending me from Italy the material which allowed me to study Pintoricchio's frescoes.

[28] In Milanesi's edition (1878) III, 497 and 579.

[29] See Schmarsow A., *Pinturicchio in Rome* (Stuttgart: 1882) 26 f., and Ricci C., *Pintoricchio* (Paris: 1903) 59 f. On stylistic grounds, Perugino's execution of the frescoes has been discarded; Cavallaro A., "Gli affreschi del Pinturicchio nella palazzina di Giuliano della Rovere ai SS. Apostoli" in *Un'idea di Roma*, ed. L. Fortini (Rome: 1993) 56 suggests, however, that Vasari's passage might refer to other paintings in the palazzina, which were later lost or replaced by other paintings.

floor, at the so-called Sala della Fontana, which was originally an open loggia.[30] The room's vault is decorated with eighteen monochrome scenes from biblical and Graeco-Roman history, each depicted in a dodecagon, a square or a medallion, the medallions being smaller than the squares and dodecagons. These geometric figures are divided into two groups of one square and two medallions, corresponding to the narrower walls, and four groups of one dodecagon and two medallions — two appearing over each of the wider walls.[31] The two groups over one of the larger walls represent episodes of the life of Judith, Esther, Samson and David. Most of the scenes above the opposite wall have not been definitively identified. The first group represents episodes of the life of Verginia and Cloelia (respectively in the dodecagon and the medallion on the left) and a horseman fighting a dragon;[32] in the following group one sees a triumphant king in the dodecagon[33], and in the medallions a young man lying down amidst the flames and a woman giving her son (?) a shield.[34] The suicide of Themistocles is depicted in the dodecagon over one of the narrower walls: the Athenian general, refusing to take up arms against his fatherland, commits suicide by poisoning himself with the blood of a bull. The fresco represents a man cutting a calf's throat and, next to him, Themistocles drinking the animal's blood from a chalice; in the background, one sees a sacrificial altar. One of the corresponding medallions depicts the Athenian hero Cinegirus stopping a Persian ship with his own teeth during the battle of Marathon, and the other medallion an unidentified scene showing a man who is about to kill a young woman with a scythe, but is stopped by two horsemen, one of them wounding him with a spear. Marcus Curtius appears, finally, in a medallion over the narrow wall opposite; Cocles is depicted in the second medallion of this group, and Scaevola in the corresponding square.

As Cavallaro points out, most of the scenes — including that of

---

[30] See Cavallaro, "Gli affreschi del Pinturicchio", 55 f.

[31] For a diagram of the wall, see Jong J.L. de, *De Oudheid in Fresco* (diss., Leiden: 1987) 274. Ricci, *Pintoricchio*, 63, gives a detailed description of the vault, including not only the geometric figures, but also the *vele* and lunettes.

[32] De Jong, *De Oudheid in Fresco*, 276, suggested he represents Atilius Regulus killing the snake, while Cavallaro, "Gli affreschi del Pinturicchio", 67, and Ricci, *Pintoricchio*, 63, identified him with St George.

[33] According to Ricci, *Pintoricchio*, 62, this should be David.

[34] Ricci, *Pintoricchio*, 63, suggests that this last medallion represents the 'Spartan mother'.

Curtius — refer to episodes mentioned by Valerius Maximus, who was probably, together with Livy, the cycle's literary source.[35] The *Factorum et dictorum memorabilium libri* were one of the main sources for the representation of Antiquity from the early Renaissance to the Baroque;[36] being the most complete ancient collection of *exempla* known in modern times, the book was frequently consulted by artists seeking to use a Graeco-Roman figure or story in order to illustrate a moral quality or conduct (usually virtuous). Perugino's frescoes at the Collegio del Cambio, showing twelve Graeco-Roman exemplary figures in two big lunettes under personifications of the four Virtues, were based on the *Factorum et dictorum memorabilium libri*,[37] as well as Beccafumi's frescoes in de Palazzo Bindi Sergardi and in the Sala del Concistoro in the Palazzo Pubblico in Siena, which similarly depict *exempla virtutis* related to patriotism.[38]

The historical figures displayed in Pintoricchio's frescoes are also meant to illustrate *exempla* of civic virtue, for both the biblical and the Graeco-Roman characters were connected with the defence of the fatherland. The representation of Themistocles's suicide seems to summarise the central idea of the whole programme: the sacrificial value of the general's death, stressed by the altar and the sacrificial scene depicted next to him, also characterizes the patriotic deeds of the other figures shown in the frescoes. The Greek characters represented over this wall are opposed by the Roman heroes displayed over the second narrow wall, thus configuring a main axis of Graeco-Roman *exempla*. The fact that the figures from the Old Testament — particularly Judith, Esther, Samson and David — were usually considered prefigurations of Christ, the Roman Church and the Virgin,[39] as well as their iconographical combination with the pagan heroes, indicate that the latter were also conceived as Christian prefigura-

---

[35] See above, note 5. The fact that Giuliano della Rovere owned an exemplar of the *Factorum et dictorum memorabilium libri* strengthens this hypothesis. Cf. Cavallaro, "Gli affreschi del Pinturicchio", 70.

[36] See Guerrini R., "Dal testo all'immagine. La 'pittura di storia' nel Rinascimento", in *Memoria dell'antico nell'arte italiana*, ed. S. Settis (Turin: 1985) II.

[37] Fabius Maximus, Socrates and Numa Pompilius stand for Wisdom; Furius Camillus, Pittacus and Trajan for Justice; Lucius Sicinius, Leonidas and Cocles for Fortitude; and Scipio Africanus, Pericles and Quintus Cincinnatus for Temperance. See Guerrini, "Dal testo all'immagine", 50-60, and Scarpellini P., *Perugino* (Milan: 1984) 43 f.

[38] See Guerrini, "Dal testo all'immagine", 60 f.

[39] See Cavallaro, "Gli affreschi del Pinturicchio", 64.

tions. The idea that both Old Testament and pagan history foreshadowed New Testament events was persistently expressed in humanist writings and Renaissance visual arts, for the relationship between the past and the present was often considered "typological". The history of ancient Rome, in particular, was constantly "read" on a typological basis. Many of its events were explained as "providential", and its characters as Christian prefigurations. In this way, 'the purpose and meaning of Rome's history, in which divine will stood revealed, remained aloof from the vicissitudes of time'.[40]

The meaning of Pintoricchio's Christianized *exempla virtutis* is enhanced if one recalls who the commissioner of the frescoes was. Since his cardinalate period, Giuliano della Rovere nourished a central political ambition which would characterize his pontificate: to recover and increase the papacy's territorial patrimony, unifying Italy under the power of the Roman Church, and driving the French invaders from the peninsula. The use of the ancient civic *exempla* in Pintoricchio's cycle could be connected to his patriotic ideas, if one considered the figures depicted in the frescoes to be Christian prefigurations related to the defence of the native country and the Church. The Roman group formed by Curtius, Scaevola and Cocles predictably occupies a preeminent position in the cycle: the heroes' sacrifice for Rome acquired a contemporary meaning in a period during which the Eternal City was again emerging both as a political and a cultural centre. When elected pope, Julius II — who was hailed as a second Julius Caesar during his pontificate[41] — was particularly committed to the task of building a renewed Rome, emulative of the ancient Empire, but at the same time destined to surpass it in grandeur and universality. The centrality and power of the Roman Church ought to be manifested through the reborn magnificence of Rome. In this context, the grandiose expression of the heroism of the three heroes could at the same time serve as a prefiguration of the Church's own "patriotic" fight, and as an example for contemporaries, who would feel stimulated to emulate the heroes' devotion.

Curtius re-appears as a Christian prefiguration in the *Adoration of the Shepherds* of the San Domenico Church in Padua, painted by the

---

[40] See Stinger C.L., *The Renaissance in Rome* (Bloomington, Ind.: 1985) 5. Cf. also Graf, *Roma nella memoria*, 1-33, and Jacks P., *The Antiquarian and the Myth of Antiquity. The Origins of Rome in Renaissance Thought* (Cambridge: 1993) 20 f.
[41] See Stinger, *The Renaissance in Rome*, 235 f.

Sienese artist Francesco di Giorgio Martini between 1485 and 1495 — that is, approximately in the same years as Pintoricchio's frescoes [fig. 1]. In the foreground, the Virgin and child appear surrounded by St Joseph, the shepherds and angels, while an enormous triumphal arch in ruins is depicted in the background. On each side of this architectonic structure, one sees a bronze medallion, representing, on the right, Scaevola burning his hand, and on the left, Curtius jumping into the chasm [fig. 2].[42] As pointed out above, ruins frequently held a symbolic meaning during the Renaissance, especially in images of the Nativity and the Infancy of Christ,[43] where they were meant to evoke the ancient world overcome by the birth of Christ and the beginning of the new Christian era. The insertion of ancient scenes as decorative features of architectonic structures — usually simulating reliefs in grisaille — in works representing Christian subjects was not something new either during the Renaissance. As noted by Warburg, this method allowed the artist to establish a relationship of harmony and reconciliation with the classical past on the one hand, while on the other keeping a safe distance between the Pagan universe — confined in a fictitious space and treated as an explicit metaphor — and the Christian "real" image, the meaning of which was emphasized through the allusive grisaille.[44]

Particularly frequent was the connection between representations of Christ or Christian martyrs and Graeco-Roman sacrifices, the latter conceived as typological prefigurations of the Christian sacrifice. Examples from the second half of the fifteenth century are Lorenzo Costa's *Madonna dei Bentivoglio* in the Church of San Giacomo Maggiore, Bologna (1488); Mantegna's *Trial of St James*, formerly in the Ovetari Chapel, Eremitani Church, Padua (c. 1451), and Giovanni Bellini's *Redeemer* in London's National Gallery (c. 1460). The latter shows, in the foreground, a standing Christ holding his cross, from which hangs the crown of thorns. His right hand is outstretched showing his scar; the left one gently presses the wound at his side, so that his

---

[42] Francesco's interest in Roman heroes is also to be noticed in his *Scipio* at the Bargello, Florence, which was part of a cycle — now lost — representing other ancient heroes. See Toledano R., *Francesco di Giorgio Martini* (Milan: 1987) 102-8, and Guerrini, "Dal testo all'immagine", 55.

[43] One of the most celebrated examples is Ghirlandaio's *Adoration of the Shepherds* in the Sassetti Chapel.

[44] In Gombrich E., *Aby Warburg. An Intellectual Biography* (London: 1970) 176, 247 and 296.

blood gushes forth, and is collected in a chalice by an angel kneeling next to him. In the background Bellini represented, as reliefs in the parapet, on the left a sacrificial scene, and on the right Porsenna and Scaevola.[45] The meaning of the sacrifice of Christ, stressed by his gesture of pressing out his blood and by the exhibition of the instruments of the Passion, is thus illustrated by the pagan scenes in the background, which are understood as prefigurations of the death on Golgotha. Also in the aforementioned painting of Francesco di Giorgio, the depiction of both Roman heroes at the ancient, ruined arch must have been conceived as a typological allusion to the sacrificial death of Christ.

Curtius is again depicted as a decorative feature of a triumphal arch in Botticelli's *The Tragedy of Lucretia* (c. 1499), now in the Isabella Stewart Gardner Museum, Boston [fig. 3]. The work represents Lucretia's story in three different scenes: at left, Tarquin threatens her; at right, she receives her father and husband, and, at the centre, she is depicted after her suicide, surrounded by Brutus and the Romans, who clamour for vengeance. Over both lateral scenes is represented a frieze with a relief; the left one shows Judith and Holophern, and the right one Horatius Cocles. At the centre, a statue of David with the head of Goliath appears on a high column; behind it, one sees the triumphal arch representing Scaevola, Achilles with the body of Hector, a Roman triumph, and, in the upper relief on the left side, Marcus Curtius. Thus, the image of the Roman hero is here combined with Old Testament and Greek characters linked to patriotic virtues in order to illustrate the story of Lucretia, whose iconographic reception during the Renaissance — as well as that of Curtius — had been characterized by her identification as a Christianized *exemplum virtutis*.[46]

As stated above, Curtius's Christianization could also be suggested through the hero's gestures and pose. Very often, Curtius's posture is likened to that of St George when killing the dragon, as for example in a Renaissance cassone produced towards the end of the fifteenth cen-

---

[45] The interpretation that the two figures on the right were Porsenna and Scaevola was originally proposed by Saxl F., "Pagan Sacrifice in the Italian Renaissance", *Warburg Journal* 2 (1938) 352.

[46] See Donaldson, *The Rapes of Lucretia*, who also indicated the interpretation according to which Lucretia's death would be related to the establishment of the Roman Republic.

tury, now in London's National Gallery [fig. 4][47]. Here Curtius is represented as an angel-like youth mounted on a horse and raising a knife in his right hand; unlike most of the versions of the scene where he is depicted in armour, in the cassone-painting the hero wears only a short Roman tunic. An interesting aspect of this work is that Curtius is not represented in the Roman Forum, as should be expected, but in the countryside. Many other Renaissance representations of the hero similarly depict him in a natural landscape, such as those of Marcantonio Raimondi or Lucas Cranach,[48] both produced in the first decades of the Cinquecento. Moreover, most sixteenth-century Italian majolicas representing the death of Curtius are also set in the countryside.[49] It is possible that this tendency stemmed from a desire to disconnect the hero's self-sacrifice from Rome and, consequently, to alienate it from its original patriotic meaning. Once its earthly motive is removed, Curtius's death seems to be plainly spiritualized in a Christian sense.

From the beginning of the Cinquecento onwards, however, the images showing Curtius in the countryside are outnumbered by those which place him, among his countrymen, in the Roman Forum. In the first years of the century, the engraver Moderno produced a bronze plaquette representing Curtius's death with an absolute archaeological correctness, a characteristic which was followed by other engravers of this period.[50] In sixteenth-century wall paintings and public buildings, too, Curtius was normally represented in a reconstructed environment. Examples are Fasolino's ceiling decoration in Palladio's Loggia del Capitaniato in Vicenza, where the hero is seen next to Horatius Cocles and Mucius Scaevola,[51]

---

[47] In the catalogue of the National Gallery this undated cassone is classified as being from the Umbrian school. Frizzoni G., "La galleria nazionale di Londra e i suoi aumenti in fatto di arte italiana", *Archivio Storico dell'Arte* (1895) 103-5, however, attributes it to Bacchiacca. See also Schubring P., *Cassoni. Truhen und Truhenbilder der italienischen Frührenaissance* (Leipzig: 1915) no 827. Curtius appeared more than once in Italian Renaissance cassoni (Schubring 263, 289, and 407). One possible reason for this is that the hero is quoted by two of the cassoni painters' favourite literary sources, that is, Livy and the *Gesta Romanorum*.

[48] See respectively *The Illustrated Bartsch* XXVI, 1, ed. K. Oberhuber (New York: 1978) 87, and *Reallexikon zur Deutschen Kunstgeschichte* III, 888.

[49] See Giacomotti, *Catalogue des majoliques*, nos 906; 999; 1000; 1041-42.

[50] See *Reallexikon zur Deutschen Kunstgeschichte* III, 888.

[51] See Venditti A., *The Loggia del Capitaniato* (University Park–London: 1971) [fig. 52].

and Pordenone's frescoes on the façade of the Palazzo d'Anna in Venice.[52]

The latter, produced around 1535, probably inspired one of the most interesting Christianized representations of Curtius, that is, Paolo Veronese's oval canvas in the Kunsthistorisches Museum of Vienna [fig. 5].[53] Veronese's painting, originally intended as a ceiling decoration, shows Curtius from an unusual viewpoint, as if the observer were inside the chasm into which the hero is throwing himself. Both Suida and Schulz[54] indicate the canvas' similarities with the *Triumph of Mordecai* in the Church of San Sebastiano (Venice), a connection that has been generally accepted by later studies. Contemporary scholars have drawn equal attention to the influence of Giulio Romano's frescoes in the Mantuan Palazzo Té.[55] The date of the canvas has not been established with certainty, but its supposed derivation from Pordenone's and Giulio Romano's works and its affinities with the *Triumph of Mordecai* would situate it around 1550.[56]

As well as the aforementioned cassone-painting, Veronese's Curtius seems to derive from the St George type. According to Rearick, the Austrian canvas could be linked to a drawing produced by Veronese in 1550, now in the Uffizi, representing the saint killing the dragon.[57] Perhaps the most startling characteristic of the painting, though, is the evident similarity between the figure of Curtius and that of another Veronesian representation of St George, namely in the *Martyrdom of Saint George* in San Giorgio in Braida, Verona.[58] Indeed, Curtius's figure has many features in common with the contemporary martyr-type: his upraised head and the eyes turned to Heaven — as if he were

---

[52] These frescoes are lost, but Curtius's representation is known through drawings and woodcuts. See Cohen C., *The Art of Giovanni Antonio da Pordenone*, 2 vols (Cambridge: 1996) II, cat. no 79, 709 f. Curtius equally appears on the façade of the Mantica palace in Pordenone; see Cohen, *The Art of Giovanni Antonio da Pardenone*, 741.

[53] The relationship between these two works was suggested by Suida W., "Zwei Bilder des Paolo Veronese", *Pantheon* 1 (1928) 128, and Pallucchini R., *Veronese* (Milan: 1984) 15-8, who relate Veronese's to Pordenone's *di sotto insù* vision of Curtius.

[54] Respectively Suida W., "Zwei Bilder des Paolo Veronese", 126, and Schulz J., *Venetian Painted Ceilings of the Renaissance* (Berkeley–Los Angeles: 1968) 127-8.

[55] See Pedrocco F. – Pignatti, T., *Veronese*, 2 vols (Milan: 1995) 48.

[56] See Suida W., "Zwei Bilder des Paolo Veronese", 124-8; Pallucchini, *Veronese*, and Pedrocco – Pignatti, *Veronese*.

[57] See Rearick W.R., *Tiziano e il disegno veneziano del suo tempo* (Florence: 1976) 158 and Idem, *The Art of Paolo Veronese, 1528–1588* (Washington: 1988) 38.

[58] See Cocke R., "Exemplary Lives: Veronese's representations of Martyrdom and the Council of Trent", *Renaissance Studies* 10, 3 (1996) 390 and 394.

communicating with the Divine at the moment of his death —, as well as his outstretched arms are typical of a martyr's attitude.[59] The bellicose attitude assumed by Curtius in most of his representations completely disappears: he is no longer holding his sword or the horse's reins, nor does he seem to have any control over the animal, which is thus transformed into the instrument of his sacrifice.

This same passive attitude may also be found in Renaissance depictions of other Christianized *exempla virtutis*. Lucretia, for instance, is often presented in the posture of a dying Christian martyr, as for example in the works of Francesco Trevisani, Marcantonio Raimondi and Veronese himself, who painted in c. 1580 a canvas which shows Lucretia 'apparently ignoring the dagger which she holds to her breast'.[60] As noted by Donaldson, 'as so often in these representations, Lucretia's death seems almost to take her unaware; the knife approaches Lucretia seemingly without her conscious knowledge or control, as though directed by some external force. It is as though her death, like Christ's, were essentially a matter of passive surrender rather than active self-destruction'.[61]

As discussed above, one of the main differences between the Roman civic self-offering and the Christian martyrdom, as they were understood by the early Church Fathers, is that the former is actively sought by the hero himself, whereas the latter is passively undergone by the martyr. What Veronese does is to practically remove from Curtius the power over his own death, to make him as passive as saints about to be martyred or animals led by the acolytes to the sacrificial altar. Moral criticism of Curtius's self-offering is thus deflected by the representation of what seems to be not the result of Curtius's personal heroic decision, but of an external determination that he humbly accepts. As depicted by Veronese, Curtius's descent to the underworld is practically an ascension to Heaven.

In sum, from the second half of the Quattrocento onwards, Marcus Curtius begins to appear frequently in the visual arts. In these representations, the hero is often associated with a Christian meaning or has his figure assimilated to that of Christian characters. This renewed

---

[59] Other Veronesian examples are the *Martyrdom of St Sebastian* in San Sebastiano and the *Martyrdom of St Justina* in the Uffizi.
[60] Donaldson, *The Rapes of Lucretia*, 27.
[61] Ibidem.

FIGURES 1-5

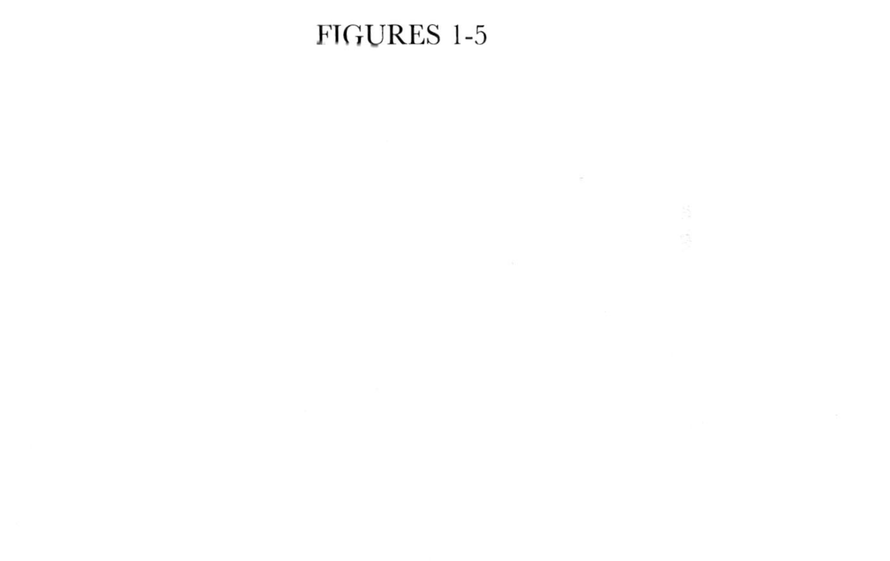

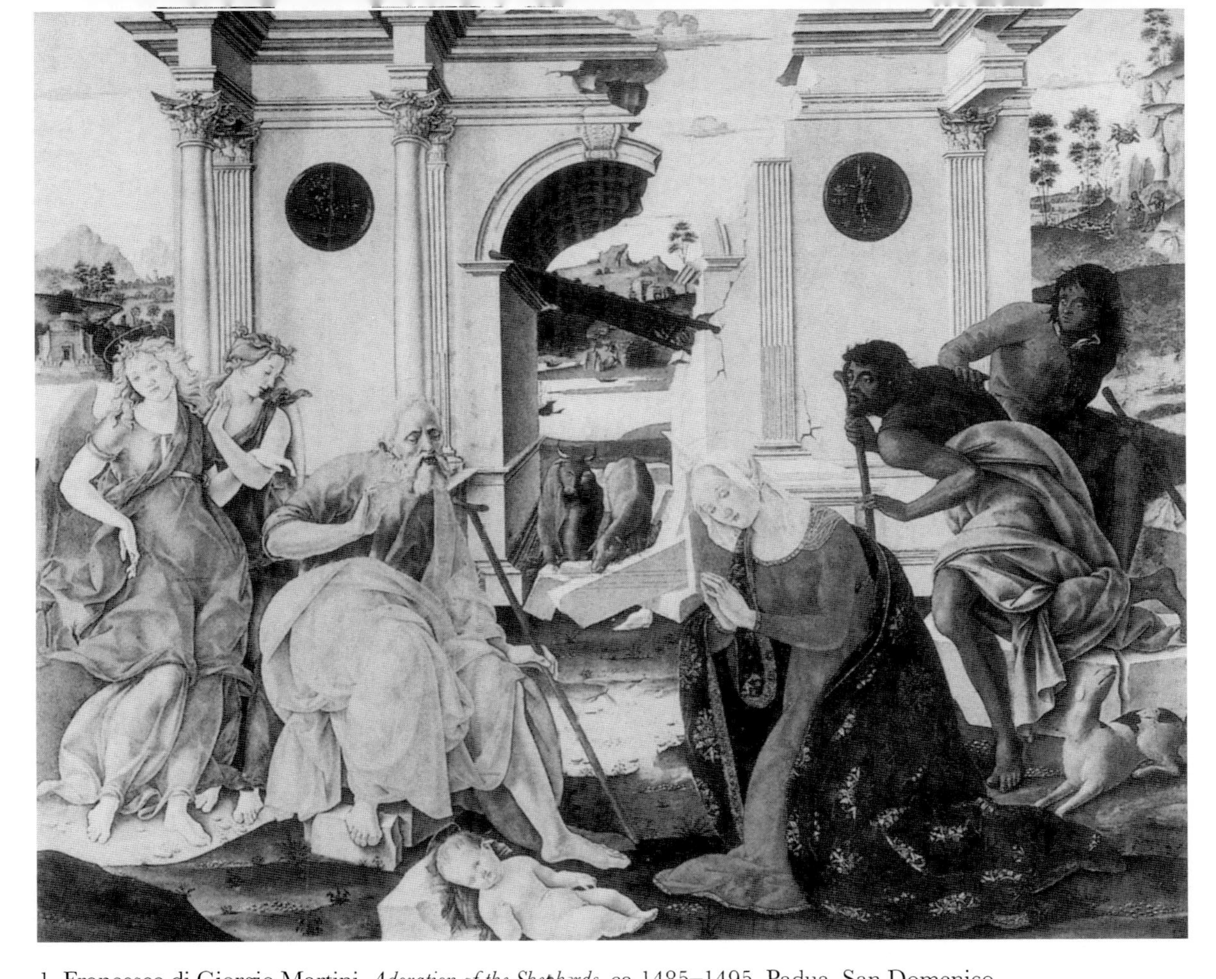

1. Francesco di Giorgio Martini, *Adoration of the Shepherds*, ca.1485–1495. Padua, San Domenico.

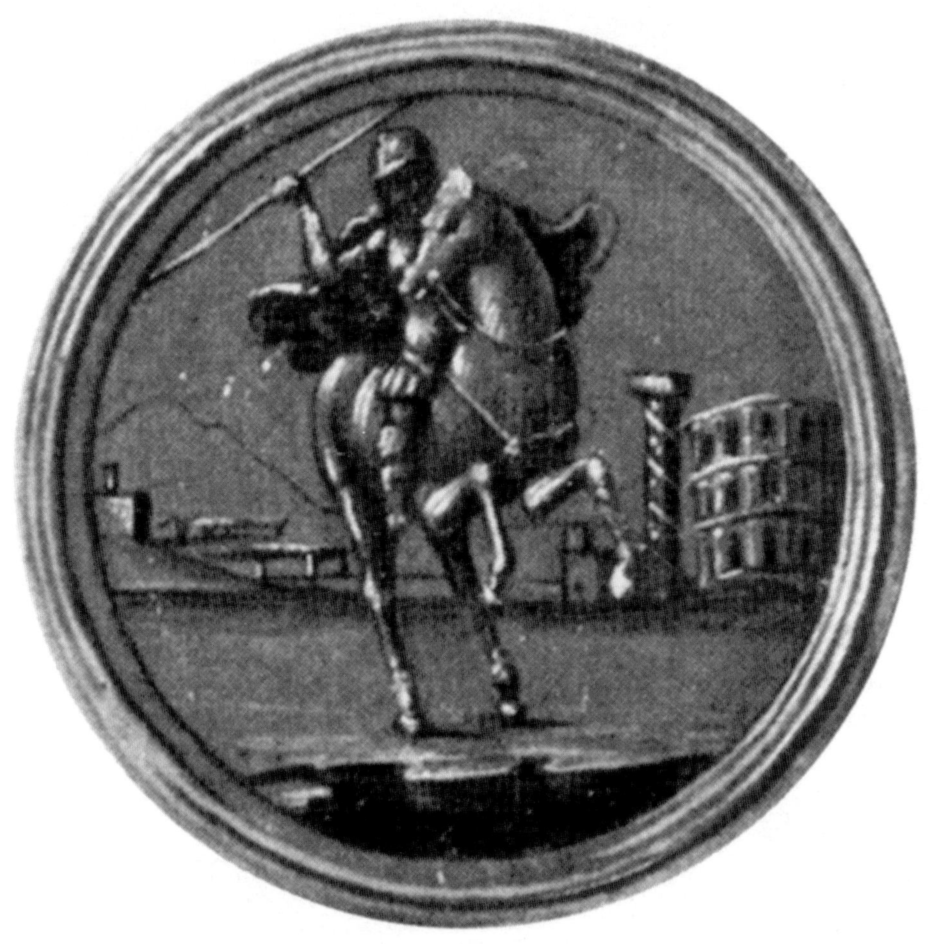

2. Detail of Fig. 1.

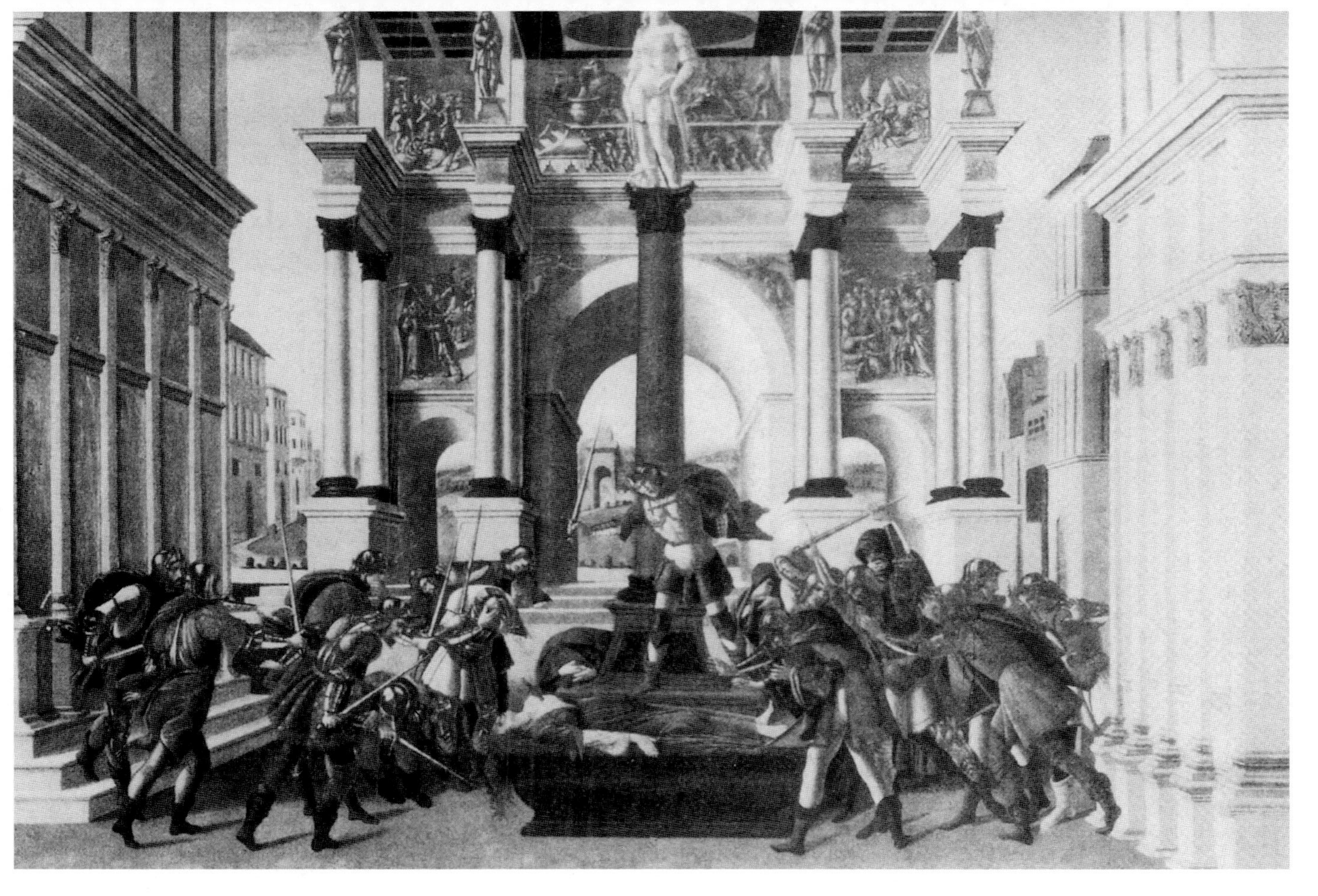

3. Sandro Botticelli, *The Tragedy of Lucretia*, ca.1499. Boston, Isabella Stewart Gardner Museum.

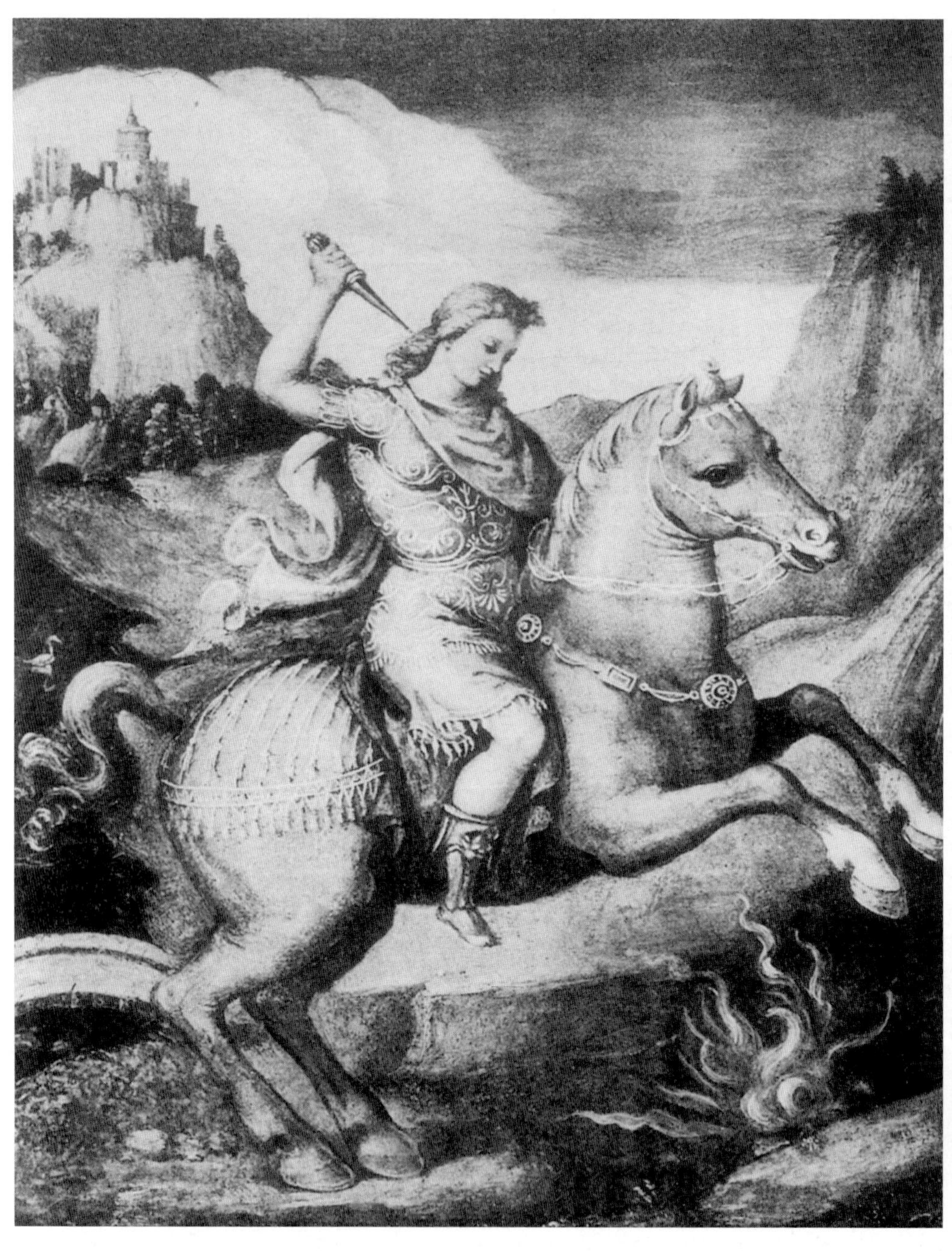

4. Anonymous, *Marcus Curtius* (cassone), last quarter of the fifteenth century. London, National Gallery.

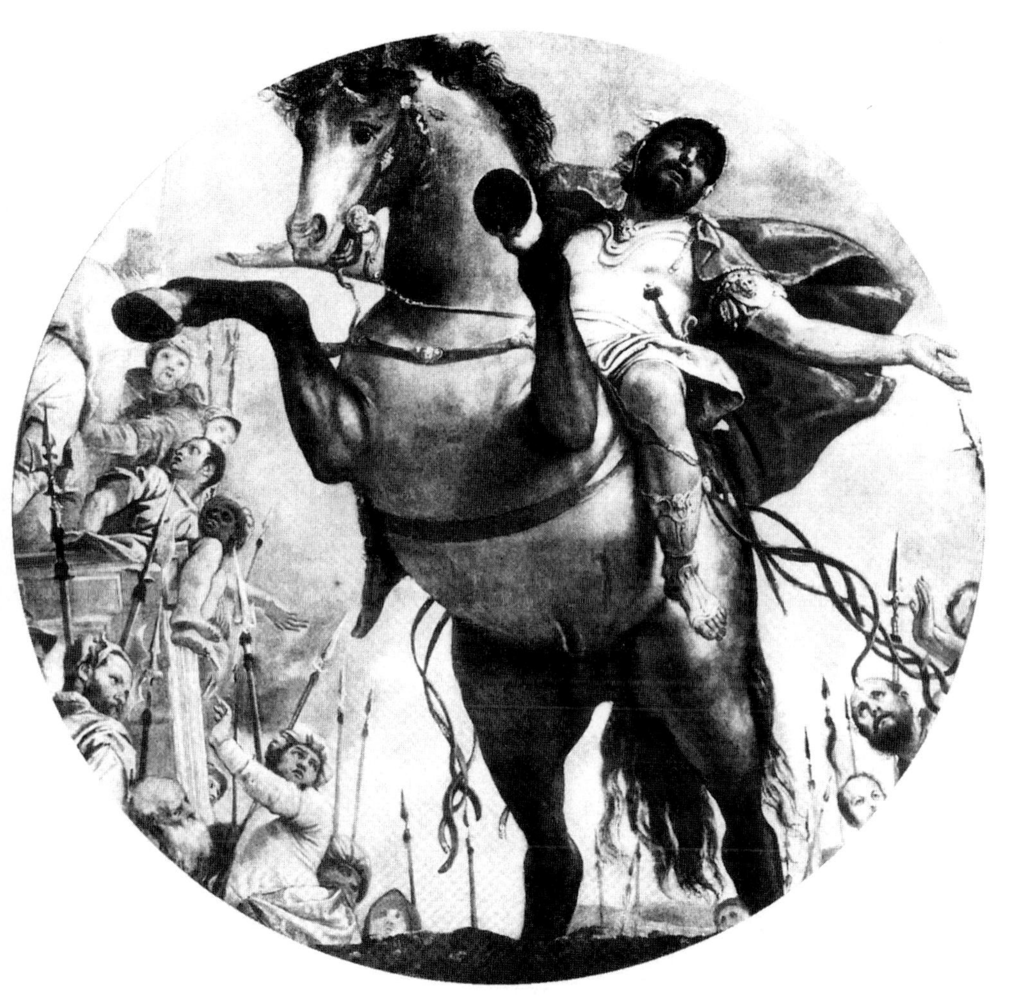

5. Paolo Veronese, *Marcus Curtius*, ca. 1535. Vienna, Kunsthistorisches Museum.

interest in Curtius can be explained within the context of the general revival of Graeco-Roman Antiquity that characterized the Renaissance. On closer examination, however, it may prove to be linked with two particular aspects of the contemporary relationship to the classical past.

Firstly, the interest in Curtius and other abnegated Roman heroes can be placed against the background of the attraction exerted by Graeco-Roman sacrifice — the civic self-offering certainly being one of its manifestations — that began to manifest itself in Italy precisely during this period. Pagan sacrificial scenes or elements were introduced into Christian works as typological allusions to the sacrifice of Christ and the holy martyrs, a process which until then had almost always involved types from the Old Testament.[62] In this context, Curtius's self-offering was also conceived as a sort of Christian prefiguration.

Secondly, his fate was closely intertwined with Rome, the Eternal City which seemed to embody at once the renewed ancient grandeur and the birth of the new Christian faith. Rome's providential origin and history were constantly acclaimed both by humanist writers and Renaissance artists, who considered the new papal Rome the culmination, rather than the antithesis, of imperial Rome.[63] In this context, heroes such as Curtius, Decius, or Cocles, who sacrificed themselves in order to save the future capital of the Roman Church from impending danger, could not but be held in the highest esteem. The ideal of patriotism that they represented, which had been so severely criticized by the Church Fathers as incompatible with true religious zeal, could now be identified with the defence of the Roman Church, whose imperial vocation was being persistently re-affirmed.

As shown by the visual arts and literary sources, therefore, the line which the Church Fathers carefully drew between the Roman heroes — including Curtius — and the Christian martyrs was eventually swept away by the intense admiration Renaissance men felt for the former, ultimately leading to their use as renewed *exempla virtutis*. For a relatively brief period — roughly speaking from the early fifteenth to the mid sixteenth century — Roman heroes could embody Christian virtues in the same way Judaeo-Christian characters could personify civic virtues; the role of both could be at the same time religious and

---

[62] Such as, for example, Isaac and Abraham.
[63] See Stinger, *The Renaissance in Rome*, 334 f.

patriotic. For the Renaissance artist, there no longer seemed to exist a contradiction between defending the celestial and the earthly city. In the particular case of Curtius, who had given his life for the future capital of the Christian world, the potential holy quality of patriotism could achieve its highest expression.

Selective Bibliography

BLUME D., "Antike und Christentum", in *Natur und Antike in der Renaissance*, Cat. exhib. in the Liebieghaus (Frankfurt a. M.: 1985)

CARLSON M.L., "Pagan Examples of Fortitude in the Latin Christian Apologists", *Classical Philology* 43 (1948) 93-104

CAVALLARO A., "Gli affreschi del Pinturicchio nella palazzina di Giuliano della Rovere ai SS. Apostoli", in *Un'idea di Roma*, ed. L. Fortini (Rome: 1993)

COCKE R. "Exemplary Lives: Veronese's representations of Martyrdom and the Council of Trent", *Renaissance Studies* 10, 3 (1996) 388-404

COHEN C., *The Art of Giovanni Antonio da Pordenone*, 2 vols (Cambridge: 1996)

DONALDSON I., *The Rapes of Lucretia* (Oxford: 1982)

FRIZZONI G., "La galleria nazionale di Londra e i suoi aumenti in fatto di arte italiana", *Archivio Storico dell'Arte* (1895) 87-105

GIACOMOTTI J., *Catalogue des majoliques des Musées Nationaux* (Paris: 1974)

GRAF A., *Roma nella memoria e nelle immaginazioni del Medio Evo* (Turin: 1923)

GUERRINI R., "Dal testo all'imagine. La 'pittura di storia' nel Rinascimento", in *Memoria dell'antico nell'arte italiana*, ed. S. Settis, II (Turin: 1985)

JACKS P., *The Antiquarian and the Myth of Antiquity. The Origins of Rome in Renaissance Thought* (Cambridge: 1993)

JONG J.L. DE, *De Oudheid in Fresco* (diss., Leiden: 1987)

LECKY W.E.H., *History of European Morals from Augustus to Charlemagne* (New York: 1876)

LIPPINCOTT K., "A Masterpiece of Renaissance Drawing: A Sacrificial Scene by Gian Francesco de' Maineri", *Museum Studies* 17, 1 (Chicago: 1991) 6-21, 42, 88-9

LITCHFIELD H.W., "National *exempla virtutis* in Roman literature", *Harvard Studies in Classical Philology* 25 (1914) 1-71

MASSMANN H.F. (ed.), *Die Kaiserchronik*, 3 vols (Quedlinburg–Leipzig: 1854)

PALLUCCHINI R., *Veronese* (Milan: 1984)

PANOFSKY E., *Early Netherlandish Painting*, 2 vols (Cambridge, Mass.: 1953)

PEDROCCO F. – PIGNATTI T., *Veronese*, 2 vols (Milan: 1995)

PIGNATTI T., *Veronese*, 2 vols (Venice: 1976)

REARICK W.R., *Tiziano e il disegno veneziano del suo tempo* (Florence: 1976)

RICHARDSON L., *A new topographical Dictionary of ancient Rome* (London–Baltimore: 1992)

SAXL F., "Pagan Sacrifice in the Italian Renaissance", *Warburg Journal* 2 (1938), 346-67

SCARPELLINI P., *Perugino* (Milan: 1984)

SCHUBRING P., *Cassoni. Truhen und Truhenbilder der italienischen Frührenaissance* (Leipzig: 1915)

SCHULZ J., *Venetian painted Ceilings of the Renaissance* (Berkeley–Los Angeles: 1968)

STINGER C.L., *The Renaissance in Rome* (Bloomington, Ind.: 1985)

SUIDA W., "Zwei Bilder des Paolo Veronese", *Pantheon*, 1 (1928) 124-8

TOLEDANO R., *Francesco di Giorgio Martini* (Milan: 1987)

VENDITTI A., *The Loggia del Capitaniato* (University Park–London: 1971)

WARDE FOWLER W., *Social Life In Rome in the Age of Cicero* (London: 1908)

WARDE FOWLER W., *The Religious Experience of the Roman People* (London: 1911).

MONTAIGNE, PLUTARCH AND HISTORIOGRAPHY

Paul J. Smith

In Book II, Chapter 32, of his *Essais*, entitled *Defence de Seneque et de Plutarque*, Montaigne joins in with the contemporary discussion about historiography. Among other things, he takes issue here with a number of views he found in an authoritative historiographical work of his time: the *Methodus ad facilem historiarum cognitionem* by Jean Bodin (first edition 1566).[1] In this work, Bodin accuses Plutarch of gullibility and unreliability. Montaigne speaks up for his favourite author in a *défense* which at first appears to be clear and straightforward but which, on closer reading, presents various problems of interpretation. In this article I will attempt to offer a close reading of this chapter, in which I not only hope to provide insight into Montaigne's view of historiography,[2] but also into his way of writing and argumentation. Before looking at the *Defence de Seneque et de Plutarque* more closely, I will first briefly consider the place that Plutarch takes in Montaigne's work and look at a number of relevant aspects of the literary genre that he inaugurated: the essay.

Montaigne as a reader of Plutarch

Isabelle Konstantinovic's recent work, *Montaigne et Plutarque* (1989), confirms something that all Montaigne's readers would already surmise: the overwhelming presence of Plutarch in the *Essais*. In her research she arrives at the following figures: Montaigne refers to or borrows from Plutarch's *Moralia* 459 times and 293 times from his *Parallel Lives*.[3] It is striking that these works, which Montaigne primarily knew through Jacques Amyot's French translation, have a constantly

---

[1] Edition consulted: Bodin J., *Oeuvres philosophiques*, ed. and transl. P. Mesnard (Paris: 1951) 99-457.

[2] Much has been written about Montaigne and his preoccupation with historiography. See for instance the recent collection *Montaigne et l'histoire* [...], ed. C.-G. Dubois (Paris: 1991). In this and other studies too little attention has been paid to chapter II, 32.

[3] Konstantinovic I., *Montaigne et Plutarque* (Geneva: 1989) 28 and 32.

high presence in all the developmental stages of the *Essais*, that is to say, both in the three published books as well as in the three layers of Montaigne's text which can be distinguished (a), (b) and (c).[4]

What was it in Plutarch that appealed so much to Montaigne? First of all, the *Moralia* as well as the *Parallel Lives* form an inexhaustible source for the innumerable quotations and anecdotes with which Montaigne larded his argument. Montaigne usually confined himself to briefly and approvingly quoting Plutarch, often more or less literally from Amyot's translation, sometimes mentioning Plutarch's name and sometimes not. At times, however, Montaigne does not agree with his *maître à penser*, and he enters into a discussion with him regarding the correct interpretation of an incident. I will confine myself to a single example, which is at the same time germane to an aspect of my argument, namely the associative character of Montaigne's writing. The chapter *Des coches* is not immediately and exclusively concerned with vehicles, as the title would seem to suggest,[5] but opens with a discussion about the multiple explanations of the *causes* of certain phenomena. As an example Montaigne takes the causes of seasickness, and cites Plutarch's authoritative opinion on the subject, which maintains that fear is the cause of seasickness. Montaigne absolutely disagrees with this, for various reasons: his own experience with seasickness, the behaviour that has been observed among pigs that have been shipped, and contemporary and classical evidence to the contrary (namely that fear can have precisely the effect of making the seasickness disappear). Montaigne sums it all up as follows:

> (b) Now I am very subject to seasickness and I know that that cause does not apply to me; and I know it not by argument but compelling experience. I shall not cite what I have been told, that animals, espe-

---

[4] I refer to the *Essais* in Montaigne's *Oeuvres complètes*, ed. A. Thibaudet – M. Rat (Paris: 1962). The letters (a), (b) and (c) designate the three most important textual layers of the *Essais*: the first edition from 1580, consisting of books I and II, is what (a) refers to; what comes after (b) are the additions of the 1588 edition (a whole, newly conceived book III, plus hundreds of additions to books I and II); finally (c) refers to the hundreds of handwritten additions which Montaigne entered in the margins of his own copy (1588 edition) between 1588 and his death in 1592. These additions were for the most part included in the posthumous 1595 edition.

[5] Elsewhere Montaigne writes: 'Les noms de mes chapitres n'en embrassent pas toujours la matiere' (III, 9, p. 973) ('The names of my chapters do not always encompass my subject-matter' (1125)). The English translations are taken from *The Essays of Michel de Montaigne*, transl. and ed. M.A. Screech (London: 1991). Following Montaigne's own usage, I use the term *chapter*, and not *essay*, as is the customary but erroneous practice.

cially pigs, which have no conception of danger, get seasick; nor what one of my acquaintances has told me about himself: he is much subject to it yet on two or three occasions when he was obsessed by fear during a great storm the desire to vomit disappeared — (c) as it did to that man in Antiquity: 'Peius vexabar quam ut periculum mihi succurreret' ('I was too shaken for the danger to occur to me'). (b) [...] I have never felt, on water [...].[6]

'That man in Antiquity', whose quotation has been added in the margin of his copy is, by the way, Seneca, who, as we shall see, is frequently bracketed together with Plutarch, although in this case he is used against him. In the continuation of the argument Plutarch vanishes from sight, and Montaigne takes his reader from *causes* to *coches* in all shapes and sizes (a play on words on the partial homophony of both words cannot be ruled out).[7] Subsequently, via sinuous argumentation, which I will not analyse here for reasons of space, Montaigne arrives at the New World and the atrocities committed there by the Spanish against the Indians. The chapter concludes with a return to the subject via the laconic formula 'retombons sur nos coches' ('let us drop back to those coaches of ours')[8], where we as readers are told how Attabalipa, the last Inca King, is pulled off his sedan chair by Francisco Pizarro. This last piece of information forms an abrupt end, the 'chute', to the chapter. Montaigne allows the fall of the Inca monarch, in the figurative as well as the literal sense (the fall from his sedan chair), to coincide with the *retombons* and the *chute* of the argumentation.

This example, in which Plutarch implicitly plays the role of discus-

---

[6] Screech, *The Essays*, 2018. 'Moy, qui y suis fort subjet, sçay bien que cette cause ne me touche pas, et le sçay non par argument, mais par necessaire experience. Sans alleguer ce qu'on m'a dict, qu'il en arrive de mesme souvent aux bestes, et notamment aux pourceaux, hors de toute apprehension de danger; et ce qu'un mien connoissant m'a tesmoigné de soy, qu'y estant fort subjet, l'envie de vomir luy estoit passée deux ou trois fois, se trouvant pressé de fraieur en grande tourmente, (c) comme à cet ancien: *Pejus vexabar quam ut periculum mihi succurreret;* (b) je n'eus jamais peur sur l'eau [...]' (III, 6, p. 876-7).

[7] For a similar word play in a similar context on *chose, cause,* and *causeur,* see *Essais,* III, 11, p. 1003: '(b) Je vois ordinairement que les hommes, aux faicts qu'on leur propose, s'amusent plus volontiers à en cercher la raison qu'à en cercher la verité: ils laissent là les *choses,* et s'amusent à traiter les *causes.* (c) Plaisans *causeurs*' [my italics] ('(b) I realize that if you ask people to account for "facts", they usually spend more time finding reasons for them than finding out whether they are true. They ignore the *whats* and expatiate on the *whys.* (c) Wiseacres!'; Screech, *The Essays*, 1161).

[8] Screech, *The Essays*, 1036.

sion partner, offers a good idea of Montaigne's writing. His argumentation is not derived from the *dispositio* scheme of classical rhetoric of which, as we shall see, Cicero is (according to Montaigne) the objectionable example. For Montaigne, it concerns a rhetorical style which adapts itself to the subject, a *rhétorique de l'objet*.[9] According to Montaigne, eloquence must be at the service of things, not of itself: '(a) When eloquence draws attention to itself it does wrong by the substance of *things*';[10] '(a) Shame on all eloquence which leaves us with a taste for itself not for its substance'.[11]

It is important for our subject that Montaigne regards Plutarch as his great example for this associative manner of argumentation. Montaigne's description of Plutarch's writing as a 'substance induc[ing] doubt, [his] purpose [being] inquiry rather than instruction'[12] can be regarded as a definition of Montaigne's essay writing. Moreover, what he says about Plutarch's *ordo neglectus* can immediately be applied to his own style of writing: '(c) [There are works of Plutarch in which] he forgets his theme, or in which the subject is treated only incidently, since they are entirely padded out with extraneous matter'.[13] Plutarch writes, according to Montaigne, 'à pieces décousues' ('in pieces not sewn together').[14] He writes about himself in similar terms: 'I pronounce my sentences in disconnected clauses'.[15] It is even the case that when he characterizes his own writing, it is likely that he deliberately uses the same qualifications as Erasmus does when talking about Plutarch. In a passage from *De la vanité* (III, 9) Montaigne rejects what is usual in an 'oraison', namely announcing precisely and explicitly what will be discussed. The reader is asked to allow himself to be carried along with the umpteenth digression: '(b) Reader: just let this ten-

---

[9] The term derives from the modern French poet Francis Ponge, who in his anti-rhetorical criticism, sides with the tradition of Montaigne. See my article on this subject "Ponge épidictique et paradoxal", in *Francis Ponge*, ed. F. Schuerewegen (Amsterdam: 1996) 35-46.

[10] Screech, *The Essays*, 194; '(a) L'éloquence faict injure aux choses, qui nous destourne à soy' (I, 26, p. 171).

[11] Screech, *The Essays*, 282; '(a) Fy de l'eloquence qui nous laisse envie de soy, non des choses' (I, 40, p. 246).

[12] Screech, *The Essays*, 568; 'forme d'escrire douteuse, enquerant plustost qu'instruisant' (II, 12, p. 489).

[13] Screech, *The Essays*, 1125; '(a) [Plutarch] oublie son theme, où le propos de son argument ne se trouve que par incident, tout estouffé en matière estrangere' (p. 973).

[14] Screech, *The Essays*, 463.

[15] Screech, *The Essays*, 1222; 'Je prononce ma sentence par articles descousus' (III, 13, p. 1054).

tative essay, this third prolongation of my self-portrait, run its course'.[16] To this Montaigne adds:

> (c) I allow myself, since it is merely a piece of badly joined marquetry, to tack on some additional ornaments. That is no more than a little extra thrown in, which does not damn the original version, but does lend some particular value to each subsequent one through some ambitious bit of precision [...]. It is a drunkard's progress, formless, staggering, like reeds which the wind shakes as it fancies, haphazardly.[17]

In his foreword to his translations of Plutarch's *De cohibenda ira* and *De curiositate*, Erasmus uses similar terms to elucidate upon what he considers to be characteristic features of Plutarch's writing:

> I had a lot of trouble with the subtlety [*subtilitas*] of Plutarch's writing and hidden significations, which he had compiled from the remote storerooms of all kinds of authors and disciplines, in such a way that one would not qualify it a coherent discourse [*orationem*] but rather a patchwork [*centonem*], or better a mosaic [*musaicum*] made from the most exquisite inlaid works [*emblematibus*]. [...] Besides this difficulty he also has a kind of concise and abrupt style, which suddenly [*subiter*] sweeps away the reader's mind in divers directions [*regionem*].[18]

The words I have placed in italics recur literally in the passage by Montaigne quoted above. The metaphor *cento* reappears in the term 'pieces décousues'; *oratio* corresponds to 'oraison', *subtilitas* to 'subtil ité', *musaicum* and *emblematibus* to, respectively, 'marqueterie' and 'embleme', and the phrase *subiter* [...] *regionem* is in accordance with the accidental being carried along which Montaigne asks of his reader.[19]

---

[16] Screech, *The Essays*, 1091; '(b) Laisse, lecteur, courir encore ce coup d'essay et ce troisiesme alongeail [...]' (p. 941).

[17] Screech, *The Essays*, 1091; '(c) [...] je me donne loy d'y attacher (comme ce n'est qu'une marqueterie mal jointe), quelque embleme supernuméraire. Ce ne sont que surpoids, qui ne condamnent point la premiere forme, mais donnent quelque pris particulier à chacune des suivantes par une petite subtilité ambitieuse [...] C'est un mouvement d'yvroigne titubant, vertigineux, informe, ou des jonchets que l'air manie casuellement selon soy' (III, 9, p. 941-2).

[18] 'Mihi certe non mediocre negotium exhibuit ipsa Plutarchicae phraseos *subtilitas*, sensusque reconditi ex retrusis omnium auctorum ac disciplinarum apothecis sic deprompti connexique, ut non *orationem* sed *centonem*, aut ut melius dicam, *musaicum* opus existimes, ex *emblematibus* exquisitissimis concinnatum. [...] Praeter hanc difficultatem habet concisum quidam et abruptum, subiter lectoris animum transmovens in diversam regionem' (Erasmus, *Opera omnia* [...], (Leiden: 1703) vol IV, 57-8).

[19] Elsewhere Montaigne allows himself to be influenced by Erasmus' qualifications of good and bad style. See Friedrich H., *Montaigne*, transl. R. Rovini (Paris: 1968) 421, n. 323.

Montaigne's View of Plutarch as Historiographer

Alongside the above-mentioned aspects — Plutarch as the source for quotations and exemplary anecdotes, and as a model of anti-rhetorical writing — it must also be said at this point that Plutarch was for Montaigne the great example of historiographic writing. In his chapter *Des livres*, Montaigne draws a distinction between two categories of historiographers, one of which is primarily preoccupied with describing great deeds and events. The second category is, according to Montaigne, superior:

> (a) Now the most appropriate historians for me are those who write men's lives, since they linger more over motives than events, over what comes from inside more than what happens outside. That is why, of historians of every kind, Plutarch is the man for me.[20]

In making this distinction between event-oriented historiography and biography, Montaigne is also influenced by Plutarch. In the opening lines of his *Alexander the Great*, Plutarch observes the following:

> We are principally looking for the signs of the soul, using them to form a natural portrait of the life and customs of everyone; we leave it to the historians to write about wars, battles and other great things.[21]

In Montaigne's reflection on Plutarch, a remarkably consistent factor can now be pointed out, which requires a little explanation: the connection that Montaigne continually makes between Plutarch and Seneca.

Symptomatic of this consistent factor is Montaigne's visit to the library at the Vatican. From the report of this visit which is given in his *Journal de voyage en Italie* it transpires that the first two works that he looked at were invaluable manuscripts of the work of Plutarch and Seneca. Naturally, naming both authors in one breath is, to put it mildly, unusual. After all, Plutarch was in his writings a strong oppo-

---

[20] Screech, *The Essays*, 467; '(a) Or ceux qui escrivent les vies, d'autant qu'ils s'amusent plus aux conseils qu'aux evenemens, plus à ce qui part du dedans qu'à ce qui arrive au dehors, ceux là me sont plus propres. Voilà pourquoy, en toutes sortes, c'est mon homme que Plutarque' (II, 10, p. 396).

[21] 'Nous allions principalement recherchant les signes de l'ame, et par iceux formans un portrait au naturel de la vie et des moeurs d'un chacun, en laissant aux historiens à escrire les guerres, les batailles et autres telles grandeurs' (Plutarch, *Les vies des hommes illustres grecs et romains* [...], ed. and transl. J. Amyot, 2 vols ([s.l.]: 1594) II, 138).

nent of the Stoa,[22] the very doctrine to which Seneca adhered. From his point of view of unconventionality and paradox (*para-doxa*: against the prevailing opinion) this difference is precisely the reason for Montaigne drawing a parallel between both authors in his chapter *Des livres*. Here, I quote from the text *in extenso*, because a number of elements in it are of importance for the rest of my argument:

> (a) Those two authors are in agreement over most useful and true opinions; they were both fated to be born about the same period; both to be the tutors of Roman Emperors;[23] both came from foreign lands and both were rich and powerful. Their teachings are some of the cream of philosophy and are presented in a simple and appropriate manner. Plutarch is more uniform and constant; Seneca is more diverse and comes in waves. Seneca stiffens and tenses himself, toiling to arm against weakness, fear and vicious appetites; Plutarch seems to judge those vices to be less powerful and to refuse to condescend to hasten his step or to rely on a shield. Plutarch holds to Plato's opinions, which are gentle and well-suited to public life; Seneca's opinions are Stoic and Epicurean, farther from common practice but in my judgement more suited (c) to the individual (a) and firmer. It seems that Seneca bowed somewhat to the tyranny of the Emperors of his day, for I hold it for certain that his judgement was under duress when he condemned the cause of those great-souled murderers of Caesar; Plutarch is a free man from end to end. Seneca is full of pithy phrases and sallies; Plutarch is full of matter. Seneca enflames you and stirs you; Plutarch is more satisfying and repays you more. (b) Plutarch leads us; Seneca drives us.[24]

---

[22] Cf. for example Babut D., *Plutarque et le Stoïcisme* (Paris: 1969).

[23] Seneca was Nero's tutor; Montaigne, Amyot and others thought mistakenly that Plutarch was Trajan's tutor.

[24] Screech, *The Essays*, 463-4; '(a) Ces autheurs se rencontrent en la plus part des opinions utiles et vrayes; comme aussi leur fortune les fist naistre environ mesme siecle, tous deux precepteurs de deux Empereurs Romains, tous deux venus de païs estrangier, tous deux riches et puissans. Leur instruction est de la cresme de la philosophie, et presentée d'une simple façon et pertinente. Plutarque est plus uniforme et constant; Seneque, plus ondoyant et divers. Cettuy-cy se peine, se roidit et se tend pour armer la vertu contre la foiblesse, la crainte et les vitieux appetis; l'autre semble n'estimer pas tant leur effort, et desdaigner d'en haster son pas et se mettre sur sa targue. Plutarque a les opinions Platoniques, douces et accommodables à la société civile; l'autre les a Stoïques et Epicurienes, plus esloignées de l'usage commun, mais, selon moy, plus commodes (c) en particulier (a) et plus fermes. Il paroit en Seneque qu'il preste un peu à la tyrannie des Empereurs de son temps, car je tiens pour certain que c'est d'un jugement forcé qu'il condamne la cause de ces genereux meurtriers de Caesar; Plutarque est libre par tout. Seneque est plein de pointes et saillies; Plutarque, de choses. Celuy là vous eschauffe plus et vous esmeut; cettuy-cy vous contente davantage et vous paye mieux. (b) Il nous guide, l'autre nous pousse' (II, 10, p. 392-3).

Once again, Plutarch is not only the subject here but also the *exemple à suivre*. In the parallel he draws, Montaigne in fact does the same as Plutarch did in the *syncrisis* parts of his *Parallel Lives*, namely compare a Greek with a Roman. To be more precise: the parallel between Plutarch and Seneca could even be suggested here by Plutarch himself; that is to say: by pseudo-Plutarch, the author of a letter to Emperor Trajan.[25] This pseudo-Plutarch writes to Trajan:

> You have exposed yourself to great dangers, and I have exposed myself to the tongues of the calumniators, because Rome could not endure a cowardly Emperor and because the common voice of the people is accustomed to blaming the masters for their disciples. Likewise Seneca has been torn by the tongues of the calumniators, because of the sins of his pupil Nero.[26]

It is interesting that Montaigne adds to his *comparatio* between both writers a *tertium comparationis*, namely Cicero. Cicero is, in all respects, inferior to both the other authors: 'his style of writing seems boring to me'.[27] To Montaigne's taste, Cicero takes too long to come to the point: His arguments 'hover about the pot and languish'.[28] For Montaigne, Seneca and Plutarch form an example of style imbued with Atticism in contrast to Cicero's ostentatious *ubertas*.

The *comparatio* between Plutarch and Seneca, from which Plutarch emerges victorious, is one of a number of places in which Plutarch is praised, and with him his translator Jacques Amyot. Chapter II, 4

---

[25] Amyot is also of the erroneous opinion that this letter was written by Plutarch himself.

[26] I translate from the French: '[...] tu t'es exposé à de grands dangers, et moy aux langues des mesdisans, pour autant que Rome ne peut endurer un lasche Empereur, et que la commune voix du peuple a tousjours ascoutumé de reietter les fautes des disciples sur leurs maistres, comme Seneque est deschiré par les langues des mesdisans, pour les pechez de son Neron' (Amyot, "Aux lecteurs", in Plutarch, *Les vies* [...], I, no pag.). Amyot considers himself Seneca's and Plutarch's successor in being a royal tutor. See for example Amyot, "Au Roy Treschrestien Charles IX. de ce nom", in *Les oeuvres morales et meslées de Plutarque*, ed. and transl. J. Amyot (Paris: 1572; rpt New York etc.: 1971): '[...] pource que comme lon tient qu'il fut iadis precepteur de Traian, le meilleur des Empereurs qui furent oncques à Rome, aussi Dieu m'auoit fait la grace de l'auoir esté du premier Roy de la Chrestienté, que nature a doué d'autant de bonté que nul de ses predecesseurs' ('Just as they say that he once was the tutor of Trajan, the best of all Roman Emperors, so God had granted that I be the tutor of the first King of Christendom, whom Nature endowed with as much goodness as any of his predecessors').

[27] Screech, 464; 'sa façon d'escrire me semble ennuyeuse'.

[28] Screech, 464: 'languissent autour du pot'. For an analysis of this anti-Ciceronian passage, see Smith P.J. – Toorn N. van der, " 'Science de gueule' et Rhétorique, ou *De la vanité des paroles* (Montaigne, *Essais* I, 51)", *Studi francesi* 32 (1988) 89-90.

begins with a lengthy eulogy to Amyot, of which here are a number of lines:

> (a) It seems to me that I am justified in awarding the palm, above all our writers in French, to Jacques Amyot, not merely for the simplicity and purity of his language in which he excels all others, not for his constancy during such a long piece of work [...], but above all I am grateful to him for having chosen and selected so worthy and so appropriate a book to present to his country. Ignorant people like us would have been lost if that book had not brought us up out of the mire: thanks to it, we now dare to speak and write — and the ladies teach the dominies.[29]

This eulogy, which is brought to a strong hyperbolic conclusion, has nonetheless a defensive undertone, which is clearly apparent in his *Journal de voyage en Italie*, in which one finds a report of a real scholarly discussion. Here are the first lines of this report:

> Dining one day in Rome with our ambassador, with Muret and other learned men present, I got on the subject of the French translation of Plutarch; and against those who esteemed it much less highly than I do, I maintained at least this: that where the translator missed the real meaning of Plutarch, he has substituted another that is possible and well in keeping with what precedes and what follows.[30]

Both the above mentioned points, the *comparatio* between Plutarch and Seneca, and the words of praise for Plutarch with a defensive undertone, occur together in the chapter which forms the main subject under consideration: the *Defence de Seneque et de Plutarque*.

---

[29] Screech, *The Essays*, 408; '(a) Je donne avec raison, ce me semble, la palme à Jacques Amiot sur tous nos escrivains François, non seulement pour la naïfveté et pureté du langage, en quoy il surpasse tous autres [...], mais sur tout je luy sçay bon gré d'avoir sçeu trier et choisir un livre si digne et si à propos, pour en faire present à son pays. Nous autres ignorans estions perdus, si ce livre ne nous eust relevez du bourbier; sa mercy, nous osons à cett'heure et parler et escrire: les dames en regentent les maistres d'escole' (p. 344).

[30] *The Complete Works of Montaigne*, transl. D.M. Frame (London: 1957) 951; 'Disnant un jour à Rome avec nostre ambassadur, où estoit Muret et autres sçavans, je me mis sur le propos de la traduction françoise de Plutarche, et contre ceus qui l'estimoient beaucoup moins que je ne fais, je meintenois au moins cela: "Que où le traducteur a failli le vrai sans de Plutarque, il y en a substitué un autre vraisemblable et s'entretenant bien aus choses suivantes et précédentes" ' (p. 1223).

The Argumentative Structure of the Defence

Before considering the problematic aspects of this chapter, I will first
provide an annotated summary. The chapter consists of three unequal
parts: in the first part, in a short and powerful manner (thus not in a
Ciceronian style), the subject and the reasons for the subject are
announced:

> (a) My intimacy with those two great men and the help they give to me
> in my old age, (c) as well as to my book which is built entirely out of
> their spoils, (a) bind me to espouse their honour.[31]

In the second and third part Seneca and Plutarch are respectively
defended.

In the part devoted to Seneca, Montaigne begins by taking a stand
against one of the many thousands of 'so-called reformed' pamphlets
('de la Religion pretendue reformée') which were written in the seven-
ties. The anonymous author proposes a comparison between 'nostre
pauvre' Charles IX and Nero and, consequently, between the Cardinal of Lorraine (one of the councillors of the French king) and Seneca.
Montaigne finds this comparison unjust, firstly because Seneca is in all
respects superior to the Cardinal of Lorraine (I will return presently to
the 'backhandedness' of this attack on the Cardinal) and secondly
because the anonymous author supports his claims by referring to an
unreliable historiographer: the Greek Cassius Dio, who was read by
Montaigne and his contemporaries in the Latin translated by Gulielmus Xylander. The rest of this section devoted to Seneca is used in
order to challenge Cassius Dio's opinion of Seneca, with the help of
the following arguments:

1. Cassius Dio is 'inconstant': one moment he is full of praise for
Seneca, and the next, he is disapproving of him;
2. The negative image that Cassius Dio offers is not in accordance
with the image which is articulated in Seneca's own writings;
3. The favourable image that Tacitus for instance gives of Seneca is
much more reliable, because Tacitus, as a Roman, was more qualified
to pass judgement;

---

[31] Screech, *The Essays*, 817; '(a) La familiarité que j'ay avec ses personnages icy, et
l'assistance qu'il font à ma vieillesse (c) et à mon livre massonné purement de leurs
despouilles, (a) m'oblige à espouser leur honneur' (p. 699).

4. Cassius Dio's 'judgement of matters Roman was so diseased that he ventured to champion the causes of Julius Caesar against Pompey, and of Antony against Cicero'.[32]

The part devoted to Plutarch is four times as long, and has a far more complicated argumentative structure. Montaigne reproaches Jean Bodin, after first praising him according to the rhetorical rules of the ironical *laus* ('Jean Bodin is a good contemporary author, endowed with far better judgement than the mob of scribblers of his time'),[33] because he twice reproaches Plutarch unjustly: firstly, that the things that he writes are 'incredible and entirely fabulous';[34] secondly, that in his *Parallel Lives* he favours the Greeks above the Romans. Bodin's first reproach of Plutarch is illustrated by Montaigne with two examples, literally translated from his *Methodus*. Here follows the passage objected to by Bodin, which is short enough to quote in full:

> [Plutarch] often tells fabulous and really incredible things, but he adds the words 'they say that' for fear of not being believed. For instance, he tells us on the subject of Lycurgus, that a Lacedemonian child bore until death the cruel ripping open, even the tearing out of his entrails in order to hide the theft of a fox. And that Agesilaus was condemned to pay a fine by the ephores, because he was the only one capable of bringing together the heart and the spirit of his fellow citizens. One should remark that, although he is reliable when comparing illustrious Greeks to other Greeks, or great Romans to other Romans, this is not the case when he compares Greeks to Romans. This can be seen clearly in his parallels between Demosthenes and Cicero, Cato and Aristides, Sulla and Lysander, Marcellus and Pelopidas. Indeed, what else is the comparison between Agesilaus and Pompey but a comparison between a fly and an elephant?[35]

---

[32] Screech, *The Essays*, 818.

[33] Screech, *The Essays*, 818; 'Jean Bodin est un bon autheur de nostre temps, et accompagné de beaucoup plus de jugement que la tourbe des escrivailleurs de son siecle'.

[34] Screech, *The Essays*, 818; 'incroyables et entierement fabuleuses'.

[35] 'Saepe incredibilia et plane fabulosa narrat, sed utitur verbo φασί, ne quis temere assentiatur. Ut in Lycurgo scribit puerum Lacedaemonium crudelissimam lacerationem et iliorum distractionem ad necem usque petulisse, ne vulpis furtum detegeretur. Et Agesilaum ab ephoris mulctatum, quod suorum civium animos et voluntates unus sibi conciliarat. Illud tamen animadversione dignum est, quod principis cum Graecis et Romanos inter se bona fide comparavit: Graecos vero cum Romanis non item. Idque facile intelligi potest in comparatione Demosthenis ac Ciceronis, Catonis ac Aristidis, Syllae ac Lysandri, Marcelli ac Pelopidae. Quid autem aliud est Agesilaum Pompeio, quam muscam Elephanto conferre?' (Bodin, *Methodus*, 132B).

Bodin's first example of Plutarch's unreliability concerns the anecdote about the Spartan boy who hides a stolen fox under his robe, and whose intestines are ripped out by the creature without the boy giving anything away. Bodin's reproach, that this anecdote is utterly unbelievable, is extensively refuted by Montaigne in a whole series of counterexamples, first from Spartan history, then more in general from the distant and recent past, all of which ostensibly demonstrate that history has been witness to many similar instances of perseverance. Bodin's second example (Plutarch's statement that Agesilaus was banished by the ephores because he was too popular with the people) is dealt with by Montaigne remarkably briefly in comparison with Bodin's first example. Montaigne concludes the chapter by refuting Bodin's second reproach to Plutarch (his pro-Hellenistic composition of the *syncrisis*).

In recapitulation, a schematic rendering of the basic argumentative structure of the chapter would read as follows:

A. introduction
B. defence of Seneca against
   a. an anonymous Protestant pamphlet
   b. Cassius Dio in four counterarguments
C. defence of Plutarch against two reproaches by Bodin:
   a. his unreliability, illustrated by two examples from Bodin:
      1. the Spartan boy and his fox (long series of counterarguments)
      2. the banishment of Agesilaus by the ephores
   b. his favouring of the Greeks above the Romans.

Praise or Blame?

Even though it is complicated, the argumentation is at first sight lucid and logical. A closer reading renders it less so. Let us start with the introduction (part A). Here, for every reader trained in humanist rhetorics, a well-known exordium topos is recognizable: the *humilitas affecta*, the feigned modesty of the rhetorician, which is further padded out by the addition of hyperbole in the (c) version: 'et à mon livre massonné *purement* de leurs despouilles' [my italics]. The formulation 'm'oblige' is revealing, for it deprives this chapter of its spontaneous character, a feature which is so typical of Montaigne's essay writing.

This artificiality, this lack of spontaneity, is also expressed in the self-exhortation which marks the transition to part C.b. (see table): 'Let us see whether we can save him from this accusation of falsehood and prevarication'.[36] We are thus dealing with a rhetorical exercise, which can be cast in rather a strange light if we care to recall Montaigne's ubiquitously expressed criticism of Ciceronian eloquence in favour of spontaneity and sincerity.

From a contextual perspective the experienced Montaigne reader is also on his guard for other reasons: when Montaigne claims that he will defend something or someone, does he then really do this? The best known example of a case in which he announces this but does not do it, and even attacks the person he says he will defend, is Book II, chapter 12 entitled *Apologie de Raimond Sebond*.[37]

This last question can also be asked of the B part of the chapter: are we really dealing here with a genuine defence of Seneca? Part B.a. deals more with the pamphlet challenged than with Seneca. Montaigne's political position is not difficult to gauge here. The phrase 'pretendue reformée' is an indication of his Catholic standpoint; the remark 'nostre pauvre feu Roy Charles' is indicative of his royalist sympathies. Yet the nuance is that the Cardinal of Lorraine will be allocated lengthy *laus* with regard to, among other things, his intelligence, his religious diligence and his loyalty to the King, but he is then floored in rather a subtle manner, according to the interpretation by David Lewis Schaefer:

> In sum, in saying that the Protestant pamphleteer did 'great honor' to Lorraine by comparing him with Seneca, Montaigne really meant that the Protestant hadn't insulted the cardinal enough: despite his numerous defects, Seneca was still far superior![38]

Montaigne's position against the Cardinal is in keeping with his aversion to the right-wing political movement which the Cardinal and other members of the De Guise clan stood for. In the meantime, however, there has been nothing substantial said about Seneca.

This does happen in part B.b., in which Cassius Dio's opinion of Seneca is criticised. The four arguments advanced by Montaigne are, however, far from convincing. The 'inconstance' which Cassius Dio is

---

[36] Screech, *The Essays*, 822; 'Voyons si nous le pourrons garentir de ce reproche de prevarication et fauceté' (p. 704).

[37] Montaigne's apology of Sebond's *Natural Theology* turns out to be a critical reading of this book.

[38] Schaefer D.L., *The Political Philosophy of Montaigne* (Ithaca–London: 1990) 266, n. 28.

accused of when Montaigne voices his opinion of Seneca (argument 1) is, on the contrary, cited elsewhere in the *Essais* as a positive point in relation to the admired Plutarch, who presents 'hundreds of [...] things, in two opposite and contrasting manners'.[39] Moreover, it will strike every reader that Montaigne himself is also at times positive and then at others much more negative with regard to Seneca.[40] Argument 2 (the negative image of Seneca sketched by Cassius Dio is not in accordance with his writings) is immediately weakened by the preceding chapter II, 31, in which it is argued that someone's writings can conceal their true nature and aims: 'Saying is one thing: doing another; we must consider the preaching apart and the preacher apart'.[41] Argument 3 is without any basis because it implies that Plutarch would also be unreliable when writing about the Romans.[42] Moreover, Montaigne indicates elsewhere in his *Essais* that even Tacitus is sometimes wrong in his historiographic writing about the Roman Empire.[43] Finally, argument 4 is literally borrowed from Bodin, who writes: 'videtur tamen ubique partes Caesaris adversum Pompeium; et Antonii adversus Ciceronem data opera tueri voluisse'.[44]

---

[39] Screech, *The Essays*, 1206; 'mille [...] choses, diversement et contrairement' (III, 12, p. 1041).

[40] Especially in III, 9, p. 939: '(b) je me desplais de l'inculcation, voire aux choses utiles, comme en Seneque, (c) et l'usage de son escole Stoïque me desplait [...]' ('(b) I hate persistent admonition even when it serves a purpose as in Seneca, (c) and I dislike the practice of the Stoic School of [...]'). See also III, 12, p. 1016: '(b) A voir les efforts que Seneque se donne pour se preparer contre la mort, à le voir suer d'ahan pour se roidir et pour s'asseurer, et se desbatre si long temps en cette perche, j'eusse esbranlé sa reputation, s'il ne l'eut en mourant très vaillamment maintenué' ('(b) To see the exertions that Seneca imposed upon himself in order to steel himself against death, to see him sweat and grunt in order to stiffen and reassure himself during his long struggles on his pedestal, would have shaken his reputation for me if he had not sustained it with such valour as he was dying'; p. 1177).

[41] Screech, *The Essays*, 811; '(a) Le dire est autre chose que le faire: il faut considerer le presche à part, et le prescheur à part' (p. 693). Elsewhere Montaigne seems to doubt Seneca's sincerity: 'Je croirois volontiers Seneca de l'experience qu'il en fit en pareille occasion, pourveu qu'il m'en voulut parler à coeur ouvert' (III, 9, p. 971), — which implies that Seneca does not always speak openly.

[42] This is another reproach Bodin makes to Plutarch: 'Interdum etiam in Romanorum antiquitate labitur: quod in homine Graeco, qui se linguam Latinam non satis intellexisse in vita Demosthenis confitetur, mirum videri non debet' ('Sometimes he is also wrong about the history of the Romans, which is not astonishing in a Greek who declares in his *Life of Demosthenes* that he is not sufficiently fluent in the Latin language'; Bodin, *Methodus*, 132B). Significantly, this argument against Plutarch as well as the convincing examples that follow, are not commented upon by Montaigne.

[43] Cf. III, 8, p. 920-2.

[44] Bodin, *Methodus*, 133B. For Screech's translation of Montaigne's translation, see above, 177.

Montaigne improperly conveys his source here. For, as it happens, Bodin gives a favourable and particularly nuanced judgement of Cassius Dio, as is apparent from the sentence which immediately precedes the above quotation: 'he was almost the only one to have reported that which Tacitus calls the secrets of the empire. For he was a diligent investigator of the public deliberations'.[45] Montaigne's tone is understandable though, for elsewhere he says that since childhood he had composed speeches defending Pompey against Caesar.[46]

This tacit borrowing from Bodin stresses once again the underlying, associative structure which the directly visible, logical structure at once confirms, then again undermines. As an authority Bodin is not only present in part C, but also in part B and in the adjoining chapters, even though he is only once mentioned by name elsewhere.[47]

Just as the argumentation advanced by Montaigne in part B strikes one as very contrived and contorted, that in part C appears to be very convincing. Part C.a. is introduced by emphasizing the seriousness of Bodin's accusations: if he had accused Plutarch of ignorance, or if Bodin had simply said that Plutarch had written things which were untrue, then Montaigne could agree with him. But accusing Plutarch of gullibility, 'is to accuse the most judicious author in the world of lack of judgement'.[48]

Bodin's criticism of the credibility of the anecdote about the Spartan boy and the fox (part C.a.2.) is introduced by Montaigne with the remark that the example was badly chosen. According to Montaigne, Bodin should have made a distinction between two categories: the capabilities of the human spirit and those of the human body. With regard to the incredibility of the second category, Bodin could have found good examples in Plutarch. The example of the Spartan boy

---

[45] 'ea, quae Tacitus imperii arcana vocat, paene solus evulgavit. Fuit enim publici consilii diligens indagator'.

[46] III, 9, p. 975: 'Or j'ay attaqué cent querelles pour la deffence de Pompeius' ('So I have begun dozens of quarrels in defence of Pompey'; Screech, *The Essays*, 1128). On the subject of Pompey Montaigne also criticises Tacitus: '(b) Je me plains un peu toutesfois dequoy il a jugé de Pompeius plus aigrement que ne porte l'advis des gens de bien qui ont vescu et traicté avec luy' (III, 8, p. 920) ('I do regret though that, [...] he judged [Pompey] more harshly than is suggested by the verdict of men who lived and dealt with him'; Screech, *The Essays*, 1066).

[47] Bodin is mentioned in chapter II, 10, p. 398. For the tacit presence of Bodin in the *Essais*, see the 'Table des auteurs cités' in the monumental edition by Strowski F. et alii, *Les Essais de Michel de Montaigne*, 4 vols (Bordeaux: 1920) IV, p. XVII.

[48] Screech, *The Essays*, 818; 'c'est accuser de faute de jugement le plus judicieux autheur du monde'.

was however more appropriate for the first category and, says Montaigne, here the bounds for human capabilities know no limitations. Plutarch's example is even not so exceptional when considered from the perspective of Spartan upbringing and culture. Furthermore, Montaigne does not accept Bodin's interpretation of the expression *Comme on dit* which Plutarch uses to precede these and other anecdotes. He reads Bodin a philological lesson at this point:

> (a) And as for the phrase, 'So they say', he does not employ it in this context with that sense: that is easy to see, since he relates elsewhere other examples touching the powers of endurance of the boys of Sparta which happened in his own time and which are even harder to accept.[49]

The following pages of the chapter are devoted to examples from the present and the past which should demonstrate what the human spirit is capable of under physical torment. It is in this part of the chapter that Montaigne writes and appends according to the procedure of textual amplification (the so-called *allongeails*), as he does elsewhere in his *Essais*. Here he also strays from his subject, in so far as his argumentation has less to do with a defence of Plutarch than with expressive examples of human cruelty and human perseverance. What is also typical of Montaigne is that all these examples are, to an increasing degree, taken from Montaigne's own times and own experience: 'Je sçay qu'il s'est trouvé [...]' ('I know that there are […]'); 'J'en ay veu un [...]' ('I myself saw one […]'); 'J'ay cogneu cent et cent femmes [...]' ('I have known hundreds and hundreds of women [...]'). It is not then surprising that the series is concluded with an extrapolation directed towards the personal I of the essayist:

> I admire the greatness of those souls; those ecstacies which I find most beautiful I clasp unto me; though my powers do not reach as far, at least my judgement is most willingly applied to them.[50]

What is relevant here is in fact what Montaigne writes in his foreword to the *Essais*: 'It is my own self that I am painting'.[51] The apology of the 'other' imperceptibly overflows into self-reflection.

---

[49] Screech, *The Essays*, 819; '(a) [...] que ce mot: *Comme on dit*, il ne l'employe pas en ce lieu pour cet effect, il est aysé à voir par ce que luy mesme nous raconte ailleurs sur ce subject de la patience des enfans Lacedemoniens, des exemples advenuz de son temps plus mal-aisez à persuader' (p. 107).

[50] Screech, *The Essays*, 822; '(a) et admire leur grandeur, et les eslancemens que je trouve très-beaux, je les embrasse; et si mes forces m'y vont, au moins mon jugement s'y applique très-volontiers' (p. 703).

[51] 'C'est moy que je peins [...] je suis moy-mesmes la matiere de mon livre' (p. 9).

That the apologetic aspect becomes lost in the background is also apparent in the remarkably few lines that Montaigne actually uses in the argumentative part C.a.2. It is not until the last part (C.b.) that Montaigne explicitly resumes the defence of Plutarch.

This brings us to the question which has already been suggested concerning the extent to which the defence of Seneca and Plutarch is paradoxical. We have already demonstrated that the defence of Seneca is in fact not a genuine one, but more a settling of scores with the right-wing Catholic De Guise clan and with Cassius Dio's historiographic opinions. Moreover, Seneca serves as a stepping-stone to Plutarch, according to the rhetorical procedure of the *syncrisis*, whereby one praises A in order to praise B all the more.[52]

Indeed, in his defence of Plutarch we can also ask ourselves whether something else can be read between the lines, such as a rejection of one or two points which are only minor ones in comparison with the whole of Bodin's argumentation in his *Methodus*. Could it perhaps be the case that Montaigne is more generally concerned with Bodin and his authorative historiographic opinions?

Such an interpretation is possible, but difficult to substantiate. I think Montaigne would patently disagree with a number of points from the *Methodus*: this is the case, for example, with Bodin's latent Machiavellianism and his mathematically determined historiography, based on a convoluted numerology. In opposition to Bodin's objectively determinable and even predictable interval of time, Montaigne advocates his sceptical view of subjectively experienced time, without fixed points, where the past, present and future overflow into each other, and where the means for measurement (years, months, days and hours) are uncertain:

> (b) And what if (as some say) the heavens as they grow old are contracting downwards towards us, thereby casting our very hours and days into confusion? And what of our months too, since Plutarch says that even in his period the science of the heavens had yet to fix the motions of the moon? A fine position we are in to keep chronicles of past events![53]

---

[52] Curtius E.R., *European Literature and the Latin Middle Ages*, transl. W.R. Trask (Princeton: 1973) 162-6 ('Outdoing').

[53] Screech, *The Essays*, 1161; (b) 'Quoy, ce que disent aucuns, que les cieux se compriment vers nous en vieillissant, et nous jettent en incertitude des heures mesme et des jours? et des moys, ce que dict Plutarque qu'encore de son temps l'astrologie n'avoit sçeu borner le mouvement de la lune? Nous voylà bien accommodez pour tenir registre des choses passées' (III, 11, p. 1003).

The principal difference between the two authors lies in their explanations of the difference between peoples. Bodin is a follower of the so-called climate theory originating in Hippocrates's doctrine of the humours, in which the difference between peoples was explained by the differences in climate. From this point of view then, the differences are determined by nature. Montaigne, on the other hand, attributes the differences between people to the power of culture, thus to the adaptability of human beings.[54] Although Montaigne does not explicitly say this anywhere, an emphasis placed on his ideas with regard to this subject would imply a position against and rejection of Bodin's authoritative views. The latter, for that matter, comes much clearer to the fore at a later stage, namely with regard to the lively discussion about witchcraft (III, 11). In this, Montaigne seems to criticise Bodin's *Demonomanie des sorciers* (1580), which is an attack on Johannes Wier's *De praestigiis Daemonum* (1563). But neither Bodin nor Wier are referred to by name here.[55]

Except for Montaigne's admiration of Plutarch and his fundamental difference of opinion with Bodin concerning historiography, another motive for writing *Defence de Sénèque et de Plutarque* can be pointed out. It so happens that the anecdote cited by Bodin about the Spartan boy and his fox is discussed by Montaigne at an earlier stage, that is, in chapter I, 14, entitled *Que le goust des biens et des maux depend en bonne partie de l'opinion que nous en avons* (*That the taste of good and evil things depends in large part on the opinion we have of them*). Plutarch's anecdote is mentioned here in a series of examples which serve to demonstrate that the experience of pain is determined mentally. The first example is an empirical fact: '(a) We feel the surgeon's scalpel ten times more than a cut from the sword in the heat of the battle'.[56] The fourth example, which, just like the other examples, is historical in nature, concerns our anecdote:

> (a) Why, a little Spartan boy had stolen a fox (Spartans were more afraid of being mocked for having botched a theft than we are of being punished for one): he stuffed it under his cloak and rather than betray himself let it gnaw into his belly.[57]

---

[54] On this subject, see Desan P., *Penser l'histoire à la Renaissance* (Caen: 1993) 136-42.

[55] For this discussion, see, e.g., Nakam G., *Les 'Essais' de Montaigne, miroir et procès de leur temps. Témoignage historique et création littéraire* (Paris: 1984) 387-90.

[56] Screech, *The Essays*, 61; '(a) Nous sentons plus un coup de rasoir du Chirurgien que dix coups d'espée en la chaleur du combat' (p. 58).

[57] Screech, *The Essays*, 61-2; '(a) Un simple garçonnet de Lacedemone, ayant desrobé un renard (car ils craignoient encore plus la honte de leur sottise au larecin

This chapter was probably written around 1571, before Montaigne had become acquainted with Bodin's *Methodus*. It so happens that one of Montaigne's principles when writing is that he never deletes or corrects, but only makes additions: '(b) I make additions but not corrections'.[58] Montaigne's defence of Plutarch against Bodin thus gives him an opportunity to return to his earlier chapter, and to render the argumentation more explicit and, in a disguised manner, defend it against Bodin (or against an imagined reader who would confront Bodin's interpretation of Plutarch with Montaigne's). His complicated argumentation against Bodin's interpretation of Plutarch and the long series of *exempla* which ostensibly support this are in fact a clarification of his main subject, namely the power of the human spirit. In this, Montaigne does not hesitate to use, once again, another anecdote borrowed from Plutarch which he had already used in chapter I, 14, but this time more expansively:

> (a) Then there is the one which Plutarch relates with a hundred other witnesses; during the sacrifice a hot coal slipped up the sleeve of a Spartan boy while he was swinging the incense; he let the whole of his arm be burnt until the smell of cooked flesh reached the congregation.[59]

The above close reading of Montaigne's *Defence de Sénèque et de Plutarque* reveals a deceptive polysemy, which not only comes to the fore in this chapter about historiography, but is typical of Montaigne's essay writing in general. This ambiguity is even, according to Montaigne himself, the most important feature of his writing:

> Neither they [= my stories] nor my quotations serve always as mere examples, authorities or decorations: I do not only have regard for their usefulness to me: they often bear the seeds of a richer, bolder subject-matter; they often sound a more subtle note on the side, both for me,

---

que nous ne craignons sa peine) et l'ayant mis sous cape, endura plustost qu'il luy eut rongé le ventre que de se découvrir' (p. 59).

[58] Screech, *The Essays*, 1091; '(b) J'adjouste, mais je ne corrige pas' (III, 9, p. 941). This statement is a mystification, as is evident from the great amount of deletions, corrections and corrections of corrections he worked into his text.

[59] Screech, *The Essays*, 819; '(a) Et ce que Plutarque aussi recite, avec cent autres tesmoins, que, au sacrifice, un charbon ardant s'estant coulé dans la manche d'un enfant Lacedemonien, ainsi qu'il encensoit, il se laissa brusler tout le bras jusques à ce que la senteur de la chair cuyte en vint aux assistans' (p. 701). Compare the earlier version: '(a) Et un autre donnant de l'encens à un sacrifice, le charbon luy estant tombé dans la manche, se laissa brusler jusques à l'os, pour ne troubler le mystère' (I, 14, p. 59) ('Another lad was carrying incense for the sacrifice when a live coal fell up his sleeve: he let it burn through to the bone, so as not to disturb the ceremony'; Screech, *The Essays*, 62).

who do not wish to press more out of them, and also for those who get my gist.[60]

I hope for Montaigne's *Defence de Seneque et de Plutarque* that I have made this 'matiere plus riche' and this 'ton plus delicat' (which exceeds the apologetic character of the chapter) perceptible.

Selective Bibliography

BABUT D., *Plutarque et le Stoïcisme* (Paris: 1969)

BODIN J., *Oeuvres philosophiques*, ed. and transl. P. Mesnard (Paris: 1951)

CURTIUS E.R., *European Literature and the Latin Middle Ages*, transl. W.R. Trask (Princeton: 1973)

DESAN P., *Penser l'histoire à la Renaissance* (Caen: 1993)

FRIEDRICH H., *Montaigne*, transl. R. Rovini (Paris: 1968)

KONSTANTINOVIC I., *Montaigne et Plutarque* (Geneva: 1989)

MONTAIGNE M. DE, *The Complete Works*, transl. D.M. Frame (London: 1957)

MONTAIGNE M. DE, *Les Essais*, ed. F. Strowski et alii , 4 vols (Bordeaux: 1920)

MONTAIGNE M. DE, *The Essays*, transl. and ed. M.A. Screech (London: 1991)

MONTAIGNE M. DE, *Oeuvres complètes*, ed. A. Thibaudet – M. Rat (Paris: 1962)

Montaigne et l'histoire [...], ed. C.-G. Dubois (Paris: 1991)

NAKAM G., *Les 'Essais' de Montaigne, miroir et procès de leur temps. Témoignage historique et création littéraire* (Paris: 1984)

PLUTARCH, *Les oeuvres morales et meslées*, ed. and transl. J. Amyot (Paris: 1572; rpt New York etc.: 1971).

PLUTARCH, *Les vies des hommes illustres grecs et romains* [...], ed. and transl. J. Amyot, 2 vols ([s.l.]:1594)

SCHAEFER D.L., *The Political Philosophy of Montaigne* (Ithaca–London: 1990).

SMITH P.J., "Ponge épidictique et paradoxal", in *Francis Ponge*, ed. F. Schuerewegen (Amsterdam: 1996) 35-46

SMITH P. J. – TOORN N. VAN DER, " 'Science de gueule' et Rhétorique, ou *De la vanité des paroles* (Montaigne, *Essais* I, 51)", *Studi francesi* 32 (1988) 82-90.

---

[60] Screech, *The Essays*, 282-3; '(c) Ny elles [= mes histoires], ny mes allegations ne servent pas tousjours simplement d'exemple, d'authorité ou d'ornement. Je ne les regarde pas seulement par l'usage que j'en tire. Elles portent souvent, hors de mon propos, la semence d'une matiere plus riche et plus hardie, et sonnent à gauche un ton plus delicat, et pour moy qui n'en veux exprimer d'avantage, et pour ceux qui rencontreront mon air' (I, 40, p. 245).

PLUTARCH'S *LIVES* AND *CORIOLANUS*:
SHAKESPEARE'S VIEW OF ROMAN HISTORY

Bart Westerweel

In addressing the issue of Shakespeare's view of history as exemplified
in his Roman plays, notably in *Coriolanus*, it is just as well to note at the
outset that the phrase 'Shakespeare's view of history' needs to be qualified before it can be said to mean anything at all. And even when one
focuses on Shakespeare's use of Plutarch for this set of history plays
one should be aware that one is faced with a set of Chinese boxes. As
Peter Saccio pointed out in a discussion of Shakespeare's English history plays — of which the Roman plays are a special branch — a
number of perspectives should be taken into account. The first is our
twentieth-century way of looking at and describing the past, which is
radically different from the way in which history was perceived and
practised in Shakespeare's day.[1]

Another complication in assessing Shakespeare from a historiographical vantage point is the fact that he relied for his Roman plays,
and for *Coriolanus* almost exclusively, on one source text, the *Parallel
Lives of the Greeks and Romans* by Plutarch (first century AD). Shakespeare did not resort to Plutarch directly but used Thomas North's
English translation of 1579. North, in his turn, had translated
Plutarch's text from the French version by Jacques Amyot of 1559.[2]

Finally, it should not be forgotten that the only means we have at
our disposal for a discussion of 'Shakespeare's ideas about history' are
his dramatic works. Geoffrey Bullough summarized the issue succinct-
ly by emphasizing that Shakespeare's adaptation of Plutarch's *Lives*
was directed first and foremost to the making of a good play, then to
're-create the characters of the hero and his associates', and, thirdly,

---

[1] Saccio P., *Shakespeare's English Kings: History, Chronicle, and Drama* (London–Oxford–New York: 1977) 13-4.

[2] All references in this article to the text of Plutarch's *Lives* are to the translations by
B. Perrin in the volumes of the Loeb Classical Library, except for *Theseus*, for which
the translation by I. Scott-Kilvert (Penguin Books) was used. Unless specified otherwise, references to the translation by Sir Thomas North are to the, slightly modern-
ized, text in *Shakespeare's Plutarch: the Lives of Julius Caesar, Brutus, Marcus Antonius, and
Coriolanus in the translation of Sir Thomas North*, ed. and introd. T.J.B. Spencer (Harmondsworth: 1964).

to 'interpret the political situation in Rome in terms suited to early Jacobean England and the conditions of 1607–1608'.[3]

Dare I add yet another snag? The meaning of the notions *history* and *historiography* themselves is by no means stable. Before doing anything else we should provide some kind of context for the way a playwright such as Shakespeare would have understood the term *history*.

An obvious text to turn to is Sir Philip Sidney's *Defence of Poetry* (c. 1579), one of the most influential treatises of its kind in the English Renaissance. That Shakespeare had read Sidney's *Defence* is undisputed.[4] Sidney, the Elizabethan embodiment of the courtly ideal of Castiglione's *Il Cortegiano*, makes clear that in his view history is a handmaiden to poetry:

> even historiographers (although their lips sound of things done, and verily be written in their foreheads) have been glad to borrow both fashion and, perchance, weight of the poets. So Herodotus entitled his History by the name of the nine Muses; and both he and all the rest that followed him either stale [stole] or usurped of poetry their passionate describing of passions, the many particularities of battles, which no man could affirm; or, if that be denied me, long orations put in the mouths of great kings and captains, which it is certain they never pronounced.
>
> So that truly neither philosopher nor historiographer could at the first have entered into the gates of popular judgements, if they had not taken a great passport of poetry.[5]

and

> [...] the best of the historian is subject to the poet; for, whatsoever action, or faction, whatsoever counsel, policy, or war stratagem the historian is bound to recite, that may the poet (if he list) with his imitation make his own, beautifying it both for further teaching, and more delighting, as it please him.[6]

Throughout the *Defence* Sidney leans on Plutarch to support his argument about the pre-eminence of poetry above history and philosophy. Sidney even quotes Plutarch as an authority on the status of tragedy:

---

[3] Bullough G., *Narrative and Dramatic Sources of Shakespeare* (London: 1964) V, 476.

[4] See, e.g., Muir K., *Shakespeare: Contrasts and Controversies* (Norman: 1985) 20.

[5] Sidney P., *Miscellaneous Prose*, ed. K. Duncan-Jones – J. van Dorsten (Oxford: 1973) 75.

[6] Sidney, *Miscellaneous Prose*, 89.

Tragedy, that openeth the greatest wounds, and showeth forth the
ulcers that are covered with tissue; that maketh kings fear to be tyrants,
and tyrants manifest their tyrannical humours; that, with stirring the
affects of admiration and commiseration, teacheth the uncertainty of
this world [...] how much it can move, Plutarch yieldeth a notable testimony of the abominable tyrant Alexander Pheraeus, from whose eyes a
tragedy, well made and represented, drew abundance of tears, who
without all pity had murdered infinite numbers, and some of his own
blood: so as he, that was not ashamed to make matters for tragedies, yet
could not resist the sweet violence of a tragedy.[7]

Sidney could have had access to a number of editions of Plutarch and
refers to his wish to acquire a copy of Amyot's French translation of
Plutarch's works in letters to his humanist mentor and friend Languet
in 1573 and 1574. Sidney's eagerness was such that he was willing to
pay five times the normal price for the two folio volumes.[8]

There is a clear line, then, from Plutarch's *Parallel Lives* through the
Latin editions by Guarino da Verona and others in the fifteenth cen-
tury, to Jacques Amyot's translation of 1559, to Thomas North's ver-
sion of Amyot's text into English in 1579, to Sidney's *Defence* of 1579–
1580, and then on to Shakespeare's *Julius Caesar*, *Antony and Cleopatra*,
Coriolanus, and *Timon of Athens* in the early seventeenth century.[9] While
Sidney's humanist leanings led him in the direction of Amyot, for
Shakespeare's theatrical interest North was all he needed.

Hermann Heuer aptly compared the French and English versions
with the original text of Plutarch. Heuer emphasizes the fact that
Plutarch wrote the *Lives* in couples and approaches his subject from
the well-known idea that Plutarch demonstrates a natural tendency to
favour the Greek Lives above the Roman ones. The couple Alcibi-
ades/Coriolanus forms no exception: 'the versatility and adaptable
smoothness of Alcibiades is admirable, as contrasted with the crudity
of Coriolanus. For him, Coriolanus exhibits a want of education'.[10]

---

[7] Sidney, Miscellaneous Prose, 96. The reference to Plutarch is to a passage in the
Vita Pelopidae, 29 in which Plutarch describes Alexander Pheraeus's response to a performance of Euripides's *Troades*.

[8] Osborn J.M., *Young Philip Sidney 1572–1577* (New Haven: 1972) 121, 135; Doherty M.J., *The Mistress-Knowledge: Sir Philip Sidney's* Defence of Poesie *and Literary Architectonics in the English Renaissance* (Nashville: 1991) 283, n. 73; Duncan-Jones K., *Sir Philip
Sidney: Courtier Poet* (New Haven–London: 1991) 77.

[9] See Highet G., *The Classical Tradition: Greek and Roman Influences on Western Literature*
(New York–London: 1949) 119 and 126.

[10] Heuer H., "From Plutarch to Shakespeare: A Study of Coriolanus", *Shakespeare
Survey* 10 (1957) 51.

If one looks more closely at some of the distinctions Plutarch makes between the two men's characters right from the start it is not only Coriolanus' lack of education that is emphasized in contrast to the close companionship Alcibiades enjoys with Socrates but his being fatherless as well: 'Caius Marcius, whose life I now write, lost his father at an early age, and was reared by his widowed mother'.[11] Volumnia, the mother, plays a crucial role in Plutarch's story as well as in Shakespeare's play. Another basic difference is in the extent of the self-knowledge of both men. While Alcibiades is said by Plutarch to have been taught by Socrates 'how great were his deficiencies and how incomplete his excellence'(17), no such restraint was imposed on Coriolanus. Alcibiades is also said to have been a very able speaker and Plutarch invokes the authority of Theophrastus who had said that Alcibiades 'was of all men the most capable of discovering and understanding what was required in a given case' (25). One of the fatal flaws in the character of Shakespeare's Coriolanus is that he is unable to speak the right words at the right time.

Shakespeare's interest in the Athenian counterpart of Coriolanus is shown in *Timon of Athens*, the last play based on material from North's Plutarch and probably written within a year after *Coriolanus*.[12] Alcibiades turns up as one of the characters in *Timon of Athens*. Although the character of Alcibiades is drawn too sketchily to make a full comparison with Coriolanus worthwhile, Shakespeare makes use of some characteristic aspects that he found in North's Plutarch. Both men return to their native cities, Rome and Athens, respectively, from exile and both men threaten to destroy those cities in revenge for the injustice done to them. However, whereas Coriolanus is prevented from

---

[11] Plutarch, *Lives*, IV: *Alcibiades and Coriolanus; Lysander and Sulla*, transl. B. Perrin, Loeb Classical Library (Cambridge, Mass.–London: 1936) 119. Perrin translates the Greek of Plutarch's 'Gaios Markios' with Caius Marcius. In the remainder of this essay I shall follow Shakespeare (and North) in referring to the hero of his play as Caius Martius Coriolanus.

[12] The story of the play is based on the section in North's translation of the Life of Marcus Antonius in which Antony is said to have retreated from public life in a house by the sea, 'saying that he would lead Timon's life, because he had the like wrong offered him that was before offered unto Timon [...]' (*Shakespeare's Plutarch*, 263). As Oliver, the editor of the the Arden edition, points out, Shakespeare's dependence on the *Life of Alcibiades* is slight and perhaps boils down to the sentence in which North summarizes the exploits of Alcibiades: '*Alcibiades* spite and malice did work great mischief and misery to his country: but when he saw they repented them of the injury they had done him, he came to himself and did withdraw his Army' (*Timon of Athens*, ed. H.J. Oliver, Arden edition (London–New York: 1959) introd., xxxiii).

executing his plans by a final plea of his mother and is subsequently stabbed to death by his enemies, Alcibiades is persuaded by the Senators to be reconciled and return to Athens in peace.

The passages quoted above indicate that Plutarch was a historian of a particular kind. As we shall see it was the particularity of Plutarch's historiography that made him so suitable for inclusion in a defence of poetry such as Sidney's and in drama such as the Roman plays of Shakespeare. Montaigne, whose essays came to Shakespeare through John Florio's translation of 1603, nicely describes the impact Plutarch made on him in his essay *Of books*:

> The historians come right to my forehand. They are pleasant and easy; and at the same time, man in general, the knowledge of whom I seek, appears in them more alive and entire than in any other place — the diversity and truth of his inner qualities in the mass and in detail, the variety of the ways he is put together, and the accidents that threaten him. *Now those who write biographies, since they spend more time on plans than on events, more on what comes from within than on what happens without, are most suited to me. That is why in every way Plutarch is my man* [italics mine].[13]

Both in the elegance of tone and in its argumentation Montaigne's text is reminiscent of Sidney, with this difference that for the latter history is the handmaiden of poetry:

> Truly, Aristotle himself, in his discourse of poesy, plainly determineth this question, saying that poetry is [...] more philosophical and more studiously serious than history. His reason is, because poesy dealeth with [...] the universal consideration, and the history with [...] the particular: now, saith he, the universal weighs what is fit to be said or done, either in likelihood or necessity [...] and the particular only marks whether Alcibiadis did, or suffered, this or that. Thus far Aristotle: which reason of his (as all his) is most full of reason [...]. If the poet do his part aright, he will show you in Tantalus, Atreus, and such like, nothing that is not to be shunned; in Cyrus, Aeneas, Ulysses, each thing to be followed; where the historian, bound to tell things as things were, cannot be liberal [...] of a perfect pattern, but, as in Alexander or Scipio himself, show doings, some to be liked, some to be disliked.[14]

---

[13] Montaigne, M. de, *The Complete Essays*, transl. D.M. Frame (Stanford: 1958) II, 303.

[14] Sidney, *Miscellaneous Prose*, 87-8.

In terms of Renaissance historiography the borderlines between history, biography, philosophy and poetry should not, therefore, be drawn too rigidly. Sir Thomas North, the English translator of Plutarch, introduces his author as 'that grave learned philosopher and historiographer, Plutarch of Chaeronea'.[15]

Have we come to the end of the series of Chinese boxes at this point? One tiny box is still rattling within the last one we opened. What about the way Plutarch saw himself as a historian? In most accounts of Shakespeare's Plutarch the emphasis is firmly on what Plutarch led up to and sample texts from Plutarch are carefully chosen to fit the pattern. Before we turn to Shakespeare proper, I want to devote some space to some of the ideas expressed by Plutarch himself on the topos of historical writing.

The passage that comes up consistently in most accounts of Plutarch's view on history and biography and his relationship with Shakespeare's plays is from the introduction of his *Life of Alexander* :

> [...] *it is not Histories that I am writing, but Lives*; and in the most illustrious deeds there is not always a manifestation of virtue or vice, nay, *a slight thing like a phrase or a jest often makes a greater revelation of character than battles where thousands fall,* or the greatest armaments, or sieges of cities. Accordingly, just as painters get the likenesses in their portraits from the face and the expression of the eyes, wherein the character shows itself, but make very little account of the other parts of the body, so I must be permitted to devote myself rather to the signs of the soul in men, and by means of these to portray the life of each, leaving to others the description of their great contests [italics mine].[16]

If one bases one's conclusion about Plutarch's ideas about historiography solely on the passage quoted here, one is bound to conclude that Plutarch clearly distinguished between the methods of the historian and that of the biographer but, as Alan Wardman argued convincingly, that is both a simplification and a misrepresentation of Plutarch's intentions.[17] For one thing Plutarch does not discuss historiography or biography *per se* but their products: 'Histories' and 'Lives', respective-

---

[15] Quoted in Hunter G.K., "Shakespeare's Reading", in Muir K. – Schoenbaum S., *A New Companion to Shakespeare Studies* (Cambridge: 1971) 61.

[16] Plutarch, *Lives*, vol VII: *Demosthenes and Cicero; Alexander and Caesar*, transl. B. Perrin, Loeb Classical Library (Cambridge, Mass.–London: 1919) 225.

[17] Wardman A., *Plutarch's Lives* (London: 1974) 4-10. I am grateful to Marlein van Raalte for pointing out Wardman's book to me and for other useful suggestions about Plutarch's views on historiography.

ly, and, as the evidence from other *Lives* suggests, he regards biography as a special mode of historical enquiry rather than as an independent branch of knowledge.[18] For another, he seems to adapt his historical method to the problem at hand and the way of going about the *Life of Alexander* seems to have been instigated by the fact that Plutarch felt he had to make a selection from the large quantity of historical material available to him in this particular case. In other *Lives* the emphasis is different, because the exigencies of those particular *Lives* require it. The *Life of Theseus*, for instance, begins with an apology:

> Now that in writing my *Parallel Lives* I have reached the end of those periods in which theories can be tested by argument or where history can find a solid foundation in fact, I might very well follow their example and say of those remoter ages, 'All that lies beyond are prodigies and fables, the province of poets and romancers, where nothing is certain or credible'.

In his attempt to find a Greek Life parallel to the *Life of Romulus*, the founder of Rome, Plutarch comes up with Theseus, the founder of Athens, but for the writing of his Life he cannot, as in the case of the Lives of other great figures, rely on firm historical evidence:

> Let us hope, then, that I shall succeed in purifying fable, and make her submit to reason and take on the appearance of history. But when she obstinately defies probability and refuses to admit any element of the credible, I shall throw myself on the indulgence of my readers and of those who can listen with forbearance to the tales of Antiquity.[19]

Here the successful telling of the tale, measured by the persuasion of the audience, is the final yardstick by which the *Life of Theseus* is to be judged, the expression of a sentiment that is frequently found at the end of Shakespeare's plays, too, where one of the actors stays behind to address the audience directly in an epilogue.[20]

Shakespeare had, of course, written a number of history plays before those for which he chose Rome as his focal point. In the late eighties and the nineties of the sixteenth century the two tetralogies on

---

18 Wardman, *Plutarch's Lives*, 5.

19 Plutarch, *The Rise and Fall of Athens: Nine Greek Lives*, transl. I. Scott-Kilvert (Harmondsworth: 1960) 13-4.

20 In *The Tempest*, for instance, Prospero addresses the audience in the epilogue: 'Now my charms are all o'erthrown, / And what strength I have's my own, / Which is most faint [...] / As you from crimes would pardon'd be, / Let your indulgence set me free' (Epilogue II, 1-3; 19-20). Cf. *A Midsummer Night's Dream*, where Puck ends the play in a similar way.

English history were written. The first tetralogy consisted of the three *Henry VI* plays and *Richard III*; the second of *Richard II*, the two parts of *Henry IV* and *Henry V*. The eight plays deal with the troubled events of the Wars of the Roses and the period that witnessed the civil strife between the white rose of the Yorkists and the red rose of the Lancastrians. It is not irrelevant to note that Shakespeare wrote these plays in a logical rather than a chronological order. It is as if Shakespeare gradually moved away from the presentation of the eventful genesis of the Tudor monarchy to the probing of character in the second series of history plays. In the *First Folio* of 1623, however, the editors had restored the chronological order of the history plays, adding *King John* before and *Henry VIII* after the tetralogies.

Members of the audience in the 1580s would have had grandfathers who had fought and died in the Battle of Bosworth of 1485, where Richard III was killed and succeeded by Henry VII, the first of the Tudor monarchs. The first tetralogy deals with England's history between 1422 and 1485, the second with the period between 1398 and 1422.

Richard III forms a borderline case between the genre of the history play and tragedy. Much more than the three *Henry VI* plays that preceded it, *Richard III* focuses on the king/protagonist and has created, not only for his compatriots but for the twentieth-century reader/ spectator as well, the image of the hunchbacked monster who was responsible for killing all those standing in his way to the crown or threatening to undermine its legitimacy, including the Princes in the Tower.[21] In this sense *Richard III* as a play is transitional, preparing the way for the second tetralogy and the later tragedies. Whereas the *Henry VI* plays conformed to the factual progression of the chronicles on which they were based, those of Hall (1548) and Holinshed (2nd ed., 1587) mainly, the later plays tend to focus more and more on the individual character as a focal point of political pressures and historical contingencies.

In short, although Shakespeare derived the substance of the English history he transformed into drama from the English chronicles he used as sources, the order in which he wrote them and the changing emphasis from events to character suggest that Shakespeare the dramatist changed gear and tack during the early nineties of the sixteenth century.

---

[21] See Saccio, *Shakespeare's English Kings*, 3ff.

In their genesis the Roman plays can be regarded as counterpoints to the English chronicle plays. In the first place they were not conceived as a unified series as the earlier plays were. They were written at various intervals: *Julius Caesar* in 1599, *Antony and Cleopatra* in 1606–1607, *Coriolanus* in 1608, and *Timon of Athens* (date uncertain, but probably 1608–1609). On the other hand, what unites them, is that they were for the greater part based on one source, Plutarch's *Lives*.

Let us, before we go any further, first consider the change of source material. Holinshed and Hall are matter-of-fact chronicles, compiled with an eye to providing the emerging unified nation and its monarchs with a sense of their own history; they did not have literary aspirations nor did they select their material to suit the creation of a particular character. As we saw before, Plutarch's aim was to write 'lives' and bring out those elements in a life that together constituted an individualized character. Obviously, Plutarch's way of dealing with historical phenomena would be congenial to a playwright and especially to a playwright like Shakespeare, who was at a juncture of his creative life where he was already turning away from a type of history that was chronicle-oriented to plays that were more character-oriented.

There is another reason for Shakespeare to turn from English chronicle plays to Roman tragedy. It is formulated in Hunter's monumental study of English drama in the age of Shakespeare:

> Shakespeare's eight interconnected plays on English history had merely skirted tragedy because the continuity of history up to his own time ruled out any sense of irreparable loss. In these plays the system always tends to exceed its representatives: the king might die, but the State goes on [...] English history had to carry a burden of teleology; the past had to be seen in terms of what it led to. But Roman history was over; [...] it had to be assumed that the end was not fulfilment but an understanding of the conditions within which the search for fulfilment was conducted.[22]

In other words, when Shakespeare wrote his English history plays, he did so under specific historical circumstances and constrained by the socio-political context of a Tudor monarchy, whose reigning representative, Elizabeth I, was a granddaughter of Henry VII, the first of the Tudor kings, who had beaten Richard III at the battle of Bosworth in 1485. It was unthinkable for Shakespeare to present a

---

[22] Hunter G.K., *English Drama 1586–1642: The Age of Shakespeare* (Oxford: 1997) 449.

dramatic version of the events preceding the accession of the Tudors that would throw a negative light on their reign. The way Richard III is presented in Shakespeare's play conforms to the negative tone of one of the sources for his play, the biography of Richard that had been written by Sir Thomas More, privy councillor in the service of Henry VIII.[23] The Tudor-friendly characterization of Richard was doubtlessly also due to the fact that the reign of Elizabeth was seen as the fulfilment of the struggles of the previous century. As Hurstfield writes, '[t]he force which destroys Julius Caesar, Coriolanus, Richard II, Richard III is a force which threatened the Tudor and Stuart monarchy'.[24] Neale, in his classic biography of Elizabeth I, recounts how the Queen responded to documents concerning the reign of Richard II, presented to her by the historian William Lambarde:

> Her thoughts flew to the Essex rising and the ominous prominence then given to this king's story. "I am Richard II", she said; "know ye not that?" When Lombarde tells her obliquely of a certain gentleman [i.e. Shakespeare] whose "wicked imagination" had made him write about Richard II, the queen answered: "He that will forget God will also forget his benefactors". This tragedy — of Richard II — was played forty times in open streets and houses.[25]

It was tricky for a playwright to create associations between the past and the present by writing about Richard II, whose throne had been usurped by Henry Bolingbroke (Henry IV). The change to Roman history allowed Shakespeare the scope that English history never could.

Whereas the English chronicle plays showed Shakespeare's craftsmanship in transforming his sources to suit his dramatic purpose, for the Roman plays the moral and dramatic patterns were already there in Plutarch, more or less ready-made. As Eliot put it: 'Shakespeare acquired more essential history from Plutarch than most men could from the whole British Museum'.[26]

It was Eliot, too, who ranked *Coriolanus* among the two plays that he considered 'Shakespeare's most assured artistic success'. Actually,

---

[23] Sir Thomas More, *The History of King Richard the thirde* (first complete printing in 1557, but incorporated for the greater part in Edward Hall's chronicle *The Union of the Two Noble and Illustrate Famelies of Lancastre and York* of 1548).

[24] Hurstfield, "The Historical and Social Background", in Muir and Schoenbaum, *A New Companion*, 168.

[25] Neale J.E., *Queen Elizabeth I* (1952; rpt Chicago: 1992) 398.

[26] Eliot T.S., *Selected Essays*, 3rd ed. (London: 1951) 17.

Eliot regards *Coriolanus* as the culminating point of his successes in writing tragedy.[27] Spencer, whose article "Shakespeare and the Elizabethan Romans" is still one of the seminal essays on the subject, wrote: 'To write *Coriolanus*, was one of the great feats of the historical imagination in Renaissance Europe'.[28] Shakespeare's choice of *Coriolanus* was different from that of the matter for the other Roman historic tragedies, *Julius Caesar* and *Antony and Cleopatra*, in that these earlier plays were about characters that were entirely familiar to the audience, while *Coriolanus* was not. Also, whereas the former two plays dealt with the highest leadership of what was, for Renaissance Europe, the most important political power that had ever been, Coriolanus was a successful general aspiring to become consul. We shall return to the consequences of this particular choice of a protagonist in *Coriolanus*. For the other plays there are dramatic precedents as well, for *Coriolanus* there are not.[29] The only contemporary plays on the same subject were a German play, of an entirely different nature than Shakespeare's and certainly unknown by him, Hermann Kirchner's *Coriolanus tragicomica* (1599) and Alexandre Hardy's *Coriolan*, that was published in 1625, well after Shakespeare's death, although it had already been written before Shakespeare's play.[30] The *Romanitas* for which Shakespeare found the basic material in Plutarch had to be recreated by him to make it stick with his audience. What was the story of Shakespeare's play?

The action is situated partly in Rome and partly in Corioli, the city of the Volscians, in the fifth century BC. The play begins, significantly, with the unrest of the citizens of Rome, who are starving and suspect the Senate of keeping away the corn from them. Menenius Agrippa, a patrician, tries to appease them but, encouraged by the tribunes Sicinius and Brutus, they direct their frustration against Caius Martius. Martius is a Roman soldier, who, although scornful of the

---

[27] Eliot, *Selected Essays*, 144. Eliot wrote an (unfinished) poem *Coriolan* in the thirties, in which the setting is the aftermath of World War I. In other poems the figure of Coriolan is mentioned as well. See Eliot T.S., *Collected Poems 1909–1962* (London: 1963) 139-43. Cf. Bergonzi B., *T.S. Eliot*, 2nd ed. (London: 1978) 142.

[28] Spencer T.J.B., "Shakespeare and the Elizabethan Romans", *Shakespeare Survey* 10 (1957) 35.

[29] See P. Brockbank's excellent introduction to *Coriolanus*, Arden edition (London–New York: 1976) 33.

[30] See Brockbank (ed.), *Coriolanus*, 75-6 and MacCallum M.W., *Shakespeare's Roman Plays and their Background* (London: 1910) 475-82. I rely on Brockbank for the reference to Kirchner.

common people of Rome, had in the past shown his valour time and again in battles of the Romans against the Volscian army. When another attack on Rome is imminent, Martius again joins the army under Cominius, the Roman general, and demonstrates an almost superhuman strength and courage in the ensuing battle, in the course of which he enters the city of Corioli by himself, killing numerous Volscians and fighting Tullus Aufidius, their military leader, in single-handed combat. In recognition of his services to Rome the honorary title of Coriolanus is bestowed on Martius by Cominius. Between these scenes of public display — for males only — the three female characters are introduced in an all-female domestic scene. Volumnia and Virgilia, mother and wife to Coriolanus, and Valeria, friend of the family. Virgilia is presented strictly in terms of Elizabethan expectations of a dutiful wife, preferring silence to speech and the retirement of home occupations like sewing to the exposure of public scrutiny. By way of contrast Volumnia immediately bursts out into a monologue of self-praise extolling her education of her son in the Roman virtue of honour as expressed in fearless martial exploits. When Coriolanus returns to Rome in triumph he is persuaded by his mother to offer himself to be elected consul. Coriolanus makes an utterly miserable impression in the ritual preceding such an election, which requires him to present himself in a humble garb and show his war wounds to the common people. The tribunes persuade the crowd, who admired Coriolanus at first because of his brave deeds, to turn against him, because of his disdainful attitude. Although persuaded by Menenius and Volumnia to apologize to the people, Coriolanus cannot bend his pride to utter words of humility. The mob gets more and more excited and now demands that Coriolanus be put to death. The senate gives in to the mob's wishes but banishes Coriolanus from Rome for life instead of sentencing him to death.

Coriolanus, embittered by what he can only see as ungrateful and undeserved treatment at the hands of his fellow citizens, now turns to the Volscians and reconciles himself with Tullus Aufidius. Together they plan an attack on Rome. When word of this reaches Rome the mob panics and turns against the tribunes who had advised them to rise against Coriolanus. In the final act Menenius and Cominius plead with Coriolanus to abandon his plan of vengeance but in vain. Coriolanus seems impervious to their appeal. As a last resort the three women, accompanied by his son, appeal to Coriolanus and it is his mother, who, by kneeling for him, finally persuades Coriolanus to spare his home city. On his return to Corioli he is killed by a group of conspirators who act at the behest of Tullus Aufidius, who feels his authority threatened by the popularity of Coriolanus with the Volscians.

In many ways *Coriolanus* is a remarkable play in the Shakespeare canon. As was indicated earlier, it is the only one of the history plays, English and Roman, whose protagonist is not the political leader of the state. Consequently, the focus of the play is different, too. Whereas the politics of the other plays involve either a tension between dynastic continuity and individual rule or between public duty and private indulgence, Coriolanus is very much his own man and, even though the mob turns against him, the moral struggle is all within his own mind. Unlike all other heroes of the history plays, with the possible exception of Richard III, he lives 'As if a man were author of himself / And knew no other kin' (V, iii, 36-7).

Terry Eagleton called Coriolanus, 'though literally a patrician [...], perhaps Shakespeare's most developed study of a bourgeois individualist'.[31] But Coriolanus is different even from Richard III in the crucial respect that, whereas the latter cuts himself loose from all natural ties of friendship and family relations, leaving himself utterly alone towards the end of the play, the former turns towards his family precisely at the point in the fifth Act when the three women plead with him not to turn against his native Rome. The scene is dominated by the famous speech of Volumnia, culminating in the three ladies kneeling for Coriolanus. At this point, Shakespeare depends especially on North's Plutarch. It is revealing for the kind of dependence of Shakespeare's play on North's Plutarch to zoom in more closely on this scene. The moment is highly dramatic because Coriolanus is fully aware that, by giving up the radical independence of spirit that had marked his behaviour so far and that had filled both his friends and his enemies with awe, he gives up his main shield against those that have reason to hate him:

> O mother, mother!
> What have you done? Behold, the heavens do open,
> The gods look down, and this unnatural scene
> They laugh at. O my mother, mother! O!
> You have won a happy victory to Rome;
> But for your son, believe it, O, believe it,

---

[31] Eagleton T., *William Shakespeare* (Oxford: 1986) 73.

> Most dangerously you have with him prevail'd,
> If not most mortal to him. But let it come (V, iii, 182-9).

North's version is:

> Oh mother, what have you done to me?' And holding her hard by the
> right hand, 'Oh mother', sayed he, 'you have wonne a happy victorie
> for your countrie but mortall and unhappy for your sonne. For I see
> myself vanquished by you alone.

Actually, the last sentence of this passage in North is a mistranslation
of Amyot's French version, who writes: '[...] car je m'en revois vaincu
par toy seule'. 'Revois' is a variant of 'revais', a literal translation of
the Greek ἄπειμι in Plutarch's text, meaning 'return'.[32]

Another instance where Shakespeare takes his inspiration from
North's (mis-)translation is his use of the word 'unnatural' in the passage just quoted. Actually, Shakespeare removed the word 'unnatural'
from Volumnia's speech, where North has her say: 'No man living is
more bounde to shewe him selfe thankefull in all partes and respects
then thy selfe: *who so unnaturally sheweth all ingratitude* [italics mine]'. In
Amyot the italicized phrase reads: 'veu que tu poursuis si asprement
une ingratitude'. The word 'asprement' is a literal translation of the
Greek πικρῶς.[33] Shakespeare follows North but, significantly, puts the
word 'unnatural' in Coriolanus' mouth instead of his mother's. The
dramatic effect of this is that it is *his* realisation of the consequences of
his actions that is emphasized rather than the accusation by the mother as in North.

As Heuer pointed out, 'nature', 'natural' and its reverse 'unnatural'
are key words in this scene. They are used no less than five times.
Heuer concludes:

> The consequence of North's modifications is that the conflict, con-
> ceived psychologically or rather logically in the French version as one
> between 'rigueur' and 'raison', is now being transferred to a different
> plane. [...] The disruption of the natural bonds and of the naturally
> inherent order of human existence has become the decisive issue.[34]

---

[32] MacCallum, in *Shakespeare's Roman Plays*, his classic study of the Roman plays,
incorporated an Appendix, printing Volumnia's speech in the Latin version of
Plutarch by Guarino of Verona, (c. 1470) and a Greek edition of 1599, side by side
with Amyot's French translation from the Greek, North's translation of Amyot's text
and Shakespeare's text (630-43). The quote in the main text is taken from MacCallum's Appendix.

[33] MacCallum 635 (Plutarch), 637 (Amyot), 640 (North).

[34] Heuer, "From Plutarch to Shakespeare", 52.

The exploration of (human) nature, the bonds of nature and the contrast between what is 'natural' and 'unnatural' behaviour in this crucial scene forms the culminating point of what constitutes one of the major fields of imagery in the play. The imagery comes to the surface not only in family relations but also as an emblem of the disrupted relations between the Senate and the citizens of Rome. The imagery of the corn, that is withheld from the common people, is telling in this respect. Perhaps surprisingly in a play that abounds with images of war and destruction, the word 'grain' is used more frequently in *Coriolanus* than in any other of Shakespeare's plays.

In comparison with all the sources — and in this case he deviates even from North — Shakespeare refers far more frequently and explicitly to the, natural, harvest of grain on the one hand and the, unnatural, famine of the people on the other. The deviation is most notable in the very first scene of the play when the mutinous citizens complain to Menenius about the neglect they suffer at the hands of the patricians. Menenius tries to appease them by referring to the patricians as 'fathers': 'You slander / The helms o'th'state, who care for you like fathers, / When you curse them as enemies' (I, i, 75-7). The citizens respond with sarcasm: 'Care for us? True indeed! they ne'er cared for us yet. Suffer us to famish, and their storehouses crammed with grain; make edicts for usury, to support usurers [...]. If the wars eat us not up, they will; and there's all the love they bear us' (I, i, 78-85). In the parallel passage in North and the earlier sources, the reference to the 'storehouses crammed with grain' is absent as is the phrase in which Menenius refers to the patricians as the people's 'fathers'. By these additions Shakespeare subtly turns the government of the state into a precarious family situation in which the parent refuses to fulfill the natural role of nourishing his children with wholesome food.

In his attempt to persuade the citizens to give up their mutinous march against the Capitol Menenius appeals to the natural order of things by telling the famous fable of the belly (I, i, 95-153), that is included in all the versions of Plutarch's text.[35] Having told the story

---

[35] The fable of the belly is the only passage in the play for which Shakespeare demonstrably relied on other sources besides North's Plutarch. Brockbank summarized the dependence of *Coriolanus* on the English translation by Philemon Holland of Livy's *Ab urbe condita* (1600), on Camden's *Remaines* (1605) and on William Averell's *A Marvailous Combat of contrarieties* (1588), in his introduction to the Arden edition of the play (29).

of the members of the body that rebelled against the belly, because
they thought that they did all the hard work for the body and the belly
did not do anything useful in return, Menenius concludes:

> The senators of Rome are this good belly,
> And you the mutinous members: for examine
> Their counsels and their cares, digest things rightly
> Touching the weal o'th'common, you shall find
> No public benefit which you receive
> But it proceeds or comes from them to you,
> And no way from yourselves (I, i, 147-53).

As Brockbank phrases it, Shakespeare's use of the fable reflects an
organic theory of the state, 'the conviction that the state is, or ought to
be, a unity made from a variety of functions, a system of mutual
responsibilities'.[36]

Later in the play, Coriolanus is seen to pervert both the political
and moral significance of the word 'grain' as a symbol for wholesome
and natural relations between a leader and his people or for those
between a man and his closest relatives and friends. When Cominius
returns from his fruitless mission to persuade Coriolanus to abandon
his plans for an outright attack on Rome, he reports:

> I offer'd to awaken his regard
> For's private friends. His answer to me was
> He could not stay to pick them in a pile
> Of noisome musty chaff. He said 'twas folly,
> For one poor grain or two, to leave unburnt
> And still to nose th'offence.

Menenius responds:

> For one poor grain or two?
> I am one of those; his mother, wife, his child,
> And this brave fellow too: We are the grains,
> You are the musty chaff [...] (V, i, 23-30).

The quoted speeches are without parallel in Plutarch and his transla-
tors. The winnowing metaphor derives from *Matthew*, 3, 12: 'he will
throughly purge his floor, and gather his wheat into the garner; but he
will burn up the chaff with unquenchable fire'.

Shakespeare's method as a playwright in dealing with his sources

---

[36] *Coriolanus*, ed. P. Brockbank, introd., 38.

becomes apparent in this brief analysis of the series of 'natural' images in the play. Although he could rely on North's Plutarch for all the basic ideas and metaphors, the way of stringing them together in a unified pattern, combining them with material from other sources and distributing them among different scenes in a dramatically effective way is uniquely his.

Another aspect of what one might call Shakespeare's imaginative historiography is the way in which he dealt with Roman customs and manners to make them appear authentic on the one hand and recognizable for his Jacobean audience on the other. Many details in *Coriolanus* bear the hallmark of authenticity. It is quite obvious that Shakespeare wished to create a Rome that his audience would find credible. As Spencer puts it:

> More than *Julius Caesar* or than *Antony and Cleopatra*, *Coriolanus* (perhaps by the rivalry or stimulation of Ben Jonson) shows a great deal of care to get things right, to preserve Roman manners and customs and allusions. We have, of course, the usual Roman officials, and political and religious customs familiarly referred to; and we have the Roman mythology and pantheon. But we are also given a good deal of Roman history worked into the background. [...] Moreover, in *Coriolanus* there is some effort to make literary allusions appropriate. The ladies knew their Homer and the Tale of Troy. The personal names are all authentically derived from somewhere in Plutarch; Shakespeare has turned the pages to find something suitable.[37]

It is quite revealing to compare the entirely different ways in which the two great friends and rivals, Jonson and Shakespeare, went about creating their respective Roman worlds. Ben Jonson, in *Sejanus* and other plays with a Roman setting, goes out of his way to create an authentic atmosphere, but what he gains in historical veracity he loses in dramatic impact. The language of his plays occasionally makes a laborious, studied impression, whereas Shakespeare invariably shapes the material to make it suit the requirements of his drama with an eye to the performance. His 'historic eye' was, Janus-like, focused not only on using his sources in such a way that his audience would be convinced that they were watching a play representing an era and culture remote from their own but, at the same time, touching on events and themes, that had 'a local habitation and a name'. Compare, for instance, the following stage direction from *Sejanus* (1605), in which a

---

[37] Spencer, "Shakespeare and the Elizabethan Romans", 34-5.

flamen (a priest of a particular deity) is instructed to perform a special ritual, with the way in which Shakespeare refers to the *flamen* in a description of Coriolanus' triumphal progress through Rome:

> While they [the *tubicines* and *tibicines* mentioned earlier, bw] sound again, the *Flamen* takes of the honey with his finger and tastes, then ministers to all the rest: so of the milk in an earthen vessel, he deals about: which done, he sprinkleth, upon the altar, milk: then imposeth the honey, and kindleth his gums, and after censing about the altar placeth his censer thereon, into which they put several branches of poppy, and, the music ceasing, proceeds (*Sejanus* V, iv, 8ff.).[38]

> All tongues speak of him, and the bleared sights
> Are spectacled to see him. Your prattling nurse
> Into a rapture lets her baby cry
> While she chats him. The kitchen malkin [wench, bw] pins
> Her richest lockram [linen fabric, bw] 'bout her reechy neck,
> Clamb'ring the walls to eye him; stalls, bulks, windows,
> Are smother'd up, leads fill'd and ridges hors'd
> With variable complexions, all agreeing
> In earnestness to see him. Seld-shown flamens
> Do press among the popular throngs, and puff
> To win a vulgar station (*Coriolanus* II, i, 203-13).[39]

The liveliness of the description could apply to any festive gathering anywhere and Shakespeare is more likely to have been inspired in writing it by a royal entry into Elizabethan and Jacobean London than by any reading of historical texts. The "authentic touch" of the Roman *flamens* is introduced ever so lightly, as part of the homely backdrop, which is probably the reason why it is so utterly convincing.

In this sense the discourse of the history play is not essentially different from travel accounts of the period in which minute proto-anthropological descriptions of the environment and of the life and manners of the newly discovered countries and their inhabitants are frequently mixed with elements from the world back home, whether they be topical, mythical or fabulous.[40] Social space is as much a determining fac-

---

[38] Jonson B., "Sejanus", in *Five Plays* (London: 1953) 185-6.

[39] I owe these quotations to Martindale C. and M., *Shakespeare and the Uses of Antiquity* (London–New York: 1990) 125-6.

[40] See Grafton A., *New Worlds, Ancient Texts: The Power of Tradition and the Shock of Discovery* (Cambridge., Mass.–London: 1992) *passim*. Cf. also Westerweel, "Richard Hakluyt en het Engelse reisverhaal" in K. Enenkel – P.A.W. van Heck – B. Westerweel (ed.), *Reizen en Reizigers in de Renaissance: Eigen en Vreemd in Oude en Nieuwe Werelden* (Amsterdam: 1998) 133-52.

tor in assigning meaning to historic texts, of which travel accounts and historic plays are only two variants, as is the reconstruction of a meaningful connection between the past and the present, or, in the case of this article, between two points in the past, one much longer ago than the other but both seen, inevitably, from a later point in time that we call the present and from a different or changed social and cultural vantage point. Such confrontations invariably involve a confrontation between the now and then, between the familiar and the unknown, and between the self and the Other.[41]

In the case of *Coriolanus* this clash entails that the play, notwithstanding its overall historical veracity, contains quite a number of anachronisms in the details of the presentation. We do not expect Coriolanus to wave his 'hat' as he is reported to do in II, iii, 165. The detail so shocked eighteenth-century editors that most of them copied Pope's emendation to 'cap'. For neo-classical readers such as Dryden and Pope, who praised Shakespeare for the authenticity of his presentation of Roman manners, the playwright's 'occasional carelessness or indifference [...] jarred against the pervading sense of authenticity everywhere else in the Roman plays'.[42] Shakespeare, I am sure, had other priorities. Similarly, when, very much against his will, Coriolanus goes through the motions of obtaining the votes of the citizens for his election, he wonders: 'Why in this wolvish toge should I stand here / To beg of Hob and Dick that does appear / Their needless vouches?' (II, iii, 114-6). Although the names 'Hob and Dick' would surely have the effect of calling to mind an Elizabethan or Jacobean crowd rather than the Roman mob, the atmosphere of Rome is saved by the mentioning of the toga.

In an earlier scene the citizens, stirred up by the tribunes, are about to start a riot in the streets of Rome. In his translation Sir Thomas North describes the occasion thus:

> Now those busy prattlers that sought the people's good will by such flattering words, perceiving great scarcity of corn to be within the city, and, though there had been plenty enough, yet the common people had no money to buy it; they spread abroad false tales and rumours

---

[41] I am borrowing the phrase 'social space' from J.D. Cox – D. Scott Kastan (eds.), *A New History of Early English Drama* (New York: 1997), especially Part II, *Early English Drama and Social Space* 131-248.

[42] Spencer, "Shakespeare and the Elizabethan Romans", 28. Martindale, *Shakespeare and the Uses of Antiquity* ,121-5 devote a useful section to anachronisms in the Roman plays.

> against the nobility: that they, in revenge of the people, had practised
> and procured the extreme dearth among them.[43]

Menenius Agrippa tries to appease the mob and Shakespeare has him say: 'What work's, my countrymen, in hand? Where go you / With bats and clubs? The matter? Speak, I pray you' (I, i, 54-5). Although the gist of the scene clearly derives from Plutarch, through the mediation of North, the particular image of the 'bats and clubs' is definitely English. They were the arms of the London apprentices, 'often called in to quieten an affray, and sometimes to start one'.[44]

Towards the end of the play Menenius, describing Coriolanus' martial prowess in witty hyperboles, says that he 'is able to pierce a corslet with his eye, talks like a knell, and his hum is a battery' (V, iv, 20-1). Here Menenius is inventing siege-guns well before they came into existence. Elsewhere Menenius refers to Galen, who lived in the second century AD. Brockbank writes: 'Technically an anachronism, the allusion nevertheless mediates aptly between the Jacobean audience and the classical past'.[45] Obviously, Shakespeare did not consult his history books for every detail of the play.

In other instances Plutarch provided Shakespeare with what might be called *historical coincidence*. That is the case with the corn riots referred to above. They were there, for the taking, in Shakespeare's Plutarch, but they would also remind his audience of similar riots caused by food shortage in Elizabethan and Jacobean England. They would be likely to think of the Oxfordshire rising of 1597 and the Midlands insurrection of 1607, events that had occurred not long before *Coriolanus* was written.[46]

What is utterly classical in the play, although only partially derived from Plutarch, is Shakespeare's recognition of the importance of rhetoric in a social context and his exploration of the moral values attached to codes of conduct. Coriolanus fails to live up to the chief social and civic duties of a Roman citizen in being unable to address his fellow citizens properly. This is not quite the same thing as Miola's delineation of Coriolanus's character in this respect: 'Differing sharply from Plutarch's Coriolanus of "eloquent tongue" [...] the inarticulate

---

[43] *Shakespeare's Plutarch*, ed. Spencer, 314-5.

[44] Shakespeare, *Coriolanus*, ed. Brockbank, 98n.

[45] Shakespeare, *Coriolanus*, ed. Brockbank, 158n.

[46] See Bullough, *Narrative and Dramatic Sources* V, 456-8, 553-8 and Pettet E.C., "Shakespeare and the Midlands Insurrection of 1607", *Shakespeare Survey* 3 (1950) 34-42.

Coriolanus on stage is Shakespeare's own creation'.[47] Coriolanus is not so much 'inarticulate' as unwilling to adapt his speech to the occasion. When he has put on the gown of humility Coriolanus protests that he doesn't know how to address the people of Rome: 'What must I say? — / 'I pray, sir,' — Plague upon't! I cannot bring / My tongue to such a pace' (II, iii, 51-3). In his encounter with the tribunes in Act III Coriolanus sins against all the basic prescriptions of successful oratory, observing neither 'orderly arrangement (*dispositio*), suitable style (*elocutio*), and graceful delivery (*actio*)'.[48] By blundering through his speeches, full of contempt for the mob and directing outright insults at the tribunes, Coriolanus throws away much of the goodwill that his heroic war actions had won him.

The exploration of the Roman virtue of 'valiantness', North's translation of the Latin *virtus*, forms a crucial key to the play's theme and to the characterization of Coriolanus:

> Now in those days valiantness was honoured in Rome above all other virtues: which they call *virtus*, by the name of virtue itself, as including in that general name all other special virtues besides. So that *virtus* in the Latin was as much as valiantness. But Martius, being more inclined to the wars than any other gentleman of his time, began from his childhood to give himself to handle weapons and daily did exercise himself therein; and outward he esteemed armour to no purpose, unless one were naturally armed within. [49]

In the play these ideas are telescoped in a speech in which the Roman general Cominius extols Coriolanus' military bravery:

> [...] the deeds of Coriolanus
> Should not be utter'd feebly. It is held
> That valour is the chiefest virtue and
> Most dignifies the haver: if it be,
> The man I speak of cannot in the world
> Be singly counter-pois'd (II, ii, 82-7).

The English word 'valiantness' as it was used in Shakespeare's day combines the notions of active bravery and courage on the battlefield with the inner quality of a worthy character or nature. By copying the notion of 'valour' in North's translation Shakespeare allowed a wider range of meaning to it than the restrictive definition that North copied

---

47 Miola R.S., *Shakespeare's Rome* (Cambridge: 1983) 185.
48 Miola, *Shakespeare's Rome*, 186.
49 *Shakespeare's Plutarch*, ed. Spencer, 297.

faithfully from his sources. In North's translation, as in Plutarch's Greek text, the Roman concept of 'virtus' (ἀρετή in Greek) is limited to manly valour in military endeavours, whereas Shakespeare's use of 'valour' clearly implies the inner virtue as well. Because of his outstanding feats of valour on the battlefield Coriolanus is expected to live up to the high moral expectations implied in the notion of 'valour' as well. The fact that he fails to live up to them only adds to the tragic quality of his downfall.[50]

For Coriolanus, the particular interpretation of valour and honour, its social corollary, which his life exemplifies, ultimately leads to an annihilation of the self, a loss of identity. Coriolanus turns out to be nothing beyond his military actions, beyond his deeds. When those end, by his death, nothing remains. Even the name, Coriolanus, which is derived from his actions, has no significance anymore. No one has summarized the starting-point of the play as tersely as Gordon: 'Name is fame, is honour, and is won by deeds; in Rome, by deeds of war'.[51] The outcome of the play is not gain, however, but loss. Coriolanus is a war machine — trained by his mother — and, machine-like, his downfall is caused by his lack of 'conversation', by his failure to fulfill the social obligations of a leader.

Coriolanus' end is bleak and does not offer any hopeful prospect. His death is different from that of the heroes of all other history plays, both English and Roman. In *Julius Caesar* and *Antony and Cleopatra* a strong sense is conveyed that, even though a great leader dies, the state will survive. In the English history plays the notion of the King's Two Bodies applies. Whereas the natural body of the king will die, the body politic survives: 'the king is dead, long live the king'.[52] This kind of dynastic or political continuity is denied in *Coriolanus*. As Brockbank puts it: 'Shakespeare perceived that in the history as

---

[50] As Karl Enenkel pointed out to me Plutarch may wilfully have narrowed down the meaning of the word ἀρετή to a purely military definition in its Roman context. This may have been done with his Greek readership in mind. The definition reflects negatively on the Roman Coriolanus, thus creating a contrast with the more positive qualities attributed to the Athenian Alcibiades. My interpretation of Shakespeare's use of the 'valour' and 'valiantness' in *Coriolanus* is equally relevant for the character of the titular hero of *Othello*.

[51] Gordon D.J., "Name and Fame: Shakespeare's *Coriolanus*", in *The Renaissance Imagination*, ed. Stephen Orgel (Los Angeles–London: 1975) 203-19, this quote 203.

[52] Cf. Kantorowicz E.H., *The King's Two Bodies: A Study in Medieval Political Theology* (Princeton: 1957).

Plutarch presents it the personal crisis coincides with the political one'.[53]

As Plutarch conceived the Lives of Coriolanus and of Alcibiades together, Shakespeare in all probability wrote *Coriolanus* and *Timon of Athens* in the same year. It can hardly be a coincidence that, whereas Coriolanus remains an outsider and does not even want to be called by his proper name by his former friends, Alcibiades is presented as a symbol of regeneration in the final speech of *Timon of Athens*. The role of the nameless character is reserved for Timon, the misanthrope, whose epitaph is read by Alcibiades, Timon's friend: '*Here lies a wretched corse, of wretched soul bereft: / Seek not my name* [...]'.[54] The final words of the play are for Alcibiades:

> Bring me into your city,
> And I will use the olive with my sword,
> Make war breed peace, make peace stint war, make each
> Prescribe to other, as each other's leech.
> Let our drums strike (V, iv, 81-5).

Timon of Athens ends with natural images of peace ('olive'), fertility ('breed'), and health ('prescribe', 'leech'). *Coriolanus* ends on a heavier note, with a mourning speech by Aufidius, who had just had Coriolanus killed:

> Though in this city he
> Hath widow'd and unchilded many a one,
> Which to this hour bewail the injury,
> Yet he shall have a noble memory.
> Assist (V, vi, 150-4).

The speech celebrates the noble general Coriolanus once was, but emphasizes at the same time the pain inflicted on the relatives of those Romans whose lives were ended untimely and unnaturally by his hand.

---

[53] Shakespeare, *Coriolanus*, ed. Brockbank, 37.

[54] The epitaph was taken literally from North's translation of the *Life of Marcus Antonius* (Spencer, *Shakespeare's Plutarch*, 265).

Selective Bibliography

BERGONZI B., *T.S. Eliot*, 2nd ed. (London: 1978)

BOAS F.S., *Shakespeare and his Predecessors* (1896; rpt New York:1968)

BULLOUGH G., *Narrative and Dramatic Sources of Shakespeare* (London: 1964)

COX J. D. – SCOTT KASTAN D. (eds.), *A New History of Early English Drama* (New York: 1997)

DOHERTY M.J., *The Mistress-Knowledge: Sir Philip Sidney's* Defence of Poesie *and Literary Architectonics in the English Renaissance* (Nashville: 1991)

DUNCAN-JONES K., *Sir Philip Sidney: Courtier Poet* (New Haven–London: 1991)

EAGLETON T., *William Shakespeare* (Oxford: 1986)

ELIOT T.S., *Selected Essays*, 3rd ed. (London: 1951)

ELIOT T.S., *Collected Poems 1909–1962* (London: 1963)

ENENKEL K. – HECK P.A.W. VAN – WESTERWEEL B. (eds.), *Reizen en Reizigers in de Renaissance: Eigen en Vreemd in Oude en Nieuwe Werelden* (Amsterdam: 1998)

GORDON D.J., "Name and Fame: Shakespeare's *Coriolanus*", in *The Renaissance Imagination*, ed. S. Orgel (Los Angeles–London: 1975) 203-19

GRAFTON A., *New Worlds, Ancient Texts: The Power of Tradition and the Shock of Discovery* (Cambridge, Mass.–London: 1992)

HEUER H., "From Plutarch to Shakespeare: A Study of Coriolanus", *Shakespeare Survey* 10 (1957) 50-9

HIGHET G., *The Classical Tradition: Greek and Roman Influences on Western Literature* (New York–London: 1949)

HUNTER G.K., *English Drama 1586–1642: The Age of Shakespeare* (Oxford: 1997)

JONSON B., "Sejanus", in *Five Plays* (London: 1953) 95-210

KAHN C., *Roman Shakespeare: Warriors, Wounds, and Women* (London–New York: 1997)

KANTOROWICZ E.H., *The King's Two Bodies: A Study in Medieval Political Theology* (Princeton: 1957)

MACCALLUM M.W., *Shakespeare's Roman Plays and their Background* (London: 1910)

MARTINDALE C. and M., *Shakespeare and the Uses of Antiquity* (London–New York: 1990)

MIOLA R.S., *Shakespeare's Rome* (Cambridge: 1983)

MONTAIGNE M. de, *The Complete Essays*, transl. D.M. Frame (Stanford: 1958)

MUIR K. – SCHOENBAUM S., *A New Companion to Shakespeare Studies* (Cambridge: 1971)

MUIR K., *Shakespeare: Contrasts and Controversies* (Norman: 1985)

NEALE J.E., *Queen Elizabeth I* (1952; rpt Chicago: 1992)

OSBORN J.M., *Young Philip Sidney 1572–1577* (New Haven: 1972)

PETTET E.C., "Coriolanus and the Midlands Insurrection of 1607", *Shakespeare Survey* 3 (1950) 34-42

SACCIO P., *Shakespeare's English Kings: History, Chronicle, and Drama* (London–Oxford–New York: 1977)

Shakespeare's Plutarch: the Lives of Julius Caesar, Brutus, Marcus Antonius, and Corio-

lanus in the translation of Sir Thomas North, ed. and introd. T.J.B. Spencer (Harmondsworth: 1964)

SHAKESPEARE W., *Coriolanus*, ed. P. Brockbank, Arden edition (London–New York: 1976)

SHAKESPEARE W., *Timon of Athens*, ed. H.J. Oliver, Arden edition (London–New York: 1959)

SHAKESPEARE W., *Hamlet*, ed. H. Jenkins, Arden edition (London–New York: 1982)

SHAKESPEARE W., *The Tempest*, ed. F. Kermode, Arden edition (London–New York: 1958)

SHAKESPEARE W., *King Richard III*, ed. A. Hammond, Arden edition (London–New York: 1981)

SIDNEY P., *Miscellaneous Prose*, ed. K. Duncan-Jones – Jan van Dorsten (Oxford: 1973)

SPENCER T.J.B., "Shakespeare and the Elizabethan Romans", *Shakespeare Survey* 10 (1957) 27-38

THOMSON J.A.K., *Shakespeare and the Classics* (London: 1952)

WARDMAN A., *Plutarch's Lives* (London: 1974).

THE RECEPTION OF PLUTARCH IN THE NETHERLANDS: OCTAVIA AND CLEOPATRA IN THE HEROIC EPISTLES OF J.B. WELLEKENS (1710)*

Olga van Marion

He had intended to lead a life as a painter in Italy, but instead, by a whim of fate, Jan Baptista Wellekens (1658–1726) ended up as a poet in the Netherlands. A southern Dutch Catholic by birth who grew up in Amsterdam and was apprenticed to the painter Anthonie de Grebber, Wellekens thought his training period should be completed abroad, so he left for Italy in 1676, at the age of eighteen. We know little of this period in the painter's life, only that his career came to an abrupt end when he became disabled by failing eyesight and then suffered a stroke. That is how Wellekens got into poetry.

After returning to Amsterdam in 1687, Wellekens earned a living by writing occasional verse, some of which was printed in a limited edition for friends. It was not until 1710 that his first collection of poetry was published, which was followed in 1715 by a translation of Tasso's *Aminta*. His daughter, Magdalena Barbara Wellekens, published two compilations of verse in 1729 and another in 1737 after her father's death.[1]

None of his paintings is left; however, his small but important literary oeuvre remains. Inspired by his eleven-year stay in Italy in a period when pastoral literature was flourishing again, Wellekens composed a large collection of pastoral songs unique in the Netherlands. He took the name *Silvander* from Sannazaro's *Arcadia* to serve as a pseudonym. In an essay on bucolic poetry Wellekens defended the value of the pastoral genre, denying that it was a light, leisurely poetic activity.[2] As a defender of less pretentious genres, Wellekens also stood

* The research project *Heldinnenbrieven in de Nederlandse letterkunde* was generously supported by the Dutch Organisation for Scientific Research (NWO). For this paper, I profited from the helpful remarks of Karl Enenkel, Paul Smith, Paul Hoftijzer, Ton Harmsen, Tijn Cuypers, Ton van der Wouden and Ellen Ilfeld.

[1] For a biography of Wellekens, see Pennink R., *Silvander (Jan Baptista Wellekens) 1658–1726* (Haarlem: 1957) 1-56. For Anthonie de Grebber, see Wurzbach A. von, *Niederländisches Künstler-Lexikon*, 3 vols (Vienna–Leipzig: 1906–1911) I, 613.

[2] For Wellekens's Arcadian poetry see Blommendaal J.L.P., *De zachte toon der herdersfluit. De pastorale poëtica van Jan Baptista Wellekens (1658–1726)* (Utrecht: 1987). The

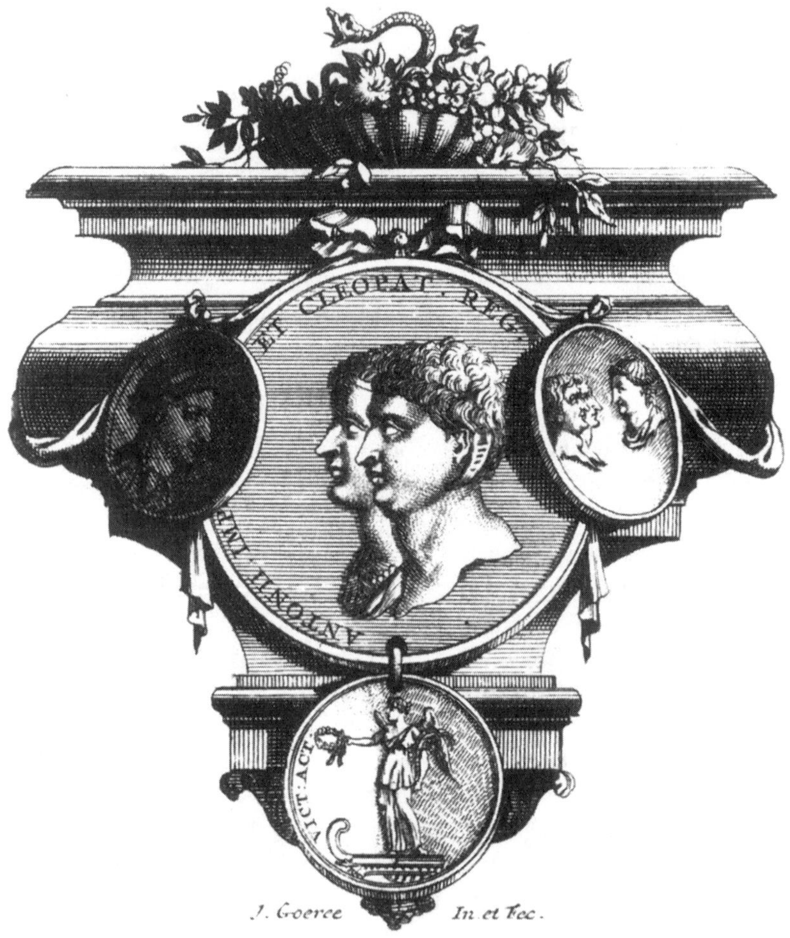

Effigy of Antony and Cleopatra. Engraved by Jan Goeree. Jan Baptista Wellekens en Pieter Vlaming, *Dichtlievende uitspanningen* (Amsterdam: 1710), 154.

up for the so-called heroic epistles. These were fictitious letters, written in imitation of the *Epistulae heroidum* or *Heroides* of Publius Ovidius Naso, in the voices of mythological heroines such as Penelope, Dido, Ariadne and Medea. Ovid's twenty-one epistles were prime examples of witty elegies written in the form of letters from lovelorn women addressing their distant husbands or lovers showing a range of emotions, from hopeful, to disappointed, to furious. As was demonstrated by Dörrie,[3] the *Heroides* inspired European literature, both in Latin and the vernacular, from fourteenth-century Italy up to the nineteenth century in the Netherlands, England, Germany and France. The genre of heroic epistles ranged from variations on the original *Heroides*, including replies to the Ovidian letters, to imitations with new characters as writers and objects of address. A wide range of figures from mythological, biblical, and historical stories, as well as contemporary kings and queens served as fictitious authors. The role of moral, religious and political themes became increasingly important.

In the Low Countries the heroic epistle experienced two waves of popularity. The first wave rose around 1535 in the humanistic circles surrounding Janus Secundus, leading up to a tradition of elegiac couplets — particularly from 1590 on at the young Leiden University and around 1640 in Jesuit circles in the Southern provinces. The second wave of heroic epistles was initiated around 1550 in a chamber of rhetoric in Antwerp, inspiring a vernacular tradition, especially among Amsterdam poets such as P.C. Hooft (1615), Joost van den Vondel (1642) and Govert Bidloo (1675).[4] But by 1700 the heroic epistle tradition seemed to have come to an end.[5]

Wellekens, however, breathed new life into the genre. He referred to the heroic epistle as 'my dearest nymph to play with, in the bloom

---

essay was published as Wellekens, *Verhandeling van het herderdicht*. For Wellekens and Sannazaro see Harmsen A.J.E., "Sannazaro nella letteratura Olandese", *Acta Conventus Neo-Latini Bariensis Proceedings of the Ninth International Congress of Neo-Latin Studies*, Bari 29 August to 3 September 1994, ed. R. Schnur et alii (Tempe: 1998), 305-13.

[3] Dörrie H., *Der heroische Brief. Bestandsaufname, Geschichte, Kritik einer humanistisch-barocken Literaturgattung* (Berlin: 1968).

[4] P.C. Hooft composed a letter from Menelaus to Helen; Joost van den Vondel imitated Jesuit *Heroides sacrae* in his twelve letters from Virgin Martyrs; Govert Bidloo imitated Vondel in his letters from the Twelve Apostles; for the latter epistles see Marion O. van, "*Heroides*-imitaties van Govert Bidloo: De Brieven der gemartelde apostelen uit 1675", *Nieuwe Taalgids* 87 (1994) 499-514.

[5] See http://www.let.LeidenUniv.nl/Dutch.Heroides.html for a database of heroic epistles in Dutch literature.

of my youth',[6] admitting that he had devoted himself to the genre at
an early age. Eventually Wellekens brought together eight of his letters in a collection of *Brieven* in 1690.[7] They were only published twenty years later in the *Dichtlievende uitspanningen*, a collective work of
Wellekens and his Amsterdam friend and maecenas, the lawyer and
poet Pieter Vlaming (1686–1734).[8] Jan Goeree (1670–1731), the poet,
bookseller and famous illustrator of Arcadian works, created thirty-
two engravings for it.[9] The *Brieven* in the 1710 edition are dedicated to
the Amsterdam merchant and maecenas Philip Moilives van der Noot
with a frontispiece designed and engraved by Goeree, representing a
woman writing and cupids carrying her letters away.

With his heroic epistles Wellekens took a new course. The *Brieven*
are made up of four pairs of letters using a variety of historically-
linked persons as fictional letter-writers,[10] a remarkable method never
used before in Dutch heroic epistles. Up until this time, pairs of letters
had stemmed from competitions between two poets, for instance
Janus Dousa Pater and Hugo Grotius in 1602, P.C. Hooft and an
anonymous author in 1615–1616, and Caspar Barlaeus and Cornelis
Keyser in 1629–1630.[11] A second innovative element on Wellekens'
part, departing from the earlier Dutch tradition, was the choice of
characters: they were selected from diverse historical periods. Traditionally heroic epistle collections were homogeneous, but Wellekens
chose his subjects from a variety of historical contexts: from the Old
Testament King David and his wife Michol, the daughter of Saul, to

---

[6] 'Myn liefste Speelnimf, in het bloeien myner jeugt'. In the dedication poem *Aan
den Heere Philip Moilives van der Noot, rechtsgeleerden* (1706) in Wellekens J.B. – Vlaming P.,
*Dichtlievende uitspanningen. Bestaande in Herders- Hoef- en Veldgezangen, Tafereelen, Brieven,
enz. Met 32 Konstplaaten door Jan Goeree* (Amsterdam: 1710) 119.

[7] *Dichtlievende uitspanningen* 118-66. Two pairs of epistles only appeared posthumously in the *Verscheiden gedichten* (Amsterdam: 1729); these letters seem to have been composed in the same period of the poet's life.

[8] For a biography of Vlaming see Cox-Andrau M.S.J., *De dichter Pieter Vlaming
(1686–1734). Een studie over zijn werk met een levensbeschrijving* (Bussum: 1976).

[9] For Goeree's illustrations see Fontaine Verwey E. de la, *De illustratie van letterkundi-
ge werken in de 18e eeuw. Bijdrage tot de geschiedenis van het Nederlandse boek* (Leiden: 1934).
For a biography see Thieme U. – Willis F.C., *Allgemeines Lexicon der bildenden Künstler*
(Leipzig: 1922) XIV, 308-9.

[10] *Michol aan David* and *David aan Michol*, *Achilles aan Polyxena* and *Polyxena aan Achilles*,
Oktavia aan Markus Antonius and *Kleopatra aan Oktavia*, *Boudewijn aan Judith* and *Judith aan
Boudewijn*.

[11] Janus Dousa Pater, *Epistola Jacobae Bavarae ad Iohannem patruum* and Hugo
Grotius, *Responsum Iohannis Bavari ad Iacobam*; P.C. Hooft, *Brief van Menelaus aen Helena*
and *Antwoorde op den brief van C.P.H.*; Caspar Barlaeus, *Epistola Ameliae ad Fredericum Henricum* and Cornelis Keyser, *Antwoort inghestelt op den Naem van mijn heer Frederick Henrick*.

the mythological Achilles and the Trojan princess Polyxena, from the ninth century Flemish count Balduinus Ferreus and his forbidden relationship with Judith, the daughter of Charles the Bold, to the Roman Republic and the triangular relationship between Antony, Octavia and Cleopatra. With the choice of this last theme, another innovation was added to the Dutch heroic epistle tradition. Up until then, Roman history had never played a role in it.

A Letter From Rome

This contribution focuses on the two final epistles. The first is a letter from Rome called "Oktavia aan Markus Antonius", consisting of 156 alexandrines in rhyming couplets.[12] Here we meet Octavia, sister of Octavian (Augustus), at the time she was married to Antony, a member of the triumvirate and responsible for the establishment of Roman authority in the eastern part of the Empire. Most of Wellekens's readers would have known the story of Antony and his relationship with Egypt's queen Cleopatra. The political rivalry between him and Octavian resulted in the Battle of Actium in 31 BC, which was disastrous for both Antony and Cleopatra. Readers not familiar with this tragedy were informed by a short *argumentum* preceding the text.

In this plot, all the prerequisites for an heroic epistle were at hand. a heroine feels lovelorn and neglected by her husband, and although she blames him fully for her feelings, she still loves him, so she argues strongly to persuade him to return. The heroine herself is, of course, impeccable. Octavia fits perfectly in this scheme.

> To purify my name in all the ages to come,
>   I send you this letter, my dear husband and lord.
> I fear the slandering tongue would cry, if I would remain silent:
>   Octavia is rightly suspected of faithfulness and honour.
> But how? For what reasons would I not be allowed to write
>   To you, my consort? To you, who is mine?
> Antony is mine, and will forever be, by the promise of faith
>   That was pledged, in spite of the adversaries.[13]

---

12 *Dichtlievende uitspanningen*, 144-9.

13 'Tot zuivring van myn naam in alle volgende eeuwen, / Zende ik u deezen brief, myn waarde Man en Heer. / Ik ducht, de lastertong, indien ik zweeg, zou schreeuwen: / Oktavia wort recht verdacht van trouw en eer. / Maar hoe? Om welke reên

Octavia's complaints and arguments easily match those of Ovid's heroines, especially the two most virtuous amongst them: Penelope (*Heroides* 1) and Laodamia (*Heroides* 13). These two examples of faithful, worried wives had the strongest influence on the creation of heroines within the Dutch heroic epistle tradition. When Caspar Barlaeus shaped his Latin epistle from the Dutch princess Amalia van Solms to Frederik Hendrik, audaciously fighting to win the city of Den Bosch from the Spanish (1629), he closely modelled the princess after Laodamia, the Ovidian heroine who urged her husband Protesilaus in her epistle to protect his life and to return home safely from the Trojan War, not knowing he was dead already (the reader of the text, of course, was well aware of that).[14]

Laodamia's cry for a hasty 'return': 'Ye gods, I pray, keep from us the sinister omen, and let my lord hang up his arms to Jove-of-Safe-Return!' is echoed in Octavia's letter.[15] Reminiscences of these lines can be heard in Octavia's words: 'Return, return Antony, Jove is still being prayed to. He waits for your remorse; ah, return while you can!'.[16] More explicit similarities between the two epistles can be found as well. In her letter to Ulysses Penelope complains about the course of events:

> O would that then, when his ship was on the way to Lacedaemon,
> The adulterous lover [Paris] had been overwhelmed by raging waters!
> Then had I not lain cold in my deserted bed [...].[17]

Octavia passes her own strictures upon history:

> Ah, had there been a quarrel with another people,
> Had you not put your sabre on Rome's breast;
> I would not have to go to sleep as a sorrowful widow [...].[18]

---

zou ik niet mogen schryven / Aan u, myn eigen deel? Aan u, die myne zyt? / Antonius is myne, en zal het eeuwig blyven, / Door duurbezwoore trouw, tot aller haatren spyt' (*Dichtlievende uitspanningen*, 145). Cf. the sarcastic opening lines as in Ovid, *Heroides* 5.

[14] *Epistola Ameliae ad Fredericum Henricum, maritum, audacius sub ipsis Sylvae-Ducis moenibus militantem* (Leiden: 1629). For this epistle see Marion O. van, "Ovid's *Heroides* in the Netherlands. A Dutch princess in a heroic epistle of Caspar Barlaeus (1629)", to be published in the *Acta of the Xth Congress of the IANLS in Avila* (1997).

[15] 'Di, precor, a nobis omen removete sinistrum, / et sua det Reduci vir meus arma Iovi!' (Ovid, *Heroides* 13, 49-50); I quote from Ovid, *Heroides and Amores*, transl. G. Showerman, 2nd ed. by G.P. Goold, Loeb Classical Library (Cambridge, Mass.–London: 1986).

[16] 'Keer: keer Antonius, Jupyn wordt noch verbeden: / Hy wacht naar uw berouw; ei keer; terwyl gy meugt!' (*Dichtlievende uitspanningen*, 147).

[17] Ovid, *Heroides* 1, 5-7.

[18] *Dichtlievende uitspanningen*, 148. Other similarities for instance in Ovid, *Heroides* 17,

The import of Octavia's letter is clarified through these lines: a faithful and honest burgher woman takes a stand against a lascivious queen.

Wellekens's Epistle *and Plutarch's* Lives

The source of the heroic epistle is indicated by the *argumentum* preceding the letter: 'For this history see Plutarch and others of that time'.[19] Plutarch's life of Antony in the *Parallel Lives* is still the most important source as regards Octavia's life.[20] Wellekens follows the blueprint of Plutarch's narrative from Octavia's marriage with Antony in Chapter 31 through Chapter 60, where Octavian had made sufficient preparations to start war. All the descriptions of warfare, however, are skipped. The story of Octavia's beseeching pleas to her husband is the only one recapitulated. Thus, Wellekens bases his plot on Plutarch's chapters 53 and 54. Here we find Octavia desirous of sailing to Antony, but when she arrives in Athens (in 35 BC) she receives letters from him in which he bids her to stay away. Nevertheless she sends her husband all the gifts she has prepared for him. Cleopatra, in her turn, is afraid Octavia will gain control over her husband and she pretends to be passionately in love with Antony herself. The rumour is spread that Octavia married Antony as a matter of political expediency, but that Cleopatra is Antony's beloved. Octavia returns to Rome, not wanting to be the reason of a civil war between Octavian and Antony. Therefore, she dwells in her husband's house and cares for his children.

Several narrative segments from these two chapters of Plutarch's *Life of Antony* are cited in Octavia's letter, for instance Chapter 54, 2. Octavia dwelt in Antony's house while he was staying abroad, as Plutarch recounts, 'just as if he were at home, and she cared for his children, not only those whom she herself, but also those whom Fulvia had borne him, in a noble and magnificent manner'.[21] This situation is echoed in Octavia's letter:

---

193 (Helen to Paris): 'Hypsipyle testis, testis Minoia virgo est' and *Dichtlievende uitspanningen*, 145: 'Getuigen zyn de Goôn [...], Getuige zy het bloet, het Kroost [...]' ('Witnesses are the gods [...], witnesses are your children [...]').

[19] *Dichtlievende uitspanningen*, 150. 'Zie van deeze geschiedenisse Plutarchus, en andre van dien tyd'.

[20] *Paulys Realencyclopädie der classischen Altertumswissenschaft*, ed. G. Wissowa – K. Ziegler (neue Bearbeitung), 83 vols (Stuttgart: 1893–1980) XVII.2, 1859-68.

[21] Plutarch, *Antony* 54, 2 (*Lives*, vol IX, transl. B. Perrin, Loeb Classical Library (Cambridge, Mass.–London: 1919, rpt 1988)).

I trained your sons in all good manners,
>   And I showed them the path of heroism, the straight path of virtue.
I waited for your commands that still give me pleasure,
>   And I lead the children in discipline.
I live in your own house, and I never left it;
>   However I was disapproved of, and slandered, doing my duties.
I take care of your goods instead of strangers.
>   I bewail your absence, although you flee my sight.[22]

Parallels like this could be easily extended, for instance Octavia summing up all the goods she sent her husband to please him, including the two thousand men with splendid armour and the clothing for his soldiers; it matches the list in chapter 53, 2. The only embellishment Wellekens added was that she had sewn these clothes herself. Octavia recounts that she had rushed into Athens to pay Antony a visit, but that she was turned back by Cleopatra (it matches chapter 53, 1-4). Some of the rumours in Wellekens's letter appear to be taken from Plutarch too: 'Are you bragging of being a descendant of Hercules?', Octavia asks (chapter 60, 3). 'Messengers told us that Cleopatra and you play Isis and Bacchus' (chapter 54, 6 and 60, 3).[23] On the basis of these similarities, the reader may well get the impression that what Wellekens basically did was reproduce in verse several sections from Plutarch's *Life of Antony*.

However, the parallel sections are outnumbered by those in which Wellekens departed from Plutarch. In addition, Wellekens's different depiction of the characters is noteworthy. According to Plutarch's reconstruction of history, Antony's whole life shows his passivity and his inferiority to Octavian. Because of Cleopatra and the flatterers at her court he has returned to his earlier excesses. Antony is enthralled by Egypt's queen, spending most of his time in her presence, neglecting his duties as a Roman statesman and acting as if he and Cleopatra were oriental rulers. Plutarch suggests that the couple formed a constant threat to Octavian and to the Roman Empire; the Battle of Actium was a direct result of Antony's insubordination. As regards

---

[22] 'Ik oeffende uwe zoons in alle braave zeden,/En wees hen 't heldespoor, de rechte deugdebaan./Ik wachtte op uw geboôn, my aangenaam tot heden,/En ben in alle tucht de kindren voorgegaan./'k Bewoon uw eigen huis, en heb het nooit verlaten;/Hoe zeer my elk misprees en lasterde in myn plicht./'k Draag zorge voor uw goed, daar anders vreemde zaten./'k Betreur uw afzyn, schoon gy vlied voor myn gezicht' (*Dichtlievende uitspanningen*, 145).

[23] On the interesting parallel Antony-Osiris and Cleopatra-Isis see Brenk F.E., "Antony-Osiris, Cleopatra-Isis. The end of Plutarch's Antony", in *Plutarch and the Historical Tradition*, ed. P.A. Stadter, (London–New York: 1992) 159-82.

Cleopatra, flatterers have their methods, using a timely frankness to win credibility, demeaning themselves when appropriate, adapting themselves to their victim's tastes: that is just how Cleopatra and her court behave.

Octavia, in Plutarch's view, is a worthy rival. As beautiful and dignified as Cleopatra, she becomes a serious challenge when she prepares to visit her husband in Athens. Cleopatra is forced to defend her claim on Antony: she

> perceived that Octavia was coming into a contest at close quarters with her, and feared lest, if she added to the dignity of her character and the power of Caesar her pleasurable society and her assiduous attentions to Antony, she would become invincible and get complete control over her husband.[24]

In an elaborate way Plutarch balances the motives of both Octavia's and Cleopatra's behaviour.[25] His Octavia seeks equilibrium and peace, fighting for the preservation of the relationship between her brother and husband, and without any feeling of resentment or reproach.

Wellekens's letter, on the other hand, ascribes different qualities to the characters. An heroic epistle by definition reduces world history to the personal and psychological history of the heroine. Political machinations, appointments and battles are all considered from the heroine's (egoistic) point of view. According to Wellekens's Octavia, she herself is not to blame: 'The gods were witness of my faithfulness to you, witnesses are the children I carried under my heart. Never was I unfaithful and my duties I always fulfilled.'[26] But in her eyes Antony is nothing but an adulterer:

> Do you, a hero, walk as a slave behind Cleopatra's state carriage now? Did you abandon our gods for a dog's head? Wake up to the fact and flee this wicked sorceress! Wake up, for all Rome, all Europe will march against you. I can see Memphis fall already; don't expect to rely on the weak Egyptians. Ah, had you not put your sabre on Rome's breast, I would not have to go to sleep as a sorrowful widow, but I would follow you in battle. If you return to your home, your city, your country, your name will ride on poet's pens forever. Antony, return!

---

[24] Plutarch, *Antony* 53, 3.

[25] For Plutarch's manipulation of his source-material see Plutarch, *Life of Antony*, transl. B. Perrin, vol IX, 33-6, and Russell D.A., *Plutarch* (London: 1972).

[26] Paraphrase of the lines 9-19; *Dichtlievende uitspanningen*, 145. The next quote is a paraphrase of the rest of the epistle, 145-9.

Octavia's remarks directed to Antony are harsher than Plutarch's. For instance, Antony did not just 'bestow the honourable and solemn rites of his native country upon the Egyptians' like he did according to Plutarch.[27] According to the epistle he left Jove and the gods of his forefathers for a dog's head, a calf or cow goddess.[28] In other words, Antony is depicted as a renegade who worships primitive gods.

The criticism of Cleopatra, however, even surpasses that of Antony. Octavia's portrayal of the queen is over-simplified. She gives her opinion straight-forwardly: 'Does this woman, Cleopatra, have the right to retain you? Is it fair that an honest heart is defeated by the cunning schemes of a whore? Will a barbarian beat a Roman woman?' Cleopatra's influence on history is compared to the detrimental effect of Helen's stay in Troy: 'Gods, help us, a filthy whore will burn an Ilium, a kingdom again!'. She is also to blame for the sabotage of Octavia's intentions to sail to Antony, about which our heroine is highly indignant, referring to Antony's mistress as 'the jealous whore' that 'withdrew me, cunning and loose'.[29]

The main differences between Plutarch's Antony and Wellekens's heroic epistle thus do not reside in the so-called historical facts of the story, but rather in the moral assessment of the characters and their deeds. In other words, Wellekens's embellishment on Plutarch's famous story was the way in which he rendered the characters' thoughts about each other, elaborating on their moral qualities, pretending to reflect the point of view of his heroine. In this way Wellekens added to Octavia's point of view a strong moral rejection of both Antony's and Cleopatra's behaviour and a strong advocacy of her own power and worth. It is not impossible that Wellekens invented these moral assessments of his characters himself. There is, however, evidence that the poet had another source of inspiration.

Plutarch's Lives *in Dutch*

Wellekens's biography turns out to be a good source of insight into his work; the poet, who had received only basic education, was unable to

---

[27] Plutarch, *Antony* 50, 4.

[28] 'En gy verlaat Jupyn, de vaderlandsche Goden,/Om eenen Hondekop, een Kalf- of Koegodin?' (*Dichtlievende uitspanningen*, 146).

[29] 'Maar de yverzieke Boel weêrhield my, loos en schuw' (*Dichtlievende uitspanningen*, 148).

read Greek or Latin. Blommendaal thinks that Wellekens only knew the classical sources he mentioned by name through translations or quotes in someone else's work. Research showed, for instance, that Wellekens used Polybius in a Dutch translation, and Vergil's *Eclogues* in a translation by the Dutch poet Joost van den Vondel. For Ovid's *Metamorphoses*, from which he drew on extensively in his epithalamia, he used the translation of Vondel as well.[30] In a sonnet entitled "Ongeleertheit" ("Illiteracy"), Wellekens wrote that the Temple of the Muses at Mount Pindus remains inaccessible for him, because

> My voice is far too low to sound in that choir.
> Ah! that I never suckled from Latin or Greek breasts,
> Nor flew on the Ida or Hymet like the sweet little bee,
> Although nature seemed to entice me there with a gentle hand.[31]

If we assume Wellekens did not read the *Parallel Lives* in Greek nor in a Latin translation, the next step is to suppose he read Plutarch in Dutch, just as he did Vergil and Ovid. The seventeenth century had brought forth two Dutch versions of the *Parallel Lives*, both published in Leiden, both in the beginning of the century: 1601 and 1603.[32] The 1601 edition was not a complete translation of the Greek *Lives*, but an abbreviated version based on *Darius Tibertus*, by Marten Everart (Martinus Everaerts). Everart had many translations to his name, mostly from Italian, German and Spanish.[33] His *Tleven ende vrome daden van de doorluchtige Griecsche ende Romeynsche mannen*[34] has limited contents and there is no indication of any direct textual link with the heroic epistle. Therefore, it is not very likely that Wellekens used this edition. The 1603 version is more promising.

---

[30] Blommendaal, *De zachte toon der herdersfluit*, 44 en 48. For Wellekens's use of the *Metamorphoses* see Arens J.C., "J.B. Wellekens idylliseert Ovidius", *Spiegel der letteren* 7, 4 (1964) 288-93.

[31] "Ongeleertheit" in *Verscheiden gedichten*, 338: 'Myn galm is veel te laag om in dat choor te klinken. / Ach! dat ik noit Latynsche of Grieksche borsten zoog, / Op Ida noch Hymet als 't lekker bietje vloog, / Schoon my natuur daar scheen met zachte hant te winken'.

[32] Of Plutarch's *Moralia* before 1600 only one translation appeared, namely of the *Praecepta coniugalia* (1575); in 1661 the *Verscheide zedige werken van Plutarchus. Door J.H. Glazemaker vertaalt* (Amsterdam: 1661). As for the *Lives*, H.L. Spiegel adapted Plutarch's *Vita Numae* around 1600 into his *Zinspel Numa* (first complete edition 1902).

[33] For instance *Magia* (1566) originally by Giambattista Dellaporta, *T'Boeck vande vroet-wijfs* (1591 and many reprints) by Jacob Ruff and *Cort onderwijs van de Conste der see-vaert* (1598) by Rodrigo Zamorano.

[34] Not mentioned in Rynck P. de – Welkenhuysen A., *De Oudheid in het Nederlands. Repertorium en bibliografische gids voor vertalingen van Griekse en Latijnse auteurs en geschriften* (Baarn: 1992; Supplement, Baarn: 1997).

Jacques Amyot's Vies *in Dutch*

The history of the more promising, more influential 1603 version of
Plutarch's *Lives* in Dutch starts with the famous French translation of
Plutarch's *Lives*, *Vies des hommes illustres* (1559 and many reprints) by
Jacques Amyot. A Dutch translation of the French original showed up
several years later, composed by A.V.Z.V.N., that is Adam van Zuylen
van Nyevelt (died c. 1596). Little is known of this man, beyond the fact
that he held several political offices in the service of the Provincial
States of Holland. None of his literary work appeared during his lifetime. Both his translation of Plutarch and two translations of Machiavelli were published after his death.[35] One way or another, the manuscript of *T'leven* came into the hands of two Leiden publishers, the Leiden University publisher Jan Paedts and his companion Jan Bouwens.
It is unknown whether they had commissioned the translation or not.[36]
Once they got hold of the text, however, Paedts and Bouwens decided
to delay the publication. The fact is, they planned to initiate an even
bigger project: publishing a fullsized Dutch version of Plutarch, incor-
porating not only Amyot's *Vies*, but also additions to the Amyot text,
including preliminaries, annotations, small fragments in verse and —
most important — moral and religious commentary in the margins.
Upon comparison it is clear that Paedts and Bouwens copied this
enlarged edition from *Les Vies des hommes illustres Grecs et Romains*, a version of Amyot's *Vies* edited by Simon Goulart (1543–1628).[37] This version appeared in 1583 and in the period 1583–1620 it went through
seventeen editions. In order to benefit from the success of this edition,
the Leiden publishers probably copied the design of the French original to make the Dutch edition look very much the same, including the
title page as well as the introduction with historical information, the
complete layout of the text including all the marginalia, and the *Lives*
from other sources that Goulart had added. The Leiden project must

---

[35] Van Zuylen van Nyevelt was governor of Schoonhoven (1583) and infantry cap-
tain of the States of Holland. Besides Amyot's *Vies* (1603) he translated Machiavelli's
Discorsi and *Il principe* (1652).

[36] Paedts (c. 1541–1622) was Leiden University publisher from 1602 to 1620;
Bouwens worked with him until 1612. The name of Van Zuylen van Nyevelt (Adam
as well as his brother Willem) shows up several times in Paedts's list.

[37] According to the preface 'the Dutch version of the text proper was composed by
A.V.Z.V. Nieuvelt, and published after his death; but all the additions of Simon
Goulart are recently translated into Dutch, both in verse and in prose, by another per-
son, being a devotee of his mother tongue' (*To the reader*, 1644 edition, f. *3v).

have been succesful too; *T'leven der doorluchtige Griecken ende Romeynen, tegen elck-anderen vergeleken* (1603) was reprinted in 1644, including a dedication to the States General on the first page.

For Paedts and Bouwens, Van Nyevelt's Dutch text formed the basis of the project, but the remaining segments still had to be translated. To achieve this, the publishers worked together with a second translator, someone they called a 'devotee' and 'a lover of his mother tongue'.[38] Extra support came from a third person involved in the publication, the most famous scholar of them all. He identified himself in the preliminary 'Poem on the contents of this book' with the initials 'P.S.', that is Petrus Scriverius.[39]

The poet states: 'This book is a theatre in which the wise Plutarch shows the play of many thousands of people, high and low, good and bad, dressed in garments of virtue and vice'. The reader is expected to draw moral lessons from these characters. Moreover, the poet warns that although it may seem that ill fate governs the lives in this work, it is in fact God in heaven who determines world history:

> Behold the great God who judges them all: how he shields the truth and bridles the lie, he slays the conceited and wants men to bend and bow under his hand. Through this, God tells them that 'The world is nothing but a dream'.

Although Scriverius's poem has for a long time been considered as a work of his own hand, it is in fact a word-for-word translation of the preliminary poem in the 1583 edition of Amyot's *Vies*.[40]

The Dutch reader is informed about the publication history of *T'leven* in the preface 'To the reader'. The anonymous author(s) — probably the publishers — explain that the book the reader holds in his hands contains more than Van Nyevelt's translation of the plain

---

[38] According to the title page: 'composed by A.V.Z.V.N. and another devotee'; the second quote is taken from the preface *To the reader*.

[39] *Gedicht op deses Boucx inhoudt*, in the 1644 edition, f. *1v. For Scriverius's life see Tuynman P., "Petrus Scriverius 12 January 1576 – 30 April 1660", *Quaerendo* 7 (1977) 4-45; for the identification of 'P.S.' see Breugelmans R., "Een rhombos voor Romboldus door de schrijver P.S.", in *De letter doet de geest leven* (Leiden: 1980). Whether the second translator can be identified with Scriverius or not is unknown, but not likely. The preliminary poem can also be found in Scriverius P., *Gedichten. Benevens een uytvoerige Beschryving van het Leeven des Dichters* (Amsterdam: 1738) 95. The text of the poem follows the preface *To the reader* in the 1603 edition; in the 1644 edition it was proudly presented at the reverse side of the title page.

[40] *Sonet sur le sujet des Vies de Plutarque*: 'Ce livre est un Theatre, où Plutarque le sage/ Ameine un million de mortels, revestus/De vestemens divers de vices et vertus' (Plutarch, *Les Vies*, ed. 1617, f. **2v).

text of Amyot. The entire work is put in a new moral framework and interpreted in a religious sense.

The impact of this editorial choice by Paedts and Bouwens cannot be overestimated. Via the philological and literary work of Amyot, Plutarch had become the moral guide of several generations in France and in England as well (through the translation by Sir Thomas North, 1579), offering an image of the *bon souverain* or *bon citoyen*. The *Vies* nourished the contempory humanistic *idéal civique* with heroic models from the past and was an inexhaustible source of such divergent literary works as novels and plays.[41] But however influential the *Vies* by Amyot may have been in France and in England, for the Low Countries, Simon Goulart's ideas provided the moral framework for understanding Plutarch from the start.

The Commentary of Goulart in Dutch

In 1583 *Les Vies des hommes illustres Grecs et Romains* appeared both in Geneva and in Paris, in the revised edition of the French theologian and historian Simon Goulart.[42] As a Protestant, Goulart had fled from France in 1566 and again in 1572 after the massacre of St. Bartholomew. He lived for a long time in Geneva as a pastor and humanistic scholar, author, and editor; one of his many achievements as an editor was an annotated version of Plutarch's *Oeuvres morales* (1581–1582). Most of his works reflect his unfaltering faith in God.[43]

---

[41] For the influence of Plutarch in eighteenth-century European literature see Walling H.M., *The Influence of Plutarch in the Major European Literatures of the Eighteenth Century* (Chapel Hill, NC: 1970), irrespective of the question which edition or translation of Plutarch the authors used. For Amyot's moral interpretation of Plutarch's *Parallel Lives* see Frazier F., *Histoire et morale dans les Vies parallèles de Plutarque* (Paris: 1996) and Aulotte R., *Amyot et Plutarque. La tradition des Moralia au XVIe siècle* (Geneva: 1965).

[42] It was not until three years later that Goulart finished the whole *Parallel Lives*. The preface of the second volume is dated 30 November 1586. Nevertheless, Goulart's biography (Jones L.C., *Simon Goulart (1543–1628). Étude biographique et bibliographique* (Genève–Paris: 1917)) lists 1583 as a complete edition. For my research I used a copy of the 1617 edition (Cologne [Geneva]) in the Leiden University Library.

[43] For Goulart's interesting life story see Jones, *Simon Goulart.* His name can easily be mistaken for 'Simon Goulart from Geneva', Goulart's son and Remonstrant pastor in Amsterdam, Antwerp, Calais and Friedrichstadt, well-known from Brandt G., *Historie der Reformatie, en andre kerkelyke geschiedenissen, in en ontrent de Nederlanden*, 4 vols (Amsterdam: 1671–1704) II, book 22). The name of Goulart the father is indicated S.G.S. on the title page of the 1603 edition, that is Simon Goulart Senliensis (from Senlis).

In the 1583 *Vies* we find him as a commentator whose moral opinions are based upon general Christian doctrines; the preliminary 'Poem on the contents of this book', for instance, comes from his hand (as we saw earlier, Scriverius translated it word for word). The idea of a god who runs world history is not a distinguishing feature of a specific religious denomination.

Goulart was quite sure about God's role in history. The illustrious characters in Plutarch's histories are judged moment by moment, condemned when they behave immorally, praised when they show their virtue. There is no getting around these judgements and appreciations in the margins of the text, either in French or in Dutch. The marginalia are translated word for word in the 1603 *T'leven*. Their position and order are followed strictly. Thus the opinions of Goulart were delivered directly to the Dutch readers. Therefore, it is most likely that it was upon Goulart's commentary that Wellekens based his heroic epistle. With the exception of the overtly religious interpretation, the moralizing of the heroic epistle corresponds closely to Goulart's commentary.

Goulart's Antony, for instance, is regarded as the simple adulterer we found in Wellekens's letter from Octavia. He committed 'obscenities with the Egyptian woman', and he is a man with lax morals:

> Antony is a prototype of those who are contaminated badly by the love of an indecent woman, and neglect their honour and duties.[44]
> Antony, who worships a concubine and is thoroughly unfaithful to his legal wife: this is an image of God's judgement on whoremongers and adulterers.[45]

This disapproval of the relationship with Cleopatra must have appealed to Wellekens: 'The love of a whore deprives every man who is smitten with it, of the love of his friends, his subordinates and servants, even of that of his housewife and children'.[46] 'Antony and Cleopatra both show that evil people are instruments of doom'.[47]

---

[44] 'Antonius is een beeldt der gene, die seer leelijcken besmet zijnde door de liefde van een oncuysche vrouwe, achterlaten hare eere ende plicht' (Plutarch, *T'leven* (Delft–Utrecht: 1603) f. 417v in marg.).

[45] F. 418r.

[46] 'De liefde van een hoer ontneemt alle man die daer mede geslagen is, de liefde van zijn eere, van sijn vrienden, sijn ondersaten, ende dienaren: ja oock van sijn huysvrouwe en kinderen' (f. 417r in marg.).

[47] 'Antonius en Cleopatra toonen dat de boose menschen instrumenten zijn van den onderganck ende verwerringe den eenen den anderen voor het rechtveerdich oordeel Godes' (f. 419v in marg.).

Cleopatra, too, found no favour at all in the eyes of Goulart. It is here that we find the description Octavia used in her letter, 'the ardent whore, cunning and loose':[48]

> Cleopatra, a true to life image of a cunning whore, who wants to keep up her dishonest prestige by means of hypocrisies, and longs in every way for satisfaction of her indecencies.[49]

This is the only designation Goulart assigns to her: 'It is nothing new that whores decorate themselves with resounding titles, because they have nothing else to decorate themselves with'.[50]

Octavia is the only one who finds favour in the eyes of Goulart: 'Octavia, a model and prime example of a true and honourable wife'.[51] This comment echoes in the opening lines of Octavia's letter where she sums up these very virtues: 'Octavia is rightly suspected of faithfulness and honour'.[52] In the fragment below Goulart praises her wish to stay in Antony's house without any feeling of resentment, as a proof of her virtue. This is echoed in Octavia's letter: 'I live in your own house, and I never left it; [...] I bewail your absence, although you flee my face'. 'A corroboration of Octavia's virtue, which condemns women who are unfaithful, and those who rejoice at the infidelity of their husbands, or want a divorce, or somehow reciprocate what he did.'[53]

It is clear that the 1603 Dutch *T'leven* contained ample material for Wellekens in search of contrasting characters for an emotional heroic epistle. The lovelorn heroine's point of view could easily be derived from it as well. From time to time the poet even amplified information from *T'leven*, for instance in the case of Antony being drugged by Cleopatra. Originally Plutarch only suggested that 'Antony had been

---

[48] 'De yverzieke Boel [...], loos en schuw' (*Dichtlievende uitspanningen*, 148).

[49] 'Cleopatra, een levendich beeldt van een loose Hoere, die door gheveynstheden onder houden wil haren oneerlijcken credijt, ende die anders niet en begeert dan om sich op alle manieren te versadigen van hare oncuyscheden' (f. 417v in marg.).

[50] 'Het is niet nieuws dat de hoeren sich vercieren met schone titelen, want sy en hebben oock anders niet daer sy sich mede connen vercieren' (f. 417v in marg.).

[51] 'Octavia, een Patroon ende sonderlingh exempel van een eerlijcke ende deuchdelijce vrouwe' (f. 417r in marg.).

[52] 'Oktavia wort recht verdacht van trouw en eer' (*Dichtlievende uitspanningen*, 145).

[53] 'I live [...] my face', the Dutch text is quoted in n. 22. 'Bevestinge van [...] de groote eerbaerheydt van Octavia, de welcke veroordeelt de ontrouwe vrouwen, ende die wel blijde zijn om de misganghen van hare mannen, ofte om sich van hen te scheyden, ofte om hem t'selve wederom te vergelden in wat manier dat het oock zy' (f. 417v in marg.).

drugged', putting the words in the mouth of Caesar who collected arguments to undermine Antony's authority.[54] In the Goulart version and its Dutch equivalent a magic element is added within the text itself: 'And Caesar argued that Antony was no longer in control of himself, but that Cleopatra had robbed him of his wit with enchantments and love potions'.[55] Wellekens in his turn expanded Caesar's accusation and embellished it with Octavia's idea of a poison scandal:

> Or did that 'Circe' enchant you with wizard's rhymes?
> Can she also satisfy her guests with gruesome brews?
> Wake up, good hero, wake up from your dreams;
> Wake up: flee this wicked sorceress:
> She gave you slobber of vipers and blood of dragons, please beware:
> She bewitched you by means of poison and spells.[56]

The Second Epistle: a Reply From Alexandria

The story of Antony, Octavia and Cleopatra includes three characters; to compose a pair of heroic epistles, one needs only two. Since Octavia's life circumstances perfectly fit the heroic epistle genre, the obvious person for her to address was her unfaithful husband. Against all expectations, it was not Antony who replied — he could have cleared himself of adultery or he could have used a commission of the gods as an excuse. This was customary in the heroic epistle genre and was the kind of reply Wellekens's readers expected. Surprisingly, Wellekens broke with the tradition. Octavia's letter was intercepted and Cleopatra responded: "Kleopatra aan Oktavia", in 116 alexandrines in rhyming couplets.[57] The letter follows Plutarch's "Antony" up to chapter 57, 2 where Antony sent men with orders to evict Octavia from his house. Cleopatra starts her letter explaining how she managed to get hold of Octavia's missive:

---

[54] Plutarch *Antony* 60,1; cf. 37,4 'as if he were under the influence of certain drugs or of magic rites'.

[55] 'Ende Caesar seyde daerbeneven dat Antonius sijn selfs meester niet was, maer dat hem Kleopatra door eenighe betoveringhen, ende drancken tot liefde verweckende, van sijn verstant vervreemt hadde' (f. 418v.).

[56] 'Of heeft die Circe uw ziel met toverrym bezongen?/Kan zy de gasten ook met gruweldranken vo'n? / Ontwaak dan, braave Held, ontwaak uit uwe droomen;/Keer in u zelve: vlucht die snoode Toverkol:/Zy schonk u adderspog en draakebloet, wil schroomen:/Zy bragt u door vergif en toverdicht op hol' (*Dichtlievende uitspanningen*, 146).

[57] *Dichtlievende uitspanningen*, 150-4.

> Your infamously fabricated letter fell into our hands.
>   Think how Antony holds the Roman woman dear:
> He was going to burn your piece of libel unseen;
>   That is what Octavia achieved with her sad screed.
> Lest you, fool, would be left without an answer,
>   I will tell on his behalf: that he hates you bitterly;
> Neither your threats nor your flattery can move his heart,
>   And he will leave you and your bed for ever.[58]

Haughty and patronizing, Cleopatra dismisses Octavia's threats and trivializes her claims on Antony. The reader's acquaintance with the tragic end of Cleopatra's life give her scornful words extra tension; her argumentation gains a hidden meaning and becomes witty. 'Silly woman, ah, spare your laments: had you been familiar with the art of love, he would still be at your side'.[59] The burgher woman from Rome, Cleopatra continues, must not think she can take a stand against an Egyptian queen; she is no match in beauty or intelligence or grace. The whole city of Rome is no match for Egypt and the threats of the Roman armies are meaningless. A majestic marble tomb will rise in honour of Antony and Cleopatra, because they have decided that one day they will die together. 'Antony is mine, and will be mine for ever'.[60]

Wellekens's choice to have Octavia's rival answer the letter enabled him to emphasize the moral oppositions between his fictional authors. Two very different kinds of women are diametrically opposed to each other. The lascivious Cleopatra provided a suitable antagonist to the virtuous Octavia — Antony was but a victim of Cleopatra's witchcraft and therefore not interesting enough.

This moral contrast is reflected in Wellekens's choice for the *iuxta-positio* as a leitmotiv of his epistles. This was similar to the contrast Ovid used in *Heroides* 16 and 17, the pair of letters from Paris and Helen, in which the splendour of Asia is contrasted to the poor Achaea, the luxurious Troy to rural Sparta, Paris is pitted against Helen, both claiming to be the highest in birth. In the early seven-

---

[58] 'Uw snô verdichte brief geraakte in onze handen./Denk hoe Antonius de Roomsche vrouw bemint:/Daar hy uw lasterschrift wou onbezien verbranden;/Zie wat Oktavia met smeekend schryven wint./Doch wyl ge, dwaaze, niet om antwoord blyft verleegen,/Zo zeg ik, uit zyn naam: dat hy u bitter haat; Uw dreigen noch gevlei zyn hart niet kan beweegen,/En hy uw zyde en bed, in eeuwigheid verlaat' (*Dichtlievende uitspanningen*, 151).

[59] 'Onnozel vrouwtje, ei wil dan uwe klachten spaaren: / Wist gy de minnekunst, hy zat noch aan uw zy' (*Dichtlievende uitspanningen*, 151).

[60] Paraphrase of *Dichtlievende uitspanningen* 152-3.

teenth century the Dutch poet P.C. Hooft had imitated this *iuxtapositio* successfully in his famous letter from Menelaus to Helen (1615). Here Menelaus criticizes the luxury of Troy and praises the simplicity of Sparta, he repudiates Paris's lascivious behaviour and commends his own honesty and faithfulness.

In Wellekens's Cleopatra epistle the *iuxtapositio* is the main ingredient as well: a marriage of slavery contrasted to a marriage of love, a Roman burgher-woman pitted against an Egyptian queen, ordinary looks contrasted to divine beauty, poor children compared to children Antony himself made kings, the losses suffered minimized in light of the victories won, the use of slaves in the army contrasted to the voluntary alliances between Eastern monarchs, a boy like Octavian in opposition to a general of Antony's stature, the parsimony in Rome set alongside the royal life-style in Alexandria, gods invented by men juxtaposed to the gods that are eternal. In fact, of course, Cleopatra turns the world upside down. The reader is supposed to understand that neither beauty nor resounding titles, wealth, temporary victories and alliances, physical strength, nor the worship of dog's heads can counterbalance the virtues Octavia represents.

Before the life stories of Octavia, Antony and Cleopatra came into the hands of the 1710 Dutch poet of heroic epistles J.B. Wellekens, they had undergone a series of interpretations. Irrespective of the authors that inspired Plutarch, the historical stories had passed through Plutarch's political presuppositions, Jacques Amyot's translation and his ideas about the heroic models of interest to the *bon citoyen*, Simon Goulart's harsh religious moral margin notes, and the Dutch translations of Van Nyevelt and an anonymous 'devotee'. In this latter version (1603) Wellekens found ample material for his choice of a heroine in the style of Ovid's *Heroides*, especially the virtuous Penelope and Laodamia. From the text of Plutarch's *Antony* he selected Octavia's life story; he concentrated upon the chapters that deal with Octavia's attempts to win her husband back, from which he derived a few narrative fragments. The image he presents of an unimpeachable woman, however, was inspired by the moral commentary in the margins, together with the heroine's outbursts of anger towards her husband; in order to create a pair of epistles with the greatest moral contrast, Antony was depicted as a plain adulterer and a lascivious man, in a way that surpassed Plutarch's portrayal of Antony as a spineless creature.

Then Wellekens needed an antagonist of loose morals, someone who greatly challenged the moral virtues of Octavia. He departed from the traditional heroic epistle scheme of male/female pairs and chose instead a female opponent. Therefore, Cleopatra could no longer be portrayed as the clever flatterer she was according to Plutarch, as beautiful and young as Antony's wife; the Romans who had seen Cleopatra 'knew that neither in youthfulness nor beauty was she superior to Octavia'.[61] Influenced by the image of the queen as a whore in the Dutch *T'leven*, and using the stylistic device of the *iuxtapositio*, Wellekens pitted 'fatal lust against marital faith', creating the moral opposition he was seeking to depict as one of the themes in his series of epistles.

Finally, without Simon Goulart and the efforts of two Leiden publishers in 1603, the contrasting characters of Octavia, Antony and Cleopatra in the 1710 heroic epistles would never have been born. Since there is evidence of the direct influence of the 1603 *T'leven* in Dutch drama,[62] it is most likely that in contrast with Plutarch's interpreters in other countries, Goulart's moral ideas were the dominating framework of Plutarch's *Lives* in the Netherlands.[63] More research is needed to determine which authors did, in fact, use Goulart's version of the *Lives*, and to what extent Goulart's edition coloured their understanding, response to, and interpretation of Plutarch's work.

---

[61] Plutarch, *Ant.* 57, 3. According to this passage in the "Life of Antony", Cleopatra and Octavia were born in the same year (69 BC).

[62] For instance the Dutch poet Joost van den Vondel modelled Jempsar, the wife of Potiphar, after Cleopatra in his play *Joseph in Egypten*. In this play he took lines from the text and from the margins of the Dutch 1603 *T'leven*.

[63] The moral acceptance, for instance, of the relationship between Antony and Cleopatra which is to be seen in English, French and German plays was unknown in Dutch ones (For the heroic epistles see Dörrie, *Der heroische Brief*, 525). In the Netherlands the theme appeared only in plays translated from French or English, for instance *Cleopatra* (1669) after a play by Isaac de Benserade, *Marcus Antonius en Kleopatra* (1685) after a play by Jean de la Chapelle, and *Marcus Antonius en Cleopatra* (1781) after Shakespeare's *Antony and Cleopatra*. See the census of Dutch drama CENETON (http://www.let.LeidenUniv.nl/Dutch/Ceneton/index.html).

Selective Bibliography

ARENS J.C., "J.B. Wellekens idylliseert Ovidius", *Spiegel der letteren* 7, 4 (1964) 288-93

AULOTTE R., *Amyot et Plutarque. La tradition des Moralia au XVIe siècle* (Geneva: 1965)

BLOMMENDAAL J.L.P., *De zachte toon der herdersfluit. De pastorale poëtica van Jan Baptista Wellekens (1658–1726)* (Utrecht: 1987)

BRANDT G., *Historie der Reformatie, en andre kerkelyke geschiedenissen, in en ontrent de Nederlanden*, 4 vols (Amsterdam: 1671–1704)

BRENK F.E., "Antony-Osiris, Cleopatra-Isis. The end of Plutarch's Antony", in *Plutarch and the historical tradition*, ed. P.A. Stadter, (London–New York: 1992) 159-82

BREUGELMANS R., "Een rhombos voor Romboldus door de schrijver P.S.", in *De letter doet de geest leven* (Leiden: 1980)

COX-ANDRAU M.S.J., *De dichter Pieter Vlaming (1686–1734). Een studie over zijn werk met een levensbeschrijving* (Bussum: 1976)

DORRIE H., *Der heroische Brief. Bestandsaufname, Geschichte, Kritik einer humanistisch-barocken Literaturgattung* (Berlin: 1968)

FONTAINE VERWEY E. DE LA, *De illustratie van letterkundige merken in de 18e eeuw. Bijdrage tot de geschiedenis van het Nederlandse boek* (Leiden: 1934)

FRAZIER F., *Histoire et morale dans les Vies parallèles de Plutarque* (Paris: 1996)

JONES L.C., *Simon Goulart (1543–1628). Étude biographique et bibliographique* (Geneva–Paris: 1917)

MARION O. VAN, "*Heroides*-imitaties van Govert Bidloo: De Brieven der gemartelde apostelen uit 1675", *Nieuwe Taalgids* 87 (1994) 499-514

MARION O. VAN, "Ovid's *Heroides* in the Netherlands. A Dutch Princess in a Heroic Epistle of Caspar Barlaeus (1629)", to be published in the *Acta of the Xth Congress of the IANLS in Avila* (1997)

PENNINK R., *Silvander (Jan Baptista Wellekens) 1658–1726* (Haarlem: 1957)

PLUTARCH, *Les Vies des hommes illustres Grecs et Romains, comparees l'une avec l'autre.* [...] *Enrichies en ceste derniere edition d'amples sommaires sur chacune vie: d'annotations morales en marge qui monstrent le profit qu'on peut faire en la lecture de ces histoires:* [...] *Plus, y ont esté aioustees de nouveau les vies d'Epaminondas, de Philippus de Macedoine,* [...] *Le tout dispose par S.G.S. Avec les vives efigies des hommes illustres soigneusement retirees des medailles antiques* [...] (Geneva: 1583; Paris: 1583)

PLUTARCH, *Tleven ende vrome daden vande Doorluchtige Griecsche ende Romeynsche mannen, met haer figuren.* [...] *int corte begrepen, ende in Latijn gestelt door Darius Tibertus.* [...] *In onse Neerduytsche sprake overgeset, door M. Everart* (Leiden: 1601)

PLUTARCH, *T'leven der doorluchtige Griecken ende Romeynen, tegen elck-anderen vergeleken. Wt de Griecsche sprake overgeset door M. Iaques Amyot* [...] *Mitsgaders het leven van Hannibal, Scipio den Africaen, uyt het Latijn verfranscht by Carolus Clusius. Voorder het leven van Epaminondas* [...] *Ende noch het leven vande negen voortreffelijcke Krijgs-oversten, beschreven door Aemilius Probus. Met een cort begryp op elcx leven: leringen op de cant, chronijck- ende Leer-registers: alles versamelt ende uytgegeven by S.G.S. Te samen van nieus tot gemeen nut verduyscht, door A.V.Z.V.N. ende ten deele by eenen anderen beminder* (Leiden: 1603; Delft–Utrecht: 1644)

PLUTARCH, *Life of Antony*, ed. C.B.R. Pelling (Cambridge: 1988)

RUSSELL D.A., *Plutarch* (London: 1972)

SCRIVERIUS P., *Gedichten. Benevens een uytvoerige Beschryving van het Leeven des Dichters* (Amsterdam: 1738)

TUYNMAN P., "Petrus Scriverius 12 January 1576–30 April 1660", *Quaerendo* 7 (1977) 4-45

WALLING H. M., *The Influence of Plutarch in the Major European Literatures of the Eighteenth Century* (Chapel Hill, NC: 1970)

WELLEKENS J.B., *Amintas. Herderspel, van Torquato Tasso. Met eenige verklaaringen. Bovendien eene verhandeling van het Herderdicht* (Amsterdam: 1715)

WELLEKENS J.B. – VLAMING P., *Dichtlievende uitspanningen. Bestaande in Herders- Hoef- en Veldgezangen, Tafereelen, Brieven, enz. Met 32 Konstplaaten door Jan Goeree* (Amsterdam: 1710; Amsterdam: 1735)

WELLEKENS J.B., *Verhandeling van het herdersdicht*, ed. J.D.P. Warners (Utrecht: 1965)

WELLEKENS J.B., *Verscheiden gedichten* (Amsterdam: 1729).

THE RECEPTION OF PLUTARCH IN FRIEDRICH SCHILLER'S LECTURES ON SOLON'S AND LYCURGUS'S LEGISLATION

Sjaak Onderdelinden

It is well known that the German *Klassik* strongly focused on Greek and Roman Antiquity. Its most important sources of inspiration were sculpture and literature, in particular tragedy. The role played by historiography is a small one and is accorded little interest in literary research. Indeed, Schiller the poet is of much greater importance than the historian of the same name. However, looking at Schiller's assimilation of Plutarch can be very instructive, if only to gain a clearer insight into the connection between his historical writing, historical philosophy, aesthetic programme, and dramaturgical practice. Our aim, therefore, is to connect his historical interest in Plutarch with Schiller's typical German classicist ideas concerning the duty and possibilities of the artist within society as expressed in his theoretical reflections on literature, while towards the end the notions thus obtained will be tested on a central dramatic text, namely the tragedy *Maria Stuart*, bearing in mind of course the main question, which is to what extent this specific form of perception contributed to the 'Nachleben' of Plutarch.

Not only was Schiller a historian, he was even a professor. Indeed not a full professor (but an extraordinary one), not for a long period of time (in fact he only really lectured during one semester after which it gradually became a honorary position — the revenues that came with it provided at least some security to the writer who was constantly plagued by illness and poverty), and unfortunately, after a sensational start, not very successful. In 1789, Goethe, through the Duke Karl August von Sachsen Anhalt, provided Schiller, who was hardly known personally to him at that time — their famous and literarily so productive friendship did not develop until 1794 — with a position as extraordinary professor in general history (or, using the impressive German term of the time: *Universalgeschichte*) at the University of Jena which is, therefore, now called Friedrich-Schiller-Universität. This was pure protectionism, although justifiable. For

Schiller already had several historical publications to his name, one of them being the comprehensive study *Geschichte des Abfalls der Vereinigten Niederlande von der spanischen Regierung*.[1] No *Universalgeschichte*, it is true, but still a historical study. Nonetheless, Schiller's appointment in Jena was a sensation, caused rather by his literary reputation (*Die Räuber*) than his scientific one. When on 26 May 1789, Schiller held his oration on the theme *Was heißt und zu welchem Ende studiert man Universalgeschichte?*, public interest was so great that the event had to be moved from a moderately sized lecture room to the largest, an expedition which led straight through the small town and caused great excitement. The non-academic civilian population feared riots and issued a fire alarm.[2] In the end, some 450 students attended the oration, and that was far more than half of the total student population of that time.[3]

The oration was a success, followed by a serenade and cheers in front of Schiller's house. But on that occasion already, a critical observer, the Prussian inspector for education Gedicke, had objections:

> Ich gestehe indessen, daß es mir schwer ward, die Ursachen seines übergroßen Beifalls zu finden. Er las alles Wort für Wort ab, in einem pathetischen, deklamatorischen Ton, der aber häufig zu den simpeln historischen factis und geographischen Notizen, die er vorzutragen hatte, gar nicht paßte. Überhaupt war die ganze Vorlesung mehr Rede als unterrichtender Vortrag. Der Reiz der Neuheit und die Begierde, einen berühmten theatralischen Dichter nun auf dem Katheder in einer ganz neuen Situation zu sehen, mochte wohl am meisten den Zusammenfluß so vieler Zuhörer bewirkt haben, zumal da nichts für das Kollegium bezahlt ward.[4]

Not surprisingly, the novelty soon wore off and the number of auditors quickly dwindled to a few dozen. A great lack of continuity, which was caused by Schiller's frequent illness, was also to blame for

---

[1] Schiller F., *Historische Schriften. Erster Teil*, dtv Gesamtausgabe vol 13 (Munich: 1966). Later (1790–1792), the extensive *Geschichte des Dreißigjährigen Krieges* would follow (dtv Gesamtausgabe vol 14 (Munich: 1966)), among other studies, often tied to the origin of his historical dramas, in the way *Don Carlos* and *Wallenstein* led to the titles mentioned. However, to Schiller historiography continued to be a means to subsistence: as he did not need the money any more after 1792, he discontinued his historiographical work.

[2] Lahnstein P., *Schillers Leben. Biographie* (Munich: 1981) 261.

[3] Herz H., *Von Schillers Berufung bis Fichtes Entlassung. Vorlesungen an der philosophischen Fakultät der Universität Jena 1789–1799* (Jena: 1989) 18 ff.

[4] Quoted from Lahnstein, *Schillers Leben*, 262.

this. After some time, a remark was regularly added to his lecture announcements: 'Si non obstiterit valetudo'[5] and so his students hardly ever saw him. Also, Schiller's interest soon shifted from historical to dramaturgic-aesthetical subjects, which was really his true vocation anyway. In fact, his role as a history professor would be restricted to that one semester in 1789, in which, after the introductory starting-points from the oration, he planned to discuss the *Universalgeschichte* by looking at the development of legislation, first the Mosaic, then the Greek. Here, the continuation is lacking also, but the ambitious plan was, of course, clear: legislation as the foundation of civilization and thus as guide for the *Universalgeschichte*. Unfortunately, however, this ambition could not be based on sufficient knowledge, as can be concluded from the account of one Franz Horn who was, otherwise, impressed by Schiller's intellectual force and ardour:

> Indessen war dabei auch eine Schattenseite, der Vortrag verweilte zu sehr im Pathetischen, die Deklamation war vorherrschend und nicht geeignet, die Lückenhaftigkeit der Kenntnisse des Redners zu verhüllen. Man sah überall, daß selbst das Beste, was er vorgetragen hatte, erst seit kurzem, vielleicht seit gestern erst erworben war.[6]

So, the later also not unfamiliar phenomenon of the tutor who is just one lesson ahead of the students does certainly apply to Schiller's lectures on Lycurgus and Solon. Therefore, it would not be right to judge Schiller's knowledge of Plutarch using strict, academic criteria. Neither are his lectures structured in a way that would justify such an analysis. Rather, they are zealous essays, providing insight into Schiller's ethical and political ideals. It is true that he gives a summary of the Lycurgian and Solonic legislation respectively, but the most interesting aspect of it is not so much the content as the tone of the presentation, and especially Schiller's comments.[7] Naturally, this is about the issue of perception. It was not Schiller's objective to reach a correct understanding of Plutarch in his time (the Roman Empire in the year 110). His focus is on the current affairs of his own time (the German Enlightened Absolutism of 1790), which is quite different. I will return to this subject later. Plutarch's focus in the *Vitae* is on the

---

[5] Herz, *Von Schillers Berufung bis Fichtes Entlassung*, 20.

[6] Quoted from Lahnstein, *Schillers Leben*, 264.

[7] The written lectures (see the criticism on the delivery!) were published by Schiller in the magazine *Thalia*, series of 1790. In this contribution, the dtv Gesamtausgabe vol 15 (Munich: 1966) is used. In it *Die Gesetzgebung des Lykurgus und Solon*, 59-88.

presentation of Great Historical Figures, a biographical procedure, which can be summarized as follows:

> According to Plutarchian methodology, the complete picture of the man and the nation will best be created through intelligent use of the imagination working upon fact, as well as upon legend or tradition. In giving the picture of a man Plutarch gives also a picture of the family from which he sprang, his nation and his antecedents, the relationship of this nation with other nations in preceding and present time, its customs, language, laws and government — in short, a kind of *Universalgeschichte*.
>
> The Plutarchian hero himself was a man who made history. Possessing both *fortitudo* and *sapientia*, his life was devoted to the interests of the state, defending the state against foreign invasion, or exerting leadership politically or militarily within the bounds of his country. The Plutarchian hero lived and died, sometimes by his own hand, for the ideals in which he believed.[8]

These characterisations of heroes were so popular during the eighteenth century that Schiller gladly made use of them for his own moralizing, idealist goal. For Plutarch was a moralist as well:

> With his biographies — which he in fact explicitly distinguished from his historical writing — Plutarch attempted to sketch the moral personality of the person he was dealing with, so that the reader would find examples, cautionary examples as well, for his own performance and attitude to life.[9]

Schiller is not interested in retelling Lycurgus's biography. That which is the starting-point for Plutarch, is no more than a side-issue for Schiller. It is true that he feels obligated to describe the historical starting point of Lycurgus's inauguration in Sparta; however, this only serves the purpose of quickly creating a framework for understanding the necessity of Lycurgus's legislation. Moreover, in this introduction, Schiller lays the foundation for his complete political proposition, of the basic idea for which he really constructed this whole argument:

> Zwischen Monarchie und Demokratie schwankte der Staat hin und wider und ging mit schnellem Wechsel von einem Extrem auf das andre über. Zwischen den Rechten des Volkes und der Gewalt der Könige waren noch keine Grenzen gezeichnet, der Reichtum floß in wenigen Familien zusammen. Die reichen Bürger tyrannisierten die

---

⁸ Howard M.W., *The Influence of Plutarch in the Major European Literatures of the Eighteenth Century* (Chapel Hill, NC: 1970) 33 ff.

⁹ Aalders G.J.D., *Plutarch's Political Thought* (Amsterdam–Oxford–New York: 1982), 9.

armen, und die Verzweiflung der letztern äußerte sich in Empörung (59).

And after this account of the precarious situation in Sparta, Schiller immediately starts summarizing Lycurgus's legislative measures. He begins with the constitutional intervention of introducing a Senate as a means of balance between tyrannical kings and anarchistic democracy: 'Eine vortreffliche Anordnung, wodurch Sparta auf immer allen den gewaltsamen inneren Stürmen entging, die es bisher erschüttert hatten' (60). This positive judgement does not change when, later, ephores have become in their turn a necessity to check the power of the Senate.

With the second Lycurgian reform too, the one during which the land was divided among the population in equal parts, Schiller keeps using positive words: 'Sparta gab jetzt einen schönen reizenden Anblick' (60). Next, the matter of the financial reforms is raised, during which gold and silver were replaced by iron, and Schiller concludes, not without satisfaction, that wealth but also theft have simply disappeared from Spartan society, as did any form of luxury (61). By now, subjects are being discussed which Schiller does still explain understandably, but of which he does not give any value judgement. The initial cheers make room for neutral statements, as in the case of the obligatory joint meals. Avoiding luxury, improving overall public health, enhancing the community spirit — Schiller understands: through the implementation of the communal kitchen 'gewann Lykurgus für seinen Zweck sehr viel' (62). But there is no room any more for positive comments, neither is there in the case of the legislation on morality where Schiller limits himself to a laconic enumeration of the facts:

> Aus der Ehe selbst wurde alle Eifersucht verbannt. Alles, auch die Schamhaftigkeit, ordnete der Gesetzgeber seinem Hauptzweck unter. Er opferte die weibliche Treue auf, um gesunde Kinder für den Staat zu gewinnen (63).

Schiller approves less and less of the way in which Lycurgus created not only laws for Spartan civilians, but also perfect civilians for his laws. During his account of the tough Spartan education of the youth, irony creeps in for the first time when he notices that war was like a form of relaxation to the Spartan youth because, during those times, discipline was not taken so strictly (64).

All neutrality comes to a definite halt when Schiller starts to discuss the subject of Spartan slavery. Right away he finds harsh words: slaves

were 'in Sparta dem Vieh gleich geachtet' (64) and 'Abscheulich war
der Gebrauch, den man in Sparta von diesen unglücklichen Menschen machte' (ibid.), and even 'die Menschheit wurde auf eine wirklich empörende Art in ihnen verspottet' (ibid.), taking into account
that 'Menschheit' has to be understood as humanness or humanity.
Next, Schiller speaks of the examples of slave-hunting and slave-mur-
der that can be found in Plutarch, and then he reaches the general
conclusion that everything served a comprehensive concept: because
of the openness of all social and public actions, everything was aimed
at the national interest, 'die Idee von Vaterland und vaterländischem
Interesse' (66), and Lycurgus, according to Schiller's evaluation, succeeded completely in the development of this concept:

> Werfen wir einen bloß flüchtigen Blick auf die Gesetzgebung des
> Lykurgus, so befällt uns wirklich ein angenehmes Erstaunen. Unter
> allen ähnlichen Instituten des Altertums ist sie unstreitig das vollendet-
> ste. [...] Kein Gesetzgeber hat je einem Staate diese Einheit, dieses
> Nationalinteresse, diesen Gemeingeist gegeben, den Lykurgus dem
> seinigen gab. Und wodurch hat Lykurgus dieses bewirkt? Dadurch, daß
> er die Tätigkeit seiner Mitbürger in den Staat zu leiten wußte und
> ihnen alle andern Wege zuschloß, die sie hätten davon abziehen kön-
> nen (ibid.).

Finally, Schiller again sums up the multitude of strategies which
enabled Lycurgus to form a completely egalitarian society, which
could count on the total dedication of all civilians. All Spartans were
so completely devoted to their home country, that Leonidas's suicide-
command at Thermopylae can be said to be its most impressive mon-
ument.

> Man muß also eingestehen, daß nichts Zweckmäßigers, nichts durch-
> dachter sein kann als diese Staatsverfassung, daß sie in ihrer Art ein
> vollendetes Kunstwerk vorstellt und, in ihrer ganzen Strenge befolgt,
> notwendig auf sich selbst hätte ruhen müssen. Wäre aber meine
> Schilderung hier zu Ende, so würde ich mich eines sehr großen Irrtums
> schuldig gemacht haben. Diese bewunderungswürdige Verfassung ist
> im höchsten Grade verwerflich, und nichts Traurigers könnte der Men-
> schheit begegnen, als wenn alle Staaten nach diesem Muster wären
> gegründet worden (67 f.).

The words of appreciation suddenly turn out to be nothing but a
rhetorical trick. The positive to neutral description quite radically
turns into severe criticism of a very fundamental nature. It is true that
Schiller recognizes the genius-like consistency of Lycurgus's concept;
however, the concept in itself is highly scandalous — hence the

rhetorically fine paradoxical confrontation of 'bewunderungswürdig' and 'im höchsten Grade verwerflich'. The reason why Schiller's judgement on Lycurgus is so hard, is of course interesting.

Lycurgus's legislation is in itself a masterpiece in behalf of a powerful and permanent state. According to Schiller, one can admire this at first sight. However, the goal is wrong. Lycurgus places the state before the people, and Schiller thinks that this is the wrong order: the state should be there for the use of the people.

> Alles darf dem Besten des Staats zum Opfer gebracht werden, nur dasjenige nicht, dem der Staat selbst nur als Mittel dient. Der Staat selbst ist niemals Zweck, er ist nur wichtig als eine Bedingung, unter welcher der Zweck der Menschheit erfüllt werden kann, und dieser Zweck der Menschheit ist kein andrer als Ausbildung aller Kräfte des Menschen, Fortschreitung (68).

This announces the next criterion which is essential to Schiller: progression. It represents an important difference between Plutarch and Schiller: the latter had a vision of 'Fortschreitung' which was totally absent in Plutarch:

> In other words, one searches in Plutarch in vain for a historical vision. History has, for him, a function as teacher of ethics and practical political activity, but for him it does not give directions toward the future. Because Plutarch does not believe in a cyclical repetition of the historical process, the meaning of history remains for him, like for the most non-Christian historians of Antiquity, limited to functioning as *exemplum*.[10]

Although Schiller could make good use of the exemplary function, the enormous difference between the conservative, static nature of Plutarch's historical conception and the progressive dynamics of Schiller's Enlightenment concept of history is obvious. The position of Plutarch can be explained as follows:

> There is a broad correlation between the expectation of progress and the actual experience of progress. Where culture is advancing on a wide front, as in the fifth century, faith in progress is widely diffused; where progress is mainly evident in specialized sciences, as in the Hellenistic Age, faith in it is largely confined to scientific specialists; where progress comes to a virtual halt, as in the last centuries of the Roman Empire, the expectation of further progress vanishes.[11]

---

[10] Aalders, *Plutarch's Political Thought*, 60.
[11] Dodds E.R., *The Ancient Concept of Progress and other Essays on Greek Literature and Belief* (Oxford: 1973) 25.

The historical period and its view are entirely different for Plutarch and Schiller. Recent research draws a parallel rather between Plutarch and the end of the twentieth century. Thus, Francis Fukuyama's book *The End of History* (1992) could give grounds for contemplating the possibility of comparing the Roman Empire and the state of the world after the demise of Marxist socialism.[12] Schiller, in his impatient desire for progress, saw things very differently. Plutarch's hero-worship, which was simplistic in his view, had to be replaced by thoughts more suitable to the bourgeois emancipatory movement. For such a structural renewal legislation is essential. Therefore, according to Schiller, the legal structure of a state should be constructed in such a way that it enables and supports the development of the human spirit. If it does not, its construction is wrong, even when the structure is as firm and durable as possible. On the contrary: the more durable it is, the more wrong it is, because intended durability of laws causes stagnation and it blocks spiritual development. Thus, Schiller formulates what may be his most important criterion for political legislation in general — it can only be right, 'insofern sie alle Kräfte, die im Menschen liegen, zur Ausbildung bringen, insofern sie Fortschreitung der Kultur befördern oder wenigstens nicht hemmen' (68). This consideration is the foundation for the idealism of the *Klassik*. Dynamics (stagnation is rigidity) and freedom (nothing is more objectionable than restraining the human spirit with legalistic shackles) — these are Schiller's surprisingly modern, main criteria.

And Lycurgus's shortcomings are now clearly visible. For him, everything is put to the use of one single virtue, patriotism. 'Diesem künstlichen Triebe wurden die natürlichsten, schönsten Gefühle der Menschheit zum Opfer gebracht' (69). Thus, much to Schiller's indignity, there was no place in Sparta for love and friendship. Even worse, humanity in general had been abandoned, which caused the absence of morality in Sparta: 'Die ganze Moralität wurde preisgegeben, um etwas zu erhalten, das doch nur als ein Mittel zu dieser Moralität einen Wert haben kann' (ibid.). Therefore, his praise of Lycurgus, namely that Sparta would flourish only as long as his laws were followed to the letter, turns against him with a vengeance. Because of the absence of all developmental dynamism, the curtailment of art and science, and the blocking of trade and international relations, Sparta

---

[12] Dillon J., "Plutarch and the End of History", in *Plutarch and his Intellectual World. Essays on Plutarch*, ed. J. Mossman (London: 1997) 233 ff.

entered a state of isolation which for Schiller is the proof of Lycurgus's legalistic failure. Naturally, this judgement has not become obsolete. There are direct parallels between Spartan legislation and the legislation in other authoritarian-dictatorial states such as Nazi Germany and the German Democratic Republic in twentieth-century European history. Both states often made use of "their" Schiller. However, they had to manipulate him to fit their purposes, and Benno von Wiese is absolutely right when he remarks in this connection: 'Als Vorläufer einer wie auch immer begründeten totalitären Staatsgesinnung kann man Schiller in keinem Fall in Anspruch nehmen'.[13]

Next, Schiller proceeds to the second part of his own Plutarchian double biography and gives an account of Solon, the explicit goal of which is the comparison of both Lycurgus's and Solon's legislations. But before he addresses Solon, he describes the Athenian form of government before his intervention. In his commentary on the shortening of the archons' rule from life to ten years, Schiller proves himself to be a veiled republican and democrat, or at least a typical child of the Enlightenment, who did not believe any more in the *Gottesgnadentum* which still prevailed in Germany at the time, and who pinned his faith to the emancipation movement of the middle classes, part of which was the notion of the sovereignty of the people. That is why the Athenian measure of appointing archons for ten years, and no longer for life, was so important. The people 'nahm alle zehen Jahre seine weggegebene Gewalt zurück, um sie nach Gutbefinden von neuem wegzugeben. Dadurch blieb ihm immer in frischem Gedächtnis, was die Untertanen erblicher Monarchien zuletzt ganz vergessen, daß es selbst die Quelle der höchsten Gewalt, daß der Fürst nur das Geschöpf der Nation ist' (72).

When, in the Athenian context, the government period of the archons was reduced to one single year and on top of that, their number was multiplied by nine, an aristocratic form of government existed marked by the real formation of factions and a complete political machinery in which, for lack of legislation, chaos and corruption were rampant. The first one to be allowed to try and bring order into it was Draco, and Schiller cannot spare a good word for his draconian measures — the only punishment was the death penalty, and such laws

---

[13] Wiese B. von, *Friedrich Schiller* (Stuttgart: 1963) 347.

did not only offend 'die heiligen Gefühle und Rechte der Menschheit' (74), but were doubly unfit for the freedom-loving people of Athens. It caused the gap between poor and rich to become bigger, and ultimately it caused anarchy. Only then does Solon enter the picture, and he is introduced as a man with an amiable character, wealthy but not overly rich, cosmopolitan through many journeys, artistic but also an outstanding military man, in short a wise man equal to his task. This immediately becomes clear from his refusal to become king, because, as he said, the monarchy was a beautiful house, but had no exit. Schiller gives him great credit for this. Solon's first measure, the remission of all debts, received much resistance but proved to be right and necessary. Next, Solon implemented a division after fortune consisting of four classes and the establishment of a National assembly, presence being compulsory. Schiller concludes:

> Athens Verfassung war auf diese Art in eine volkommene Demokratie verwandelt; im strengsten Verstande war das Volk *souverän* und nicht bloß durch *Repräsentanten* herrschte es, sondern in *eigner* Person und durch sich *selbst* (78).

Schiller has to admit that such a roll-call democracy caused much excitement and tumult which could not even be stopped definitely through the intervention of a Senate. Still, he continues to prefer the personal engagement of each citizen of Athens in the affairs of his city-state to the opposite principle of being governed. Something similar can be said of the complicated legal system which Solon designed. Schiller talks of it with admiration, although the ostracism goes too far for him.

But then, Schiller arrives at a topic which in fact interests him much more than all politics and jurisdiction. During Antiquity, legislators, he says, were much more able to connect laws and people with each other and thus exercise much more influence on the moral character of the social process:

> Bei uns stehen die Gesetze nicht selten in direktem Widerspruch mit den Sitten. Bei den Alten standen Gesetze und Sitten in einer viel schöneren Harmonie. Ihre Staatskörper haben daher auch so eine lebendige Wärme, die den unsrigen ganz fehlt; mit unzerstörbaren Zügen war der Staat in die Seelen der Bürger gegraben (81 f.).

However, having said that, Schiller continues by making a characteristic note. He does not approve of the way in which the Greek legislator connected moral duties to legislative coercion. Loyalty towards friends, generosity towards enemies, gratitude towards parents should not be regulated through coercion, they should be 'eine freie moralische Empfindung' (82).

When, for all that, he goes back to judging the Greek legislation, Schiller appears to prefer a middle course between a roll-call democracy that has been pushed too far and aristocratic despotism. Although he is hinting that he believes in a form of representative democracy, he is realistic enough to understand that the absolutist orientation of his own time inhibits the speedy establishment of such a democracy: 'Zwischen beiden eine glückliche Mitte zu treffen, ist das schwerste Problem, das die kommenden Jahrhunderte erst auflösen sollen' (84). The phrasing is aimed at an idealistic and, for Schiller's own time, utopian future. The point of view also clarifies the different political preferences of Schiller and Plutarch. The latter's way of thinking is static and conservative, although there is some room for variation of his ideas within that framework:

> Also with regard to Plutarch's political ideal various poles can be found between which his thought oscillates, viz. the ideal of a harmonious polis community, which he deems best realized in the Sparta of Lycurgus, which he idealized, the ideal of a state ruled by philosophers, inspired by Plato, and the ideal of an enlightened world ruler. He oscillates equally so with regard to the question which political system he prefers the most, between a moderate aristocratic republic, the model for which is supplied by the Sparta of Lycurgus, and a philosophically orientated kingdom.[14]

In this ideological perspective, however, Plutarch's preference really seems to be for a city-state ruled by the aristocracy:

> The best example of this [aristocratic polity] is the Sparta of Lycurgus, highly admired by Plutarch; [...] for Plutarch an aristocratic government, and that is by definition a good and temperate government, deserves preference over a democratic polity, and [...] he abhors an aristocracy that had degenerated into an oligarchy.[15]

The reasons for Plutarch's preference are simple and can be found in his idealizing and positive judgement of tough dictatorial measures which, in his view, were beneficial to the steady development of Sparta:

---

[14] Aalders, *Plutarch's Political Thought*, 11.
[15] Aalders, *Plutarch's Political Thought*, 32.

> Lycurgus has had the possibility to carry through a number of far-reaching radical measures, not the least of which were in the sphere of the equality of possessions. In Plutarch's eyes extreme differences in possessions will not exist in a good political system. This rules out both extreme poverty and greed.[16]

His aristocratic conservatism makes Plutarch turn a blind eye to the Spartan harshness, which was criticized so much by Schiller. Although Plutarch also advocates a developed and cultural society, characterized by peace and humanity, he still holds the opinion that the strict leadership of Lycurgus provides for a better result than the flexible wisdom of Solon. He therefore prefers

> geometric equality, on the strength of which power and privileges are distributed in proportion to the capacities and merits of the individual. This conception is (moderate) aristocratic in principle and in origin; it is said of Solon [...], that he went too far in the direction of arithmetic equality which confers equal rights and privileges to everyone. [...] This idea of the geometric equality [...] goes back to Lycurgus. Plutarch prefers this form of equality (which could also be called an inequality), not because it is politically efficient, and not because he is a conservative (although he is that), but because he considers this a just principle which answers to divine justice.[17]

For Schiller on the other hand, the contrary is true. The Enlightenment thought of the bourgeois emancipatory movement tried to dissociate itself from dictatorial absolutism. So, it is clear that he prefers Solon rather than Lycurgus by far. In the final part of his lecture, Schiller makes a comparison in which, again, his arguments are more interesting than the choice in itself. Lycurgus's laws were meant to last for eternity whereas Solon's had a maximum period of validity of one hundred years; in this, Schiller saw proof of Solon's greater wisdom. Because he did that, Solon programmed the dynamic of political, legal, social and cultural development which Schiller thought to be so desirable, whereas Lycurgus provided stagnation. Joined with it is Solon's primate of the individual against Lycurgus's rigid belief in the state:

> [Solons] Gesetze waren laxe Bänder, an denen sich der Geist der Bürger frei und leicht nach allen Richtungen bewegte und nie empfand, daß sie ihn lenkten; die Gesetze des Lykurgus waren eiserne Fesseln, an denen der kühne Mut sich wund rieb, die durch ihr drückendes Gewicht den Geist niederzogen (ibid.).

---

16 Aalders, *Plutarch's Political Thought*, 38.
17 Aalders, *Plutarch's Political Thought*, 44.

The resulting difference is that in Athens all qualities of the civilians were continuously mobilised, whereas in Sparta idleness prevailed during peace-time. That is why there was only dictatorship and militarism in Sparta, whereas art, literature, philosophy and cosmopolitanism could unfold in Athens. Schiller can see the ethical system of the Enlightenment being prefigured in Athens, and the existentialist optimism of his time is also a part of that; when he sings the praises of the Athenian 'Tugenden', he starts to allegorize in a dithyrambic manner:

> Um den atheniensischen Gesetzgeber steht die Freiheit und die Freude, der Fleiß und der Überfluß — stehen alle Künste und Tugenden, alle Grazien und Musen herum, sehen dankbar zu ihm auf und nennen ihn ihren Vater und Schöpfer (85).

Compared with that, Sparta offers a dark view of appalling tyranny.

At the same time, Schiller is not blind to the Athenian weaknesses. He recognizes a certain arrogance, frivolity and cruelty; he certainly does not idealize Athens. He misses the harmonious balance which sometimes causes the Athenian spiritual mobility to degenerate into a frantic pursuit of innovation, thus overshooting the mark.

Schiller's system of categorization is very recognizable. What he is searching for is harmony and balance on behalf of optimum development of the individual, and from there a form of government which guarantees enough freedom for human virtues to revive and prosper. As a matter of consistency, the historian Schiller demonstrates the same thought-world as the aesthetic theorist. The way in which he uses Plutarch does not at do all justice to the biographer from Antiquity. Whether or not this was due to the pressure of the time-shortage he experienced in the preparation of his lectures, Schiller considers Plutarch to be a primary source for constitutional history and he does not care much for the actual biographic intentions of that source. Here, one could say that Schiller fails as a historian:

> The genre is biography, and time and again Plutarch protests against any suggestion that he is writing history. A clear understanding of this contrast is essential not merely to judge his work, but also to enjoy it.[18]

But no matter how much one emphasizes the 'contrast' between the biographer and the historian, the boundaries are, of course, not very

---

[18] Wilamowitz-Moellendorf U. von, "Plutarch as Biographer", in *Essays on Plutarch's* Lives, ed. B. Scardigli (Oxford: 1995) 61.

clear. Thus, in the same essay on "Plutarch as Biographer" the writer has to admit that precisely in the biographies of Lycurgus and Solon, the legislative aspects play a greater part than what would seem to be right for a biographer. That is also open to discussion. But it is a fact that Schiller can make good use of those legislative parts and, by doing so, neglects the actual biography. This is, of course, common procedure when using authors and texts from the past instrumentally. Reception is primarily a matter of adaptation to one's own needs. And Plutarch seems to have been useful in this way to many in the eighteenth century:

> Those who were indebted to him constitute an impressive list of the eighteenth-century intellectual community — in Germany Lessing, Herder, Schiller, and Goethe; in France Montesquieu, Voltaire, and Rousseau; in Italy Vico, Alfieri and Foscolo, and in England Addison, Pope, Swift, Goldsmith, Johnson, and Boswell. Other men, too, of perhaps lesser stature, used the Greek writer's works.[19]

Indeed, during the eighteenth century, Plutarch was promoted to the status of a kind of forerunner of the Enlightenment, because everybody who made use of him did so in an identifying and approving way. There is no criticism. Plutarch's range is so wide that it enables the projection of totally different ideals. An instance of this is the Plutarchian worshipping of heroes which made it possible for both Frederick the Great, King of Prussia, and Napoleon to carry the biographies of heroes by Plutarch with them to their battles.[20] Plutarch was used as a guide in the field of upbringing as well. One of his greatest advocates in the eighteenth century is Rousseau who makes the reading of Plutarch's *Vitae* compulsory for the title-character in his "Bildungsroman" *Emile* (1762).[21] This had an autobiographical, as well as an ideological background:

> Jean-Jacques Rousseau (1712–1778), who had expressed his affection for Plutarch in his *Confessions* [...], praised Plutarch's presentation of the Spartan constitution in his *Discours sur les sciences et les arts* (1750). The sciences and arts, said Rousseau, had not improved morals and customs. The *Discours* glorifies the simple life, Roman virtues, and the Spartan constitution.[22]

---

19 Howard, *The Influence of Plutarch*, 195.
20 Howard, *The Influence of Plutarch*, 189.
21 Howard, *The Influence of Plutarch*, 144.
22 Howard, *The Influence of Plutarch*, 132.

It is striking that the Plutarchian worshipping of Lycurgus was commonly shared in the eighteenth century as well. Only Friedrich Schiller designs an ideological structure which, through his radical choice for aesthetic harmony and humanity, puts a distance between himself and the otherwise so praised Plutarch. Where Plutarch praises Lycurgus for his pedagogical radicalism and criticizes Solon for his democratic gentleness, Schiller's judgement is just the reverse. This is quite understandable since his interest lies rather in the current value of the legislative work of Antiquity. His main interest, therefore, is not the tension between historiography and biography — he is trying to find the relation between historiography and aesthetics, very much as he tried to unite his historical view with his aesthetic ideals in his writings on literary theory. As a son of the Enlightenment, with a positive attitude towards mankind's infinite capacity to improve, Schiller considers the common objective of all disciplines, historiography or biography, aesthetics or drama, to be the propagation of a moral system of virtues, not in Immanuel Kant's philosophical abstractness, but in a very practical way. However, the fact that this practical morality is contrary to the political possibilities of Schiller's time, makes things more complicated. It causes his combination of history and aesthetics to acquire the aspect of a moralizing, idealizing utopia, with high hopes yet not very realistic, despite the practical moralization. Titles of writings such as *Über die ästhetische Erziehung des Menschen* (1795) or *Über das Erhabene* (1801) already indicate the idealizing character; however, it is in the no less famous *Über naive und sentimentalische Dichtung* (1796) that we find the best example of historical development and aesthetic idealization being related to each other. 'Naiv' means: original, natural, unspoiled by culture. It is a spiritual state dating from Greek Antiquity, which can still be found in some of the few contemporaries of genius such as Goethe. 'Sentimentalisch' is the intellectual who has really lost his touch with nature, but can still strive for it in his thoughts. It is the state of Schiller's own era. For the future, he predicts a reunion of naturalness and spirit; this is the aim of the 'aesthetic education'. The attempt to bind historical and aesthetic idealism together into one great concept ends in a graphic formulation (for the literary genre of the idyll): the poet leads his audience from Arcadia, to which returning happens to be impossible, 'bis nach Elysium'.[23] Indeed, it is the same Elysium as in the well-known ode "An die Freude":

---

[23] Schiller F., *Über naive und sentimentalische Dichtung*, dtv Gesamtausgabe vol 19 (Munich: 1966) 169.

Freude, schöner Götterfunken,
Tochter aus Elysium,
Wir betreten feuertrunken
Himmlische, dein Heiligtum.[24]

Where it should be localized exactly, next to Atlantis or in heaven, does not become clear; however, it is clear that it symbolizes the utopian quality of the absolute ideal. This ideal of happiness and freedom is not a part of Schiller's time. It is a projection, only to be reached in the hereafter or in an indefinite future. Yet, it is also an instruction to every human to strive for those virtues of enlightenment in the present; these moralizing didactics are a characteristic of the German *Klassik* and they have an illustrious example in the Athens of Solon. Applied to an inadequate present, which is harassed by a disturbing discrepancy between nature and culture, and also between sentiment and reason, Athens' ideal can be realized in the future in a new humanity full of harmony and spiritual balance.

That is the theoretical road from Plutarch's Solon to Schiller. But Schiller also tries to give educational examples of his projected 'erhabene Seele' in his practice of dramaturgy. It is true that in the genre of the historical tragedy, that ideal is connected with the physical end of the tragic hero (or heroine), but Schiller trusts in the effect of catharsis — first in the case of the hero or heroine, then the spectator. The chastening of the leading character into an 'erhabene Seele' will always serve as an example for the touched spectator. In this respect, there is no doubt that Maria Stuart, in the tragedy of the same name (1801), was a serious sinner in her youth, but, after a long period of suffering, penance and confession, she reaches unprecedented spiritual levels, unlike her opponent Elisabeth. The fact that Maria Stuart, in the extreme situation of imprisonment, agony and conviction, is chastened into an 'erhabene Seele', naturally does not make her a Baroque martyr (as in the most important type of drama of the seventeenth century), and there is no point either in seeing her as a new Catholic saint (the Protestant Schiller attaches no value to Catholicism in itself); as an 'erhabene Seele', Schiller's Maria Stuart has without a doubt gained access to Elysium.

Thus, it has been shown that Schillers's thinking and writing is highly consistent. In itself this is no great surprise, considering his

---

[24] Schiller F., "An die Freude", dtv Gesamtausgabe vol 1 (Munich: 1965) 115.

philosophical and moral rigidity. But the issue here was the conceptual connection of his historical and philosophical, ethical and theoretical, lyrical and dramatic writings. The lines Schiller dares to draw from Antiquity to the Future are not without pathetic grandeur. The all-embracing idealism did not always do him good, and in postmodern relativistic times, such a pathetic idealist loses even more of his splendour. In this respect, none of the *Klassiker* (and not only those belonging to the German *Klassik* around 1800) can escape the fate pronounced on Bertolt Brecht by Max Frisch in 1964: 'die durchschlagende Wirkungslosigkeit eines Klassikers'.[25] But that is of course only a witticism. It is true that in literature, 'durchschlagende Wirkung' is not very likely. However, it is very difficult to measure *Wirkung*, and therefore I think that this 'durchschlagende Wirkungslosigkeit', which, by the way, applies to Friedrich Schiller and Max Frisch as much as to Brecht, is not such a serious problem after all. It becomes already more realistic if the ambitious notion of *Wirkung* is replaced by the considerably more tranquil *Nachleben*. And the example discussed here also gives reason for optimism: Friedrich Schiller, as a historian, was not so academically impeccable in his treatment of his source Plutarch. But what he derived from Plutarch found an integrated place in the impressive structure of Schiller's optimistic philosophy of idealism. His treatment of Plutarch is an example of *Nachleben* in the best sense of the word: a construction built upon an example in a creative and constructive manner.

---

[25] Frisch M., "Der Autor und das Theater" (1964), in *Öffentlichkeit als Partner* (Frankfurt a. M.: 1967) 73. After the fine cynicism that has been quoted, Frisch formulates a more realistic version of the function of literature in the same essay: 'Gäbe es die Literatur nicht, liefe die Welt vielleicht nicht anders, aber sie würde anders gesehen, nämlich so wie die jehweiligen Nutznießer sie gesehen haben möchten: nicht in Frage gestellt' (87).

Selective Bibliography

AALDERS G.J.D., *Plutarch's Political Thought* (Amsterdam–Oxford–New York: 1982)

DILLON J., "Plutarch and the End of History", in *Plutarch and his Intellectual World. Essays on Plutarch*, ed. J. Mossman (London: 1997)

DODDS E.R., *The Ancient Concept of Progress and other Essays on Greek Literature and Belief* (Oxford: 1973)

FRISCH M., "Der Autor und das Theater" (1964), in *Öffentlichkeit als Partner* (Frankfurt a. M.: 1967) 68-89

HERZ H., *Von Schillers Berufung bis Fichtes Entlassung. Vorlesungen an der philosophischen Fakultät der Universität Jena 1789–1799* (Jena: 1989)

HOWARD M.W., *The Influence of Plutarch in the Major European Literatures of the Eighteenth Century* (Chapel Hill, NC: 1970)

LAHNSTEIN P., *Schillers Leben. Biographie* (Munich: 1981)

SCHILLER F., *Sämtliche Gedichte. Erster Teil*, dtv Gesamtausgabe vol 1 (Munich: 1965)

SCHILLER F., *Historische Schriften*, dtv Gesamtausgabe vols 13-5 (Munich: 1966)

SCHILLER F., *Theoretische Schriften. Dritter Teil*, dtv Gesamtausgabe vol 19 (Munich: 1966)

WIESE B. VON, *Friedrich Schiller* (Stuttgart: 1963)

WILAMOWITZ-MOELLENDORF U. VON, "Plutarch as Biographer", in *Essays on Plutarch's "Lives"*, ed. B. Scardigli (Oxford: 1995), 47-74.

MARC ANTON IRONISCH?
ZU FORM UND ERFINDUNG SEINER LEICHENREDE
IN SHAKESPEARES *JULIUS CAESAR* (III, 2)*

Wilfried Stroh

And Brutus is an honourable man: der immer wieder, mit einigen Varian-
ten geradezu refrainartig wiederholte Vers und mit ihm die gesamte
Leichenrede Marc Antons bei Shakespeare (*Julius Caesar* III, 2) —
wohl die berühmteste und jedenfalls demagogisch wirkungsvollste
Rede der Weltliteratur — gilt spätestens seit dem letzten Jahrhundert
als ein Ausdruck der 'Ironie' (*irony*), ja als deren geradezu idealtypische
Verkörperung. Marc Anton sagt ja, wie für diese *Redefigur* der klassischen Rhetorik erforderlich, das Gegenteil von dem, was er meint —
so definiert etwa Quintilian die *ironia* an berühmter Stelle (*Institutio oratoria* IX, 2, 44): 'contrarium ei quod dicitur intellegendum est' ('Man
muß das Gegenteil von dem, was gesagt wird, verstehen') — , und seine Absicht ist es, die Zuhörer, die, von Brutus' 'Ehrbarkeit' überzeugt,
die Tötung Caesars für gerechtfertigt halten, von dieser Ansicht abzu-
bringen und sie zu eben seiner wirklichen, im geraden Gegensatz zum
Gesagten stehenden Meinung zu führen. Diese Absicht hat er zum
größten Teil in dem Augenblick erreicht, wo ihm auf seine Äußerung
geheuchelter Besorgnis (153 f.)

> I fear I wrong the honourable men
> Whose daggers have stabb'd Caesar; I do fear it[1]

einer der Zuhörer empört zuruft: 'They were traitors. Honourable
men!', und ein anderer einstimmt: 'They were villains, murderers',
worauf es dann dem Redner nicht mehr schwer ist, in sein Publikum
die Fackel einer lodernden, am Ende besinnungslos wütenden Em-

---

* Für förderliche Hinweise danke ich Ingeborg Boltz, Werner von Koppenfels und
Georg Ott.

[1] Text und Verszählung nach: *The Arden Edition of the Works of William Shakespeare:
Julius Caesar*, ed. T.S. Dorsch (London etc.: 1955[6]). Wertvoll war mir daneben: *A New
Variorum Edition of Shakespeare: The Tragedie of Iulius Caesar*, ed. H. Howard Furness, Jr
(Philadelphia: 1913) wegen der mitgeteilten Proben aus älterer Erklärungsliteratur.
Für die Beurteilung der Marc-Anton-Rede sind daneben besonderes instruktiv die bei
Coles B., *Shakespeare Studies: Julius Caesar* (New York: 1940) 199-204 abgedruckten
Äußerungen früherer Gelehrter.

pörung zu schleudern. An dieser Stelle also wird das zuvor nicht
Gesagte, aber Gemeinte offen ausgesprochen, somit die 'Ironie',
glaubt man, deutlich als solche markiert.

Und sie beschränkt sich, wie es scheint, nicht auf diesen einen Satz.
Vielmehr sagt Marc Anton zumal am Anfang seiner Rede immer wie-
der Dinge, die jedenfalls der Leser bzw. Zuschauer leicht als das
Gegenteil seiner wirklichen Ansicht oder Absicht erkennen kann. Dies
betrifft etwa die bedeutungsvoll klingende, aber evident unrichtige[2]
Sentenz (77 f.):

> The evil that men do lives after them,
> The good is oft interred with their bones [...].

Es betrifft vor allem die Äußerungen, die Marc Anton über den
Zweck seiner Rede macht (76; 102):

> I come to bury Caesar, not to praise him.
> [...]
> I speak not to disprove what Brutus spoke,
> But here I am to speak what I do know.

Jeweils das Gegenteil davon ist wahr; und dasselbe gilt für den geheu-
chelten Irrealis in (123-5) :

> O masters! if I were dispos'd to stir
> Your hearts and minds to mutiny and rage,
> I should do Brutus wrong, and Cassius wrong

oder für seine vorgebliche Absicht, dem Volk Caesars Testament vor-
zuenthalten (132 f., 152):

> Let but the commons hear this testament,
> Which, pardon me, I do not mean to read
> [...]
> I have o'ershot myself to tell you of it.

Ja selbst, als Marc Anton, im zweiten Teil seiner Rede (159 ff.), das
Volk in gemeinsamer Empörung schon hinter sich weiß und, von der
Rednerbühne zum Leichnam Caesars herabgestiegen, für einen
Augenblick unverhüllt vom 'envious Casca' (177) oder vom 'cursed
steel' (179) des Brutus spricht und darüber klagt, daß 'bloody treason

---

[2] So m. E. zu Recht Azzalino W., "Stilkundliche Betrachtung der Reden des Brutus und des Antonius in Shakespeares 'Julius Caesar' (III, 2)", *Neuphilologische Monatsschrift* 11 (1940) 249-71 (dort 252); dies gilt wohl auch, wenn, wie manche Kommenta-
re zu zeigen versuchen, der Gedanke sprichwörtlich ist.

flourish'd over us' (194), bleibt er doch dabei, seinen Hörern eben diese von ihm selbst erregte Empörung zu verweisen und so die eigene
Redeabsicht zu verbergen (211-3):

> Good friends, sweet friends, let me not stir you up
> To such a sudden flood of mutiny.
> They that have done this deed are honourable

und schließlich, auf dem Höhepunkt seiner demagogischen Rhetorik,
diese Redekunst selber biedermännisch in Abrede zu stellen (219-
25):

> I am no orator, as Brutus is;
> But (as you know me all) a plain blunt man,
> That love my friend; and that they know full well
> That gave me public leave to speak of him.
> For I have neither wit, nor words, nor worth,
> Action, nor utterance, nor the power of speech
> To stir men's blood: I only speak right on.

Sein Virtuosenstück am Ende ist es, daß er, in alter Rednermanier das
Visuelle miteinbeziehend,[3] zunächst die Wunden Caesars für sich
reden läßt, um das Volk aufzuwiegeln (226-8):

> I tell you that which you yourselves do know,
> Show you sweet Caesar's wounds, poor poor dumb mouths,
> And bit them speak for me.[4]

und dann im selben Atemzug eben dies, was er gerade getan hat, in
den Irrealis verweist und damit für ihm selber unmöglich erklärt (V,
228-32):

> But were I Brutus,
> And Brutus Antony, there were an Antony
> Would ruffle up your spirits, and put a tongue
> In every wound of Caesar that should move
> The stones of Rome to rise and mutiny.

Diese durchgängige Diskrepanz also zwischen dem Gesagten und
Gemeinten bzw. Beabsichtigten pflegt man, wie oben erwähnt, unter
dem Begriff der *Ironie* zu fassen. Fast sämtlichen Interpreten der unend-

---

[3] Vgl. Pöschl V., "Zur Einbeziehung anwesender Personen und sichtbarer Objekte
in Ciceros Reden", in *Ciceroniana (Festschrift K. Kumaniecki)* (Leiden: 1975) 206-26.

[4] Vgl. zur literarischen Tradition dieses aufwühlenden *Concetto*: Koppenfels W.
von, "Plutarch, Shakespeare, Quevedo und das Drama der Ermordung Caesars",
Germanisch-romanische Monatsschrift 51 (1970) 1-23.

lich oft behandelten Rede scheint dieser Begriff unentbehrlich;[5] und gar die neueren Handbücher und Nachschlagewerke sind froh, wenigstens für die Urbedeutung der schillernden, zumal durch die Romantiker bis zur Unkenntlichkeit vieldeutig gewordenen Vokabel *Ironie* einen griffigen, jedem Literaturkenner verständlichen Beleg zu haben. So wird z. B. im neuesten *Lexikon der Literatur- und Kulturtheorie* (1998) die 'Ironie als literarischer Tropus' exemplifiziert an 'der als Lob getarnten Verunglimpfung *Brutus is an honourable man*'[6] und, mit Ausdehnung auf die ganze Rede, heißt es etwa in der *Brockhaus-Enzyklopädie* (s. v. "Ironie"): 'Literarisches Beispiel für Ironie als Mittel der Rhetorik ist die Rede des Marcus Antonius in Shakespeares *Julius Caesar*'.[7]

Und doch ist diese Bestimmung schon nach gängigem Sprachgebrauch unrichtig. Wenn wir von jemandem sagen, daß er *ironisch* spreche, so meinen wir damit ja nicht eigentlich, daß er seine Ansicht verberge, sondern daß er sie nur scheinbar verberge, in dem er nämlich zwar das Gegenteil sage von dem, was er meine — so weit entspricht dem Marc Antons Ausdrucksweise —, es aber in der Weise sage, daß man deutlich erkennen solle, er meine eben das Gegenteil. Klar sieht man, daß letzteres bei Marc Anton nicht der Fall ist. Allenfalls an der schon erwähnten einen, späteren Stelle, wo die Rede ist von den 'honourable men/Whose daggers have stabb'd Caesar' könnte man denken, daß Marc Anton für einen Augenblick seine Äußerung durch ein leises Tremolo der Empörung als nicht so gemeint und damit als

---

[5] Vgl. besonders Müller W.G., *Die politische Rede bei Shakespeare* (Tübingen: 1979) 127-49 (127: Der Redner arbeite 'mit Mitteln der Verstellung und Vortäuschung [...], die man unter dem Oberbegriff Ironie zusammenfassen kann'), daneben jetzt Weiss N., *Die Szene III, 2 in William Shakespeare's Trauerspiel "Julius Caesar": Bauformen, Rhetorik und Ironie in den Leichenreden des Brutus und Mark Anton* (Nordenham–Duisburg: 1995), besonders 81 ff. Weiss (s. Fußnote zu Vers 92) betrachtet allerdings (wie auch einige andere Interpreten; vgl. Müller, *Die politische Rede*, 132 f. und besonders Kurka E., "Zur Darstellung von Redner und Rede in Shakespeares Dramen", *Shakespeare-Jahrbuch* [Ost] 104 (1968) 175-91, besonders 181 und 184) die anfängliche Verwendung von *And Brutus is an honourable man* noch nicht eigentlich als ironisch. Vgl. besonders die Arbeit von Azzalino, besonders 269 f. und Welsh A., "Brutus is an Honourable Man", *Yale Review* 64 (1975) 496-513; Greene G., "'The Power of Speech/To Stir Men's Blood': the Language of Tragedy in Shakespeare's Julius Caesar", *Renaissance Drama* 11 (1980) 67-93 (dort 85-8).

[6] Müller, W.G., Art. "Ironie", in *Metzler Lexikon Literatur- und Kulturtheorie*, A. Nünning (Hrsg.) (Stuttgart–Weimar: 1998), 244. Idem Art "Ironie" in *Reallexikon der deutschen Literaturwissenschaft*, H. Fricke (Hrsg.), vol 2 (Berlin–New York 2000) 184-9;*Der Literatur Brockhaus*, vol 2 (Mannheim: 1988) 226, s. v. "Ironie"; *Meyers Kleines Lexikon: Literatur*, (Mannheim etc.: 1986) 219, s. v. "Ironie"; Wilpert G. von, *Sachwörterbuch der Literatur* (Stuttgart: 1969[5]) 361, s. v. "Ironie".

[7] *Brockhaus Enzyklopädie*, vol 10 (Mannheim: 1989[19]) 642, s. v. "Ironie".

ironisch im üblichen Sinn kennzeichnet[8] — auch das ist keineswegs eindeutig oder sehr wahrscheinlich; im übrigen gilt aber für die Rede, daß Marc Anton so gut wie nie in dem Sinn ironisch spricht, daß seine Zuhörer eine Diskrepanz von Gesagtem und Gemeintem empfinden sollen. Er verbirgt seine Redeabsicht wirklich[9] und führt seine Hörer in eine Richtung, die er ihnen gerade nicht angibt: Ohne es auch nur ironisch zu sagen, erweckt er in ihnen von Anfang an Zweifel daran, daß Brutus ein 'honourable man' sei; und er treibt sie in den Sturm der Empörung, indem er, völlig unironisch, eben dies zu tun leugnet (so daß sie gewissermaßen glauben müssen, sie seien schlauer als der Redner selbst). Eher noch als mit *Ironie* wäre sein Verfahren mit Vokabeln wie *Verstellung* oder *Irreführung* zu beschreiben;[10] aber man fühlt leicht, daß solche Bezeichnungen zwar wohl ungefähr richtig, aber doch viel zu allgemein sind, um dieses Besondere von Marc Antons Redetaktik zu erfassen.

Oder wäre der wissenschaftliche Begriff der *Ironie* weiter zu fassen als der der Umgangssprache? Durchaus nicht. Auch die gute Tradition der Rhetorik und Literaturwissenschaft spricht dagegen, Marc Antons Rede als ironisch zu bezeichnen.[11] Als Anaximenes, ein Zeit-

---

[8] Siehe die *A new Variorum Edition of Shakespeare*, ad loc.: 'Here, I think, for the first time Antony uses these words with a distinct sneer; and then fairly hurls the next line in the faces of the crowd' (vgl. auch die oben in Anm. 5 erwähnten Ansichten von Kurka, Müller und Weiss, die dazu tendieren, erst hier die eigentliche Ironie beginnen zu lassen). Dagegen meinte etwa der dort zitierte treffliche Hudson, daß die (auch von ihm angesetzte) *Ironie* von der schauspielerischen Interpretation der Rede ganz fernzuhalten sei: 'I have heard speakers and readers utterly spoil the effect of this speech by specially emphasizing the irony; the proper force of which, in this case [!], depends on its being so disguised as to seem perfectly unconscious'. Man kann es kaum besser sagen (und damit zugleich dartun, warum die Rede eben gerade nicht ironisch ist).

[9] Vor allem in der Arbeit von Müller werden die Mittel der *simulatio* und *dissimulatio* in der Rede herausgearbeitet; den Widerspruch zum üblichen Etikett 'ironisch' fühlend, setzt er eine 'dissimulierend-ironische Methode' (S. 127) an und bringt damit den Widersinn der üblichen Deutung sozusagen auf den Begriff.

[10] Zur Begriffsklärung Müller W.G., "Ironie, Lüge, Simulation, Dissimulation und verwandte rhetorische Termini", in *Zur Terminologie der Literaturwissenschaft*, C. Wagenknecht (Hrsg.) (Stuttgart: 1989) 189-208 (201 zu Marc Anton).

[11] Zur Begriffsgeschichte am informativsten ist jetzt wohl Behler E., Art. "Ironie", in *Historisches Wörterbuch der Rhetorik*, G. Ueding (Hrsg.), Bd. IV (1998) 599-624 (zur Antike 603 f.; vgl. idem, *Klassische Ironie – Romantische Ironie – Tragische Ironie*, (Darmstadt: 1972); idem *Ironie und literarische Moderne* (Paderborn etc.: 1997) [idem 36]); eigenwilliger Weinrich H., Art. "Ironie", in *Historisches Wörterbuch der Philosophie*, J. Ritter – K. Gründer (Hrsg.), Bd. IV (1976) 578-82 (vgl. idem, *Linguistik der Lüge* (Heidelberg: 1970) besonders 59 ff.); für die römische Antike war mir am wertvollsten der Artikel "ironia" von Centlivres im *Thesaurus linguae Latinae*, Bd. VII, 2, 381 f.

genosse des Aristoteles, der seinerseits *eironeia* nur als Charaktereigen-
schaft (im Sinne der Selbstverkleinerung) kennt,[12] den Begriff zum *terminus technicus* der rhetorischen Stilistik macht, definiert er ihn zwar
nur allgemein als die Redeweise, bei der 'wir die Dinge mit den entge-
gengesetzten Wörtern bezeichnen',[13] aber seine Beispiele (wie 'Wir,
die Schlechten') sind so gewählt, daß die Absicht, konträr zum Wort-
sinn verstanden werden zu wollen, offensichtlich ist. Cicero sodann,
der die Vokabel als Fremdwort im Lateinischen einbürgert und meist
mit *dissimulatio* übersetzt, gebraucht sie, sowohl im älteren, aristoteli-
schen, vor allem auf die Person des sich selbst herabsetzenden Sokrates bezogenen Sinn (*Brutus* 292; *Academica* II, 15) als zugleich auch in
dem des 'cum alia[14] dicuntur ac sentias' ('anderes sagen als man
meint', *De oratore* II, 269), wobei freilich nicht der punktuelle Tropus
des *contraria dicere* (wie bei Anaximenes) gemeint ist — ihn bezeichnet
Cicero mit 'verba invertere' (*De oratore* II, 262: 'pulchellus puer' (schö-
nes Knäblein', für einen Häßlichen[15]) — als vielmehr ein durchgängi-
ges, dem scheltenden Spott dienendes Sichverstellen (*De oratore* II, 269
'cum toto genere orationis severe ludas, cum aliter sentias ac loquare';
'wenn man in der ganzen Art des Redens auf ernste Weise spottet,
indem man anderes denkt, als man sagt'). Wiederum zeigen neben
der Definition auch die von Cicero gegebenen Beispiele, daß die Diskrepanz von *sentire* und *loqui* dabei eine offenkundige zu sein hat: Wer
ironisch spricht, lügt nicht.

Eindeutig in diesem Sinn äußert sich der größte Meister exakter
Begrifflichkeit auf diesem Feld, Quintilian. Er lehnt die Übersetzung
mit *dissimulatio* als zu speziell ab (*Institutio oratoria* IX, 2, 44), läßt das
ciceronische *verba invertere* als Tropus der *ironia* zu, ergänzt diesen aber

---

[12] Das Problem der ursprünglichen Bedeutung von *eironeia* (s. Bergson L., "Eiron und
Eironeia", *Hermes* 99 (1971) 409-22 und Markantonatos G., "On the Origins and Meanings of the Word EIRONEIA", *Rivista di Filologia e di Istruzione Classica* 103 (1975) 16-
21) sowie ihrer Beziehung zu Sokrates muß hier fast völlig außer Betracht bleiben; gele-
gentlich zu lesende Sätze, wie daß der Begriff der *Ironie* in der Geschichte unzertrennbar
mit Sokrates verbunden gewesen sei, klingen imponierend, sind aber nicht richtig.

[13] Anaximenes 21 (1434 A). Eine andere Bedeutung, die *eironeia* bei ihm hat ('etwas
sagen, indem man so tut als sage man es nicht', eine Verwendungsweise der *praeteritio*),
scheint für die spätere Entwicklung der Terminologie belanglos.

[14] Auf den für die Geschichte der Terminologie an sich nicht unerheblichen Gegensatz, ob Ironie in weiterem Sinn als 'aliud sentire ac loqui' (Cicero) oder im engeren als
'contrarium sentire ac loqui' (Quintilian) zu verstehen sei, muß ich in unserem Zusammenhang, wo es nur um die Markiertheit der Ironie geht, nicht näher eingehen.

[15] Der Verfasser der (m. E. nachciceronischen) Herenniusrhetorik sagt von dieser
Form der Ironie, die er (wie zwei andere Arten allegorischer Rede) mit *permutatio*
übersetzt: 'ex contrario ducitur' (*Rhetorica ad Herennium* IV, 34, 46).

(IX, 1, 3; 2, 44) durch die gleichnamige Figur (die etwa Ciceros *dissimulatio* entspricht). Entscheidend ist, daß Quintilian nicht nur zum ersten Mal ausdrücklich das erwähnt, was bisher nur implizit selbstverständlich war: daß nämlich die Ironie als solche verstanden werden müsse ('contrarium ei, quod dicitur, intelligendum est'), sondern daß er auch schon Zeichen nennt, die die Diskrepanz von 'intellegi' und 'dicere' kenntlich machen, also, was wir als "Ironiesignale" bezeichnen (VIII, 6, 54): 'aut pronuntiatione intellegitur [ironia] aut persona aut rei natura: nam si qua earum verbis dissentit, apparet diversam esse orationi voluntatem', d. h. entweder 'die Art des Vortrags', oder die 'Person' des Redners oder schließlich die 'Natur der Sache' selbst müssen so im Widerspruch zum Gesagten stehen, daß die Ironie (als 'Verschiedenheit von Rede und Absicht') unverkennbar wird. In der Tat: eine Ironie ohne 'Signale' könnte *eo ipso* keine mehr sein.[16]

Den Rhetorikern, genauer gesagt: Quintilian, folgen die Literaturwissenschaftler der Spätantike. Schon Plotius Sacerdos, in der ersten (uns erhaltenen) *Ars grammatica*, betont bei seiner Definition von *ironia* noch stärker als Quintilian die entscheidende Bedeutung des Vortrags (*pronuntiatio*) bzw. Tonfalls;[17] dasselbe sagt, mit demselben Textbeispiel (einer ironischen Verspottung der siegreichen Venus durch Vergils Juno [*Aeneis* IV, 93 f.]), der für die spätere Tradition so wichtige Donatus (*Grammatici Latini* IV, 401, 30 ff.): "ironia est tropus per contrarium quod conatur ostendens, ut 'egregiam vero laudem et spolia ampla refertis,/tuque puerque tuus" et cetera. Haec nisi gravitas pronuntiationis adiuverit, confiteri videbitur quod negare contendit' ('Die Ironie ist der Tropus, der, was er sagen will, durch das Gegenteil zeigt, wie in "Wahrlich gar herrlichen Ruhm gewinnt ihr und große Trophäen,/du sowohl wie dein Sohn" und so weiter. Wenn hier nicht der bittere Ernst im Tonfall zu Hilfe kommt, scheint sie [die Sprecherin] das zuzugeben, was sie doch zu leugnen bemüht ist').[18] Auch hier ist klar vorausgesetzt, daß die Ironie erkennbar sein muß. Ebenso hebt Augustinus auf die Wichtigkeit der *pronuntiatio* ab in seinem christli-

---

[16] Dieser Satz scheint unbestritten (vgl. aber oben in Anm. 8 das Zitat aus Hudson!), wird jedoch selten explizit formuliert (wie etwa bei Weinrich, *Linguistik der Lüge*, 60 f.; vgl. Müller, "Ironie, Lüge, Simulation", 200; Lapp E., *Linguistik der Ironie* (Tübingen: 1992) 28.

[17] *Grammatic Latini* VI 461, 13 f.: 'Ironia est oratio cum inrisione, pronuntiatio dictionis in contrarium redigens intellectum'.

[18] Ähnlich Diomedes, *Grammatic Latini* I 462, 7 ff., der durch 'pronuntiando et affectu' verdeutlicht.

chen Lehrwerk der Hermeneutik und Rhetorik (*De doctrina Christiana* III, 29, 41: 'Sed hironia pronuntiatione indicat, quid velit intellegi, ut cum dicimus homini mala facienti, "res bonas facis"' ('aber die Ironie gibt durch den Tonfall zu verstehen, was verstanden werden soll, wie wenn wir zu einem Menschen, der Schlechtes tut, sagen "Du tust Gutes"'); ihm folgt vor allem der im Mittelalter viel gelesene Isidorus (*Origines* I, 37, 25; vgl. II, 21, 42).

Wir können darauf verzichten, die Definitionen des mittelalterlichen und neuzeitlichen Ironiebegriffs (bis zu seiner Verunklärung im 19. Jahrhundert) im einzelnen weiter zu verfolgen.[19] Bis heute gilt, jedenfalls für den rhetorischen Ironiebegriff, was vor zwanzig Jahren der Anglist und Shakespearespezialist Wolfgang G. Müller in einer klärenden Abhandlung über "Ironie, Lüge, Simulation, Dissimulation und verwandte rhetorische Termini"[20] festgestellt hat, daß 'bei der Ironie die semantische Inversion durchsichtig und die eigentliche Bedeutung rekonstruierbar', dagegen 'bei der Lüge die semantische Inversion undurchsichtig und die wahre Meinung des Sprechers nicht rekonstruierbar' ist.[21] Und dabei sollte es auch, schon im Hinblick auf den außerwissenschaftlichen Sprachgebrauch, in aller Zukunft bleiben. 'Ironie muß bemerkt werden',[22] sagt, soweit sehr vernünftig, eines der neuesten zahlreichen Handbüchlein der "Literaturwissenschaft".

Warum aber spricht man dann — um endlich zum Thema zurückzukehren — der Rede des Marc Anton gegen alle Evidenz, Tradition

---

[19] Erhellend ist neben den oben (Anm. 11) zitierten Arbeiten bes. Knox N., *The Word Irony and its Context, 1500–1755* (Durham, NC: 1961). Die zusammenfassende Einführung zu diesem Buch ist ins Deutsche übersetzt in Hass H.-E. – Mohrlüder G.-A. (Hrsg.), *Ironie als literarisches Phänomen* (Köln: 1973) 21-30; einige Belege zur Wortgeschichte in der frühen Neuzeit auch in *The Oxford English Dictionary*, VIII (1989²) 87. Erst nach Abschluss dieser Untersuchung wurde mir zugänglich Knox D., *Ironia: Medieval and Renaissance Ideas on Irony* (Leiden etc.: 1989); 51 ff. zu Ironie vs. Lüge; noch unbekannt ist mir Hutcheon L., *Irony's Edge: The Theory and Politics of Irony* (London: 1995).

[20] S. oben Anm. 10, Zitat dort 191 (vgl. auch 192 die Kritik an der Darstellung in Lausbergs bekanntem Handbuch).

[21] Vgl. die von Müller, "Ironie, Lüge, Simulation" zitierte, besonders knapp treffende Definition von C. Kerbnarat-Orecchioni. Etwas anders als üblich bestimmt jetzt der Sprachwissenschaftler Lapp (*Linguistik der Ironie*, besonders 153 und 169) Lüge als 'Simulation der Aufrichtigkeit', Ironie als 'Simulation der Unaufrichtigkeit', aber auch bei ihm gilt selbstverständlich, daß die Simulation der Ironie eine zum Durchschauen bestimmte ist (besonders 155).

[22] Schäfer-Willemborg M., "Form und Rhetorik", in *Literaturwissenschaft*, in Fuhrmann J. – Müller H. (Hrsg.) (München: 1995) 217-48. Freilich gilt dies nur für die Intention des Sprechers; ansonsten kann Ironie auch unverstanden bleiben.

und Vernunft eine "Ironie" zu, die sie nicht oder allenfalls nur punktuell hat und mit der gerade das Wesentliche ihrer Taktik nicht beschrieben werden kann? Versteht man darunter etwa eine Ironie nicht Marc Antons selber, sondern seines Erfinders Shakespeare, der seinem Publikum, also nicht dem der Rede, sondern dem des Stücks, in der Tat deutlich zu erkennen gibt, daß der Redner anderes meint als er sagt?[23] Ein Blick in die gelehrte Literatur zeigt, daß dies keineswegs der Fall ist, daß die "Ironie" vielmehr durchweg Marc Anton selber zugeschrieben wird, um — und dies scheint ja auch sinnvoll — seine rednerische Leistung zu würdigen. Selbst ein so scharfsinniger Interpret wie der zitierte Wolfgang Müller, dem wir die eindringlichste Analyse der Rede verdanken, glaubt ja hier auf den doch offenkundig schiefen Terminus nicht verzichten zu können. Warum? Ich antworte: Weil die heutige Literaturwissenschaft das rhetorische Instrumentarium nicht mehr hat, mit dem sie einer solchen Rede gerecht werden könnte. Wir müssen, nicht nur weil *Julius Caesar* zufällig in Rom spielt, zurück zur klassischen Antike, *ad fontes*.

Man unterscheidet nämlich in der antiken Rhetorik zwischen der *Ironie* und der *oratio figurata* (griech.: λόγος ἐσχηματισμένος), was mit 'figurierter Rede' zu übersetzen wäre. Ihren ersten literarischen Beleg hat diese 'figurierte Rede', deren Theorie und Praxis erst neuerdings von Georg Ott systematisch aufgearbeitet wurde,[24] schon im zweiten Buch der homerischen *Ilias* (110 ff.), wo Agamemnon den Versuch macht, das griechische Heer dadurch zum stürmischen Angriff auf Troia zu motivieren, daß er den Soldaten vorschlägt, nunmehr, nach zehn Jahren, doch den Krieg abzubrechen und nach Hause zu fahren, wobei er aber diesen Vorschlag mit Argumenten begründet, die eher für die energische Fortführung des Kriegs sprechen. In eben dieser Diskrepanz zwischen wahrer und vorgeblicher Absicht besteht die 'Figuriertheit' der

---

[23] Wie schon Donat im Terenzkommentar bemerkt hat (Müller, "Ironie, Lüge, Simulation", 193), kann in einem Drama die Ironie einer Äußerung vom unmittelbaren Rezipienten auf der Bühne verkannt und nur vom Publikum verstanden werden. Aber der dort behandelte Fall ist ganz anders als der unsere.

[24] Ott G., *Oratio figurata: Formen verschlüsselten Sprechens in der Antike*, (Wiss. Zulassungsarbeit zum Staatsexamen, masch., München: 1994). Da Georg Ott dabei ist, eine Dissertation zum selben Thema abzuschließen (wobei auch die 'Trugrede' eine Rolle spielt, auf die hier nicht einzugehen ist), beschränke ich die Angaben auf das Allernotwendigste. Eine kurze Zusammenstellung der einschlägigen Quellen gab ich selbst schon in *Taxis und Taktik: Die advokatische Dispositionskunst in Ciceros Gerichtsreden* (Stuttgart: 1975) 74 Anm. 74, die wichtigste moderne Gesamtdarstellung findet man noch immer (nicht ersetzt durch neuere Handbücher) bei Volkmann R., *Die Rhetorik der Griechen und Römer* (1885²; 1963) 111-23.

Rede,[25] wobei die Parallele zu Marc Anton auf der Hand liegt[26] — mit dem einen Unterschied, daß Agamemnon erfolglos ist: seine Soldaten reagieren nämlich programmwidrig, indem sie in der Tat nach Hause wollen (nebenbei ein Hinweis darauf, daß die Technik dieser 'figurierten Rede' wohl schon älter als die *Ilias* ist: die Darstellung des erfolglosen Manövers scheint die eines erfolgreichen vorauszusetzen). Die Theorie zu dieser Praxis dürfte ursprünglich schon in der Sophistenzeit, also zusammen mit dem Aufkommen einer systematisch gelehrten Rhetorik, entstanden sein; sie liegt uns zuerst vor in einer fälschlich dem Demetrios von Phaleron zugeschriebenen Schrift *Über den sprachlichen Ausdruck* (Περὶ ἑρμηνείας) aus dem dritten oder zweiten vorchristlichen Jahrhundert, dann vor allem bei Quintilian (also am Ende des ersten Jahrhunderts nach Christus) und in einer ausführlichen Spezialabhandlung *Über figurierte Reden*, die unter dem Namen des zur Augusteerzeit lebenden Dionysios von Halikarnaß überliefert ist, in Wirklichkeit aber später verfaßt wurde. Diese und manche anderen Autoren verstehen unter 'figurierter Rede' ein verhülltes Sprechen, bei dem man insgeheim etwas anderes meint oder beabsichtigt, als man den Worten nach sagt. Die Abgrenzung von der Ironie findet sich vor allem bei Quintilian, der zugleich die außerordentliche Beliebtheit dieser Redeweise, die er auch schlechtweg *figura* (oder *schema*) nennt, im rhetorischen Unterricht der Kaiserzeit bezeugt (*Institutio oratoria* IX, 2, 65): 'iam enim ad id genus, quod et frequentissimum est et exspectari maxime credo[!], veniendum est, in quo per quandam suspicionem quod non dicimus accipi volumus, non utique contrarium, ut in ironia, sed aliud latens et auditori quasi inveniendum' ('Damit kommen wir zu der Art, die besonders häufig ist und deren Behandlung man [von mir], wie ich glaube, vor allem erwartet, nämlich die, wo wir durch sozusagen eine Art von Verdächtigung erreichen wollen, daß etwas verstanden wird, was wir nicht sagen, nicht unbedingt das Gegenteilige, wie in der Ironie,[27] sondern

---

[25] Diagnostiziert von Ps. Dionysios (*De oratione figurata* I, 15) und Eustathios (s. Ott, *Oratio figurata*, 92-5).

[26] Hinweis darauf schon bei Ott, *Oratio figurata*, 37 f., der allerdings nur den ersten Teil der Rede (bis 153) für 'figuriert' halten möchte, aus ähnlichem Grund wie dem, der etwa Müller, *Die politische Rede bei Shakespeare*, dazu bestimmt, nur den zweiten Teil der Rede als eigentlich ironisch anzuerkennen.

[27] Dies berührt einen zweiten Gegensatz zwischen *Ironie* und *oratio figurata* (den wir in unserem Zusammenhang vernachlässigen, vgl. oben Anm. 14): daß die Ironie, was Cicero anders sah, auf ein *contrarium* geht, die *oratio figurata* nicht ebenso, sondern auch auf ein bloßes *aliud* (womit das *contrarium*, das ja immer auch ein *aliud* ist, natürlich nicht ausgeschlossen wird: *non utique!*).

etwas anderes, Verborgenes, das der Hörer gewissermaßen selbst finden muß'). Schon diese Definition trifft genau zu auf die Rede Marc Antons, dem es ja in der Tat gelingt, ohne Einsatz von Ironie 'durch eine Art *suspicio*' bei seinen Hörern Zweifel an der (den Worten nach nicht in Frage gestellten) Ehrenwertheit des Brutus zu wecken, so daß diese von selbst allmählich auf den vom Redner verborgenen Gedanken kommen, daß die Mörder Caesars Verräter und Verbrecher sind.

Die Übereinstimmung geht weiter. Quintilian nennt drei Gründe, die es geben kann, um die *figura* anzuwenden: das persönliche Sicherheitsbedürfnis des Redners ('si dicere palam parum tutum est'), die Rücksichtnahme auf die Schicklichkeit ('si non decet [sc. dicere palam]'), die Freude an der Anmut der 'Figur' als solcher ('venustatis modo gratia'). Sogleich ist klar, daß der Fall Marc Antons zur ersten, wichtigsten Kategorie gehört, von der Quintilian sagt, daß sie besonders dann vorliege (ibid., IX, 2, 68), 'wenn uns mächtige Personen im Wege sind, deren Tadel aber nötig ist, um unsere Sache behaupten zu können' ('cum personae potentes obstant, sine quarum reprehensione teneri causa non possit') — bei Marc Anton wäre dies der durch sein Ansehen und seine moralische Autorität mächtige Brutus —: Hier gelte es natürlich mit größter Vorsicht zu agieren, um nicht durchschaut zu werden, weil (ibid., IX, 2, 69) 'die offenbare "Figur" ja eben dies verliert, daß sie "Figur" ist' ('aperta figura perdit hoc ipsum, quod figura est', im Gegensatz zu anderen Figuren wie auch der Ironie); so verfährt ja auch Marc Anton, wenn er, um sich nicht zu gefährden, bis zum Ende die Form der *oratio figurata* durchhält. Quintilian warnt vor allem vor allzu suggestiven Zweideutigkeiten der Formulierung (ibid. IX, 2, 71): 'Die Sachen selbst (d. h. nicht die Wörter) sollen den Richter[28] auf den Verdacht bringen' ('res ipsae perducant iudicem ad suspicionem'); dabei sei 'sehr hilfreich auch der Ausdruck der Gefühle' ('multum etiam adfectus iuvant') sowie das 'Unterbrechen der Rede durch Schweigen sowie das wiederholte Zögern' ('et interrupta silentio dictio et cunctationes'): 'So nämlich wird es kommen, daß der Richter selber nach dem gewissen Etwas nachforscht, das er vielleicht nicht glauben würde, wenn er es zu hören bekäme, und daß er dem glaubt, auf das er selbst gekommen zu sein meint' ('sic enim fiet ut iudex quaerat illud nescio quid ipse, quod fortasse non crederet, si audiret, et ei, quod a se inventum existimat, credat'). Von der Prozeß-

---

[28] Quintilian denkt wie alle antiken Rhetoriker an den Gerichtsprozeß als Normalfall der Rede.

situation abgesehen paßt auch dies genau zur Rede Marc Antons. Er
manipuliert die Gedanken seines Publikums gerade dadurch, daß er
immer wieder innehält, sich zurückruft, Dinge nicht gesagt haben
will, die er gesagt hat; und wenn er gleich nach dem ersten Absatz seiner Rede behauptet, eine Pause einlegen zu müssen, weil sein Herz
bei Caesar sei:

> My heart is in the coffin there with Caesar,
> And I must pause till it come back to me,[29]

in Wirklichkeit aber, weil er die Wirkung seiner bisherigen Worte
testen und vor allem seinen Hörern Gelegenheit geben will, ihre
Gedanken in der von ihm gewünschten Weise weiterzuspinnen, um
schließlich selber auf jenes *nescio quid* zu kommen, das er ihnen vor-
enthält (was ja am Ende auch geschieht) — dann hat man vielleicht
nicht ohne Grund den Eindruck, daß dieser Marc Anton Quintilian
mit seiner Empfehlung der 'interrupta silentio dictio' gelesen hat.
Denn eben diese Stelle zeigt ja nebenbei auch schon, wie es vor allem
die Kraft seiner Emotionen (*affectus*), d. h. zunächst die Glut seiner
unverhohlen zur Schau gestellten[30] Liebe zu Caesar, ist, die seine
Hörer in Harnisch gegen dessen Mörder bringt,[31] wobei sie aber
immer doch das Gefühl haben, sich ihr Urteil selbständig bilden zu
können.

Es geht mir nicht darum nachzuweisen, daß Shakespeare, über dessen klassische Bildung ich kein Urteil habe, das neunte Buch von
Quintilians *Institutio* gekannt oder gar studiert hat — obschon das
nach den Forschungen des peniblen T.W. Baldwin keineswegs für
unmöglich gelten kann.[32] Meine Gelehrsamkeit reicht auch leider

---

[29] Der Gedanke geht letztlich zurück auf ein erotisches Epigramm des römischen
Staatsmanns und Hobbydichters Lutatius Catulus, das bei Gellius überliefert ist
(XIX, 9, 14); imitiert bzw. übersteigert ist dort Kallimachos, wo nur die Hälfte der
Seele zum Geliebten entflohen ist.

[30] Daß der Redner für seinen Freund eintritt, ist etwas, das man ihm immer, auch
wenn er in schlechtester Sache zu sprechen scheint, zugute hält.

[31] Mit anderen Interpreten meine ich, daß das Emotionslose den Hauptmangel der
in mancher Hinsicht ja brillianten Rede des Brutus ausmacht. In genialer Weise hat
Shakespeare dessen fein pointierten, aber allzu kühlen Redestil, wie wir ihn aus man-
chen Äußerungen vor allem auch Ciceros erschließen können, rekonstruiert oder
intuitiv erfaßt.

[32] Baldwin T.W., *William Shakespere's Small Latine and Lesse Greeke* (Urbana: 1944) II,
197-238: *The Rhetorical Training of Shakespeare: Quintilian, the Supreme Authority* (dort 231-3:
zum 9. Buch). Das Material ist beeindruckend, wenn auch nicht durchweg beweis-
kräftig. Neuere Arbeiten über Shakespeares Verhältnis zur Theorie der Rhetorik

nicht aus, um zu beurteilen, ob der Dichter sonst durch irgendwelche
Kanäle der Überlieferung mit der antiken Theorie der *oratio figurata*
bekannt sein könnte (wobei diese, wenn ich nicht irre, in der engli-
schen Rhetorik seiner Zeit keine Rolle spielt) oder ob ihn etwa gar die
erwähnte Rede Agamemnons bei Homer hätte inspirieren können,[33]
so daß er dann vielleicht in Marc Anton einen rhetorisch erfolgreichen Agamemnon hätte agieren lassen wollen. Für die literarkritische
Beurteilung der Rede, um die es uns bisher ausschließlich gegangen
ist, wäre das natürlich gleichgültig.

Im übrigen ist es aber wohl gar nicht so schwer zu sehen, wie Shakespeare selbst die Form seiner Rede erfunden haben dürfte, auch
wenn er dafür keine Vorschriften bzw. Vorbilder in Theorie und Praxis der antiken Rhetorik kannte. Der Refrain seiner Rede 'And Brutus
is an honourable man', stammt jedenfalls, wie schon vor fast andert-
halb Jahrhunderten entdeckt,[34] von Antonius selbst, von dem Cicero
in der zweiten *Philippica* bezeugt, daß er vom Caesarmörder Brutus
mit dem vorsichtigen Zusatz 'quem ego honoris causa nomino' ('den
ich ehrenhalber erwähne') gesprochen habe (was Shakespeare
unzweifelhaft, auf welchem Weg auch immer, bekannt geworden sein
muß).[35] Cicero behauptet, daß er darin einen Beweis für die unglaub-
liche Dummheit des Antonius habe, der den Widerspruch zwischen
seiner Verwerfung des Attentats und der 'ehrenhaften' Nennung des
Attentäters gar nicht bemerke.[36] Das wird ihm Shakespeare so wenig

---

Struever N., "Shakespeare and Rhetoric", *Rhetorica* 6, 2 (1988) 133-44 und Plett H.F.,
"Shakespeare and the 'Ars Rhetorica' ", in *Rhetoric and Pedagogy (Festschr. James J. Mur-*
phy), W.B. Horner – M. Leff (Hrsg.) (Mahwah, N.J. – Hove: 1995) 243-59) sind für solche Fragen weniger ergiebig. Im allgemeinen ist immer noch wertvoll Schirmer W.F.,
"Shakespeare und die Rhetorik", *Shakespeare-Jahrbuch* 71 (1935) 11-31. Zur Frage von
Shakespeares Lateinbildung s. jetzt Boltz I., in *Shakespeare Handbuch*, I. Schabert (Hrsg.)
(Stuttgart: 2000[4]) 139ff., dort 145-147 zu den neuen Forschungen von Richard Wilson.
[33] Insgesamt scheint ja Homer (etwa in der Übersetzung von Chapman, in der
schon 1598 das zweite Buch der *Ilias* vorliegt — *Julius Caesar* wurde wohl 1599 aufge-
führt [*The Oxford Shakespeare: Julius Caesar*, ed. A. Humphreys (Oxford: 1984) 1-5]) für
Shakespeare kaum eine Rolle zu spielen (Baldwin, *William Shakespere's Small Latine and*
Lesse Greeke, 658-61).
[34] Watkiss, W.L., *Essays on the Life and Plays of Shakespeare* (London: 1858) (Kapitel
über *Julius Caesar*, ohne Paginierung): 'The ambiguous tones in which he [sc. Antony]
harps upon his consideration for Brutus especially and then his associates, come down
from Cicero; the second *Philippic* (XII) furnishes his very words'.
[35] Anders Kytzler B., *William Shakespeare: Julius Caesar* (Frankfurt a. M.–Berlin:
1963), 120: 'Daß Shakespeare diese Notiz Ciceros gekannt und bewußt verwendet
hätte, ist jedoch kaum anzunehmen'. Dann war Shakespeare ein Hellseher.
[36] Cicero, *Philippica* II, 30: 'Sed stuporem hominis vel dicam pecudis attendite. Sic
enim dixit: "Brutus, quem ego honoris causa nomino, cruentum pugionem tenens

geglaubt haben, wie wir es tun; aber auf der Suche nach einer auch historisch glaubhaften Rede im Munde Marc Antons muß er sich überlegt haben, wie denn dieser dazu gekommen sein konnte, so ehrerbietig vom Mörder des geliebten Freundes zu reden. Es könne nur Verstellung gewesen sein, sagte er sich offenbar: Antonius habe insgeheim die Menschen gegen den allseits angesehenen und verehrten, von Cicero geradezu gefeierten Brutus aufbringen wollen. Und so zeigte denn Shakespeare in seiner Leichenrede, von den Nachrichten Plutarchs (und vielleicht Appians) ausgehend[37] — mit oder ohne Kenntnis der antiken *oratio figurata* —, wie ein genialer Demagoge,[38] der alle Mittel seiner Kunst einsetzt, ein solches Meisterstück in bedenklichster Situation fertigbringen konnte.

Die Richtigkeit unserer Interpretation hängt auch nicht an dieser, wie mir scheint, plausiblen genetischen Hypothese. Nach ihr *ist* vielmehr die Leichenrede Marc Antons, wie auch immer entstanden, ein fast idealtypisches Beispiel der *oratio figurata* im Sinn der antiken Theorie, die hier zeitlose Gültigkeit hat, einfach darum, weil sie dem für unterschwellige Demagogie so empfänglichen Mechanismus der menschlichen Seele entspricht. Auf alle Fälle kann die moderne Sprach- und Literaturwissenschaft von ihr und an Shakespeare lernen, daß es für die Diskrepanz von Gesagtem und Gemeintem nicht nur die Alternative Lüge oder Ironie gibt.

Ciceronem exclamavit: ex quo intellegi debet eum conscium fuisse". Ergo ego sceleratus appellor a te quem tu suspicatum aliquid suspicaris: ille qui stillantem prae se pugionem tulit, is a te honoris causa nominatur?'.

[37] Die antiken Quellen analysiert Kennedy G., "Antony's Speech at Caesar's Funeral", *The Quarterly Journal of Speech* 54 (1968) 99-106.

[38] 'Nowhere else in literature is the procedure of a demagogue of genius set forth with such masterly insight' (*Study-Aid Series: Notes on Shakespeare's Julius Caesar* (London: 1965) 29) — was, zur Ehre von Demosthenes und Cicero, natürlich auch an den Möglichkeiten der dramatischen Bühne liegt, wo die Wirkung auf das Publikum sichtbarer wird als in einer publizierten Rede.

Selective Bibliography

AZZALINO W., "Stilkundliche Betrachtung der Reden des Brutus und des Antonius in Shakespeares 'Julius Caesar' (III, 2)", *Neuphilologische Monatsschrift* 11 (1940) 249-71

COLES B., *Shakespeare Studies: Julius Caesar* (New York: 1940) 199-204

GREENE G., "'The Power of Speech / To Stir Men's Blood': the Language of Tragedy in Shakespeare's Julius Caesar", *Renaissance Drama* 11 (1980) 67-93

KENNEDY G., "Antony's Speech at Caesar's Funeral", *The Quarterly Journal of Speech* 54 (1968) 99-106

KNOX D., *Ironia: Medieval and Renaissance Ideas on Irony* (Leiden etc.: 1989)

KNOX N., *The Word Irony and its Context, 1500–1755* (Durham, N.C.: 1961)

KOPPENFELS W. VON, "Plutarch, Shakespeare, Quevedo und das Drama der Ermordung Caesars", *Germanisch-romanische Monatsschrift* 51 (1970) 1-23

KYTZLER B., *William Shakespeare: Julius Caesar* (Frankfurt a. M.–Berlin: 1963)

LAPP E., *Linguistik der Ironie* (Tübingen: 1992)

MULLER W.G., *Die politische Rede bei Shakespeare* (Tübingen: 1979) 127-49

MULLER W.G., "Ironie, Lüge, Simulation, Dissimulation und verwandte rhetorische Termini", in *Zur Terminologie der Literaturwissenschaft*, C. Wagenknecht (Hrsg.) (Stuttgart: 1989) 189-208

OTT G., *Oratio figurata: Formen verschlüsselten Sprechens in der Antike* (Wiss. Zulassungsarbeit zum Staatsexamen, masch.; München: 1994)

SCHABERT I. (Hrsg.), *Shakespeare-Handbuch* (Stuttgart: 2000⁴)

SHAKESPEARE W., *Julius Caesar*, ed. T.S. Dorsch, Arden Edition (London etc.: 1955⁶)

A New Variorum Edition of Shakespeare: The Tragedie of Iulius Caesar, ed. H. Howard Furness Jr (Philadelphia: 1913)

STROH W., *Taxis und Taktik: Die advokatische Dispositionskunst in Ciceros Gerichtsreden* (Stuttgart: 1975)

WEINRICH H., *Linguistik der Lüge* (Heidelberg: 1970)

WEISS N., *Die Szene III, 2 in William Shakespeare's Trauerspiel "Julius Caesar": Bauformen, Rhetorik und Ironie in den Leichenreden des Brutus und Mark Anton* (Nordenham–Duisburg: 1995).

THE USES OF ANCIENT HISTORY IN THE EMBLEMS OF JOANNES SAMBUCUS (1531–1584)*

Arnoud Visser

Firmly embedded in the humanist tradition of Neolatin epigrams, the genre of the emblem book played constantly with the classics of Greek and Latin literature. The first example of the genre is Andreas Alciatus's *Emblematum libellus* (Augsburg: 1531), consisting of epigrams, partly translated from the *Greek Anthology*, to which the German publisher Heynrich Steyner had added illustrations. The book was a great success, resulting in a rapidly increasing number and variety of emblem books. The popularity of the genre reached its peak in the seventeenth century, when hundreds of different editions in Latin and the vernacular languages were produced. By the end of the eighteenth century, the production of emblem books had gradually decreased. Humanist emblem writers used the genre for the most part as learned play, reworking mythological, allegorical and natural subjects to confirm and reformulate a humanist ethic. Prominent influences include Neoplatonism and the symbolic interpretation of hieroglyphs.

Joannes Sambucus's emblem book, printed some thirty years after the publication of Alciatus's collection of emblems, is one of the most influential examples in the genre. To define the aim of his emblems Sambucus uses the analogy of history: 'Most importantly, I want them to teach about life, like history does [...]'.[1] This may not be a surprising statement from the perspective of an early modern conception of history, but it clarifies the instrumental role history played for the emblematist.

This article will address the way in which Sambucus transformed

---

* I am grateful to Jan Frans van Dijkhuizen, Karl Enenkel and Bart Westerweel for their critical comments on earlier drafts of this article.

[1] Sambucus J., *Emblemata cum aliquot nummis antqui operis* [...] (Antwerp, Plantin: 1564): 'sed imprimis vitam, ut historiae, volo erudiant, ut quemadmodum illae sunt Philosophia εἰδωλοποιός, ita haec in oculos notis quibusdam incurrant animumque auditoris agunto [...]' ('But above all I would have them teach good living, like histories, so that, just as the latter are wisdom in the form of illustrations, so emblems should strike the eye with their signs [i.e. images]; let them stimulate the mind of the hearer'); translated by Drysdall D.L., "Johannes Sambucus, *De Emblemate*", *Emblematica* 5, 1 (1991) 114-5.

                    ARNOUD VISSER

traditional accounts of ancient history in his emblems. As the epigrams made by Sambucus formed the starting point for the construction of the emblems, the *pictura*, made by several designers, could in fact be seen as a first reception of the epigrams. The textual parts will therefore be the main point of attention in this article. I shall start by giving a short survey of emblem poetics in order to define the margins within which historical topics could be set. After this the focus will shift to the role of history in these emblems. Sambucus used historical anecdotes as *exempla* for conveying a specific moral message. Seen as rhetorical instruments, how do these *exempla* work? An analysis of the selected examples will show how the classical sources and their subsequent *Nachleben* are imitated and transformed into an emblematic epigram. This investigation of the ways in which Sambucus reworked his classical sources is not intended as an autonomous interpretation of separate emblems. It will shed light on the function of these historical anecdotes as carriers of a specific message. Hence, it enables us to explore the reasons for their selection. Finally, I shall investigate the relation between ancient history in these emblems and the audience the book intends to address. Before turning to the historical emblems, the origin of the *Emblemata* and the activities of its author deserve to be outlined briefly.

Sambucus and his Emblem Book

Joannes Sambucus (Zsámboky János, 1531–1584) was born in the then Hungarian town of Nagyszombat (Tyrnau), today's Trnava in Slovakia.[2] His *peregrinatio academica* brought him to many universities in Germany, France and the Italian cities of Padua and Bologna. In the autumn of 1563 he stayed in Ghent and Antwerp. In Ghent he finished the composition of his emblems, probably in close cooperation with Lucas d'Heere, the main designer of the illustrations.[3] In August

---

[2] For a detailed biography see Gerstinger H., "Johannes Sambucus als Handschriftensammler", in *Festschrift der Nationalbibliothek in Wien herausgegeben zur Feier des 200jährigen Bestehens des Gebäudes* (Vienna: 1926) 251-90.

[3] Waterschoot W., "Lucas d'Heere und Johannes Sambucus", in *The Emblem in Renaissance and Baroque Europe. Tradition and Variety. Selected Papers of the Glasgow International Emblem Conference 13-17 August, 1990*, ed. A. Adams, A.J. Harper (Leiden: 1992) 45-52. Other designers are Geoffroy Ballain, Pieter Huys, and — for the extended editions — Peeter vander Borcht.

1564 Plantin published the *Emblemata cum aliquot nummis antiqui operis*. More editions followed. Apparently, there was a favourable market for this type of emblem book which allowed Plantin to publish an edition in French and Dutch in 1566, as well as an extended version of the Latin collection. This Latin edition was reprinted four more times in Antwerp and Leiden before the end of the century.[4]

Early in 1564 Sambucus established himself in Vienna, after a period of twenty-two years of travelling. Probably the next year he was appointed court historian at the court of Maximilian II.[5] Here he would serve the Habsburg Emperor — from 1576 this was Rudolf II — and work as a historiographer, philologist, physician, numismatist, and cartographer. He died in Vienna in 1584.

The publication of his emblem book came at a crucial moment in Sambucus's career. At the Habsburg court Sambucus still had no clear and secure position. The emblem book is also to be seen as a tool in this social context. The copy of the *Emblemata* that Sambucus presented to the Emperor is still kept in the Nationalbibliothek. It is luxuriously bound, and includes a manuscript dedication by the author.[6] In his dedicatory emblem to Maximilian II, Sambucus presents himself as an ideal scholar-poet for the Emperor. He promises to magnify the imperial glory by writing an epic and by collecting ancient treasures and old manuscripts. At the same time this opening emblem can be seen as a specimen of his capacity to eulogise: Maximilian is portrayed as a new Augustus who will bring peace to the Holy Roman Empire in a new golden age [fig. 1].[7] In the *pictura* Maximilian II is enthroned on the top of the temple of Janus; the closed doors of this temple and the olive branch symbolise the new *pax Romana*. The eagle of Jupiter brings to Maximilian the three crowns, representing three-

---

4 See Voet L., *The Plantin Press (1555–1589). A Bibliography of the Works Printed and Published by Christopher Plantin at Antwerp and Leiden*, 6 vols (Amsterdam: 1980–1983) V, nos. 2168-74 (p. 2024-39; the 1599 edition is not included here). Of the first edition from 1564, two fac-simile editions have been published: J. Sambucus, *Emblemata* [...] *Antverpiae 1564*, introd. A. Buck (Budapest: 1982), and Voet L. – Persoons G., *De emblemata van Joannes Sambucus* [...] *Reproductie van de Latijnse editie van 1564 en van de tekst van de Nederlandse vertaling van 1566 en van de Franse vertaling van 1567* (Antwerp: 1980–1982). The most detailed account of the printing history remains Rooses M., "De Plantijnsche uitgaven van *Emblemata Joannis Sambuci*", *Het Boek. Tijdschrift voor Boek- en Bibliotheekwezen* 1 (1903) 3-15.

5 Gerstinger, "Johannes Sambucus als Handschriftensammler", 277.

6 The dedication is dated Vienna, 26 September 1564; Österreichische Nationalbibliothek, 74W95, Rara 5.

7 Sambucus, *Emblemata* [ed. 1564] 9-12.

fold regal authority: before he became emperor, Maximilian was King of Bohemia, Hungary and Rome. Romulus and Remus with the nurturing wolf not only signify the power Maximilian formally exerts over Rome, but also mark his reign as the beginning of a second Roman Empire.

Towards a Poetics of Sambucus's Emblems

It is difficult to provide a uniform definition of the emblem book. A reason for the somewhat elusive character of emblem poetics is the relative artificiality of the notion itself. In the two centuries when most emblem books were published, a large variety of styles can be discerned: emblems with or without illustrations and with different kinds of epigrams; emblems with extensive commentary or only *picturae* accompanied by a biblical quotation; subjects taken from daily life, from mystical themes or amorous life. Therefore it seems wise to restrict the scope of the poetics here to those aspects which are relevant for the use of history in Sambucus's emblems.

The form of Sambucus's emblems is the same as those of Alciatus. There are three recurring parts: a motto providing either a general moral, for example a proverb, or a description of the story that will be told, a *pictura*, in this case a woodcut illustration, and finally an epigram, written in a variety of (Horatian) metrical forms. In the epigram the general motto is explained, mostly by means of a graphic example. The epigram as poetic form limits the range of stories that can be narrated, and their length. As a result, an emblem does not lend itself to the telling of intricate stories with a long sequence of events. Therefore in most cases the history Sambucus used in his emblems is anecdotal, representing a particular historical scene. Similarly, the representation of history in a *pictura* implies a focus on particular moments of a story.

In the preface to his emblems entitled *De emblemate* Sambucus introduces the reader to his work.[8] Rather than being a poetic treatise, this

---

[8] Apart from the translation by Drysdall, two other editions of the preface have been published recently: O. Scholer provides a copious commentary in his "Ein Text hart wie ein Diamant oder *De Emblemate* des Joannes Sambucus Tirnaviensis", *Études classiques, publiées par le Centre Universitaire de Luxembourg* 5 (1993) 69-209, and Ari Wesseling deals with the first three paragraphs in his "Testing Modern Emblem Theory: the Earliest Views of the Genre (1564–1566)" in *The Emblem Tradition and the Low*

text is an introduction with what might be said to be a commercial slant. The poetic observations Sambucus makes, are all connected to his desire to elevate the status of the book. Nonetheless, some of these indicate how Sambucus wanted emblems to be seen. As such, these comments deserve to be mentioned here.

According to Sambucus, the language and imagery ideally suited to conveying the emblematic lesson should be veiled and enigmatic. It will render the emblems (in accordance with the conventional humanist use of the Horatian adage *utile dulci* (not only more pleasing, but also more useful).[9] This element is present in the epigrams in the use of ambiguous wording and *exempla* with multiple meanings. The pictorial equivalent of this enigmatic aspect is the use of symbols, allegories and hieroglyphs. In his preface Sambucus specifies the implied cryptic nature of emblems by using the Greek rhetorical terms εἰρωνικά, which can be paraphrased as 'investing a word or phrase with a meaning different from the immediately apparent one' and παραδοξότερα, 'contrary to appearance'.[10] The important emblematic feature of paradox can be considered to function on both a rhetorical level as a means of surprising the reader by an extraordinary invention, and on a metaphysical level as a way of revealing a hidden truth.

This short survey of the main poetical characteristics may well be illustrated by the emblem *Heroes divini* (*Divine heroes*) [fig. 2], dealing with an episode from Vergil's *Aeneid* about Aeneas and his Italian enemy Turnus. In this story, Juno is trying to save Turnus from a fatal confrontation with Aeneas.[11] She lures him from the battlefield to a ship by creating a fake Aeneas out of a cloud. Turnus eagerly fights the phantom and when it seems to retreat, he triumphantly follows it, eventually finding himself on the ship sailing away from the battlefield.

Countries. Selected Papers of the Leuven International Emblem Conference 18-23 August, 1996, Imago Figurata Studies 1b, ed. J. Manning – K. Porteman – M. Van Vaeck (Turnhout: 1999) 3-22.

[9] In the 1564 edition p. 3-4 [A2a-b]: 'Itaque tecta, arguta, iucunda, et varie significantia sint [...]' ('So let them be veiled, ingenious, pleasing, and with variety of meaning [...]') and p. 5 [A3a]: 'Quare selecta, et ὀγκώδη erunt, nec minus, quam caecae, et singulares Aegyptiorum, et Pythagoreorum illae notae mentem exerceant [...]' ('By these means [emblems] will be select, pregnant with meaning, and may exercise the mind no less than those obscure and extraordinary symbols of the Egyptians and the Pythagoreans'); translated by Drysdall, "*De Emblemate*", 116-7.

[10] Ibid., 5.

[11] Vergil, *Aeneid* X, 633-89.

Of the three parts of the emblem the motto indicates the theme of the emblem, in this case two keywords rather than a moral dictum. The epigram argues that leaders should act cautiously. With divine grace and wisdom, as Sambucus asserts, their rule can be fortunate. Turnus is mentioned as an example of imprudent behaviour: a leader should not run after his enemies without knowing what to expect. Then, it seems, even divine support cannot help. The limits of the help Turnus received are reflected in his ambiguous victory over Aeneas. Turnus thinks Aeneas makes a retreat, but in fact it is he who is fleeing from Aeneas. It is to this scene that the word 'fugacem' in Sambucus's verse ambigously refers: Aeneas seems to 'flee' from Turnus, but in fact he is *elusive*, a phantom. The episode from the *Aeneid* is used here as an exemplum to underscore the two-sided form of divine help and the primacy of fate.

The *pictura* represents the battle scene: we see Turnus attacking the phantom of Aeneas emerging from a cloud. In the upper left corner Juno watches the fight, accompanied by her attribute, the peacock. The narrative space for the designer is always restricted to the depiction of a fixed scene. Nevertheless, the designer has tried to reveal the outcome of Turnus's actions by displaying a cancer on the shield of Turnus as a symbol for walking backwards.[12]

The Function of History and Exempla

Two commonplace characteristics of the early modern conception of history are its emphasis on personal actions and on its practical moral use, or, in the words of Felix Gilbert: 'History can encourage man by calling into his mind the achievement of the *viri illustri*. Nevertheless, history in the Renaissance was not important *per se*; it provided illustrative material for the teaching of moral philosophy'.[13] By taking a historical example a general, abstract message is made explicit in a concrete and therefore helpful way.

---

[12] Cf. the emblem *Cur sues cancris vescantur* (*Why swines eat cancers*) in the 1564 edition (emblem 61): 'gradus retro, quomodo cancer [...]' ('walking backwards, like cancers').

[13] Gilbert F., "Renaissance interest in history", in *Art, Science, and History in the Renaissance*, ed. C.S. Singleton (Baltimore: 1967) 376; see also: Landfester R., *Historia magistra vitae. Untersuchungen zur humanistischen Geschichtstheorie des 14. bis 16. Jahrhunderts* (Geneva: 1972), passim and Stierle K., "Geschichte als Exemplum — Exemplum als Geschichte. Zur Pragmatik und Poetik narrativer Texte", in *Geschichte — Ereignis und Erzählung*, ed. R. Koselleck and W.-D. Stempel (Munich: 1973) 358.

MAXIMILIANO II.

IMPERATORI AVGVSTO,

Germaniæ, Hungariæ, Bohemiæ, Dalmatiæ
Croatiǽq; Regi optimo, Archiduci Auſtriæ,
Duci Burgundiæ, Comiti Tirolis, &c. Do=
mino ſuo clementiſſimo.

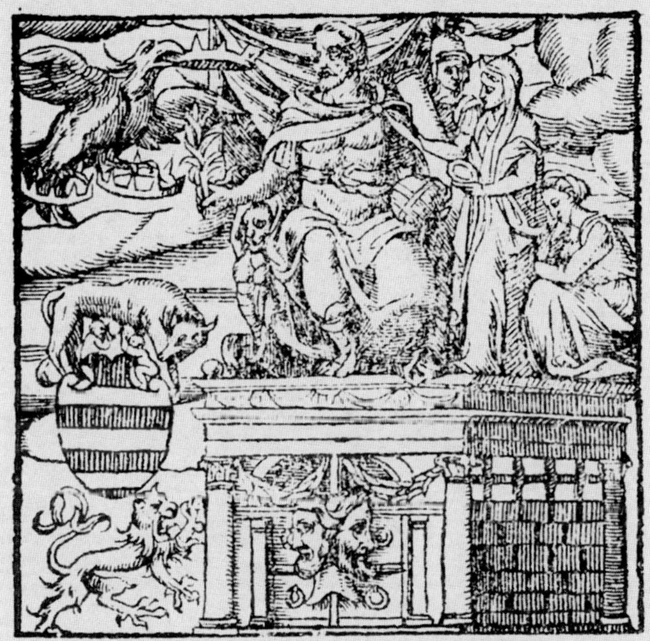

1. Joannes Sambucus, *Emblemata, et aliquot nummi antiqui operis* [...] (Antwerp: 1569), f.
A3r. Photo: Koninklijke Bibliotheek, The Hague.

Vno omnes cupiunt pro Cicerone loqui.
Vel quos exercent lites, ac iudicis ira:
Vna vbi finita est caussa, decem redeunt.

Heroës diuini.

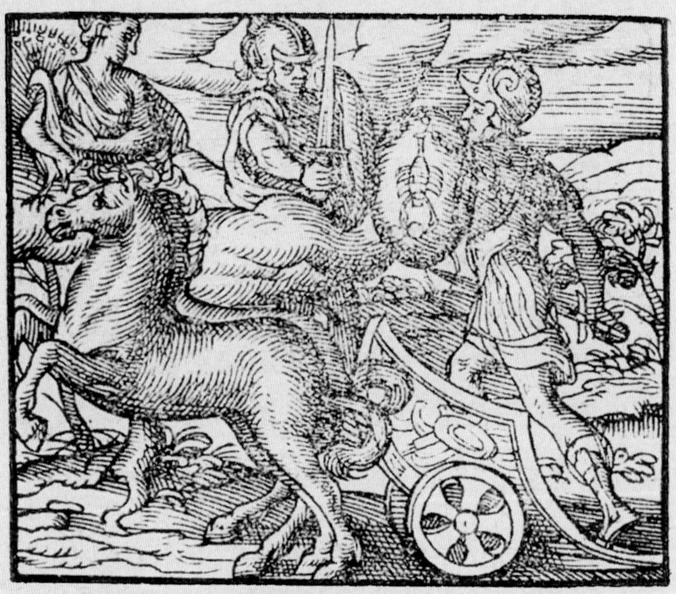

EST Ducibus præsto Diuûm præsentia, cuius
 Consilio, & nutu prosperiora gerunt:
Non ruit imprudens aduersos semper in hostes,
 Sed cauet, occultu & manifesta notat.
Aeneas quoties vmbris subducitur, inque
 Prælia seruatur, dum sua fata sinunt:
Ardua res cautè geritur, tibi, Turne, fugacem
 Id facit Aeneam, at Iupiter hostis erat.

Stu-

2. Joannes Sambucus, *Emblemata, et aliquot nummi antiqui operis* [...] (Antwerp: 1569) 128.
Photo: Koninklijke Bibliotheek, The Hague.

Curis tabescimus omnes.

Ad Ioan. Hartungum, &c.

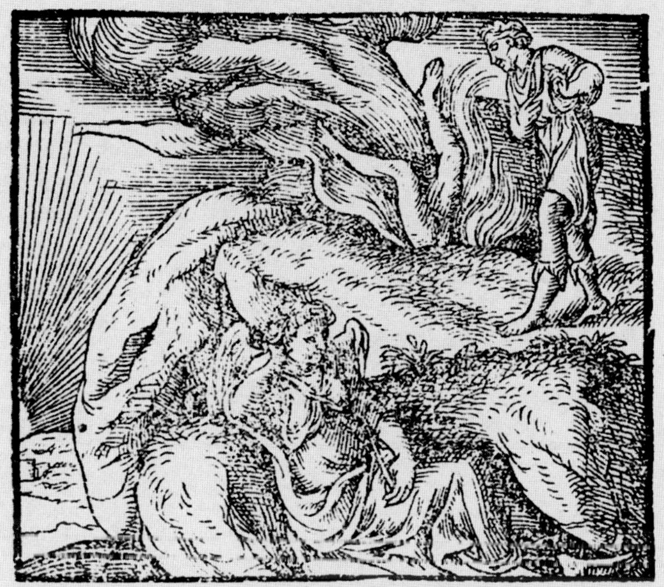

VESVIVS ardentes dum moles spirat in auras,
　Faucibus accurrens Plinius obstupuit.
Dumque nimis caussas scrutatur, forte vorago,
　Et circum exusti corripuere loci.
Debuerat mortis Siculi mentor esse poëtæ,
　Qui dedit Aetneis frigida membra focis.
Incidit heu quantus, propius spectacula rerum!
　Dumque fidem quærit, materiam ipse fouet.
Num hic quoque Cyclopes formabant, Iuppiter, arma,
　Ignibus, aut incus verbere quassa sonat?
Error quisque suus, nimium quos cura lacessit,
　Et nisi consumit sollicitudo bonos.

Mu.

3. Joannes Sambucus, *Emblemata, et aliquot nummi antiqui operis* [...] (Antwerp: 1569) 150.
Photo: Koninklijke Bibliotheek, The Hague.

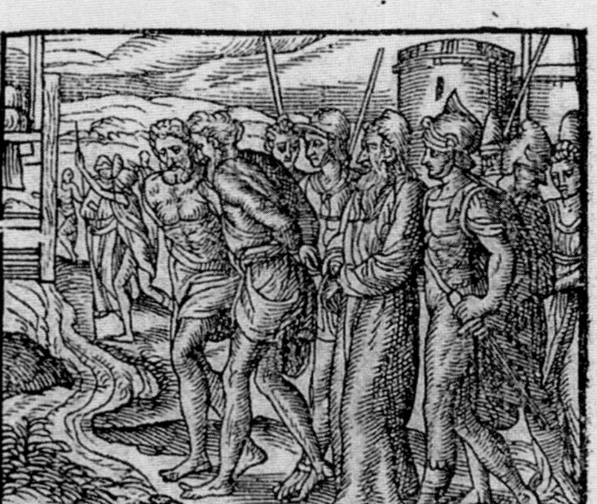

Sola culpa præstanda.

De Antiphonte poëta à Dionysio damnato.

NVLLIVS sceleris qui conscius esse putatur,
   Cur fugiat mortem? funere maior erit.
Namque bonus culpam si præstitit, omnia soluit,
   Sunt reliqua exigui temporis, acta fluunt.
Labe igitur vacuus vates, quem sæua tyrannis
   Supplicio addixit, corripuit socios:
Qui faciem vt sontes velabant: Quid pudet huius,
   Cras ne quis videat forte timetis, ait?
Præte eunt hora crudelia iussa tyranni,
   Morte breui longam cur vereare diem?
Tantus amor veri, tantum sibi conscia virtus

                    M 2   Fidit,

Fidit, & oblitum non sinit esse sui.
Socratis en quantum se mors diffudit in æuum,
   Solamenque mali noxia nulla grauans.

Simile à simili non læditur.

EST quibus in furias animus, dentesque paratus,
   Morsibus haud inter se appetiere canes.
Semper & imbelles mordent, quos sedere vires,
   Aut anni cogunt, vt superare queant.
Piratæ raro sese, prædoque latrones
   Offendit, metuunt conditione pari.
Crescit at in duris virtus, maiora meretur,
   Abstinet à victis, inque superba ruit.

                                    Ius

4[a+b]. Joannes Sambucus, *Emblemata, et aliquot nummi antiqui operis* [...] (Antwerp: 1569) 179-80.
Photo: Koninklijke Bibliotheek, The Hague.

Οὐ χρὴ παννύχιον εὕδειν, &c.

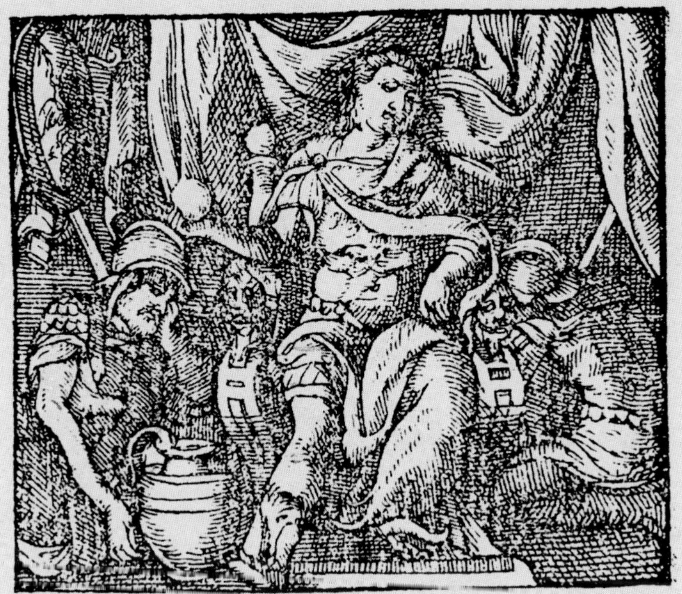

EXERCITVS *curam gerens somno leuis*
    Est nec profundè dormiens :
N *egotiosus semper, & paratior*
    Ad arma primus prodiens.
V *ictorias celebres tulit Macedo vigil,*
    Laudes, trophæa maxima.
S *opore nunquam passus est se comprimi :*
    Sed altera globus manu
D *etentus, æreum incidebat vasculum,*
    Quiete mox se colligens.
D *e Iulio fertur minus nec Cæsare,*
    Ad singulas vigili vices.

Con~

5. Joannes Sambucus, *Emblemata, et aliquot nummi antiqui operis* [...] (Antwerp: 1569) 29.
Photo: Koninklijke Bibliotheek, The Hague.

Μισάνθρωπος Τίμων.

Ad Hierony. Cardanum.

O D E R A T *hic cunctos, nec se, nec amabat amicos,*
    Μισῶν ἀνθρώπους *nomina digna gerens.*
Hoc vitium, & morbus de bili nascitur atra,
    Anxiat hæc, curas suppeditatq́; graues.
Quapropter cecidisse piro, fregisseq́ue crura
    Fertur, & auxilium non petijsse malo.
Suauibus à socijs, & consuetudine dulci
    Qui se subducunt, vulnera sæua ferunt.
Conditio hæc misera est, tristes suspiria ducunt,
    Cumq́ue nihil causæ est, occubuisse velint.

A₃

At tu dum poteris, noto socieri sodali,
    Subleuet vt pressum, corq́ue dolore vacet.
Quos nulla attingunt prorsus commercia, grato
    Atque sodalitio, subsidijsq́ue carent:
Aut Dij sunt proprij, aut falsus peruertit inanes
    Sensus, vt hos stolidos, vanaq́ue corda putes.
Tu vero tandem nobis dialectica sponte
    Donata, in lucem mittito, si memor es.

H 3   Volu-

6. Joannes Sambucus, *Emblemata, et aliquot nummi antiqui operis* [...] (Antwerp: 1569) 116-117.
Photo: Koninklijke Bibliotheek, The Hague.

I. SAMBVCI

Importuna adulatio.

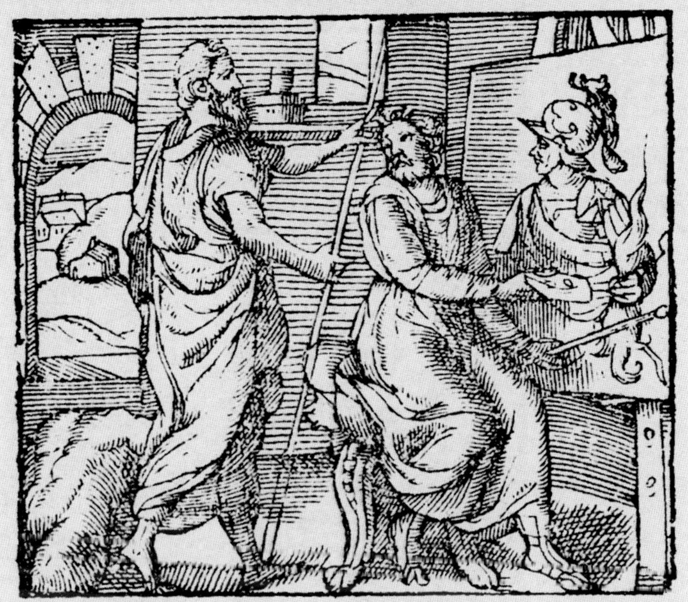

MAGNVS Alexander patulum qui subdidit Orbē,
  Vt natus esse crederetur è pclo:
Illius effugiem insignem picturus Apelles,
  Addidit adulator trisulca fulmina.
Sed nimium fuit hoc, & res suspecta modestos
  Habuit reprensores negotij leuis.
Lysippus plastes qui Regem duxerat ære,
  Hastam decere nam magis Reges ait.
Iulius exceptus victor, non Regis honores,
  Vult imperatoris sed vsque nomina.
Fulmina mortales terrent, sunt fulmina cælo.
                                    Benignius

7. Joannes Sambucus, *Emblemata, et aliquot nummi antiqui operis* [...] (Antwerp: 1569) 34.
Photo: Koninklijke Bibliotheek, The Hague.

Ridicula ambitio.

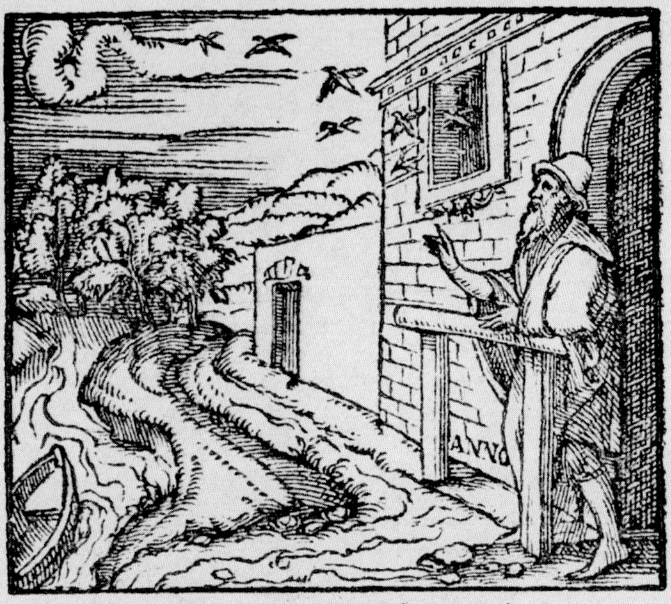

QVID *non ambitio persuadet dedita vanis,*
  Dum ex leuibus certum capiat inepta decus?
Annon ex auium cantu, quas gutture nomen
  Fingere consueuerat, notior esse cupit.
His igitur tandem missis vt spargere in Orbe
  Nomen heri possent, atque sonare procul:
Pristina continuò repetebant carmina syluis,
  Annonis & votum docta fefellit auis.
Ficedulas etiam religatas pertrahit esca,
  Stamina sirumpant, libera rura petunt.
In leuibus quæso firmam ne ponito laudem:
  Sola fugit virtus tristia fata rogi.

Cus

8. Joannes Sambucus, *Emblemata, et aliquot nummi antiqui operis* [...] (Antwerp: 1569) 58.
Photo: Koninklijke Bibliotheek, The Hague.

The use of *exempla* in emblems should be interpreted in this light. The message is constituted by moral philosophy, the *exemplum* serves as its carrier, and history is the field from which the *exemplum* is taken. The fact that the emblematist uses history for moral instruction means that the historical examples need to be set in a particular moral context. This leads to the next step in our investigation: how did Sambucus formulate *exempla* from ancient history? In what way did he adapt the *exempla* to the intended moral message and to the poetical framework we sketched before?

Curis tabescimus omnes (*We are all consumed by worries*) [fig. 3], may serve as a case in point.[14] The epigram warns against the consuming effects of anxiety. As support for this warning Sambucus gives two *exempla*. Firstly, he mentions the death of Pliny the Elder, who was killed at the eruption of Mount Vesuvius in 79 A.D. According to Sambucus, the cause of the accident lay in Pliny's inclination to ponder. A second *exemplum*, the death of Empedocles, should strengthen the message about the consuming effects of worries. As the argument goes, Pliny could have learnt from Empedocles, who died by leaping into the crater of Mount Etna.[15] Here Sambucus explicitly refers to the didactic function of *exempla*. The emblematist compares worrying to the consuming powers of a volcano. Pliny serves here as an example of a melancholic genius, who has to keep the balance between his creative potential and his inclination to worry. His intellectual capacities can suddenly turn into a destructive madness. The moral interpretation of Pliny's death in this emblem is constructed by Sambucus, as we will see in the analysis of the sources.

---

[14] The source for the motto is Ovid, *Tristia* V, 1, 69: 'Nolumus assiduis animum tabescere curis' ('we do not want to waste our mind with constant worries'); the omission of *animus* (mind) as object for *tabescere* (to waste), in Sambucus's motto clears the way for the change of mental agony into a more complete, even physical danger.

[15] The description of this episode is derived from Horace's *Ars poetica*. This text was edited by Sambucus and published by Plantin in the same year as the emblems. In Horace, Empedocles is mentioned as a typical enraged poet. In both Horace and Sambucus the antithesis of the cold body, signifying here Empedocles' insensitive brain, and the burning vulcano he jumped into is emphasised. Horace, *Ars poetica* 453-67; in particular 464-6: 'deus inmortalis haberi/dum cupit Empedocles, ardentem frigidus Aetnam/insiluit [...]' ('wanting to be considered an immortal god, the cold Empedocles jumped into Mount Etna [...]'); Sambucus, 159: 'Debuerat mortis Siculi memor esse poetae,/Qui dedit Aetneis frigida membra focis' ('He should have thought of the death of the Sicilian poet, who threw his cold body in the fire of Mount Etna').

In the picture the theme of the emblem is displayed by means of a personification of melancholy. The figure of Melancholy is clearly fashioned after Dürer's famous engraving *Melencolia I* that is, it is portrayed in the *caput manui innixus* gesture, and is holding a pair of compasses. The two exempla are also shown in the picture: Pliny is seen walking towards the crater and looking into it, while Empedocles has almost disappeared in the volcano. The figure of Melancholy is the pictorial allusion to the theory of the four humours, which is also referred to in the epigram. The cold limbs ('frigida membra') of Empedocles refer to a saturnine, melancholic disposition.[16] Melancholy represents both intellectual creativity and pathological destruction.[17]

Transforming Discourses

The anecdotes from ancient history figuring in the emblems derive from classical sources. They are moulded by the author into an emblematic discourse and thereby often set in a new moral context. Thus the rhetorical function of ancient history as a repository of ethical *exempla* can be gauged by comparing the emblematic *exemplum* to its classical sources. This becomes clear in the case of Pliny's death.

In Sambucus's emblem Pliny's death is said to be caused by scholarly curiosity. From the ancient source for this episode, Pliny the Younger's famous letter to Tacitus, a very different picture arises. At Tacitus's request he described in detail the course of events concerning his uncle's death during the eruption of Mount Vesuvius. Curious about the phenomenon of the fuming volcano, as his nephew relates,[18] Pliny set out in a galley to investigate the event. When he was asked to help people in danger, his exploration turned into a rescue operation.[19] At the same time, this did not prevent him from writing down all the peculiarities of the volcano's activity.[20] He died

---

[16] On the subject of melancholy and specifically Dürer's engraving, see Panofsky E. – Saxl F., *Dürers "Melencolia I". Eine Quellen- und Typengeschichtliche Untersuchung* (Leipzig: 1923).

[17] For a recent study of the reception of this melancholy theme as set out foremost by Ficino, see Tersch H., "Melancholie in Österreichischen Selbstzeugnissen des Späthumanismus. Ein Beitrag zur Historischen Anthropologie", *Mitteilungen des Instituts für Österreichische Geschichtsforschung* 105 (1-2) (1997) 130-55.

[18] Pliny, *Epistulae* VI, 16, 7.

[19] Ibid., VI, 16, 9.

[20] Ibid., VI, 16, 10.

eventually from suffocation; his body was found, completely intact, three days later.[21]

Pliny's behaviour is characterised by his nephew as brave and cool-headed. His courage, his lack of fear and panic are stressed.[22] One should note that Pliny's description for Tacitus is not necessarily a reliable historical report. It has to be regarded from a different rhetorical perspective. For him, this accident forms an excellent example of the virtue of his uncle, in addition to his work as a writer. In his writings, Tacitus will confirm the immortal fame of Pliny's uncle.[23]

Another, more complex example of the construction of history in emblems is *Sola culpa praestanda* (*One is only responsible for his guilt*) [fig. 4], specified by the subtitle "About the conviction of the poet Antiphon". This tragedian was said to be sentenced to death after insulting Dionysius, tyrant of Syracuse (430–367 BC). The epigram opposes the immortality of virtue to the mortality of man. Why should one be afraid of death, Sambucus asserts, if one has a clear conscience? Antiphon even addresses his friends in the epigram and rebukes them for their fear of death, a scene that alludes to the death of Socrates as described in the famous passage in Plato's *Phaedo*.[24] Socrates is also explicitly mentioned in the epigram (consequently, he seems to be the other prisoner in the *pictura* beside Antiphon). Sambucus uses Antiphon as a second Socrates to point at the relativity of death in the face of moral integrity. How did he shape this anecdote to illustrate the theme of moral responsibility?

The story of Antiphon is reported on two occasions by Plutarch in

---

[21] Ibid., VI, 16, 19-20.

[22] Cf. VI, 16, 10 'solutus metu' ('free from fear'); 'fortes Fortuna iuvat' ('Fortune assists the brave'); in VI, 16, 11 'utque timorem sua securitate leniret' ('so that he alleviated the fear by his calmness'); in VI, 16, 12 'cenatque hilaris aut, quod aeque magnum, similis hilari' ('and when eating he was cheerful, or, what is equally great, he seemed cheerful') and 'et apud illum quidem ratio rationem, apud alios timorem timor vicit' ('and indeed in him reason overcame reason, while in others fear prevailed over fear').

[23] Ibid., VI, 16, 2: 'Quamvis enim pulcherrimarum clade terrarum, ut populi, ut urbes, memorabili casu quasi semper victurus occiderit, quamvis ipse plurima opera et mansura conciderit, multum tamen perpetuitati eius scriptorum tuorum aeternitas addet' ('For notwithstanding he perished, as did whole peoples and cities, in the destruction of a most beautiful region, and by a misfortune memorable enough to promise him a kind of immortality; notwithstanding he has himself composed many and lasting works; yet I am persuaded, the mentioning of him in your immortal writings, will greatly contribute to eternize his name'); transl. W.M.L. Hutchinson, Loeb Classical Library (Cambridge, Mass.–London: 1923).

[24] Plato, *Phaedo* 117 C 5 – E 4.

different moral settings. The treatise *Quomodo adulator ab amico internoscatur* (*How to Tell a Flatterer from a Friend*) relates the anecdote in some
detail. At a convivial gathering Antiphon had been asked to give his
opinion on the matter of the best kind of bronze. Antiphon had
answered that he considered that bronze best 'from which they fashioned the statues of Harmodius and Aristogeiton at Athens'.[25] This
reference to the tyrannicides of Athens was a grave insult to Dionysius, who could only see it as a hidden condemnation of his own position. Antiphon serves here as an example of blunt behaviour. Honesty
and frankness are important virtues, but they should be combined
with tact. As Plutarch puts it: 'Let us purge away, as it were, and eliminate from our frankness all arrogance, ridicule, scoffing, and scurrili-
ty, which are the unwholesome seasoning of free speech'.[26] The
behaviour shown by Antiphon obviously lacked tact. It even showed
signs of arrogance, ὕβρις, and contempt, σκῶμμα, and is therefore to
be rejected.

In his work criticising the Stoics, *De stoicorum repugnantiis* (*Stoic Self-
Contradictions*), Plutarch mentions Antiphon in a different, perhaps
even opposite, moral context. Discussing the theme of the cause of evil
in the world, Plutarch observes a contradiction in the thought of the
Stoic philosopher Chrysippus (c. 281–c. 208 BC):

> Moreover, although he has often written on the theme that there is
> nothing reprehensible or blameworthy <in the> universe since all
> things are accomplished in conformity with the best nature, yet again
> there are places where he does admit instances of reprehensible negli-
> gence.[27]

The situation is compared by Chrysippus to the management of a large
household, where sometimes 'some husks get lost and a certain quantity of wheat also though affairs as a whole are well managed'. This comparison does not go down well with Plutarch. He denounces the comparison of 'husks that get lost [with] the accidents to upright and virtuous men such as were the sentence passed upon Socrates and the burning alive of Pythagoras by the Cyloneans and the torturing to death of

---

[25] Plutarch, *Moralia*, 68A (*Quomodo adulator ab amico internoscatur*); transl. H. Cherniss,
Loeb Classical Library (Cambridge, Mass.–London: 1976); cf. Plutarch, *Moralia*: 1051
C-D (*De Stoicorum repugnatione*). In the Pseudo-Plutarchean *Vitae decem oratorum Moralia*,
833 B-C and in Pilostratus's *Vitae sophistarum* I, 15, 3 Antiphon the tragician is mistak-
en for the rhetor Antiphon of Rhamnus.

[26] Plutarch, *Moralia*: 67 E (*Quomodo adulator ab amico internoscatur*).

[27] Plutarch, *Moralia*: 1051 B (*De Stoicorum repugnatione*).

Zeno by the tyrant of Demylus and of Antiphon by Dionysius'.[28] The four examples named by Plutarch should shatter Chrysippus's argument. Antiphon is mentioned here as an example of a morally upright man, victimised by a capricious tyrant. Since Antiphon is not the strongest example in the list of famous victims of 'heavenly negligence', men like Socrates and Pythagoras are named first, but his appearance in this sequence confirms his status as a virtuous man.

Sambucus seems to have been directly influenced by this passage in the *Stoic Contradictions*. In the emblem, Antiphon exemplifies an innocent, conscientious man, an independent, fearless poet-prophet who dares to criticise the immorality of tyranny and for this reason is sentenced to death. His fate is also in this aspect compared to that of Socrates: in the end the fame resulting from their actions may serve as comfort to those who are innocent victims.

Sambucus fits Plutarch's anecdote into an argument against the transient power of tyranny and in favour of perpetual truth.[29] The emblematist argues that a poet will attain immortal fame for telling the truth. The opposition between the virtuous poet and the unjust tyrant is emphasised here, not the way in which criticism should be presented, which was the main focus of Plutarch's *How to Tell a Flatterer from a Friend*. Considering that Antiphon's criticism of tyranny was the cause of his execution, one can even perceive a political statement in this emblem. Sambucus's portrayal of Antiphon as a truth-loving hero contains signs of a martyr victimised by censorship. This was as delicate in Europe during the 1560's as at the court of Dionysius. This political interpretation raises questions about the reasons for selecting these particular histories. This will be investigated in the next section.

Selection of Subjects: Why were these Histories Used?

An important criterion for selecting a particular story is the potential authority of the *exemplum*. This authority will depend on the moral Sambucus wants to convey and the audience he intends to address. We will first consider the criteria for selection in relation to the message Sambucus wanted to transmit.

---

[28] Ibid., 1051 C-D.
[29] Sambucus, 193: 'saeva tyrannis'; 'crudelia iussa tyranni'; 'vacuus vates'; 'tantus amor veri'.

A suitable example is the emblem with the Homeric motto *Οὐ χρὴ παννύχιον εὕδειν* etc. (*One should not sleep all night*) [fig. 5].[30] The poem contends that a (military) leader should only sleep lightly, that is, he should always be on his guard. Alexander the Great, for example, secured his vigilance by holding a ball above a bronze vessel, in order to wake himself when he fell asleep. Sambucus also mentions Julius Caesar of whom similar stories are told.

In the classical sources I have not found any reference to the story of Alexander holding a ball. The same act is, however, told about Aristotle by Diogenes Laertius in his *Life of Aristotle*.[31] Yet, there is the traditional topos of the *grus vigilans*, the vigilant crane: a crane watches over a crowd of fellow-cranes, while holding a stone in its feet.[32] The moment that it falls asleep, the falling stone wakes the bird.[33] It seems that in the emblem elements of two different stories have been merged and applied to the persona of Alexander.[34] The reason for this mix of elements is probably the extraordinary appeal of Alexander as a military leader. Alexander serves as a positive role model strengthening the argument for vigilance. In this way the emblem can be seen as an attempt to emulate the *grus vigilans*-theme. The substitution of the crane by Alexander provides a more immediately attractive example to the intended reader, who in this case may be the Emperor himself.

The logical counterpart to a positive role model is a negative one. This can be found in the emblem about Timon of Athens, called

---

[30] The scene in the *Iliad* from which the motto is derived, tells the story of Zeus sending a dream to Agamemnon to deceive him. This personified dream addresses the leader of the Greeks in the guise of old Nestor, saying: ʽ*εὕδεις, ᾽Ατρέος υἱὲ δαΐφρονος ἱπποδάμοιο; οὐ χρὴ παννύχιον εὕδειν βουληφόρον ἄνδρα, ᾧ λαοί τ᾽ ἐπιτετράφαται καὶ τόσσα μέμηλε!*ʼ (ʽYou're asleep, O son/Of fiery Atreus, breaker of horses. But to sleep/All night is not good for a man in charge of an army/And laden with so many cares' [Homer, *Iliad* II, 23-5, transl. E. Rees, Oxford: 1991²]).

[31] Diogenes Laertius, *De claropuum philosophorum vitis* V, 16.

[32] Apart from classical sources like Aristotle, Plutarch, Aelian and Pliny, the theme appears in Horapollo's *Hieroglyphica* II, 94 (ʽA man guarding himself against the plots of his enemies', ed. Boas, 1993³); see Erffa H.M. von, "Grus vigilans. Bemerkungen zur Emblematik", *Philobiblon* 1, 4 (1957) 297-304.

[33] Sambucus's emblem 200 (in the 1564 edition) shows the coat of arms of the author's family, consisting of two cranes together holding one stone, while they clasp a bracelet between their beaks. This emblem, entitled *In labore fructus* (*Fruits by labour*) plays with the association of vigilance, within the context of leading an industrious and virtuous life.

[34] The theme of Alexander as the ideal of a vigilant ruler is also expounded by J.P. Valerianus under the heading *custodia* in his *Hieroglyphica* (Basle: 1556) liber 17. Here Valerianus treats the image of the crane holding a stone.

Μισάνθρωπος Τίμων [fig. 6]. The emblem relates the story of Timon who avoided social contact with others and consequently denied himself medical help and died after falling over a pear tree.[35] In the epigram his misanthropy is presented as a disease caused by black bile. The addressee of the emblem, Girolamo Cardano, is advised to accept help from his friends when he needs it. Apart from this, Sambucus asks him to publish his treatise on dialectics. In the end Sambucus does not condemn all misanthropes, but distinguishes two sorts: they are either characterised as more god-like than other humans or as utter fools.[36] Here, as in the case of the Pliny *exemplum*, the ambiguous nature of melancholy is used to convey a specific moral. Melancholy can be a sign of divine talent and genius, but it can also show destructive sides and madness. Timon's unnecessary death is used as an illustration of the destructive character of melancholy. The reader should see this as a warning not to follow this example.

Positive and negative role models can be combined in the same emblem, as is the case in *Importuna adulatio* (*Improper flattery*) [fig. 7]. The epigram tells the story of the famous painter Apelles who painted a portrait of Alexander bearing a thunderbolt, an attribute exclusively used for Jupiter. This form of flattery upsets his colleague, the sculptor Lysippus, who consequently protests against such blasphemy and suggests the spear as a more proper attribute. The comment of the epigram argues that the signs of honour should befit the status of the person concerned. By showing his understanding of the order between man and god, Lysippus exemplifies moral integrity. Apelles, however, is characterised as a flatterer, *adulator*, a strongly pejorative term.[37]

Instead of authoritative role models, the author could also base his selection on the rhetorical force of humour. An example of this type of selection is *Ridicula ambitio* (*Ridiculous ambition*) [fig. 8]. The epigram relates the story of Hanno the Carthagian as told by Aelian in his *Varia historia*.[38] Hanno had taught some birds he kept in his house to call his

---

[35] Cf. *Suidae Lexicon*, ed. A. Adler (Leipzig: 1935) s.v. ἀπορεῶγας and Τίμων.

[36] Sambucus, *Emblemata*, 127: 'Quos nulla attingunt prorsus commercia, grato / Atque sodalitio, subsidiisque carent: / Aut Dii sunt proprii, aut falsus pervertit inanes / Sensus, ut hos stolidos, vanaque corda putes'.

[37] Flattery was vigorously condemned by Sambucus in *Cedendum, sed non adulandum* (*One should avoid, not flatter him*, = emblem 192 in the 1564 edition), where he compares the flatterer to the pest: 'Pestis adulator, morsque inimica siet' ('the flatterer is the pest and a hostile death').

name in praise. In this way he wanted to become famous wherever the birds would fly. But as soon as the birds were freed, they took up their old song again. In the picture we see Hanno portrayed as an old man, waving at the birds as they are flying out of his house. In the epigram the vanity of ambition is stressed. Sambucus urges the reader not to try to achieve fame by vain activities, because only virtue will last.

The comic effect of the story is anticipated in the adjective 'ridiculous' in the motto. This humorous aspect of the emblem is not free of moral implications. Although the reader can hardly accept any historical authority from Hanno as a role model, he is forced to laugh at the behaviour. The effect is the same as that of a negative role model.

Selection and Audience

The selection of *exempla* gives us interesting information about the type of audience the author intended to reach. One should distinguish two kinds. The primary audience is specified in dedications occurring in more than eighty of the emblems. Sometimes the person mentioned beneath the motto is also addressed in the epigram, as in the case of the Timon-emblem for Cardano. Consequently in these emblems the personal message is felt more strongly than in the emblems where this is not the case, like the Pliny-emblem. The publication of the emblem book, of which 1,250 copies were printed for the first edition,[39] presupposes at the same time a wider audience.

Evidently the Pliny-emblem playfully teaches a moral lesson to the scholarlily oriented reader. The figure of Pliny the Elder, the writer of the widely used encyclopedia *Naturalis historia*, could exert some historical authority on humanists. It is not surprising therefore to find that Johann Hartung (1505–1576), the addressee, was a member of this scholarly circle.[40] This professor of Greek at Freiburg University and his colleagues there — the *et ceteros* in the motto refers to Hartung's

---

[38] Aelian, *Varia historia* XIV, 30; Aelian's work consists of anecdotes in which the moral is made explicit each time. In this case, Aelian begins the story with a moral statement, indicating the direction in which the story should go: 'Hanno the Carthaginian in his arrogance was not prepared to accept the limitations of humanity'; transl. N.G. Wilson, Loeb Classical Library (Cambridge, Mass.–London: 1997).

[39] Rooses, "De Plantijnsche uitgaven", 8.

[40] Jöcher, C.G., *Allgemeines Gelehrten-Lexicon* (Leipzig: 1750) s.v., mentions that Hartung also fought against the Ottomans in Hungary, which would certainly have been appreciated by the Hungarian patriot Sambucus.

milieu — are likely to have appreciated the subtlety of the argument. Although the *exemplum* presents the addressees with a negative role model, it is a very attractive one. The melancholic genius of Pliny leaves the reader space for a positive identification. The warning against too much intellectual activity thus presupposes an acknowledgement of Hartung's scholarly capacities.

Antiphon represents the ethical conscience of a man of letters. Again the intended readership is constituted by the humanists of the Republic of Letters. The focus here is on the political attitude of a morally responsible individual. Personal responsibility is held to be more important than a stable political life. Keeping the delicate dependence of most humanists on patronage in mind,[41] this morally correct attitude may easily be challenged by more pragmatic behaviour.

The position of most members of the humanist community required a constant balancing of political dependence on the one hand and their intellectual and artistic thoughts on the other. Especially during the turbulent times of the religious conflicts in the second half of the sixteenth century, the margins within which humanists could express political opinions were narrow, as they were often employed by parties actively engaged in these conflicts.[42] Accentuating the primacy of virtue over death, Antiphon was meant to be seen as a comforting example of the relativity of their dependence.

The way Sambucus constructs his emblems in order to address a scholarly oriented audience modifies his explicit aim of teaching lessons. The historical exempla used by him are not merely illustrations of a moral message. The emblem also serves as a way of confirming friendship, expressing admiration and communicating erudition. Ancient history provided Sambucus with a rich repository of anecdotes which he could combine and vary to stress these aspects in his emblems.

---

[41] Cf. *Avaritia huius saeculi* (*The avarice of these times* = emblem 197 in the 1564 edition) dedicated to Marc-Antoine Muret, complaining about the lack of financial support from new Maecenases.

42 An illuminating example in this context is the pragmatic political attitude of Justus Lipsius compared to his self-fashioning in his autobiography; see Enenkel K., "Humanismus, Primat des Privaten, Patriotismus und Niederländischer Aufstand: Selbstbildformung in Lipsius' Autobiographie" in *Lipsius in Leiden, Studies in the Life and Works of a Great Humanist*, ed. K. Enenkel and C.L. Heesakkers (Voorthuizen: 1997) 13-42

Selective Bibliography

BARNI G.L., *Le lettere di Andrea Alciato Giureconsulto* (Florence: 1953)

DRYSDALL D.L., "Joannes Sambucus, *De Emblemate* (text and translation)", *Emblematica* 5, 1 (1991) 111-20

ENENKEL K., "Humanismus, Primat des Privaten, Patriotismus und Niederländischer Aufstand: Selbstbildformung in Lipsius' Autobiographie" in *Lipsius in Leiden, Studies in the Life and Works of a Great Humanist,* ed. K. Enenkel and C.L. Heesakkers (Voorthuizen: 1997) 13-42

ERFFA H.M. VON, "*Grus vigilans.* Bemerkungen zur Emblematik", *Philobiblon* 1, 4 (1957) 286-308

GERSTINGER H., "Johannes Sambucus als Handschriftensammler", in *Festschrift der Nationalbibliothek in Wien herausgegeben zur Feier des 200jährigen Bestehens des Gebäudes* (Vienna: 1926) 251-90

GERSTINGER H., *Die Briefe des Johannes Sambucus 1554–1584,* Sitzungsberichte der Österreichischen Akademie der Wissenschaften, Philologisch-Historische Klasse 255 (Vienna: 1968)

GILBERT F., "Renaissance interest in history" in *Art, Science, and History in the Renaissance,* ed. C.S. Singleton (Baltimore: 1967) 373-87

LANDFESTER R., *Historia magistra vitae. Untersuchungen zur humanistischen Geschichtstheorie des 14. bis 16. Jahrhunderts* (Geneva: 1972)

PANOFSKY E. – SAXL F., *Dürers "Melencolia I". Eine quellen- und typengeschichtliche Untersuchung* (Leipzig: 1923)

ROOSES M., "De Plantijnsche uitgaven van *Emblemata Joannis Sambuci*", *Het Boek. Tijdschrift voor Boek- en Bibliotheekwezen* 1 (1903) 3-15

SAMBUCUS J., *Emblemata cum aliquot nummis antqui operis* [...] (Antwerp: 1564). Fac-simile editions: Sambucus J., *Emblemata* [...] *Antverpiae 1564,* introd. A. Buck (Budapest: 1982) and Voet L. – Persoons G., *De emblemata van Joannes Sambucus* [...] *Reproductie van de Latijnse editie van 1564 en van de tekst van de Nederlandse vertaling van 1566 en van de Franse vertaling van 1567* (Antwerp: 1980–1982)

SCHOLER O., "Ein Text hart wie ein Diamant oder *De Emblemate* des Joannes Sambucus Tirnaviensis", *Études classiques, publiées par le Centre Universitaire de Luxembourg* 5 (1993) 69-209

STIERLE K., "Geschichte als Exemplum — Exemplum als Geschichte. Zur Pragmatik und Poetik narrativer Texte" in *Geschichte — Ereignis und Erzählung,* ed. R. Koselleck and W.-D. Stempel (Munich: 1973) 347-75

TERSCH H., "Melancholie in Österreichischen Selbstzeugnissen des Späthumanismus. Ein Beitrag zur Historischen Anthropologie", *Mitteilungen des Instituts für Österreichische Geschichtsforschung* 105 (1997) 130-55

VOET L., *The Plantin Press (1555–1589). A Bibliography of the Works printed and published by Christopher Plantin at Antwerp and Leiden,* 6 vols (Amsterdam: 1980–1983)

WATERSCHOOT W., "Lucas d'Heere und Johannes Sambucus" in *The Emblem in Renaissance and Baroque Europe. Tradition and Variety. Selected Papers of the Glasgow International Emblem Conference 13-17 August, 1990*, ed. A. Adams, A.J. Harper (Leiden: 1992) 45-52

WESSELING A., "Testing Modern Emblem Theory: the Earliest Views of the Genre (1564–1566)", in *The Emblem Tradition and the Low Countries. Selected Papers of the Leuven International Emblem Conference 18-23 August, 1996*, Imago Figurata, Studies 1b, ed. J. Manning – K. Porteman – M. Van Vaeck (Turnhout: 1999) 3-22

THE EMPEROR HADRIAN AS AN ARTIST
IN KAREL VAN MANDER'S *SCHILDER-BOECK**

Francesca Terrenato

Up to our present day the ineffable personality of the emperor Hadrian (who reigned from 117 to 138) has been the object of many inquiries and speculations. Contemporary scholars and writers have frequently underlined his 'humanistic' qualities as a statesman.[1] With his philhellenism he embodies the Graeco-Roman cultural unity, an ideal created to counter the disintegration of the empire. This is also reflected in his preoccupation with the defence of the borders and the administration of all the provinces of the empire.

Hadrian, first in a line of philosopher-emperors including also Marcus Aurelius, appears to us as an historical character enjoying a mostly favourable press: he is depicted as a man-at-arms who advocated peace, an indefatigable traveller interested in the culture and traditions of the Roman provinces, and a practising man of letters. Even if his early biographers condemned his ambition and jealousy, the volatility of his behaviour and his ruthlessness with domestic political enemies, on the whole in ancient literature he comes across as a positive character.

In the early modern period his life and deeds were recast in a number of works on Roman emperors. In these, a set of qualities for the righteous ruler were defined, converging in the tradition of the panegyrics of statesmen and of the *specula principis*.

That biographical practice is connected to the rise of individuality in the Renaissance is a historical commonplace which has its share of truth. The book market in those days was flooded with *vitae*. Biographies of medieval and early modern rulers were modelled on the lives of Roman and Greek statesmen, but the range of suitable characters, besides religious and political leaders, also included, as it

---

* Thanks to Karl Enenkel for his kind advice and help in the realisation of this paper, as well as to Jan de Jong and Paul Smith for their suggestions.

[1] See, on this subject, Mazzarino S., *L'Impero romano*, 2 vols (Bari–Rome: 1988) 316-34 and Calandra E., *Oltre la Grecia. Alle origini del filellenismo di Adriano* (Naples: 1996) 15-7; 163-6.

X V.

SIC GESTVRVS SVM PRINCIPATVM,
VT SCIAM REM POPVLI ESSE,
NON MEAM PRIVATAM.

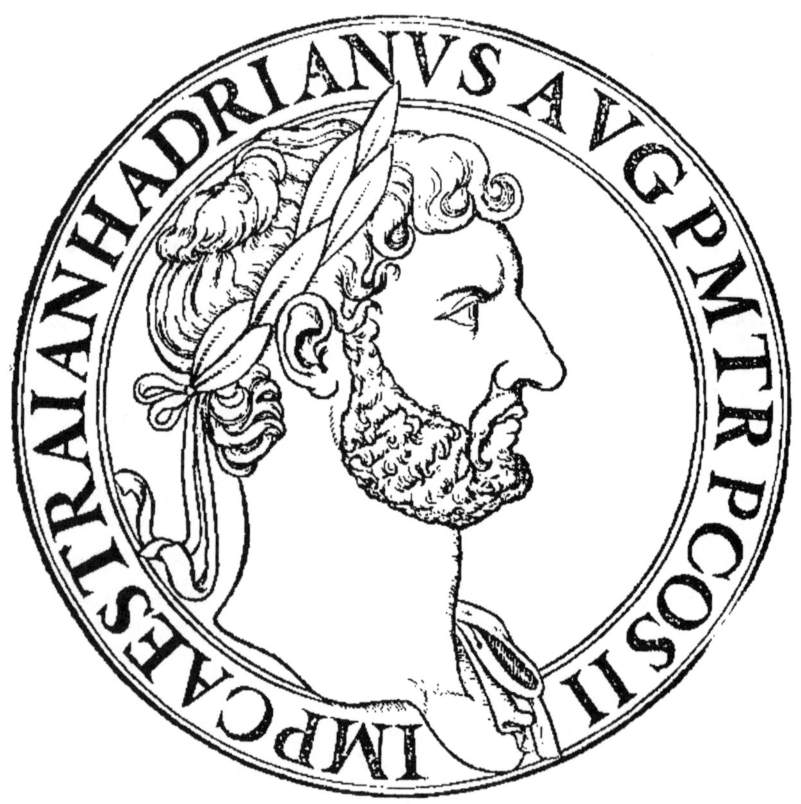

Cùm regnaſſet annis XXI. & vixiſſet LXII. interijt.

The Emperor Hadrian. Engraving by Hubert Goltzius. Idem, *Vivae omnium fere imperatorum imagines* (Antwerp: 1557).

did in earlier times, scholars and writers. Artists became part of this repertory with Vasari in Italy and Van Mander in the Low Countries.

The classic texts offered patterns of action, which, isolated and/or placed in new narratives, could be made available for the present and the future. It is in this cultural and literary context that the emperor Hadrian makes his rather unexpected appearance as an artist in a Renaissance work dealing with the art of painting and the painters: Karel van Mander's *Schilder-boeck* (*Book of Painting*, editio princeps Haarlem: 1603–1604). The unconventional characterisation of the philhellene emperor in this work provides a convenient example to illustrate the reshaping of a classical figure for a new audience. This paper will be devoted to reviewing the main ancient sources for Hadrian's biography, as well as the treatments of his life in two mid-sixteenth century collections, read in the light of the peculiar role he plays in the *Schilder-boeck*, which is a milestone in Dutch and Flemish art history.

Van Mander's *Schilder-boeck* contains, besides the more famous collection of the lives of Flemish, Dutch and German painters, a series of lives of ancient Greek and Roman painters, *Het leven der oude antijcke doorluchtige Schilders*. In the series, opening with Gyges (the first and only Egyptian painter), and closing with the Roman emperor Hadrian, all the material on ancient painters available at that time is arranged in the form of a collection of biographies, on the model of Vasari's *Le vite de' più eccellenti pittori, scultori e architetti* (Florence: 1550 and 1568). Information on the style and the works of the painters of Antiquity was derived by Van Mander mainly from Pliny's *Naturalis Historia*, though partly also from other sources, such as Plutarch's Βίοι Παράλληλοι (*Parallel lives*).[2] Book 35 of Pliny's work represents the most extensive source of information on Greek and Roman artists that has come down to us from Antiquity. All the ancient artists mentioned in the *Schilder-boeck* are treated in the *Naturalis Historia*, with one exception: Hadrian. His biography closes the section, thereby announcing

---

[2] The editions of the sources consulted by the author for this compilation have been identified and edited, together with a reprint of the original text in Mander K. van, *Het leven der oude antijcke doorluchtige Schilders*, ed. H. Miedema (Amsterdam: 1977). Miedema gives convincing evidence of the close connection between the biographies of ancient painters and passages in the works of Pliny, Plutarch, and the other sources. With regard to the *Life of Hadrian*, as we will see, the identification of the source used by Van Mander is more problematic.

the following one, on Italian painters, largely indebted to Vasari's work.

In his *Life of Hadrian*, Van Mander gives his interpretation of this historical character, focusing on his own field of interest. The title reflects the author's preoccupation with the artistic achievements of the emperor, apart from his political role: "Of Hadrian, fifteenth Roman emperor, painter, sculptor and poet".[3] It is in fact both his literary and his artistic talent that are highlighted, together with his other intellectual abilities:

> He was a man of great erudition, experienced in both languages, Latin and Greek, and talented and skilled in all arts and sciences. He was a good mathematician, geometer, astrologer, a very clever musician, and not ignorant in medicine. He was also a very accomplished writer of comedies, in which he employed with great rhetorical skill many striking sentences. He was an extraordinarily good painter, and he made many beautiful pieces with his hand, and he was unbelievably patient in his work [...]. He was also a good sculptor, and he made many beautiful statues, valuable and appreciable, in marble and copper.[4]

The description of Hadrian's artistic abilities is followed by the remark that the arts underwent a revival during his reign, as testified by Trajan's column, which Van Mander believes to have been erected by him (it was in fact erected in 113, when Trajan was still alive; Hadrian was only responsible for the placing of Trajan's bones at the base of the column).[5] A brief report of Hadrian's illness and death closes the biographical part proper of the text. The author then goes on to some general conclusions: it is known that some other emperors

---

[3] "Van Hadrianus, den 15en. Roomschen Keyser/Schilder/Beeldtsnijder/en Poeet", in Mander K. van, *Het Schilder-boeck* (Haarlem: 1603–1604) 90r, 43 - 90v, 38.

[4] 'was een Man van grooter gheleertheyt/ervaren in beide spraken/Griecx en Latijn/en in alle Consten en wetenschappen gheschickt en gheoeffent. Hy was goet Mathematicus, Geometrus, Astrologus, seer behendich Musicien/en in de Medecine niet onwetende. Een seer constigh Dichter van Cluchtspelen: in welcke hy veel treflijcke Sententien met groote welsprekendheyt te weghe bracht. Hy was een uytnemende goet Schilder/en heeft veel aerdighe stucken met zijner handt gedaen/en was in zijner arbeydt wonder verduldigh [...]. Hy was oock een goet Beeldtsnijder/en heeft van Marmer en Coper veel constighe Beelden ghedaen/die weerdigh en loflijck waren' (Van Mander, *Het Schilder-boeck*, 90v, 5-17).

[5] See Cassius Dio LXIX, 2, 3: Τὰ δὲ τοῦ Τραιανοῦ ὀστᾶ ἐν τῷ κίονι αὐτοῦ κατετέθη (*Dio's Roman History*, ed. E. Cary, Loeb Classical Library, 9 vols (London–Cambrige, Mass.: 1968), vol 8). For an early Latin translation and manuscripts circulating amongst early humanists see Bolgar R.R., *The Classical Heritage and its Beneficiaries* (Cambridge: 1963) 435 and 470.

and kings painted,[6] but being unable to mention specific works by them, Van Mander prefers to end the section dealing with ancient painters, ready to begin with the 'illustrious modern' Italian painters, who in their turn revived the arts.

The two main ancient sources for Hadrian's life are book 69 of Cassius Dio's *Roman History* and *De vita Hadriani* in the *Historia Augusta*. The *editio princeps* of the extant books of Dio's *Roman History* dates back to 1548, but lacks the treatment of Hadrian's reign, which could instead be found in the works of epitomizers. An edition which aimed at reconstructing the work as a whole is *Dionis Cassii Nicaee Romanae historiae libri (tot enim hodie extant) XXV. Nunc primum de Graecis Latini facti Guglielmo Xilandro interprete* [...] *additum est Ioannis Xiphilini e Dione Compendium Guil. Blanco Albiensi interprete* (Basle: 1558 and Lyon: 1559). In the sixteenth century Dio was also known through the *Suidas-Lexicon* (*editio princeps* Milan: 1499). Hadrian's life in the *Historia Augusta* had been printed in *Scriptores Historiae Augustae* (*editio princeps* Milan: 1475). Furthermore, both were combined in a compilation by Giorgio Merula,[7] in the edition of *Johannis Baptistae Egnatii Veneti De Caesaribus l[ibri] III*, printed by Aldus Manutius in Venice in 1516,[8] which also appeared two years later in Erasmus's edition of Suetonius and other authors.[9]

Cassius Dio worked on his 'Ρωμαικὴ ἱστορία (*Roman History*) in the period 200–222.[10] His strong commitment to the senatorial class and

---

[6] In the (unnumbered) page of *errata* which closes the biographical part of the *Schilder-boeck* Van Mander mentions Marcus Aurelius, the seventeenth Roman emperor, whose education, according to his biographer, included painting.

[7] Giorgio Merula (1430/31–1494), humanist and historiographer born in Alexandria, studied in Milan, and taught in Padua and Venice. He provided many editions of classical authors, Cicero and Plautus among them, and wrote the *Historia Vicecomitum* (unfinished) for the Duke of Milan, Lodovico il Moro.

[8] *Nervae et Traiani atque Adriani Caesarum Vitae* [...]. For a detailed list of editions of the *Historia Augusta* (many of them combined with Dio's lives of Nerva, Trajan and Hadrian) see Schweiger F.L.A., *Bibliographisches Lexicon der gesamten Literatur der Römer*, 2 vols (Leipzig: 1834; Amsterdam: 1962) I, 382-6. Schleier mentions a previous publication which I have not been able to find: *Index operum quae in hoc volumine continentur: Censorini de die natali liber aure(us)* [...], *Nervae Traianique et Adriani Caesaris vitae ex Dione in latinum versae: a Georgio Merula, Item Vesuvi montis conflagratio ex eodem Merula interprete, Cebetis Thebani tabula, Plutarchi libellus de differentia inter odium et invidiam, Basilii oratio de invidia, Basilii espistola de vita solitari* [...] (Milan: 1503), see Schleier R., *Tabula Cebetis oder "Spiegel des Menschlichen lebens/ darin Tugent und untugent abgemalet ist"* (Berlin: 1973) 16.

[9] *Suetonius (Caius) Tranquillus, ex recognitione Desiderii Erasmi Roterodami* [...] (Basle: 1517, 1518 and 1533).

[10] Cassius Dio was born in Bithynia between 155 and 164 AD.

his interest in the relationship between the emperor and the senate overshadows his preoccupation with historical accuracy; nevertheless, for emperors like Augustus, Hadrian and Severus, he refers to their own memoirs. The method followed by the historian to deal with the imperial age includes, as a deviation from the annalistic arrangement, the biographical technique: a collection of material dealing with the character and behaviour of the emperor is placed at the beginning and end of each reign. The illustrative section is quite extensive in Hadrian's case. From the point of view of the emperor's artistry, the relevant passage in Dio's description of the life and attitudes of Hadrian is the following:

> By nature he was fond of literary study in both the Greek and Latin languages, and has left behind a variety of prose writings as well as compositions in verse. For his ambition was insatiable, and hence he practised all conceivable pursuits, even the most trivial; for example, he modelled and painted, and declared that there was nothing pertaining to peace or war, to imperial or private life, of which he was not cognizant.[11]

The historian's opinion of Hadrian as a man and statesman is reasonably balanced between his qualities and his faults: these last, however, in particular envy, which caused his injustice towards learned and capable men, such as the architect Apollodorus, are more underlined than the first.

The other basic source for Hadrian's life is his biography contained in the *Historia Augusta*. As to the date and authorship (one author, anonymous, or many, as the text itself asserts) of this collection of emperors' lives, covering the years 117–284, the debate is still ongoing.[12] Programmatic statements in the *Historia Augusta* connect this work to that of Suetonius and other biographers (as opposed to the historians), and express a greater concern with accuracy in information than with style. In Hadrian's *vita* chronological framing is lacking, but neither has the alternative arrangement *per species* (categories) been

---

[11] Cassius Dio, *Roman History*, LXIX, 3, 1-2: Ῥύσει δὲ φιλολόγος ἐν ἑκατέρᾳ τῇ γλώσσῃ· καὶ τινα καὶ πεζὰ καὶ ἐν ἔπεσι ποιήματα παντοδὰ καταλέλοιπε. Φιλοτιμίᾳ τε γὰρ ἀπλήστῳ ἐχρῆτο, καὶ κατὰ τοῦτο καὶ τ᾽αλλα πάντα καὶ τὰ βραχύτατα ἐπετή δευε· καὶ γὰρ ἔπλασσε καὶ ἔγραφε καὶ οὐδὲν ὅτι οὐκ εἰρηνικὸν καὶ πολεμικὸν καὶ βασιλικὸν καὶ ἰδιωτικὸν εἰδέναι ἔλεγε᾽.

[12] Benario H.W., *A Commentary on the Vita Hadriani in the Historia Augusta* (Ann Arbor: 1980) summarizes the state of the question, and agrees with the option of a single author, who composed the work around 395 AD. The name of Aelius Spartianus, indicated as the author of Hadrian's life, would just be one of the pseudonyms used by the anonymous writer of the *Historia Augusta*. See Benario, *A Commentary on the Vita Hadriani*, 1.

consistently followed.[13] The combination of diverging traditions and sources results in an unmethodical juxtaposition of feats and anecdotes partly favourable, partly unfavourable to the emperor. Hadrian's life in the *Historia Augusta* offers a good example with regard to the shaping in literary form of the personality of the good (and the bad) prince. The passage dealing with Hadrian's erudition and artistic talent is counterbalanced by his criticism of those who surpassed him in knowledge and skill, as we read in these two passages:

> Hadrian was greatly interested in poetry and in letters. [...] In arithmetic, geometry, and painting he was very expert. Of his knowledge of flute-playing and singing he even boasted openly. [...] He wrote much verse about the subjects of his passion [...].[14] And although he was very deft at prose and at verse and very accomplished in all the arts, yet he used to subject the teachers of these arts, as though he were more learned than they, to ridicule, scorn, and humiliation.[15]

In sharp contrast with this attitude, the author of his biography reports that he also used to honour them. But the most prominent characteristic of the emperor, throughout this report, is his inconstancy. In the *virtue canon*[16] proposed throughout the *Historia Augusta*, which presents the emperors as specimens of the *princeps bonus*, the *princeps medius* or the *princeps malus*, Hadrian clearly straddles all of the categories.

Hadrian's biography was available in Latin in a number of editions after the late fifteenth century and by the middle of the sixteenth-century treatments in the vernacular also appeared. These were contained in collections of the lives of emperors, books generally intended to reinforce the idea of a continuity of the empire, from ancient to modern times, and to disseminate useful historical knowledge among a larger public. One of them is the Spanish *Historia imperial y cesárea* by Pedro

---

[13] See Benario, *A Commentary on the Vita Hadriani*, 3.

[14] 'Fuit enim poematum et litterarum nimium studiosissimus, [...] arithmeticae, geometriae, picturae peritissimus. Iam psallendi et cantandi scientiam prae se ferebat. [...] Nam et de suis dilectis multa versibus composuit' (*De vita Hadriani*, 14, 8-9; I used the edition *Scriptores Historiae Augustae*, with an English transl. by D. Magie, Loeb Classical Library, 3 vols (London–Cambridge, Mass.: 1953)).

[15] 'Et quamvis esset oratione et versu promptissimus et in omnibus artibus peritissimus, tamen professores omnium artium semper ut doctior risit, contempsit, obtrivit' (*De vita Hadriani*, 15, 10-1).

[16] 'Tugend-Kanon'; see Scheithauer A., *Kaiserbild und literarisches Programm. Untersuchungen zur Tendenz der Historia Augusta* (Frankfurt a. M.–Bern–New York–Paris: 1987) 24.

Mexía (Seville: 1497–1551).[17] Printed for the first time in Seville in 1545, the book, reprinted many times in Spain, also appeared in an Italian translation in Venice in 1558. It is a compilation containing the lives of emperors from Julius Caesar to Maximilian I, grandfather of Charles V, dedicated to prince Philip but meant as a propitiatory gift for Charles, who in fact designated Mexía as imperial chronicler in 1548. A learned humanist, Mexía consulted a wide range of sources, dutifully listing them at the end of each biography, together with the names of illustrious men and the popes who lived under the reign of the various emperors. The connection established between Charles V and the ancient and medieval Roman empire provides 'an historical argument for the justification of the absolutist form of government of this monarch'.[18] At the same time, the dedication of the *Historia imperial* to the prince, the future Philip II, reminds us of the didactic function that such collections of historical examples exerted. The tradition of the *speculum principis* mingles here with biographical art.

In Mexía's *Historia imperial y cesárea*, the two Spanish emperors, Trajan and Hadrian, are both honoured with a long and laudatory biography. Trajan's kindness, wisdom and liberality are great, but he lacks erudition. His successor combines virtue and knowledge. Hadrian's intellectual qualities (together with the reference to his artistic practice) are described as follows: 'He was very learned in both languages, Latin and Greek, and wrote and composed in verse and in prose', and, besides his musical talent and his knowledge of mathematics, geometry, astrology and medicine, he also 'drew and painted as the most knowledgeable practitioner of that art'.[19] Miedema identifies this as the source of Van Mander's life of Hadrian, as the material's arrangement is close to that followed by the *Schilder-boeck*'s author. Van Mander's life of Hadrian diverges from Mexía's treatment in sev-

---

[17] Information on the life and the works of this Spanish humanist is to be found in Mexía, *Silva de varia lección*, 9-52. See also Bataillon M., *Erasme et l'Espagne*, 3 vols (Geneva: 1991, first ed.: 1937) I, 678-9; Praag J.A. van, "Sobre la fortuna de Pedro Mejía", *Revista de filología hispanica* 19 (1932) 288-92; Costes R., "Pedro Mexía, chroniste de Charles-Quint", *Bulletin Hispanique* 22 (1920) 1-36; Morel-Fatio A., *Historiographie de Charles-Quint* (Paris: 1913) 75.

[18] 'Un argomento histórico para justificar la fórmula absolutista de gobierno de esto monarca' in Mexía, *Silva de varia lección*, ed. A. Castro (Madrid: 1989) 40.

[19] 'muy docto en ambas lenguas, Latina y Griega, y escriuio y compuso en verso y en prosa'; 'debuxaua y pintaua como el que mas sabio artifice era de équel arte' (Mexía P., *Historia imperial y cesárea* (Seville: 1542) 65v). The passage is reprinted in Mander K. van, *Het leven der oude antijcke doorluchtige Schilders*, page opposite to 90v.

eral respects, however, some of which cannot even be ascribed to a direct knowledge of the ancient sources.

An interesting detail: the 1558 Italian translation of the *Historia imperial y cesaréa*,[20] which is a relatively accurate rendering of the original, was provided by Lodovico Dolce, author of the famous *L'Aretino, o dialogo della pittura* (*The Aretino, or dialogue on painting*) (Venice: 1557). In this dialogue Hadrian is mentioned notably as an historical *exemplum* of a great man who cherished and practised the arts.[21] Roskill, in his study on Dolce, underlines the singularity of this appearance, for none of the other well-known and influential fifteenth and sixteenth-century Italian writers on the arts (Alberti, Paolo Pino, Castiglione, Vasari) ever mentions Hadrian's name.[22]

Mexía's biography of Hadrian was not unique in the contemporary literature. A written portrait of the emperor is contained in a work by the Flemish numismatist and engraver Hubertus Goltzius (1525–1583),[23] *Vivae omnium fere imperatorum imagines*.[24] The book was printed in Antwerp in 1557 in three different editions — Latin, Italian and German — and is dedicated, like Mexía's *Historia*, to Philip, king of Spain, who later designated Goltzius as court historian and court painter. The series, which extends from Julius Caesar to Charles V and his brother, Ferdinand, includes engraved portraits, in the form of a large medal or coin, coupled with biographical notices.

This *Vivae omnium fere imperatorum imagines*, and the flourishing production of numismatic works at that time deserve a closer look. Hubertus

---

[20] *Le Vite di tutti gl'Imperadori da Giulio Cesare insino a Massimiliano, tratte per M. Lodovico Dolce dal libro spagnuolo del nobile Cavaliere Pietro Messia* [...] (Venice: 1558). A second Venetian edition appeared in 1561, containing the *Life of Charles V* by Dolce.

[21] See Dolce L., *Dialogo di pittura intitolato l'Aretino* (first edition Venice: 1557), in *Trattati d'arte del Cinquecento. Fra Manierismo e controriforma*, ed. P. Barocchi, 3 vols (Bari: 1960–1962) I, 160.

[22] See Roskill M.W., *Dolce's 'Aretino' and Venetian Art Theory of the Cinquecento* (New York: 1968) 257. Other emperors, such as Nero, Valentinianus and Alexander Severus are mentioned as lovers and practitioners of painting in Alberti L. B., *De pictura* (Rome–Bari: 1975; first edition Basle: 1540) II, 27 and in Lomazzo G. P., *Trattato della pittura*, in *Scritti d'arte del Cinquecento*, ed. P. Barocchi (Milan–Naples: 1971–1977) III, 430-8.

[23] On the life and works of Hubertus Goltzius (or Goltz) see: Mander K. van, *The Lives of the Illustrious Netherlandish and German Painters*, ed. H. Miedema, 5 vols (Doornspijk: 1994ff.), I (1994) I, 247v-9r; IV, 100-8; Dekesel C.E., *Hubertus Goltzius. The Father of Ancient Numismatics. Venlo-Weertsburg 30.10.1526–Bruges 24.10.1583* (Ghent: 1988) (with bibliography on 197-213); Loup W. Le, *Hubertus Goltzius en Brugge 1583-1983*, catalogue of the exposition at Gruuthuse-museum (Bruges: 1984).

[24] Quoted here is the Latin edition; the Italian edition has been consulted too.

Goltzius, uncle of the engraver Henricus Goltzius, had inherited from his master Lambert Lombard an antiquarian passion. In the sixteenth century coin collecting was a growing field of interest, and Goltzius visited local collections (among which that of the cartographer Ortelius), to produce his portraits of emperors. The *Imagines* was the first book of its kind to be produced in the Low Countries, although other numismatic works appeared in France, Germany, and Italy around 1550.[25] In the following years, during which his book was translated into French and Spanish, Goltzius visited collections abroad, and produced more works which combined historical reports with engravings based on coins and medals. From 1558 on, he collaborated with Marcus Laurinus, Lord of Watervliet (1530–1581).[26] Laurinus was not only his patron, but also probably the author of the texts of the series of books on Roman history illustrated by Goltzius in the following years: *C. Julius Caesar* (Bruges: 1563); *Fasti magistratuum et triumphorum Romanorum* (Bruges: 1566), *Caesar Augustus* (Bruges: 1575). The preparation and publication of the *Imagines* however, antedated the meeting and agreement between the numismatist and his learned patron. We might, therefore, consider Goltzius himself as the author of the biographies contained in the *Imagines*, as the title page suggests: in it we read that Hubertus Goltzius, painter, dedicates to King Philip both the images and the 'lives, acts, habits, virtues, vices, depicted in their own colours with historical brush' ('vitae, acta, mores, virtutes, vitia, suis coloribus historico penicillo delineatae'). The author states in the dedication the double aim of the book, which both glorifies the Holy Roman Empire, and is at the same time profitable and useful for antiquarians. An introduction describes the origins and the republican period of Rome. In an appendix, at the end of the book, Goltzius gives a list of the authors he used in his compilation: Dio and Aelius Spartianus (indicated as the author of *De vita Hadriani* in the *Historia Augusta*) are among these, together with another eighty ancient and modern authors. Goltzius has freely elaborated on both the standard ancient sources for Hadrian's life.

---

[25] Guillaume Rouillé's *Promptuaire des medailles* (Lyon: 1553), Jacopo Strada's *Epitome du Thrésor des Antiquitez* (Lyon: 1553), Guillaume du Choul's *La Religion des anciens romains* (Lyon: 1555–1556), Enea Vico's *Discorsi sopra le medaglie degli antichi* (1555) immediately preceded the publication of Goltzius's *Imagines*. See Haskell F., *History and its Images. Art and the Interpretation of the Past* (New Haven: 1993) 14. For more information about the first generation of numismatic works, see the whole chapter "The Early Numismatists", 13-25.

[26] See De la Fontaine Verwey, "The first private press in the Low Countries", 294-310.

Goltzius's treatment of Hadrian's life[27] has its peculiarities. In the first part, dealing with the intellectual qualities and habits of the emperor, we read that he 'embellished his writings and comedies with beautiful sentences' ('qui scripta sua ac Comoedias venustis gravibusque sententiis, verbisque elegantibus ornarit'). The emperor's pictorial activity is particularly underlined ('tantum denique a pictura et sculptura valuit, ut ipse plurimas imagines sua manu depinxerit'), as well as his ability as a sculptor ('et quadam etiam in aere ac lapide artificiose caelaverit'). In the beginning of his reign, reports Goltzius, he erected Trajan's column ('columnam altitudinem pedum centum et quadraginta exstruxit. [...] Hanc exstrinsecus praeclare Traiani gestis exornavit'). The biography continues with a report of the political activity and journeys of the emperor. In connection with the Jewish rebellion Hadrian had to cope with, it is asserted that he protected the Christians. Furthermore, his *moles* and the bridge on the Tiber (*Pons Aelius*) are presented as examples of the grand architectural works realised under his reign.

The text pertaining to Hadrian's portrait shows a closer correspondence with Van Mander's life of the emperor than any other previously analysed. The emperor's resiliency ('laboris patiens fuit'), noted by Goltzius in regard to his frequent journeys, is applied by Van Mander to his artistic activity, as well as his retentive memory ('memoriae fuit tenacis'). Having been to Rome himself, Van Mander develops the description of the column with an explanation of the *gesta* represented in the bas-relief: Trajan's victories against Parthians, Dacians and Germans, and other peoples. The named cause of death is the same in Goltzius's ('in diutinum morbum incidit, tandemque hydropicus vita decessit') and in Van Mander's treatment.[28] The *Imagines* is briefly described in the fourth section of the *Schilder-boeck*, dedicated to Northern painters, together with other numismatic-historical works by Goltzius. Van Mander clearly expresses his appraisal of Goltzius's books, although no mention is made of them as a source. The thematic and formal correspondence between the two texts testifies to the fact that Van Mander had direct

---

[27] Goltzius H., *Vivae omnium fere Imperatorum imagines, a C. Julio Caes. usque ad Carolum V ex antiquis veteribus numismatis adumbratae* (Antwerp: 1557) C3v. Hadrian's portrait is on the opposite page, C4r.

[28] It merits attention that a mistake which also remained unnoticed in the errata, occurs in these lines of the *Schilder-boeck*: the text reads *Trajanus* instead of *Hadrianus*; this is probably due to the discussion of Trajan's column in the preceding lines.

knowledge of this book.[29] Possibly inspired by Dolce's mention of Hadrian among the artist-emperors, and surely by the presence of explicit reference to Hadrian's artistic activities in Goltzius's work, he decided to introduce Hadrian as an *artifex doctus*, whose life would represent a worthy conclusion for the *Schilder-boeck*'s section on ancient painters.

A ruler educated in all the liberal arts and actively practising painting and sculpture, such as Hadrian, represents an excellent exemplar for Van Mander who, like his predecessor Vasari, strives to include the art of painting among the noble disciplines. The curriculum of a great master such as Dürer,[30] for instance, follows almost the same pattern. The capacity to come up with striking sentences, one of the intellectual abilities of the emperor, is also a typical trait of the witty artist. Throughout the *Schilder-boeck* many are the quotations of wise or humorous answers given by the artist to the ignorant or disrespectful colleague, commissioner or merchant. Eloquence is an ability Van Mander associates with good manners and erudition.[31] The other qualities of the emperor, patience and tenacious memory, also recur in the lives of the Northern masters.[32]

By including an emperor among the practitioners Van Mander confirms and underlines a recurring theme in his treatment of ancient painting: the dignity attached to pictorial practice in antiquity. In his *Life of Pamphilus* Van Mander reminds us that drawing was at that time taught to the children of noble families, while the practice of all kinds of figurative arts was forbidden to the lower classes and slaves.[33] This in turn becomes an argument against those who, in his times, still considered painting vile manual work. Hadrian is in fact also cited in the fourth section of the *Schilder-boeck*, in the life of Anthonis Blocklandt. Here Van Mander tells of a disciple of his, a young nobleman, a very good portraitist, who refuses to bear this name as dishonourable:

---

[29] It is true, as Miedema suggests, that Van Mander's erroneous conviction that the *Caesar Augustus* comprised two volumes gives rive to the suspicion that he collected information on Goltzius's books without having seen them. He might, indeed, have seen and read just the *Imagines*. For the relevant passage in the text see Van Mander, *The Lives* I, 248r, 38; for Miedema's comment see Van Mander, *The Lives* III, 100-3.

[30] See Van Mander, *The Lives* I, 208v, 1-5.

[31] See Van Mander *The Lives* I, 231v, 1-2; 244v, 21-2.

[32] Patience and memory are among the qualities of Hubert van Eyck sung in the ode to the *Lam Gods* by Lucas d'Heere in Van Mander, *The Lives* I, 201v, 22. See also 219v, 12-4; 171v, 43-5; 285v, 15-7.

[33] See Van Mander, *Het Schilder-boeck*, 72r, 18-35.

being of a different feeling and opinion than the illustrious old noble family of the Fabii, who so proudly wore the name Painter as a beautiful ornament[...]. Not to talk of the knight Turpilius, the emperor Hadrian, and others, who sought to attach illustrious fame to their families and names with the brush.[34]

Hadrian serves as an exemplar not only with regard to artistic practice but also with regard to the role of kings and rulers as patrons: Trajan's column is presented as a testimony of Hadrian's love for the arts. The theme of the art-loving and expert Maecenas recurs in the *Schilder-boeck*. Patronage governing artistic production and the art market is less developed in the Low Countries than in contemporary Italy and in ancient Greece and Rome: Hadrian embodies the ideal relationship between authority and the arts, one which is often focused on in the book.[35]

Hadrian's appearance in the *Schilder-boeck* finds its motivations, as we have seen, in the context of Van Mander's *magnificatio* of painting. Biographical information was chosen and rearranged for a specific purpose, developing one of the aspects of the emperor's manifold personality; his exemplarity loses its political value to acquire an artistic one. We have thus isolated just some moments in the long and complex evolution of this character in history and art literature: this description presents an example of how past experience can profitably be 'recycled' for present needs.

Appendix: Hubertus Goltzius, Vivae omnium fere imperatorum
imagines *(Antwerp: 1557) C3v*

Hadrianus, Traiani consobrinus, ab eodemque adoptatus, Imperator eligitur ab Senatu Populoque Rom[ano] anno post Christum natum centesimo decimonono. Vir fuit hic magnae erudtionis, atque adeo Romanus; qui id semper operam dedit, ut modis omnibus Athenienses imitarentur. Ornamentum sese praebuit utriusque linguae, Graecae ac Latinae; et poetam eiusmodi, qui scripta sua ac Comoedias venustis gravibusque sententiis, verbisque quam

---

[34] 'anders van sin en ghevoelen wesende/als t'heerlijck oudt Roomsch gheslacht der edel Fabij, die den naem Schilder tot een pracht en cieraet soo moedigh voerden. [...] Ick laet dan staen den ridder Turpilius, keyzer Adrianus, en ander/die door den Pinceel hun gheslacht en naem hebben ghesocht eerlijck gherucht by te voeghen' (Van Mander, *The Lives* I, 255r, 16-21).

[35] See the pages devoted to this subject in Miedema H., *Kunst, kunstenaar en kunstwerk bij Karel van Mander. Een analyse van zijn levensbeschrijvingen* (Alphen a.d. Rijn: 1981) 251-84 (particularly 251, 254-6, 259-60).

elegantibus plurimum ornarit; atque id quidem Graece praecipue, adeo ut Graeculus vulgo appellatus sit. In respondendo atque interrogando adeo fuit promptus, adeo acutus, ut ad graviter interrogata graviter etiam responderit; ad iocose item iocose, ac breviter, sic sua responsa temperarit, ut vel ex tempore ad quaevis interrogata promptissime responderit, non aliter atque si singula diligenter praemeditatus fuisset. In omni disciplinarum genere plurimum fuit exercitatus, mathematicus insignis, astrologus et geometra acutissimus, musicus, ac medicinae minime ignarus. Tantum denique a pictura et sculptura valuit, ut ipse plurimas imagines sua manu depinxerit, et quasdam etiam in aere ac lapide artificiose caelaverit. Rarum quiddam profecto fuit, et quod nemo non alienum ab huiusmodi homine putaret. Supra quam credibile cuiquam est, laboris patiens fuit, ut qui regiones ac civitates ipse frequentissime peregrarit. Memoriae adeo fuit tenacis, ut quo quid loco et tempore gestum fuisset, nominaque singulorum absentium militum, facile meminisset. Circa initium principatus, auctoritate Senatus Populique, columnam altitudine pedum centum et quadraginta extruxit, quae etiamnum hodie superest. Hanc extrinsecus praeclare Traiani gestis exornavit, cuius etiam busta sub eadem recondidit, referens ipsum inter Divos: locumque in quo columnam istam statuerat, forum appellavit Divi Traiani. Sub id temporis incommodissima in Africa seditio passim inter Iudaeos pullulabat, qui tantam multitudinem in Libya, Aegypto et Alexandria interemerunt, ut nisi Adrianus aliunde secum qui agros colerent eo advexisset, terra inculta ac plane deserta permansisset. Postquam vero miserabilem istam seditionem composuisset, ac penitus extinxisset, Athenas in Graeciam profectus est, ibique leges suas et statuta renovavit; Atheniensibus leges Solonis ac Draconis, ut petierant, confirmavit. Cumque isthic hyemaret, obtulerunt ipsi Quadratus atque Aristides (qui Apostolorum fuerant discipuli) libros quosdam in Christianae religionis defensionem a sese conscriptos, inter quos et Apologetici aliqui fidei christianae eidem oblati fuere. His autem commotus ac iam aliquantulum in fide Christiana eruditus, probeque in iisdem per Serenum Gravium, legatum suum, instructus, rescripsit indignum esse Christianos religionis causa passim occidi; effectusque est ea instructione mirus fautor Christianorum. Scripsit ad Asiae Proconsulem Minutium Fondanum literas, quibus ne deinceps Christiani comprehenderentur, nisi aliorum scelerum rei testibus convicti, mandavit. Quum vero Cothebas, Iudaicae factionis princeps, patriam suam caedibus contaminaret, ac Christianos variis multisque cruciatibus insequeretur, eo quod arma adversus Romanus movere nolebant, Adrianus omnes passim Iudaeos interfici curavit, iussitque ne Iudaeorum cuiquam aditus ad Hierosolymam pateret donavitque civitatem moenibus probe munitam Christianis, eam de suo praenomine Aeliam appellans. Deinde necessitate compulsus, in Sarmatas, qui iam ab Imperio desciverant, expeditionem paravit: quibus post multa bella devictis, profectus est in Germaniam et Galliam, ubi illud summopere conatus est, ut paci potius quam bello consuleretur; studuitque milites in ea expeditione magis in officio continere, quam ut armis quicquam tentarent. Posteaquam iam regiones et provincias omnes pacatas tranquillasque fecisset, maximo sane triumpho Romam reversus a Senatu Populoque *Pater patriae* salutatus est, uxorque eius Sabina *Augusta* nominata.

Atque ita quidem pace terra marique parta, Romam magnificis multisque aedificiis deinceps ornare aggressus, quorum etiamnum hodie quaedam supersunt, Castrum videlicet Angelicum, quod Moles Adriani dicitur; et pons quidam, quem etiam nunc Pontem Aelium appellamus. Hac tempestate res Romanae in summo loco fuerunt constitutae. Reges enim magno pacem ad Adriano redimebant; ita ut hinc ille saepenumero dicere solitus est, plura se in otio fuisse consecutum, quam armis et caedibus potuerant alii. Hic ergo ubi orbem universum civitatemque Romam legibus ac constitutionibus late exornasset, in diutinum morbum incidit, tandemque hydropicus in fata concessit. Et quia Imperio Rom[ano] ab omnibus Princeps facile utilissimus eorum qui ab Augusti temporibus usque fuerant habitus erat, inter optimos Caesares relatus est.

Selective Bibliography

ALBERTI L. B., *De pictura* (Rome–Bari: 1975; first edition Basle: 1540)

BATAILLON M., *Erasme et l'Espagne*, 3 vols (Geneva: 1991, first edition: 1937)

BENARIO H.W., *A Commentary on the Vita Hadriani in the Historia Augusta* (Ann Arbor: 1980)

BERSCHIN W., "Sueton und Plutarch im 14. Jahrhundert", in *Biographie und Autobiographie in der Renaissance*, ed. A. Buck (Wiesbaden: 1983) 35-43

CALANDRA E., *Oltre la Grecia Alle origini del filellenismo di Adriano* (Naples: 1996).

CASTRO A., Introducción, in P. Mexía, *Silva de varia lección*, ed. A. Castro (Madrid, 1989)

COSTES R., "Pedro Mexía, chroniste de Charles-Quint", *Bulletin Hispanique* 22 (1920) 1-36.

De Vita Hadriani Aelii Spartiani, in *Scriptores Historiae Augustae*, with an English translation by D. Magie, 3 vols (London–Cambridge, Mass.: 1953), I

De Vita Hadriani Aelii Spartiani, in *Scrittori della Storia Augusta*, ed. P. Soverini, 2 vols (Torino: 1983) I, 134-227

DIHLE A., "Antike Grundlagen", in *Biographie zwischen Renaissance und Barock. Zwölf Studien*, ed. W. Berschin (Heidelberg: 1993) 1-22

DIO CASSIUS, *Dio's Roman History*, ed. E. Cary, 9 vols (London–Cambridge, Mass.: 1968), LXIX (vol 8)

DOLCE L., *Dialogo di pittura intitolato l'Aretino* (first edition Venice: 1557), in *Trattati d'arte del Cinquecento. Fra Manierismo e controriforma*, ed. P. Barocchi, 3 vols (Bari: 1960–1962)

EBERHARDT O., *Der Fürstenspiegel Smaragds von St. Michiel und seine literarische Gattung* (Munich: 1977) 267-320

GENTILI B. – CERRI G., *Storia e biografia nel pensiero antico* (Bari: 1983) 65-108

GOLTZIUS H., *Vivae omnium fere Imperatorum imagines, a C. Julio Caes. usque ad Carolum V ex antiquis veteribus numismatis adumbratae* (Antwerp: 1557)

GREVE H.E., *De bronnen van Carel van Mander voor 'Het leven der Doorluchtige Nederlandtsche en Hoogduytsche Schilders'* (The Hague: 1903) 104-8

HAMPTON T., *Writing from History. The Rhetoric of Exemplarity in Renaissance Literature* (Ithaca–London: 1990)

HASKELL F., *History and its Images. Art and the Interpretation of the Past* (New Haven: 1993)

HENDRICKS W.T.M., "Hubertus Goltzius van Venlo, schilder, graveur, geschiedschrijver, drukker en numismaticus. 1526–1583", *Spiegel der Historie* 3 (1968) 322-5

LOMAZZO G. P., *Trattato della pittura*, in *Scritti d'arte del Cinquecento*, ed. P. Barocchi (Milan–Naples: 1971–1977)

LOUP W. LE, *Hubertus Goltzius en Brugge 1583–1983*, catalogue of the exposition at Gruuthuse-museum (Bruges: 1984)

MANDER K. VAN, *Het Schilder-boeck* (Haarlem: 1603–1604)

MANDER K. VAN, *Het leven der oude antijcke doorluchtige Schilders*, ed. H. Miedema (Amsterdam: 1977)

MANDER K. VAN, *The Lives of the Illustrious Netherlandish and German Painters*, ed. H. Miedema, 5 vols (Doornspijk: 1994ff.), I (1994), 247v-9r; IV (1997) 100-8

MAZZARINO S., *L'Impero romano*, 2 vols (Bari–Rome: 1988), I, 316-34

MEXÍA P., *Historia imperial y cesaréa* (Seville: 1542)

MEXÍA P., *Vite di tutti gl'imperadori romani, composte in lingua spagnuola da Pietro Messia et da M. Lodovico Dolce nuovamente tradotte e ampliate[…] alle quali da Girolamo Bardi Fiorentino[…] sono state in questa quinta impressione agiunte le vite di Ferdinando Primo e di Massimiliano Secondo Imperadori* (Venice: 1578; first edition Venice: 1558)

MIEDEMA H., *Kunst, kunstenaar en kunstwerk bij Karel van Mander. Een analyse van zijn levensbeschrijvingen* (Alphen a.d. Rijn: 1981)

MILLER F., *A Study of Cassius Dio* (Oxford: 1964) 60-72

MONBALLIEU A., "De schilderscarrière van Hubertus Goltzius (1526–1583)", *Jaarboek van het Koninklijke Museum voor Schone Kunsten Antwerpen* 1984 203-18

MOREL-FATIO A., *Historiographie de Charles-Quint* (Paris: 1913) 73-5; 148-51

NARDONI D., *La Colonna Ulpia Traiana* (Rome: 1986)

PFLAUM H.-G., "Le valeur de la source inspiratrice de la vita Hadriani et de la vita Marci Antonini à la lumière des personnalités contemporaines nommément citées", in *Historia-Augusta-Colloquium* (Bonn: 1970) 173-232

PLEW J., *Quellenuntersuchungen zur Geschichte des Kaisers Hadrian* (Strasbourg: 1890)

PLUTARCH, *Les Vies des hommes illustres, traduites du grec de Plutarque, par J. Amyot*, Nouvelle ed. (Paris: 1826) I, CXLIII-CLXX

PRAAG J.A. VAN, "Sobre la fortuna de Pedro Mejía", *Revista de filología hispanica* 19 (1932) 288-92

PRICE ZIMMERMANN T.C., "Paolo Giovio and the Rhetoric of Individuality", in *The Rhetorics of Life-Writing in Early Modern Europe*, ed T.F. Mayer – D.R. Woolf (Ann Arbor: 1995) 39-62

ROSKILL M.W., *Dolce's 'Aretino' and Venetian Art Theory of the Cinquecento* (New York: 1968)

SCHLEIER R., *Tabula Cebetis oder "Spiegel des Menschlichen lebens/ darin Tugent und untugent abgemalet ist"* (Berlin: 1973)

SCHWEIGER F.L.A., *Bibliographisches Lexicon der gesamten Literatur der Römer*, 2 vols (Leipzig: 1834; Amsterdam: 1962).

TYRANT OR STOIC HERO?
MARC-ANTOINE MURET'S *JULIUS CAESAR*

Jan Bloemendal

The figure of Julius Caesar has appealed to the imagination for many centuries. The end of his life has contributed to this considerably. The general who had conquered all Europe, the victor of the civil war, the dictator at the height of his power, vilely stabbed by a group of conspirators, among them Brutus, so favoured and supported by him — it is indeed a moving story. Its attraction is heightened even further by the moralising interpretations that seemed to be ready at hand, for instance "Pride will lead to a fall", or "Do not revolt against lawful authorities". Dramatists especially liked the story of the murder: it offered a tragic conflict between two powerful personalities, Caesar and Brutus. There was a clash that could easily be raised to a general level: monarchy could be opposed to tyranny or to republicanism, clemency to rigour, good to evil. Furthermore, there were certain elements that must have appealed to a dramatist: a dream, omens, prophecies and a deification. Shakespeare wrote one of his most famous dramas on this theme, and the French dramatists Jacques Grévin and Robert Garnier, among others, treated the story which itself was famous enough, since Caesar was one of the *Nine Worthies*.[1]

---

[1] A survey of the images of Caesar during the centuries is given by Christ K., *Caesar. Annäherungen an einen Diktator* (Münich: 1994). See also Frenzel E., *Stoffe der Weltliteratur. Ein Lexikon dichtungsgeschichtlicher Längsschnitte* (Stuttgart: 1976⁴) 112-6 and Gundolf F., *Caesar. Die Geschichte seines Ruhms* (Berlin: 1924). For the early modern stage see especially Ginsberg E.S., "The Legacy of Marc-Antoine de Muret's Julius Caesar", in *Acta Conventus Neo-Latini Lovaniensis* (Leuven: 1977) 247-52; Morgan Ayres H., "Shakespeare's *Julius Caesar* in the light of some other versions", *Publications of the Modern Language Association of America*, NS 18 (1910) 202-12; Dutertre E., "A propos de quelques tragédies de la mort de César des XVIe et XVIIe siècles", *Littératures Classiques* 16 (1992) 199-227; Collischonn G.A.O., *Jacques Grévins Tragödie "Caesar" in ihrem Verhältniß zu Muret, Voltaire und Shakespeare*, Ausgaben und Abhandlungen aus dem Gebiete der romanischen Philologie (Marburg: 1886). On the 'Nine Worthies' (Hector, Alexander the Great, Julius Caesar, Joshua, David, Judas Maccabaeus, King Arthur, Charlemagne and Godfrey of Bouillon) see Schroeder H., *Der Topos der Nine Worthies in Literatur und Bildender Kunst* (Göttingen: 1971) and his own addenda (1981), and Anrooij W. van, *Helden van weleer. De Negen Besten in de Nederlanden (1300–1700)* (Amsterdam: 1997).

Marc-Antoine Muret

The first to present the murder of Caesar on the stage, and one of the very few to do so in Latin, was the French humanist Marc-Antoine Muret (1526–1585), who taught classical languages at Poitiers and Bordeaux.[2] After 1550 — during his stay in Paris, Toulouse and, from 1554 on, in Italy — Muret was to publish many text editions, translations and commentaries, including Aristotle's *Ethica Nicomachaea* and *Topica*, Cicero's *Orationes in Catilinam* and *Tusculanae Disputationes*, the poetry of Horace, Tibullus and Propertius and the comedies of Terence. In 1547 Muret arrived in Bordeaux, where he succeeded the Scottish humanist George Buchanan at the famous Collège de Guyenne. Probably in the same year Muret wrote and published his neo-Latin tragedy *Julius Caesar* to be played by his pupils at the Collège. The exact date of its publication is uncertain, which is partly due to the fact that Muret's biography is based on information given by Josephus Justus Scaliger (1540–1609), who, at the end of his life, recorded what he had heard from his father, who was visited by Muret in Agen.[3] According to Scaliger Jr *Julius Caesar* was first published in 1544. On the other hand, in one of his *Essais* Montaigne (born 1533) says, quoting Vergil's *Eclogue* VIII, 39: 'Already when I was scarcely twelve years old, I represented the chief parts in the Latin tragedies of Buchanan, Guérente and Muret, which were played with dignity in our Collège de Guyenne',[4] suggesting that *Julius Caesar* was staged not earlier than 1545. If Montaigne's remark means that he

---

[2] The standard biography of Muret is Dejob C., *Marc-Antoine Muret. Un professeur français en Italie dans la seconde moitié du xvie siècle* (Paris: 1881; rpt 1970). An alternative, convincing chronology of Muret's youth is suggested by Trinquet R., "Recherches chronologiques sur la jeunesse de Marc-Antoine Muret", *Bibliothèque d'Humanisme et Renaissance* 27 (1965) 272-85. The most recent, short biography is by Mouchel C., in *Centuriae Latinae. Cent une figures humanistes de la Renaissance aux Lumières offertes à Jacques Chomarat*, ed. C. Nativel, (Geneva: 1997) 575-9. Another Latin drama which has Caesar as its subject is Nikodemus Frischlin's curious play *Iulius redivivus* (1584). See Rädle F., "Einige Bemerkungen zu Frischlins Dramatik", in *Acta Conventus Neo-Latini Guelpherbytani* (Binghamton, NY: 1988) 289-97.

[3] Scaliger gives his information in *Confutatio stultissimae Burdonum fabulae* (Leiden: 1608) 387-9. This is a controversial defence of the Scaliger family against a lampoon by Caspar Schoppe, *Scaliger hyperbolimaeus, hoc est Elenchus epistolae Jos. Burdonis Pseudoscaligeri de vetustate et splendore gentis Scaligerae* (Mainz: 1607).

[4] 'Avant l'âge *alter ab undecimo tum me vix ceperat annus*, j'ai soutenu les premiers personnages ès tragédies latines de Buchanan, de Guérente et de Muret, qui se représentèrent en notre collège de Guyenne avec dignité', Montaigne, *Essais* I, 26, ed. P. Michel (Paris: 1972) 254.

played in a tragedy each year, respectively those by Buchanan, Guérente and Muret, this would support the assumption that 1547 was the year it was staged. Probably it was performed at the anniversary of the Collège, on 25 August.[5]

Julius Caesar — *Characteristics*

Muret's tragedy *Julius Caesar* has the same formal features as the ten tragedies which are assigned to Seneca (4 BC–65 AD): the play is divided into five acts, the first four of which are concluded by a chorus; monologues prevail over dialogues; the drama also contains many *sententiae* (aphorisms). Frequently a dream sequence occurs in Seneca's plays, often told in a dialogue between a mistress and her nurse, a *domina-nutrix* scene. In the tragedies of Seneca much attention is paid to emotions.[6] Stylistically they are characterized by *repetitio* and *anaphora*, a tendency to *brevitas* and a visualisation of passions.[7] These features occur in *Julius Caesar* too: there is a dream sequence told by Caesar's wife Calpurnia to her nurse, attention is paid to the passions, and the

---

[5] The first extant edition of *Julius Caesar* is part of the *Juvenilia*, printed in Paris (widow M. a Porta), 1553. It might have been published earlier, but such an earlier edition is now lost. Recently the *Juvenilia*, including *Julius Caesar*, were edited and translated into German by D. Schmitz: Marcus Antonius Muretus, *Caesar Juvenilia* (Frankfurt a. M. etc.: 1995). Schmitz, however, fails to mention the edition on which his was based. Without explaining he assumes that *Julius Caesar* was written in 1544.

[6] I will not take a stand in the many discussions concerning the authorship of these tragedies (were they, yes or no, or were only some of them written by the philosopher Seneca), the staging (were they, yes or no, written to be staged) or their aims (do they express stoic lessons, and if they do, in what manner; why the enormous attention paid to pathos and horror). Of the extensive literature on *Seneca tragicus* I mention Costa C.D.N., *Seneca* (London, etc.: 1974); Mayer R., "Personata Stoa: Neostoicism and Senecan Tragedy", *Journal of the Warburg and Courtauld Institutes* 57 (1994) 151-74; Liebermann W.L., *Studien zu Senecas Tragödien* (Meisenheim a. Glan: 1974); Sutton D.F., *Seneca on the Stage* (Leiden: 1986) and Zwierlein O., *Die Rezitationsdramen Senecas mit einem kritisch-exegetischen Anhang* (Meisenheim a. Glan: 1966). Schmitz, Marcus Antonius Muretus, mentions some Seneca-parallels with passages of *Julius Caesar*, but he discusses the play merely, and anachronistically, in terms of Aristotelic and French classicist dramatic concepts.

[7] Emotions are visualised by, among others, repetition, see for example *Julius Caesar* verses 449 ('Hac, hac manu atque hoc, hocce gladio') and 474 ('Sic, sic'); by *anaphora*, for example *Julius Caesar* verses 445-6: ('En [...] en'); and by *brevitas*, see for example *Julius Caesar* verse 26 ('Caelum petendum est: terra iam vilet mihi'). For a visualisation of passions see *Julius Caesar* verses 240-5.

For Seneca's stylistic visualisation of emotions see, among others, Liebermann, *Studien*, 85-110.

features of Seneca's style are present as well. Finally the play contains some direct quotations of and allusions to Seneca's dramas, while some scenes of *Julius Caesar* seem to be inspired directly by Senecan scenes.[8] Just as in classical tragedy the murder itself is not shown on stage.

In spite of these Senecan features *Julius Caesar* is not a completely classical tragedy, but it remained more or less a school drama. Its style for instance is less elaborate than the style of Seneca's plays, in which metaphors and periphrases are used lavishly and in which the sentence structure is sometimes far from transparent. Muret uses these stylistic features sparingly, apparently to keep his drama comprehensible to the young audience.[9] Its length — half the length of a tragedy by Seneca — seems to be adapted to the audience too. Moreover some of the authors whom Muret read with his pupils are alluded to or quoted in the play. The opening lines of the second act, for example, are a variation on the beginning of Cicero's first Catilinarian, undoubtedly read by Muret's students. The agreeable *Aha-Erlebnis* will certainly have contributed to make them extra *attenti* and *benevoli*. At the end of the drama the pupils will have been struck by, among others, a phrase of Propertius and a line of Horace they knew from their lessons.[10]

---

[8] The literal quotations and the imitation of complete scenes give the play the status of "classical, Senecan tragedy". The first monologue of the play already has such a function: the first act of several dramas by Seneca consists of a monologue.

[9] For example *Julius Caesar*, 98-108 is an example of the very lucid style of the play:
'*Quousque tandem*, Brute, virtutem tuam
Dormire *pateris* otiosam degener?
Quousque differs, civitatem liberam
Tua videre vindicatam dextera?
Nihilne te virtus tuorum *commovet*,
Nomenque Bruti? *nihil* gementis patriae,
Pressae a tyranno, opemque poscentis tuam
Conditio dura? *nil* libelli supplices,
Queis Brutum abesse civitatis vindicem
Cives queruntur? Haec parum si te *movent*,
Tua iam, vir ut sis, te satis coniunx monet [...]'. [italics mine]
('In heaven's name, weak Brutus, how long will you let your virtue sleep inactively? How much longer yet will you postpone seeing the state free, avenged by your hand? Are you not at all impressed by the virtue of your ancestors, not at all by the name of Brutus? Not at all by the hardship of your groaning country, oppressed by that tyrant and begging for your help? Not at all by the petitions in which the citizens lament the fact that Brutus fails to avenge the state?').

[10] For the passage reminiscent of Cicero's *In Catilinam* see the previous footnote. The words and phrases quoted (almost) literally are printed in italics. Besides, compare *Julius Caesar* 551 'sunt manes aliquid' to Propertius IV, 7, 1 'sunt aliquid manes' and *Julius Caesar* 552-3 'est aliquid tamen quod vitat Libitinam' ('there is yet some-

Not unexpectedly parallels to contemporary plays also occur. Muret would have continued the stage tradition that Buchanan had started at the Collège de Guyenne in Bordeaux by staging tragedies and writing them; it is therefore likely that Muret knew the dramas of this humanist and playwright, admired them and used their material. Indeed direct reminiscences of Buchanan's *Jephthes* are traceable in the dream sequence Calpurnia told to her nurse in *Julius Caesar*.[11]

The structure of the play is fairly simple. The action takes place on the last day of Caesar's life, 15 March 44 BC. At the beginning Caesar is portrayed as an unassailable hero at the height of his power and very conscious of it. He has conquered the whole world; the only thing he has not accomplished yet is being admitted to heaven. He is not afraid of death, even when disaster is prophesized. The chorus puts this attitude in a stoic perspective by reflecting on the vicissitudes of fortune: he who was raised high, can be brought low; it was also fortune that made Caesar defeat Pompey. In the second act the conflict becomes apparent: Marcus Brutus plots against Caesar, urged on, so he says, by his country, which considers Caesar a tyrant. His fellow conspirator Brutus also urges him on and makes it clear that the latter is the actual leader of the rebellion. The chorus also supports Brutus in his fight against Caesar.

---

thing escaping death') to Horace *Carmen* III, 30, 6-7 'multaque pars mei vitabit Libitinam' ('an important part of me will escape death'). Schmitz in his edition of the *Julius Caesar* does not mention the passages reminiscent of Propertius and Horace.

[11] This dream sequence (*Julius Caesar* 240-305) is full of intertextuality: it is based on the one hand on the historical data given by, among others, Plutarch, *Life of Caesar*, 63 and Suetonius, *Life of Caesar*, 81; on the other hand such a dream sequence to a nurse is a typical scene in Seneca's drama and the tragedies based on it. The scene in *Julius Caesar* in some expressions resembles Buchanan's *Jephthes*, cf. 'horror artus concutit, corpusque totum frigidus sudor lavat, quoties recordor' (*Julius Caesar* 242-4) with *Jephthes*, 88-90: 'sed metus, veluti recens, quoties recordor, concutit formidine mentem; visa noctis proximae me terruerunt; *Julius Caesar* 255-6 with *Jephthes*, 76: 'nocturna sic me visa territant; sopor timores saepe vanos obiicit [...] fallaxque mentem imago turbavit tuam'. 'Sed vana mentes saepe ludunt somnia [...] Abiice ex animo metum' (*Julius Caesar* 263, 279, 288, 301) with *Jephthes*, 85, 118-9 'Vanaeque causas abiice aegritudinis [...] Nisi vano mens augurio credula nimium pectora fallit'. See also Lebègue R., *La tragédie religieuse en France. Les débuts (1514–1573)* (Paris: 1929) 244-7. Muret must have seen Buchanan's *Jephthes* in manuscript, since this tragedy was first published in 1554. It was certainly performed at Bordeaux, and perhaps in Paris, Coimbra and Cambridge, see Lebègue, *La tragédie religieuse*, 245. The play has been edited and translated by P. Sharratt and P.G. Walsh: George Buchanan, *Tragedies* (Edinburgh: 1983) 21-94. On *Jephthes* and its tremendous influence on European drama, see especially McFarlane I.D., *Buchanan* (London: 1981) 190-205. Schmitz in his edition of the *Julius Caesar* completely overlooks these allusions to Buchanan's play.

In Act III Caesar's wife Calpurnia tells her nurse that she has had a frightening dream in which she saw her husband die; she will beg him not to leave the house. The nurse tries to dispel her terror by arguing that nobody would dare oppose Caesar or would even want to do so, considering his clemency. The chorus celebrates the festival of Anna Perenna, an old Roman year-goddess, adding the plea that it will be celebrated in peace for many years to come. In act IV Calpurnia indeed asks her husband to stay home, or at least to postpone the meeting of the senate that he is going to attend. Decimus Brutus, one of the other conspirators, prevents this by a subtle speech in which he appeals to Caesar's honour. The chorus, which implicitly comments on the action, sings the praises of sensible women who predict the future. Those who do not listen to them — it is not explicitly said that Caesar did not listen to Calpurnia at the end — will be brought to ruin.

The murder itself is not shown on the stage, but it is over when, in Act V, Marcus Brutus briefly addresses the citizens: they can breathe freely again because the tyrant Caesar has been killed. Calpurnia and the chorus join in mourning: the wife wants to die with her husband. The chorus, consisting of Roman citizens, calls on everything and everybody to feel sorry with them. Then from heaven they hear the voice of Caesar: because he has been deified they need not mourn at all.

The chorus ends the play with the reflection that there is life after death and that whoever has lived a pure life without doing wrong will be raised to heaven.

Sources

Muret could draw on several sources for his information about Caesar, though he will no doubt already have known the principal facts. After all Caesar was famous as one of the *Nine Worthies*. Furthermore, he consulted the biographies of Caesar, Marcus Brutus and Antony in Plutarch's *Βίοι Παραλλήλοι* (*Parallel Lives*), Suetonius's *De vita Caesarum* (*The Lives of the Caesars*) and Velleius Paterculus's second book of his *Historia Romana* (*History of Rome*).[12] Of these texts Plutarch's *Life of Caesar* appears to be Muret's main source.

---

[12] Moreover Cassius Dio Cocceianus (c. 155–235) wrote a detailed *Roman History* (*Ῥωμαικὴ ἱστορία*). The *editio princeps*, however, dates from 1548 so the chance that Muret knew this work is small.

The works of these biographers and historians were well-known. Plutarch's *Parallel Lives* especially enjoyed an extensive circulation in manuscripts and printed editions alike. There were a few Latin translations by Italian humanists, such as Lapo da Castiglionchio, Donato Acciaiuoli and Guarino Guarini.[13] In this edition the *Life of Caesar* was translated by Jacopo Angelo de Scarparia, the *Life of Brutus* by Guarino.

In his *Parallel Lives* of famous Greeks and Romans the Greek biographer attributes to the persons described an exemplary value and presents them as instructive examples of political and social virtues or vices, from which we should learn good and avoid morally reprehensible behaviour.[14]

Plutarch is rather positive about Caesar: he 'sets Caesar forth as above everything else astute, a man marked to rule, thrusting his way with unerring political sagacity into popular favor; cultivated, brave, of inhuman energy, and renowned for a clemency designed to be something more than its own reward; a man of humor and of pithy utterance; toward the close of his life somewhat under the domination of his adherents, and restless in the desire for futher achievement'.[15] Caesar is versatile, witty, competent and merciful. The leitmotiv of this biography of Caesar is his road to tyranny. Plutarch's moral aim in connection with this *Life* seems to be that pride will lead to a fall. Muret gives this lesson a more tragic effect by presenting Caesar as much more than only a villain.

In 1547 Suetonius's *De vita Caesarum* (*The Lives of the Caesars*) had already gone through several editions as well. The first printed edition was published in Rome in 1470, by Giannantonio Campano. The Paris edition by Robert Estienne dates dates from 1543.[16] The biographies by Suetonius are arranged partly chronologically, partly thematically (descent, military and political pursuits, private life, death, funeral

---

[13] *Plutarchi Chaeronei Graecorum Romanorumque illustrium vitae* (Basle: 1553). The translations have been collected by Hieronymus Gemusaeus: the *Life of Caesar* can be found on f. 268r-79r, the *Life of Brutus* on f. 305v-14r. Standard work on the *Nachleben* of Plutarch is Hirzel R., *Plutarch* (Leipzig: 1912). See further the article "Plutarchos" by Ziegler K., in *Realencyclopädie der classischen Altertumswissenschaft*, ed. G. Wissowa – K. Ziegler (neue Bearbeitung), 83 vols (Stuttgart: 1893–1980) vol 12, col. 947-62 and Aulotte R., *Amyot et Plutarque. La tradition des Moralia au XVIe siècle* (Geneva: 1965) 155-62.

[14] See for example Scardigli B., *Essays on Plutarch's* Lives (Oxford: 1995). More information on Plutarch, his methods and aims can be found in Westerweel's article in this volume.

[15] Morgan Ayres, "Shakespeare's *Julius Caesar*", 189; cf. also Krist, *Caesar*, 99-101.

[16] See Suétone, *Vies des douze Césars*, transl. H. Ailloud I (Paris: 1954) XLVI.

and testament). Suetonius's main purpose is to delineate the human being behind the emperor — the man behind the mask, with his qualities and defects, with his virtues and vices. The final judgement is left to the reader. Thus his Caesar is a man of strong contrasts: on the one hand he is just and mild and sober with regard to wine and housing, on the other hand he indulges in sexual debauchery and is hungry for money, which gives him a bad reputation. He is lenient and indulgent, but also arrogant and without shame, courageous, but also effeminate. Both in Suetonius' biography and in the one by Plutarch Caesar's aspirations to monarchical power are the dominant theme.[17]

The *editio princeps* of Velleius's history, for a long time the only one available in print, was made by J.A. Burer, a pupil of Beatus Rhenanus (Basle: 1520). Velleius's work is a compendium of Roman history from the beginning up to his own time, the early Principate. In the second book the author deals with the period of Caesar and the late Republic. He gives a concise description of the most important political, military and biographical events in Caesar's life, mixed with anecdotes and simple maxims. His attitude to Caesar is very positive: he regards him as an adroit politician and a clever strategist.[18]

Back to Muret's main source. Plutarch describes the events on the Ides of March and on the day after as follows:[19]

> Caesar [...] noticed that Calpurnia was in a deep slumber, but was uttering indistinct words and inarticulate groans in her sleep; for she dreamed, as it proved, that she was holding her murdered husband in her arms and bewailing him. [...] At all events, when day came, she begged Caesar, if it was possible, not to go out, but to postpone the meeting of the senate; if, however, he had no concern at all for her dreams, she besought him to enquire by other modes of divination and by sacrifices concerning the future (Plutarch, *Life of Caesar*, 63).

But at this juncture Decimus Brutus, surnamed Albinus, who was so trusted by Caesar that he was entered in his will as his second heir, but was

---

[17] See for example Krist, *Caesar*, 101-3; Cizek E., *Structures et idéologie dans "Les Vies des Douze Césars" de Suétone* (Paris: 1977) 66-77; Gugel H., *Studien zur biographischen Technik Suetons* (Vienna–Cologne–Graz: 1977).

[18] See for example Starr J.R., "The Scope and Genre of Velleius' History" in *Classical Quarterly* 31 (1981) 162-74. On the Velleian image of Caesar see Krist, *Caesar*, 92-3.

[19] He also gives a description of the murder itself. As Muret does not show it on stage Plutarch's description of it can be omitted here. The translations are quoted from *Plutarch's Lives*. Translated by B. Perrin, Loeb Classical Library (Cambridge, Mass.–London: 1967) 591, 593 and 601.

partner in the conspiracy of the other Brutus and Cassius, fearing that if Caesar should elude that day, their undertaking would become known, ridiculed the seers and chided Caesar for laying himself open to malicious charges on the part of the senators, who would think themselves mocked at; for they had met at his bidding, and were ready and willing to vote as one man that he should be declared king of the provinces outside of Italy [...], but if some one should tell them at their session to be gone now, but to come back again when Calpurnia should have better dreams, what speeches would be made by his enemies? (Plutarch, *Life of Caesar*, 64).

On the next day Brutus came down and held a discourse, and the people listened to what was said without either expressing resentment at what had been done or appearing to approve of it; they showed, however, by their deep silence, that while they pitied Caesar, they respected Brutus (Plutarch, *Life of Caesar*, 67).

Other details Muret also derived from Plutarch's work. In the second scene of Act II Brutus is exhorted by his fellow conspirator Cassius; a similar scene can be found in Plutarch's *Life of Brutus*. Other details — an allusion to the self-mutilation of Brutus's wife Porcia, the two tribunes Flavius and Marcellus who remove the laurel-wreaths from Caesar's busts, Caesar who refuses the crown offered him by Antony — can all of them be found in Plutarch's work.[20]

It may be assumed that Muret also consulted Velleius Paterculus's *Historia Romana*.[21] Particularly striking is the way in which both Velleius Paterculus and Muret comment on the death of Pompey, who was killed in Egypt. The parallel makes it clear that Muret knew the *Roman History*, at least partially:

The leader [Pompey] who used to put others to flight, himself now took to flight in panic and on his way to the south he perceived that in troubles loyalty quickly disappears (*Julius Caesar* 21-3).[22]

---

[20] For Porcia's self-inflicted wound in *Julius Caesar* 108-13 ('If all this doesn't impress you, it must be enough stimulation that your wife who has pledged her fidelity to you with her own blood and doing so has shown to be a true daughter of your uncle, incites you to be a man') see Plutarch, *Life of Brutus*, 13, 5-11: 'Porcia, a daughter of Cato, took a little knife and made a deep gash in her thigh, to show that she was superior to pain and make her husband Brutus faithful to her'; for the deposed tribunes see *Julius Caesar* 137 and Plutarch, *Life of Caesar*, 61, 4-5; for the refusal of the crown see *Julius Caesar* 135-6 and Plutarch, *Life of Antonius*, 12, 4.

[21] For example concerning the deposition of the tribunes see *Julius Caesar* 137 and Velleius Paterculus II, 68, 4; for the dream of Calpurnia see Velleius Paterculus II, 57, 2; for other bad omens see Velleius Paterculus II, 57, 2; for the *clementia Caesaris* see Velleius Paterculus II, 56, 3 and for the battle of Pharsalus in Thessaly see Velleius Paterculus II, 52.

[22] 'Ductor ipse exterritus,

When does loyalty not change together with fate?[23]

Plutarch's biography has been Muret's main source, but Suetonius's *Life of Caesar* has been used as well. An important element in the play, Caesar's apotheosis, is only briefly and indirectly described by Plutarch but extensively by Suetonius:

> He died in the fifty-sixth year of his age, and was numbered among the gods, not only by a formal decree, but also in the conviction of the common people. For at the first of the games which his heir Augustus gave in honour of his apotheosis, a comet shone for seven successive days [...], and was believed to be the soul of Caesar, who had been taken to heaven.[24]

Muret had to make rather a lot of choices with regard to his Caesar.[25] The biographies by Plutarch and Suetonius ascribe widely divergent character traits to him. Add to this the fact that in the tradition too he was judged differently according to the monarchical or republican inclination of the judge. Thus, for instance in Sienna about 1400, Caesar was depicted as a horrifying example of ambition, while in the palaces of princes pictures of a triumphant Caesar abounded.[26]

---

     fugare suetus, fugit, et notos petens,
     sensit manere raram in aerumnis fidem'.

[23] 'Aut quando fortuna non mutat fidem?' (Velleius Paterculus II, 53, 2). A similar comment, though in another context, in Lucan, *Pharsalia* II, 460-1: 'Facilis sed vertere mentes / Terror erat, dubiamque fidem fortuna ferebat' ('But danger was quick to change men's minds, and the turn of events swept away wavering allegiance'; transl. J.D. Duff, Loeb Classical Library (Cambridge, Mass.–London: 1977) 91). It is the more likely that this expression stems from Lucan, since there is an obvious reminiscence of Lucan in *Julius Caesar* 18-9: '[Pompeius] quemque noluerat parem, tulit priorem' ('Pompey endured as his superior the man whom he had not wanted to have as an equal'). Cf. Lucan, *Pharsalia* I, 125-6: 'nec quemquam iam ferre potest Caesar priorem Pompeiusve parem' ('Caesar could no longer endure a superior, nor Pompey an equal', transl. J.D. Duff, 13). That another interpretation of this murder is also possible, or even more plausible, is made clear by Cassius Dio's comment that the event proves the weakness and the strange fate of humanity (Cassius Dio, *Roman History* XLII, 5).

[24] Suetonius, *Caesar*, 88, transl. J.C. Rolfe, Loeb Classical Library (Cambridge, Mass.–London: 1960) I, 119. Plutarch (69) only mentions the comet. He also speaks of a voice that Brutus heard, but this was the voice of his own evil spirit, not of Caesar.

[25] It is not quite clear why Muret does not use the fact that Brutus may have been an illegitimate son of Caesar's: it would have resulted in a beautiful intrigue.

[26] See for example Mantegna's *Caesar's triumph* (c. 1490). The glorification or vilification of Caesar is often inversely proportional to the vilification or glorification of Cicero. The explanation is of course their contrasting political positions: the one a monarchist, the other a republican.

Muret's Caesar: a Stoic Hercules

There are different sides to the Caesar pictured in *Julius Caesar*. In the beginning of the play he is represented as very sure of himself:

> Even the conqueror of the world, Rome, has submitted to me (*Julius Caesar*, 14-5).

> What remains, or what can the subjected world show aught more, worthy of Caesar? I have to go to heaven: the earth is yet too small for me (*Julius Caesar*, 24-6).[27]

On the other hand his opening monologue gives evidence of a certain resignation and loss of vitality: 'Iam vel mihi, vel patriae vixi satis' ('I have lived long enough, for myself and for my country', *Julius Caesar*, 34).[28] In the play refence is also made, by Calpurnia's nurse, to the well-known *clementia Caesaris*.[29]

In the play Caesar's uncertainty of mind is stressed, when he is wavering between the fears of his wife Calpurnia, who bids him to stay at home, and the exhortations of Brutus to go to the senate:

> Uncertain of mind I am distracted to both sides as a ship, off its course upon the roaring sea, caught by the raging winds (*Julius Caesar*, 379-82).[30]

On the other hand Caesar is shown as a man with stoical contempt for any circumstances, when he says·

> Caesar never feared. A coward without experience is afraid for the uncertain day of his death; a man with a noble mind, by no crime defiled, is always free of fear (*Julius Caesar*, 47-51).[31]

---

[27] Respectively 'Ipsa victrix gentium/Mihi Roma cessit' and 'Quid ergo restat, quidve dignum Caesare/Subacta tellus exhibere ultra potest?/Caelum petendum est: terra iam vilet mihi'.

[28] This is in line with a remark by Suetonius (86): 'Caesar left in the minds of some of his friends the suspicion that he did not wish to live longer and had taken no precautions, because of his failing health. [...] Some, too, say that he was wont to declare that it was not so much to his own interest as to that of his country that he remain alive; he had long since had his fill of power and glory' (transl. Rolfe, 117 and 119).

[29] As a matter of fact the *clementia Caesaris* was not seen as a private virtue in Antiquity, but as the gracious demeanour of a sovereign to his subjects. On Caesar's clemency see Suetonius, *Caesar*, 75 and Velleius Paterculus II, 52, 6; furthermore: Dahlmann H., "Clementia Caesaris", *Neue Jahrbücher für Wissenschaft und Jugendbildung* 10 (1934) 17-26; Treu M., "Zur clementia Caesaris", *Museum Helveticum* 5 (1948) 197-217.

[30] 'Incertus animi, et huc et illuc distrahor/Qualis per aequor concitum bacchantibus/Deprensa ventis fertur incerto ratis/Agitata cursu'.

[31] At enim timere Caesaris nunquam fuit,/Ignava mens rebusque non exercita/Vereatur atrae mortis incertum diem:/Generosus animus, quique se nullo videt/Scelere impiatum, semper est liber metu'.

Muret especially emphasizes stoic notions in Caesar. He possesses a *generosus animus*, a noble mind. This no doubt alludes to the stoic virtues, and he is a model of the stoic sage, who is sure of himself, undaunted in danger and master of his emotions. Such a sage loyally serves his country, led by his *virtus*, which embraces the four cardinal virtues *prudentia* (practical wisdom), *fortitudo* (bravery), *temperantia* (self-control) and *iustitia* (justice). He regards everything, even death, as *indifferentia* (neither good nor bad, but indifferent) and therefore does not fear death.[32]

There is a literary example, to wit the Hercules from Seneca's *Hercules Oetaeus*, which contributes to this philosophic vision of Caesar. Just like Seneca's Hercules, Caesar is — among other things — represented as the stoic hero who 'keeps his cool' in times of stress.[33] That this Hercules figure must be taken into account is clear from several allusions to *Hercules Oetaeus* in *Julius Caesar*. The opening monologue resembles that of Seneca's play in various respects: in both the hero reflects on his glorious exploits and prays that he may be given his proper place in heaven, and there are many similarities in phrasing.[34]

---

[32] On the stoic sage see for example Sandbach F.H., *The Stoics* (London: 1975) and Pohlenz M., *Die Stoa. Geschichte einer geistigen Bewegung* I (Göttingen: 1948) especially 153-8; Rist J.M., *Stoic Philosophy* (London–New York–Melbourne: 1969).

[33] On Hercules as stoic hero, see for example Bassett E.L., "Hercules and the Hero of the *Punica*", ed. L. Wallach, *The Classical Tradition. Literary and Historical Studies in Honor of Harry Caplan* (Ithaca etc.: 1966) 258-63, especially 259; Enenkel K.A.E., "*Hercules in bivio* en andere tweesprongen: de geschiedenis van een idee bij Petrarca", *Lampas* 22 (1989) 111-39; Enenkel K.A.E., *Petrarca, De vita solitaria Buch I. Kritische Textausgabe und ideengeschichtlicher Kommentar* (Leiden etc.: 1990); Galinsky G.K., *The Herakles Theme. The Adaptations of the Hero in Literature from Homer to the Twentieth Century* (Oxford: 1978), ch. 8 "Seneca's *Herakles*" and 9 "Exemplar virtutis".

[34] Compare Muret, *Julius Caesar* 1, 7-8 ('Iam tota pene terra Romanos timet, [...]/ Quacunque Nereus margines terrae premit Reges vel ipsi Caesaris nomen timent; 'Now nearly the whole world fears the Romans, [...] and wherever the sea touches the boundaries of the earth even kings fear the name of Caesar') with Seneca, *Hercules Oetaeus*, 4-6: 'Quacumque Nereus porrigi terras vetat./Non est tonandum: perfidi reges iacent, Saevi tyranni' ('Wherever the sea forbids the land to extend its bounds. Thou needst not thunder now; false kings lie low, and cruel tyrants'; transl. F.J. Miller, Loeb Classical Library (Cambridge, Mass.,–London: 1987) II, 187) and *Julius Caesar* 27-8 ('Supreme Rector, qui verendo fulmine, iratus, orbis utrumque perterres polum'; 'Sovereign Lord, who with thy fearful thunderbolt in anger frighten both skies [East and West]') with *Hercules Oetaeus*, 1-2: 'Sator deorum, cuius excussum manu Utraeque Phoebi sentiunt fulmen domus' ('O sire of gods, hurled by whose hand both homes of Phoebus [East and West] feel the thunderbolt'; transl. Miller II, 187). Also compare Muret, *Julius Caesar*, 24-5 ('Quid ergo restat, quidve dignum Caesare/Subacta tellus exhibere ultra potest?'; 'What remains, or what can the subjected world show aught more, worthy of Caesar?') with Seneca's other Hercules play, *Hercules furens*, 613-5: 'Quid restat aliud? Vidi et ostendi inferos. Da si quid ultra est' ('What else remains? I have seen

Just like Hercules, Caesar suffers from a kind of ἄτη, blindness, and he despises the gods:

> Not even when Jove himself with his own voice would warn me of the danger and advise me to stay here, would I be held back (*Julius Caesar*, 388-90).[35]

The deification of Caesar is of course attested by the historians.[36] But demonstrating this by the sound of Caesar's voice bidding Calpurnia to cease bemoaning his transition to the stars is also a reminiscence of Senecan drama: in *Hercules Oetaeus* it is the voice of Hercules that comforts Alcmena.[37]

It is clear that in *Julius Caesar* the picture of Caesar is conditioned by the fact that the biographical elements are tailored to a Senecan model. Formal adaptations are therefore necessary. For instance, in a tragedy the number of characters is limited. This seems to be the reason why the various augurs who warned Caesar just before the critical moment, or the seer Artemidorus, who handed him a letter, do not appear in the play.[38] The presentation of Caesar himself is also determined by the tragic conventions. Thus Caesar's uncertainty is emphasized in his discussions with Calpurnia and Brutus about whether or not to go to the senate. However, we also become aware of his stoic imperturbability in the face of death. Both indecision and imperturbability are characteristic for certain characters in Seneca's tragedies. For instance Medea is desperate in the drama of that name, as is Clytaemnestra in *Agamemnon*.[39] But Hercules in *Hercules Oetaeus* does

---

and revealed the lower world. If aught is left to do, give it to me'; transl. F.J. Miller I, 57). The idea that the earth is too small (*Julius Caesar* 24-6) can be found in Seneca, *Hercules furens*, 955-61. See also Morgan Ayres, "Shakespeare's *Julius Caesar*", 203-7.

[35] 'Non si ipse voce propria praesens Deus/Moneat pericli, atque hic manendum suadeat,/Me continebo'; cf. Seneca, *Hercules furens*, 965-7: 'I will free Saturn from his bonds, and against my unfilial father's lawless sway I will loose my grandsire' (transl. F.J. Miller I, 85).

[36] For example Plutarch, *Life of Caesar*, 69; Suetonius, *Life of Caesar*.

[37] Seneca, *Hercules Oetaeus*, 1940-3: 'Quid me tenentem regna siderei poli caeloque tandem redditum planctu iubes sentire fatum? Parce; iam virtus mihi In astra et ipsos fecit ad superos iter' ('Why, since I hold the realms of starry heaven and at last have attained the skies, dost by lamentation bid me taste of death? Give over; for now has my valour borne me to the stars and to the gods themselves', transl. F.J. Miller II, 337; compare Muret, *Julius Caesar* 532 ('Quid caelitum me fletis adiunctum choro?'; 'Why do you mourn me since I am admitted to the gods?') and 545: ('Ego ad alta caeli tecta stellantis feror'; 'I am hastening to the lofty dwellings of the sky').

[38] The personages are mentioned in for instance Plutarch, *Caesar*, 65.

[39] Respectively Seneca, *Medea* 123-4 and *Agamemnon* 131-44.

not know any fear of death. A hero who on the surface seems undecided, but is essentially imperturbable, certainly fits the view of Senecan drama held in Renaissance times. It was regarded as containing stoic lessons in the field of ethics which could easily be transposed to the total view of characters.[40] The stoic ideals of ἀπαθεία (imperturbability) and *constantia* (constancy) determine how the personages were seen.

The Aims of the Play

Philosophic notions also dominate the end of the play, where the chorus points to the moral. It argues that there is life after death in a Platonic (and also stoic) sense:[41] the soul, liberated from the prison of the body, flies to heaven and there takes its place among the stars and the gods. That reward can only be earned by being good in this life.

> Shades do exist: when cruel death has brought the last day there is something which stays out of death's clutches and which escapes cremation. If this something has lived a pure life and has not contaminated itself with crime it will, as soon as it is free of its bodily prison, hasten to the stars, where Juno has fashioned a road with her milk, and there, amidst the gods, feed on heavenly ambrosia and drink cups of sacred nectar.
> You can be certain of these rewards if you honour virtue and venerable faith with sincerity and a clear conscience (*Julius Caesar*, 551-70).[42]

---

[40] See Mayer, "Personata Stoa".

[41] For the stoic view of the soul see for example Rist, *Stoic Philosophy*, 256-72.

[42] 'Sunt manes aliquid: cumque diem ultimum
Adduxit fera mors, est aliquid tamen,
Quod vitat Libitinam
Exstructosque fugit rogos.
Id si, dum vegetat membra, datum sibi
Vitae curriculum pariter egerit,
Nec se turpificarit
Impuris scelerum notis.
Mox, ut corporeo carcere liberum est,
Rursus sidereas convolat in domos,
Qua Saturnia lacte
Signavit proprio viam:
Atque illic, numero caelicolum additum,
Caelesti ambrosiae gramine vescitur,
Et carchesia sacri
Plena nectaris ebibit.
Haec olim haud dubie praemia vos manent,
Quicunque innocuo pectore simplices
Virtutemque tenetis,
Et canam colitis fidem'.

The good life, therefore, consists of *virtus* and *fides*, i.e. imperturbability and faith, especially loyalty to one's country.[43] This is the lesson *Julius Caesar* impresses upon the audience, the young Bordeaux pupils at the Collège de Guyenne. Caesar's life is exemplary: he has always loyally served his country and kept his impassiveness, or at least did not fear death. As in the case of Hercules his reward was certain: the tyrant received eternal life.[44]

Selective Bibliography

BASSETT E.L., "Hercules and the Hero of the *Punica*", ed. L. Wallach, *The Classical Tradition. Literary and Historical Studies in Honor of Harry Caplan* (Ithaca etc.: 1966) 258-63

CHRIST K., *Caesar. Annäherungen an einen Diktator* (Munich: 1994)

CIZEK E., *Structures et idéologie dans "Les Vies des Douze Césars" de Suétone* (Paris: 1977) 66-77

COLLISCHONN G.A.O., *Jacques Grévins Tragödie "Caesar" in ihrem Verhältniß zu Muret, Voltaire und Shakespeare* (Marburg: 1886).

COSTA C.D.N., *Seneca* (London, etc.: 1974)

DAHLMANN H., "Clementia Caesaris", *Neue Jahrbücher für Wissenschaft und Jugendbildung* 10 (1934) 17-26

DEJOB C., *Marc-Antoine Muret. Un professeur français en Italie dans la seconde moitié du xvie siècle* (Paris: 1881; rpt 1970)

DUTERTRE E., "A propos de quelques tragédies de la mort de César des XVIe et XVIIe siècles", *Littératures Classiques* 16 (1992) 199-227

ENENKEL K.A.E., "*Hercules in bivio* en andere tweesprongen: de geschiedenis van een idee bij Petrarca", *Lampas* 22 (1989) 111-39

GALINSKY G.K., *The Herakles Theme. The Adaptations of the Hero in Literature from Homer to the Twentieth Century* (Oxford: 1978)

GINSBERG E.S., "The Legacy of Marc-Antoine de Muret's Julius Caesar", in *Acta Conventus Neo-Latini Lovaniensis* (Leuven: 1977) 247-52

GUGEL H., *Studien zur biographischen Technik Suetons* (Vienna–Cologne–Graz: 1977)

---

[43] 'Canam [...] fidem' is an allusion to Vergil, *Aeneis* I, 292. *Virtus* and *Fides* are old Roman goddesses, who can be worshipped.

[44] Transl. by W.J. van Tent.

GUNDOLF F., *Caesar. Die Geschichte seines Ruhms* (Berlin: 1924)

LIEBERMANN W.L., *Studien zu Senecas Tragödien* (Meisenheim a. Glan: 1974)

MAYER R., "Personata Stoa: Neostoicism and Senecan Tragedy", *Journal of the Warburg and Courtauld Institutes* 57 (1994) 151-74

MORGAN AYRES H., "Shakespeare's *Julius Caesar* in the light of some other versions", *Publications of the Modern Language Association of America,* NS 18 (1910) 202-12

RÄDLE F., "Einige Bemerkungen zu Frischlins Dramatik", in *Acta Conventus Neo-Latini Guelpherbytani* (Binghamton, NY: 1988) 289-97

SCHMITZ D., German translation of Marcus Antonius Muretus, *Caesar. Juvenilia* (Frankfurt a. M. etc.: 1995)

SUTTON D.F., *Seneca on the Stage* (Leiden: 1986)

TREU M., "Zur clementia Caesaris", *Museum Helveticum* 5 (1948) 197-217

ZWIERLEIN O., *Die Rezitationsdramen Senecas mit einem kritisch-exegetischen Anhang* (Meisenheim a. Glan: 1966).

CAESAR THE FATHER IN MARIE-ANNE BARBIER'S
LA MORT DE CÉSAR (1709)

Alicia Montoya

In her monumental work *L'accès des femmes à la culture (1598–1715)*, the late Linda Timmermans argued that, towards the end of the seventeenth century, French literature was transformed by the growing acceptance of a new genre system which reflected perceived differences between masculine and feminine modes of writing. This gendered genre system codified what until then had merely been literary practice: literary domains in which female authorship had always been rare (notably the great genres of Antiquity: tragedy, epic, etc.) were increasingly perceived to be somehow incompatible with femininity, while emerging genres such as the novel, which had from the beginning enjoyed a large proportion of female practitioners, were declared in one way or another to be quintessentially feminine. The idea gained ground that what women were best at was producing texts in which they could give free rein to their imagination and to their *style naturel et naïf*, while men were by right the custodians of genres which demanded scholarly precision and familiarity with classical authors. Women's admittance into the *République des lettres* was facilitated by the recognition that their works had their own unique merits, but was, at the same time, predicated on their prior acceptance of a gender-based division of labour.[1]

The introduction of new, gendered genre systems meant that the use of classical sources and literary models, which had been standard practice among authors up to the middle of the seventeenth century, had by the beginning of the eighteenth century become problematic for women writers in particular. Women who studied Latin and Greek became one of the stock characters of classicist comedy; following Molière's example, dramatists such as Fatouville and Regnard ridiculed women scholars (Fatouville, *La Fille sçavante*, 1690) or highborn women who wished to learn Greek (Regnard, *La Critique du Légataire*, 1708).[2] To the traditional obstacles which had to be over-

---

[1] Timmermans L., *L'accès des femmes à la culture (1598–1715)* (Paris: 1993), especially 152-236.

[2] Ibid., 342.

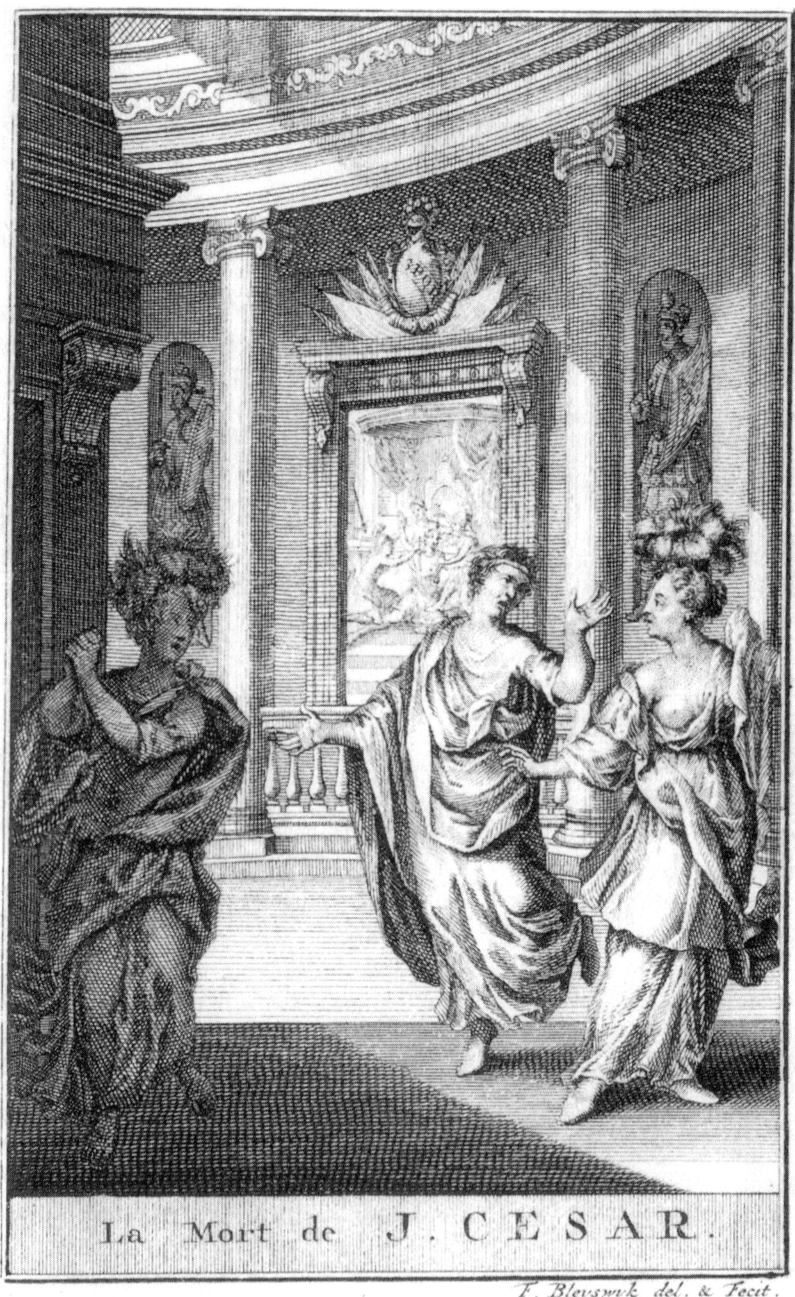

Scene from Marie-Anne Barbier's La Mort de César. Engraving by F. Bleyswyk.

come by the woman writer in order to gain a classical education was now added a new problem: once classically oriented literature had been effectively defined as being not only a male preserve but also masculine in its very essence, the woman writer who sought to link her work to the classicist tradition was perceived to de-sex herself by the very act of writing.

Timmermans's argument raises questions about the few French women who *did* persist after the end of the seventeenth century in linking their literary work to the classical tradition. How did these women manage to reconcile their apparently masculine literary activity with the new genre system, and was their use of classical sources really notably different from that of their male colleagues? The evidence so far suggests that while some *femmes savantes* studiously avoided any reference to their own sex and to the gendered genre system — one thinks, for example, of the classical scholar Anne Dacier (1651–1720) who, while never saying a word about her own unique position as a woman, *did* vehemently attack modern literary theory — others made at least some attempt, whether strategically motivated or proceeding from sincere literary considerations, to reconcile the classical tradition with the emerging feminine tradition in literature. A good example of the latter approach is the little-known dramatist Marie-Anne Barbier (c. 1670 1745)[3], whose tragedies were regarded by some eighteenth-century critics as models of classicism,[4] but who also sought to introduce a specifically female viewpoint, consistent with her avowed intention to demonstrate 'the merit of our sex',[5] into her work.

Marie-Anne Barbier, eighteenth-century femme de lettres

Marie-Anne Barbier was, with her eight published plays and operas (four tragedies, one comedy, and three opera librettos), the most prolific French woman dramatist before George Sand in the nineteenth

---

[3] For biographical details, see Titon du Tillet E., *Second supplément du Parnasse françois* [...] (Paris: 1755) 27-8, and Couret de Villeneuve L.F., *Tribut de la société nationale des neuf soeurs* (Paris: 1791) 75-88.

[4] Notably in Germany, where Luise Gottsched's translation of Barbier's second tragedy, *Cornelia, Mutter der Gracchen*, was produced for inclusion in the second volume of her husband's *Deutsche Schaubühne* (1741), whose avowed purpose was to furnish Germans with suitable models for the creation of a national neo-classicist theatre.

[5] Gethner P. (ed.), *Arrie et Pétus*, in *Femmes dramaturges en France (1650–1750). Pièces choisies*, Biblio 17 (Paris–Seattle–Tübingen: 1993) 259.

century. One of only a handful of women whose tragedies reached performance in seventeenth and eighteenth-century France,[6] she saw all her known plays produced either by the prestigious Comédie-Française, both in their Paris theatre and at court, or by the Académie Royale de Musique (the Paris *Opéra*). Later in the century, Barbier's work was performed abroad and translated into Dutch, German, Italian and Russian.

Although Marie-Anne Barbier's tragedies are sometimes uneven and, on occasion, facile in their use of literary convention, their very conventionality (which is sometimes only apparent) furnishes the modern reader with a better entry into characteristic period concerns and literary values — the stuff, finally, of *histoire des mentalités* — than the often more atypical works of her more celebrated contemporaries. Thus, I will be arguing that Marie-Anne Barbier's last published tragedy, *La Mort de César* (1709), owes its relevance to its attempt to articulate a certain conception of monarchy which, not coincidentally, corresponded to a new 'feminine' emphasis on the language of the heart in eighteenth-century France.

La Mort de César: *history or family drama?*

La Mort de César, Barbier's fourth tragedy to be staged by the Comédie-Française, had like all her previous dramatic work to contend with the masculine status of tragedy itself, which was based at least in part on its use of classical sources.[7] French theorists had invariably held that the proper subject of tragedy was events drawn from Greek or Roman history or mythology and described by the well-known classical historiographers (although, on occasion, exception could be made for a suitable biblical theme). History's function in tragedy was rhetorical: by relying on the *auctoritas* of the Ancients and by referring to the factual nature of the events portrayed, dramatists gave weight to the moral or political

---

[6] For a bibliography of French women dramatists, see Beach C., *French Women Playwrights before the Twentieth Century* (Westport, CN: 1994).

[7] Other supposedly typically masculine attributes of tragedy included its political subjects (as suggested by Corneille when writing that '[la tragédie] demande quelque grand intérêt d'État ou quelque passion plus noble et plus *mâle* que l'amour') and its elevated style (described by La Mesnardière as 'pur, grave, *mâle*, continu, vigoureux et magnifique' [my italics]). Cf. Corneille P., *Discours de l'utilité des parties du poème dramatique*, in *Oeuvres complètes* III, ed. G. Couton (Paris: 1987) 124 and La Mesnardière J. de, *La Poétique* (Paris: 1640) 390.

concerns which were often at the core of their work.[8] References to classical authors contributed both to tragedy's perceived role as a *miroir des princes* and to its standing, along with epic, at the summit of the literary genre-hierarchy. That this link between tragedy and classical historiography could, however, exclude women and the uneducated from writing it, was sometimes recognized, for example by Corneille when, commenting on his Latin sources in his first preface to *La Mort de Pompée*, he added as an afterthought: 'Les dames se les feront expliquer'. While classical historiography's link to gender was often left implicit, it did sometimes surface in popular reactions to particular plays. Racine, a dramatist notorious among his detractors for the 'ahistorical' and 'novelistic' elements he supposedly introduced into his tragedies, was said also to write only for women and *galants*.[9] Bad tragedies were, in critical parlance, *romanesque* (read: overly feminine?), whereas good tragedies were true to their historiographic sources, and were regularly praised for their *force* and for their *mâle* character.

Marie-Anne Barbier's first task in *La Mort de César* was thus to prove to a potentially sceptical audience that she knew her sources, and this she does conscientiously. In the preface, she informs us that it is to Amyot's translation of Plutarch's *Parallel Lives* — which she quotes briefly: '[que] je dois les principales beautez de ma Tragédie' (p. 249).[10] Her quotations of Caesar's famous 'The die is cast' (*Le sort en est jetté*) and his dying words to Brutus 'Et toi, mon fils, aussi' suggest at least some recourse to Suetonius and/or Cassius Dio, authors she had previously used when writing her first tragedy, *Arrie et Pétus* (1702). In at least one passage in the play itself (p. 262; I, 4) it is obvious that Barbier is paraphrasing a passage from Plutarch's *Life of Cesar* (63, 2-3), just as the notes addressed to Brutus by his critics (III, 3) follow the exact wording of Amyot's translation (*César* 80). Barbier's depictions of Porcie and Octavie, finally, suggest that she also used Plutarch's lives of Brutus and Antony in the writing of her tragedy. Whether she was herself able to read Greek and/or Latin remains a moot point.

----

[8] See, in relation particularly to Corneille and Racine, Forestier G., "Théorie et pratique de l'histoire dans la tragédie classique", *Littératures classiques* 11 (1989) 95-107 and Vuillemin J.-C., "Histoire et dramaturgie classique au XVIIe siècle", in *Actes de Columbus*, ed. C.G.S. Williams, Biblio 17 (Paris–Seattle–Tübingen: 1993) 229-44.

[9] Descotes M., *Histoire de la critique dramatique en France* (Paris–Tübingen: 1980) 78 passim.

[10] All page references are to *Les Tragédies et autres poésies de Mademoiselle M.A. Barbier* (Leiden: 1719).

Yet, despite this evidence of her use of classical sources, the plot of Barbier's tragedy is far removed from any known historical account of the events leading up to Julius Caesar's murder. Caesar, worried that his political opponent Brutus may pose a threat to him, decides to ensure his political allegiance by marrying him off to his niece Octavie. Brutus, who loves Caton's daughter Porcie instead, sees Caesar's proposed marriage deal as yet another sign of his political tyranny, and is strengthened in his oppositional role by Porcie's insistence that he avenge her father's death, which she blames on Caesar. Antoine, who loves Octavie, is angered by Caesar's plan to deprive him of his beloved. Caesar is warned by an oracle consulted by Calpurnie that he should fear for his life and, in an attempt to discover the identity of his aspiring murderer, he confronts Brutus and Antoine, thereby uncovering the discontent occasioned by his marriage plans. Repenting of his previous dictatorial behaviour, he gives Porcie to Brutus and Octavie to Antoine, and embraces Brutus as his 'son', but it is too late. Although he is torn between his growing admiration for Caesar and his sense of political justice, Brutus, urged on by Porcie, finally carries through with his original plan to kill Caesar. Antoine, recounting the deed to Octavie, brings the tragedy to a close with a statement not completely bereft of ambiguity:

> Octavie
> Cruels! tant de fureur sera-t-elle impunie?
> > Antoine
> Non, je les perdrai tous. Mais voyons Calpurnie;
> Et *faisant au tombeau succeder les autels*,
> Plaçons le grand César entre les Immortels (p. 324; V, 10 [my italics]).

Indeed, in the light of the marital drama which had dominated the play, there is a lurking possibility that these *autels* Antoine refers to are not necessarily sacrificial altars but, perhaps, marriage altars, playing thereby on a semantic confusion between marriage and death which Barbier had exploited in her previous work and which, before her, had constitued an important element in the dramatic work of Racine.[11] Caesar the dictator had to die, perhaps, in order to make the marital fulfilment of his subjects possible.

By reading the political murder of Caesar as a family drama, Marie-Anne Barbier was following the literary conventions of her day and, in passing, illustrating the relativity of the gendered genre system

---

[11] Mauron C., *L'Inconscient dans la vie et l'oeuvre de Racine* (Paris: 1957) 36.

described by Timmermans. Right from the beginning, authors of classicist tragedies had tended, inspired by Plutarch's own example but also by contemporary novelistic practice and especially by the unofficial *histoires secrètes* of the period, to graft secret love affairs and intrigues onto well-known historical fact in an attempt to explain history in a manner in keeping with current sensibilities.[12] Cinna's plot against Augustus was motivated, in Corneille's *Cinna* (1643), as much by his love for Emilie, a character invented by the dramatist, as by deep-seated political conviction. Nero's elimination of Britannicus was, according to Racine in *Britannicus* (1670), a move to eliminate not a political rival but a rival for the love of Junie. Classicist tragedy's receptivity to techniques and themes issuing from other genres — including characteristically 'feminine' ones such as the novel — was so essential to the genre's continuing ability to speak to contemporary audiences that it would have been difficult, in actual literary practice if not in theory, to close it off as a truly masculine preserve — a fact Barbier was able to turn to her own advantage in her *César*.

Caesar, the ruler besieged

If, in *César* as in most of the drama of the period, contemporary and ancient history merged imperceptibly on stage, turning Roman rulers into bewigged and perfumed *mondains*, Barbier would probably have been one of the first to recognize this. In her dedication of the play to her friend Marc-René d'Argenson, Louis XIV's enlightened *Lieutenant général de police* (who, not unhelpfully, was also responsible for theatrical censorship), she uses the common *translatio imperii* topos (which figured also in her other prefaces) to contrast d'Argenson's loyalty to Louis XIV to Brutus's betrayal of Caesar, and to wish her friend: 'Puisse au gré de mes voeux un choix encor plus juste / Te donner pour Mecene à ce nouvel Auguste!' (p. 247). Identifying Louis XIV with Julius Caesar and Augustus was of course nothing new in 1709,[13] but if the comparison is intended, then it is all the more curious that Caesar is portrayed in Barbier's tragedy as a wavering, melancholy ruler whose words at times, especially when he suspects his friends of plotting against him, have a distinctly pathetic ring to them:

---

[12] Truchet J., *La Tragédie classique en France* (Paris: 1975) 126-9.
[13] Burke P., *The Fabrication of Louis XIV* (New Haven–London: 1992) 115 passim.

Moi Tyran! ce nom seul me fait fremir d'horreur.
Albin, tu lûs cent fois dans le fond de mon coeur,
Rien ne me fut plus cher que de regner sur Rome.
[...]
Mais je crûs que le Peuple et le Senat lui-même
Viendroit me présenter le sacré diadème,
Et loin de m'égarer en d'injustes projets,
Je comptois tous les coeurs pour mes prémiers Sujets.
N'y pensons plus; le Ciel autrement en ordonne,
Peuple, Senat, amis, enfin tout m'abandonne:
Et sur qui me fier? où trouver de la foi,
Lorsqu'Antoine et Brutus conspirent contre moi?
Je les attens, mais non pour les charger d'outrages,
Non pour briguer encor leurs indignes suffrages,
Ni pour les effrayer, ni pour les attendrir,
Je ne veux que les voir, les confondre, et mourir (p. 301-3; IV, 3).

Caesar, attacked on all sides, comes to feel that he has failed as a ruler. He is successively harangued by Porcie (II, 2), threatened by Antoine (III, 6), and told by Octavie that, once married to Brutus, she will do nothing to prevent his murder (III, 8). It is, however, Porcie who he fears the most; his misgivings about Brutus, which are the starting-point of the dramatic action, are in fact a barely contained fear not of his possible supplanter, but of the formidable mistress '[qui] tient son ame asservie':

Car enfin sur mes jours s'il osoit attenter,
A la seule Porcie il faudroit l'imputer.
Je sçai que dans son coeur cette fiere Romaine
De Caton contre moi fait revivre la haine;
Et si de ses beautez Brutus est trop épris,
Sans doute de ma mort sa main sera le prix (p. 263-4; I, 4).

If Porcie is feared by Caesar, then it is for good reason, for she represents the last in a line of formidable seventeenth-century *femmes fortes* to be brought to the stage by Marie-Anne Barbier.[14] Like Arrie, Cornélie and Tomyris before her (the protagonists of Barbier's previous tragedies), Porcie is a powerful female figure playing a political role in a man's world and, in introducing her into the drama, Barbier stays true to her own declared intention in her earlier tragedies to portray women whose deeds were 'glorious to our sex'.[15] As in Plutarch's *Bru-*

---

[14] For an analysis of the seventeenth-century *femme forte* tradition and its key texts, see MacLean I., *Woman Triumphant. Feminism in French Literature 1610–1652* (Oxford: 1977).

[15] Gethner, *Arrie et Pétus*, 257. See also Barbier's preface to *Cornélie, mère des Gracques*, in which she states that, in portraying the deeds of Cornélie: 'J'ai cru ne pouvoir rien mettre sur la Scène qui fut plus glorieux à notre sexe' (p. 88).

tus and in the seventeenth-century moralists' accounts Barbier probably knew,[16] Porcia must put pressure on Brutus to make him reveal
the conspiracy to her but, once she has learned of it — and, at this
juncture, Barbier's account diverges significantly from her predecessors' — it is Porcia who becomes the driving force in the conspiracy
and who urges Brutus to fulfill his pledge when he seems to falter.
Even before Brutus's revelation, Porcia assumes a political role by
directly confronting Caesar and accusing him, in no uncertain terms,
of depriving Rome of her liberty:

> [...] quel fruit Rome en peut-elle attendre [de vos exploits],
> Lorsqu'elle perd un bien que rien ne peut lui rendre?
> Non, la noire Discorde, et toute sa fureur,
> Ces champs semez de morts, ce theatre d'horreur,
> Et tout ce qu'a d'affreux une guerre intestine,
> N'approche pas des maux que la paix nous destine,
> Malgré tant de malheurs, Reine de l'Univers,
> Rome donnoit des loix; on lui donne des fers (p. 272; II, 1).

Caesar's reaction to Porcie is interesting: not only does he attribute
her words to 'les transports d'une Amante' (p. 273), but:

> A travers vos discours j'entrevois vôtre haine,
> Je vois mon ennemi, le plus cruel de tous,
> L'implacable Caton revivre encor en vous (p. 272)

By aiming his response as much at Caton as at Porcie, Caesar suggests
that his arranged marriage between Brutus and Octavie, which he
announces to Porcie in this scene, is not only intended to thwart Porcie (as he had himself admitted), but goes even further and is ultimately directed at another man, Caton. Porcie and Octavie are made the
central objects in a male system of exchanges in which the ruler actually interacts with other men *through* women (Caesar interacts with
Caton through Porcie, and with Brutus through Octavie). As a pawn
in the male political marriage market, Porcie becomes, like the female
protagonists of so many tragedies (Camille in *Horace*, Emilie in *Cinna*)
the focal point of resistance to what is perceived as a tyrannical
regime. As she makes clear in her threat to Caesar, family and state

---

[16] Notably Madeleine de Scudéry's *Femmes illustres ou les Harangues héroïques* (1642),
Jacques du Bosc's *La femme heroïque* (1645), and Pierre Le Moyne's *Gallerie des Femmes
Fortes* (1647), all of which dwell at length on Porcia's role in the conspiracy against
Caesar.

power must be equated with one another: 'déja sur les coeurs portant la tyrannie / ne vous flattez pas de la voir impunie' (p. 273; II,2).

While Barbier's handling of the theme of woman-as-rebel does not differ much from male dramatists' handling of the same theme (even down to her inclusion of a male figure behind the female rebel — Caton — who legitimizes her unusually confrontational role), Barbier suggests no final reconciliation between the female rebel and the male ruler. Although Porcie resembles Emilie in *Cinna* (as did Arrie in Barbier's *Arrie et Pétus*), she is not 'recuperated' by the male authorities as is her counterpart in Corneille's play when Auguste, forgiving Emilie for having participated in the conspiracy, wins her loyalty. Likewise, Barbier's play offers the reader no equivalent of Corneille's Livie, the wise woman behind the ruler Auguste who steers the political conflict towards a peaceful resolution. *César*, truer to the hopeless situations of Racinian tragedy, ends up as a kind of *Cinna* gone wrong, in which the estrangement between the male and female protagonists admits of no resolution but in which there is no real reflection either, on the part of the female protagonist, on her own political role as being anything other than oppositional and, ultimately, ideologically immobile.

Caesar, father of the nation

Caesar's answer to his fear of Brutus and Porcie is, of course, to separate them by arranging a political marriage between Brutus and Octavie, thereby going against Antoine's previous advice to 'eliminate' Brutus in some more direct way. Caesar's choice of political weapon — marriage — is unsurprising given his well-established dramatic reputation for clemency, but it furnishes Barbier with a starting-point for her own reflection on the nature of his political power, which is portrayed as familial and sentimental. Not only does Caesar confess, in his pathetic outburst, that 'Je comptois *tous les coeurs* pour mes prémiers Sujets' [my italics] but, when telling Porcie of his marriage plans, he mixes the language of politics with the language of sentiment:

> Je rappelle à regret la Discorde fatale,
> Qui, ne nous rassemblant dans les champs de Pharsale
> Que pour voir les Romains triompher des Romains,
> Dans nôtre propre sang nous fit tremper nos mains.
> De nos divisions si malgré ma clemence

> Il reste dans les coeurs encor quelque semence,
> Apprenez quels chemins je prens pour l'y chercher.
> [...]
>
> Je veux les reünir [les Romains], mais sans les déchirer.
> Que l'hymen entre nous forme ces douces chaines;
> Dans nos embrassemens qu'il étouffe nos haines;
> Qu'aux vaincus à jamais unissant les vainqueurs,
> Dans une paix profonde il tienne tous les cours (p. 270; II, 2).

The political marriages planned by Caesar are presented as examples of his benevolence, even as he glosses over the fact that the discord he refers to ('les champs de Pharsale') was of his own making. His choice of political vocabulary, particularly his use of the word 'coeur', is noteworthy. If the word had originally denoted manly courage in classicist tragedy, as when Don Diegue famously asks his son in *Le Cid* (1637), 'Rodrigue, as-tu du coeur?' (I,5; l. 261), when Caesar talks of 'les coeurs' in conjunction with 'les embrassemens' and 'l'hymen [qui] entre nous forme ces douces chaînes', the term seems to have acquired the affective connotations which linked it, in the eyes of early eighteenth-century readers, with a specifically feminine, novelistic influence in literature.[17] The cumulative effect of Barbier's frequent use of the word 'coeur' in her tragedy, coupled with Caesar's protestations of love towards Brutus and Antoine — 'Brutus, je vous aime toujours' (p. 265; I,5), 'je vous ai trop aimez' (p. 303; IV,4), etc. — subtly feminizes the ruler, even as Porcie, whose 'coeur indomptable' really *is* courageous, is presented in a virile stance, for example when Caesar addresses Brutus:

> Que je serois heureux, si ce coeur indomptable,
> A force de bienfaits rendu plus équitable,
> Pouvoit enfin pour moi desarmer ses rigueurs!
> Je n'aspire, Brutus, qu'à regner sur les coeurs,
> Et Rome vainement m'offre un superbe Empire,
> S'il faut qu'un seul Romain en secret en soupire.
> A de si beaux desseins prêtez vôtre secours,
> Faites benir par-tout et mes lois et mes jours;
> Prévenez le Senat, et faites-lui connoitre,
> Que *César en ces lieux est plus Pere que Maitre* (p. 289; III, 5 [my italics]).

---

[17] The changing meanings of the word 'coeur' in this period are discussed by DeJean J., *Ancients against Moderns. Culture Wars and the Making of a Fin de Siècle* (Chicago–London: 1997) 108-23.

The image of the ruler as benevolent father is one of the central metaphors in the tragedy's sentimentalization of politics, as indeed it was in Marie-Anne Barbier's own time, where learned debate on the paternal essence of kingship had produced such works as Sir Robert Filmer's *Patriarcha* (1680), Locke's refutation of Filmer in his *Two Treatises of Government* (1690, French translation 1691) and, in France, Bossuet's *Politique tirée des propres paroles de l'Ecriture sainte*, published a mere three months before the première of Barbier's *Mort de César*. The metaphor had, in literature, been expressed most concisely in 1692 by La Bruyère: 'Nommer un roi PÈRE DU PEUPLE est moins faire son éloge que l'appeler par son nom, ou faire sa définition'.[18]

Given the immediate historical context of Barbier's tragedy, it is impossible — and perhaps unimportant — to establish whether her portrayal of the ruler as benevolent father is inspired by the tradition within classical historiography which commonly presented Caesar as a *pater patriae*, or whether it is a response to more contemporary conceptions of kingship. That the two should coincide is fortuitous, and a good example of the manner in which ancient and modern history could fuse completely in classicist tragedy, mutually reinforcing and recreating one another. In Barbier's *César*, the author underlines the metaphor in various ways. Antoine, at the very beginning, announces that 'Tous appellent César du tendre nom de Pere' (p. 257; I, 2), and both Octavie and Brutus consider themselves spiritual children of Caesar, Octavie because her uncle, following Roman kinship laws, '[lui] tient lieu de pere' (p. 256; I, 1), and Brutus because he sees in Caesar, unconsciously at first, a powerful father figure. The most effective dramatization of the ruler-as-father theme, however, is that produced by Barbier's portrayal of the oedipal conflict which opposes Caesar and Brutus to one another.

As tragic irony will have it, Caesar begins to really fulfill the role of benevolent father-ruler, rather than merely using the conventional political metaphor for his own ends, as Brutus is inexorably driven towards his fatal deed. Caesar repents of his previous dictatorial behaviour in the fourth act (IV, 4) and, vowing to reform, makes Brutus an honest offer:

> Obtiens le premier rang entre tous mes amis,
> Et consens que du moins je t'appelle mon fils (p. 307).

---

[18] La Bruyère J. de, *Les Caractères ou les Moeurs de ce siècle*, in *Oeuvres complètes*, ed. J. Benda (Paris: 1951) 284.

Caesar's words to Brutus and Antoine, which overflow with expressions of affection — 'Helas! je vous ai trop aimez', 'malgré tout mon amour', 'je les aime, et c'est moi qui les rens malheureux' — provoke within Brutus an anguished conflict between his political conviction that 'La seule liberté rend les Romains heureux' (p. 308; IV, 5), and his love and admiration for the man he wants to see as his father.

> Touché de mes regrets, il m'a rendu Porcie.
> J'ai vu dans ce moment ses pleurs prêts à couler;
> Du nom de fils sa bouche a daigné m'appeler,
> Et je pourrais encore, inhumain et perfide,
> Sous ce beau nom de fils cacher un parricide!
> Ah! que plutôt cent fois ma main, ma propre main,
> Si Rome veut du sang, en cherche dans mon sein (p. 313; V, 1).

Although the final decision has already been taken, Brutus, finding himself on the verge of abandoning the conspiracy in order to re-enter the aegis of his spiritual father, begs Caesar one last time, in a moving scene later imitated by Voltaire in his own *Mort de César* (1735; III,5), not to go to the Senate:

> O ciel! où courez-vous?
> Permettez moi, Seigneur, d'embrasser vos genoux:
> Ne me refusez pas la grâce que j'implore;
> Et si du nom de fils vous m'honorez encore,
> En ce fatal moment souffrez qu'à mon secours
> J'appelle un nom si cher pour conserver vos jours (p. 316; V, 3).

Brutus's words come dangerously close to revealing the entire conspiracy to Caesar, demonstrating the remarkable capacity of Caesar's politico-paternal discourse to win over his political enemies. It is finally Porcie, the outsider in the family drama, who must push Brutus to carry out his promise, suggesting that while patriarchal politics may work among men, it is the women who invariably end up feeling excluded (as is also suggested, intriguingly from a psychological point of view, when a jealous Porcie complains that Brutus loves Caesar more than her, p. 269; II, 1). This gendered reading of the plot of *Caesar* is reinforced by another character in the tragedy whose actions also subtly undermine the central political metaphor, namely Octavie, Caesar's adopted daughter.

Octavie: feminine obedience on display

That Octavie does not, like Porcie, immediately stand out in *César* is due to her obedience and apparent refusal to rebel against Caesar's tyranny, a role in keeping with Plutarch's and later descriptions of her as a model wife, who remains faithful to her husband even throughout his widely publicized escapades with Cleopatra.[19] When she learns from Antoine that she must marry another man, her reaction is a curt 'Helas!' which appeared excessively cold and lacking in 'sensibilité naturelle' to Barbier's audiences.[20] Antoine, expecting a more emotional outburst, is informed by her, again with remarkable crispness, that:

> Par de suprémes loix Brutus est mon époux;
> Et vous n'avez, Seigneur, que mes soupirs pour vous (p. 278-9; II, 6).

In fact, as she hastens to explain to Antoine and as Barbier herself underlined in her preface when answering her critics, she is doing no more than fulfilling her duty towards Caesar, 'un Héros, qui me tient lieu de pere' (p. 280). As Barbier explained to her readers:

> Le terme d'*adoption*, qu'elle employe au troisieme Vers, peut-il laisser le moindre doute là-dessus? Et cette adoption, qui la rend fille de César, lui permet-elle un autre langage? Elle fait plus; elle ajoute qu'Octavien a transmis à César tous les droits qu'il avoit lui-même sur son sort. En faut-il davantage pour la tenir indispensablement dans l'obeïssance qu'elle doit à ce pere d'adoption? (p. 253).

One may suspect Barbier in her attempt to justify herself of some specious argumentation. Strictly speaking, of course, Octavie's daughterly obedience is laudable, but it is so extreme (and so obviously so to Barbier's audience, as their critical reactions demonstrate) that it seems to acquire an ironic edge in the hands of an author who had, after all, already shown herself a skillful user of irony in her previous work. This suspicion of ironic intent is strengthened by the second scene in which Octavie distinguishes herself, namely when, to Caesar's announcement of his decision to marry her to Brutus, she replies:

---

[19] See in particular Madeleine de Scudéry's elaboration on this theme in her *Femmes illustres* – and, for Dutch variations on the theme, Olga van Marion's article in this volume.

[20] For example the anonymous critic D.E., quoted in Parfaict F. and C., *Histoire du théâtre françois depuis son origine jusqu'à présent*, XV (Paris: 1748), 32.

Vous formez entre nous [Brutus et moi] d'indissolubles noeuds,
Qu'allons-nous devenir, s'il nous trompe tous deux?
Que serait-ce, grands Dieux! si la triste Octavie
Découvrait des complots, et contre votre vie?
Par ma bouche, Seigneur, seraient-ils déclarés?
Ses intérêts alors me seraient trop sacrés.
    CÉSAR
Qu'entends-je? Si Brutus tramait un jour ma perte,
Malgré sa perfidie à vos yeux découverte,
Vous pourriez sans remords le laisser achever?
    OCTAVIE
Je réponds de mourir, mais non de vous sauver (p. 293; III, 8).

Octavie's acceptance of the social conventions whereby women must remain at all times under the authority of a male counselor, whether father or husband, is so complete that, once having become Brutus's wife, she would not break her husband's trust even to save her own 'father's' life. Her excessive obedience and apparent submission to male authority thus acquire a critical edge, and her refusal to speak in the event of a conspiracy against Caesar seems to be a wry reference to her own political voicelessness in a patriarchal state. Although Octavie ostensibly participates in the same politico-familial discourse as Brutus, her attitude emphasizes the real difference between them: where Brutus's growing admiration for Caesar offers him the possibility of inclusion within Caesar's political system, Octavie must always, despite her best efforts, remain a political outsider. Whether her self-conscious attitude towards Caesar *can* however really 'force the patriarchy to self-destruct by a "work-to-rule" adherence to [her] subordinate status', as English Showalter contends,[21] remains questionable. Caesar does finally die in *La Mort de César*, but it would be difficult to see in his death a harbinger of female emancipation, as Barbier's female characters, locked in their oppositional role, can do nothing but endlessly (re)cite the prevalent politico-familial discourse.[22]

---

[21] Showalter E. Jr, "Writing Off the Stage. Women Authors and Eighteenth-Century Theater", *Yale French Studies* 75 (1988) 95-111 (esp. p. 101).

[22] I have borrowed this term from Terdiman, R. *Discourse/Counter-Discourse: The Theory and Practice of Symbolic Resistance in Nineteenth-Century France* (Ithaca, NY: 1989), who considers (ironic) 're/citation' a first stage in the articulation of a critical counter-discourse.

Writing women into history

We seem to have drifted away from Plutarch and Suetonius in Marie-Anne Barbier's family drama, where sons and daughters struggle against tyrannical fathers, and yet the author makes a conscious effort to integrate her own reading of the events into the known historical accounts. Her *César* is in fact punctuated by a series of quotations and recurring references to her classical sources which, at crucial moments, help to push the action forward. One of these recurrent motifs is the linguistic predetermination which makes Brutus Caesar's inevitable murderer. As Caesar himself, before his own change of heart, says of his political rival:

> Son nom m'est odieux, et me le rend suspect.
> Oui, je me sens fremir aussi-tôt qu'on le nomme.
> Un Brutus autrefois chassa les Rois de Rome;
> Ce Brutus, cher Antoine, étoit de ses Ayeux.
> Je sçai que sur lui seul Rome entiere a les yeux.
> J'ignore s'il prétend me servir ou me nuire:
> Mais je ne vois que lui qui puisse me détruire (p. 260; I, 3).

At six regularly spaced intervals in the course of the action (I, 3 ; I, 4; II, 1; III, 3; IV, 4, and V, 5) different characters — Caesar, his confidant Albin, Porcie, and Brutus himself — link Marcus Brutus to Junius Brutus, his legendary ancestor according to Plutarch (*Marcus Brutus* I, 1). The function of these references to Brutus's prophetic name is to tie the action to its historiographical source but, more importantly, to use the *auctoritas* of the Ancients to legitimize Barbier's own reading of the political events. Thus, in the scene where Brutus reveals the conspiracy to Porcie, thereby inaugurating the female protagonist's heroic intervention, the voice of the classics is very present:

> si l'aspect du rang, où César m'a placé,
> Impose aux plus hardis un silence glacé,
> Empruntant d'autres voix pour me crier vangeance,
> Ils sement des écrits dont ma gloire s'offense;
> Ces mots y sont tracez, à mes regards confus,
> Tu dors Brutus, tu dors, & n'és pas vrai Brutus.
> Ah! d'un courroux trop lent puisque l'on se défie,
> Il est temps que j'éclate, et que je justifie
> Et le fameux Romain dont je porte le nom,
> Et l'amour de Porcie, et le choix de Caton (p. 285-86; III, 3).

Not only had the central event of the scene — Brutus's revelation of the conspiracy — constituted an important episode in Plutarch's *Brutus* (14), but the accusing notes addressed to him — 'Tu dors Brutus, tu dors, et n'és pas [le] vrai Brutus' — are, down to the sixteenth-century grammatical construction, lifted directly from Amyot's translation (*César* 80) —, as of course is the reference to Brutus's putative ancestor. However, classical authority serves not to support a historically faithful rendering of the events, but to justify a characterization of Brutus as courtly lover: Brutus's words and Barbier's allusions to her historiographical sources, after all, lead up to his climactic declaration that it is for Porcie and for her father that he is prepared to kill Caesar. Barbier literally and symbolically writes her female characters into history by suggesting that her feminocentric reading of the political assassination, in which it is Porcie rather than Brutus who is the real motor of the action, has its roots in classical historiography; once again, contemporary concerns and history — Barbier's position as an eighteenth-century woman anxious to prove 'the merit of our sex' — are subtly juxtaposed onto ancient history.

A close examination of Barbier's *César* reveals that every act contains its own set of allusions to classical sources which in a similar manner help to legitimize Barbier's own version of the family drama. The well-known topoi of classical accounts are all integrated into the tragedy either through indirect narrative or in action, from Antoine's attempt to crown Caesar and Caesar's refusal of the honour (III, 6) to the exchange between Caesar and Albin on the day of his death (Caesar and the diviner, in Plutarch's version) to the effect that, though the Ides of March have arrived, they have not yet passed (IV, 3). The overall effect produced by Barbier's references to her classical sources is one of fragmentation and highly strategic use of classical *auctoritas* which recalls the royal historiography of her time. Like the official history of Louis XIV's reign,[23] which simply consisted of a collection of medals illustrating his exploits accompanied by Latin inscriptions, Barbier's *César* invokes the authority of the Ancients even while emphasizing events which, although nominally historical, were contemporary in their sentimental appeal and possible political implications. If, as Peter Burke contends, the year 1709 marks 'a remarkable change of emphasis' in the portrayal of Louis XIV, characterized by a

---

[23] *Médailles sur les principaux evenements du regne de Louis le Grand, avec des explications historiques* (Paris: 1702).

renewed attention to his role as 'father of his people'[24], then it is note-worthy not only that Marie-Anne Barbier and the Comédie-Française turned their attention to the same subject in 1709, but also that, in doing so, Barbier seems to make use of some of the same techniques as Louis's historiographers royal, Boileau and Racine.

Barbier's use of classical sources, characterized both by their frag-mentation and by the juxtaposition of ancient and modern history, reaches its apogee in the last scene of *César*, in which Antoine recounts Caesar's death. Caesar's dying words to Brutus 'Et toi, mon fils, aussi!' (p. 324; V, 10) are both a reference to Cassius Dio and Suetonius, and a recapitulation and legitimization, through recourse to ancient *auc-toritas*, of the tragedy's central concern with political patriarchy. The intervening juxtaposition of a family drama and sentimentalization of politics onto the events leading up to Caesar's death, indeed, mean that by the time Barbier's spectators reach Caesar's legendary words, the author has problematized patriarchal politics itself by suggesting that its ultimate losers are women. Although it is ostensibly Caesar and classical authority — Cassius Dio and Suetonius — who speak at this moment, Marie-Anne Barbier has, by a feat of ventriloquism not unlike Octavie's ironic re/citation of patriarchal rules, insinuated her own version of the events and, especially, her own female protago-nists, into the supposedly historical account.

Classical historiography's function as a rhetorical tool which pro-vides both an example and a means for introducing new, sentimental elements into tragedy is thus much the same in *César* as in other tragedies of the period, but the actual object of its persuasion, as in any tragedy, lies finally with the author. In her representation of the death of Julius Caesar, Marie-Anne Barbier effects a double inscrip-tion: not only does she write a female reflection on patriarchal politics into history by suggesting that this reflection was already present in classical historiography but, in the process, she literally writes herself, too, into history as perhaps the last woman, decades before Voltaire's triumphs and before the tragedies of the French revolution, to write true classicist tragedies for the French stage.[25] While Barbier's lack of successors is probably attributable in part to the process, whose begin-

---

²⁴ Burke, *The Fabrication of Louis XIV*, 112-3.

²⁵ There were other women authors of tragedies after Barbier, notably Mme de Gomez between 1714 and 1717, and Mme Du Boccage in 1749 (with *Les Amazones*), but their tragedies depart so much from the classicist model that I would argue that Barbier was the last true imitator of Corneille and Racine among women authors.

nings Timmermans had documented, of the progressive closing off of the genre to female participation, *La Mort de César* demonstrates how, despite increasing theoretical attempts to define tragedy as a masculine genre by its use of classical historiography, the very *auctoritas* of the classics could, in actual literary practice, be put to the service of a feminine voice in literature just as easily as a masculine one.

Selective Bibliography

BARBIER M.-A., *Les Tragédies et autres poésies* (Leiden: 1719)

BEACH C., *French Women Playwrights before the Twentieth Century: A Checklist* (Westport, CN: 1994)

BURKE P., *The Fabrication of Louis XIV* (New Haven–London: 1992)

CORNEILLE P., "Discours de l'utilité des parties du poème dramatique", in *Oeuvres complètes* III, ed. G. Couton (Paris: 1987)

DEJEAN J., *Ancients against Moderns. Culture Wars and the Making of a Fin de Siècle* (Chicago–London: 1997)

DESCOTES M., *Histoire de la critique dramatique en France* (Paris–Tübingen: 1980)

FORESTIER G., "Théorie et pratique de l'histoire dans la tragédie classique", *Littératures classiques* 11 (1989) 95-107

GETHNER P. (ed.), *Femmes dramaturges en France (1650–1750). Pièces choisies*, Biblio 17 (Paris–Seattle–Tübingen: 1993)

LA BRUYÈRE J. DE, *Les Caractères ou les Moeurs de ce siècle*, in *Oeuvres complètes*, ed. J. Benda (Paris: 1951)

LA MESNARDIÈRE J. DE, *La Poëtique* (Paris: 1640)

MACLEAN I., *Woman Triumphant. Feminism in French Literature 1610–1652* (Oxford: 1977)

MAURON C., *L'Inconscient dans l'oeuvre et la vie de Racine* (Paris: 1957)

PARFAICT F. and C., *Histoire du théâtre françois depuis son origine jusqu'à présent*, XIV (Paris: 1748)

SHOWALTER E. Jr, "Writing Off the Stage. Women Authors and Eighteenth-Century Theater", *Yale French Studies* 75 (1988) 95-111

TERDIMAN R., *Discourse/Counter-Discourse: The Theory and Practice of Symbolic Resistance in Nineteenth-Century France* (Ithaca, NY: 1989)

TIMMERMANS L., *L'Accès des femmes à la culture (1598–1715)* (Paris: 1993)

TITON DU TILLET E., *Second supplément du Parnasse françois, ou ordre chronologique des poètes et des musiciens que la mort a enlevés depuis le commencement de l'année 1743 jusu'à cette année 1755* (Paris: 1755)

COURET DE VILLENEUVE L.F., "Vie de Mademoiselle Barbier", *Tribut de la société nationale des neuf soeurs* (Paris: 1791) 75-88

TRUCHET J., *La Tragédie classique en France* (Paris: 1975)

VUILLEMIN J.-C., "Histoire et dramaturgie tragique au XVIIe siècle", in *Actes de Columbus*, ed. C.G.S. Williams, Biblio 17 (Paris-Seattle–Tübingen: 1993) 229-44.

THE DUTCH REPUBLIC BETWEEN HAUTEUR AND GREED:
LAMBERT VAN DEN BOSCH AND HIS DRAMA
*L. CATILINA**

Bettina Noak

'History is the mother and nurse of all human knowledge, be it in the area of nature, philosophy, or theology', according to Gerardus Vossius (1577–1649).[1] History possesses a special influence on ethical conduct and is thus, in the *politica*, indissolubly connected with the practice of statecraft. For she provides examples in which the results of human actions under the most varied historical circumstances may be seen, but she also spurs on to imitation. She bestows knowledge, but she also awakens will power. Thus she makes us not only into spectators, but into actors. In this way she forms the basis, and at the same time becomes the highest perfection of statecraft.[2]

Vossius refers here to the principle of Renaissance *imitatio*, the imitation of great historical examples that he derives by preference from Antiquity. This idea, of course, never means the slavish copying of the deeds of ancient protagonists, but rather an active adoption of the lessons that may be drawn from their fates.[3] This principle of imitation played an important role in the historical perception of the Renaissance. Examples worthy of imitation, as well as their opposites — those historical personalities whose scandalous conduct must be avoided — are provided especially by Roman history. Every class, as is emphasized in a Dutch edition of Livy, can draw suitable lessons from them.[4] The Roman State itself was regarded as a model particularly worthy of imitation, since it was assumed then that it united with-

---

• For the translation of this article I am grateful to Don McFarlane. I profited from the remarks of Karl Enenkel and Alicia Montoya.

[1] Vossius G., *Geschiedenis als wetenschap*, ed. C. Rademaker (Baarn: 1990) 51.

[2] Vossius, *Geschiedenis als wetenschap*, 55-9.

[3] Vossius emphatically demands that a politician not only possesses knowledge and virtue, but also reflect actual prevailing circumstances in his measures, as well as being able to react flexibly to human frailties. *Imitatio* thus becomes a creative process. Cf. Vossius, *Geschiedenis als wetenschap*, 55-6.

[4] Livy, *Romainsche Historien van Titus Livius, sedert de bouwing van Romen tot aan d'ondergang van 't Macedonische Rijk*. [...] *Nieuwelijks uit de Romainsche Historie van M. Scipio Dupleix vertaalt en met nieuwe Bladwyzers verrijkt* (Amsterdam: 1646), f. *3v.

in itself, under consular rule, the three classical forms of statehood: monarchy, aristocracy and democracy. This conception, going back to Polybius, possessed a particular importance for political debate in the Netherlands, as it was exactly this mixed form of state, by means of which the single components balanced each other out, that some theorists saw as the most fitting for the Dutch Republic.[5] In this context they laid emphasis on the harmonious coordination between the monarchist and the aristocratic principle that one identified with the rule of the Stadholder and also of the States.[6]

Hugo Grotius (1583–1645) argued in favour of this type of government in his *Tractaet vande Oudheyt vande Batavische, nu Hollantsche Republique* (*Treatise on the Antiquitiy of the Batavian, now the Dutch Republic*, 1610) in order to provide the young Dutch State with a historical tradition that reached back into Antiquity.[7] In his opinion it was no accident that the Batavian State, whose direct heir was the Dutch Republic, won its first glory in its dispute with the Roman Empire, against whose attempts at expansion it successfuly defended its freedom. The stability of the Batavian community lay for Grotius precisely in this mixed form of government: 'Indien by dit gebiedt van de treffelijcksten, wesende 't samenghevoeght uyt de Staten, noch toe-komt een wettelijck Vorstendom, alsulcken regeringe moet geacht werden voor de best uytverkoren, ende wel gematight'.[8] As will be seen later the discussion concerning the mixed form of state has a direct relevance for Van den Bosch's tragedy.

Historical drama, the genre to which Van den Bosch's *L. Catilina*

---

[5] Cf. Livy, *Romainsche Historien*, f. ***1v. Regarding the interpretations of Polybius, their Nachleben and the theory of the mixed form of government, compare also Bodin J., *Über den Staat*, ed. G. Niedhart (Stuttgart: 1994) II, 1, 46-50.

[6] Concerning political theory in the Netherlands see, in general, Blom H., "Politieke Filosofie in het Nederland van de zeventiende eeuw", *Geschiedenis van de Wijsbegeerte in Nederland* 4 (1993) 167-78; Klashorst G.O. van de, "*Metten schijn van monarchie getempert*. De verdediging van het stadhouderschap in de partijliteratuur 1650–1686", in *Pieter de la Court in zijn tijd (1618–1685). Aspecten van een veelzijdig publicist* (Amsterdam–Maarssen: 1985) 93-137; Kossman E.H., *Politieke theorie in het zeventiende-eeuwse Nederland* (Amsterdam: 1960); Lademacher H., *Die Niederlande. Politische Kultur zwischen Individualität und Anpassung* (Berlin: 1993); Vrankrijker A.J.C. de, *De staatsleer van Hugo de Groot en zijn Nederlandsche tijdgenooten* (Utrecht: 1937).

[7] This work was simultaneously published in Latin as *De antiquitate Reipublicae Batavicae*; in the seventeenth century there were a further six Latin and six Dutch editions. Cf. the bibliography in Grotius H., *De oudheid van de Bataafse nu Hollandse Republiek*, ed. G.C. Molewijk (Weesp: 1988) 93.

[8] 'If a legitimate principality is also added to this rule of the best, comprised from the States, then this form of government must be regarded as the best chosen and most harmonious' see Grotius, *De oudheid van de Bataafse nu Hollandse Republiek*, 44.

(1669) belongs, played an important part in the forming of modern Europe's ideology. The notion of imitation again plays a defining role because the plays seek to inspire, by means of their representation of human behaviour, as through the historical examples, an imitation of virtuous behaviour or a flight from the vices.[9] Precisely this Roman material was of vital importance for European drama of the seventeenth century; indeed it belonged to the 'national consciousness' of this period.[10] In the Dutch dramatic literature of the seventeenth century dramatists such as J. Bouckart, H. Verbiest and J. van Someren, as well as L. van den Bosch, are also concerned with Roman themes, a preoccupation which is evident in the fifties and sixties.[11]

In the first century BC Roman society went through a deep crisis. Historians such as Livy and Sallust ascribed the sequence of catastrophies to an implied moral decay. The fall of the old, once so praiseworthy Republic was deemed a punishment for the decline of Roman morals.[12] Thus we read in Livy:

> But either I am deceived by the love of the assumed task, or no state was ever greater, more honourable and richer in good examples, and amongst no other citizenry made greed and the love of extravagance so late an entry, and nowhere stood poverty and thrift so high and so long in honour. So much so that the less one possessed, the less one desired. Only lately has wealth brought avarice to us and the excess of longing for pleasures has brought with it the desire, through debauchery and extravagance, to go towards destruction, and destroy everything.[13]

---

[9] Concerning *imitatio* as a constitutive principle of drama see Smits-Veldt M.B., *Het Nederlandse renaissancetoneel* (Utrecht: 1991) 48-50.

[10] Cf. Lindenberger H., *Historical Drama. The Relation of Literature and Reality* (Chicago–London: 1975) 8 and Duits H., *Van Bartholomeusnacht tot Bataafse opstand. Studies over de relatie tussen politiek en toneel in het midden van de zeventiende eeuw* (Hilversum: 1990) 27.

[11] The following dramas are mentioned here in chronological order: R.O. van Zonhoven, *Blyeindig-Treurspel Van 't Gevecht Der dry Horatien ende Curiatien, ende der Zuster moord Horatij* [...] (1616); J. Michaelius, *Iulius Caesar, Ofte Kaiser-Moorders* (1645); M.F. Besteben, *De 'tsamensweringe Catalina* (1647); H. Verbiest, *De Doodt Van Julius Caezar* (1650); J. Lemmers, *Scipio. Bly-Endigh-Spel* (1651); J. Bouckart [Boukart], *De Nederlaagh van Hannibal* (1653); idem, *De Ballingschap van Scipio Africanus* (1658); J. Neuye, *Eneas of Vader des Vaderlandts* (1667); L. van den Bosch, *L. Catilina* (1669); J. Neuye, *De gewroke Lucretia, of Romen in Vryheit* (1669); J. van Someren, *C. Iulius Caesar, ofte wraeck van vermande vryheydt* (1670); cf. Meeus H., *Repertorium van het ernstige drama in de Nederlanden 1600–1650* (Leuven: 1983); Worp J.A., *Geschiedenis van het drama en van het toneel in Nederland*, 2 vols (Rotterdam: 1903–1907), vol I.

[12] Cf. here also the prologue to the Livy edition of 1646: Livy, *Romainsche Historien*, f. *4r as well as Hogers T., "Vertoog van dat Julius Caesar een Tyran heeft geweest", in *De Gemene Vryheit*, ed. R.H. Schele [...] (Amsterdam: 1666) H f. 8r-v.

[13] Livy, *Ab urbe condita* Prologue, 34.

Sallust in his *De coniuratione Catilinae* (*The Conspiracy of Catiline*) depicted Catiline as an exponent of the process of decay, as he sullied his patrician origins through his abominable deeds and placed no restraints on his power mania and his unbridled greed.[14] As well as Van den Bosch's play, M.F. Besteben's *De 'tsamensweringe Catalinae* (*The Conspiracy of Cataline*, 1647) is an example of the dramatical reinterpretation of the subject matter.[15] In it Catiline appears totally in the spirit of man's unbridled strife for power. The play especially rejects Catiline's intention to introduce a new form of government and to destroy the old and trustworthy constitution of the Roman Republic.[16] Tradition in particular is valid, as we have seen with Grotius, as a guarantee for the stability of a state, and the theoreticians of the Dutch Revolt constantly referred to the restoration of old rights in opposition to the newly introduced reforms of Philip II.[17] Thus these thoughts, publicly uttered in the Netherlands, were well known and did not lack an actual reference.

By means of L. van den Bosch's drama *L. Catilina* I shall now explain in more detail how the interpretation of historical subject matter might also be of use in taking up a position in the Dutch political debate.

Lambert van den Bosch, or Lambertus Sylvius, (1620–1698), teacher, poet, publicist and translator, was one of the most productive Dutch authors of the seventeenth century. He was born in Amsterdam in 1620. His family came originally from the Southern Netherlands and was of humble origin. After he had practiced his original profession of apothecary for some years, he became the headmaster of the grammar school at Helmond and was, from 1655 to 1671, assistant headmaster of the grammar school at Dordrecht, which was quite a respected institution. Legend has it that he was dismissed due to his drunkeness and licentious lifestyle. However, archival research has not confirmed this, nor was it able to reveal the real reason for his dismissal. Possibly he underwent political difficulties due to his con-

---

[14] On Catiline, cf. Livy, *Romainsche Historien*, f. Bb5v–Cc2v.

[15] The drama is preserved solely in a manuscript in the City Library of Haarlem, catalogue number 187 B 33; cf. the introduction to Besteben M.F., *De 'tsamensweringe Catalinae*, ed. G. van Emeren (Leuven–Amersfoort: 1988) 9.

[16] Besteben, *De 'tsamensweringe Catalinae* II, vs. 465-83 and 671-2.

[17] Concerning the political theory of the uprising, see Gelderen M. van, *The Political Thought of the Dutch Revolt 1551–1590* (Cambridge: 1992).

firmed allegiance to the House of Orange, as the town was in the hands of the De Witt family and their clientele. He later ran grammar schools at Heemstede and Vianen, where he died in 1698. Of his immense oeuvre, which places him in the ranks of prolific authors in the style of Simon de Vries (c. 1624–1708), the following titles should be mentioned: the first Dutch translation of Cervantes's *Don Quixote*: *Den verstandigen vroomen ridder Don Quichot de la Mancha* (1657), the first original Dutch epics, *Belgias* (1646), *Mauritias* (1646), *Baeto* (1648) and *Britannias* (1661), the historical dramas *Carel de negende anders Parysche bruiloft* (1645), *Wilhem of Gequetste Vryheyt* (1662) and *L. Catilina* (1669), as well as various historiographical and publicist writings, such as *Het leeven van Maria Stuart, koninginne van Schotland* (1647), *Het Treur-Toonneel Der Doorluchtige Mannen Onser Eeuwe* (1650), *Het Vorstelyck Treur-Toonneel, of Op- en Onder-gangh Der Grooten* (1652) and the continuation of Aitzema's *Saken van Staet en Oorlogh* under the title *Historien onses tyds* (1685).[18]

The author used historical subject matter in many of his works to support his arguments. In order to do this he employed different genres, such as historiography, epic poems and historical drama. It was for him, as for the majority of his contemporaries, a matter of course that this preoccupation with the past had a primarily moral meaning. Through the fall of the mighty it demonstrated the transience of earthly fortune and by this means helped to instill detachment towards temporal things.[19] Besides this ethical meaning given to his torical description, a political statement frequently appeared. In this plays the two historical dramas, *Carel de negende anders Parysche bruiloft* (*Charles IX or the Parisian Wedding*, 1645) and *Wilhem of Gequetste Vryheyt* (*William or Tormented Freedom*, 1662) were, for example, most probably

---

[18] Cf. Duits H., "Lambert van den Bosch als pleitbezorger van het stadhouderschap", in *'t Ondersoeck leert. Studies over middeleeuwse en 17de-eeuwse literatuur ter nagedachtenis van Prof. dr. L. Rens*, ed. G. van Eemeren – F. Willaert (Leuven–Amersfoort: 1986) 341-52; Idem, *Van Bartholomeusnacht tot Bataafse opstand*, 50-1; Lechner J., "Vertaler, bewerker, bederver. Jacob Campo Weyerman en *Don Quijote*", *Mededelingen Stichting Jacob Campo Weyerman* 18 (1995) 42-50; Oey-de Vita E., "De wanen van Caspar Barlaeus ten tonele gevoerd in de herfst van 1648?", in *'t Ondersoeck leert*, 329-39; Smit W.A.P., "Het Baeto-Epos dat geschreven werd", *Verslagen en Mededelingen Vlaamse Academie* 1 (1971) 11-26; Vliet R. van – Niet M. de, "Van ridders en andere Dordtse helden. De *Don Quichot*-vertaling van Jambert van den Bos", *Mededelingen Stichting Jacob Campo Weyerman* 18 (1995) 10-20; Wilke F.A.S., *Lambert van den Bos. Biografie. Dordrechtsche Arcadia. Zuydt-hollandtsche Thessalia. Bibliografie* (unpublished undergraduate thesis, Amsterdam: 1969).

[19] Cf. the preface to *Het Treur-Toonneel der doorluchtige Mannen onser eeuwe*, f. ***3v (1650).

written as a direct reaction to a contemporary political conflict. *Carel de negende* contains a warning against the political threat posed to the Dutch Republic from an ever more powerful France, shortly before the Peace of Münster. In *Wilhem of Gequetste Vryheyt* Van den Bosch takes the side of the party supporting the House of Orange, which concerned itself during the first Stadholderless period (1650–1672) with the reintroduction of the office of Stadholder that was to be occupied by the young Prince of Orange.[20] As shall be shown afterwards, Van den Bosch's drama *L. Catilina* might also be examined for its political content.[21] In it the author intended to display certain parallels between the Roman and Dutch Republics. The difficulties that the aristocratic mode of government brought the Roman Republic were to be held up in particular as a warning before the eyes of the contemporaries.

As to the dramatic action, Van den Bosch sticks very closely to his sources: Sallust's *De coniuratione Catilinae* and Cicero's *In Catilinam Orationes* (*Speeches against Catiline*).[22] Some Roman nobles, among them Catiline, Lentulus and Curius, agree to end a period of rule in which, according to their way of thinking, the highest authority lies in the hands of a few persons who are abusing the old nobility. They plan a coup d'état with the murder of Cicero as its starting point. Yet Curius betrays their intentions to his lover Fulvia in order to impress her. She warns Cicero, who takes the necessary precautions to render the conspirators harmless. In the meantime the conspirators have attempted to form an alliance with the Gallic tribe of the Allobroges. These, however, betrayed them to the Romans. By means of his famous speech before the Senate, Cicero forces Catiline to leave Rome. The remaining conspirators are arrested and must, convicted by the irrefutable evidence, admit their guilt. According to the demands of the uncompromising Cato they are sentenced to death. Lastly a messenger describes the execution and the downfall of Catiline during the battle of Pistoria. He dies, so says the reporter, a heroic death. It is the sad fate of Rome,

---

[20] See Van den Bosch, *Carel de negende anders Parysche bruiloft* (1645 and *Wilhem of Gequetste Vryheyt* (1663); cf. Duits, *Van Bartholomeusnacht tot Bataafse opstand*, 50-66 and 122-53.

[21] I used the edition which is to be found in the Royal Library in the Hague (no 448 K 132).

[22] Cf. Worp, *Geschiedenis van het drama* I, 330.

concludes Cicero, that it always has to gain the bloodiest victories against itself.

If one wishes to approach the political content of the play, it is relevant to pose the question as to why the author at the time of writing, around 1669, should have chosen just this historical material. If one primarily peruses Sallust's *De coniuratione Catilinae*, one notices that he not only presents a picture of the conspiracy but also, at the same time, attempts to explain how it has come to such a situation in the Roman Republic. His conclusion is that, above all, the extravagant lifestyle of the Romans and the degeneration of the values of their forefathers are responsible for the decay of society. A craving for riches rules the Roman aristocracy. Holding public office serves only the enrichment of a tiny minority, which has grabbed all political power for itself. Nowhere does the old willingness to make sacrifices exist that was shown during the glorious campaigns against Carthage and which envisaged solely the welfare of the people. The result is civil war, at present the greatest threat to the Roman state.[23]

Those who have knowledge of the political situation in the Netherlands during the first Stadholderless period and the discussions that were current at this time concerning the future of the Republic, should be somewhat familiar with these thoughts.[24] The publicists' quarrel conducted in those days turned principally on the question of which form of state was best suited to the Dutch Republic. The adherents of the circle of regents around the De Witt brothers ("staatsgezinden") regarded a purely aristocratic government as the best guarantee for welfare and stability. With the *Eternal Edict* of 1667, through which the office of Stadholder in Holland was abolished forever, they believed themselves to have taken a significant step on the road to totally aristocratizing the Dutch Republic. The adherents of the young Prince of Orange ("prinsgezinden"), on the other hand, defended the idea of a mixed form of government. With that concept they meant a state which would be balanced out by the interaction of three powers: the royal, the aristocratic and the bourgeois.[25] This is a form of government, therefore, by which the Stadholder, as the

---

[23] Cf. Sallust, *De Coniuratione Catilinae*, 9-21; for the dramatization of these complaints in van den Bosch's drama see II, ii, p. 11-2.

[24] See e.g. Israel J., *De Republiek 1477–1806*, 2 vols (Franeker: 1996–1997) II, 799-904; Van de Klashorst, *"Metten schijn van monarchie getempert"*.

[25] Cf. Van de Klashorst, *"Metten schijn van monarchie getempert"*, 103.

monarchist element, curbs the power of the representatives of states and cities, that is, the aristocratic element. In the debate criticism of the conception of the opposition party naturally played an important role. Therefore the adherents of the De Witts underlined the disadvantages of a monarchically tinged form of government, while the partisans of Orange sniped at the aristocracy. Against this background the political implications of Van den Bosch's play can be more closely discerned.

The playwright clearly took up a pro-Orange position in his drama *Wilhem of Gequetste Vryheyt*. In it he defended the services rendered by the House of Orange to the Dutch state and formulated the necessity of reintroducing the office of Stadholder.[26] In *L. Catilina*, however, relevant to the contemporary discussion, he highlights the problems that an aristocratic model of government brings with it. As for Sallust, the threat to society manifests itself for him, too, in two aspects: the downfall of morality goes along with the downfall of the political system.

In his speech before the Senate, directed against Catiline, it is Cicero himself who cites the alteration in the Roman customs as the cause of the problems:

> Beschreven Vaderen; onse Ouderen wel eer
> Gebruyckten voor de Roem en vryheyt hun geweer,
> Eer door huns selfs gewicht 't gebiedt, de Staet, dees wallen
> Door boosheyt ondermijnt, dus sloegen aen 't vervallen.
> Maer zedert dat de pracht en dartelheyt te met
> Sich in de plaets van deught en vroomheyt heeft geset,
> En niet, 't gemeen belangh, de voorstant van de wetten,
> En gulde vryheyt sich tot tegen-weer versetten;
> Maer eygen baet, en hoop tot snoot en vuyl gewin,
> Nam sulck een droef verval sijn aenvangh en begin,
> En steegh na desen trap (III, i, p. 17).[27]

The ancestors fought for the fame and freedom of the country. They remained undefeated until the evil at the core of the state raised its

---

²⁶ Cf. Duits, *Van Bartholomeusnacht tot Bataafse opstand*, 122-53.

²⁷ 'Senators, our ancestors of yore, used their weapons for glory and freedom before, through their own weight, the rule, the state, these walls, through evil undermined, in such fashion began to wobble. Since, however, pomp and frivolity have simultaneously taken the place of virtue and piousness, and the general good, the sense of justice and golden freedom did not defend themselves against self-interest and anticipation of shameful and dirty gain, such a sad decay began and reached this stage of development'.

head. When welfare and voluptuousness took the place of virtue and steadfastness, and self-interest and the pursuit of profit started to determine dealings among citizens, the distressing decay of society began. The desire for riches is the source of all evil. Before this background the motto of the drama is to be easily apprehended: an exclamation that only allows one basis for the actions of Catiline and his followers: 'Quid non mortalia pectora cogis,/Auri sacra fames'. ('What was there that ye mortal hearts, shameful with greed for gold, were not capable of?').[28]

Moreover, so Cicero claimed, it is not the humblest citizens over which the pernicious passions have gained mastery, for it is only those of quality who are tainted by this stain:

> Ghy hoort Quiriten, uyt soo naeckten waerheyt heden,
> Hoe ver 't verderf sich streckt door d' edelste onser leden,
> Hoe ver de moetwil dat verrotte deel vervoert,
> Aen wie het hanght dat gantsch de stadt wordt omgeroert (II, iii, p. 14).[29]

Harmful effects such as envy and greed were, according to the Orangist pamphleteers, at the origin of the possible degeneration of the aristocracy. The author of the pro-Orange *Haeghs Hof-Praetje* (*Hague Court Conversation*, 1662), for example, regards ambition as the most important motive for human activity in the oligarchy:

> 't Herte van een Mensch is Hoveerdich ende begeerigh, trachtende daerom dickwils meer haer eygen, als het gemeene beste ende welvaert. [...] In summa, is men geen Hooft, men soeckt het te worden, door Dach en Nacht te kuypen, corruptie en andere vuyligheden te plegen, waer door het seer lichtelijck gebeurt, dat inde Steden [...] groote Geslachten alleen een-hoofdigh, ende gelijck als Princelijck Regeren, ja weten de selve Regeringh, onder die bedeckten Naem van populaire, aen haer ende haer geslachten alleen te brengen.[30]

Thus it was, he maintained, in Rome and thus it also is in the Dutch Republic.

---

[28] Cf. the title page. The verse is taken from Vergil *Aeneid* III, 56-7.

[29] 'You hear today, citizens of Rome, the naked truth, how very greatly the corruption has infected our noblest limbs, how far the malignance of this rotten body seduces. It is due to this that the whole city has been won over to insurrection'.

[30] 'The heart of man is haughty and covetous, therefore tending more often to its own well-being than to the common good. [...] On the whole if one is not a commander, one strives to become one by scheming day and night, employing corruption and other abominations through which it very easily comes about that in the cities [...] only great families rule absolutely, as it were, princely, indeed striving, under the false

The inclination towards riches and power is, therefore, the cause of the degeneration of the Republic into an oligarchy. Van den Bosch conveys the political consequences this has for the state by means of the emissary of the Allobroges. In a conversation with the conspirator Lentulus he describes the misery of his own land. Not only does the heavy tribute demanded of them by the Romans oppress the people, the greatest problem is their own government:

> Eylaes! ons ongeval valt des te swaerder uyt,
> Dat het haer eygen last, als in sich selfs besluyt.
> Sy die den Hemel schickt tot heerschen en gebieden,
> Tot voorstant van de Staet, en van bedruckte lieden,
> Sijn oorsaeck van het leet, dat ons ter neder druckt,
> Na dat we ellendigh zijn geschoren en gepluckt.
> Hier leyt de gront: men gaet elck eer-ampt-loos bekuypen,
> En koomt soo van ter zij het kussen te bekruypen,
> En 't eereloos verschot, de prijs van dese Staet,
> Ontgelt de goe Gemeent op 't bitterste: men laedt
> Hen sware lasten op, en pluckt haer kloeckste veren,
> Tot datse macht'loos zijn, en sich niet konnen weren.
> Dan rooft men op het seerst, elck slaet sijn hant daer an,
> Elck is een Koninck, en elck Koninck een Tyran,
> Een yeder, om terwijl sijn banden vast te maecken,
> Maeckt aenhanck, om niet weer van 't kussen af te raecken.
> Daer kant men tegen een, die sich het meeste stijft,
> Met macht van magen, is 't die eynd'lijck boven drijft.
> Terwijl verwaerloost, door soo snoode kuyperijen,
> Loopt alle winst in 't riet, de Staet kan niet bedijen.
> Men acht op scha noch winst, stelt self fortuyn te leur,
> En komt ons voordeel toe, men wijst het self de deur (II, ii, p. 10-1).[31]

---

name of government for the people, to secure government for themselves and their families alone'; *Haeghs Hof-Praetje, ofte 'tSamen-spraeck tusschen een Hagenaer, Amsterdammer ende Leydenaer* [...] (Leiden: 1662) 9. Cf. Van de Klashorst, "*Metten schijn van monarchie getempert*", 113.

[31] 'Alas! Our misfortune is all the greater that it bears its own burden within itself. Those who heaven destines to rule and command us, as protectors of the state and oppressed people, are the origin of the misfortune which weighs on us after we are wretchedly driven and plundered. And this is the reason: men scheme unscrupulously for each position of honour and thus reach, by devious means, the prize of the state, while the dishonourable perquisites, the price for this post, must be paid most bitterly by the good community. One weighs them down with heavy burdens and plucks out their best feathers until they are powerless and can no longer defend themselves. Now the robbery really begins. Each has his share in it. Each is a king and every king a tyrant. Each and every one acquires partisans in order to strengthen his own position of power and in order not to lose it again. One stands in hostility against the other and he who is able to strengthen himself the most with the support of allies finally remains

Not the Romans, but rather their own government is the cause of the suffering of the people. Although the divine mandate of their office is the protection of the state and the support of the good community, the regents pursue nothing more than their own advantage. The honorary posts are purchasable and each attempts, through perfidious practices, to assume power or to hold on to power. Corruption and partisan rivalry are the order of the day, while the subjects must pay the price for this power struggle. In truth, it is not a concern of aristocracy, that is to say the united rule of the best, but each rather wants to rule for himself, as king. This kingdom however degenerates into a tyranny. The strong position of one's own family or party is more important for these regents than the welfare of the state. Furthermore the Gaul complains that they have no respect for religion:

> De Gods-dienst boven dat loopt schaloos, eertijts waren
> De hooghste sorgh van Staet de Kercken en Altaren,
> En dees Druuyden, die den waren wegh ter deught,
> Met kommer en met sweet, vertoonen aen de jeught,
> Nu acht men dit noch dat, men loopt in 't wilt daer henen,
> En d'Altaers onberoockt die schijnen te beweenen
> De kommer van t' gemeen, de vreckheyt van den Raet,
> Die 't liever doorbrenght in haer pracht en overdaet,
> Als tot hun eygen nut, aen konsten te besteden,
> Of Tempels om ten dienst hunne Altaers te bekleden.
> 't Verwildert volck ontsiet noch Godt noch menschen meer,
> Men acht op geen bevel, elck wordt sijn eygen Heer,
> En d'armoe, die gemeen de wanhoop heeft als eygen,
> Schijnt yeder uur de Staet het uyterste te dreygen (II, ii, p.10-1).[32]

The protection of religion and its servants was formerly the most important task of government. Now the altars are deserted and

---

the victor. In the meantime all advantages are lost, neglected due to such vile intrigues, and the state cannot flourish. Men have regard neither for injuries, nor for profit and disappoint Fortuna herself; when fortune is kind men send her away again themselves'.

[32] 'Above all religion receives injury. Earlier the churches and altars as well as the Druids, those who showed youth the true way to virtue through grief and sweetness, were the most important concern of the state. Now men are concerned neither with this nor that, they run wild, and the unincensed altars appear to mourn the grief of the people and the avarice of the council, that prefers to squander everything in pomp and superfluity instead of dedicating their riches, also for its own advantage, to the arts or to the temple, for the upkeep of the altar service. The people grown wild no longer fear either God or man. Men follow no command, each is become his own master and the poverty that commonly gives rise to despair appears every hour to threaten the state to the outmost'.

nobody is present any more to direct youth to the path of virtue. The people run wild and become, by this means, a threat to the concord of society, as whoever fears neither God nor the law, and is impoverished due to the intrigues of the regents, will easily become an insurgent.

This passage possesses a special meaning as Van den Bosch can only construct the speech of the Allobroges without reference to any original source. Concerning this Gallic tribe, in fact, almost nothing is known.[33] Proceeding from known general facts about the Gauls, he presumes an aristocratic government that he ultimately blames for those mistakes which are also illuminated in the pro-Orange literature of the period. The emissary of the Allobroges holds up a mirror to the conspirator Lentulus, and Lentulus admits that the Roman Republic suffers equally from these defects. It has therefore forfeited its role as guardian of international law.[34] More important however is that the Dutch reader could recognize the situation described by the Gaul. According to the pro-Orange publicists, discord, factional quarrel and neglect of state interests were characteristic of the aristocratic system. Above all, the tendency to raise oneself above the members of one's own class provoked these authors repeatedly to criticize what in their eyes appeared to be the damaging social ambition of the rulers.[35] Furthermore the supposed discrimination against religion, that is the Reformed Church, by the regents to whom were attributed Arminian and Libertarian tendencies, was an especially sore point for Van den Bosch. He was a Calvinist and had made this, as well as his anti-Catholic prejudices, unmistakably clear in his publicistic quarrel with Vondel and his "Catholic" drama *Maria Stuart* (1646).[36] It is therefore not surprising that in his play the protective role of government in respect to the church, as well as the usefulness of religion for the stability of rule, should be given a certain emphasis.

---

[33] On the Allobroges, see *Der kleine Pauly, Lexikon der Antike. Auf der Grundlage von A.F. Pauly's Realencyclopädie der classischen Altertumswissenschaften*, ed. K. Ziegler – W. Sontheimer, 5 vols (Stuttgart: 1964–1975) I, 275.

[34] See II, ii, p. 11-2.

[35] Cf. Van de Klashorst, *"Metten schijn van monarchie getempert"*, 113-4.

[36] Cf. Van den Bosch, *Geest Vande Coningin Elisabeth, Uyt den Grave opgeweckt, Door Toover-veersen van haren Laster-dichter* (1647), a polemical poem directed directly against Vondel, as well as his own biography of Mary Stuart, *Het leeven van Maria Stuart, koninginne van Schotland* (1647). See also Duits, *Van Bartholomeusnacht tot Bataafse opstand*, 51.

In summing up it may be stated that Van den Bosch, by means of his treatment of the Catiline material, saw a possibility to take part in the criticism of pro-Orange circles concerning the dominant political power structures that existed in the Netherlands. He was, moreover, not the only one who adapted the material in this way. The author of *Den herstelden prins* (*The Restored Prince*, 1663) draws two conclusions in particular from Catiline's conspiracy: in an aristocracy unworthy individuals often attempt to gain power by violence which can lead to unrest and disunity in the state, therefore those governing must take care to distribute power equally among the oldest and most distinguished families in order to remove the basis for dreaded partisan warfare:

> Gelijck men in 't brede inde historie van *C. Salustius* vande tsamensweeringe van *Catalina* wel leest, ende bevind dat beroyde behoeftige ende bedorven luyden de meeste roervincken en stooke-branden sijn aller muyterijen en 'tsamen-sweeringen [...] want om datse hovaardich zijn, ende veel behoeven, soeckense hun in de Regeringe te dringen, ende om dat hun de deucht ende de qualiteyten daar toe vereyst, en na 's Lands wetten nodich, onbreecken, traghtense door veranderinge vande Regeringe ofte oproer daar toe te komen.
>
> Tot dien eynde word Staat en baatzucht vermomt en met de eerlicke naam van 't gemene-best op-gepronckt, om die tot hun voornemen te gebruycken, dat verhaalt den voornoemden Salustius, die mede te kennen gecft dat de Regeerders de oudste en trefflickste Geslachten [...] behoorden op te trecken, ende die Regeringe meerder onder die te verdeelen, alse ten tijde van Catalina deden: want doen sochten daar eenige de gansche Regeringe tot hun te trecken, ende alle profijtelicke ampten onder hun te verdeelen.[37]

Naturally the adherents of the Prince of Orange knew only one remedy against these problems: the restoration of the office of Stadhold-

---

[37] 'As one reads at length the history of C. Sallust concerning the conspiracy of Catiline and recognises that impoverished, penniless, and degenerate people are the greatest insurgents and incendiaries in all munities and conspiracies [...]. Because as they are ambitious and have many needs, they attempt to seize the reins of government, but, as the virtue and the qualities that are thus needed and demanded by the laws of the land are wanting, they attempt to attain it through altering the regime, or through insurrection.

To this purpose ambition and greed are concealed and covered with the honest name of common good in order to use it for their own intentions. Thus reports the said Sallust, who also demonstrates that those who govern should honour the oldest and most excellent families [...] and that the Government should be more equally divided among these, as it was in the time of Catiline. Because then, a small number attempted to turn the whole government to its own hand and to divide all profitable offices among themselves'; *Den herstelden prins*, 5-6 (1663).

er. It is the task of the Stadholder to curb the dishonest ambitions of the regents, to resolve their internecine strife, and to uphold the unity of the land.[38] Although Van den Bosch, as mentioned, explicitly supported the restoration of the office of Stadholder in his play *Wilhem of Gequetste Vryheyt*, he allows of no alteration in his drama *L. Catilina*, which enables one to conclude that he considers a mediating influence, in the sense of the delineated position of the Stadholder, necessary for the removal of the difficulties in the Roman state. The wise policies of Cicero, the leader of the Roman aristocracy, are on the contrary to be welcomed for enabling the state to survive the severe trials of the conspiracy period. For this he is emphatically praised:

> Men noemt u Heylandt, en behouder van de Staet,
> Die Romens Borgery verbystert, t'eynden raet,
> Door sulck een trouw beleyt geredt hebt, en getoogen
> Uyt hare dienstbaerheyt, soo schijnbaer voor haer oogen (IV, i, p. 23).[39]

As we saw above it was precisely Cicero who criticized the decay of the old customs and denounced them as the origin of the crisis. His administration is accordingly responsible for bringing the Senate to reason and for restoring that venerable virtue.[40] With this attitude towards the character of Cicero Van den Bosch thus follows the same perspective as his sources concerning the role of the Consul during the suppression of the conspiracy.[41]

Although the drama contains no criticism of Cicero's personality one is able nonetheless to discern a clear warning in the address of he who, with the suppression of Catiline's conspiracy, stood at the zenith of his power. Shortly before his execution the conspirator Lentulus has a prophetic vision. He fears the future loss of Roman freedom and predicts a tragic fate for the Consul Cicero:

> Ick sie die hant (indien ick hachlijck niet en dool)
> Beneffens 't wijse hooft, gehecht voor 't Capitool.
> Misschien van hen (doch 't valt wat hachelijck om te raden)
> Die nu uytvoerders zijn, van sijn verwoede daden.

---

[38] Concerning these ideas in pro-Orange literature see Van de Klashorst, "*Metten schijn van monarchie getempert*", 114.

[39] 'Men call you Saviour and Preserver of the State who, through your faithful exercise of office, rescued the Roman citizens who, ineffectual and no longer knowing where to turn, were unable to withstand the slavery which lay before their very eyes'.

[40] Cf. V, i, p. 35.

[41] Cicero, *In Catilinam Orationes*, especially underlines this role.

> Die nu hij noemen derft sijn hant en beste stut,
> En de betrachters van het algemeene nut (V, i, p. 37).[42]

The messenger who reports Lentulus's execution to Cicero attempts to convince him that this prophecy must be an admonition for caution. Perhaps greater dangers for the state lay hidden in the future. The Consul, however, haughtily disregards this.

Van den Bosch employs here a procedure favoured in Renaissance drama, that is using a prophecy to introduce events that, as far as the plot is concerned, lie in the future but, nonetheless, binds them to the dramatic action. The grisly death of Cicero furnished the author, moreover, with a possibility for employing once again oft-recited ideas concerning the transitory nature of worldly power. Possibly this addition to the actual Catiline material also had its own political implications. The outstanding position of Cicero, the leader of the Roman political scene, entices one to draw further comparisons with Johan de Witt, the most powerful man in the Dutch Republic at that time. In spite of his partially explicit criticism of the aristocratic ruling class Van den Bosch withheld his censure from the head of the system. It is impossible to divine if this was an act of caution (Van den Bosch, the father of a family, was still assistant headmaster of the grammar school in Dordrecht where the De Witt family ruled) or if the author's attitude towards Johan de Witt had changed with the course of time.[43] Van den Bosch's sharp attacks against the Great Pensionary after the latter's death in 1672, as a result of which Bosch became involved in a literary feud with Joachim Oudaan (1628–1692), have grown familiar.[44] Nev-

---

[42] 'I see the hand (if I am not greatly mistaken) nailed on the Capitol beside the wise head, perhaps by those (but this is difficult to tell), who now carry out his gruesome deeds. By those, who he now ventures to name his allies and his best support, as well as protectors of the general benefit'.

[43] The hint in the preface to *Wilhem of Gequetste Vryheyt*, to the effect that the drama contains no political statement was probably also a precautionary measure, whereas, in fact, the content of the play proves the contrary; cf. Duits, *Van Bartholomeusnacht tot Bataafse opstand*, 122-4. Yet Van den Bosch had, with his welcome for Cornelis de Witt returning victorious from the second Anglo-Dutch Naval War, sung the praises of the De Witt family: *Welkomst van den Wel-edelen achtbaren, gestrengen Heer, de Heer Cornelis de Wit, tot Dordrecht by Simon onder de Linde*; cf. Van Vliet – De Niet, "Van ridders en andere Dordtse helden", 13.

[44] Cf. Oudaan J., *Aanmerkingen op de beschuldigingen, raakende de heeren gebroederen De Witten; van Lambert van den Bos. in zijnen Reysende Mercurius De Selve Heeren te last gelegt* (1574 [*sic*]). See the bibliography in Oudaan J., *Haagsche Broeder-Moord of Dolle Blydschap. Treurspel [1672], ingel. en geannot. door een werkgroep van Utrechtse neerlandici* (Utrecht: 1984) 142. On Joachim Oudaan see Melles J., *Joachim Oudaan. Heraut der verdraagzaamheid (1628–1692)* (Utrecht: 1958).

ertheless, the warning in Cicero's address could equally apply to Johan de Witt. Even a great victory and the apparent peace and stability of the state do not protect it from a possible change in the political situation. Those in government must be constantly on guard lest, while they enjoy their power, decay in the state quietly grows and they be toppled from their seemingly secure height some day.

In conclusion one can ascertain that a political reading of the drama seems justified due to the correspondence between the two political systems: the Roman state at the time of Catiline and the Dutch state around 1669 are both aristocratic republics. Van den Bosch saw here possibilities for formulating criticism of the aristocratic form of government. He thus found himself, although he does not take up the theme of the Stadholdership here, in agreement with the pro-Orange publicists of his time. The politically powerful, be they Roman consuls or Dutch pensionaries, are warned against arrogance and unconcern. No throne stands so firm that it cannot be endangered through hauteur and greed.

Selective Bibliography

Besteben M.F., *De 'tsamensweringe Catalinae* [1647], ed. G. van Emeren (Leuven–Amersfoort: 1988)

Blom H., "Politieke Filosofie in het Nederland van de zeventiende eeuw", *Geschiedenis van de Wijsbegeerte in Nederland* 4 (1993) 167-78

Bosch L. van den, *L. Catilina. Treur-spel* (Dordrecht: 1669)

Duits H., "Lambert van den Bosch als pleitbezorger van het stadhouderschap", in *'t Ondersoeck leert. Studies over middeleeuwse en 17de-eeuwse literatuur ter nagedachtenis van Prof. dr. L. Rens*, ed. G. van Eemeren – F. Willaert (Leuven–Amersfoort: 1986), 341-52

Duits H., *Van Bartholomeusnacht tot Bataafse opstand. Studies over de relatie tussen politiek en toneel in het midden van de zeventiende eeuw* (Hilversum: 1990)

Gelderen M. van, *The Political Thought of the Dutch Revolt 1551–1590* (Cambridge: 1992)

Grotius H., *De oudheid van de Bataafse nu Hollandse Republiek*, ed. G.C. Molewijk (Weesp: 1988)

Haeghs Hof-Praetje, ofte 'tSamen-spraeck tusschen een Hagenaer, Amsterdammer ende Leydenaer [...] (Leiden: 1662)

HOGERS T., "Vertoog van dat Julius Caesar een Tyran heeft geweest", in *De Gemene Vryheit*, ed. R.H. Schele [...] (Amsterdam: 1666)

ISRAEL J., *De Republiek 1477–1806*, 2 vols (Franeker: 1996–1997)

KLASHORST G.O. VAN DE, "*Metten schijn van monarchie getempert. De verdediging van het stadhouderschap in de partijliteratuur 1650–1686*", in *Pieter de la Court in zijn tijd (1618–1685). Aspecten van een veelzijdig publicist* (Amsterdam–Maarssen: 1985) 93-137

KOSSMAN E.H., *Politieke theorie in het zeventiende-eeuwse Nederland* (Amsterdam: 1960)

LADEMACHER H., *Die Niederlande. Politische Kultur zwischen Individualität und Anpassung* (Berlin: 1993)

LECHNER J., "Vertaler, bewerker, bederver. Jacob Campo Weyerman en *Don Quijote*", *Mededelingen Stichting Jacob Campo Weyerman* 18 (1995) 42-50

LINDENBERGER H., *Historical Drama. The Relation of Literature and Reality* (Chicago–London: 1975)

MEEUS H., *Repertorium van het ernstige drama in de Nederlanden 1600–1650* (Leuven: 1983)

MELLES J., *Joachim Oudaan. Heraut der verdraagzaamheid (1628–1692)* (Utrecht: 1958)

OEY-DE VITA E., "De wanen van Caspar Barlaeus ten tonele gevoerd in de herfst van 1648?", in *'t Ondersoeck leert. Studies over middeleeuwse en 17de-eeuwse literatuur ter nagedachtenis van Prof. dr. L. Rens*, ed. G. van Eemeren – F. Willacrt (Leuven–Amersfoort: 1986) 329 39

OUDAAN J., *Haagsche Broeder-Moord of Dolle Blydschap. Treurspel [1672], ingeleid en geannoteerd door een werkgroep van Utrechtse Neerlandici* (Utrecht: 1984)

Romainsche Historien van Titus Livius, sedert de bouwing van Romen tot aan d'ondergang van 't Macedonische Rijk. [...] Nieuwelijks uit de Romainsche Historie van M. Scipio Dupleix vertaalt en met nieuwe Bladwyzers verrijkt (Amsterdam: 1646)

SMIT W.A.P., "Het Baeto-Epos dat geschreven werd", *Verslagen en Mededelingen Vlaamse Academie* 1 (1971) 11-26

SMITS-VELDT M.B., *Het Nederlandse renaissancetoneel* (Utrecht: 1991)

Het Treur-Toonneel der doorluchtige Mannen onser eeuwe. Waer op den val der Grooten levendigh vertoont wordt. Het eerste deel. Vertaelt door I.H.G. [Glazemaker] en ten dele uyt verscheydene schryvers 't samen getrocken door L.v.B. [van Bos]; [...] (Amsterdam: 1650)

VLIET R. VAN – NIET M. DE, "Van ridders en andere Dordtse helden. De *Don Quichot*-vertaling van Lambert van den Bos", *Mededelingen Stichting Jacob Campo Weyerman* 18 (1995) 10-20

VOSSIUS G., *Geschiedenis als wetenschap*, ed. C. Rademaker (Baarn: 1990)

VRANKRIJKER A.J.C. DE, *De staatsleer van Hugo de Groot en zijn Nederlandsche tijdgenooten* (Utrecht: 1937)

WILKE F.A.S., *Lambert van den Bos. Biografie. Dordrechtsche Arcadia. Zuydt-hollandtsche Thessalia. Bibliografie* (unpublished undergraduate thesis, Amsterdam: 1969)

WORP J.A., *Geschiedenis van het drama en van het toneel in Nederland*, 2 vols (Rotterdam: 1903–1907).

LIST OF ILLUSTRATIONS

Figures 1-10 (belonging to the article by A. Boschloo), and figures 1-16 (belonging to the article by J.L. de Jong) can be found between pages 26 and 27:

[Boschloo]
1. Arnoldo de Vuez (Ducci), *Alexander the Great Cuts the Gordian Knot*, drawing, 1677. Rome, Accademia Nazionale di San Luca.
2. Ludovico Bologna, *Alexander the Great Cuts the Gordian Knot*, drawing, 1677. Rome, Accademia Nazionale di San Luca.
3. Tommaso Nasini, *Polistratos Finds the Dying King Darius*, drawing, 1682. Rome, Accademia Nazionale di San Luca.
4. Francesco Boccaccini, *Polistratos Finds the Dying King Darius*, drawing, 1682. Rome, Accademia Nazionale di San Luca.
5. Francesco Boccaccini, *Hannibal Crossing the Alps*, drawing, 1683. Rome, Accademia Nazionale di San Luca.
6. Pietro Paolo Petrucci, *Hannibal Crossing the Alps*, 1683. Rome, Accademia Nazionale di San Luca.
7. Giovanni Battista Armilli, *Romulus Killing King Amulius*, drawing, 1704. Rome, Accademia Nazionale di San Luca.
8. Angelo de Coster, *Romulus Killing King Amulius*, drawing, 1704. Rome, Accademia Nazionale di San Luca.
9. Agostino Masucci, *Battle between the Horatii and the Curatii*, drawing, 1707. Rome, Accademia Nazionale di San Luca.
10. Giovanni Battista Calandrucci, *Battle between the Horatii and the Curatii*, 1707. Rome, Accademia Nazionale di San Luca.

[De Jong]
1. Sala di Costantino. Vatican Palace, Rome.
2. Raphael, *The Apparition of the Cross*, 1519–1520. Sala di Costantino, Vatican Palace, Rome.
3. Raphael, Giulio Romano and Gianfrancesco Penni, *The Battle at the Milvian Bridge*, ca. 1520. Sala di Costantino, Vatican Palace, Rome.
4. Giulio Romano and Gianfrancesco Penni, *The Baptism of Constantine*, ca. 1523–1524. Sala di Costantino, Vatican Palace, Rome.
5. Giulio Romano and Gianfrancesco Penni, *The Donation of Constantine*, ca. 1523–1524. Sala di Costantino, Vatican Palace, Rome.

6. Donatello, *The Miracle of the Mule*, ca. 1446–1447. S. Antonio, Padua.

7. Donatello, *The Miracle of the Speaking Babe*, ca. 1446–1447. S. Antonio, Padua.

8. Raphael, *The Transfiguration*, ca. 1518–1520. Rome, Pinacoteca Vaticana.

9. Raphael, *The Expulsion of Heliodorus*, ca. 1512–1513. Stanza di Eliodoro, Vatican Palace, Rome.

10. Raphael, *The Miracle of the Mass at Bolsena*, ca. 1512–1513. Stanza di Eliodoro, Vatican Palace, Rome.

11. Raphael, *Pope Leo III Repelling Attila*, ca. 1513–1514. Stanza di Eliodoro, Vatican Palace, Rome.

12. Raphael, *The Fire in the Borgo*, ca. 1516–1517. Stanza dell'Incendio, Vatican Palace, Rome.

13. Livio Agresti, *King Peter of Aragon Offering His Kingdom to Pope Innocent III*, ca. 1564. Sala Regia, Vatican Palace, Rome.

14. Cesare Nebbia and Giovanni Guerra, *The Donation of Constantine*, ca. 1588. Sala di Costantino, Lateran palace, Rome.

15. Giovanni Battista Ricci, *Pope Sylvester Consecrating the High Altar of the Lateran*, ca. 1599–1600. St John in Lateran, Rome.

16. Tommaso Laureti, *The Justice of Brutus*, ca. 1586–1592. Sala dei Capitani, Conservators' Palace, Rome.

Figures 1-16 (belonging to the article by M. Morford), and figures 1-10 (belonging to the article by K. Enenkel) can be found between pages 74 and 75:

[Morford]

1. Otho Vaenius, *Batavorum cum Romanis Bellum* (Antwerp: 1612), Title-Page.

2. Antonio Tempestà, *Romanorum et Batavorum Societas* (Rome: 1611).

3. *Battle at the Bridge.* Antonio Tempestà, Plate 31, *Romanorum et Batavorum Societas* (Rome: 1611).

4. *Cerialis and Civilis at the Bridge.* Antonio Tempestà, Plate 36, *Romanorum et Batavorum Societas* (Rome: 1611).

5. Otho Vaenius, *Cerialis and Civilis at the Bridge.*

6. *The Fleets on the Rhine.* Antonio Tempestà, Plate 33, *Romanorum et Batavorum Societas* (Rome: 1611).

7. *The Oath in the* Sacrum Nemus. Antonio Tempestà, Plate 4, *Romanorum et Batavorum Societas* (Rome: 1611).

8. Otho Vaenius, *The Feast in the Garden.*

9. Otho Vaenius, *The Oath in the* Sacrum Nemus.

10. *Women at the First Battle of Vetera.* Antonio Tempestà, Plate 8, *Romanorum et Batavorum Societas* (Rome: 1611).

11. Otho Vaenius, *Women at the First Battle of Vetera.*

12. *Germans at the Siege of Vetera.* Antonio Tempestà, Plate 13, *Romanorum et Batavorum Societas* (Rome: 1611).

13. Otho Vaenius, *Germans at the Siege of Vetera.*

14. *Batavians Attacking Vetera.* Antonio Tempestà, Plate 14, *Romanorum et Batavorum Societas* (Rome: 1611).

15. Cluverius, *A Batavian Man and Woman.*

16. *Cerialis Receives the Returning Legionaries.* Antonio Tempestà, Plate 26, *Romanorum et Batavorum Societas* (Rome: 1611).

[Enenkel]

1. *Retiarius and Secutor.* Lipsius, *Saturnalium sermonum* [...] (Antwerp: 1585).

2. *Retiarius and Secutor.* Lipsius, *Saturnalium sermonum* [...] (Antwerp: 1604).

3. *Myrmillo and Thr[a]ex.* Lipsius, *Saturnalium sermonum* [...] (Antwerp: 1604).

4. *Meridiani.* Lipsius, *Saturnalium sermonum* [...] (Antwerp: 1585).

5. *Catervarii.* Lipsius, *Saturnalium sermonum* [...] (Antwerp: 1585).

6. *Big Battle Scene.* Lipsius, *Saturnalium sermonum* [...] (Antwerp: 1585).

7. *Big Battle Scene.* Lipsius, *Saturnalium sermonum* [...] (Antwerp: 1604).

8. *Women and Dwarfs Fighting as Gladiators.* Lipsius, *Saturnalium sermonum* [...] (Antwerp: 1604).

9. *Meridiani.* Lipsius, *Saturnalium sermonum* [...] (Antwerp: 1604).

10. *Postulaticii and Catervarii.* Lipsius, *Saturnalium sermonum* [...] (Antwerp: 1604).

Figures 1-5 (belonging to the article by Maria Berbara) can be found between pages 162 and 163:

1. Francesco di Giorgio Martini, *Adoration of the Shepherds*, ca. 1485–1495. Padua, San Domenico.

2. Detail of Fig. 1.

3. Sandro Botticelli, *The Tragedy of Lucretia*, ca. 1499. Boston, Isabella Stewart Gardner Museum.

4. Anonymous, *Marcus Curtius* (cassone), last quarter of the fifteenth century. London, National Gallery.

5. Paolo Veronese, *Marcus Curtius*, ca. 1535. Vienna, Kunsthistorisches Museum.

Page 214 (figure belonging to the article by O. van Marion):

Effigy of Antony and Cleopatra. Engraved by Jan Goeree. Jan Baptista Wellekens en Pieter Vlaming, *Dichtlievende uitspanningen* (Amsterdam: 1710), 154.

Figures 1-8 (belonging to the article by A. Visser) can be found between pages 274 and 275:

1. Joannes Sambucus, *Emblemata, et aliquot nummi antiqui operis* [...] (Antwerp: 1569), f. A3r. Photo: Koninklijke Bibliotheek, The Hague.

2. Joannes Sambucus, *Emblemata, et aliquot nummi antiqui operis* [...] (Antwerp: 1569) 128. Photo: Koninklijke Bibliotheek, The Hague.

3. Joannes Sambucus, *Emblemata, et aliquot nummi antiqui operis* [...] (Antwerp: 1569) 150. Photo: Koninklijke Bibliotheek, The Hague.

4. [a+b]. Joannes Sambucus, *Emblemata, et aliquot nummi antiqui operis* [...] (Antwerp: 1569) 179-180. Photo: Koninklijke Bibliotheek, The Hague.

5. Joannes Sambucus, *Emblemata, et aliquot nummi antiqui operis* [...] (Antwerp: 1569) 29. Photo: Koninklijke Bibliotheek, The Hague.

6. Joannes Sambucus, *Emblemata, et aliquot nummi antiqui operis* [...] (Antwerp: 1569) 116-117. Photo: Koninklijke Bibliotheek, The Hague.

7. Joannes Sambucus, *Emblemata, et aliquot nummi antiqui operis* [...] (Antwerp: 1569) 34. Photo: Koninklijke Bibliotheek, The Hague.

8. Joannes Sambucus, *Emblemata, et aliquot nummi antiqui operis* [...] (Antwerp: 1569) 58. Photo: Koninklijke Bibliotheek, The Hague.

Page 288 (figure belonging to the article by F. Terrenato):
The Emperor Hadrian. Engraving by Hubert Goltzius. Idem, *Vivae omnium fere imperatorum imagines* (Antwerp: 1557).

Page 320 (figure belonging to the article by A. Montoya):
Scene from Marie-Anne Barbier's La Mort de César. Engraving by F. Bleyswyk.

INDEX NOMINUM

Abraham: 163
Acciaiuoli, Donato: 309
Achilles: 13, 59, 159, 217
Aelian: 280-2
Aelius Donatus: *see* Donatus
Aelius Lampridius: 88
Aelius Spartianus: 292-3, 296
Aemilia: 325-8
Aeneas: 13, 36, 42, 191, 273-4, 341
Afranius, Lucius (consul 60 BC): 121
Agamemnon: 261-2, 265, 280, 315
Agesilaus: 14, 177
Agresti, Livio: 51
Aitzema, Lieuwe van: 343
Albert of Austria, Archduke: 58, 134, 140
Alberti, Leon Battista: 1-9, 14, 39-41, 295
Albertini, Francesco: 129
Albin(us): 334-5
Alciato, Andrea: 269, 272
Alcibiades: 189-191, 208-9
Alcmena: 315
Alexander the Great: 12, 14, 17, 172, 191-3, 280-1, 303
Alexander of Pherai: 189
Alexander Severus: 295
Alfieri, Vittorio: 248
Alfonso II, Duke d'Este: 104
Amalia of Solms: 218
Ammianus Marcellinus: 128-9
Amulius: 19, 21
Amyot, Jacques: 167-8, 172-5, 187, 189, 200, 224-6, 231, 323, 335
Anaximenes: 257-8
Ancus Martius: 22
Anna Perenna: 308
Antichrist: 31
Antiphon of Ramnus: 278
Antiphon, the tragician: 277-9, 283
Antonello da Messina: 154
Antoninus Pius: 49
Antony St: 38, 152
Antony: *see* Marc Antony
Apelles: 281
Apollodorus: 292
Appian: 8-9, 266
Archimedes: 18
Argenson, Marc-René d': 325
Ariadne: 215, 219
Aristides: 45, 177, 300

Aristogeiton: 278
Aristotle: ix, xi; 34, 44-8, 191, 258, 280, 304
Armenini, Giovanni Battista: 8, 23-4
Arnobius: 96
Arria the Elder (wife of Caecina Paetus): 60, 321, 326, 328
Artemidorus: 315
Arthur, King: 303
Ascham, Roger: 125
Aspertini, Amico: 154
Assonleville, Christophe d': 127
Atilius Regulus: 155
Atreus: 191
Attabalipa, Inca King: 169
Atticus: 65
Attila: 51
Auctor ad Herennium: 258
Aufidius, Tullus: 198-9, 209
Augustine, St: xii; 130, 134, 149-51, 259-60
Augustus (Octavian): 33, 86, 88, 110, 152, 217, 219-20, 292, 296, 298, 301, 325, 328, 332
Ausonius: 96
Averell, William: 201
Averroës: 47

Bacchiacca, Francesco Ubertini: 160
Bacchus: 220
Baeto: 343
Balaam: 42
Balduinus Ferreus, Count: 217
Baldwin, T.W.: 264
Ballain, Geoffroy: 270
Barbier, Marie-Anne: xiii; 319-37
Barlaeus, Caspar (Baerle): 59, 216, 218
Bartoli, Cosimo: 39
Basilius Magnus: 291
Batavia, personification of: 68
Beccafumi, Domenico: 156
Bellini, Giovanni: 158-9
Bellori, Giovanni Pietro: 1-10, 13, 16, 43, 49
Benedictus Canonicus: 129
Benserade, Isaac de: 232
Bessarion, Card.: 103
Besteben, Marten Frank: 341-2
Bidloo, Govert: 215
Billaeus, Carolus: 107
Bingham, Johannes: 112

Biondo, Flavio: 75-8, 80-1, 129, 133, 136
Blancus, Gulielmus: 291
Blocklandt, Anthonis: 298
Boccaccini, Francesco: 18
Boccaccio, Giovanni: 8-9
Boccage, Le Page, Marie-Anne du: 336
Bodin, Jean: 167, 177-8, 180-5, 340-2
Boel, Cornelius: 60
Boileau, Jean Jacques: 336
Bolingbroke, Henry: *see* Henry IV
Bonaparte: *see* Napoleon
Borcht, Peeter vander: 60, 93, 109, 270
Borghini, Raffaello: 5
Borgia, Alfonso: *see* Callistus III
Borromeo, Carlo, Card.: 131
Bosc, Jacques du: 327
Bosch, Lambert van den (Sylvius): xiii; 339-55
Bossuet, Jacques Bénigne: 330
Boswell: 248
Botero, Giovanni: 134
Botticelli, Sandro: 40, 159
Bouckart, Jan (Boukart): 341
Bouwens, Jan: 224-6
Brecht, Bertolt: 251
Breen, Adam van: 117
Britannicus: 325
Brockbank, P.: 206, 208
Bruni, Leonardo: 102-3
Brunt, Peter: 63
Brutus, Decimus Albinus: 303, 308, 310, 334-5
Brutus, Lucius Junius (consul 509 BC): 159, 334
Brutus, Marcus Junius: 7, 253-5, 257, 263-6, 303, 306-9, 311-3, 315, 323-36
Buchanan, George: 304-5, 307
Buchell, Arend van: 118-9, 123
Bullough, Geoffrey: 187
Burer, J.A.: 310
Burke, Peter: 335
Burmannus, Petrus (Burman): 58, 60
Busbequius, Augerius Gislenus: 95

Caesar, Gaius Julius: xii-xiii; 6-7, 12, 65, 112, 121, 128, 157, 173, 177, 181, 189, 195-7, 208, 228-9, 253-67, 280, 294-7, 303-37, 341
Calandrucci, Giovanni Battista: 19
Calgacus: 66
Callimachus: 264
Callistus III, Pope (Alfonso Borgia): 77
Calpurnia, wife of Caesar: 305, 307-8, 310-1, 313, 315, 324

Cambiaso, Luca: 7
Camden, William: 201
Camilla: 327
Campano, Giannantonio: 309
Capito, Fonteius: 64
Cardano, Girolamo: 281-2
Carlos, Don: 236
Carondelet, Jacques de: 107
Casaubon, Isaac: 103, 110
Casca: *see* Servilius
Cassiodorus: 129
Cassius: 7, 311
Cassius Dio: 85, 88, 96, 110, 176-1, 183, 290-2, 296, 308, 312, 323, 336
Castiglionchio, Lapo da: 309
Castiglione, Baldassare: 50, 188, 295
Catiline: 304, 328, 339-55
Cato the Elder: 75, 177
Cato of Utica: 65, 311, 324, 327-8, 344
Cavalcanti, Bartolomeo: 103
Cavallaro, Anna: 154-6
Censorinus: 291
Cerialis, Petilius: 57, 64-6, 69-70, 72-3
Cervantes: 343
Cesari d'Arpino, Giuseppe: 20, 53
Chapelle, Jean de la: 232
Charlemagne: 6, 54, 303
Charles V, Emp.: 6, 294-5, 297
Charles IX of France: 174, 176, 179, 343-4
Charles the Bold: 217
Choul, Guillaume du: 296
Christina of Sweden: 9
Chrysippus: 278-9
Cicero: x, xii; 45-7, 60, 61, 65-6, 82-3, 96, 98, 128, 148, 151, 170, 174, 177, 179, 258-9, 262, 264-6, 291, 304, 306, 312, 344-7, 352-4
Cid: 329
Cincinnatus, Lucius Quinctius, dictator: 156
Cinegirus (Kynaigeros), brother of Aeschylus: 155
Cinna, Lucius Cornelius: 325, 327-8
Civilis: *see* Julius
Classicus: *see* Julius
Claudius Civilis: *see* Julius
Claudius Paulus: *see* Julius
Clement I, Pope: 29
Clement VII, Pope: 27, 29-30
Cleopatra: xii; 189, 195, 208, 213-34, 332
Cloelia: 155
Cluverius, Philippus (Clüver): 71-2, 124
Clytaemnestra: 315

Cocles: *see* Horatius
Codrus, King of Athens: 150
Colonna, Marcantonio: 154
Colonna, Sciarra: 154
Columella: 128
Cominius, Postumus Auruncus, consul
    501 and 493 BC: 198, 202, 207
Constantine the Great: ix, xi; 23, 27-
    34, 37, 39-40, 42, 45, 48-9, 52-5
Constantine VII Porphyrogenitus, Byz.
    Emp.: 102
Constantius II, Emp.: 128
Coornhert, Dirck Volckertsz.: 73
Coriolanus, Gnaeus Marcius: 187-211
Corneille: 322-3, 325, 328, 336
Cornelia, mother of the Gracchi: 321,
    326
Costa, Lorenzo: 158
Cothebas: 300
Cranach, Lucas: 160
Crassus: 121
Curiatii: 19-22, 341
Curii: 87
Curio: *see* Curtius, Marcus
Curius, Quintus, supporter of Catiline:
    344
Curtius, Marcus, Roman hero (Iovinus:
    152; Curio: 152; Martinus: 152;
    Marcus Tuitius: 152): xii; 8, 147-65
Curtius Rufus, Quintus: 112
Cyrus: 191

Dacier, Anne: 321
Daedalus: 47
Danti, Vicenzo: 5-6
Darius of Persia: 18
Darius Tibertus: 223
David: 147, 155-6, 159, 216, 303
David, Jacques-Louis: 24
Decii: 150
Decius Mus: 147, 163
Dellaporta, Giambattista: 223
Demaratus of Corinth, father of
    Tarquinius Priscus: 21
Demetrius of Phaleron: 262
Demosthenes: 177, 180, 266
Dido: 13, 36, 215
Diego, Don: 329
Dillius Vocula: 64
Dio Cassius: *see* Cassius
Diogenes Laertius: 280
Diomedes: 259
Dionysius of Halicarnassus: 103, 137,
    262
Dionysius, tyrant of Syracuse: 277-9
Discenet, Alessandro: 21
Dolce, Lodovico: 3-4, 295, 298

Domenichi, Lodovico: 39
Donaldson, Ian: 162
Donatello: 38-9
Donatus, Aelius: 259, 261
Dörrie, Heinrich: 215
Dousa, Janus Sr: 82-3, 216
Draco (Drakon), Athenian legislator:
    243, 300
Dryden, John: 205
Dürer, Albert: 276, 298
Duyck, Anthonis: 117-8
Duystius, Johannes: 125

Egnatius, Johannes Baptista: 291
Eliot, T.S.: 196-7
Elizabeth I of England: 195-6, 250,
    350
Empedocles: 275-6
Erasmus, Desiderius: 47, 170-1, 291
Ercole II, Duke of Ferrara: 103
Ernest, Prince Bishop of Bavaria: 60,
    106
Esther: 155-6
Estienne, Robert (Stephanus): 309
Euripides: 189
Euryalus: 43
Eusebius: 42
Eustathius: 262
Evander: 43
Everart, Marten (Everaerts): 223
Eyck, Hubert van: 298

Fabii: 156, 299
Fabius Maximus Cunctator: 156
Fabricii: 87, 118
Fabricius: 118
Farnese, Alessandro, Duke of Parma:
    58-60
Fasolino, Benedetto: 160
Fatouville, Nolant de: 319
Fazio: *see* Uberti
Félibien, André: 9-16
Ferdinand I, Emp.: 295
Festus, Sextus Pompeius: 96, 112
Ficino, Marsilio: 276
Fides, goddes: 317
Filmer, Robert: 330
Fiorini, Giovanni Battista: 52
Flaccus: *see* Hordeonius
Flavius, tribune: 311
Flavius Josephus: 89, 109, 112, 121
Florentius, Nicolaus: 133-4
Florio, John: 191
Fortuna: 248-349
Foscolo, Ugo: 248
Frederick the Great of Prussia: 248
Frederik Hendrik of Nassau: 216, 218

Frisch, Max: 251
Frischlin, Nikodemus: 304
Fuffetius, Mettius, King of Alba Longa:
    21-2
Fukuyama, Francis: 242
Fulvia: 219, 344
Furius, Johannes: 107
Furius Camillus: 156-7
Furor, personification of: 36

Galba, Emp.: 64
Galen: 206
Garnier, Robert: 303
Gedicke, Friedrich: 236
Gellius, Aulus: 112, 264
Gemusaeus, Hieronymus: 309
Gentileschi, Artemisia: vii
George, St: 159-61
Germanicus: 10, 13
Gheyn, Jacob de: 117
Ghirlandaio, Domenico: 40, 53, 147,
    158
Gilbert, Felix: 274
Gilio, Giovanni Andrea: 4-5, 11, 13,
    16, 35-7
Giotto: 40
Giselinus, Victor: 82
Giudice, Armannino: 152
Giulio Romano: 7, 23, 27, 31, 33-4,
    39, 49, 52, 54, 161
Glazemaker, Jan Hendrik: 223
Godfrey of Bouillon: 303
Goeree, Jan: 216
Goethe: 235, 248-9
Goldsmith: 248
Goliath: 147, 159
Goltzius, Henricus: 295
Goltzius, Hubertus: 295-9
Gomez, Madeleine Angélique de: 336
Gora, Lucrezia: 154
Gordius, King of Phrygia: 17
Gordon, D.J.: 208
Gottsched, Luise: 321
Goulart, Simon: 224, 226-9, 231-2
Gozzoli, Benozzo: 40
Gracchi: see Cornelia
Graces: 60
Grebber, Anthonie de: 213
Gregory I, Pope: 28
Gregory XIII, Pope: 131
Greve, Willem de: 61
Grévin, Jacques: 303
Grotius, Hugo: 71-2, 216, 340, 342
Grucchius, Nicolaus: 110
Guarini, Guarino: 309
Guarino da Verona: 189, 200
Guérente, Guillaume: 304-5

Guerra, Giovanni: 53
Guise, Charles de, Card. of Lorraine:
    176, 179, 183
Gyges: 289

Hacqueville, Nicolas de: 137-8
Hadrian, Emp.: xii; 33, 287-302
Hadrian VI, Pope: 29
Hall, Edward: 194-6
Hall, Joseph: 126
Hannibal: 18, 341
Hanno: 281-2
Hardy, Alexandre: 197
Harmodius: 278
Hartung, Johann: 282-3
Hector: 13, 159, 303
Heere, Lucas d': 270, 298
Helen: 215, 219, 222, 230-1
Heliodorus: 38, 42-3
Henry IV of England (Henry
    Bolingbroke): 196
Henry VI of England: 194, 196
Henry VII of England: 194-5
Henry VIII of England: 196
Hercules: xiii; 314-5, 317
Herder, Gottfried: 248
Herod: 40, 89
Herodotus: 188
Heuer, H.: 200
Hippocrates: 184
Holinshed, Ralph: 194-5
Holland, Philemon: 201
Holophern: 159
Homer: 35, 42, 203, 261-2, 265, 280
Hooft, Pieter Cornelisz.: 215-6, 231
Horace: ix; 59, 275, 304, 306-7, 327
Horapollo: 280
Horatii: 8, 19-24, 341
Horatius Cocles: 75, 148, 153, 155-7,
    159-60, 163
Hordeonius Flaccus: 64
Horn, Franz: 237
Horror, personification of: 36
Hutten, Ulrich von: 30-1
Huys, Pieter: 270
Hygeia: 83
Hypsipyle: 219

Icarus: 47
Innocent III, Pope: 51-2
Iovinus: see Curtius, Marcus
Isaac: 163
Isabella, Archduchess of Austria: 58
Isidorus of Seville: 260
Isis: 220

James, St: 158

Janus: 271
Janus Secundus: 215
Jempsar: 232
Jepthes: 307
Jerome, St: 149-150
Jesus Christ: 4, 33-34, 48, 131, 148-
    152, 156, 158-159, 162-163
Joab: 7
John the Baptist: 52, 91-92
John, King of England: 194
Jonson, Ben: 203-204
Joseph, St: 158
Joseph: 232
Joshua: 303
Jove (Jupiter): 218, 222, 271, 281
Judas Maccabaeus: 303
Judith: 155-6, 159
Judith, daughter of Charles the Bold:
    217
Julius Caesar: *see* Caesar
Julius Civilis: 57-74
Julius Classicus: 64
Julius Paulus (Claudius Paulus): 64
Julius Sabinus: 64
Julius Tutor: 64
Julius II, Pope: 154, 156-7
Junia: 325
Juno: 259, 273-4, 316
Jupiter: *see* Jove
Justina, St: 162

Kant, Immanuel: 249
Karl August, Duke of Sachsen Anhalt:
    235
Keyser, Cornelis: 216
Kirchner, Hermann: 197
Konstantinovic, Isabelle: 167
Kynaigeros: *see* Cinegirus

La Bruyère, Jean de: 330
Lactantius: 150
La Font de Saint-Yenne, Etienne: 24
Lairesse, Gerard de: 11-3, 23
Lambarde, William: 196
Lampridius: *see* Aelius
Lampsonius, Dominicus: 58, 60-1, 107
Langhius, Carolus (de Langhe): 58, 61
Languet, Claude: 189
Lannoy, Philippe de: 124-5, 137
Laodamia: 218, 231
Lapo da Castiglionchio: *see*
    Castiglionchio
Lascaris, Janus: 47, 103, 108, 110
Laureti, Tommaso: 54
Laurinus, Marcus, Lord of Watervliet:
    296
Lausus, son of Mezentius: 43

Lecky, W.E.H.: 151-2
Lemmers, J.: 341
Lentulus, Publius Cornelius Sura,
    supporter of Catiline: 344-5, 348,
    350, 352-3
Leo I, Pope: 29
Leo III, Pope: 51
Leo X, Pope: 27-31, 47
Leonardo da Vinci: 2-3, 6-7, 40-2, 46
Leonidas, King of Sparta: 156, 240
Lernutius, Janus: 82, 98, 128
Lessing: 248
Liberale da Verona: 153-4
Libitina: 306-7, 316
Lippi, Filippo: 40
Lipsius, Justus: x-xi; 57-146, 283
Livia: 328
Livy: x; 8-9, 18-20, 22-3, 84, 89, 96,
    103, 109-12, 120-1, 147, 156, 160,
    201, 339-42
Locke, John: 330
Lodovico il Moro, Duke of Milan: 291
Lomazzo, Gian Paolo: 6-8, 18, 23, 295
Lombard, Lambert: 296
Louis XIV of France: 325, 335-6
Loyola, Ignatius of, St: 115
Lucan: 128, 311-312
Lucretia: 149, 159, 162, 341
Lucumo: *see* Tarquinius Priscus
Lupercus: *see* Munius
Lutatius Catulus: 264
Luther, Martin: 30-1
Lycortas: 101
Lycurgus: xii; 177, 235-52
Lysander: 177
Lysippus: 281

Maas, personification of: 68
Machiavelli, Niccolò: 103, 113, 224
Macrobius: 80, 82-3
Mander, Karel van: xiii; 287-302
Manlius: 121
Mantegna, Andrea: 154, 158, 312
Manutius, Aldus: 291
Marc Antony: xii; 177, 189-90, 195,
    197, 208-9, 217-22, 227-32, 253-
    67, 308, 311, 323-4, 328-32, 334-5
Marcellus, Marcus, tribune: 177, 311
Marcellus, Marcus Claudius, consul
    287: 177
Marcius Coriolanus: *see* Coriolanus
Marcus Aurelius: 9, 23, 287, 291
Mariano da Firenze: 129
Martialis: 87
Martini, Francesco di Giorgio: 158-9
Martinus: *see* Curtius, Marcus
Martius, Gaius: *see* Coriolanus

Martius Coriolanus: *see* Coriolanus
Mary, Virgin: 4, 156, 158
Mary Stuart: 235, 250, 343, 350
Masucci, Agostino: 19-20
Maurits of Nassau, Prince of Orange: xi; 116-9, 344-5, 351
Maxentius: 28, 49
Maximilian I, Emp.: 294
Maximilian II, Emp.: 63, 271-2
Mazzocco, Angelo: 76
Medea: 215, 315
Medici, family: 28
Medici, Maria: 59
Medusa: 91
Melancholy, personification of: 276
Meleager: 1
Menelaus: 215, 231
Menenius Agrippa Lanatus, consul 503 BC: 197-8, 201-2, 206
Merula, Giorgio: 291
Messina, da: *see* Antonello
Mettius: *see* Fufetius
Mexía, Pedro: 293-5
Mezentius, King of Caere: 43
Michaelis, J.: 341
Michelangelo Buonarotti: 5, 36, 43, 52
Michol, daughter of Saul: 216
Minucius Felix: 149
Minucius Fondatus: 300
Miola, R.S.: 206-7
Moderno: 160
Molière: 319
Montaigne: xii; 167-86, 191, 304
Montesquieu: 248
More, Thomas: 196
Moretus, Johannes: 105-6
Moyne, Pierre Le: 327
Mozart, Constance: vii
Mozart, Wolfgang Amadeus: viii
Mucius Scaevola: 8, 148-9, 153, 155, 157-60
Müller, W.G.: 260-261
Munius Lupercus: 57
Muret, Marc-Antoine: xiii; 175, 283, 303-18
Muses: 60, 188, 223

Napoleon: 248
Nebbia, Cesare: 53
Neptune: 62
Nereus: 314
Nero, Emp.: 27, 132, 173-4, 176, 295, 325
Nerva, Emp.: 291
Nestor: 280
Neuyed, J.: 341

Nicolas V, Pope (Tommaso Parentucelli): 77, 103
Nicomachus, Virius Flavianus: 83
Nisus: 43
Noot, Philip Moilives van der: 216
North, Thomas: 187, 189-90, 192, 199-201, 203, 205-7, 209, 226
Numa Pompilius: 156, 223

Octavia: xii; 213-34, 323-4, 326-7, 330-3, 336
Octavian: *see* Augustus
Oestreich, Gerhard: 115
Opsopaeus, Vincentius: 103
Oranus, Petrus (d'Heur): 107
Origen: 148
Orosius: 149
Ortelius, Abraham: 59, 66, 72, 105, 125, 296
Osiris: 220
Othello: 208
Oudaan, Joachim: 353
Oultremannus, Henricus: 60
Outremeuse, Jean d': 152
Ovid: 47, 62, 77, 110, 152, 215, 218, 223, 230-1, 275

Paedts, Jan: 224-226
Pagani, M.: 20
Paleotti, Gabriele: 53
Palladio, Andrea: 160
Pallas: 43
Pamphilus of Sicyon, teacher of Apelles: 298
Parentucelli, Tommaso: *see* Nicholas V
Paris: 218-9, 230-1
Patrizi, Francesco: 103-4, 109
Paul, St: 33, 51-2, 153
Paul III, Pope: 36, 52
Paulinus, Bernardinus, papal finance minister: 124
Paulus: *see* Julius
Pazzi, Alessandro (Paccius): 47
Pelopidas of Thebes: 177
Penelope: 215, 218, 231
Penni, Gianfrancesco: 27, 31, 34, 54
Pericles: 14, 156
Perino del Vaga: 7
Perotti, Niccolò: 103
Perseus, King of Macedonia: 89
Perugino, Pietro: 154, 156
Peter, St: 28, 33, 51, 53
Peter, King of Aragon: 51-2
Petrarch: 8-9, 152
Petronius: 96
Philip II of Spain: 106, 116, 127, 294-6, 342

Philip III of Spain: 106, 115
Phoenix: 59
Piccolomini, Enea Silvio: *see* Pius II
Pighius, Stephanus (Wijnants): 82
Pino, Paolo: 295
Pintoricchio, Bernardo (Pinturicchio): 53, 154, 156-8
Piombo, Sebastiano del: 29
Pittacus: 156
Pius II, Pope: 77
Pizarro, Francisco: 169
Plantin, Christopher: 93, 270-1, 275
Plato: 173, 245, 277
Plautus: 96, 291
Pliny the Elder: ix; 45, 96, 111, 128, 275-7, 280-3, 289
Pliny the Younger: 276-7
Plotius Sacerdos: 259
Plutarch: x, xii; 8, 14, 23, 72, 121, 167-252, 266, 277-80, 289, 307-12, 315, 323, 325-6, 332, 334-5
Polybius: xi; 101-22, 134-6, 223, 340
Polystratus: 17
Polyxena, Trojan princess: 217
Pompey: 65, 121, 177, 181, 307, 311-2, 323
Ponge, Francis: 170
Pontanus, Johannes: 71
Pope, Alexander: 205, 248
Porcia: 311, 323-4, 326-9, 331-2, 334-5
Pordenone, Giovanni Antonio: 161
Porsenna, Lars, King of Clusium: 148, 159
Poseidonius: 134
Potiphar: 232
Poussin, Nicholas: 10-1, 13
Primaticcio, Francesco: 7
Procopius: 112
Propertius: 304, 306-7
Protesilaus: 218
Pyrckmair, Hilarius: 132
Pythagoras: 278-9

Quadratus (Kodratos): 300
Quednau, Rolf: 29
Quinctii: 87
Quintilian: 44-5, 49-50, 137, 253, 258-9, 262-4
Quixote, Don: 343

Rabus, Jakob: 131-133
Racine, Jean: 323, 336
Raimondi, Marcantonio: 42, 160, 162
Raphael: 14, 27-31, 34, 36-43, 45, 47-52, 54
Rearick, William R.: 161

Refinger, Ludwig: 153
Regnard, Jean François: 319
Rembrandt: 70
Remus: 19, 21, 68, 272
Reyd, Everhard van: 116-8
Reynolds, Joshua: 9-16
Rhenanus, Beatus: 310
Rhine, personification of: 68
Richard II of England: 194, 196
Richard III of England: 194-6, 199
Rodrigo, Don: 329
Roma, personification of: 68
Romano: *see* Giulio Romano
Romulus: 12, 19, 33, 68, 193, 272
Rosinus, Johannes: 78
Rosso Fiorentino: 7
Rouillé, Guillaume: 296
Rousseau, Jean-Jacques: 248
Rovere, Giuliano della: *see* Julius II
Rubens, Pieter Paul: 59
Rudolph II, Emp.: 106, 271
Ruff, Jacob: 223

Sabina, wife of Hadrian: 300
Sabinus: *see* Julius
Saccio, P.: 187
Salieri, Antonio: vii
Sallust: x; 341-2, 344-6, 351
Salome: 91
Salviati, Francesco: 36-7
Sambucus, Johannes (Zsámboky János): xii; 269-85
Sammachini, Orazio: 52
Samson: 155-6
Sand, George: 321
Sandelinus, Gerardus: 117
Sannazaro, Jacopo: 213
Saturn: 315
Saul: 42, 216
Scaevola: *see* Mucius
Scaliger, Julius Caesar: 304
Scaliger, Josephus Justus: 71, 304
Scarparia, Jacopo Angelo de: 309
Schaefer, David Lewis: 179
Schedel, Hartmann: 153
Schiller, Friedrich: xii; 235-51
Schmarsow, August: 154
Schoppe, Kaspar: 124, 304
Schottus, Franciscus: 123-4
Schulz, Jürgen: 161
Scipio, Publius Cornelius Africanus: 8, 12, 75, 101, 156, 158, 191, 341
Scriverius, Petrus (Schrijver): 63, 66, 225, 227
Scudéry, Madeleine de: 327, 332
Sebastian, St: 154, 162
Sebond, Raimond: 179

Secundus: *see* Janus
Segni, Bernardino: 47
Sejanus: 203-4
Senacherib: 7
Seneca the younger: 96, 136, 148, 167, 169, 172-6, 178-80, 183, 305-7, 314-5
Septimius Severus, Emp.: 292
Serenus Gravius: 300
Servilius, Publicus Casca Longus: 254
Servius: 83, 85
Servius Tullius: 22, 111
Sforza, Francesco, Card.: 126
Shaffer, Peter: vii
Shakespeare: x, xii; 187-211, 232, 253-67, 303
Sicinius, Lucius Vellutus, tribune: 156
Siciolante da Sermoneta, Girolamo: 52
Sidney, Philip: 188-9, 191
Sigonio, Carlo: 80, 110
Silvander: *see* Wellekens
Socrates: 156, 190, 258, 277, 279
Solms, Amalia van: *see* Amalia van Solms
Solon: xii; 235-52, 300
Someren, Johan van: 341
Sophonisba: 13
Spalatin, Georg: 31
Spartianus: *see* Aelius
Spencer, T.J.B.: 203
Spiegel, Hendrik Laurensz.: 223
Stapleton, Thomas: 124
Statius: 68
Stephanus: *see* Estienne, Robert
Stevin, Simon: 119
Steyner, Heynrich: 269
Strada, Jacopo: 296
Stradling, Joseph: 125
Suetonius: 77, 84-6, 91, 132, 152, 291-2, 308-10, 312-3, 323, 334, 336
Suida, William: 161
Sulla: 177
Swanenburgh, Isaac van: 58
Sweertius, Franciscus: 59, 105
Swift, Jonathan: 248
Sylvester, St: 30, 152
Sylvester I, Pope: 27-8, 30, 53-5
Symmachus, Quintus Aurelius: 83

Tacitus: 57, 62-72, 88, 96, 112, 135, 176, 181, 276-7
Tantalus: 191
Tarpeia, daughter of Titus Tatius: 19, 21
Tarquinius Priscus: 21-2
Tarquinius Superbus: 22, 159
Tasso, Torquato: 91, 213

Tempestà, Antonio: 57, 64, 67-70
Terence: 304
Tertullian: 78, 84-6, 95-7, 149, 151
Testa: 13
Themistocles: 155-6
Theophrastus: 190
Theopompus: 128
Theseus: 193
Tiber, personification of: 68
Tibullus: 96, 304
Timmermans, Linda: 319, 321, 337
Timon of Athens: 189-90, 195, 209, 281-2
Titus, Emp.: 90
Tollius, Jacobus: 96
Tomyris, Queen of the Massagets: 326
Torrentius, Laevinus (van der Beke): 58, 62
Trajan, Emp.: 9, 12, 23, 49, 90, 142, 156, 173-4, 290-1, 294, 297, 299-300
Trevisiani, Francesco: 162
Tuitius, Marcus: *see* Curtius, Marcus
Tullus Hostilius: 22
Turnus: 273-274
Turpilius, Roman knight and painter: 299
Tutor: *see* Julius

Uberti, Fazio degli: 152
Uccello, Paolo: 40
Ulysses: 191, 218
Urbini, Carlo: 7

Vaenius, Otho (van Veen): xi; 57-74, 93-4
Vaenius, Peter: 62
Vaga, del: *see* Perino
Valentinianus, Emp.: 295
Valeria: 198
Valerianus, Joannes Pierius: 280
Valerius Maximus: 8-9, 148, 155
Valla, Lorenzo: 30-1, 47
Varro: 96, 136, 147
Vasari, Giorgio: 5, 22-3, 33, 36-40, 42-3, 47, 49, 51-2, 154, 289-90, 295, 298
Vegetius, Flavius Renatus: 107, 112, 117
Veleda: 68
Velleius Paterculus: 308, 310-3
Venus: 13, 42, 259
Verbiest, Hendrik: 341
Vergil: 35-6, 42-3, 49-50, 83, 223, 259, 273, 304, 317, 347
Verginia: 155
Verona, da: *see* Liberale

Veronese, Paolo: 161-2
Vespasian, Emp.: 63-4, 66
Vico, Enea: 296
Vico, Giambattista: 248
Victoria, goddess of: 68
Vindicor, Tommaso: 28
Virgilia, wife of Coriolanus: 198
Virtus, goddess: 317
Vitellius, Emp.: 63-4
Vlaming, Pieter: 216
Vocula: *see* Dillius
Voltaire: 248, 331
Volumnia, mother of Coriolanus: 190,
    198-200
Vomanius: 42
Vondel, Joost van den: 215, 223, 232,
    350
Vossius, Gerardus: 339
Vries, Simon de: 343

Waal, Henry van: 70
Wallenstein: 236
Wellekens, Jan Baptista (Silvander): xii;
    213-34
Wellekens, Magdalena Barbara: 213

Wier, Johannes: 184
Wiese, Benno von: 243
Wilhelm IV of Bavaria: 153
Willem Lodewijk, Stadholder of
    Friesland: 116-7, 119
William of Orange: 343-4, 353
Witt, Cornelis de: 343, 345-6, 353
Witt, Johan de: 343, 345-6, 353-4

Xenophon: 112
Xiphilinus, Johannes: 291
Xylander, Guilielmus (Xilander): 103,
    176, 291

Zacheus: 34
Zamorano, Rodrigo: 223
Zeno: 279
Zeus (cf. Jove): 280
Zonhoven, R.O. van: 341
Zuccaro, Federigo: 37
Zuccaro, Taddeo: 37
Zuylen van Nyevelt, Adam van: 224-5,
    231
Zuylen van Nyevelt, Willem van: 224

LIST OF CONTRIBUTORS

Maria BERBARA, Ph.D. in Art History, University of Hamburg, is specialized in the reception of Graeco-Roman art in sixteenth-century northern Italy.

Jan BLOEMENDAL is Scientific Project Researcher at the Constantine Huygens Institute in The Hague. He specializes in Renaissance poetics and Neo-Latin drama. His recent publications include *Daniel Heinsius, Auriacus, sive Libertas saucia* (1997); *Een handvol Huygens. Vijf Latijnse gedichten van Constantijn Huygens vertaald en toegelicht* (1997).

Anton BOSCHLOO is Professor of Art History at Leiden University. He specializes in Italian art of the early modern period and his recent publications include *The Prints of the Remondinis. An Attempt to Reconstruct an Eighteenth-Century World of Pictures*, Amsterdam University Press, 1998.

Karl ENENKEL teaches Latin and Neo-Latin Literature in the Department of Classics at Leiden University. He is the author of *Francesco Petrarca: De vita solitaria, Buch 1. Kritische Textausgabe und ideengeschichtlicher Kommentar* (1990), of *Kulturoptimismus und Kulturpessimismus in der Renaissance* (1995), and of numerous articles on Italian and Dutch humanism. He is the editor of *Lipsius in Leiden* (1997), and *Modelling the Individual Biography and Portrait in the Renaissance* (1998).

Jan L. DE JONG, Ph.D. (1987) in Art History, Leiden University, is Assistant Professor of Italian Renaissance Art at Groningen University, The Netherlands. He has published numerous articles on sixteenth-century Italian history painting.

Jeanine DE LANDTSHEER, Ph.D. in Classical Languages (1993), Research Fellow at the Catholic University of Leuven, focuses on Neo-Latin studies, especially on the correspondence of Justus Lipsius. Recent publications (Brepols, Turnhout) include *Iusti Lipsi Epistolae, V–VII (1592–1594)*.

Marc LAUREYS is Professor of Medieval and Neo-Latin at the University of Bonn. He specializes in historiography and antiquarian studies from the late Middle Ages through the Baroque period. He edited Giovanni Cavallini's *Polistoria* (1995) and a collective volume on *The World of Justus Lipsius* (1998).

Olga VAN MARION teaches Dutch Studies at Leiden University. She prepares a thesis on the genre of the heroic epistle in Early Modern Dutch literature, and has published several articles on the same subject.

Alicia MONTOYA is Research Fellow in the Department of French Studies, Leiden University. She prepares a thesis on Marie-Anne Barbier.

Mark MORFORD is Emeritus Professor of Classics at the University of Virginia and Visiting Professor of Classics at Amherst College. He was formerly Kennedy Professor of Renaissance Studies at Smith College. He has written books on *The Poet Lucan* (1967; 2nd. ed. 1996); *Persius* (1984); *Lipsius and the Cicrcle of Rubens* (1991), and he is co-author of *Classical Mythology* (1971; 6th ed. 1999).

Bettina NOAK (Hartlieb), M.A., is Scientific Assistant at the Dutch Department of the Freie Universität of Berlin. She specializes in Dutch Renaissance tragedy.

Sjaak ONDERDELINDEN teaches German literature in the German Department, Leiden University. He is the author of several articles on classical (Goethe) and modern drama (Bertolt Brecht, Peter Weiss, Rolf Hochhuth, Tankred Dorst, Christoph Hein); he is the editor of *Interbellum und Exil* (1991) and *Brecht in Holland* (1998).

Paul J. SMITH is Professor of French Studies at Leiden University. He has written a thesis on Rabelais, and has published numerous articles on Rabelais, Montaigne, and French fable literature.

Wilfried STROH is Professor of Latin Philology at Munich University. He has published several books and articles on Cicero's Speeches, the Latin Love Elegy and on Neo-Latin poetry.

Francesca TERRENATO, Research Fellow at the Institute of Comparative Literature, University of Rome, has written a thesis on Vasari's *Vite* and Van Mander's *Schilder-boeck*.

Arnoud VISSER, Research Fellow at Leiden University, is preparing a thesis on the emblems of Joannes Sambucus.

Bart WESTERWEEL is Professor of English Renaissance Literature at Leiden University. He has written numerous articles on emblem studies and Shakespeare. He edited *Anglo-Dutch Relations in the Field of the Emblem* (Leiden: 1997), 189-212, and co-edited *Emblem Books in Leiden: A Catalogue of the Collections of Leiden University Library, the 'Maatschappij der Nederlandse Letterkunde' and Bibliotheca Thysiana*, ed. Arnoud Visser, co-ed. Paul Hoftijzer (Leiden: 1999).